W9-CLN-264

THE ECONOMICS OF LABOR AND COLLECTIVE BARGAINING

THE ECONOMICS OF LABOR AND COLLECTIVE BARGAINING

William H. Miernyk
University of Colorado

D. C. HEATH AND COMPANY BOSTON

FOR
JAN, JUDY
JEANNE
AND
JAMES

Copyright ©, 1965 by

D. C. HEATH AND COMPANY
Boston Englewood Chicago Dallas
San Francisco Atlanta London Toronto

No part of the material covered by this copyright may be reproduced in any form without written permission of the publisher.

Library of Congress Catalog Card Number: 65–12693

Printed in the United States of America. (6L4)

THIS BOOK IS PUBLISHED IN ASSOCIATION WITH TEXTBOOK ASSOCIATES, INC., NEW YORK

Preface

This book is intended for the conventional full-year course in labor economics and industrial relations. The second half, starting with Chapter 13, can also be used in a one-semester course in collective bargaining if supplemented by appropriate case material. In writing this text I tried to keep the student in mind. An effort was made to keep the book compact without sacrificing breadth of coverage. Topics which are discussed in introductory economics texts have been largely avoided. Aggregative or Keynesian employment theory, for example, has not been included since this is now covered by most textbooks on the principles of economics. By avoiding such duplication, I have been able to introduce the rudiments of various theories directly related to the processes of union growth and collective bargaining without making the book excessively long.

The organization of a textbook is less important than its scope, since the individual instructor can assign sections in any order he wishes if each section is relatively self-contained. I would like to think, however, that the organization of this book follows a logical sequence. The first part deals with the history of organized labor on the assumption that it is easier to understand today's labor problems if the student is informed about labor problems of the past and has some knowledge of the evolution of a labor movement in the United States. The labor history is followed by a discussion of the development of labor law and social legislation. The next section deals with the structure, government and objectives of trade unions. With this background the student is ready for an analysis of the process of collective bargaining and a discussion of the issues involved. Part 5 deals with labor economics; it includes discussions of the labor force, labor markets, productivity, and wage determination. This is followed by a chapter on manpower management. The book concludes with a discussion of the present state of the American labor movement, and the views of a number of experts about its future.

Economics is a discipline in which the winds of controversy blow strong, and this is certainly true of labor economics. I have made no effort to avoid controversial issues, but have endeavored to present various points of view. The object has been to avoid indoctrination while providing an analytical framework which will permit better understanding of some of the complex issues faced by unions, management, and the public.

This book combines historical, institutional, and theoretical approaches. These are not compartmentalized but are integrated insofar as this can be done in a book which treats a wide variety of topics. Theories of union growth, for example, are included as part of the section on labor history. The student is introduced to theories of collective bargaining early in the discussion of this process, and wage theory is included in the section on labor economics. It would be misleading to imply that this is a heavily theoretical book, however. Much of labor economics and industrial relations fits well into the institutional framework, and evidence of this will be found throughout the present text. The object was not to emphasize any one approach, but to introduce the student to the ideas of a number of scholars who have studied labor economics and industrial relations from different points of view.

The author of a textbook is subject to many influences. In my case these include my former teachers at the University of Colorado and Harvard. The thinking of my former colleagues at M.I.T. and Northeastern University is also reflected in these pages, and I have drawn heavily upon the work of scholars at a number of other institutions. There might be some objection to the extensive documentation in some chapters, but the numerous references are an indication of the extent of my intellectual debts. While acknowledging these debts, I alone am responsible for the interpretations and conclusions in this volume.

For permission to use copyrighted materials I would like to thank Macmillan and Company, Ltd., the RAND Corporation, McGraw-Hill, The National Bureau of Economic Research, Inc., and the American Economic Association. Specific acknowledgments of sources and authors are given in the text. It is a pleasure to acknowledge the secretarial assistance provided by Mrs. Marilyn Martello and Mrs. Charlotte Warren at Northeastern University, and by Mrs. Rose Gowen and Mrs. Mig Shepherd at the University of Colorado. Mr. Robert Britt kindly assisted with some of the proofreading. I am also grateful to the publisher's anonymous reviewers of an earlier draft. They eliminated several errors and helped clarify the exposition in a number of places.

Writing this book was a rewarding experience, but this would not have been so without the understanding and support of my family. My children, to whom this volume is dedicated, were remarkably tolerant about a work schedule which at times conflicted with their plans. My wife was a constant source of encouragement and also provided material assistance in the preparation of the index.

Boulder, Colorado

WILLIAM H. MIERNYK

Contents

Chapter 1 Introduction 1

PART 1 HISTORY OF AMERICAN UNIONISM
Chapter 2 Colonial Times to the A.F. of L. 13
Chapter 3 The Era of the A.F. of L. 26
Chapter 4 The American Labor Movement Comes of Age 46
Chapter 5 Theories of the Labor Movement 58

PART 2 TRADE UNIONS AND PUBLIC POLICY
Chapter 6 From Repression to Non-Intervention 85
Chapter 7 Government Encouragement of Trade Unions 100
Chapter 8 The Emergence of Restrictive Labor Legislation 113
Chapter 9 Social Security and the Protection of Labor Standards 140

PART 3 THE STRUCTURE, GOVERNMENT, AND OBJECTIVES OF TRADE UNIONS
Chapter 10 Trade Union Structure 167
Chapter 11 Trade Union Government 180
Chapter 12 Trade Union Philosophy and Objectives 199

PART 4 COLLECTIVE BARGAINING—PROCESSES AND ISSUES
Chapter 13 The Negotiation of Labor-Management Agreements 217
Chapter 14 Nonwage Issues in Collective Bargaining 242
Chapter 15 The Prevention or Settlement of Disputes 260
Chapter 16 The Structure of Collective Bargaining 283
Chapter 17 The Stages of Collective Bargaining 303

PART 5 LABOR ECONOMICS: THE LABOR MARKET AND WAGE DETERMINATION

Chapter 18 The Labor Force and the Labor Market 321
Chapter 19 Wage Determination—Theory and Policy 345
Chapter 20 The Economic Consequences of Trade Unions 370
Chapter 21 Productivity 393
Chapter 22 Unemployment 419

PART 6 MANPOWER MANAGEMENT—THE STATE OF THE AMERICAN LABOR MOVEMENT

Chapter 23 Manpower Management 453
Chapter 24 The Present State and the Future of American Unions 473

Index 489

List of Charts

Map of AFL-CIO Membership as Per Cent of Labor Force by State, 1960 6

Membership of National and International Unions, 1930–60 75

Membership as a Per Cent of Total Labor Force and of Employees in Nonagricultural Establishments, 1930–60 76

Map of State "Right-to-Work" Laws Showing Year Adopted 123

How the Social Security Law Works 146

History of the Social Security Law Passed in 1935 150

Structural Organization of the A. F. of L. and C. I. O. 168

Size Distribution of Unions, 1960 177

Trends in Work Stoppages 277

The Labor Force, 1955–1960 Averages 323

Civilian Labor Force, Total Employment, and Gross National Product 326

Employment in Goods-Producing Industries 327

Production and Nonproduction Workers in Manufacturing 328

Employment in Service-Producing Industries 329

Employment of White Collar and Blue Collar Workers 330

Employment for Major Occupational Groups 331

Trend of Earnings in Manufacturing, and Consumer Price Index 371

Consumer Price Index 387

Indexes of Real Product per Man-Hour in the Total Private Economy, Agriculture, and Nonagriculture, 1909–1962 395

Per Cent Change in Output per Man-Hour, Production, and Man-Hours, 1919–1926 397

Indexes of Productivity in the United States, 1889–1957 400

Indexes of Productivity in Five Major Industrial Divisions 402

Output per Man-Hour and "Real" Hourly Earnings: Manufacturing, 1914–1939 403

Total and Long-Term Unemployed 421

Seasonally-Adjusted Short- and Long-Term Unemployment Quarterly Averages, 1953–62 429

Rates of Unemployment, 1951–62 444

Chapter 1 Introduction

LABOR IN A DYNAMIC ECONOMY

A century ago the United States was predominantly an urban-agrarian economy. The total population in 1870, for example, was less than 40 million, and more than half of the nation's residents were concentrated in three regions: New England, the Middle Atlantic states, and the Great Lakes region. The rest of the nation was sparsely populated. The labor force at that time included about 12.5 million persons. Of these, more than half (53 per cent) were engaged in farming, fishing, forestry, and mining; about one-fourth were employed in providing services; and 21 per cent were in manufacturing.[1]

By 1962, the population of the United States had passed the 180 million mark. There were almost 72 million workers in the civilian labor force, but only slightly more than five million, or 7.2 per cent of the total, were in agriculture. America had become a heavily urban (and suburban) society. The nature of work was also vastly different than it had been in the 19th century. In 1962, only 36 per cent of all wage and salary workers outside agriculture were engaged in the production of goods; the rest were employed in a wide range of professional and service occupations.

The American economy has grown rapidly during the past century, and there have been significant changes in economic organization. When our society was predominantly rural—with the economy heavily dependent upon agriculture—there were few large enterprises. While we will see in the following chapters that trade unionism has a long history in the United States, there were no strong or well-entrenched unions in this country a century ago.

[1] Harvey S. Perloff, *et al.*, *Regions, Resources, and Economic Growth*, Baltimore: The Johns Hopkins Press (1960), pp. 12–13, 131.

America in the 1870's was not a highly structured society. There were few laws dealing with the activities of businessmen, and none dealing with organized labor. Indeed, government activity of all kinds was minimal. The prevailing philosophy was that "the government which governed least governed best." The economy was also relatively simple. Transportation was slow, and this limited the speed of communication. Under these circumstances many markets were local in character; there was much less specialization and exchange than there is today.

It is easy to exaggerate the joys of life in 19th century America. Many of the problems which leaders of government, business, and labor wrestle with today were unheard of at that time, but so were many of the material advantages which we take for granted in the more highly specialized and institutionalized society of today. Hours of work were long, and work itself was usually arduous, only the well-to-do had the time and means to take advantage of the available cultural and recreational facilities.

THE EMERGENCE OF LARGE-SCALE ORGANIZATIONS

One important institutional change in the economy was well under way before the end of the 19th century. This was the rise of the corporation, and an increase in the size of many enterprises. This change in the form of business organization eventually led to a separation of ownership and control. As corporations grew in size and complexity a class of professional managers emerged to guide their destinies, and this in turn led to a change in the relationship between employers and employees.

In an earlier day there had been personal contact between the owner-manager of a firm and his workers. The owner did the hiring, he supervised training and maintained discipline on the job, and it was up to him to make job assignments and promotions. He dealt directly with disgruntled workers either by settling their grievances or by dismissing them. From the point of view of the worker, this was not necessarily the best of all possible worlds, but he always knew where he stood. If the employer was interested in making a profit—and in economics this is the standard assumption we make about employers—he paid close attention to the actions and attitudes of his employees. He served his own best interests by trying to keep his workers satisfied.

As some firms grew in size and adopted the corporate structure, the personal relationship between employer and employee disappeared. The growth of the corporation was one factor contributing to the development of stable trade unionism in the United States. Workers recognized that as individuals they had to accept wages, hours, and working conditions on a take-it-or-leave-it basis, and they sought to match the strength of large employers by dealing with them collectively through representatives of their choosing.

The Great Depression of the 1930's brought another change in economic organization. For the first time in our history, excluding wartime periods, government began to play an increasingly important role in economic life. Among other things, the government laid down the rules governing labor-management relations, and this, as we will see, had an important impact on the growth of trade unions. The change from an economy made up of many small farms, small businesses, and small government to one in which business, government and labor have all become big was gradual. But viewed over a fairly long period of time—a century or even a half-century—the contrasts are dramatic indeed.

The principal focus of this book is on one of the major institutions in our modern industrial society; namely, trade unions. This is not because most workers belong to unions. As a matter of fact, union members in the United States are a minority of the work force. In 1960, union members in this country accounted for only 23 per cent of the labor force, and 32 per cent of workers employed in nonagricultural establishments. But the influence of unions is greater than their minority status might suggest. They have some effect upon the wage structure, and wage levels, in the entire economy. Also, in a society in which many decisions are made by representatives of organizations, the political and social influence of unions cannot be ignored.

A PROFILE OF AMERICAN TRADE UNIONISM

There were about 17.5 million union members in the United States in 1960. Most of these—approximately 16.9 million—were members of the 184 national or international unions with headquarters in the United States, and 14 million belonged to the 134 unions affiliated with the AFL-CIO.[2]

Most American unions are relatively small. In 1960, 110 of the nation's unions, or about 60 per cent of the total, claimed fewer

[2] *Directory of National and International Labor Unions in the United States, 1961*, U.S. Department of Labor, Bureau of Labor Statistics, Bulletin No. 1320 (March 1962), pp. 45–46.

than 50,000 members each. Collectively they accounted for less than 8 per cent of total union membership. Another 53 unions reported membership ranging between 50,000 and 200,000. The unions in this size group accounted for 29 per cent of the total, and they also accounted for 29 per cent of all members. Finally, there were 21 unions—or 11 per cent of the total—with 200,000 or more members each. Yet this relatively small number of unions combined claimed 63 per cent of all organized workers in the United States.

For some time women have constituted a growing proportion of the labor force, but the American labor movement is predominantly made up of male workers. In 1960, women accounted for almost one-third of total employment in the nation, but there were only 3.3 million women union members accounting for slightly less than 19 per cent of total union membership.

Another major trend in the labor force has been an increase in the proportion of white-collar workers. Most American union members, however, are blue-collar or manual workers. About 46 per cent of all employed workers in 1960 were in the white collar category, while an estimated 2.2 million white-collar union members accounted for only 12 per cent of total union membership.[3]

It is difficult to make an industrial classification of union membership since some unions cut across industry lines; they have members in two or more industries. The following table shows the approximate distribution of union membership in 1960 by industrial classification. The figures in Table 1-1 are approximations only. The right-hand column, in particular, is subject to some error. Different industrial classifications are used to compile data on employment and union membership, especially in the manufacturing sector, and some rearrangement was required to derive the figures in the table. Also, the union membership figures include *all* members of unions with headquarters in the United States while the employment data apply only to establishments in this country. Since about 94 per cent of the total membership of these unions is in the United States the errors are not large. The figures in the right-hand column, however, overstate to some extent the degree of organization by industrial classification. In the absence of more reliable data these figures have been used to give at least some notion of the extent to which unions have been able to organize the various sectors of the economy.

[3] Carol A. Barry, "White Collar Employment: Trends and Structure," *Monthly Labor Review* (February 1961), p. 12.

TABLE 1–1

Industry Group	Number of Unions[a]	Members[b] (in thousands)	Per Cent of Total	Union Members as Approximate Per Cent of Employment[c]
Manufacturing	106	8,591	47.6	52.6
Durable goods	96	5,285	29.3	57.8
Nondurable goods	83	3,158	17.5	49.8
Not classifiable	21	147	.8	17.3
Nonmanufacturing	103	8,375	46.4	22.9
Mining, quarrying	11	593	3.3	89.3
Contract construction	23	2,271	12.6	82.0
Transportation	48	2,566	14.2	98.0
Service industries	31	1,281	7.1	19.3
All other	36	1,664	9.2	7.0
Government	41	1,070	5.9	12.7

[a] Figures in this column *are not additive* since some unions have members in more than one industrial classification.

[b] Detailed figures add to more than 17.5 million since they include all members of unions with headquarters in the United States.

[c] Computed from employment data in Robert L. Stein and Herman Travis, "Labor Force and Employment in 1960," *Monthly Labor Review* (April 1961), p. 347.

Source of union data: *Directory of National and International Labor Unions in the United States, 1961*, U.S. Department of Labor, Bureau of Labor Statistics, Bulletin No. 1320 (March 1962), pp. 51–52.

Unions have been most successful in mining, construction, and transportation. Elsewhere in the non-manufacturing sector they have had only meager success. More than half of all factory workers belong to unions, however, and unions have made more headway in the durable goods sector than in nondurables. Unions have not been highly successful in organizing workers in trade and financial establishments, and only a relatively small number of government workers (federal, state, and local) have become union members. These, it might be noted, are the most rapidly growing sectors of the economy. Also, government workers who belong to unions rarely have the right to strike, so the effectiveness of their organizations is severely limited by law.

The geographical distribution of union members is far from even. This is indicated by Map 1-1 which shows AFL-CIO membership as a percentage of the labor force in each state. Total membership figures would have been preferred, but unions not affiliated with the AFL-CIO do not report membership to state labor bodies. Unlike Table 1-1, which slightly overstated union organization

MAP 1–1
AFL-CIO MEMBERSHIP AS PER CENT OF LABOR FORCE BY STATE, 1960

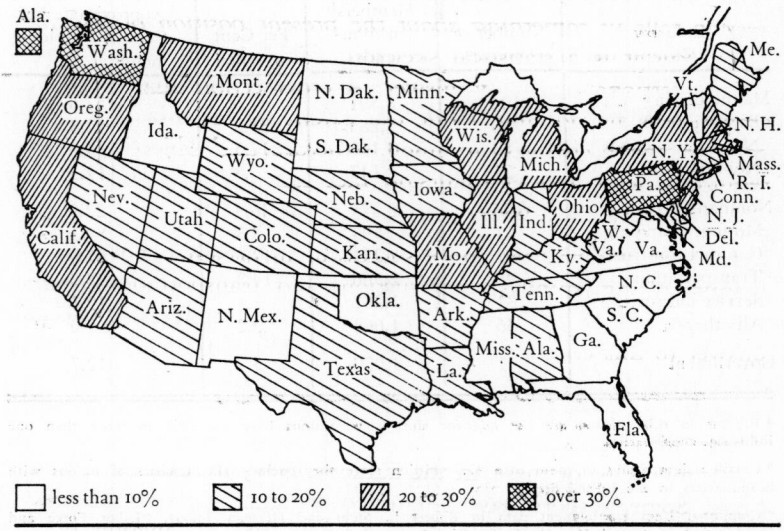

Source: Membership data, Department of Labor, *Directory of National and International Labor Unions*, 1961, p. 53; labor force data, U.S. Census of Population 1960, *U.S. Summary General Social and Economic Characteristics*, Final Report PC (1)–1C pp. 1–264—1–265.

by industrial classification, Map 1-1 understates somewhat the degree of union organization in the various states. However, the *relative* distribution of union members throughout the nation is probably not distorted significantly by the exclusion of unaffiliated union members.

Unions have been least successful in organizing workers in the Southeast, and in a scattering of other states with predominantly rural populations. With few exceptions, the states in which 20 per cent or more of the labor force belong to unions are highly industrialized, or—as in the case of Montana—heavily dependent upon mining as a source of employment. There are some exceptions to this. West Virginia, for example, is a state in which mining is important, but only about 12 per cent of the workers in this state belong to unions. Indiana is a borderline state, and here membership in AFL-CIO unions amounted to a fraction less than 20 per cent in 1960. If total membership figures were available on a state basis, however, Indiana would fall in the same category as most of its neighboring states.

THE SYSTEMATIC STUDY OF LABOR ECONOMICS AND INDUSTRIAL RELATIONS

The brief profile of American unions sketched in the preceding section tells us something about the present position of organized labor. But it is a statistical skeleton, and bare statistics can raise more questions than they answer. A cross-section analysis, for example, tells us nothing about the extent of organization in the past, or about changes in union structure and objectives. These require at least a brief excursion into labor history—the starting point of the present book.

Why have unions been more successful in organizing workers in manufacturing, mining, construction, and transportation than in other sectors of the economy? There is no universally-accepted answer to this question. Since the early days of trade unions, however, scholars have speculated about the motives which lead some workers to organize, and those which keep others from doing so. There are a number of theories of the labor movement, and the most important of these, in the author's view, are examined in this book. Some authors have attempted to analyze various kinds of trade unionism; others to develop a unified explanation of this particular phenomenon of industrial society, and in recent years a number of theorists have concentrated on the question of union growth. What forces—economic, political, and social—contribute to rapid union growth at times and to little or no growth at others?

In a democracy, all of us live under the rule of law, but there is nothing static about the legal system. The law has changed vastly since the days of Hammurabi, and it will continue to change in the future. Labor law is a fairly new addition to jurisprudence in this country, but in recent decades it has become an important, if controversial, part of the legal system. An introduction to labor law is an integral part of a systematic study of trade unionism.

The essence of trade unionism is collective action, and collective bargaining today is a highly complex process. One who relies entirely upon news media for information about collective bargaining is likely to obtain a distorted image. Strikes and labor unrest are reported with meticulous attention to detail, but peaceful collective bargaining is not regarded as newsworthy. One cannot hope to have an understanding of industrial relations, however, without some knowledge of the techniques of contract negotiations, contract administration, and dispute settlement. Like many other social processes, collective bargaining has been evolutionary. To understand this process it is not enough to examine current practices; these must be viewed against the changes which have occurred as unions have grown, and as their position vis-à-vis management has been altered.

There are some obvious questions which a student of labor economics and industrial relations will ask. How are wages determined? Do unions affect the wage level? What effect do they have on wage structure? Have unions changed the pattern of income distribution? These questions are the raw material of wage theory, a branch of economics with a long history. New theories have been advanced as our analytical tools have been refined, as new evidence for the testing of hypotheses has become available, and as the world has changed around us.

In recent years various economists have developed theories of bargaining which examine the behavioral aspects of negotiations. Wage and bargaining theories do not, of course, provide definitive answers to the questions listed above. They have the virtue, however, of showing that simple answers—usually based upon personal predilections—are not likely to be convincing. In an introductory text many of the refinements of wage theory and of the theory of bargaining must be ignored, but enough can be said about them to show how the analytical tools of economics can be applied to problems which are of central interest to economists and policy makers alike.

It is not uncommon for textbooks on labor to begin with a discussion of "labor problems," a convention which has not been followed in this volume. But there certainly are labor problems, and these are not ignored in this book. There are the problems of labor-management disputes and of tensions which stop short of overt economic warfare, and there are economic problems which directly affect the behavior of union leaders and management in collective bargaining.

Problems

One of the most intractable problems in the United States in recent years has been that of relatively high-level unemployment even at the peaks of business cycles. And during much of the period since the end of World War II there has been concern about "creeping inflation." Interest in these problems is not limited to those who engage in collective bargaining. There has been a tendency in recent years for the government to become involved in various ways in major labor-management disputes. Also, our government is committed to a policy of maintaining "full" employment, although there is far from complete agreement about just what this means or how it is to be accomplished. While there is at present no legal commitment to do so, the government has an interest in maintaining price stability.

The "correct" solutions to these and other labor problems will not be found in this book. In a society made up of many groups with diverse interests there are no solutions to social and economic problems which will satisfy everyone. The object has been to discuss the problems fully, and to present various points of view about them.

The emphasis in this book is upon trade unions, but even an introductory text should have something to say about the other party to collective bargaining. A detailed analysis of personnel adminstration would go beyond the scope of this book. It does contain a brief examination of various management attitudes toward unions, and some discussion of how managerial decisions concerning personnel administration and labor relations are made.

Finally, the historical portions of this book show that there have been major changes in unions, in the collective bargaining process, in labor laws, and in the reactions of management to trade unionism. Little imagination is required to realize that there will be further changes. Only a prophet could foretell what these changes will be, and reliable economic prophets are in short supply. Projections of the future of trade unionism can be made, however, based upon various assumptions about long-run trends in the American economy. A few of the more interesting projections made in recent years are examined in the concluding chapter.

PART 1

history of american unionism

Chapter 2 Colonial Times to the A.F. of L.

Most general histories of the United States touch only briefly on the trade-union movement. Because unions have had an impact on our political and economic lives only in fairly recent times, few students are likely to be well informed about the somewhat obscure beginnings of trade unionism in the United States. Labor unions existed in the early days of our history, however, although a labor movement as such did not get started in the United States until the second quarter of the nineteenth century.

The broad outlines of labor history are sketched in this and the following two chapters. In this tightly compressed treatment only the highlights can be touched upon, but it is hoped that this will provide a framework for later discussions of trade union policy, labor law, the structure and government of unions, collective bargaining, and labor economics—topics which make up the bulk of the text.

Early Labor Organizations in the United States

The first labor organizations formed in this country bore little resemblance to a modern trade union. In colonial America there were organizations, strongly reminiscent of the medieval guilds, which included both masters and journeymen, but there were others, typically charitable and benefit societies, which consisted of journeymen alone. Both types of organizations consisted of workers in the skilled trades only. One of the earliest of these organizations was the Carpenters Society of Philadelphia which was established in 1724. This organization engaged in both charitable activities and bargaining. Among other things, it maintained a secret wage scale, imposing fines on its members for disclosing the list of wages to non-members.[1]

Similar organizations were established by journeymen printers, shoemakers, tailors, hatters, bricklayers, and coopers. Many of these, first established as charitable societies, gradually became involved in a form of bargaining, although in those days this was typically limited to the establishment of a "price list" or scale of wages. There was also some effort, however, to exert control over apprentices in order to protect the job security of the journeymen, but there was no counterpart in those days to modern collective bargaining agreements.

The first labor organizations in this country were not exceptionally stable. The colonial period was one of great flux. One day a man might be a journeyman in one of the skilled trades, and the next an independent businessman. The skilled worker did not consider himself part of a wage-earner class. There were cases where master and journeyman cooperated to by-pass the "merchant capitalist," a middleman who performed the function of today's retail store.

Toward the end of the eighteenth century, however, organizations were formed which bore a stronger resemblance to today's trade unions. They were made up entirely of wage earners, and their objective was solely that of improving the economic condition of employees. The Federal Society of Journeymen Cordwainers was such an organization. It was established in 1794 by the Philadelphia shoemakers and survived until 1806. Similar societies were established by the carpenters and shoemakers of Boston in 1793 and 1794. The printers of New York also organized in the latter year.

Although some of these organizations lasted for a number of years, their members still did not consider themselves to be part of a working class. While they practiced their trades, however, they felt the need for mutual protection both from merchant capitalists and employers. They sought to negotiate joint agreements with the masters and in a few cases even demanded a closed shop. To achieve their ends they used the weapon of the strike. There are records of strikes for the 10-hour day, for the closed shop, and even some instances of sympathy strikes. The first labor dispute of a modern character was evidently conducted by the Philadelphia printers who went on strike for a minimum wage of six dollars a

[1] Norman Ware, *Labor in Modern Industrial Society,* Boston: D. C. Heath and Company (1935), page 27.

week. The union was sufficiently well organized to pay strike benefits at that time.[2]

The early unions did not go unchallenged. A number of militant employers associations were formed specifically to deal with organized workers. Some agreed to negotiate with the unions, but by and large they set out to destroy the unions by recruiting non-union workers, and by turning to the courts for protection from what they considered to be "labor conspiracies." The courts were sympathetic. Between 1806 and 1815 there were at least six conspiracy cases, and in four of these organized workers were found guilty of conspiring to injure their employers. One of the verdicts also concluded that labor organizations were adverse to the best interests of the community.

But it was not so much employer opposition or the courts which limited the growth of early American trade unions. Economic instability was their greatest enemy. They could not achieve sufficient strength to withstand the shocks of the short but severe depressions which were commonplace at that time. For example, following the end of the Napoleonic Wars there was a severe and prolonged depression which reached its depth in 1820. Few of the early labor organizations were able to survive this economic onslaught.

The Beginning of a Labor Movement

The existence of trade unions in a handful of skilled trades does not constitute a labor movement. This comes into being only when wage earners develop a feeling of solidarity which extends beyond the members of a single occupation. This feeling did not exist among the early charitable and benefit societies which were eliminated by the depression of 1820. The revival following the depression was spirited but short-lived. By the middle of the 1820's the nation was again in the grip of an industrial depression. Discontent was more widespread than ever before, and it found expression in increased political activity which culminated, in 1828, in the election of Andrew Jackson as President—an event which signalized the rise of the "Common Man."

Jacksonian democracy was the result of more than industrial depression. The average citizen and wage earner had many grievances. "Economic and political inequality between citizens of different classes, the length of the work day, imprisonment for debt, absence

[2] Harry A. Millis and Royal E. Montgomery, *Organized Labor,* New York: McGraw-Hill Book Company (1945), p. 21.

of mechanics' lien laws . . . the Pennsylvania compulsory militia system under which the wealthy could avoid service, lack of free public education . . . , governmental favoritism toward the banks and other corporations, the issue of banknote currency of unstable purchasing power and the monopoly of credit maintained by the banks . . ."[3] were among the complaints of those who supported Jackson in his campaign against the "aristocrats" of New England and Virginia.

There was general agreement that all of the problems of the Common Man were not solved by the introduction of Jacksonian democracy, but there was much less agreement about how reforms should be achieved. Some thought the answer lay in the direction of agrarian reform, a few were intrigued by Robert Dale Owen's proposal of "public guardianship," and others believed that the wage earner would receive equitable treatment only if workers organized for political action. Property qualifications for voting had been removed in most states by 1821. The first American Labor Party was organized in Philadelphia in May, 1828, and a second workingman's party was organized in New York the following year. These parties were not led by laborers, however, but by reformers or small businessmen. The platforms of the labor parties demanded the 10-hour day, the abolition of imprisonment for debt, an end to prison contract labor, enactment of mechanics' lien laws, abolition of discriminatory militia sytems, curbs on licensed monopolies, especially banks, and universal education. The labor parties in the United States did not survive, however. They were gradually absorbed by the two major parties with some segments splintering off into small factions like the "Loco-Focos" or the "Equal Rights" group.

The reform organizations were so badly divided that they accomplished little. However, during this era of agitation, trade unionism was revived again. This time the individual organizations of skilled craftsmen did not operate in a vacuum. We can trace the beginning of a labor *movement* in the United States to the late 1820's. For example, in 1827 the Philadelphia Mechanics Union of Trade Associations was formed. This is believed to be the first coordinated movement of several trade unions to accomplish a common objective. It grew out of a strike by workers in the Philadelphia building trades for the 10-hour day. The 10-hour movement also sparked formation of The New England Association of

[3] Millis and Montgomery, *ibid.*, pp. 24–25.

Farmers, Mechanics and Other Workmen which, as the name suggests, was somewhat broader than a trade union. It was both a political and an economic organization. Some of the leaders of the new labor movement also supported the labor parties which had been formed, but the association between the unions and the political organizations was not close. The unions were much more intent upon achieving job security than political power.

The First Attempts at Federation

Some of the unions organized during the early days of Jacksonian democracy were able to survive for a number of years. They resembled modern trade unions much more than any of the organizations formed before the 1820's. From 1832 to 1837, partly due to the expansion of state banks and the circulation of irredeemable currency, the cost of living surged upward. The number of local trade unions began to increase rapidly as workers made an effort to protect their real income by seeking higher wages. By 1833 it is estimated that there were twenty-nine unions in New York, twenty-one in Philadelphia, and seventeen in Baltimore. Skilled craftsmen in a number of other eastern cities were also organized. In addition to higher wages, most of these unions demanded the 10-hour day, control of apprenticeship, and the closed shop.

More important, the individual unions did not try to carry on alone. The individual societies combined into what were then called "trades' unions"—later to be designated city centrals. And local unions in the various trades began to form national organizations. Finally, in March 1834, the National Trades Union was formed—the first federated labor body in the United States. It was headed by Eli Moore, who was also a labor candidate for Congress. But from the beginning, all efforts to turn the National Trades Union into a political movement were effectively squelched. For the next two years the trade union movement in the United States grew and gained in strength. A number of conventions were held by the national unions, and viable trade unionism appeared to have come to the United States. But then came the panic of 1837, one of the worst financial disasters in our history, and during the depression which followed this panic virtually every labor organization in the nation was wiped out.

For the next decade the American economy was in the grip of a severe depression. Reform of our unstable monetary system was slow in coming. Wage earners, farmers, and small businessmen, were all victims of the deflationary pressures strongly at work during this decade. Workers had organized during an earlier period of inflation to protect their real earnings, but they seemed incapable of concerted action during a period of widespread unemployment.

Following the crash of 1837, a number of reform movements were started or revived. The brand of socialism advocated by Robert Owen (and practiced at New Harmony in the mid-1820's) was revived by his son, Robert Dale Owen and the latter's associate, Frances Wright. The disciples of Fourier advocated his program of Association. Both groups were critical of the waste and inefficiency which they claimed stemmed from the competitive system. There were also demands for producers' and consumers' cooperatives, and for agrarian reform. All of these movements gained adherents during the "hot air forties," but they failed to attract wage earners in significant numbers. Indeed, most labor historians are of the opinion that these and other reform movements impeded the growth of job-conscious unionism during this decade of economic stagnation in the United States.

The Emergence of Stable Trade Unionism

As the economy emerged from the depression in the late 1840's, trade unionism again appeared on the American scene. The experience of the 1840's indicated quite clearly that wage earners in this country were not interested in humanitarian schemes designed to alter the structure of American society. But as business conditions improved, and as prices began to rise again, a number of national trade unions were formed. The National Typographical Union was established in 1852—the first national union to survive to the present day. It was followed in 1854 by the Hat Finishers, in 1855 by the Journeyman Stonecutters Association, and in 1856 by the United Cigar Makers, a union destined to play an important part in subsequent trade union history. Two other national unions, the Ironmoulders, and the Machinists and Blacksmiths, were established in 1859.

The long depression following the panic of 1837 was followed by an equally long period of prosperity. This was a period of rapid population growth, rising prices, and of growing industrialization —all of which contributed to an increase in trade union membership. In addition, the rapid expansion of a network of rails led to broadened markets. Indeed, the growth of the railroad system was one of those innovations, like the subsequent growth of the automobile industry, which had far-reaching economic ramifications. Under these conditions, the trade union movement grew steadily, if not spectacularly. But trade unionism in the United States was far from strong enough to withstand the impact of a severe depression, and such a depression struck again in 1857. During this depression most of the weaker unions in the nation were once again wiped out.

Most of the unions which survived the crash of 1857 disappeared soon after the outbreak of the Civil War. But by 1863, wartime conditions were stimulating economic growth. The cost of living rose sharply and there was a labor shortage. These conditions have generally been a stimulus to union growth in the United States.

The trade unionism which emerged during the Civil War followed the pattern established before the crash of 1857. Local unions were formed in the skilled trades, and these were combined into city centrals or trades' assemblies. As these grew in number, national unions were formed. The growth of unions continued after the Civil War ended. Before the end of the 1860's there were about thirty national unions in existence. Some of the unions formed during the Civil War and the post-Civil War period have survived to the present day. The Brotherhood of Locomotive Engineers was founded in 1863. The conductors organized in 1868, and the Brotherhood of Firemen and Enginemen was founded in 1873. The unions that grew during this period were pragmatic craft organizations primarily interested in bargaining. As had been true of earlier unions, many joined in the movement for a shorter work day, but there was at least some modest flirtation with more radical reform schemes.

The post-Civil War period was similar to the 1830's and 1840's in terms of general confusion and lack of direction in the American economic system. It was a time of rapid growth in the manufacturing sector, and a period of increased concentration of ownership and control. Broadened markets had stimulated competition, and many businessmen sought to evade the uncertainties of aggressive price competition through collusion or consolidation. Agriculture also grew rapidly, and after the Homestead Acts were passed land prices soared while farm production increased and farm prices fell. The real wages of industrial workers thus went up, but the plight of the farmers again stimulated a host of agrarian reform movements. It was during this time that Henry George advanced his proposal for the Single Tax to appropriate unearned increments in land. The existing unions steered clear of this and other reform movements during the 1860's.

There was another severe panic in 1873 followed by a sustained depression. By this time, however, some of the national trade unions were sufficiently strong to be able to withstand a depression of some duration. During the depression of the 1870's there was some labor support for Greenbackism, and a heightened interest in consumer's cooperation. Despite their flirtation with reform movements, however, most unions continued to emphasize bargaining, and considerable collective bargaining as we know it today was practiced in the occupations in which unions had achieved a measure of strength.

There were a number of strikes during the 1870's, some of which were quite violent. Much of the violence, however, was initiated by a terrorist organization known as the Molly Maguires which Millis and Montgomery have called "a kind of labor Ku Klux Klan." Never a large group, the Molly Maguires "terrorized the community with a success entirely disproportionate to their strength and numbers. . . . Between 1871 and 1879 the Pennsylvania coal strikes gravitated, to a considerable extent, into the hands of the Molly Maguires, and several of the Mollys, in turn, gravitated into the hands of the Pinkerton Detectives."[4]

Few of the strikes during this period succeeded, however. The courts came to the aid of employers and granted injunctions liberally. Where physical violence occurred or threatened, Federal troops were used to settle industrial disputes.

A second attempt at national federation had been started before the panic of 1873. The National Labor Union had been founded in 1866. This was a federation of trade unions, but it had strong political overtones. Organizationally, it was a rather loose structure, composed of city centrals, national trade unions, and individual local unions. It also included in its membership, however, some reform organizations which ranged all the way from anarchists to women suffragists, and included a few socialist groups. When the first convention was held in 1866, unemployment was a major problem, and the federation urged legislative enactment of the 8-hour day. Partly as the result of this agitation, the 8-hour day for federal government employees was established in 1868. However, the general 8-hour movement failed, as did many other objectives of the National Labor Union and its member organizations.

[4] Millis and Montgomery, *ibid.*, p. 49.

There was some support in the National Labor Union for producers cooperatives. Indeed, the national shoemakers' union—the Order of the Knights of St. Crispin—had as one of its objectives the ultimate self-employment of its members. The Ironmoulders, led by William H. Sylvis, went beyond the mere advocacy of producers cooperatives, and set up at least ten cooperative foundries after losing strikes in 1867 and 1868. None of these survived for any length of time. A number of other trades also attempted producers cooperatives with an equal lack of success. The flirtation with such radical reform movements undoubtedly contributed to the relatively short life of the National Labor Union.

The trade unions formed during the 1860's bore a close resemblance to today's craft unions. At the local level, skilled workers in a common trade—carpenters, ironmoulders, and the members of the railroad Brotherhoods, for example—banded together to protect their job security and earnings. This was done both through control of apprenticeship and the establishment of wage lists. In a number of skilled trades, as local unions multiplied, national organizations were formed. This was partly a consequence of the extension of market areas which had led some craft union leaders to believe that it was necessary to broaden their geographic jurisdictions. With the improvement of transportation facilities, as the nation's railroad network expanded, local unions often could not stand alone against employers. If they went on strike, products, or even at times workers, could be imported from other communities. Local unions provided the funds for national treasuries through per capita taxes. This permitted the national to support local unions in strike activities and to exert some control over competition from other areas when a local union went on strike.

The national union could also try to establish wage and other standards extending beyond a single community. Under these circumstances, a growing amount of power and authority gravitated into the hands of the national union leaders. Local union leaders often did not relinquish authority readily. But in time, as organization in specific crafts spread, the locus of power in American trade unionism gradually shifted from the local to the national union.

Early attempts at federation with the formation of the National Trades Union (1834), and the National Labor Union (1866) had failed. But even when the second of these federations collapsed, many of the national unions survived.

The Knights of Labor

There was a new development in 1869 which was to lead to one of the most turbulent eras in the history of American trade unionism. In that year, the Knights of Labor was founded. The purpose of this organization was to establish "One Big Union." Even when they had banded into federations, leaders of the national craft unions had jealously guarded their power and prerogatives. The emergence of a new "federation" in which power was to be centralized at the top set the stage for a period of internecine warfare in the American labor movement.

The founder of the Knights of Labor was Uriah Stephens who as a young man had been trained for the Baptist ministry. Although the original nucleus of the Knights of Labor consisted of seven tailors, Stephens had come to the conclusion that craft unionism was not the right approach to organization because of what he considered to be its divisive effects on the labor movement. He wanted to bring together into a single organization all workers, including farmers, without regard to occupation, nationality, sex, or creed.

The Knights of Labor was initially a secret society. During most of the tenure of Uriah Stephens as Grand Master Workman the organization grew slowly although it continued to expand even after the crash of 1873. Many workers who might otherwise have joined stayed out of the organization, however, because of the vow of secrecy which each member had to swear. Catholic workers, for example, could not join a secret society. When Terrence V. Powderly became Grand Master Workman in 1879, he eliminated the secret vow. Up to that time Cardinal Gibbons had opposed the Knights of Labor, not only because of the vow but also because he believed it had socialistic tendencies. Powderly convinced him that this was not so, and the Cardinal's opposition ended. Following this, Catholic workers felt free to join the Order. Its membership then grew more rapidly. For example, on October 1, 1879, there were slightly more than nine thousand workers in the Order. By July 1, 1883 this number had increased to almost fifty-two thousand.

The most powerful impetus to the growth of the Knights of Labor came in 1885. There was a strike that year against a wage cut on the Wabash, and the Missouri, Kansas and Texas railroads, both of which were controlled by Jay Gould, one of the most powerful financiers in the nation at that time. The railroad shopmen went out first and were supported by the running crafts. At the Moberly, Missouri, shops a series of layoffs were interpreted as a lockout, and the Knights of Labor threatened to call a general strike on all Gould railways. Because he was engaged in the manipulation of his railroad stocks at that time, Gould felt that he could not afford a strike. Not only did Gould capitulate to the demands of the striking workers, but he firmly avowed his belief in trade unions. Following this, there was a virtual stampede into the Knights of Labor. Membership in 1885 stood at slightly more than 111,000. The following year it leaped to almost 730,000 and was a power that had to be reckoned with by employers in many industries and areas. But after this upsurge membership in the Knights of Labor declined, at first gradually, then precipitously. By 1890, membership was down to an estimated one hundred thousand and the Knights of Labor clearly was on the way out.

Conflict Between the Knights and the National Unions

Why did the Knights of Labor fail to survive? Essentially, the answer is that the notion of "One Big Union" came into conflict with the various national unions of skilled craftsmen. The Knights had wanted to organize everyone, excluding lawyers, bankers, gamblers, stockbrokers, and saloon keepers. But workers were not to be organized along occupational lines. Obviously, in an organization of any size, there must be some hierarchical arrangement, and this was recognized by the Knights. The organization which was planned was quite simple. At the top was the National Assembly. Below this were District Assemblies made up of Local Assemblies. The Local Assemblies could consist of existing local unions, most of which were made up of skilled craftsmen. But the leaders of the Knights did not intend that all Local Assemblies were to be limited to the members of a single craft. Some could follow industrial lines, and others could be mixed.

Relatively few District Assemblies actually came into existence. The first was established in Philadelphia, in 1873, made up of about eighty locals. A second was planned for the anthracite coal region, but was never actually formed. The third assembly covered locals in western Pennsylvania. Basically, the leaders of the Knights wanted the District Assemblies to be geographical in character—not limited to members of a specific craft or industry. However, some of the District Assemblies were made up almost entirely of workers in a specific industry and geographic area. Finally, following the upsurge to membership in 1886, National Assemblies were authorized. But this authorization came after the Knights of Labor had passed its apogee and was on the way down.

Throughout the period of rapid growth of the Knights of Labor there was a running battle between the leaders of the national craft unions and those who were dedicated to the notion of "One Big Union." In part, the rapid growth of the Knights of Labor from 1883 to 1886 was facilitated by the absorption of local unions already in existence. Some of these locals found themselves torn between two loyalties. If they belonged to a national union the officers of the national wanted to direct their bargaining and other activities. There was no place for the national union in the Knights of Labor table of organization, although it could accommodate locals of skilled craftsmen. Also, the leaders of the Knights wanted to have the final say on all union matters.

This conflict was apparent from the outset, and as early as 1881 the national unions—with support from some disaffected members of the Knights of Labor—had established the Federation of Organized Trades and Labor Unions of the United States and Canada. This organization was originally set up, among other things, to engage in political action, but it soon became embroiled in the growing controversy between the leaders of the Knights and the national unions. Throughout this controversy there were workers who belonged to both a national union and the Knights of Labor, but these workers could not give their complete loyalty to either.

The growing friction came to a head in 1886. On May 18 of that year a conference was held between the leaders of the Knights and the national unions which was expected to lead to a "treaty of peace." It was agreed that the Knights were not to attract local unions without the consent of national headquarters. The charter of any local joining the Knights without this consent was to be revoked. At the same time the Knights proposed an exchange of cards which would have permitted the continuation of dual membership. This was unanimously rejected by the leaders of the national unions. Little came out of this conference, and at their convention of 1886, the leaders of the Knights ordered all members of the Cigarmakers' Union—one of the more powerful craft unions—to resign from their union. The conflict was now out in the open. In December, 1886, at Columbus, Ohio, a convention of national unions was held. Although only about half of the national unions then in existence, plus a few City Centrals, were represented, the American Federation of Labor was formed at this convention. All national unions were urged to join, and the break with the Knights was complete.

After 1886, the membership of unions affiliated with the American Federation of Labor began to grow slowly, and membership in the Knights of Labor began to decline. The decline was accelerated when the Knights called a number of strikes which they lost. Continued resistance within the Knights to the formation of National Assemblies along craft or occupational lines also contributed to its eventual demise. Craft unions began to leave the Knights *en bloc* and to reaffiliate with nationals in the A.F. of L. The Knights of Labor was never formally disbanded, but after 1890 this organization was no longer a significant part of the American labor movement.

Chapter 3 The Era of the A.F. of L.

When the A.F. of L. was founded in 1886, its constituent national unions had a total membership of roughly 175,000, about one-fourth the membership of the Knights of Labor. Membership in the Knights declined sharply after 1886, while the number of workers in the A.F. of L. increased slowly. It was not until the turn of the century that the A.F. of L. could claim more members than the Knights of Labor had signed up at peak strength. However, membership in the A.F. of L. continued to grow slowly throughout the time it was the only federation of national trade unions in the United States.

Further efforts were made to conciliate the differences between the declining Knights of Labor and the slowly growing A.F. of L. As late as 1888, the Knights proposed a mutual recognition of membership cards which would have permitted a worker to belong to both a trade union and the Order. But at the same negotiations, leaders of the A.F. of L. proposed that the Knights revoke all charters of trade districts, and thus become a purely benevolent, educational, and humanitarian order. Under such conditions, leaders of the A.F. of L. averred, they were quite willing to have union members also belong to the Knights of Labor, but they completely rejected the notion that a worker who belonged only to the Knights was a union man. The practical effect of this was to keep members of the Knights who did not belong to one of the national trade unions out of closed shops.

The unions which banded together to form the A.F. of L., and those which subsequently joined, were organized along craft lines, and their membership consisted of skilled workers.[1] By the time the A.F. of L. was formed, the center of power in the craft unions had gravitated to their national headquarters. In setting up the A.F. of L., the leaders of the craft unions made sure that this power would not be surrendered to the offices of the Federation. It was also agreed by the national union leaders that there would be only one legitimate union in each occupation or industry. These agreements formed the two basic principles upon which the A.F. of L. was founded.

The Principle of Autonomy

The American Federation of Labor, it was hoped, would be the spokesman for all organized workers on some matters. But partly because of their prior experience with the Knights, and partly because of the structure of the unions which initially formed the Federation, it was agreed that there would be no interference from the outside with the activities of each of the individual national unions.

This meant that each national union would be free to determine which workers it would attempt to organize, the dues to be paid by each member, the tactics to be employed in organization, and the formulation of bargaining demands. Each of the craft unions was to be free to make its own plans with respect to its members. The Federation could take a stand on various issues of *public* policy, but it was not to tamper with the internal affairs of its constituent unions.

The Principle of Exclusive Jurisdiction

The second of the major principles upon which the A.F. of L. was founded called for one legitimate union in each trade. The great fear of the leaders of the national unions—and of the A.F. of L.—throughout the era under discussion was that of "dual" unionism, i.e. more than one union competing for membership within a single occupation.

This principle was at variance with that adopted by unions in other parts of the world. The British trade unions at that time, for example, held to the notion that no union had the exclusive right to organize any given group of workers. In the United States, while the craft unions which predominated by the end of the nineteenth century were anxious to limit their members to skilled

[1] There were two major exceptions; the United Mine Workers and the Brewery Workers—both industrial unions—enrolled all workers under their jurisdictions without regard to skill or occupational classifications.

tradesmen, they were equally anxious to avoid the splintering of these tradesmen into various competing groups. During the early stage of the development of the A.F. of L., the principle of exclusive jurisdiction posed relatively few problems. But later, as the complexity of economic life increased, it was to lead to a considerable amount of strife of the kind which most outsiders consider to be the least defensible, that is, jurisdictional disputes.

Somewhat surprisingly, the principle of exclusive jurisdiction worked fairly well during the early years of the A.F. of L. Dual unionism could not be entirely suppressed. There were, for example, dual unions in the clothing and shoe industries. Elsewhere, however, dual unionism failed to survive.

It was originally thought that one of the functions to be performed by the Federation would be the prevention of jurisdictional disputes. But it was not clear exactly how this was to be accomplished if the Federation was to be kept weak—and this was something the leaders of the national unions insisted upon.

There were a few cases, after the turn of the century, in which the A.F. of L. intervened to settle jurisdictional controversies by recommending amalgamation. This approach was most successful when the disputants consisted of one strong and one weak union. The leaders of a weak union could readily see that it would be the better part of valor to merge with their stronger brethren. But there were also cases of disagreement between two strong unions, when neither was willing to accept the A.F. of L.'s jurisdictional award. In a case decided in 1903, for example, the A.F. of L. ruled that the Operating Engineers were to have jurisdiction over all members of this craft wherever employed. Most other unions went along with this, but the Brewery Workers refused to give up their operating engineers who, incidentally, did not want to leave this union. Four years later, despite repeated gestures by the A.F. of L., the Brewers were still adamant. The A.F. of L. then revoked the charter of the Brewery Workers. The Brewers had many friends in the labor movement, however, and when the A.F. of L. met in convention that year the delegates ordered the restoration of the Brewery Workers' charter. They went beyond this to amend the A.F. of L. constitution relieving the Executive Council of its right to revoke charters, which henceforth could be done only by a two-thirds majority of delegates to the annual convention.

There were other difficulties with jurisdictional awards between pairs of strong unions, such as the Teamsters versus the Brewery

Workers, and the Carpenters opposing the Machinists, when both unions were represented on the Executive Council. Some of the A.F. of L.'s jurisdictional awards led to mergers. Some involving pairs of strong unions were never really settled. Others led to the withdrawal of unions from the Federation. Those who seceded were usually relatively weak unions. Of the fifty unions which withdrew from the A.F. of L. prior to 1933, for example, only a dozen were to survive their secession. This is at least a rough measure of the success which the relatively weak A.F. of L. had in enforcing the principle of exclusive jurisdiction.

No Political Involvement

The two basic principles of what some have termed "the A.F. of L. settlement" were autonomy and exclusive jurisdiction. A further assumption upon which the A.F. of L. operated was that American trade unions would have to rely upon economic power to achieve their ends. The American trade union movement was to avoid political alliances or entanglements. It must be remembered that by the time the A.F. of L. was formed, there was a fairly long history of labor organization in the United States, and that some of the earlier organizations had been basically reformist in character.

The leaders of the A.F. of L. made it clear that they had no intention of overthrowing the capitalistic system. The leaders of the craft unions wanted to improve the economic lot of their members. This was to be done by tightly sewing up each craft or trade so that strictly economic pressures—such as strikes and boycotts—could be brought to bear on recalcitrant employers who resisted their demands. The approach of A.F. of L. leaders was entirely pragmatic. The kind of unionism they forged was called "business unionism" by their critics both in this country and abroad. This term, which was used contemptuously by Socialists and others who condemned the A.F. of L. approach, was an appropriate one. Trade unions, their leaders insisted, were designed to get "more here and now" for their members. They were not to be concerned with ultimate goals and lofty aspirations. They were to achieve their stated goals by a show of their own economic muscle, not by relying upon political action.

This did not mean that trade union members were to ignore politics. It did mean, as the first president of the A.F. of L. succinctly put it, that American trade unions would "reward their friends and punish their enemies" without respect to party affiliation.

The Founders of the A.F. of L.

Who were the men who formed the first successful federation of national trade unions in the United States? Among the most active leaders of the movement were Adolph Strasser, P. J. McGuire, W. H. Foster, and Samuel Gompers. Strasser, who had emigrated to the United States from Germany, was president of the Cigarmakers Union, a powerful craft union in its day. P. J. McGuire was the founder and leader of the Brotherhood of Carpenters and Joiners, which was also a power in the late 19th-century labor movement. But the man who undoubtedly did more than anyone else to hold the new organization together was Samuel Gompers, formerly a vice president of the Cigarmakers Union. Perhaps the most important step taken at the Columbus convention at which the A.F. of L. was organized was the election of Gompers as president of the new Federation (at a salary of $1,000 per year). From that time on, Samuel Gompers devoted his life to the A.F. of L. He aspired to no public office, and refused to use his position in later years to add to his own income. He was totally devoted to the trade-union cause.

Both Strasser and Gompers had been reared in the tradition of German Socialism. They continued their study of this doctrine while they practiced their craft in New York. To ease the monotony of their tasks, the cigarmakers would designate one of their group to read aloud while the remainder worked. Each member would make a contribution to make up for the wages lost by the reader. Gompers, who was considered to have had a pleasant and resonant voice, was often designated as the reader. He would read aloud from Karl Marx's *Das Kapital,* or from other Socialist literature of the day.

Strasser and Gompers recognized, however, that socialism had little appeal for the average American worker who was job-conscious but not class-conscious. Indeed, many workers hoped to remain at their jobs only long enough to accumulate a stake which would permit them to go into business for themselves, or to move west in search of land. Though well grounded in socialist theory, both Strasser and Gompers rejected it as a guide line to the American labor movement. Although Strasser and Gompers continued to have an interest in the welfare of all workers, they felt that there was only one formula which could lead to trade-union success in the United States. This was the organization of skilled workers along craft lines in national unions which would manage their own internal affairs. Their objectives were to be achieved through economic strength rather than political action. The basic goal was the immediate improvement of wages, hours, and working conditions.

The craft unionists were anxious to be accepted by the society in which they operated, and they went to great pains to emphasize that they had no plans for the transformation of that society. This is illustrated by an excerpt from the testimony of Strasser before the U. S. Senate Committee on Education and Labor during a hearing held in 1883. The chairman of the committee had asked Mr. Strasser what ultimate ends were sought by trade unions. In reply, Strasser said: "We have no ultimate ends. We are going on from day to day. We are fighting only for immediate objects—objects that can be realized in a few years." Somewhat later, the chairman said, ". . . you are a little sensitive lest it should be thought you are a mere theorizer." To which Strasser replied: "Well, we say in our constitution that we are opposed to theorists, and I have to represent the organization here. We are all practical men."[2]

More than three decades later, Samuel Gompers was to reiterate these views. He stressed that the A.F. of L. was guided by the lessons of history; that it was bound to no theory of social reform, and that it sought only the immediate improvement of the economic conditions of workingmen. The founders of the A.F. of L. were thoroughly familiar with earlier unsuccessful attempts to establish even a moderately radical form of trade unionism in the United States. They were convinced that a successful trade union movement in this country had to be essentially conservative in its aims.

Gompers became president of the A.F. of L. in 1886, and was to continue in this office, with the exception of a single year (1894–95), until his death in 1925. He guided the A.F. of L. through its formative period during the years after the turn of the century when employer resistance hardened, and later when opposition from dissidents within some of the unions threatened to alter the fundamental character of American trade unionism by urging the adoption of a socialist program.

[2] J. B. S. Hardman, *American Labor Dynamics,* New York: Harcourt, Brace and Company, Inc. (1928), p. 99.

THE A.F. OF L. FROM 1886 TO 1920

A decade after the A.F. of L. had been formed, its leaders could feel that they had found the formula for a stable and successful brand of American trade unionism. The intervening years had not been easy. In 1892, for example, the Association of Iron and Steel Workers led a strike against the Carnegie Homestead Plant. It was a bitter strike, conducted with much violence, and the union was utterly defeated. By this time the Carnegie Corporation was the dominant firm in the steel industry, and when it broke off relations with the union other companies in the Pittsburgh area followed suit.

The following year saw the nation once again plunged into a severe financial panic, but fortunately for the A.F. of L. the depression which followed was relatively short. The next year, 1894, was also a bad one for the trade union movement. In that year the American Railway Union, led by Eugene V. Debs, went on strike against the Pullman Company. This union, which was making an effort to unite all railroad workers into a single organization, was not affiliated with the A.F. of L., but there was some pressure within the Federation for support of the Pullman strike. Gompers urged all A.F. of L. affiliates to stand clear of the strike which eventually collapsed when President Cleveland sent federal troops to Chicago, ostensibly to protect the U. S. mails but effectively to break the strike.

The violence of the Homestead and Pullman strikes, which led some to consider that it was necessary for the government to intervene in the latter dispute, caused many citizens to view the growing labor movement with alarm. Some of the public alarm died down, however, as economic conditions improved and the craft unions adhered fairly closely to the new brand of business unionism.

The Victory of Craft Unionism

The relative success of the older unions which had formed the A.F. of L., and their ability to survive the crash of 1893, stimulated the formation of an increasing number of new craft unions. Between 1897 and 1904, for example, the number of national and international unions affiliated with the A.F. of L. rose from 58 to 120. This number was to decline during the following decade, partly as a result of union mergers but also due to the liquidation of a few of the weaker unions.

After 1904, there was continued growth although it was quite slow. From 1897 to 1904, the number of union members in the United States increased from 447,000 to slightly more than two million. By 1914, however, this figure had increased to only 2.7 million. Much of the growth which occurred after 1904 was concentrated in a few of the stronger unions; the most rapid growth was in the building trades, transportation, communications, and in mining. In 1914, the unions in these industry groups accounted for 55 per cent of total union membership in the United States. Thus, craft unionism was limited to relatively few lines of economic activity. Most manufacturing industry was predominantly unorganized, and the same was true of virtually all service activities. The craft form of organization appeared to be particularly suitable in building construction and transportation. The major union in the coal industry, however, was organized along industrial lines. It was one of two unions in the country which had succeeded in establishing and maintaining this form of organization.

Emergence of the Labor-Management Agreement

By the late 1890's one of the goals of the craft unions was well along the road to realization. This was the signing of labor-management agreements which were the result of negotiations between union leaders and employers. Although there was no legal compulsion to do so at that time, a growing number of employers had "recognized" unions.

In 1890 an agreement was negotiated in the glass container industry, and in 1891 the National Union of Ironmoulders and the Stove Founders Defense Association signed an agreement which has often been characterized as the precursor of the modern labor-management agreement. The bituminous coal miners succeeded in negotiating an agreement in 1897, and the following year the anthracite miners also reached agreement with the operators. Organized printers signed a contract with an association of employers in 1898. Agreements between some of the building craft unions and employers, and also between the operating crafts and the railroads, had been signed as early as 1880, but these were exceptions, not the rule. By the turn of the century, however, a growing number of employers entered into agreements with unions representing craftsmen in their employ. When a trade union had achieved sufficient strength to negotiate a signed agreement with an employer—or better still with a group of employers—it had "arrived." The negotiated trade agreement was, of course, the hallmark of successful business unionism.

THE I.W.W.—A NEW THREAT OF RADICAL UNIONISM

Everything considered, the period from 1897 to 1904 was a good one for the A.F. of L. These were years of prosperity, and of rapid growth for the trade unions which experienced almost a four-fold increase in seven years. The craft unions were not without their problems, however, and during the decade following 1904 their problems were to multiply. Part of their troubles were due to the establishment of a rival labor organization in 1905—an organization which had an impact far out of proportion to its numerical strength.

The early growth of the craft unions was largely concentrated in the urban East where the building trades were important, and where there was a large number of railroad and other transport workers. The Miners, who were organized along industrial lines, were also highly successful in the East. But farther west, in the hard-rock mining communities and the scattered coal towns of the Mountain States, the threat of dual unionism had been raised as early as 1898 when the American Labor Union was established as a rival to the A.F. of L. This grew out of an earlier organization known as the Western Federation of Miners, which initially sought to organize only hard-rock miners and smelter employees.

The leaders of the American Labor Union were extremely militant, and they sought to broaden the scope of their organization to include all laborers in one big union. In June 1905, this group met with representatives of the Socialist Labor and Trade Alliance, and with leaders of a few dissident A.F. of L. locals. A scattering of intellectuals, members of various socialist parties, and some disgruntled trade unionists also attended this convention which was held in Chicago. The one feature that bound the delegates together was their militancy and revolutionary outlook.

Out of this assembly grew the Industrial Workers of the World, a revolutionary organization which was the complete antithesis of the conservative, job-conscious A.F. of L. Several of the more colorful radical leaders of the day played leading roles at this meeting including "Wild Bill" Haywood, of the Western Federation of Miners; Mother Jones, an organizer for the United Mine Workers; Daniel DeLeon, leader of the revolutionary Socialist Labor Party; and Eugene Debs, who headed the more moderate Socialist Party. But while these and other leaders of the I.W.W. could agree on the revolutionary ends of the new organization they were far from agreed on means. They wanted to abolish the wage system, but could not agree on whether this would best be accomplished through political action or by more direct measures. Almost from the start there were serious differences of opinion between the intellectual revolutionaries and the somewhat more pragmatic leaders of the miners. Within a few years, the Western Federation of Miners withdrew from the new organization it had helped create to became once again a relatively conservative trade union.

The leaders of the I.W.W. were exuberant in their revolutionary zeal. Organizers would move into a mining community and urge the local miners to go on strike. They were ruthless in their treatment of employers, and were not in the least averse to violence. After reaching a "settlement" the organizers would move on. After a time, without the leadership needed to hold them together, the miners were often persuaded to go back to their former terms of employment. Thus, while the I.W.W. created considerable stir throughout the West, its long-run achievements were negligible.

During the early days, when the I.W.W. limited its activities to the mining areas of the West, the leaders of the A.F. of L. were not seriously concerned, although they always opposed dual unionism. In 1912, however, the I.W.W. began to move into some of the industrial centers of the East, such as Lawrence, Massachusetts, and Paterson, New Jersey, where it led to bitter strikes whose scars were not eradicated for many years. The Paterson strike was a failure, and the I.W.W. left no lasting establishment in Lawrence. Following this unsuccessful incursion into the industrial Northeast membership in the I.W.W. declined sharply. Indeed, it has been estimated that total membership in the "Wobblies" never reached 60,000. However, the short-term impact of this turbulent and radical organization was far out of proportion to the number of card-carrying members it was able to sign up. The decline which started when the I.W.W. failed to achieve lasting trade agreements was hastened when its leaders opposed American entry into World War I. Our society has never been hospitable to radical organizations, and this has been especially true when emotions become highly-charged during wartime. While it seems likely that the I.W.W. would have disappeared in any event, our entry into World War I completed the decimation of this organization.

Leaders of the A.F. of L. became alarmed by the activities of the I.W.W., particularly after its brief foray into the East. Employers, and those sympathetic to the employers' point of view, used the record of the I.W.W. as a propaganda tool to combat the conservative A.F. of L. unions. The A.F. of L.'s leaders reacted by becoming even more conservative. Samuel Gompers, and other leaders of the A.F. of L., missed no opportunities to publicize the pragmatic, nonrevolutionary basis of craft unionism. They not only denounced the dual unionism of the I.W.W., but condemned its revolutionary goals and violent tactics. There is little evidence that these denunciations won the applause of many employers, or of the community at large, however. By the time the I.W.W. had started its campaign, employers, including many who recognized the conservatism of the A.F. of L., were organizing to resist the spread of unionism, especially in manufacturing.

GROWING JOB CONSCIOUSNESS

One obstacle to the formation of lasting trade unionism during the 19th century was the mobility of workers. There was a steady stream of immigrants, many of whom would stop in urban areas only long enough to accumulate sufficient savings to permit them to move westward. After the turn of the century, however, although the number of immigrants continued to rise, opportunities for self-employment and land ownership diminished. This strengthened the job-consciousness of craft unionists who felt that they had to protect themselves from the competition of the new immigrants; at first by limiting their organization to the skilled trades, but eventually by urging that restrictions be imposed upon the flow of immigrants into the nation. Partly because of technological developments, employers were not at first willing to go along with such restrictions.

The trend toward fewer and larger industrial units had started long before the advent of the A.F. of L. It was accelerated during the first quarter of the twentieth century by the development of mass production techniques. As the size of plants increased, employers found that they could break skilled jobs into their component parts so that the work could be performed by semi-skilled or, in some cases, unskilled laborers. In the building trades, transportation, and in mining, there was little opportunity to do this, and these were the sectors in which trade unionism grew. The assembly line technique was spreading throughout the manufacturing sector, however, especially in the heavy industries. This development effectively barred the entry of craft unions which limited their membership to the skilled trades.

Some employers actively recruited immigrants for the semi-skilled and unskilled jobs in their plants. In plants which could be departmentalized, the departments were staffed by workers of different national origins. This practice was followed in some of the gigantic textile mills of New England, for example, where the selection of workers for different departments was not left to chance. Many of the immigrants brought with them their antipathies toward other nationalities. They continued to speak their native language, and to follow many of their native customs, after coming to this country. This was not discouraged by employers since it was an effective bar to communication, and since it precluded solidarity of action by all the workers in the plant. Unions raised no objections to these practices; indeed, they made no overtures toward the growing number of semi-skilled and unskilled workers in manufacturing.

Coupled with growing employer opposition, and the side-effects of the activities of the I.W.W., this self-limitation to the skilled trades contributed to slow union growth from 1904 until our entry into World War I. In 1904, total union membership in the United States amounted to 6.4 per cent of the civilian labor force. In 1916, on the eve of our entry into World War I, this proportion had increased to only 6.9 per cent.

TRADE UNIONISM DURING WORLD WAR I

Most of the trade unions which had been founded before the formation of the A.F. of L. were unable to withstand economic adversity. Recurring financial panics often spelled their ruin, and the initial effects of the Civil War on unions were disastrous. By the time we were preparing to enter World War I, however, there had been vast changes. By that time federated craft unions had been able to survive for three decades. While their membership had increased only slowly there were relatively few years of actual decline. A growing number of employers had been forced to recognize unions, and this had been achieved without legal sanctions. Public acceptance of trade unionism was far from a reality, but at the same time public hostility had clearly diminished. There had been organized attacks by employers in some areas, and the well-publicized activities of the I.W.W. had no doubt contributed to the slow rate of union growth. But in spite of these obstacles, trade unions had expanded. A labor movement had been firmly established in the United States.

An important deterrent to rapid union growth throughout the life of the A.F. of L. was the structural rigidity of federated craft unions. The growing number of unskilled and semi-skilled workers in manufacturing were largely untouched by the unions in the A.F. of L. The building trades, transportation, and mining were the strongholds of organized labor. The great manufacturing enterprises of the nation had resisted trade unionism, and the craft unions were not flexible enough to override the opposition of the manufacturers.

Wartime Union Growth

From the turn of the century until the beginning of World War I, total union membership in the United States just about tripled, but it must be remembered that this growth was from a relatively small base. There was a strong upsurge in union membership during the war and the immediate postwar period, however. The number of workers belonging to unions almost doubled between 1916 and 1920 when there were more than five million union members in the nation. At that time they accounted for 12 per cent of the civilian labor force.

There were a number of reasons for this rapid growth. As thousands of young men entered the various services, labor shortages developed. At the peak of our war effort more than five million men had been drawn from the civilian labor force into the services. Also, the supply of labor had been sharply curtailed by our growing restrictions on immigration.

The leaders of the A.F. of L. strongly supported the war effort. The generally conservative views of union leaders encouraged the government to seek their wartime support, and also encouraged some employers to enter into agreements with them. Government operation of the railroads, and government administration of some other sectors of the economy, provided a further stimulus to union growth since the administrative agencies adopted policies which, by and large, encouraged union membership. Employers faced with an unprecedented demand for their products were reluctant to run the risk of strikes or other labor disturbances. They were also much more agreeable to union demands for higher wages than they had been in the past. This no doubt resulted less from altruistic or patriotic motives than the innovation of the cost-plus contract. Higher costs meant a larger "plus" and thus higher profits.

The growth of union membership was not widespread. As might be expected, most of this occurred in those industries, such as the metal-working, machinery, shipbuilding, and garment industries, most closely associated with the war effort. It has been estimated that about three-fourths of all union growth between 1915 and 1920 was concentrated in these industries.[3] Thus, growth was largely limited to existing craft unions.

Unions after the Armistice

Although there was a brief business recession shortly after announcement of the Armistice of November, 1918, union membership continued to grow. Indeed, there were large gains in total membership both in 1919 and 1920. The drop in business activity was very brief, and the labor market remained tight until demobilization was completed. Also, the demand for American products remained at a high level while the war-torn economies of the European combatants were being restored. Due to favorable economic conditions, and partly no doubt due to inertia, unions continued to sign up new members. For a time it seemed as though broadly-based trade unionism might be realized in the United States, but the immediate postwar prosperity was relatively short-lived. The economy took a downward plunge in 1920, and this marked an end to the growth of federated craft unionism in the United States.

TRADE UNIONS DURING THE 1920's

Union Membership in the Twenties

After five years of steady and rapid growth, union membership began to decline in 1920. This decline continued in every year but one until 1934. It would be going too far to say that the institution of trade unionism had been widely accepted during World War I. But active resistance to unionism was at a minimum when the overriding concern of the nation was the defeat of Germany. The postwar reaction to the inevitable dislocations of war came slowly, but when it came it did so with a vengeance.

World War I had involved America in a large-scale international venture for the first time. By the end of 1919, however, it was quite clear that the mood of international cooperation had passed. The forces of isolationism were victorious in Congress, and they succeeded in keeping us out of the League of Nations. On the domestic scene there was a resurgence of conservatism. The successful Bolshevik Revolution in Russia added to the alarm of those who, without looking carefully into the matter, suspected

[3] Leo Wolman, *Ebb and Flow in Trade Unionism*, New York: National Bureau of Economic Research (1936), p. 28.

all trade unions of radical leanings. There were, to be sure, a few radical political parties in the nation—including the Communist Labor and the Communist parties. Competent scholars have estimated, however, that the membership of all the radical parties lumped together at that time would account for scarcely one-tenth of one percent of the nation's adult population. There was great concern about the "Red Menace," however. Anything which appeared to threaten the "return to normalcy" was often linked in the public mind with the threat of revolution, and the press rarely did anything to disabuse the public of this notion.

The Postwar "Strike Wave"

During World War I and the immediate post-Armistice period there was little strike activity. Late in 1919, however, there were a few widely publicized strikes. These were cited by opponents of trade unionism as examples of the growing threat which unions posed to the American way of life. The Boston Police Strike, which began in September 1919, provided a great deal of propaganda for those preaching the alleged threat of trade unionism to the American system.

The Boston police had a number of grievances. Their minimum pay was less than $100 per month, and out of this the officers had to buy their own uniforms. Following the lead of the nation's craftsmen, the Boston police organized a union and affiliated with the A.F. of L. They did this despite an injunction from Police Commissioner Curtis not to affiliate with an outside organization. Charges were brought against a number of officers known to be union members and, following a hearing on police union activities, nineteen officers were suspended by the Commissioner. The remainder of the force then threatened to strike. The mayor of Boston appointed a committee to settle the dispute, and this committee suggested a compromise. Commissioner Curtis refused to consider a compromise settlement, however, and on September 9 a large proportion of the force failed to show up for evening roll call. The press quickly announced that Boston was almost entirely without police protection. The city's hoodlums—recognizing an unparalleled opportunity when they saw one—thereupon had a field day. Windows were smashed, stores were looted, and there were numerous incidents of violence. The mayor asked Governor Calvin Coolidge for assistance from the National Guard, and on the following day this was provided. A call was also issued for volunteer police. Both the Guardsmen and the volunteers were inexperienced, however, and the city remained in a state of virtual anarchy.

The Boston Central Labor Union briefly considered calling a general strike in support of the policemen's demands, but recognizing that public opinion was overwhelmingly against the police strike, the trade union leaders decided against this action. Commissioner Curtis then began to deal with the strike on his own terms. He discharged the nineteen officers who had been suspended, and began to recruit a new force. Samuel Gompers protested to Governor Coolidge who then issued the dictum that there was "no right to strike against the public safety by anybody, anywhere, anytime." This clearly spelled the end of the Boston Police Strike. It also made Coolidge a national figure, and undoubtedly played an important part in his subsequent election as vice-president.

Although local in character, the Boston Police Strike attracted national attention. To the public it seemed that this was only the beginning of a wave of strike activity. Shortly after the beginning of the Boston Police Strike, there was a large-scale walkout in the steel industry involving several hundred thousand workers. Although subsequent investigation revealed that the steel workers had a number of genuine grievances, steel management quickly labeled the strike as Communist inspired. One of the leaders of the strike was William Z. Foster—at that time a Syndicalist—who subsequently became a leader of the American Communist Party.

There was little mention of the real issues involved in press accounts of the steel strike. At that time the standard shift in the steel industry was twelve hours, and when a worker changed shifts he was on the job for twenty-four consecutive hours without rest. The pay of steel workers was low, and working conditions were often deplorable. These factors seemed much less important to the newspapers than the fact that Foster was seeking to organize the workers along industrial lines. Steel management—led by Elbert H. Gary of U.S. Steel—refused to have any dealings with union spokesmen, and the strike eventually collapsed. Even before the steel strike had ended, however, there was a major strike in the coal fields which added to the public alarm. The miners had an industrial union, and some of their spokesmen had advocated nationalization of all coal mines. This seemed to clinch the case for those who equated unionism with radicalism.

There were growing demands that the government "do something" to halt the wave of "labor terrorism." Attorney General A. Mitchell Palmer, whose name had been prominently associated with the "Red Scare" which followed World War I was quick to respond to what he considered the pressure of public opinion. President Wilson, by then too ill to keep in touch with daily affairs was not aware of what was going on, and could not restrain his Attorney General. The day before the coal strike was scheduled to begin, Mr. Palmer secured an injunction from a federal court enjoining the leaders of the miners' union from doing anything to further the strike. In spite of the injunction, almost four hundred thousand coal miners walked out of the pits. Their leaders could not participate in the strike without running the risk of criminal contempt of court and the strike collapsed.

There can be no doubt that by the beginning of the 1920's the public had grown increasingly fearful about trade unionism. There were other factors, however, which contributed to the decline of the federated craft unions in the United States. These included important shifts in the composition of the work force as the result of growing mass production, a new and energetic "open shop" campaign, and general prosperity which, however, concealed a substantial amount of unemployment—much of it concentrated in the skilled crafts which had been highly organized by A.F. of L. unions.

The American Plan

In the early 1920's anti-red hysteria, and a number of major strikes made it relatively easy for certain employers to openly attack trade unions. "Yellow-dog" contracts, which bound workers not to join a union as a condition of employment, were widely used by employers to combat what they termed the "un-American" institution of trade unionism. The main attack was on the closed shop. Under this form of agreement employers hired union members only, and obtained workers from union hiring halls rather than going directly into the labor market. A housing shortage after World War I was attributed by some to the high wages of construction workers and the allegedly restrictive practices of building trade unions. The slow pace of construction cut sharply into the ranks of the construction unions. In three years, according to Wolman's estimates, membership in construction unions dropped by almost one hundred thousand from the peak of nearly nine hundred thousand which had been reached in 1920.[4]

A substantial number of employers proclaimed their acceptance of the principle of trade unionism, but many of them argued that unions should not be "outside" organizations. According to this

[4] *Ibid.*, p. 30.

employer-sponsored approach, unions should be restricted to the workers of a single company; they should free themselves from the clutches of "dues hungry outsiders." In a number of industries this appeal was successful. Local unions broke away from their national organizations and became "company unions." The term "company union" eventually came to have a definite connotation. It meant a company-*dominated* union which engaged in little if any collective bargaining.

Why did workers in some industries break away from the national unions which contributed to their collective strength? Some employers were rather outspoken about their preference for company unions. And they could point out that growing unemployment in some areas would make it relatively easy for them to recruit non-union workers. Also, many workers fortunate enough to remain steadily employed, accepted the arguments that the United States had reached a state of permanent prosperity, and that their ability to share in this depended upon labor-management "cooperation."

This prosperity was not reflected in a rising wage level. One sector of the economy which failed to share in the new prosperity of the "twenties" was agriculture. Farm prices fell, so that the real earnings of industrial workers went up. Increasingly aggressive competition in the textile and garment industries also led to reduced prices for clothing. Industrial workers were able to obtain the necessities of life on better terms than they had in the past. Under such circumstances there was little pressure for wage increases, and indeed the A.F. of L. unions were often unable to forestall wage cuts.

Finally, the 1920's will be remembered as the decade of unrestrained speculation. Many workers were induced to share in the promised riches of the stock market by purchasing shares in the companies which employed them. Since these workers became capitalists, although rather small ones, they could be convinced that their best interests were tied to the fortunes of the company. Many workers took a somewhat dim view of the unions which allegedly were hampering managerial efficiency and curtailing company earnings. Such workers could be easily induced to switch from a bona fide trade union to a company union.

The Acceleration of Mass Production

Another factor which contributed to the decline of craft unions during the 1920's was the rapid spread of mass-production techniques. The automobile industry began to grow rapidly during this decade and, as the demand for automobiles increased, manufacturers turned increasingly to assembly line methods. These techniques spread to other industries engaged in continuous production, such as steel. Jobs in the mass production industries were carefully engineered to reduce them to the lowest skills. Some jobs which had formerly been performed by skilled craftsmen were broken into components; each of the operations could then be handled by semi-skilled, or at times unskilled, workers after brief on-the-job training.

The A.F. of L. responded by stepping up its organizational activities in steel, the nation's largest industry in terms of value of output, and in the automobile industry. But the craft unionism of the A.F. of L. did not accommodate itself to the growing number of unskilled and semi-skilled workers in these industries. There was also an effort to organize the rapidly expanding southern textile industry, and to bring within the A.F. of L. the growing number of women workers in industry in general. All of these organizing campaigns ended in failure.

The A.F. of L. could not cope with the new era of prosperity. Its leaders refused to adapt the rigid structure of their craft unions which might have permitted a greater amount of organization in the mass-production industries. Instead of becoming more militant, the union leaders tried to adapt to their changing environment by becoming more conservative. Even more than in the past, they preached the gospel of "business unionism." Wages, they urged, should be tied to increasing productivity, and they promised that organized labor would cooperate with management to increase overall efficiency. But these pleas, directed both to the unorganized workers and to management, fell on deaf ears. The blandishments of "bread and butter" unionism had little appeal for the employed industrial workers whose real wages were rising. This made it relatively easy for employers to resist the sporadic attempts by unions to organize the unorganized. By 1929, the total number of union members in the country had dropped to 3.4 million. This represented a decline of about 33 per cent from 1920, despite the fact that the nation's labor force had grown during this period.

Then came the financial crash of October, 1929 which rocked the foundations of American capitalism. The new era of "permanent" prosperity had come to an end. Unrestrained speculation had greatly inflated the book value of stocks, and the dizzying upward spiral of equity prices stopped abruptly, then plunged downward.

Within a matter of months, unemployment was widespread. Much of this was concentrated among the unorganized workers in mass production industries. To a lesser extent it also affected the nation's skilled craftsmen. Union membership continued to decline after 1929 as unemployment spread throughout the nation. By 1933, total membership had dropped below the three million mark, and fewer than 6 per cent of the nation's civilian workers belonged to trade unions. In numerical terms, trade unionism in the United States was weaker than it had been at any time since 1917.

Chapter 4 The American Labor Movement Comes of Age

The stock market crash of 1929 ushered in the longest and deepest depression in American history. It was some time after the crash, however, before it was widely recognized that this depression was different from those which our economic system had successfully weathered in the past. After the first precipitous drop in economic activity in the fall of 1929 there was a slower decline which continued until 1933. During much of this period many businessmen and economists confidently predicted that there would be an upturn, but the upturn did not come.

The political campaign of 1932 dealt largely with the depression and with means of combatting it. The New Deal government was swept into office by an alarmed electorate which looked to the federal government to get the economic machine back on the track once again. The first measures taken by the new government were largely of an emergency nature. During the early days of the New Deal there was little thought of fundamental reform in our economic system; it was only after the depression had persisted for a number of years that lasting reforms were initiated. Among these reforms were some which had a profound effect on union growth and on the role which unions were to play in our economic system. The first New Deal legislation to deal specifically with the trade union issue was a jerry-built law, passed in 1933, known as the National Industrial Recovery Act.

The National Industrial Recovery Act was the result of a somewhat frantic effort by Congress to attack the depression on a broad front. Its major purpose was to stimulate a revival of the economy. But Section 7(a) of the Act stipulated that workers had the right to organize unions and to bargain collectively through representatives of their own choosing without fear of employer interference, restraint, or coercion. Many employers, however, refused to take this section of the law seriously since they were advised by their attorneys that it would be declared unconstitutional. Also, the Act failed to distinguish clearly between employer-dominated company unions and independent labor organizations. As a consequence, while there was considerable union growth between 1933 and 1935 —when the NIRA was declared unconstitutional—most of this was in company unions. It has been estimated that membership in company unions amounted to about 1.3 million in 1932, and that the number of workers in such organizations increased to approximately 2.5 million by 1935.[1] By 1935, the members of company unions amounted to about 60 per cent of the number in independent trade unions.

About three-fifths of all company unions were formed between 1933 and 1935. Although much of the membership in independent unions was concentrated in the nation's smaller industrial plants, company unions were formed in some of the nation's larger enterprises. The liberal senators and congressmen who had insisted upon including Section 7(a) in the NIRA were concerned about the growth of employer-dominated company unions and the failure of independent unions to make headway under the law. There was relatively little dismay in Congress when the Supreme Court ruled that this entire piece of hastily-constructed legislation was unconstitutional.

There were two subsequent developments which were to have a profound effect upon the trade union movement. These were enactment of the National Labor Relations Act—better known as the Wagner Act—and a split in the A.F. of L. which was to lead to the subsequent formation of a new federation, the Congress of Industrial Organizations.

The National Labor Relations Act of 1935

Some of the detailed provisions of the Wagner Act will be discussed in a later chapter which deals with public policy toward trade unions. But it would be difficult to understand trade union development in the United States during the latter half of the 1930's without specific reference to this law.

The Wagner Act, unlike the earlier NIRA, dealt only with the matter of trade union organization, and it was far more carefully thought out than the law which had been declared unconstitutional.

[1] Millis and Montgomery, *Organized Labor,* New York: McGraw-Hill (1945) p. 194.

Two provisions of the law in particular, Sections 7 and 8, guaranteed that if workers in a company wished to form an independent union they were free to do so. For example, Section 7 declared that: "Employees shall have the right to self-organization, to form, join, or assist labor organizations, to bargain collectively through representatives of their own choosing, and to engage in concerted activities, for the purpose of collective bargaining or other mutual aid or protection." For the first time in our history the complete legality of trade unions was established by this section of the Wagner Act.

Equally important was Section 8 of the law which outlawed company-dominated unions. Among the provisions of this section was one which prohibited employers from dominating or interfering with the formation or administration of any labor organization. Employers were prohibited from contributing financial or other support to any labor organization to forestall the formation of company unions. Another provision of this section prohibited discrimination against workers for union activity. And finally, the provision which put teeth into the law was one which made it an unfair labor practice for an employer "to refuse to bargain collectively with the representatives of his employees . . ." It is important to stress that the National Labor Relations Act did not *compel* an employer to enter into a union agreement; all that the employer was compelled to do was to meet and negotiate with representatives of his employees chosen by them for collective bargaining purposes.

To administer the Wagner Act, Congress provided for a three man National Labor Relations Board. The Board had the assistance of a sizeable staff of investigators, including field examiners, attorneys, and review officers operating through regional offices, who helped them administer and enforce the law.

At first, many employers thought that the Wagner Act would go the way of the earlier NIRA—that it would be declared unconstitutional. This issue was not decided until 1937 in *NLRB v. Jones & Laughlin Steel Corp.,* when the Supreme Court upheld the constitutionality of the Act. Trade union leaders were jubilant; henceforth there could be no question about the legality of trade unions, and employers could no longer avoid meeting and negotiating with trade union leaders if a majority of the employees voted for union representation.

Union membership started to grow again in 1935, and it grew rapidly and steadily until the end of World War II. There can be no doubt that the Wagner Act was a powerful stimulus to union growth. It is difficult to assess the effects of this Act in isolation, however, since another event occurred in 1935 which permitted unions to penetrate the mass-production industries which had heretofore successfully resisted organization. This was the split in the A.F. of L. which led to a new federation of industrial unions, the result of a long-smoldering debate which had gone on among the top leaders of the Federation for many years.

The A.F. of L. Split and the Formation of the C.I.O.

Even before the Wagner Act was passed, a faction within the American Federation of Labor had been urging structural reform to permit organization of the vast number of workers in mass-production industries who were not eligible for membership in the existing craft unions. But the principle of craft unionism was so firmly imbedded in the thinking of those who controlled the A.F. of L. that the radical change needed to organize workers along industrial lines was not seriously considered. At the 1933 convention of the A.F. of L., a conference was authorized to study the problem of organizing the unorganized. In January of the following year this conference proposed the establishment of "federal unions" to be affiliated directly with the A.F. of L. in those industries where craft unions had made no progress. The language of the proposal was somewhat equivocal, however, on the issue of craft versus industrial unions.

At the 1934 convention the issue was discussed intensively and debated heatedly. Once again the Executive Council of the A.F. of L. reiterated the urgent necessity of organizing workers in the automotive, cement, aluminum, and steel industries. But the leaders of craft unions, jealously guarding their prerogatives, would not yield on the issue of structural change. Workers in the mass-production industries, according to the resolution passed, would be organized into federal unions. It was assumed that these workers would be channeled into the appropriate craft unions at a later time. There were some efforts during the following year to put this plan into practice, but it met with limited success. Meanwhile, those leaders in the A.F. of L. who urged unrestricted industrial unionism, were becoming increasingly dissatisfied. The issue finally came to a head at the Atlantic City Convention of 1935.

At Atlantic City, a minority of the Committee on Resolutions submitted a report which bluntly called for the establishment of industrial unionism. After bitter debate the convention voted by a substantial margin to reject the report. However, even before the convention was adjourned, those who supported industrial unionism held an informal conference and agreed to keep in touch with each other on this issue. On November 10, 1935, shortly after the A.F. of L. convention had ended, the officers of eight unions, representing slightly more than 900,000 workers, met to form the Committee for Industrial Organization. Although this was initially a somewhat loose organization, its avowed purpose was the organization of workers in mass-production industries without regard to craft jurisdiction. Shortly afterwards, six other unions joined the original eight in the C.I.O.

In a program adopted at the November 10 meeting, the leaders of the new committee stated that they had no intention of forming a "dual" federation, and indicated that they would continue to work within the A.F. of L. But in January, 1936, the Executive Council of the A.F. of L. expressed concern about the new organization and suggested that it be immediately dissolved. The organizers of the Committee refused to comply, and the member unions of the C.I.O. were suspended from the A.F. of L. in July. Later that year, at the A.F. of L. convention, the Executive Council's suspension order was overwhelmingly accepted, partly because the rebellious industrial unions were not represented. Although the Committee did not become a permanent organization until two years later—at which time it changed its name to the Congress of Industrial Organizations—the American labor movement was definitely split in two at that time.

The unions which had left the A.F. of L. then began a sustained drive to organize workers in the clothing, printing, textile, and hat industries, as well as in glass, steel, autos, rubber, and electrical machinery. They moved into oil fields and refineries and into the nation's shipyards. Spearheading the drive for industrial unionism was John L. Lewis, President of the United Mine Workers of America. His union required no structural reorganization since it had always been organized along industrial lines.

In each industry, special organizing committees were set up which eventually became national or international unions. The organizing committees met stiff resistance. They moved into industries which had long resisted union organization, except among some of the more highly skilled craftsmen. There was considerable violence and bloodshed. This often alarmed many citizens who recognized that the advocates of industrial unionism were less conservative than the leaders of the A.F. of L. The public was further led to believe by press reports that the leaders of the vigorous organizing committees were Communists, or at least "fellow travelers."

The radicalism of the early C.I.O. leaders was greatly exaggerated, however. Some of the organizing committees made use of young Communists during the early days of their forays into open-shop industries. But with very few exceptions, the leaders of the C.I.O. organizing committees accepted the American economic system quite as fully as their A.F. of L. counterparts. Once they had successfully penetrated the industries they set out to organize, the C.I.O. conducted a successful purge of Communists in strategic positions. Some of the tactics employed—such as the "sit down" strikes in the automobile industry—added to the public alarm. But once the major firms in the mass-production industries had recognized the new unions, the latter settled down to the tactics which had been employed by earlier trade unions.

The A.F. of L. unions did not simply sit by and watch the progress of the new industrial C.I.O. unions. The earlier philosophy of "voluntarism," which had relied on the grass roots formation of unions by workers with a common skill, was largely scrapped by the A.F. of L. which stepped up its own organizing activities. Many of the principles to which the A.F. of L. leaders had clung before the split were gradually ignored as the craft unions which remained in the older Federation stepped up their organizing activities to match the gains of the C.I.O. unions. There can be little doubt that the formation of a new and competing federation did much to revitalize the A.F. of L. Under the stimulus of competition from the industrial unions, and aided by the sanctions provided by the Wagner Act, the A.F. of L. unions conducted a strenuous campaign to add to their membership. In spite of the fact that the economy remained depressed with widespread unemployment, when World War II broke out total union membership in the United States had reached an all-time peak of 8.6 million.

Trade Union Growth during World War II

World War II provided a powerful impetus to union growth. When the attack on Pearl Harbor suddenly plunged the nation into a full-scale world conflict, labor-management differences were subordinated to the broader goal of military success. There was a tremendous amount of slack in the economy when Pearl Harbor was attacked, but the rapid mobilization of millions of young men, coupled with an all-out production effort, quickly eliminated unemployment. Labor shortages developed, particularly in strategic industries, and labor and management cooperated to meet the wartime emergencies. Federal agencies were set up to control wages and prices, and the War Labor Board was established to handle labor-management disputes which might affect the war effort. Technically, the status quo was to be maintained with respect to union organization. Wartime regulations were supposedly designed to neither encourage nor discourage union membership. The device adopted to maintain this state of affairs was known as the "maintenance-of-membership" agreement. Such agreements required that workers who were union members at the time the agreement went into effect had to maintain their membership as a condition of employment. The object was to prevent workers who had been union members from leaving their unions in a tight labor market, but these agreements were not supposed to force new workers entering the labor market to join unions. However, the sharp upsurge in employment during a time when employers offered little resistance to trade unions led to a rapid rise in membership. By 1945 when World War II ended, there were about 12.7 million union members in the nation, and they accounted for almost 23 per cent of the civilian labor force. World War II consolidated the gains which had been initiated by the twin forces of the Wagner Act and the A.F. of L.-C.I.O. split in 1935.

The Post-War Reaction to Trade Unions—the Taft-Hartley Act

American trade unions emerged from World War II as a powerful force in our society. Unions had participated wholeheartedly in the war effort, and opposition to trade unions was negligible during the war. But following World War II—as had been the case after the first World War—a wave of conservatism swept the country. While some of the excesses which had followed World War I were avoided, there was mounting alarm over the tactics of trade unions during the post-war period. A conservative Congress enacted a new law governing labor-management relations which many believed to be less one-sided than the earlier Wagner Act—the Labor-Management Relations Act of 1947, better known as the Taft-Hartley Act. This law retained the basic provisions of Sections 7 and 8 of the Wagner Act which protected the rights of workers to organize unions, and required management to meet and negotiate with union representatives where a majority of workers voted for representation. But in addition, it specified a series of unfair labor practices for unions, and eliminated some of the restrictions on management's ability to express its opinion of unions, so long as such expression contained no threats of reprisal or coercion.[2]

During the hearings preceding enactment of the Taft-Hartley Act, union spokesmen refused to make any concessions. They insisted that the Wagner Act was entirely satisfactory and that no changes were required. Spokesmen for organized business groups argued to the contrary, however, and in the climate of the times their views prevailed. Once the law was enacted it was denounced as a "slave labor" act by union leaders and some predicted that this was only the first step in a broader onslaught on the American trade union movement. The so-called "right to work" provision of the Taft-Hartley Act was particularly objectionable to union leaders. It permitted those states which chose to do so to outlaw the union shop, under which workers are required to join the union after accepting a job. They felt that this would make it more difficult for unions to organize the unorganized in those areas, such as the South, where unions had made little headway.

The rate of union growth was definitely slowed down after 1947, but the extent to which this was due to the Taft-Hartley Act alone is debatable. There were undoubtedly other factors which contributed to the declining rate of union growth, but these were largely ignored by union spokesmen who continued to demand total repeal of the new Labor-Management Relations Act. During subsequent election campaigns union political activity was stepped up. Representative Hartley was defeated when he ran for office again, and the unions worked hard to defeat Senator Taft when he came up for re-election in Ohio, but without success.

Some union leaders undoubtedly feared a loss of membership, similar to that of the 1920's, under the Taft-Hartley Act. But this did not happen. Although unions had already succeeded in organizing a large proportion of the nation's manufacturing workers—with the notable exception of textiles, chemicals, and a few smaller industries—total membership in trade unions continued to rise. The growth rate was much slower than it had been in the past, however. For several years union leaders continued to press for repeal of the Taft-Hartley Act, but when the likelihood of this became increasingly remote, they settled for the removal of certain objectionable features—such as elimination of the non-communist affidavit formerly required of unions wishing to use the machinery of the National Labor Relations Board.

[2] Further details of the Taft-Hartley Act will be discussed in Chapter 8.

Slowly union leaders came to recognize that their position in our society had changed. They were no longer regarded as the underdogs; their power was now recognized even by legislators and others basically sympathetic to the trade union cause. Partly because of the changing climate of public opinion, and partly because of the decline in the rate of union growth, the leaders of the A.F. of L. and C.I.O. began to reexamine their respective positions and to consider the prospect of merging into a single federation. Some union leaders believed that the fragmentation of union power resulting from the split in the House of Labor in the 1930's was not serving the best interests of the American labor movement. They began to hold preliminary discussions to consider the prospects of reuniting the two federations.

Even before World War II, there had been some preliminary—if highly tentative—discussions about the feasibility of a reunified labor movement. While these early efforts were unsuccessful they were renewed from time to time even during the war years. By the end of the 1940's, it became apparent that the chances for a successful merger were increasing. One of the obstacles to reunion was removed when the C.I.O. expelled some of its unions which had been charged with Communist-domination. Meanwhile, the issue of craft versus industrial unions had diminished in importance. While the A.F. of L. was still broadly characterized as a federation of craft unions and the C.I.O. as a federation of industrial unions, some of the differences had disappeared. During the period of active rivalry between the two federations some of the A.F. of L. unions had modified their structures to such an extent that they came to resemble industrial unions. The leaders of the two federations began to suggest that the differences which divided them were less important than the threat of outside opposition to a divided labor movement.

Leaders of the A.F. of L. and the C.I.O. began to work together on political and legislative matters. From the beginning, the C.I.O. had played an active part in political affairs, and leaders of the A.F. of L. gradually abandoned their opposition to political action. The Korean War during the early 1950's brought the two federations closer together when their leaders worked jointly to develop an emergency defense program. A further step toward unity was taken in 1953 when a "no-raiding" agreement was negotiated by the two federations and ratified by their conventions.

The movement toward merger gained impetus in 1954 following the establishment of "unity committees" by each of the federations.

The basic agreement to merge was reached as early as October, 1954, but the details of the proposed merger—including the jurisdictions of competing unions in the two federations—were not worked out at that time.

The executive boards of the A.F. of L. and the C.I.O. approved the terms of the merger in February, 1955. Their last conventions were held on December 1 and 2 of that year. These conventions approved the merger agreement and an "implementation agreement" which was designed to bring the two federations together without formally dissolving either organization. A constitution for the merged federation was also approved at these conventions.

The American Federation of Labor and Congress of Industrial Organizations (AFL-CIO) was founded on December 5, 1955. At the first convention George Meany, who had led the A.F. of L. into the merger, was elected president. Walter Reuther stepped down from the presidency of the C.I.O. to become one of 27 vice presidents and head of the Industrial Union Department of the new federation. Under the constitution of the AFL-CIO, the president, the secretary-treasurer, and the vice presidents make up the twenty-nine-man Executive Council which governs the federation between its biennial conventions.

Under the terms of the merger, state and local bodies were required to combine within two years. The affiliated unions of the former A.F. of L. and C.I.O. were also encouraged to combine in those circumstances where a single national union seemed appropriate. But such mergers were not made mandatory by the new federation and only a few have taken place. Conflicts between competing unions were also to be settled on a voluntary basis.

Both sides had made genuine concessions in arriving at the merger agreement. The new federation is a conglomerate of unions organized predominantly along craft lines, alongside others which have organized workers without respect to occupation. It is significant of the changes that had taken place in the older federation that more than half of the affiliates of the new Industrial Union Department had formerly belonged to the A.F. of L. As members of a common parent body the affiliated unions agreed to continue to abide by the earlier no-raiding agreement and a few signed mutual assistance pacts. Long before the merger, the A.F. of L. had departed from its earlier position of avoiding political action to establish Labor's League for Political Education, a counterpart to the C.I.O.'s Political Action Committee. In the merged federation these activities have come together under the Committee on Political Education (COPE).

The rivalry between A.F. of L. and C.I.O. unions during the twenty years of their separate existence no doubt contributed to the growth of total union membership. The A.F. of L., which had been unwilling to change its structure prior to the split, was forced to depart from earlier practices when the C.I.O. began its explosive growth. The split definitely settled the question of how to go about organizing the mass-production industries. Once a large proportion of workers in manufacturing had been organized, however, the going became more difficult for both federations. By the middle of the 1950's their leaders were convinced that they had more to gain than to lose from a merger.

At the time of the merger it was announced that the reunited labor movement would step up its organizing activities, particularly outside of manufacturing where union growth had been proceeding very slowly. The hopes expressed at that time have not been realized, however. In 1955, there were about 17.7 million union members in the United States, accounting for approximately 27 per cent of the civilian labor force. Slightly more than one out of three workers in non-agricultural employment belonged to trade unions. Growth continued to be slow during the first five years of the merged federation; by 1960 there were only slightly more than 18 million union members in the nation, and union membership had grown at a slower rate than the labor force. In relative terms there had been a modest decline since 1955. Little headway was made in organizing white-collar and professional workers, and declining employment in some industries led to net losses in some of the national unions.

The merger had solved problems which had plagued the American labor movement for some time, but clearly it had not paved the way for a revival of rapid union growth. While the new organization is likely to endure, not all of the personal and jurisdictional rivalries in the House of Labor have been resolved. New problems arose to plague the leaders of organized labor in the United States during the relatively prosperous decade of the 1950's. Some of the more important of these will be discussed in the concluding section of this book.

REFERENCES

BOOKS

Commons, J. R., and Associates, *History of Labor in the United States,* four volumes, New York: The Macmillan Company (1918–1935).

Galenson, Walter, *The CIO Challenge to the AFL,* Cambridge, Massachusetts: Harvard University Press (1960).

Millis, Harry A., and Royal E. Montgomery, *Organized Labor,* New York: McGraw-Hill Book Company (1945).

Perlman, Selig, *History of Trade Unionism in the United States,* New York: The Macmillan Company (1937).

U.S. Department of Labor, *Brief History of the American Labor Movement,* Bureau of Labor Statistics Bulletin 1000, revised, Washington: U.S. Government Printing Office (1957).

Ware, Norman, *Labor in Modern Industrial Society,* Boston: D. C. Heath and Company (1935).

Wolman, Leo, *Ebb and Flow in Trade Unionism,* New York: National Bureau of Economic Research (1936).

ARTICLES

Bernstein, Irving, "The Growth of American Unions," *The American Economic Review,* XLIV (June 1954), pp. 301–318.

———, ———, "The Growth of American Unions, 1945–60," *Labor History,* Vol. 2 (Spring 1961), pp. 131–157.

Ulman, Lloyd, "The Development of Trades and Labor Unions," and "Unionism and Collective Bargaining in the Modern Period," Chapters 13 and 14 in Seymour E. Harris, *American Economic History,* New York: McGraw-Hill Book Company (1961), pp. 366–482.

Chapter 5 Theories of the Labor Movement

The preceding chapters have sketched the development of trade unions in the United States from colonial times to the AFL-CIO merger. Many details have been omitted; only the highlights have been given, and these have been related to the broad changes which have taken place in the American economy.

Interest in worker organizations is almost as old as the institution of trade unionism. Various scholars have attempted to explain the reasons for the existence of unions and their impact—actual or potential—upon society. Their views, of course, have differed widely depending upon the authors' predilections and social philosophies. Some have considered unions a threat to the economic system of their time, others as a benign influence. A few who have espoused the overthrow of capitalism—such as Karl Marx—have argued that unions can do little to improve the workers' status. According to this view, unions should be the vehicle for revolutionary economic and social change.

EARLY VIEWS OF UNIONS

Adam Smith on Labor Organization

When Adam Smith published his monumental *Wealth of Nations* (1776), the rudimentary forms of labor organizations were far different from the unions we know today. Smith pointed out, however, that wages depend upon an agreement between the worker and his master "whose interests are by no means the same." This agreement, in his opinion, was the result of a continuous contest between the two parties. "Workmen," he wrote, "desire to get as much, the masters to give as little as possible. The former are disposed to combine in order to raise, the latter in order to lower the wages of labour." But in this contest, Smith pointed out, all the advantage was on the side of the masters since the law ". . . authorises or at least does not prohibit their combinations, while it prohibits those of the workmen."[1]

Any combination of workers designed to raise their wages was widely publicized and generally deprecated in Smith's day. But as the founder of modern economics pointed out, employers also combined to keep wages down and "to violate this combination is everywhere a most unpopular action, and a sort of reproach to a master among his neighbors and equals." The public is not aware of employer combinations, however, since their discussions are held in secret.

At times, Smith wrote, employers agreed to depress the wage level. And this led to a "contrary defensive combination" of the workmen. Workers, however, sometimes combined without such provocation in an effort to raise the price of their labor. But whether the workers combined for offensive or defensive purposes, Smith pointed out, their combinations were always "abundantly heard of." The reason, he stated, is that "they have always recourse to the loudest clamour, and sometimes to the most shocking violence and outrage. They are desperate, and act with the folly and extravagance of desperate men, who must either starve, or frighten their masters into an immediate compliance with their demands."

Whenever there is an outbreak of labor unrest, however, the employers are just as clamourous as the workers, "and never cease to call aloud for the assistance of the civil magistrate, and the rigorous execution of these laws which have been enacted with so much severity against the combinations of servants, labourers, and journeymen."[2] Thus labor combinations were not highly successful in Adam Smith's day. The legal barriers to labor organization—which did not extend correspondingly to employers—effectively prevented concerted action on their part. Labor uprisings generally resulted in nothing more than the punishment or ruin of their ring-leaders. As a result of the legal restrictions on workers, labor combinations could have no effect on wages in Smith's view. On the other hand, employers could not depress wages below the basic subsistence level if they hoped to maintain the necessary supply of labor.

[1] Adam Smith, *The Wealth of Nations,* Modern Library Edition, New York: Random House, Inc. (1937), p. 66.
[2] *Ibid.,* p. 67.

Adam Smith was the great apostle of a policy of laissez faire. To him the ideal economy was one in which a free market place would determine the allocation of resources, and the distribution of returns to workers, employers, landlords, and investors. He clearly condemned the unequal treatment of labor and employer organizations before the law, but he felt that market forces, in the long-run, would determine the level of wages. Employers, even acting in combination, could not depress wages below the "natural" rate, nor could workers, even if they were permitted to combine, keep their wages above this level.

Karl Marx on Trade Unions

The policy of laissez faire did not, as its advocates claimed it would, lead to the best of all possible worlds. By the middle of the 18th century the industrial revolution was in full swing in Great Britain. The unfettered market place did not, however, lead to an equitable distribution of income. Manufacturers became enormously wealthy, but wages failed to rise and working conditions were generally deplorable. Marx attributed the conditions he saw to private ownership of the means of production. The only solution to this problem, in Marx's view, was the complete overthrow of capitalism and the substitution of communism.

Neither in the *Communist Manifesto* which Marx wrote with Friedrich Engels in 1848 nor in *Capital,* his major work, did Marx discuss trade unions extensively. He was more than skeptical, however, that unions could accomplish anything for workers within the framework of capitalism—a position held by devout Marxists to the present day. Despite the rapid advances in production which the industrial revolution had produced, and was producing, Marx argued that workers would be unable to raise their wages above the level of subsistence. Capitalists would insist on appropriating all returns from gains in productivity. Workers were aware of gains in productivity, Marx noted, but he concluded that any efforts on their part to share in these gains would be resisted. "The capitalist politely knocks on the head such pretensions as gross errors as to the nature of wage-labour," Marx wrote. "He cries out against this usurping attempt to lay taxes on the advance of industry, and he declares roundly that the productiveness of labour does not concern the labourer at all."[3] As long as workers felt that they could improve their conditions by combining into unions without overthrowing capitalism, Marx believed, they were deluding them-

[3] Karl Marx, *Capital,* Modern Library Edition, New York: Random House, Inc. (1906), pp. 610–611.

selves. The full force of law and government was on the side of employers. Although a small minority, the latter controlled the nation's wealth. Workers could only improve their position by revolting against the capitalists and the governments which the capitalists controlled.

Marx did not oppose the formation of trade unions. Indeed, he conceded the necessity for worker organization. Even under capitalism, such organization would reduce somewhat the severe competition for available jobs engendered by the high level of unemployment which he believed would always be present under capitalism. More important, Marx also thought in tactical terms; labor organizations, in his view, could spearhead the attack on capitalism. But unions could not be depended upon to revolt against their masters. Without proper leadership, from the Marxist point of view, workers would combine in an effort to improve their conditions under capitalism. Thus it would be necessary for communists to "educate" the leaders of trade unions so that when the time was ripe they would be prepared to dispossess the exploiters of labor and establish the "dictatorship of the proletariat."

Marx did not live to see the development of powerful free trade unions in democratic countries. His followers, however, have continued to level attacks on the notion that satisfactory earnings and working conditions are compatible with capitalism in any form. They have been contemptuous of "business unionism," and have labeled the leaders of free trade unions as willing tools of the greedy capitalists. Leaders of the free unions have returned Marxist insults in kind and have refused to listen to their blandishments. They point to the gains which unions have won through democratic means and insist that the Marxist conception of trade unionism is not only completely erroneous but a snare and delusion which would cost workers their freedom if they were to follow the path of the Marxists.

James Thorold Rogers—An Early View of "Business Unionism"

When Adam Smith wrote about the economic effects of trade unions—or rather the lack of such effects—he did so largely in hypothetical terms since labor combinations were forbidden by law. The British Combination Acts were repealed in 1824 and 1825, however, so that by the time Karl Marx wrote unions were tolerated in Great Britain. But Marx denied categorically that unions would be able to improve the lot of the working man within the framework of capitalism—a belief consistent with his view that capitalism as a system was doomed to perish. When Thorold Rogers venturned a few remarks about unions in 1884, however, he presented an entirely different view. Most economists at that time considered any interference with the free operation of market forces as socially undesirable. But Rogers considered unions to be, on the whole, a benign influence. "A trade union conducted on legal and peaceful principles," he wrote, "by which I mean moral forces only, and with an entire abstention from violence, both in its inception and its administration, does not economically differ from any other joint stock partnership." He preferred the term "labour partnership" to trade union and he pointed out that while successful businessmen were termed "merchant princes, pioneers of industry, creators of public wealth, benefactors of their country, and guarantors of its progress,"[4] labor leaders were denounced for trying to achieve the same thing as the successful businessman. In discussing unions, Rogers used the terminology of the business world, and drew a parallel between the behavior of union leaders and businessmen. Rogers was critical of John Stuart Mill for accepting the notion of a fixed wage fund. He also criticized Mill for arguing that an increase in wages must necessarily raise the cost of production and consumer prices. He argued that "in point of fact, if trade unions do or can raise wages, they may do so to the ultimate benefit of producers and consumers." This would follow, Rogers argued, if a trade union could reduce the number of competing capitalists and improve efficiency in a given market. Unions could also successfully raise wages, he further argued, if in their dealings with employers they would reduce the number of middlemen who he felt "do mischief instead of service, are parasites, and not, in any sense, producers."[5] Rogers clearly had little love for the middleman, and felt that such intermediaries between trade and production did more to destroy producers' profits than union efforts to raise wages.

In a sense, Rogers developed a reverse notion of Galbraith's concept of "countervailing power."[6] Galbraith argued that the countervailing power of unions was induced by the growth of original power on the product side of the market. Rogers suggested that the growth of unions would lead to fewer but larger producers in a given market and have the further side effect of cutting into the ranks of

[4] James Thorald Rogers, *Six Centuries of Work and Wages,* London: Swan Sonnenschein and Co., Ltd. (1903), p. 400.
[5] *Ibid.,* pp. 402–403.
[6] John Kenneth Galbraith, *American Capitalism,* Boston: Houghton Mifflin (revised edition, 1956), pp. 114–117.

middlemen—a development which he considered would be altogether beneficial.

Rogers was critical of some union tactics. He believed that strikes could seldom be successful, although he considered them to be analogous to speculative purchases by sellers who hoped to control the market by reducing supply. He condemned union violence as "indefensible and suicidal." But even undesirable union behavior he attributed in part to the position which the early unions occupied under British law. Rogers wrote after repeal of the Combination Acts, and noted that unions were no longer forbidden by law. But the union, he went on, "was not, indeed, under the protection of laws; and I conceive that much of the savagery which for a long time characterized the conduct of trade unions was due to the outlawry under which those wholesome institutions were placed."[7]

In addition to supporting the early trade union movement as such, Thorold Rogers was one of the early advocates of labor-management cooperation. He considered unions to be socially desirable institutions which would help improve the efficiency of capitalism, and would thus be beneficial to workers, producers, and consumers alike. An unparalleled optimist, Rogers also hoped that the growth of an international trade union movement would diminish the warlike instincts of governments. "I confess that I look forward to the international union of labour partnerships as the best prospect the world has of coercing those hateful instincts of governments, all alike, irresponsible and indifferent, by which nations are perpetually armed against each other, to the infinite detriment, loss and demoralization of all."[8]

TRADITIONAL TRADE UNION THEORY

The term "traditional analysis" has been applied by Clark Kerr and Abraham Siegel to the writings of a number of scholars who dealt with the question of trade unionism. These writers are classified on the basis of their *approach* to the discussion of unions; Kerr and Siegel do not suggest that they reach similar conclusions about the nature of trade unions or their effects upon society.[9] The ideas of some of the leading "traditional theorists" are discussed in this section.

[7] Rogers, *op. cit.*, p. 439.
[8] *Ibid.*, p. 402.
[9] Clark Kerr and Abraham Siegel, "The Structuring of the Labor Force in Industrial Society: New Dimensions and New Questions," *Industrial and Labor Relations Review*, Vol. 8, No. 2 (January 1955), pp. 151–168.

Sidney and Beatrice Webb

Sidney and Beatrice Webb (1859–1947, 1858–1943)—later Lord and Lady Passfield—were among the founders of Fabian Socialism. They are usually included among the relatively small number of "institutional" economists who have made important contributions to economic thought. Fabian socialism is the evolutionary approach to social reform which eventually led to a system of democratic socialism in Great Britain. Institutional economics is less easy to define. Essentially it is descriptive rather than theoretical, and institutional analysis is built around careful study of the various organizations which play an important role in the life of society at any given time. Among other things, the Fabian Society favored the strengthening of trade unions. Unlike Marxists, who believe that trade unions can play a useful role if they spearhead a revolution designed to establish the dictatorship of the proletariat, the Fabians believe that trade unions can improve wages, hours, and working conditions by democratic collective action. As John Dunlop has shown, however, the Webbs did not have a fully rounded theory of the labor movement.[10] They did not concern themselves with the reasons for the emergence of trade unions or with patterns of union development. But they made important contributions to our understanding of trade union government, and were among the pioneers of labor history.

The Webbs were critical of classical economists, such as Nassau Senior, who stressed the social benefits of vigorous competition. They recognized that aggressive price competition often led to sub-standard wages. In their view one of the most important objectives of a trade union was that of guarding its members from the evil effects of unrestricted competition.

To the Webbs, a trade union was "a continuous association of wage-earners for the purpose of maintaining or improving the conditions of their working lives."[11] Unions, the Webbs believed, were not a passing phenomenon in the historical sweep of forces. They felt that labor organizations are essential to the preservation of democratic society.

Broadly speaking, the Webbs believed that unions could pursue one of two courses of action to improve conditions for their mem-

[10] "The Development of Labor Organizations: A Theoretical Framework," in *Insights into Labor Issues,* Richard A. Lester and Joseph Shister, eds. New York: The MacMillan Company (1948), p. 168.

[11] Sidney and Beatrice Webb, *History of Trade Unionism* (1920), p. 1; quoted by Dunlop, *ibid.,* p. 166.

bers. The first was to pursue a policy of restrictionism; that is, to control the supply of labor. The second was to work toward the establishment of minimum wage and working standards for the entire work force. The Webbs were critical of unions which tried to restrict labor supply in order to raise wages, however. They strongly favored union efforts to establish a "Common Rule" based on the notion of a "living wage" for all workers. Such minimum standards would be achieved, according to the Webbs, through collective bargaining, political action, and through establishment of schemes of mutual insurance.

Through collective bargaining, unions would seek to raise wages and press for a gradual extension of fringe benefits. The Webbs were convinced that the establishment of a Common Rule would be beneficial not detrimental to industry. Once minimum standards for labor were established, they believed, employers would seek to increase productivity through technological progress. If this followed, all of society would benefit.

It is somewhat surprising, in view of their socialistic predilections, that the Webbs would advocate mutual insurance schemes for the payment of sick benefits and unemployment compensation. Such schemes are administered by governments today through programs of social security. Unions support such programs and are spared the problems of administration which mutual insurance plans would have involved.

The Webbs were critical of the autocratic attitudes of employers in their day. In their view the spread of trade unionism would lead to more democratic relations in industry. They anticipated to some extent what Sumner Slichter was later to refer to as a system of "industrial jurisprudence."[12]

The Webbs did much to provide intellectual support for the trade unions which were emerging in Great Britain at the time they wrote. Public resistance to union growth was strong, and the doctrines of the classical economists went largely undisputed. There was still widespread acceptance of the notion of a fixed "wage fund" and it was argued that if unions "artificially" raised wages there could only be one consequence—unemployment. The Webbs recognized the argument that if trade unions made headway in a particular sector of the economy only there could be a flight of capital to non-union sectors which would lead to unemployment.

[12] Sumner H. Slichter, *Union Policies and Industrial Management,* Washington, D.C.: The Brookings Institution (1941), p. 1.

But they countered this argument by insisting that trade union pressure would lead to improved technology, and that both workers and society would gain from effective trade union action.[13] They also acknowledged that there were upper limits to which unions could push wages at a given time without causing employers to either go out of business or to relocate their establishments. However, they thought that there were lower limits to wages below which workers would desert particular employers and seek jobs elsewhere. Within these limits unions could have an effect upon the wage level. In this respect, the Webbs' theory of wage determination under trade unions was remarkably close to the notions of certain modern wage theorists.

Robert F. Hoxie and Functional Unionism

Robert Hoxie, (1868–1916), who had been a student of the iconoclastic Thorstein Veblen, was interested in both the structure and functions of unions. He regarded unions as only one of the institutions devised by men—acting collectively—to alter their environment. Workers faced with common problems reacted by banding together to form a union which would serve their specific needs. This led him to question monocausal explanations of the rise of trade unions, and to advance his own notion of unions as functional types.[14] He distinguished four major types of unions, each designed to serve a different function.

Business unionism, according to Hoxie, is the type which develops among skilled craftsmen. Their specific interest is in improving wages, hours, and working conditions for their own membership. They tend to be conservative and to rely primarily on collective bargaining for the achievement of their goals. Hoxie's description of business unions applied to many of those in the A.F. of L. at the time he wrote.

Some workers are not interested in immediate economic gains, however. These tend to band together in *uplift unions.* Such unions support movements for broad social reform. They often align themselves with radical reform groups in search of a panacea for the ills of society. Those attracted to such unions are easily swayed by rhetoric, and their goals are not narrow but broadly inclusive. Uplift unionists have been inclined to think in terms of producers and

[13] Sidney and Beatrice Webb, *Industrial Democracy,* New York: Longmans, Green and Company (1897), pp. 615–616.

[14] Robert F. Hoxie, *Trade Unionism in the United States,* New York: D. Appleton-Century, Inc. (1917), Chapter 1.

consumers cooperatives, radical schemes of monetary reform, and elimination of the wage system of payment. There were some elements in the Knights of Labor with a strong uplift tinge. But as Millis and Montgomery have pointed out, uplift unionism has rarely found much of a following in the United States.[15]

Revolutionary unionism, as the name implies, is dedicated to the overthrow of capitalism. It is the kind of unionism advocated by Marxists. The ideology of the I. W. W. was also revolutionary. This type of unionism has been strongly condemned by American labor leaders, and it has made relatively little headway in other nations of the western world.

Predatory unions, according to Hoxie, are entirely non-ideological. Their members are interested in obtaining "more here and now," and they are not particular about the means used to obtain this end. The leaders of predatory unions are often corrupt and some have close ties to the underworld. The McClellan Committee's investigation, conducted during the late 1950's, revealed that there was some predatory unionism in the United States. It also revealed that there were some employers who raised no objections to dealing with predatory unions.

In discussing the structure and function of trade unions, Hoxie was reluctant to generalize. But in his discussion of collective bargaining, he reached a rather sweeping conclusion:

> Collective bargaining and arbitration . . . are steps toward full labor control. They are an entering wedge toward industrial democracy and abolition of the profit system. Recognition of the union is the first step, since individual bargaining gives the worker no voice. This, then, is the important thing—not the lack of a principle of justice. Collective bargaining is not an instrument of peace, primarily, it is a step in the process of control. Indeed, the significant thing about unionism is the development of a process of control. This is the larger aspect of unionism and in this sense collective bargaining is a solution of the labor problem.[16]

Tannenbaum's View of the Union as a Response to the Challenge of the Factory System

To Frank Tannenbaum (1893–), the trade union is more than an economic institution. During medieval times, for example, the skilled artisan belonged to a guild. While the guilds were not fore-

[15] Harry A. Millis and Royal E. Montgomery, *Organized Labor,* New York: McGraw-Hill Book Company, Inc. (1945) pp. 33–45.
[16] Hoxie, *op. cit.* from Joseph Schister, *Readings in Labor Economics and Industrial Relations,* New York: J. P. Lippincott Company (second edition, 1956), p. 178.

runners of trade unionism—they were more nearly akin to business organizations—the worker identified himself with his organization. This sense of belonging disappeared with the rise of Mercantilism and the cottage system of production. It was completely destroyed by the Industrial Revolution which created a class of wage workers.

The rise of trade unions in modern times, according to Tannenbaum, is the result of the worker's need to feel a strong identification with his job. The factory system poses a threat to the worker's security. It is large and impersonal and the worker, as an individual, can do little to protect his own interests. Workers react collectively by joining forces to gain as much security as possible in an essentially insecure world.[17] But it is not just economic security which the worker seeks. In the modern world, workers "belong to nothing real, nothing greater than their own impersonal pecuniary interests."[18] The trade union provides the worker not only with greater security than he could expect as an individual under the factory system, but it provides a nexus with his job and his source of income. Whether he realizes it or not, a worker who joins a trade union is trying to fulfill his need for a sense of belonging.

Tannenbaum feels that trade union values are not unlike those of management. The individual worker joins the union to protect himself against the vagaries of the market. But management often also seeks to avoid the consequences of unrestrained competition by entering into collusive arrangements. Both trade union leaders and businessmen are responding to acquisitive instincts when they seek to strengthen their security and add to their income. Thus "trade unionism is often monopolistic, restrictive, arbitrary, often at war within itself, costly, and in contradiction of all theories of a free unrestricted market. So is the corporation."[19]

If there is a strong similarity between the trade union and the business organization, what is the most likely outcome of the contact between these two institutions? In his earlier views, at least, Tannenbaum felt that the trade union would ultimately lead to a radical transformation of our economic system. He felt that trade unions

[17] Frank Tannenbaum, *The Labor Movement, Its Conservative Functions and Social Consequences,* New York: G. P. Putman Sons (1921), p. 32; cf. John T. Dunlop, *op. cit.* p. 166.

[18] Frank Tannenbaum, *A Philosophy of Labor,* New York: Alfred A. Knopf (1951), p. 53.

[19] Frank Tannenbaum, "The Social Function of Trade Unionism," *The Political Science Quarterly* (June 1947), p. 176, quoted by Paul Sultan, *Labor Economics,* New York: Henry Holt and Company (1957), p. 214.

would eventually create a system of "industrial democracy" which would displace the existing capitalistic system.

John R. Commons—Trade Unions as Part of "Collective Democracy"

John R. Commons (1862–1945) was one of the small group of "institutional" economists who made important contributions to American economic thought. A prodigious scholar, he directed publication of the eleven-volume *Documentary History of American Industrial Society* (1910–1911). With his associates he published the first two volumes of *History of Labor in the United States* in 1918. The remaining two volumes of this classic history of American unions were published in 1935 by his associates, D. D. Lescohier, Elizabeth Brandeis, Selig Perlman, and Philip Taft.

Commons believed that the trade union could not be analyzed in isolation. The origin, development, and impact of trade unionism could only be understood within the broader framework of general history, including political history. He was not alarmed by the tendency toward group organization which he saw. The rise of a single, powerful pressure group would be cause for alarm. But collective action on one side of the market faced by similar action on the other side is part of what Commons referred to as "collective democracy."[20]

To Commons, American trade unionism was not a protest against the factory system.[21] "Whatever may have been its origin in other countries, the labor movement in America did not spring from factory conditions. It rose as a protest against the merchant-capitalist system."[22]

Commons was the first major labor historian to point out the obstacles to union growth in the United States. The labor force was made up of immigrants from many countries. Workers had difficulty in communicating, not only because of language barriers, but because of differences in their cultural backgrounds. The fluidity of the labor force and universal male suffrage prevented the formation of the rigid class lines found in Europe. And as industrialism developed in the United States, the mass production system led to a dilution of labor skills.

[20] In this respect his ideas are similar to some of those advanced by John K. Galbraith in *American Capitalism, The Concept of Countervailing Power,* Boston: Houghton Mifflin Company (1956).
[21] Contrast this view with that of Tannenbaum discussed in the preceding section.
[22] *A Documentary History of American Industrial Society,* Vol. V, p. 23, quoted by Dunlop, *op. cit.,* p. 165.

Competitive pressures, however, eventually forced workers with common interests to form trade unions. Commons was not alarmed by the interference with market forces which trade unions were bound to produce. He disagreed quite strongly with those economic theorists who felt that unrestrained markets would produce ideal equilibrium solutions to economic problems. This disagreement, incidentally, went back to his days as a graduate student, and caused him considerable trouble in his courses dealing with orthodox economic theory. Instead of searching for ideal solutions based on the concept of an atomistic society, Commons believed that economists should recognize the collective nature of human behavior in a group society. Within this framework, he saw the trade union representing the interests of the working man. He felt that unions and business organizations would be able to accommodate their differences and to work out areas of agreement which would permit both to survive.

John R. Commons has had wide influence on labor economists, and upon specialists in industrial relations, whether or not they accept all of his views. He was a prodigious worker and left an important heritage of books and scholarly articles. Some of his students, such as Edwin Witte, Sumner Slichter, and Selig Perlman, continued the Commons tradition and made important contributions of their own to the field of labor economics.

Selig Perlman and "Job Conscious" Unionism

Selig Perlman (1888–1959), a protégé of John R. Commons, had a long and distinguished career at the University of Wisconsin. He collaborated closely with Commons, and in his *History of Trade Unionism in the United States,* published in 1922, provided a great deal of detail about the early days of American trade unionism. Later, in *A Theory of the Labor Movement* he developed his concept of job conscious unionism based upon the argument that there is a continuous scarcity of job opportunities. He explained the delayed development of a trade union movement in the United States by a lag on the part of workers in recognizing that good jobs are scarce. Once this was recognized, however, job conscious craftsmen banded together to stake out a property right on the jobs available to them.

Stable trade unionism could not develop, Perlman believed, until the worker recognized that he stood to gain as an individual through the union's administration of job opportunities for the group as a whole. A union cannot become strong until "it has educated the members to put the integrity of the collective 'job territory' above the security of their individual job tenure."[23] Thus the union may at times demand sacrifices from individual members, and the latter cannot stop to count too closely the costs involved to themselves.

Perlman anticipated the rise of industrial unionism. As technological change broke down the partitions between various grades of labor in an industry, it would lead to a broadening of the "job territory." When this happens, Perlman said, "the now expanded job-territory will sooner or later be taken over by an *industrial* union or by an *amalgamated* union bordering upon the industrial type."[24] The new industrial unions, Perlman believed, would display the same kind of solidarity as had the earlier craft unions.

Perlman felt that the trade union movement in the United States is affected by three groups of influences. These are: (1) the "resistance power of capitalism" based upon the confidence of employers in their ability to satisfy customers and workers alike; (2) the role of the intellectual who typically underestimates the resistance power of capitalism and overestimates the desire of workers to alter the system, and (3) the "manualist" sentiment of workers which leads to their concern about the scarcity of job opportunities. All of these influences are important, but Perlman seemed to attach the greatest importance to job consciousness. He also recognized that the control of job territories was not simple. "Many are the influences affecting union job control: the legal status of unionism, the policies of the government, a favorable public opinion, and others. Thus every union soon discovers that the integrity of its 'job-territory' like the integrity of the geographic territory of a nation, is inextricably dependent on numerous side relationships."[25]

THE NATURE OF TRADE UNIONS

The theories discussed in the preceding section were formulated at a time when unions were relatively weak and predominantly of the craft variety. The authors of the early theories were concerned with the answers to one or more of the following questions:

[23] Selig Perlman, *A Theory of the Labor Movement,* New York: The MacMillan Company (1928), p. 273.
[24] *Ibid,* p. 275.
[25] *Ibid.,* p. 276.

1. How is one to account for the origin or emergence of labor organizations?
2. What explains the pattern of growth and development of labor organizations?
3. What are the ultimate goals of the labor movement?
4. Why do individual workers join labor organizations?[26]

Dunlop points out that there are a number of similarities in the trade union theories described briefly in the last section, but there are also sharp differences. A particularly sharp cleavage is that between the writers (such as the Webbs and Commons) who explain the rise of trade unions in terms of *economic developments,* and those (such as Hoxie and Perlman) who emphasize worker attitudes or psychology. This cleavage, in Dunlop's view, "represents a fundamental failure in the formulation of 'theories of the labor movement.' " In his opinion, four *interrelated* factors must be considered in exploring the development of trade unions. These are: (1) technology, (2) market structures and the character of competition, (3) community institutions of control, and (4) ideas and beliefs. Instead of seeking a single or a few causes of union development, Dunlop believes that the rise of a labor movement must be viewed in the context of its *total* environment. It is his view that labor organization emerges "among employees who have strategic market or technological positions." The organizations of workers in strategic positions then become "growth cones," which facilitate the organization of workers in less strategic positions.[27]

Dunlop's thesis that trade unions spread from a strategic nucleus is particularly applicable to the emergence of a labor movement prior to the Wagner Act. "Organization by ballot rather than by the picket line places much less emphasis upon strategic employees in the technological and market scene."[28] Thus he feels that his theory is a less satisfactory explanation of the rise of industrial unionism in the United States following the advent of the CIO.

Are Trade Unions Basically "Economic" or "Political" Organizations?

In an important book entitled *Wage Determination Under Trade Unions,* first published in 1944,[29] John T. Dunlop examined the ways in which trade unions affect wage levels and the wage structure within the framework of economic theory. Dunlop did not,

[26] John T. Dunlop, *op. cit.,* pp. 164–165.
[27] *Ibid.,* pp. 174–180.
[28] *Ibid.,* p. 183.
[29] All references here are to the second edition of John Dunlop, *Wage Determination under Trade Unions,* New York: Augustus M. Kelley, Inc. (1950).

however, insist that wage determination could be explained entirely in economic terms. "The fundamental tenet of the following pages," he stated in the introduction, "is that modes of behavior that are broader than economic theory contribute materially to the understanding of wage determination."[30] But he did develop an economic model of a trade union, and examined bargaining power under varying degrees of competition and monopoly both in labor markets and product markets.

A few years after Dunlop's book appeared, Arthur M. Ross published his *Trade Union Wage Policy,*[31] in which he stated that "many of the most interesting questions concerning union behavior cannot be answered by any strictly economic analysis . . ."[32] He went on to state that among all the participants in economic life "the trade union is probably the least fitted to purely economic analysis." After considering the various criteria used by labor and management in wage negotiations, and the pressures to which those responsible for wage determination are subjected, Ross concluded that "a trade union is a *political* agency operating in an economic environment." He did not intend, however, to analyze union behavior exclusively in political terms. This, he asserted, would be just as unsatisfactory as an explanation based entirely upon economic analysis. Ross explicitly recognized the interdependence between political and economic influences. On balance, however, he appeared to grant primacy to the political process. "The economic environment is important to the unions at the second remove: because it generates political pressures which have to be reckoned with by the union leader."[33]

In the preface to the 1950 edition of *Wage Determination Under Trade Unions,* Dunlop replied that "the thesis must be rejected that wage determination under collective bargaining is to be explained most fundamentally or fruitfully in terms of a political process."[34] This is so, in Dunlop's view because:

1. Emphasis upon the political process reflects the experience of newer unions in which there have been factional struggles.
2. Those who stress political wage setting are preoccupied with the short run, and largely ignore more persistent factors.

[30] *Ibid.*, p. 5.
[31] Arthur Ross, *Trade Union Wage Policy,* Berkeley and Los Angeles: University of California Press (1948).
[32] *Ibid.*, p. 4.
[33] *Ibid.*, pp. 7–14.
[34] Dunlop, *Wage Determination,* p. iii.

3. The political approach underestimates the knowledge which labor leaders have of technology and the "economic facts" of an industry.
4. Emphasis upon political wage setting leads to excessive concern with internal union and management affairs and neglects "the stubborn facts of the external world."[35]

It is worth repeating that neither Dunlop nor Ross insisted that union behavior could be explained *only* in economic or political terms. Dunlop chose to emphasize the economic aspects of wage determination under trade unions while acknowledging that non-economic factors must also be considered. Ross, for his part, conceded that economic factors cannot be ignored in explaining union behavior, but emphasized the political pressures to which union leaders are subjected. Economic factors are important, Ross admits, but largely because they will have an influence on those political pressures.

THEORIES OF TRADE UNION GROWTH

Labor theorists and labor historians have long been interested in the process of union growth. John R. Commons, for example, associated fluctuations in union growth with business cycles. He claimed that during periods of prosperity there was union growth, and that during depressions the labor movement contracted.[36] This appears to have been the pattern during the early days of American trade unionism discussed in Chapter 2. Commons based his conclusions on rather scanty statistical data. Indeed, until 1936, with the publication of Leo Wolman's *Ebb and Flow in Trade Unionism,*[37] there was no consistent series of union membership figures covering a long time period, and Wolman's data go back only to 1897. These have now been supplemented by figures collected annually by the U. S. Department of Labor. And while there are some weaknesses in the data, it is possible to project a statistical picture of union growth covering a period of more than seventy years. Chart 5-1 shows the trend in membership of American unions from 1930 through 1958.[38] Most of the growth, of course, has occurred since 1935.

[35] *Ibid.,* pp. iii–iv.
[36] See John R. Commons, *A Documentary History of American Industrial Society,* Glendale, California: Arthur H. Clark Co. (1910–11) Vol. V. p. 19.
[37] Leo Wolman, *Ebb and Flow in Trade Unionism,* New York: National Bureau of Economic Research (1936).
[38] For the period 1897–1930, see Irving Bernstein, "The Growth of American Unions," *American Economic Review* (June 1954), pp. 303–307.

CHART 5–1
MEMBERSHIP OF NATIONAL AND INTERNATIONAL UNIONS, 1930–60

Source: U.S. Department of Labor, Bureau of Statistics, Bulletin No. 1320 (March 1962), p. 46.

The labor force has also increased substantially since 1930, however. Thus a measure of "real" membership must make allowances for the growth of employment and the labor force. This can be done by expressing union membership as a percentage of either non-agricultural employment or the total labor force. The growth curve is then not as steep, as indicated by Chart 5-2.

Once fairly reliable statistical data on trade union membership were available, a number of scholars began to analyze the figures. It is not surprising that they did not all reach the same conclusions. In recent times there has been a lively debate about union growth.[39] Virtually everyone agrees that union growth has not been steady. There have been times when union membership has grown rapidly, and other times when the rate of growth has slowed down or when union membership has declined. But there seems to be relatively little agreement about the causes of such fluctuations in the growth of union membership.

It will be recalled that John R. Commons felt that union growth was closely related to the business cycle; that membership increased during good times and declined during depressions. Others have

[39] The precision of union membership figures has also been the subject of considerable controversy. For an excellent analysis of some of the weaknesses of union membership figures see Albert Epstein, "Union Records as Statistical Sources," 108th Annual Meeting, American Statistical Association, December 29, 1948.

CHART 5–2
MEMBERSHIP AS A PER CENT OF TOTAL LABOR FORCE AND OF EMPLOYEES IN NONAGRICULTURAL ESTABLISHMENTS, 1930–60

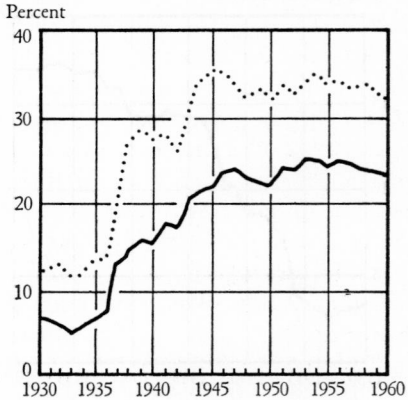

PERCENT OF NONAGRICULTURAL EMPLOYMENT ·····
PERCENT OF TOTAL LABOR FORCE ——

Source: U.S. Department of Labor, Bureau of Labor Statistics, Bulletin No. 1320 (March 1962), p. 46.

related it to the business cycle, but have come to different conclusions.

Wars and Depressions as Causes of Union Growth

In a rather sketchy discussion of short-term fluctuations in union growth, John T. Dunlop identified seven major periods of rapid union expansion between 1827 and 1945.[40] He divided these seven periods into two groups: (1) wartime periods, and (2) periods of fundamental unrest. He noted that unions grew during the Civil War, the Spanish-American War, and the two World Wars. Union expansion during wartime, in Dunlop's view, is explained by labor market developments. Labor shortages and rising prices stimulate union membership.

The remaining three periods of union growth in Dunlop's schema coincided with the low points of major depressions. He feels that at the bottom of depressions, worker dissatisfaction rises to a crest and workers respond by joining unions.

Irving Bernstein, who has made extensive statistical studies of union growth, has also concluded that "in the short run member-

[40] John T. Dunlop, "The Development of Labor Organization: A Theoretical Framework," in Lester and Shister, *Insights into Labor Issues*, p. 190.

ship has expanded sharply as a consequence of wars and very severe depressions. Unions, in other words, have been the beneficiaries of disaster."[41]

A Critique of the Disaster Theory

The short run variations in union growth advanced by Dunlop and Bernstein have come under sharp criticism from Julius Rezler. Rezler points out, for example, that Bernstein attributes union growth early in this century to the depression of 1893 while Dunlop relates it to the Spanish-American War. In Rezler's opinion, however, "the growth was initiated by a twenty-four months' expansion of business activity starting in June 1897 and augmented by an exceptionally friendly attitude of Americans toward unionism." He also disagrees that World War I itself led to growth, and attributes growth during this period to "the friendly attitude of the Federal Government toward unionism."[42] He supports this argument by pointing out that union membership continued to grow *after* World War I when, presumably, the conditions favorable to union growth during wartime no longer existed.

The Role of Inertia in Union Growth

Horace B. Davis has argued that, whatever causes an upsurge or decline in union membership, there is considerable inertia once the movement has started. Davis is of the opinion that while union membership fluctuates, the waves of membership "are not closely synchronized with those of the business cycle."[43] By and large, however, Davis's theory would tend to support the Dunlop thesis, although there might be some differences of opinion on timing. "A major wave of growth, if not brought on by a war, will nearly always be found to have been preceded by an accumulation of wage-earners' grievances, as during a major depression, while the accumulation of employer resistances during the wave of growth is a factor in the ensuing period of absolute or relative decline."[44]

Multicausal Theories of Union Growth

There has been considerable debate about short-run fluctuations in union membership. When one examines various theories of

[41] Irving Bernstein, "The Growth of American Unions," *American Economic Review* (June 1954), p. 317.
[42] Julius Rezler, *Union Growth Reconsidered: A Critical Analysis of Recent Growth Theories,* New York: The Kossuth Foundation, Inc. (1961) pp. 4–8.
[43] Horace B. Davis, "The Theory of Union Growth," *Quarterly Journal of Economics* (August 1941), pp. 611–637, Reprinted in Francis S. Doody, Ed., *Readings in Labor Economics,* Cambridge, Massachusetts: Addison-Wesley Press, Inc. (1950). Page references are to this volume.
[44] *Ibid.,* p. 22.

long-term union growth, however, there seems to be considerable agreement that many causes are involved. For example, while Davis relates waves of union growth to wars and depressions, he also takes into account the effects of union leadership, the growth of industrialism, and technological change particularly as it leads to the displacement of labor. Dunlop has mentioned the influences of technology, market structures and the character of competition, community institutions, and ideas and beliefs. And in a final summation, Rezler has mentioned ten major factors affecting union growth which include variations in business activity, changes in the composition of the labor force, technology, union leadership, the legal framework, the structure of union organization and the value system of society.[45] Bernstein has also concluded that long-run growth cannot be explained in terms of a single cause, and that single explanations are "only sporadically helpful" in explaining short-term fluctuations. Among the primary forces that have shaped long-term growth he includes expansion of the labor force, growing social acceptability of unionism, increasing homogeneity in the working class, and the extension of collective bargaining provisions for union security.[46]

THE STAGNATION THESIS

There has been considerable debate about the causes of union growth, especially about the causes of short-term fluctuations in growth, but there has been an even more lively debate about the prospects of future growth. A number of economists and historians have been involved in this discussion, but the major ideas have been developed by two of the outstanding antagonists—Irving Bernstein and Daniel Bell.

The Stagnation Thesis

The stagnation thesis was first advanced by Daniel Bell in *Fortune* magazine, April 1953. It was elaborated the following year after it had been criticized by Bernstein.[47]

The basis of Bell's argument is "that because something once grew in a specific way in the past, there is no guarantee, logically or empirically, that it will develop in the same manner, or respond to the same stimuli, in the future."[48] Bell argued that in the past,

[45] *Op. cit.*, p. 16.
[46] *Op. cit.*, p. 317.
[47] *Proceedings of the 7th Annual Meeting of Industrial Relations Research Association*, December 28–30, 1954, pp. 231–236.
[48] *Ibid.*, p. 231.

unions had grown by *eruption, extension,* and *enforcement.* The most important of these, in Bell's view, is *eruption.*

An eruption in union membership occurs, as in the latter half of the 1930's, when some factor or combination of factors leads to a large scale willingness on the part of workers to join unions. There was clearly an eruption of membership after 1935, the year in which the Wagner Act was passed and the AFL-CIO split occurred.

The extension of union membership occurs after the initial breakthrough when some of the hold-out firms are brought into line, and unorganized workers begin to feel that they could benefit from unionism. There can also be an extension of union membership during wartime when government agencies adopt a benign attitude toward unions, and employer resistance is diminished by cost-plus contracts and the necessity of meeting production schedules.

The phase of enforcement occurs when unions have become strong enough to negotiate union security provisions such as those calling for the closed shop or union shop. This tends to bring all workers in a bargaining unit into the union whether or not they would willingly join as individuals.

After this brief description of union growth in the past, Bell considered the effect of these forces on future growth. He concluded that the prospects for further growth were dim. He could see no reason why there might be another eruption similar to that of the late 1930's. The problem of union growth, in his view, is primarily one of *extension.* And here, he insisted, unions would encounter difficulties. In manufacturing, with the notable exception of the textile and chemical industries, most industries were between 80 and 100 per cent organized at the time he wrote. The same was true in mining and rail transportation. These are the areas of successful union penetration, and they have been largely saturated, according to Bell's thesis. Also, there is a high degree of organization in large enterprises, and it is easier for a union to sign up members in a single large firm than in many scattered small establishments. There has been little growth of trade unionism among supervisory and white collar workers.

The only areas in which there can be large-scale union growth in the future will be the so-called "white collar" trade and service occupations; yet in these occupations, Bell feels, unions will make little headway. For one thing "in office and financial institutions unionism has failed to take hold because its language and actions are cast in the mold of the industrial worker and unions have failed to find a language appropriate to white collar workers."[49] Also, many workers in such establishments are relatively young women who do not expect to remain in the labor force permanently.

In addition, Bell feels that management has learned a great deal since the eruption of union membership in the 1930's. It has developed personnel practices and has granted benefits to workers which have made unionism relatively unattractive to them. He also feels that government policy was less conducive to union growth after World War II than it had been during the 1930's. While Bell did not pretend to make a projection into the indefinite future, he concluded after examination of these factors that the tide of unionism in the United States had reached a high-water mark. In the immediate future, he concluded, there would be no significant growth in trade unionism.

Bernstein's Critique of the Stagnation Thesis

Shortly after Bell's initial article appeared in *Fortune,* Irving Bernstein wrote that the stagnation thesis had "only surface plausibility."[50] This was so, he argued, because despite Bell's gloomy prognosis unions had in fact continued to grow. In a later article which included union membership figures through 1959, with his own estimates for 1960, Bernstein insisted that American trade unionism continued to exhibit growth. He distinguished between short-term and long-term growth, and repeated the points he had made in his earlier article. Short-term growth tends to come in sharp spurts following wars and depressions. But long-term growth, in Bernstein's view, is due to expansion of the labor force, the increasing social acceptability of unionism, the growing homogeneity of the working class, and the extension of union security provisions in labor-management agreements.[51] Bernstein's figures, which have been subject to some criticism, show a slow growth of union membership through 1960. But his measure of "real" membership, i.e. union membership as a per cent of the civilian labor force, shows a modest but fairly sustained decline since 1953. In

[49] *Ibid.,* p. 235.
[50] Irving Bernstein, "The Growth of American Unions," *American Economic Review* (June 1954), p. 301.
[51] Irving Bernstein, "The Growth of American Unions, 1945–1960," *Labor History* (Spring 1961), pp. 131–132.

that year union membership amounted to 28 per cent of the labor force. By 1960, there had been a decline of 26.2 per cent.

Charts 5-1 and 5-2 show that there was a sharp spurt of membership from 1935 until 1945. This was followed by five years with little or no change. Another spurt, although a smaller one, occurred from 1950 until 1955, with a modest drop after 1956. Chart 5-2 shows that "real" membership has declined modestly since 1954.

There are other authors, such as Solomon Levine and Bernard Karsh, who are optimistic about future union growth. And, of course, the "stagnationists" have supporters as well. Those who have participated in the debate about future union growth do not pretend to be able to give definitive answers. Competent scholars have examined the same body of data, and have come to different conclusions about what these figures portend for the future. These debates are more than interesting academic exercises, however, since they focus attention on the various factors which have contributed to the process of union growth in the past.

REFERENCES

BOOKS

Commons, John R., *A Documentary History of American Industrial Society,* eleven volumes, Glendale, California: Arthur H. Clark Company (1910–1911).

———, ———., and Associates, *History of Labor in the United States,* four volumes, New York: The Macmillan Company (1918–32).

Dunlop, John T., *Wage Determination Under Trade Unions,* New York: Augustus M. Kelley, Inc. (1950).

Gompers, Samuel, *Labor and the Employer,* New York: E. P. Dutton and Company (1920).

Hoxie, Robert F., *Trade Unionism in the United States,* New York: D. Appleton (1922).

Marx, Karl, *Capital,* Modern Library Edition, New York: Random House, Inc., Copyright 1906, by Charles H. Kerr and Company.

Millis, Harry A., and Royal E. Montgomery, *Organized Labor,* New York: McGraw-Hill Book Company, Inc. (1945).

Perlman, Selig, *The Theory of the Labor Movement,* New York: Macmillan Company (1928).

Rezler, Julius, *Union Growth Reconsidered,* New York: The Kossuth Foundation, Inc. (1961).

Rogers, Thorold, *Six Centuries of Work and Wages,* London: Swan Sonnenschein and Co., Ltd., (1903).

Ross, Arthur M., *Trade Union Wage Policy,* Berkeley and Los Angeles: University of California Press (1948).

Sultan, Paul, *Labor Economics,* New York: Henry Holt and Company (1957).

Tannenbaum, Frank, *The Labor Movement, Its Conservative Functions and Social Consequences,* New York: G. P. Putnam Sons (1921).

Tannenbaum, Frank, *A Philosophy of Labor,* New York: Alfred A. Knopf (1951).

U. S. Department of Labor, Bureau of Labor Statistics, *Directory of National and International Labor Unions in the United States, 1959,* Washington, D.C.: Bulletin No. 1267 (December 1959).

Webb, Sidney and Beatrice, *History of Trade Unionism,* New York: Longmans, Green and Company (1894).

———, ——— — ———, *Industrial Democracy,* New York: Longmans, Green and Company (1897).

ARTICLES

Bernstein, Irving, "The Growth of American Unions," *American Economic Review,* Vol. XLIV (June 1954), pp. 301–318.

———, ———, "The Growth of American Unions, 1945–1960," *Labor History,* Vol. 2, No. 2 (Spring, 1960), pp. 131–157.

———, ———, "Union Growth and Structural Cycles," *Proceedings,* Industrial Relations Research Association (December 28–30, 1954), pp. 202–320, and "Discussion," by Daniel Bell, *idem.,* pp. 231–236.

Davis, Horace B., "The Theory of Union Growth," *Quarterly Journal of Economics,* Vol. LV (August 1941), pp. 611–637, reprinted in Frances S. Doody (Editor) *Readings in Labor Economics,* Cambridge, Massachusetts: Addison-Wesley Press, Inc. (1950).

Dunlop, John T., "The Development of Labor Organization: A Theoretical Framework," *Insights Into Labor Issues,* Richard A. Lester and Joseph Shister (Editors), New York: The Macmillan Company (1948), pp. 163–193.

Kerr, Clark, and Abraham Siegel, "The Structuring of the Labor Force in Industrial Society: New Dimensions and New Questions," *Industrial and Labor Relations Review,* Vol. 8, No. 2 (January 1955), pp. 152–168.

Marx, Karl, and Friedrich Engels, "Manifesto of the Communist Party," in Earl L. Sikes *Contemporary Economic Systems* (Revised edition), New York: Henry Holt and Company (1951), pp. 659–679.

PART 2

trade unions and public policy

Chapter 6 From Repression to Non-Intervention

In this chapter and the three which follow we shall consider the evolution of labor law in the United States. It will be helpful perhaps to list the broad stages through which our public policy toward trade unions has passed. These are:

1. A period of repression during which unions were denied the right of legal existence.
2. A stage of sufferance, in which unions were tolerated, however grudgingly, but in which union activities were severely limited.
3. A period of non-intervention during which a few of the major restrictions on union behavior were curtailed.
4. Full legal recognition, and a period of encouragement and assistance by government.
5. A stage of growing control over union activities in which, however, the full legal rights of unions have been protected.[1]

Our discussion will go beyond the laws and court decisions which deal directly with trade unions. There is a considerable body of legislation, most of it dating from the 1930's, which deals with labor standards, and the provision of a minimum of protection against the vicissitudes of life in a modern industrial society. The laws which provide this protection are often referred to collectively as *social legislation* to distinguish them from the labor laws which in one way or another have affected or now affect trade unions.

Common Law and Statutory Law

There are a number of ways in which systems of law can be classified. For present purposes, however, it will be sufficient to distinguish between *common* law and *statutory* law.

[1] The first four stages are based upon a similar classification by Ludwig Teller in *A Labor Policy for America,* New York: Baker, Voorhis and Co., Inc. (1945), pp. 3–5.

Laws which are specifically enacted by the Congress and by state legislatures are known as statute laws. Much of our law, however, is known as common law—part of our Anglo-Saxon heritage—which consists of the gradual accumulation of court decisions.

Statute laws typically are the result of political pressures. Such laws generally represent a change either in earlier statute law or in the common law. Common law also changes over time, however. Many court decisions are based upon earlier judicial precedent. From time to time, however, a court will make a path-breaking decision which departs from earlier precedent, and which might be cited subsequently as precedent for later decisions.

The Period of Union Repression

As noted in an earlier chapter, the first unions in the United States did not find the political and economic climate particularly hospitable. The British doctrine of laissez faire, enunciated by Adam Smith in 1776, was largely accepted in this country by the beginning of the nineteenth century. One of the strongest unions in existence at that time consisted of a group of Philadelphia shoemakers producing high-grade boots and shoes largely made of cordovan leather. The journeymen cordwainers, or employees in the shoe shops, had organized a club. Eventually they got around to drawing up a schedule of rates which they presented to their employers, the master cordwainers. The journeymen's demands came at a time when the Philadelphia shop owners were trying to depress prices to compete with shoemakers in other cities for the expanding markets of the country. The journeymen demanded that the masters meet their schedule "or else." The masters accepted the latter alternative.

The masters immediately took the case to court. The journeymen were charged with "contriving, and intending unjustly and oppressively, to increase and augment the prices and rates usually paid and allowed to them and other artificers," and with preventing "by threats, menaces, and other unlawful means," others from working as cordwainers for wages below the rates they had set. Basically, the journeymen cordwainers were charged with engaging in a criminal conspiracy. And criminal conspiracies were at variance with the British common law which had been adopted virtually intact in this country.

The counsel for the defense argued bravely that the British common law conflicted with the goals of the Revolution, but the judge who heard the case, Recorder Levy, was not impressed. The Recorder, it seems quite clear, was determined to defend the best interests of businessmen and property owners in Philadelphia. An obvious disciple of Adam Smith, he castigated the journeyman cordwainers for interfering with the natural forces of supply and demand. There could be no objection, he said, to an individual workman's demand for a higher wage. But in a widely quoted passage he concluded that: "A combination of workmen to raise their wages may be considered in a two-fold point of view: one is to benefit themselves . . . the other is to injure those who do not join their society. The rule of law condemns both." The redoubtable Recorder made it abundantly clear that society could not tolerate conspiracies of workmen whose goal was to disturb the equilibrium of wages set by the forces of a free market.

The precedent set in the *Philadelphia Cordwainers* case of 1806 was widely followed for the next three decades. Similar restrictions were not placed on the combination of capital. In other cases which reached the courts during this time, judges decided that combinations of businessmen were permissible since this would permit them to engage in ventures "too weighty for an individual."[2] The courts continued to decide, however, that if workers organized to raise wages they were guilty of criminal conspiracy. And the New York legislature obligingly passed a conspiracy law which though vaguely worded could be cited by the courts in conspiracy cases.

The workers of the day did not accept the conspiracy doctrine with equanimity. Public resentment against what many people considered to be the unfair treatment of wage-workers was growing. In some cases juries refused to convict workers charged with conspiracy, and the press was critical of judges who hewed closely to the conspiracy doctrine.

Commonwealth v. Hunt—The End of the Conspiracy Doctrine

The upshot of the growing resentment against conspiracy decisions came in 1842 in a decision handed down by Chief Justice Shaw of the Massachusetts Supreme Court. Shaw had no strong sympathy for labor organizations. But he knew that Massachusetts employers were becoming increasingly concerned about the reactions of workers—not always peaceful—when they were called criminals for attempting to better their wages. The textile and shoe industries were beginning to expand rapidly at that time in the Bay State,

[2] Charles O. Gregory, *Labor and the Law,* New York: W. W. Norton & Company, Inc. (1946), pp. 22–26.

and the employers wished to avoid worker unrest. There were political implications in *Commonwealth v. Hunt* as well since industrialists were then seeking tariff protection to guard the nation's "infant industries."

This case again involved a group of shoemakers, a craft which seemed to have a penchant for organizing and even for calling strikes despite the legal climate of the day. The workers involved had been convicted of conspiracy by a lower court. Chief Justice Shaw did not attack the conspiracy doctrine head-on. Instead, in a neat bit of judicial toe-dancing he sidestepped the issue, concluding that the organization of workers as such could not be considered as socially undesirable.[3] Indeed, his decision went so far as to deny that a closed shop, an arrangement under which union workers only were hired, could be considered illegal.

While Justice Shaw did not actually abolish the doctrine of criminal conspiracy his decision established an important precedent, and there were no subsequent decisions in which unions as such were held to be conspiracies.

UNION RESTRAINT THROUGH USE OF INJUNCTIONS

For the remainder of the nineteenth century there were no pathbreaking cases comparable to the *Philadelphia Cordwainers* case which started a train of conspiracy decisions, and *Commonwealth v. Hunt* which effectively ended the conspiracy doctrine. This is not to say that there were no labor cases; in fact there were many involving specific strikes, union efforts to restrain employers from having work done off the premises, and some cases comparable to modern jurisdictional disputes. These cases were concerned with specific issues, however, and did not result in decisions that were precedent-setting. This does not mean that the nation's judges regarded unions as benign institutions. Indeed, well before the end of the nineteenth century a new legal weapon had been forged which effectively restrained trade union activity—this was the device of the restraining order or injunction.

The first labor injunction appears to have been issued by an equity court handling a railroad bankruptcy case. A receiver was appointed to take over the road, and one of his first problems was that of a threatened strike. The strike was forestalled, however, when the judge involved issued a restraining order, and as a by-

[3] *Ibid.*, p. 29.

product discovered a powerful device for restraining labor disputes.

Injunctions are issued by equity courts as distinguished from courts of law. The same judge might sit on an equity court and a court of law, but he follows different rules in the two cases. Both in Great Britain and the United States, equity courts evolved to deal with cases where money damages would not solve the problem at issue. In an equity case the judge will issue an order either to do something or refrain from doing something, and in labor disputes it was such negative orders which became important. If a union were enjoined from performing a specific act—and went ahead with the act anyway—its leaders could be held in contempt of court. Their punishment under the criminal law could then include imprisonment. This was indeed an effective device for calming down the obstreperous labor leader who might threaten to do damage to property by calling a strike. Following the initial use of an injunction in the 1880's, similar orders were willingly issued by numerous equity courts. The initial purpose of the injunction was to protect property, but many able scholars feel that the injunction was severely abused. One of the strongest critics of the unrestrained use of labor injunctions was Justice Felix Frankfurter, then a law professor at Harvard.[4]

Injunctions were generally granted upon request, and many courts failed to look into the legality or illegality of the action which they were restraining. Even many conservatives early in the present century were strongly critical of the courts for the way in which they granted injunctions against organized labor. As noted in an earlier chapter, Samuel Gompers and many other union leaders thought that the Clayton Act of 1914 outlawed the use of the injunction, but subsequent events showed them to be wrong. It was not until the Norris-LaGuardia Act of 1932 that effective restraints were imposed upon courts in issuing labor injunctions.

UNIONS AND ANTITRUST LAWS

The Sherman Act of 1890

Between the Civil War and the 1880's, there was a marked transformation in the ownership and control of American industry. In many industries there was a decline in the number of independent establishments, and an increase in the size of those which re-

[4] Felix Frankfurter and Nathan Greene, *The Labor Injunction,* New York: Macmillan (1930).

mained. This was often brought about through mergers and other forms of consolidation, and by the 1880's a number of markets were largely controlled by one or a few firms. New corporations were set up to hold the stock of formerly competing establishments "in trust." Their objective was to restrain price competition and to ensure profits for the operating corporations which had turned over a controlling share of their voting stock to the trust.

A considerable hue and cry about the activities of the trusts was raised in the press. In the campaign of 1888 both the Democrats and the Republicans solemnly professed their opposition to monopolistic practices. When the Republicans won, President Harrison asked Congress to enact the anti-monopoly plank in the Republican platform. Several bills were introduced, one by Senator Sherman of Ohio. Congress displayed only minor interest in the proposed legislation which was enacted with little dissent and signed by the President on July 2, 1890.

The Sherman Act is an unusually short and simple piece of federal legislation. Its major provisions are covered by the first two sections of the Act. Section 1 states that "every contract, combination in the form of trust or otherwise, or conspiracy, in restraint of trade or commerce among the several States or with foreign nations, is hereby declared to be illegal." The second section simply states that any person who monopolizes or attempts to monopolize trade or commerce shall be guilty of a misdemeanor. During the early years of the law, violations were punishable by fines up to $5000, maximum imprisonment of one year, or both. The law also contained a provision—which later had an important bearing upon a case involving a trade union—which permitted persons injured by illegal restraint to sue for triple damages. Whether or not the Congress which enacted the Sherman Act intended that it should apply to trade unions has long been a matter of controversy. In 1890, however, the courts evidently did not regard the bargaining functions of unions as restraints of trade. For the first 18 years that the Sherman Act was in existence—while there was much argument about the intentions of Congress—the law was not applied to unions as such. The debate was settled, for a time at least, in 1908 in the case of *Loewe v. Lawlor,* better known as the Danbury Hatters' case. In this case the Supreme Court stated that Congress had intended that the Act apply to unions as well as to business combinations. "The Court then proceeded to do so, applying the act adversely to a union in a way that didn't seem sensible and thereafter refusing to apply it in many ways that would have made sense."[5]

The union involved in this case was relatively strong. It had organized most of the large felt hat manufacturers in the country, but the few unorganized companies made life difficult for the union by engaging in aggressive price competition. One of the outstanding recalcitrants, from the union's point of view, was the Loewe Hat Company of Danbury, Connecticut. Despite the union's best efforts, including a series of local strikes, Loewe's remained unorganized. The union therefore imposed a nation-wide boycott on Loewe hats. Following a slump in orders, Loewe brought suit against the union under the Sherman Act and the court awarded the company triple damages of more than half a million dollars.

This came as a severe shock not only to the organized hatters, but to the leaders of the A.F. of L. as well. Recognizing that the Supreme Court had read into the Sherman Act a provision which allowed it to be applied against unions, the leaders of the A.F. of L. departed from their long-established principle of no political involvement and campaigned actively for legislation which would specifically declare the immunity of trade unions to the antitrust law.

The Clayton Act of 1914

The unions' campaign appeared to bear fruit when a new Congress under President Wilson passed the Clayton Act. The new law—an amendment to the Sherman Act—was intended to clarify, among other things, the status of unions under the nation's antitrust laws. Section 6 stated that "the labor of a human being is not a commodity or article of commerce. Nothing contained in the antitrust laws shall be construed to forbid the existence and operation of labor, agricultural or horticultural organizations . . . or to forbid or restrain individual members of such organizations from lawfully carrying out the legitimate objects thereof; nor shall such organizations, or the members thereof, be held or construed to be illegal combinations or conspiracies in restraint of trade, under the antitrust laws." Section 20 went on to state that "no restraining order or injunction shall be granted by any court in the United States, or a judge or the judges thereof, in any case between an employer and employees . . . involving, or growing out of, a dispute concerning terms or conditions of employment . . ." Had Section 20 stopped at this point the most effective anti-union

[5] Gregory, *op. cit.*, p. 206.

weapon of the time might have been nullified. But it went on to hedge this initial statement with a number of conditions under which injunctions could be issued.

Samuel Gompers hailed the Clayton Act as "Labor's Magna Carta," but his jubilation was premature. In reply to Section 6, many judges stated that no one had ever supposed that labor was a commodity or article of commerce. And there was a great deal of latitude in the language of Section 20 which permitted them to grant injunctions as freely after the Clayton Act as they had before. Thus the Clayton Act did not give unions relief from the dreaded injunction. The authors of the Clayton Act carefully refrained from stating that unions were specifically immune from prosecution under the antitrust laws. There was still room for considerable judicial leeway even in this respect. This was demonstrated in two cases involving a single labor-management incident.

The Judicial Control of Union Activities

In 1914, the year of the Clayton Act, the Coronado Coal Company of Arkansas which had signed agreements with the United Mine Workers of America decided to terminate its contracts. To do this, the company closed down a number of unionized mines and announced that they would open them on a non-union basis. The workers at one of the Coronado Company's mines went on strike in an effort to force the company to reverse this decision. The strike was bitter and violent, and the mine itself was virtually destroyed by fire and dynamite. The company brought suit under the Sherman Act claiming damages of $740,000. After long litigation in the lower federal courts the case reached the Supreme Court, which handed down its decision in what is now known as the *first Coronado* case in June 1922, almost eight years after the strike had occurred. The Court denied the damages which the company sought on the grounds that the company had not been able to prove that the union intended to restrain commerce within the meaning of the Sherman Act. But this was not the end of the Coronado case.

The case was reopened when a disgruntled union official offered to testify for the company. In the *second Coronado* case this witness testified that the union had intended to keep the company's coal "from getting into the market,"—an objective which should have seemed rather obvious to the court at the first trial. With this "new evidence" the court ruled that the union was guilty of violating the Sherman Act, and conceivably would have awarded triple damages if the union had not effected a settlement out of court. In the first Coronado case the Court ruled that a labor organization engaged in a strike did not come under the Sherman Act, and this appeared to reverse the *Danbury Hatters* decision—although boycott was an issue in the first case, a strike in the second. But in the second Coronado case the court ruled, as in *Loewe v. Lawlor,* that the union was subject to the terms of the Sherman Act.

The second Coronado case made it clear that unions were not exempt from the potent triple damage provision of the Sherman Act. Moreover, in a case decided in 1921, the court made it quite clear that unions were not exempt from injunctions. This case, involving the Duplex Printing Press Company of Michigan and the International Association of Machinists, contained many elements similar to the *Danbury Hatters* case. Only four companies made presses of the kind sold by the Duplex Company. Three of these were organized, but Duplex was not. The other three companies notified the union that unless Duplex could be organized and their labor costs brought into line, they would break off relations with the union. The IAM called a strike at the Duplex plant, but only a handful of workers responded. They then instituted a secondary boycott in an effort to hamper the sale of Duplex presses. Union members were ordered not to install or repair Duplex presses, and the union took other steps to hamper the company's sales.[6] The company responded by seeking an injunction, and despite the Clayton Act, the injunction was granted. It was this decision which made it clear that Gompers' enthusiastic response to the Clayton Act was not justified.

A similar decision was reached by the Court in the *Bedford Cut Stone* case of 1927. This case came about when union stonecutters refused to handle non-union limestone coming from Indiana which led to a virtual end of out-of-state shipments. The Court once again restrained the union from continuing its boycott.

In other cases the courts continued to invoke the antitrust laws to restrain union action. Some of these, such as the Brims case decided in 1926, involved agreements between unions and employers to protect each others' interests, and thus exclude outsiders from specific markets. The latter decisions, most legal scholars agree,

[6] For a lucid and concise discussion of the secondary boycott see Albert Rees, *The Economics of Trade Unions,* Chicago: The University of Chicago Press (1962), pp. 43–46.

were fully justified by the Sherman and Clayton Acts. Even Justice Brandeis, who had dissented in the Bedford case, concurred with the decision in the Brims case. But long after the Clayton Act was passed, the status of unions under the antitrust laws remained ambiguous. Whatever the intent of Congress had been—and the Act is sufficiently vague to permit differences of opinion about this —the courts continued to exercise considerable control over labor-management relations.

Within the framework of antitrust legislation the courts hampered union progress after 1914. This was done by granting injunctions against unions when they attempted to use the secondary boycott as an organizational tactic. There was also the continued threat of the triple damages provision of the Sherman Act if unions appeared to be acting in restraint of trade. Another way in which the courts supported employer efforts to ward off union organization was by upholding the legality of "yellow dog contracts."

The term "yellow dog contract" was union-inspired. It was applied to agreements exacted from workers that, as a condition of employment, they would not join a union.[7] There were various kinds of "yellow dog contracts," some oral and some written. Until 1917, such agreements were not considered to be enforceable in the equity courts, but a decision rendered that year changed this.

The case involved the West Virginia Mine of the Hitchman Coal Company and the United Mine Workers. The mine had been organized, but relations between the union and management had never been good. Finally, a strike was called. The management held out until individual workers sought reemployment. This was granted upon the condition that they would not join the union as long as they were employed by The Hitchman Company.

Organizers from the United Mine Workers began to obtain promises from individual workers that they would join the union, however. The plan was to line up enough union workers to strike the mine again. Management learned of this, and obtained an injunction against all organizational activity. The case was carried to the Circuit Court of Appeals, and then to the Supreme Court. In *Hitchman Coal Company v. Mitchell* (1917), the Supreme Court ruled that the union was engaged in an effort to induce breach of contract, and that it had been appropriate for the lower court to issue an injunction. Thus the enforceability of

[7] See Millis and Montgomery, *Organized Labor,* New York: McGraw-Hill (1945), pp. 512–513.

"yellow dog contracts" was upheld by the highest court of the land.

LIMITING THE JUDICIAL CONTROL OF LABOR-MANAGEMENT RELATIONS

For a time, after the first *Coronado* case, it appeared that the courts were taking a somewhat more lenient attitude toward the activities of trade unions. But this notion was dispelled by the second *Coronado* decision. The courts, relying partly on the antitrust laws and partly on common law, continued to issue restraining orders. The law was still used to repress union activities under a wide variety of circumstances. But the relief from blanket injunctions, which the unions thought they were going to receive from the Clayton Act, finally was granted when Congress passed the Norris-LaGuardia Act in 1932. This law ushered in a brief period of virtual non-intervention by the government in labor matters. It should be noted that it was put on the books *before* the New Deal Administration and a liberal Congress were swept into office in the election of 1932.

The Norris-LaGuardia Act

One of the purposes of this law, which is sometimes referred to as the anti-injunction act, was to limit the jurisdiction of courts sitting in equity cases. It will be recalled that it was equity courts which granted injunctions, and typically they did so without hearings or investigation upon the complaint of an aggrieved employer. The Norris-LaGuardia Act did not prohibit courts from granting injunctions. What it did was to spell out in considerable detail the conditions under which injunctions could be granted and only "after hearing the testimony of witnesses in open court (with opportunity for cross-examination) in support of the allegations of a complaint made under oath, and testimony in opposition thereto, if offered . . ." After such hearings, an injunction could be granted if the court found that:

(a) Unlawful acts had been threatened, or would be committed unless restrained, or had been committed and would be continued unless restrained.

(b) Such acts would then be enjoinable only if the court found that substantial and irreparable injury to the complainant's property would follow.

(c) The court also had to be satisfied that failure to grant injunctive relief would lead to greater injury to the complainant than would be inflicted upon the defendant by the injunction.

(d) The complainant would also have to demonstrate that he had no adequate remedy at law and that "the public officers charged with the duty to protect complainant's property are unable or unwilling to furnish adequate protection."

Under emergency conditions a court would be able to issue a temporary restraining order upon the sworn testimony of the complainant, but it could be effective for no more than five days. If such an emergency injunction should be issued, the complainant was required to be prepared to compensate those enjoined for any "damage caused by the improvident or erroneous issuance of such order or injunction."

The Act also listed specific conditions under which courts could not issue temporary or permanent injunctions. Broadly speaking, injunctions could not be granted while workers were conducting a peaceful strike. Also, workers could not be prevented from publicizing the issues involved in a dispute provided their message did not involve fraud or violence.

The Norris-LaGuardia Act also put an end to "yellow dog contracts" by declaring that they were not enforceable at law. This removed one of the barriers to union activity widely used at various "growing points" of union organization in the past.

The new law did not explicitly sanction the use of secondary boycotts. But Section (a) of the Act was sufficiently general to permit both primary and secondary boycotts if a union could demonstrate an economic interest in such actions. The qualification that an economic interest had to be shown excluded secondary *sympathetic* boycotts from this interpretation. The law was not entirely clear on the matter of secondary *consumption* boycotts. But Section 4(e) permitted unions to publicize any labor dispute. By inference, at least, this permitted unions to seek public support for their position without fear of an injunction provided they could demonstrate an economic interest in a dispute. This appeared to be sufficient for the courts to sanction consumption boycotts in some later cases.

Section 2 of the Norris-LaGuardia Act is a declaration of public policy in labor controversies. This section points out that the government had authorized property owners to organize corporations and other forms of association.

But the individual worker, the Act pointed out, is "commonly helpless to exercise actual liberty of contract and to protect his freedom of labor, and thereby to obtain acceptable terms and conditions of employment." The worker should be free to refuse to join a union. But "it is necessary that he have full freedom of association, self-organization, and designation of representatives of his own choosing, to negotiate the terms and conditions of his employment, and that he shall be free from the interference, restraint, or coercion of employers . . ."

This statement of policy, embodied in statute law, indicated a marked change in the status of organized labor in the United States. In more emphatic terms than those used in the Clayton Act, the law made it clear that workers had the right to organize into unions and to select bargaining representatives of their own choosing. This was a far cry from the days when unions were considered as conspiracies. There was one major loophole in the law, from organized labor's point of view, since while Congress had specifically declared that workers had the *right* to form unions, nothing was said about the *obligation* of management to recognize these unions or to bargain with their chosen representatives. After the Norris-LaGuardia Act, however, it could no longer be said that unions were the victims of judicial repression. Public policy toward labor organizations by this time had clearly moved into the stage of non-intervention. There was nothing in the Act to provide a positive stimulus to union growth, but unions were allowed to enter the "self help" stage of their development.

A New Judicial View of Unions and the Antitrust Laws

Organized labor had achieved one of its goals, with respect to the antitrust laws, when the Norris-LaGuardia Act was passed. This was the end of the dreaded blanket labor injunction. But the labor injunction, it will be recalled, had not originated in antitrust law. It was the somewhat accidental discovery of the equity courts. The danger of prosecution under the Sherman Act still existed if unions could be found guilty of acting to restrain trade. The lessons of the *Danbury Hatters* case and the second *Coronado* case were not lost upon the nation's labor leaders. They recognized that an unfavorable court ruling could still lead to punitive triple damages. The unions were still not out of the woods as far as the antitrust laws were concerned. A firm ruling was needed on the status of organized labor under the antitrust laws. This was finally achieved in the case of *United States v. Hutchison* decided in 1941.

The *Hutchison* case involved a jurisdictional dispute between the Carpenters Union and the International Association of Machinists over which was to install and dismantle machinery in the Anheuser-Busch plant in St. Louis. The job had been awarded to the IAM, and the Carpenters not only called a strike at that plant but refused to permit their members to work on Anheuser-Busch property. Finally, through a publicity campaign, the Carpenters Union called upon its members and friends to refrain from buying or selling Anheuser-Busch beer.

Although by this time the Supreme Court was favorably inclined toward organized labor, the Hutchison case led to a split decision with three justices dissenting. The Hutchison case involved a secondary boycott of the kind which had led to an adverse ruling, from the union point of view, in the *Danbury Hatters* case. The Court ruled that because of the Norris-LaGuardia Act such union behavior was no longer enjoinable. As might be expected, following a split decision, legal scholars have differed in their interpretations of the *Hutchison* decision. Some feel that Congress did not intend to prevent courts from enjoining secondary consumption boycotts. And Justice Roberts in his dissent pointed out that while the Norris-LaGuardia Act forbade the use of injunctions there remained the triple damages and criminal prosecution provisions of the Sherman Act. Some lawyers agreed with Justice Roberts that the Anheuser-Busch Company should have had an opportunity to recover damages suffered as a result of the boycott. Others, it must be pointed out, felt that the Supreme Court acted according to the strict letter of the law.

Although the *Hutchison* decision provided lawyers with ample ammunition for further debate, it appeared to settle the issue of the status of trade unions under the antitrust laws. Since the *Hutchison* case it appears that "a union, acting in its own self-interest and not in combination with non-labor groups, is immune from antitrust legislation. If, on the other hand, a union combines with non-labor groups to monopolize, it is no longer immune."[8] Also, subsequent decisions indicate that unions are subject to the antitrust laws if their activities do not occur within the setting of a labor dispute or in situations where the employer-employee relationship is not involved. Thus, as Douglass Brown has pointed out, when unions become involved in the *product* market they are on the same footing as any other group and are subject to the antitrust laws. But anti-

[8] Douglass V. Brown, "Labor and the Antitrust Laws," *American Bar Association Proceedings* (August 1955), p. 23.

trust legislation does not apply to union activities in the *labor* market. This is a widely accepted view among economists and lawyers today, but it should be hastily added that there are many who dissent from it. Some critics of the *Hutchison* decision do not believe that union action should be entirely unrestrained. They suggest that cases involving secondary boycotts, and problems that might arise out of jurisdictional disputes, should be handled by legislation dealing specifically with these issues rather than under the antitrust laws.

Industrywide Collective Bargaining and the Antitrust Laws

The *Hutchison* case was a precedent-setting decision. Since 1941, courts have applied the antitrust laws to trade unions only when the latter have become involved in product markets, but the matter has not rested there. Since the end of World War II, bills have been introduced into virtually every session of Congress which if enacted would make unions subject to the antitrust laws even if their activities were limited to the labor market. Spokesmen for conservative business groups have argued that business monopoly has been outlawed by the Sherman Act and subsequent antitrust legislation, but that unions have become powerful "labor monopolies." This issue will be discussed in a later chapter in connection with other issues involved in collective bargaining since the end of World War II.

REFERENCES

BOOKS

Chamberlin, Edward H., *et. al., Labor Unions and Public Policy,* Washington: American Enterprise Association (1958).

Gregory, Charles O., *Labor and the Law,* New York: W. W. Norton and Company, (revised edition, 1949), and (second revised edition, 1961).

Millis, Harry A., and Royal E. Montgomery, *Organized Labor,* New York: McGraw-Hill Book Company, Inc. (1945).

Radin, Max, *The Law and You,* New York: Mentor Books (1948).

Teller, Ludwig, *A Labor Policy for America,* New York: Baker, Voorhis and Company, Inc. (1945).

Wilcox, Clair, *Public Policies Toward Business,* Chicago: Richard D. Irwin, Inc. (1955).

ARTICLES

Brichner, Dale J., "Labor and Anti-Trust Action," *Industrial and Labor Relations Review,* Vol. 13, No. 2 (January 1960), pp. 245–253.

Brown, Douglass V., "Labor and the Antitrust Laws," *American Bar Association Proceedings* (August 1955), pp. 23–29.

Chapter 7 Government Encouragement of Trade Unions

The Norris-LaGuardia Act of 1932 resulted in a brief period of non-intervention in labor-management affairs. Prior to that our public policy toward trade unions had been one of repression. This was due to an absence of protective labor legislation, and the judicial interpretation of existing law which permitted unrestrained use of the labor injunction. The Norris-LaGuardia Act was the first law to provide unions with a measure of security. The Act did not give them protection against a variety of tactics used by employers to forestall union organization, but for the first time they were given equality under the law. This description of our labor policy through 1932 applies to unions in general. Long before the Norris-LaGuardia Act, however, Congress had granted legislative protection to a limited group of workers—namely, the nation's railroad employees.

The Erdman Act of 1898

The objective of the Erdman Act was to encourage and promote interstate commerce. To accomplish this goal, the members of Congress reasoned, it would be necessary to reduce labor disputes on the nation's railroads. The Erdman Act was to a large extent an outgrowth of the *Pullman* strike of 1894. This strike started when employees of the Pullman Company tried to force management to recognize their union, and eventually spread to the railroads themselves. The strike was broken by a blanket injunction prohibiting virtually any activity by the union, and it resulted in the jailing of Eugene V. Debs, a well-known Socialist labor leader. There was a great deal of bitterness among the nation's railroad workers following the Pullman strike, and Congress attempted through the Erdman Act to minimize this discontent and to encourage stable labor-management relations on the nation's railroads.

The most important provision of the Erdman Act was Section 10, which, in essence, outlawed "yellow dog contracts" for railroad employees, and made it a misdemeanor for railway employers to threaten workers with loss of employment, or to discriminate against any employee because of membership in a labor organization. The law also provided for mediation and arbitration of railroad labor-management disputes.

The Erdman Act no doubt made it somewhat easier for the nation's operating crafts to strengthen their unions. There was nothing in the law to preclude the formation of company-dominated unions, however, and it did not effectively ban the various methods used by anti-union employers to prevent the organization of workers or to break strikes where unions existed. There was nothing in the Erdman Act which required employers to recognize railroad unions and to bargain with their elected representatives. Thus the law was much less effective than later railway labor legislation.

The weakness of the Erdman Act was due to the failure of Congress to incorporate in this law any provisions for enforcement. In the absence of enforcement machinery, it was up to the courts to see that the law was obeyed. At a time when most judges had strong anti-union predilections it is not at all surprising that employers won out in most of the court proceedings under the Erdman Act.

Between 1898 and 1926 unions representing the railroad operating crafts grew in numbers and strength. But it is probably fair to say that this happened in spite of the Erdman Act rather than because of it. In 1926, however, Congress took further steps to reduce labor conflict on the nation's railroads. In that year it passed the Railway Labor Act which some writers have considered ever since to be a "model" piece of labor legislation.

The Railway Labor Act of 1926

One of the major provisions of the Act was contained in Section 2. This section provided for the settlement of railway labor-management disputes by representatives of the two parties who were to be selected "in such manner as may be provided in their corporate organization or unincorporated associations, or by other means of collective action, without interference, influence, or coercion exercised by either party over the self-organization or designation of representatives by the other." In an early test case, a railroad attempted to win court approval of its preference for dealing with a company-dominated union rather than one of the independent Brotherhoods. In cases decided before the Railway Labor Act was passed, the courts had supported this position. But in the *Texas and New Orleans Railway* case, the Supreme Court unanimously ruled that railway employees had a right to organize and bargain through representatives *of their own choice* without interference or coercion by their employers. In effect, this meant that if the workers chose to be represented by an independent union the companies could not insist upon bargaining with a company-dominated union.

In spite of this decision, however, there was a considerable amount of employer interference with union activities. In 1934, Congress passed several important amendments to the 1926 law which made it increasingly difficult for employers to avoid dealing with independent unions. One amendment established the National Mediation Board to administer the Railway Labor Act. This board was authorized to conduct elections to determine which union was to represent the workers. The union receiving a majority of votes was certified as the lawful representative of railroad workers, and employers were compelled to bargain with the union thus certified. Here was a major step forward for the nation's railroad workers, and it came at a time when Congress was preparing to enact legislation which would encourage the growth of trade unions in general.

As noted earlier, the Railway Labor Act has been hailed by some writers as a "model" labor law. There can be no doubt that it had an influence on subsequent state and federal labor legislation. This favorable judgment of the law has been based on the small number of railway labor-management disputes from the early thirties until World War II, a period characterized by widespread labor strife in manufacturing industry as the new C.I.O. unions swung into their organizing campaigns. It has been pointed out, however, that the railroads were already well organized by the beginning of this period. There was "an absence of great organizing drives and new unionism on the railroads at a time when industry generally was involved in the difficult task of adjusting to unionism for the first time."[1]

Some critics of the Railway Labor Act feel that it is too highly structured, and that the parties have been all too willing to allow federal boards to settle disputes rather than resolving them through the bargaining process. An even more stinging criticism, however, is that, especially after the 1934 amendment, the Railroad Brotherhoods used their political power to effect more favorable settlements than those recommended by emergency boards. This was particularly true during World War II and the immediate postwar period.[2] Even the critics of the Railway Labor Act agree, however, that its provisions for mediation and arbitration have contributed importantly to the settlement of any disputes which otherwise might have resulted in work stoppages.

The National Industrial Recovery Act of 1933

The National Industrial Recovery Act was not limited to labor-management relations. It was an attempt by the New Deal Congress to enact legislation which would speed recovery from the Great Depression. In many ways it was a jerry-built law, and there was relatively little mourning when it was declared unconstitutional by the Supreme Court two years later. But there was one provision of the NIRA which was to play an important part in subsequent legislation for the encouragement of union growth. This was the famous Section 7 (a) which required "that employees shall have the right to organize and bargain collectively through representatives of their own choosing, and shall be free from the interference, restraint, or coercion of employers of labor, or their agents, in the designation of such representatives, or in self-organization or in other concerted activities for the purpose of collective bargaining . . ." The law went on to specify that no worker or no one seeking employment would be required as a condition of employment to join a company union. It also specified that employers had to pay stated minimum wages, and it established maximum hours and other conditions of employment which were prescribed by the various codes of this Act.

The NIRA was enacted in 1933, and it was followed by a spurt in union membership. The number of union members increased by

[1] Gordon F. Bloom and Herbert R. Northrup, *Economics of Labor and Industrial Relations,* Philadelphia: The Blakiston Company (1950), p. 627.
[2] See Herbert R. Northrup, "The Railway Labor Act and Railway Labor Disputes in Wartime," *American Economic Review* (June 1946), pp. 324–343.

almost one-third between 1933 and 1935 when the NIRA was held to be unconstitutional.

The National Labor Relations Act of 1935

Congress responded to the Supreme Court's ruling which outlawed the NIRA by passing the National Labor Relations Act of 1935, better known as the Wagner Act after its principal author. This law, unlike the NIRA, was limited to labor-management relations, and it contained much more stringent provisions than the broader law which the court had overruled.

Many employers were led to believe that the Wagner Act would go the way of the NIRA, but this did not happen. A series of court cases culminated in the *Jones and Laughlin* decisions of 1937 when the Supreme Court upheld the constitutionality of the National Labor Relations Act. The Wagner Act then became the law of the land in labor-management relations whenever interstate commerce was involved.

Section 7 (a) of the Wagner Act was a counterpart of Section 7 (a) of the defunct NIRA. It specified that "employees shall have the right to self-organization, to form, join, or assist labor organizations, to bargain collectively through representatives of their own choosing, and to engage in concerted activities, for the purpose of collective bargaining or other mutual aid or protection."

The Wagner Act, however, went far beyond the NIRA. In Section 8, it specified a list of unfair labor practices for employers which made it unlawful for an employer to "interfere with, restrain, or coerce employees in the exercise of the rights guaranteed in Section 7." Employers were also forbidden to dominate or interfere with the formation or administration of any labor organization or contribute financial or other support to it . . . " It became unlawful for employers to discriminate against union members in employment, or to discharge workers because of union activity. Finally, it became an unfair labor practice for the employer to "refuse to bargain collectively with the representatives of his employees . . ."

This was the strongest piece of labor-management legislation enacted by Congress. Its intent was clearly that of encouraging the growth of independent trade unions. To administer the law, the Wagner Act set up the National Labor Relations Board which was authorized to determine union representation by conducting elections. The union receiving a majority vote was certified as the bargaining agent, and employers were required to bargain collectively with this union.

Not all employers gave in easily. The court dockets were crowded with cases involving the National Labor Relations Board and recalcitrant employers who sought to avoid one or more provisions of the Act. But the courts continued to rule that employers would have to recognize the principles of this Act, and as case after case was decided its coverage was broadened. The *Jones and Laughlin* case had made it clear that the law applied to manufacturing industry. As other cases were decided, mining, newspaper offices, the telegraph service, the lumber industry, department stores and chain stores were brought within the purview of the law. The courts took a liberal view of what constituted interstate commerce, and applied the law to many businesses which had formerly been considered to be "local" in character, despite the fact that they operated across state lines. Within a few years it became clear that virtually all workers except agricultural laborers and domestic servants—who were specifically excluded—came under the protection of the National Labor Relations Act or the Railway Labor Act provided the businesses involved were not completely local in character.

As noted in Chapter 4, there was a virtual explosion of trade union membership in the United States after 1935, but this was not due entirely to the Wagner Act. The split between the A.F. of L. and the C.I.O. came in that year. The formation of the C.I.O. was followed by massive organizational drives in the nation's mass-production industries. With a divided labor movement in which some unions sought to organize along craft lines and others to bring within their ranks all workers in an industry, the question of which type of union was to represent a company's workers became of paramount importance. The A.F. of L. unions insisted that they had an historical right to organize on the basis of a common skill, while the C.I.O. unions split off from the parent organization because they wanted to ignore occupational lines.

The National Labor Relations Board was faced with a thorny problem. How was it to determine what the appropriate bargaining unit should be? If the members of a specific occupational group were permitted to choose their union, those in the more highly skilled occupations would be inclined to vote for a craft union. If, on the other hand, the Board had insisted that all workers in a specific company vote for a single union, it would appear to be favoring the C.I.O. approach. In practice, the Board took a number of factors into account including the prior history of collective bargaining, management practices in making wage adjustments, and the numerical importance of particular occupational groups.

Following a court decision involving the *Globe Machine and Stamping Company,* in 1937, the Board applied the "Globe doctrine" in deciding on bargaining units. In a nutshell, this doctrine permits the members of a craft group to vote for union representation as a body. While the Board made an effort to avoid interpretation of the "Globe doctrine," a number of scholars feel that it tended to favor the A.F. of L. unions over the C.I.O.

The question of the appropriate bargaining unit has continued to be a troublesome one, and it was not completely ended when the A.F. of L. and C.I.O. merged into a new federation. For some time after the Wagner Act was passed, the Board was accused of favoring industrial unions. But following the *Globe* case the charge was more often made that the Board was favorably inclined toward craft unions. Once the great surge of organization in the mass-production industries had ended, the growth of the A.F. of L. unions began to outpace that of the C.I.O. But this could have been due to a number of factors, such as different growth rates in various occupations and industries, and a less doctrinaire attitude on the part of the A.F. of L. leaders toward organization along strictly craft lines. Whatever the effects of the Wagner Act on the growth rate of A.F. of L. versus C.I.O. unions, there is no question that this law provided a powerful stimulus to overall union growth. It was soon followed by another law designed to prevent employer interference with labor disputes.

The Anti-Strikebreaker Law of 1936

This law, frequently referred to as the Byrnes Act, made it a felony to "transport in interstate commerce any person employed for the purpose of interfering by force or threats with: (a) peaceful picketing during any labor dispute affecting wages, hours, or working conditions, or (b) exercise of employee rights of self-organization or collective bargaining." The law is not aimed at the common carriers by which such strike breakers might be transported, but at those persons who "wilfully transport" or cause them to be transported for the purposes of breaking a strike. The Department of Justice is charged with the prosecution of violators who are subject to fines up to $5,000, imprisonment up to two years, or both.

Labor Legislation During World War II

By the end of the 1930's, legislation favorable to trade unionism, coupled with the A.F. of L.-C.I.O. split, had led to a prodigious growth of union membership in the United States. Total membership more than doubled between 1935 and 1939. As the new unions gained in power they redoubled their efforts to organize workers in those industries which continued to resist union penetration. There was a great deal of strike activity, and the press seemed more than willing to give it front-page billing. Conservative elements in Congress felt that unions had been given too much encouragement, and there were efforts to rescind the public policy which encouraged union organization and the practice of collective bargaining. In June of 1940, the House of Representatives passed the Smith Amendments to the Wagner Act which would have accomplished this objective, but the Senate failed to take action and the House bill died as the 76th Congress adjourned.

Strike activity remained at a high level as the national economy was tooled up for the defense effort. And early in 1941, President Roosevelt, whose sympathy for the trade union movement had been made apparent, publicly condemned the jurisdictional disputes which were interfering with defense activity. In March 1941, the President established the National Defense Mediation Board by executive order, and charged it with the responsibility of minimizing industrial conflict. Some unions—especially those affiliated with the C.I.O.—took a dim view of the newly established Board and charged that it was an effort to slow down their organizational activities. But with the German attack on Russia in 1941, and the growing belief that our entry into the war was inevitable, much of this opposition was dissipated. After this, the National Defense Mediation Board was able to settle a great many labor disputes.

Then came Pearl Harbor. On January 12, 1942, the President signed Executive Order No. 9017 establishing the National War Labor Board. Originally the Board was made up of four union representatives, four employer representatives, and four representatives of the public; later, in 1944, the number of public members was increased to eight.

Shortly after our entry into the war, unions voluntarily made a no-strike pledge, but there was plenty of work for the War Labor Board to do. The most important issues which it faced were those dealing with union security and wages. To restrict the output of consumer goods, so that our resources could be devoted to the war effort, the government had instituted a policy of price controls and rationing. An inevitable corollary was that wages would also be subject to control. And one of the duties of the War Labor Board was to see that the line was held on wages although the Board was also given the right to make adjustments to correct inequities, and to eliminate substandard rates.

Despite the efforts of the Office of Price Administration, prices rose about 10 per cent between 1941 and 1942. Following this, prices continued to rise slowly through 1945. The War Labor Board could not ignore these price increases and in a decision involving the International Harvester Company it proposed reasonable protection of real wage levels negotiated through collective bargaining. In practice, the Board permitted fairly large increases to be granted in the lower wage brackets, and restrained increases in higher brackets. There was some confusion about the base from which wages were to be raised, however. This led to adoption of the "Little Steel Formula" in July of 1942.[3] Under this formula, the Board was to decide on wage increases in the light of price increases made since January 1, 1941, rather than since the last wage adjustment. Otherwise stated, real hourly earnings were to be maintained at the January 1941 base. Wage increases were to be limited to 15 per cent, the amount by which prices had gone up between January 1941 and July 1942. The Board was still permitted to eliminate inequities and substandard rates, however.

As the war progressed, there were growing pressures on the Board to grant further wage increases, and these were not resisted by employers, especially those who were faced with a serious labor shortage. Following an order issued by the Director of Economic Stabilization in May 1943, the Board was given authority to make further adjustments to bring low rates up to the minimum going rate in specific labor market areas. The Board was further authorized to set up a series of wage-rate brackets for particular occupational groups in each labor market area. This permitted some further maneuvering within the "little steel" formula, and wage increases were granted perhaps more liberally than the Director of Economic Stabilization had anticipated.

The problem of holding the line on wages was one of two major problems which confronted the War Labor Board from the beginning. The other was the issue of union security. Union security involves

[3] The formula was based on decisions involving the Bethlehem, Republic, Youngstown Sheet and Tube, and Inland Steel Companies, sometimes referred to as the "little steel" companies to distinguish them from the nation's larger producers.

the type of agreement which has been negotiated by labor and management. The tightest form of union security is the closed shop, under which union members only are hired, typically through a union hiring hall. Next comes the union shop, a provision which specifies that all employees in a given concern must join a union within a certain number of days after accepting employment with the company. Following this is the "open" shop—which union leaders regard as no security at all—under which, technically, both union and non-union workers are to be given similar treatment.

Theoretically, the War Labor Board was charged with maintaining the status quo on union security—it was not supposed to either encourage or discourage the two parties in their efforts to arrive at an agreement. But a compromise of some sort seemed inevitable, and this was developed early in the Board's life through awards of "maintenance of membership" provisions. Under a maintenance of membership provision, a worker who had belonged to a union as of a given date was required to maintain his membership in that union as a condition of employment. But newly-hired workers would not be required to join the union, and the union was not to coerce any employee into joining. This led to a number of difficulties, however. In a case decided in August 1942, a new formula was announced, which provided for maintenance of membership provisions after a fifteen-day waiting period during which workers could withdraw from the union if they wished to do so. The maintenance of membership provision was based on the theory that by adopting no-strike pledges, unions had given up their most powerful weapon for achieving both union security and wage increases. To stabilize labor-management relations, therefore, the Board announced that maintenance of membership awards were both equitable and essential, and the Board continued to follow this policy throughout the period of hostilities.

Although it was the announced public policy that the government would attempt to maintain the status quo insofar as labor-management relations were concerned, the wartime handling of union security provisions did nothing to discourage union membership. And there was a further increase in membership of roughly 30 per cent between 1941 and 1945.

Management, of course, made little effort to stem the rising union membership, and there is some evidence that some managements were more than willing to go along with the wage increases which were permitted within the bracket system established by the War

Labor Board. This was not because management had suddenly recognized the benefits of trade unionism, but was rather a consequence of the tight labor market situation. With some twelve million men between the ages of eighteen and thirty-five under arms, the problem of unemployment which had lingered throughout the Great Depression evaporated and was replaced by one of labor shortages. Thus many companies which had displayed a marked coolness toward trade unionism before World War II were quite willing to accept a limited form of union security, and did little if anything to discourage their workers from joining a union if they wished to do so.

The War Labor Disputes Act of 1943

One piece of wartime labor legislation will be discussed at this point although its provisions might seem at variance with the title of this chapter. This is the War Labor Disputes Act, better known as the Smith-Connally Act, which was passed in June 1943 over President Roosevelt's veto. The law was ostensibly designed to prevent interference with the war effort although its authors managed to slip in one provision which bore no relationship to wartime emergency affairs. Briefly, the Smith-Connally Act empowered the President to seize an essential facility threatened by a shutdown, if this were necessary, to prevent interference with the war effort. The law required a thirty-day notice before the start of any strike which would interrupt war production. At the end of this period the National Labor Relations Board was to conduct a secret election to determine if the workers involved wished to go ahead with the strike. Penalties were also provided for anyone attempting to instigate a strike in a seized plant or other defense facility. In addition, the Act outlawed political contributions by unions in any national election. As Melvin Reder has pointed out this "was completely unrelated to the war effort and was simply a gratuitous insult to the labor movement."[4]

In practice, the Smith-Connally Act had little effect on the relatively small unions involved in strikes between its passage and the end of World War II. If a union wished to strike it simply gave notice, and at the end of the thirty-day waiting period its members would overwhelmingly support the union position. About all that the law accomplished was to add to the already heavy load of the National Labor Relations Board which had to supervise the elections. In some ways the law might even have been helpful to unions although this

[4] Melvin W. Reder, *Labor in a Growing Economy,* New York: John Wiley and Sons, Inc. (1957), p. 225.

certainly was not the intent of its authors. Most employers were anxious to avoid seizure. Within the limits of the wage and price stabilization programs, which both parties were expected to respect, the threat of seizure might have made them somewhat more amenable to union demands. There was also a basic incongruity in the law which permitted both seizure and strikes under certain circumstances. The objective of seizure is to prevent strikes, yet the law permitted strikes after a waiting period and an election. Union officials justifiably grumbled about the vagueness of the law which could have made them innocent victims of militant employers or dissident minorities within their own organization.[5] Fortunately, as wartime legislation, the Act expired six months after the formal cessation of hostilities.

The fact that the Smith-Connally Act was passed is not without significance, however. Even in the Congress which passed the Wagner Act there was a vocal anti-union minority which continued to press for a return to restrictive labor legislation. The amount of labor strife between 1935 and the outbreak of World War II alarmed many citizens, and the number of Congressmen and Senators who viewed unions as a threat to established society grew. Under the emotional stress of wartime conditions they were unable to convince a majority in Congress that union power had to be curbed to protect the war effort. The legislation they enacted was ineffective, but it indicated the beginning of a change in public opinion toward unions which subsequently was to have an effect on public policy.

There can be no doubt that between 1935 and 1940 public policy in the United States encouraged the growth of trade unions. While it might be going too far to say that wartime policies provided a further spur to the growth of union membership, it seems clear that nothing was done to discourage union growth. The unions for their part behaved admirably during the wartime emergency. There were a few strikes, to be sure. These were widely publicized, and they led to the ineffective but distasteful Smith-Connally Act. By and large, however, unions observed the no-strike pledge and worked mightily to further the war effort.

By the end of the second World War, trade unions in the United States claimed over twelve and one-half million members. The labor movement had become a mighty colossus. Union demands during the war had been moderate, and labor-management relations

[5] Harry A. Millis and Royal E. Montgomery, *Organized Labor,* New York: McGraw-Hill (1945), p. 602.

—under the guidance of the War Labor Board and the National Labor Relations Board—were relatively stable and peaceful. All was not sweetness and light, however. Some union leaders grumbled at wage restraints and some employers were resentful at having to deal with union leaders at all. Their differences could be temporarily subordinated to the common goal of winning the war, but these differences set the stage for an eruption of labor-management disturbances once the war had ended and the economy began rapidly to shift back to a peacetime basis.

Chapter 8 The Emergence of Restrictive Labor Legislation

The word "restrictive" in the title of this chapter is intended to be descriptive rather than deprecating. An unbiased observer has to admit that the Wagner Act was "pro-labor." The intent of the law was to foster the growth of unions, and it contained few limitations on union behavior. By listing a series of unfair labor practices, however, the Wagner Act clearly placed a number of restraints on management.

The Wagner Act was widely accepted by the public when it was passed. This was at a time when union members accounted for less than 7 per cent of the nation's civilian labor force. By the end of World War II, however, unions included almost 25 per cent of the civilian work force, and their status had changed markedly during a decade of protection under the Wagner Act.

Many union leaders had chafed under wartime restrictions. They had gone along with the wage stabilization program so long as prices remained relatively stable, and at a time when everyone was concerned with the common goal of bringing the war to a successful conclusion. But the government, in its haste to return to peacetime conditions, eliminated price controls prematurely and prices shot upward in 1946 and 1947. There followed a series of strikes during which unions won successive "rounds" of wage increases, only to be followed by similar rounds of price increases.

Given the huge volume of savings, industry was anxious to re-tool for civilian production. There were some hard-fought strikes, but in most cases management was forced to capitulate since it wished to produce the goods for which consumers were clamoring.

The long days of New Deal and Fair Deal control of Congress ended as the Republican Party seated a majority in the 80th Congress. Since the postwar strikes produced a considerable amount of public resentment, legislation to impose restrictions upon union behavior was high on the agenda when the new Congress convened.

The first law to impose restraints upon union practices dealt with a relatively small and specific union group. This was the Unlawful Practices in Radio Broadcasting Act of 1946 sometimes referred to as the Lea Act, but more generally as the "Anti-Petrillo" Act.[1] This Act, which is still in force, prohibits certain types of coercive labor practices in the radio industry. There had been instances where unions had compelled radio stations to employ workers who were not needed and to restrict the use of recorded programs. The Lea Act outlawed such activities, and made it a criminal offense for anyone to use or threaten to use force or violence to compel a radio station to hire extra workers or to pay for services which were not performed. The Act also outlawed the use of pressure to restrict the use of recordings and transcriptions. While highly restricted in coverage, and not entirely successful in achieving its intent, this Act marked the first break with the prewar policy of encouraging union growth without restraints upon union behavior.

THE TAFT-HARTLEY ACT

The major change in the nation's public policy toward trade unions came when the Labor-Management Relations Act of 1947 was passed. This Act is better known by the names of its two principal sponsors in the Senate and the House, Senator Taft and Representative Hartley.

During the extensive hearings held while the Taft-Hartley bill was being debated, management witnesses testified that the Wagner Act restricted their behavior without placing corresponding restraints upon union leaders. Union leaders also appeared before Congressional committees to discuss the bill, but they insisted that there was no need to change the terms of the Wagner Act. Some legislators and others sympathetic to the trade union movement urged union leaders to make some concessions since it was impossible to deny that the Wagner Act was one-sided in character. The union leaders were adamant. The Wagner Act, in their view, was all the labor legislation this country needed. It is evident, how-

[1] James C. Petrillo was president of the American Federation of Musicians at the time this Act was passed, and it was this union which was the target of the Lea Act.

ever, that union leaders misjudged the temper of the times. Congress passed the Taft-Hartley bill which was then sent to President Truman for his signature. The President vetoed the bill, but Congress overrode the veto and the Taft-Hartley bill became law.

The Taft-Hartley Act contains the provisions essential for the protection of trade unions found in the Wagner Act. It guarantees the right of workers to organize and bargain collectively. It also gives workers the right to refrain from all union activities. It places certain limits on the activities of employers, but it also restricts some of the activities of labor organizations.

The new law, as was true of the Wagner Act, is administered by the National Labor Relations Board which consists of five members, and the General Council of the Board. Members of the Board are appointed by the President for terms of five years, and the General Council for a term of four. The Taft-Hartley Act does not apply to workers covered by the Railway Labor Act, nor to agricultural laborers, domestic servants, government employees, independent contractors or employees of non-profit hospitals. Supervisors are also excluded from the terms of the Act. Section 7 of the Taft-Hartley Act is largely a carryover from Section 7(a) of the Wagner Act, with the added proviso that workers shall have the right to refrain from any or all union activities unless the union and management have negotiated a union shop agreement. This is an agreement specifying that each member of a bargaining unit must become and remain a union member—typically after a brief waiting period—as a condition of employment.[2]

Unfair Labor Practices for Employers

The Taft-Hartley Act, as was true of its predecessor, also lists unfair labor practices for employers. There are six general types of unfair practices which employers are forbidden to engage in:

(1) *Interference, restraint, or coercion of employees in the exercise of rights as guaranteed by Section 7.* For example, employers are forbidden to threaten employees with the loss of jobs or benefits if they should join a union, or to threaten to close down a plant if a union should succeed in organizing it. Under the terms of this unfair labor practice, employers are forbidden to question employees about their union activities or membership if this will tend to re-

[2] The union shop must be distinguished from the *closed* shop. Under the latter form of union security, a worker must be a union member *before* being hired. In the past this generally meant that employers with closed shop agreements obtained workers through a union hiring hall.

strain or coerce the workers. Also, employers cannot spy on union meetings or grant increases deliberately timed to defeat the self-organization of workers.

(2) *Illegal assistance or domination of a labor organization.* Employers are forbidden to take an active part in organizing a union or a committee to represent their workers; to bring pressure upon their employees to join a particular union, or to indicate favoritism if two or more unions are seeking to represent their employees. This is a continuation of the earlier ban on company-dominated unions, and also an effort to prevent an employer from favoring a particular outside union.

(3) *Discrimination in employment for union activities.* Any form of discrimination in hiring or tenure of employment, or the terms or conditions of employment, which would tend to encourage or discourage membership in any labor organizations is prohibited by the Taft-Hartley Act. One result of this provision is that the "closed shop" was outlawed. The closed shop, it will be recalled, is a form of union security under which only those workers who already belong to a union can be hired by an employer.[3] Unions and employers are permitted to negotiate union shop agreements, however, under which employees may be required to join the union within thirty days of their employment. In building and construction, employees may be required to join after seven days. Types of discrimination forbidden by this section of the law include: demoting or discharging a worker for urging others to join or organize a union; refusing to reinstate an employee because he took part in a lawful strike; refusing to hire a qualified applicant because he belongs to a union, or because he belongs to one union rather than another. Employers are not, of course, prevented from firing, transferring, or laying off workers for economic or disciplinary reasons.

(4) *Discrimination for participation in NLRB proceedings.* The law specifically makes it an unfair labor practice for an employer to fire a worker because he has filed charges or given testimony under the terms of the Taft-Hartley Act.

(5) *Refusal to bargain in good faith.* Examples of unfair labor practices forbidden by this section include: granting wage increases without consulting union representatives; granting larger wage

[3] In practice, many employers in a number of industries continued to obtain workers through union hiring halls. This was especially true in industries (such as construction and longshoring) where employment tends to be casual or intermittent.

increases than the amount offered to union representatives; refusal to put an agreement with employees' representatives into writing, and refusing to deal with the representatives of employees because the latter are on strike.

(6) *"Hot Cargo"* Agreements. Employers were forbidden by the Taft-Hartley Act to make an agreement to stop handling another employer's products, or to stop doing business with any other person. Certain exceptions were made to this provision in the case of subcontractors in the construction industry and jobbers in the apparel and clothing industries.

Unfair Labor Practices for Unions

The basic rights of workers to belong to unions have been protected by the Taft-Hartley Act. Further, employers are prevented from discriminating against union members. As under the Wagner Act they must also bargain with the freely chosen representatives of their workers after the National Labor Relations Board has certified a union as the employees' bargaining representative. The Taft-Hartley Act also specifies a series of unfair labor practices for unions which are covered under eight broad headings:

(1) *Restraint or coercion.* This provision states that it "shall not forbid the right of a labor organization to prescribe its own rules with respect to the acquisition or retention of membership." But unions are forbidden to restrain or coerce employees in the selection of bargaining representatives, or of no representatives at all, except after a union shop provision has been negotiated. For example, unions are forbidden to engage in mass picketing which would physically bar non-striking employees from entering a plant. Acts of force or violence on the picket line or in connection with strikes; threats to do bodily injury to non-striking workers, or threats to employees that they will lose their jobs unless they support the union's activities are also outlawed by the Act.

(2) *Attempts to cause discrimination for union activities.* Under this provision, for example, a union cannot force an employer to fire a worker who has urged a change in the union's method of selecting shop stewards. Nor can the union enter into an agreement which requires the employer to hire only those persons "satisfactory" to the union.

(3) *Refusal to bargain in good faith.* This is a counterpart to the provision relating to employers. For example, union officials cannot refuse to make written contracts of reasonable duration, and

they cannot insist upon the inclusion of an illegal provision (such as a closed shop) in an agreement.

(4) *Secondary boycotts and certain types of strikes and picketing.* One of the more complex provisions of the Taft-Hartley Act attempted to control various forms of union activity against employers not directly engaged in a dispute with the union. Under its terms, the Board has found that it is illegal for a union to picket the plant of an employer who continues to deal with a company with which the union has a dispute. It is also illegal to picket an entire construction project because one of the subcontractors on the project employs non-union workers. The Board has also ruled that a union official who contacted members in a retail market to tell them that a wholesaler had been placed on the union's "unfair list" was guilty of an unfair labor practice. It is *not* an unfair labor practice, however, for a union to picket the plant of an employer with whom it has a direct dispute even though such picketing might discourage other workers from entering the plant. This section does ban "sympathy" strikes or boycotts to force recognition of an uncertified union, however. It also prohibits strikes over jurisdictional disputes, or disputes involving work assignments.

The problem of secondary union pressure is a complicated one, and the Taft-Hartley Act did not settle it.[4] Some unions continued to refuse to handle "hot cargoes," that is, the products of an employer with whom the union had a dispute. The Board upheld this action in some cases. The picketing of trucks at a neutral site was upheld in some cases while in others it was considered a violation of the Taft-Hartley Act. The reasoning behind these decisions is not easy to follow. This is an indication that the language of the Act was not sufficiently precise to give the Board a clear mandate on how to deal with a variety of secondary union activities.

The NLRB was given authority to decide jurisdictional disputes by the Taft-Hartley Act. The unions involved in such a dispute are given ten days to reach a settlement following the filing of a charge. If they do not do so the Board steps in to make the decision for them. To avoid this provision of the Act some unions, such as those in the building trades, have set up private machinery to make jurisdictional awards. This typically involves an outside "umpire" whose decisions are final and binding, and in recent years, has led to a drop

[4] For discussion of some of the issues involved, with reference to a number of cases, see Charles H. Tower, "A Perspective on Secondary Boycotts," reprinted from *Labor Law Journal* (October 1951) in George P. Shultz and John R. Coleman, *Labor Problems: Cases and Readings,* New York: McGraw-Hill (1953), pp. 424–434.

in the number of jurisdictional disputes—an indirect but generally welcomed consequence of the Taft-Hartley Act.

(5) *Charging excessive or discriminatory initiation fees.* In determining what constitutes a discriminatory initiation fee the Board considers practices and customs of labor organizations in the particular industry, and the wages currently paid to employees affected. The Board found, for example, that it was an unfair labor practice when a union charged old employees—who failed to join the union before a union-shop agreement took effect—a fee of $15.00 while charging employees hired after that date only $5.00.

(6) *"Featherbedding."* The Taft-Hartley Act declared it an unfair labor practice for unions to cause or attempt to cause an employer to pay for services which are not performed or are not to be performed. This was an attempt by the framers of the Act to eliminate "featherbedding" by legislative fiat, but it has had little practical effect upon union policies. The Act mistakenly assumed that "make work" rules are easily identified, and that they could be abolished by declaring them to be unfair labor practices.

Some kinds of "make work" can be identified. The practice of setting "bogus type" or "dead horse" in some branches of the printtrades is a clear-cut example of what Paul Jacobs has called "unwork."[5] This is work which is performed and paid for, but which serves no useful purpose. Other types of work rules have been labeled as "featherbedding," however, when it is far from clear that they have been imposed by a union solely for the purpose of maintaining its members' income or to avoid unemployment. Whether or not a specific rule is designed to make work calls for detailed and specific analysis, but as Norman Simler has pointed out, there are cases where even careful observation cannot provide a definite answer.[6]

The Taft-Hartley Act attempted to deal with one of the most complex issues in collective bargaining by the simple declaration that "featherbedding" is an unfair labor practice. Thus the Act had little effect upon existing work rules. As will be noted in a later chapter, work rules have become one of the central issues in collective

[5] Paul Jacobs, *Dead Horse and the Featherbird,* Santa Barbara, California: Center for the Study of Democratic Institutions (1962), p. 4.
[6] Norman J. Simler, "The Economics of Featherbedding," *Industrial and Labor Relations Review* (October 1962), p. 119. See also, Morris A. Horowitz, *Manpower Utilization in the Railroad Industry,* Boston: Northeastern University, Bureau of Business and Economic Research (1960).

bargaining in recent years. But where changes have been made they have been due to negotiations, arbitration awards, or the recommendations of fact-finding boards.

(7) *Recognition and organizational picketing.* Under the Taft-Hartley Act a union cannot picket an employer in an effort to force him to bargain with the union (unless the union has been certified by the National Labor Relations Board as the representative of the firm's employees) if that employer has already lawfully recognized another union under the terms of the Taft-Hartley Act. The union also cannot picket the employer if there has been a valid representation election within the last twelve months. This provision does not, however, prevent informational picketing, i.e., advising the public that the employer does not employ members of a union, unless the effects of such informational picketing would be to prevent the delivery of goods to or by the firm, or the performance of services in the firm. Unions are permitted, under the terms of this provision, to picket an employer who has no labor agreement at all if the purpose of their picketing is simply to discourage customers from patronizing the firm.

(8) *"Hot cargo" and subcontracting agreements.* It is an unfair labor practice for any union and employer to make an agreement (written or implied) under which the employer would agree not to handle, use, sell, transport or otherwise deal in the products of any other employer, or to cease doing business with any other person. This is a counterpart of the unfair labor practice for employers which makes specific exceptions in the case of subcontracting in the construction industry, or relations with jobbers or subcontractors in the apparel and clothing industries. As noted earlier, however, the Board has not always held refusal by other unions to handle "hot cargoes" to be illegal.

The "Free Speech" Provision

One of the provisions of the Wagner Act which was most bitterly criticized by employers was that which, in their view at least, limited employers' freedom of speech. The law stated that employers could not "interfere with, restrain, or coerce employees" in exercising their rights to self-organization. The interpretation of this provision was, of course, somewhat tricky. What might be considered coercion by one person might simply be accepted as an expression of opinion by another. It must have been recognized at the outset that there would have to be considerable latitude in the interpretation of this provision, but it remained a hotly debated one. The Supreme Court expressed its opinion on this provision in the case of *NLRB v. Virginia Electric and Power Company* in 1941.

In that case the court said: "Neither the Act nor the Board's order here enjoin the employer from expressing its view on labor policies or problems, nor is a penalty imposed upon it because of any utterances it has made. The sanctions of the Act are imposed not in punishment of the employer but for the protection of the employees. The employer in this case is as free now as ever to take any side it may choose on this controversial issue." The court made it clear that the employer was free to express his opinions about trade unions. But the decision went on to assert that "certain *conduct,* though evidenced in part by speech, may amount in connection with other circumstances to coercion within the meaning of the Act."[7] It was the conduct of the employer, in the court's view, and not simply his opinions which might be considered as coercive. However, the line between speech and action is not always a simple one to draw, and the court concluded that "if the *total activities* of an employer restrains or coerces his employees in their free choice, then those employees are entitled to the protection of the Act and . . . pressure exerted vocally by the employer may no more be disregarded than pressure exerted in other ways."[8]

Although in subsequent opinions, the courts continued to insist that the Wagner Act did not interfere with the employer's basic constitutional right of freedom of speech, the charge was regularly made that this was the case. The Taft-Hartley Act attempted to clarify this thorny issue in Section 8(c): "The expression of any views, argument, or opinion, or the dissemination thereof, whether in written, printed, graphic, or visual form, shall not constitute or be evidence of an unfair labor practice under any of the provisions of this Act, if such expression contains no threat of reprisal or force or promise of benefit."

In interpreting this provision of the Taft-Hartley Act, the National Labor Relations Board has held that the section applies only to unfair labor practice cases and not to conduct affecting elections. The Board has ruled, for example, that Section 8(c) does not cover cases where employers threaten workers with the loss of benefits in the event a union wins an organizational election.

[7] *National Labor Relations Board v. Virginia Electric and Power Company,* 314 U.S. 469 (1941), italics added.
[8] *Ibid.,* italics added.

This provision has also been used to restrain unions. The Board has held that picket signs claiming that an employer is "unfair," when making an effort to induce his workers to engage in a secondary boycott, is a violation of Section 8(c). Moreover, statements by union officials to employees that the latter would lose their jobs if a union won an organizational election have also been ruled as a violation of the "free speech" provision of the Taft-Hartley Act.

Changing or Terminating a Contract

The Taft-Hartley Act provides for four basic steps when a contract is renegotiated. If either party desires to change or to terminate its existing agreement, it must: (1) serve written notice at least sixty days before the termination date; (2) offer to meet with the other party to discuss a new contract; (3) if agreement is not reached within thirty days, notify the Federal Mediation and Conciliation Service that a dispute exists, and (4) maintain the status quo on all terms and conditions of the existing contract until sixty days after notice is given or until the contract expires, whichever occurs later. Any worker who goes on strike during the sixty-day waiting period automatically loses his status as an employee under the terms of the Act.

These rather formal arrangements were designed to reduce the number of strikes but they have been of relatively little consequence. They assume that an element of surprise is important in changing a contract, and that if this can be eliminated the chances of a peaceful settlement will be improved. There seems to be little support for this assumption, however, and the formal steps required to terminate or change a contract have had no apparent effect upon collective bargaining behavior.

STATE "RIGHT-TO-WORK" LAWS

There is one provision of the Taft-Hartley Act which unions have criticized bitterly. This provision permits unions and employers to reach union-shop agreements except in states where such agreements are forbidden by state law. It is somewhat unusual since it is not customary for Congress to permit state laws to take precedence over federal law. At the time the Act was passed, some union spokesmen said that the inclusion of this provision was an open invitation to states where unions were relatively weak to pass laws prohibiting this form of union security. They were quite right. By 1963 twenty states had general "right-to-work" laws, and one other—Louisiana—had a right-to-work law which affected agricultural

MAP 8–1
STATE "RIGHT-TO-WORK" LAWS SHOWING YEAR ADOPTED

State with "Right-to-work" law limited in application. Affects agricultural and certain processing workers only.

States with "Right-to-work" laws.

Source: *State "Right-to-Work" Laws,* U.S. Department of Labor, Bureau of Labor Standards, Bulletin 204 (May 1959), facing p. 1, and *Business Week* (February 16, 1963), p. 56.

and certain processing workers only.[9] The geographical distribution of these states is shown on the *following map.*

Most of the southern states adopted such legislation as did some of the more sparsely populated and relatively non-industrial states in the Mountain West and the middle-western Farm Belt. The one state with a substantial amount of industry to adopt legislation with restrictions on union security is Indiana which passed a "right-to-work" law in 1957. States in which industry and mining are of considerable economic significance, and in which unions wield considerable political power, have refused to enact such legislation.

State right-to-work laws also prohibit "maintenance of membership" agreements, widely negotiated during World War II, requiring those workers who belong to a union at the beginning of a contract period to remain members during the life of the contract. The latter provision is of relatively little consequence since main-

[9] Under a 1951 amendment to the Railway Labor Act, union shops are permitted for railroad workers even in "right-to-work" states.

tenance of membership agreements were largely a wartime expedient.

The closed shop was banned everywhere by the Taft-Hartley Act. In practice, the ban has had little effect. There was not much change in hiring arrangements in previous closed shops. Enactment of state "right-to-work" laws may have had some effect on union membership, however. The loss of a union shop agreement, even if union recognition is maintained, will cause some workers to drop out of a union. Not all workers covered by union shop agreements are ardent union supporters. Given the opportunity, some will prefer to "ride the gravy train," particularly if they feel reasonably sure that a majority will continue to vote for the union. This gives them the protection of union standards without having to pay union dues. On balance, however, the "right-to-work" laws probably have not been as damaging to unions as some employers might have wished, or as some union spokesmen insist they have been.

Some unions responded to the union shop prohibition in "right-to-work" states by negotiating, or attempting to negotiate, "agency shop" contracts. An agency shop agreement requires those workers in the bargaining unit who refuse to join the union to pay a fee in lieu of union dues. Where such a provision can be negotiated the union might suffer a loss of membership, but it can at least maintain its financial strength. It can also be argued by proponents of the agency shop that such an agreement meets the criticism of compulsory union membership.

Unions have made relatively little headway with the agency shop, however. In 1959, only 15 of more than 1,600 agreements studied contained an agency shop provision.[10] Indeed, eleven of the state "right to work" laws specifically prohibit the payment of union dues as a condition of employment.[11] And in other states, Arizona and Florida, for example, the courts have ruled that the agency shop violates state "right-to-work" laws. Indiana is a notable exception. In this case courts ruled that its "right-to-work" law does not ban the agency shop. This position was upheld by the Supreme

[10] Paul E. Sultan, "The Union Security Issue," in Joseph Shister, *et al.*, eds., *Public Policy and Collective Bargaining,* New York: Harper and Row (1962), p. 99.

[11] *Ibid.*, p. 106. Nebraska became the eleventh "right-to-work" state to prohibit the denial of employment because of refusal to pay a fee through a 1961 amendment to its law. See U. S. Department of Labor, *Annual Digest of State and Federal Labor Legislation,* 1961-1962, Bureau of Labor Standards Bulletin 253, Washington: U. S. Government Printing Office (1963), p. 88.

Court, although the latter went on to say that other state laws may prohibit this form of union security.[12]

THE TAFT-HARTLEY ACT IN EMERGENCY DISPUTES

Emergency disputes are defined as those which might jeopardize national health or safety. The Taft-Hartley Act attempted to avert such disputes by setting up a number of steps which unions and employers are required to follow.

If the President believes that a threatened or actual strike (or lockout) will constitute a national emergency he can:

(1) Appoint a board of inquiry to prepare a written report on the facts of the dispute, but which does not have authority to make recommendations.
(2) After reviewing the report, the President can direct the Attorney General to seek an injunction to prevent the strike or lockout.
(3) If the court which was asked to grant the injunction agrees that the national health or safety will be threatened by a strike, it may issue the injunction.

If the issues are still unsettled at the end of a sixty-day waiting period, the board of inquiry is asked to make another report on the status of the dispute, and the positions of the parties, which is to include a statement of the employer's "last offer of settlement." Within fifteen days after this report is submitted, the National Labor Relations Board is directed to hold a secret election on the employer's "final offer of settlement." As a final step, within five days after this election, the Attorney General is directed to seek discharge of the injunction, and the court is directed to lift the injunction.

The basic assumption behind the emergency dispute proceedings under the Taft-Hartley Act is that if unions and managements are forced to go through a "cooling-off" period they might reconsider their actions and call off an existing or proposed dispute. A number of writers have been critical of this assumption. It is their contention that neither union leaders nor management decide to initiate a strike or lockout in the heat of anger, and that "cooling-off" periods are not the appropriate remedy. There is evidence that this machinery has not been effective in averting strikes which might constitute "national emergencies." Between 1947, when the Taft-

[12] *Business Week* (June 22, 1963), p. 48.

Hartley Act was passed, and 1953, twelve labor-management disputes were judged to be of an emergency nature. In five of these cases strikes occurred after the last provisions of the law were invoked, and in the three cases where an election was held on the employer's "final offer" it was rejected. In the words of Sumner Slichter, this record "cannot be regarded as a 'good batting average' for the law."[13]

The most widely-publicized application of the emergency procedures of the Taft-Hartley Act was in the steel strike of 1959. However, the use of the injunction, and an enforced "cooling-off" period, had little to do with the ultimate settlement of the most serious strike—in terms of man-days of idleness—since the wave of disputes which followed the end of World War II. The basic issue involved in this strike was that of work rules. Management insisted that it needed greater freedom to make work assignments if it was to grant "non-inflationary" wage increases. The union denied that existing work rules interfered with technological progress, and pointed to the industry's excellent record of productivity gains in support of this position. Other issues were involved but they were of secondary importance.

After prolonged negotiations, which made little headway, more than one-half million steelworkers went on strike on July 14, 1959. In general, industry stockpiles of steel were high since the strike came after more than a year of recovery from the 1958 recession. The strike had been in progress for 116 days before the emergency provisions of the Taft-Hartley Act were invoked. A fact-finding board was appointed on October 9, and issued its report on October 19. On the same day President Eisenhower requested a district court at Pittsburgh to issue an injunction. This decision was the President's since the board had no authority to make recommendations. The union asked for and obtained a stay on the injunction arguing that in view of the substantial amount of steel in inventory the defense program was not affected. This request was carried to a Circuit Court of Appeals and thence to the Supreme Court. On November 7, the latter upheld the District Court decision, and the injunction went into effect. The striking workers were ordered by the union to return to their jobs.

The steel companies made their "final offer of settlement" on November 15 but it was never voted on. A number of informal polls of steelworkers had indicated that they would reject the

[13] Sumner H. Slichter, "Revision of the Taft-Hartley Act," *Quarterly Journal of Economics* (May 1953), p. 170.

offer. This meant that the strike could have been resumed in January of 1960. Negotiations continued during the "cooling off" period, however, and agreement on all major economic issues was reached on January 4, 1960. Vice President Nixon and Secretary of Labor James P. Mitchell had participated in the discussions prior to the settlement. This, in the union's view, permitted the steel industry to save face: "What the companies were reluctant to offer voluntarily, they were ready to do if requested by a high officer of the government."[14]

The union achieved virtually all its demands, and the hotly-disputed work rules provision in the earlier agreement remained unchanged. It was agreed that a joint committee, headed by a neutral chairman, would be appointed to study the issue and to make recommendations. But the union had won the major point which led to this protracted and costly strike.

The 1959 steel strike offered further evidence that the Taft-Hartley Act does not contain adequate provisions for the settlement of so-called "emergency disputes." There is considerable agreement that the steel industry has a "high emergency potential."[15] But it is doubtful that the 1959 situation was a critical one. The union has contended that the defense program was not affected and that the companies might have reached an earlier settlement if the injunction had not been granted. Economic pressures, rather than government intervention, would have brought about the settlement. This method, in the view of a number of authorities, has much to commend it in a free society.[16]

As it stands the Taft-Hartley Act can only postpone a strike which might imperil the nation's health and safety. One suggestion to improve the Act's effectiveness would be to permit the board of inquiry to make recommendations for a settlement. The President could then be authorized to put these into effect for a stated period of time. This would put pressure upon both sides, it has been argued, to reach a settlement through collective bargaining.[17] Another suggestion calls for "flexibility and uncertainty" in the handling of emergency disputes. In essence, this means asking Congress to work out a solution to the particular problems in-

[14] *The 1959 Steel Strike,* The United Steelworkers of America, International Affairs Department (no date), p. 56.
[15] See Irving Bernstein, *et al.,* eds., *Emergency Disputes and National Policy,* New York: Harper and Brothers (1955), pp. 16 and 27ff.
[16] See, for example, Clyde W. Summers, "A Summary Evaluation of the Taft-Hartley Act," *Industrial and Labor Relations Review* (April 1958), p. 412.
[17] Sumner H. Slichter, *op. cit.,* pp. 178–179.

volved. Since the parties would not know what action Congress might take, they would be under pressure to settle their differences through negotiations.[18]

THE REACTION OF UNIONS TO THE TAFT-HARTLEY ACT

Union leaders, as noted earlier, unanimously opposed the Taft-Hartley bill while it was being debated. When the law was passed it was roundly denounced by many union leaders as a "slave labor" law. Some predicted that it would mean an end to the growth of trade unions. An objective appraisal of the law cannot avoid the conclusion that it is restrictive on certain types of union behavior, and it is certainly a far cry from the earlier Wagner Act in terms of its treatment of the two parties in labor-management relations. But despite its restrictive features the Taft-Hartley Act did not spell the end of union growth.

During the first few years the Taft-Hartley Act was on the books union membership failed to increase. There was even a modest decline between 1947, the year the Act was passed, and 1950. This was followed by a spurt in union membership which lasted until 1953 and there was a further moderate increase between 1955 and 1956. Whether or not union membership would have increased more rapidly in the absence of the law is something which has been debated. As noted in an earlier chapter, a number of influences have acted on union growth in recent years. The provision which permits states to enact "right-to-work" laws is probably the one which could affect union growth most. Enforced union membership through union security provisions has contributed to union growth in the past. But unions had met with limited success in most states with "right-to-work" laws even before Taft-Hartley.

It seems clear that the failure of unions to grow since the mid-1950's is due to a number of factors. This point is conceded by some writers with a pro-labor point of view. Solomon Barkin, who was associated with one of the nation's larger industrial unions for many years, feels that the Taft-Hartley and other restrictive labor laws have impeded union growth. But he points to a number of other influences which have contributed to declining union membership.[19] These include worker satisfaction with social conditions, the sullied image of trade unions due to the exposure of corruption

[18] Arthur J. Goldberg and Jack Barbash, "Labor Looks at the National Emergency Provisions," in Bernstein, *et al., op. cit.,* pp. 114–120.

[19] Solomon Barkin, *The Decline of the Labor Movement,* Santa Barbara, California: Center for the Study of Democratic Institutions (1961).

by The McClellan Committee, and the apathy of workers. Apathetic union leadership, structural difficulties in some cases, inadequate union organizing staffs, and the use of obsolete organizing techniques are also included by Barkin in his list of impediments to union growth.

For a number of years after the Taft-Hartley Act was passed, union leaders vowed to fight for its total repeal. In the first Congressional election following enactment of the law, Representative Hartley, one of the co-authors of the Act, was defeated. Union activity during the election was credited in part for his failure to return to Congress. Despite their best efforts, however, unions could not unseat Senator Taft. Even in subsequent Congresses, with substantial Democratic majorities, unions could not generate sufficient pressure to bring about repeal of the law. Once they recognized that repeal was highly improbable, some union leaders began to agitate for major revisions, but even these more limited efforts have been largely unsuccessful. There have been amendments of a relatively minor nature, but the Taft-Hartley Act, with only a few modest changes, remains the basic law of labor-management relations in the United States.

The failure of unions to dislodge the Taft-Hartley Act does not mean that there is general satisfaction with this legislation. Union leaders continue to regard the spirit of the Act as basically hostile toward trade unionism, while some employer spokesmen are equally critical because in their view it did not go "far enough." A symposium of papers prepared by economists, lawyers, and other specialists in the field of labor-management relations, ten years after passage of the Taft-Hartley Act, suggests that the law had failed to completely satisfy all parties concerned. Some contributors pointed out what they considered to be the weaknesses of the Act, but most of them appeared to agree with one contributor who stated that: "Ten years of experience under the Taft-Hartley Act have made one point crystal clear: It is certainly not a 'slave labor law' and it has certainly not destroyed trade unionism and collective bargaining. In terms of both economic and non-economic gains, trade unionism has flourished in the last decade as never before. While union membership has not grown as rapidly as it would have in the absence of Taft-Hartley, it has nevertheless risen by over three million—which is hardly symptomatic of a labor movement in the process of disintegration."[20]

[20] Joseph Shister, "The Impact of the Taft-Hartley Act on Union Strength and Collective Bargaining," *Industrial and Labor Relations Review* (April 1958), p. 350.

Legislation restricting certain trade union practices did not end with the Taft-Hartley Act. The philosophy behind this Act was that unions had become powerful institutions—that they were no longer the underdogs which the earlier Wagner Act had sought to support. It was also noted after the end of World War II that unions had become the guardians of substantial treasuries. They had been restricted during the war years from pressing for wage increases, but had been permitted to bargain for various kinds of "fringe benefits" since deferred payments would not disturb wage stability. Partly as a consequence of this, the larger unions negotiated welfare and pension plans to which employers contributed. As these funds grew there was growing public concern about their administration, and in 1958, Congress enacted a law requiring unions to follow certain reporting practices in the handling of these funds.

WELFARE AND PENSION PLANS DISCLOSURE ACT OF 1958

This law is described as a "disclosure statute" rather than as a regulatory measure. It makes it a duty of the administrator of every employee welfare and pension plan—with certain specific exceptions noted below—to publish a description of the plan together with an annual report. It applies in all cases covered by federal statutes which means that more than one state must be involved. Exemptions include: (1) plans which cover twenty-five or fewer employees; (2) plans administered by government agencies; (3) plans directly connected with workmen's compensation or unemployment compensation disability insurance laws; and (4) plans involving non-profit charitable, religious or educational organizations.

The plans and annual reports must be available for examination in the main office of the organization by a participant or beneficiary, and two copies of each must be filed with the Secretary of Labor where they are available for public inspection.

While the provisions of this Act are not unduly stringent, since the law calls only for public disclosure of funds which many consider to be of a quasi-public nature, there was some resentment about the law since it seemed to carry the implication that not all unions were competent enough or honest enough to handle such funds. It should be noted, however, that the Act was passed by Congress only after prior investigation had revealed a limited number of cases where there was misuse of union welfare and pension funds.

THE LABOR-MANAGEMENT REPORTING AND DISCLOSURE ACT OF 1959

In January 1957, a Select Committee was appointed by the U.S. Senate to investigate corrupt influences in labor-management relations. For a year and a half the investigation of the American labor-management scene by the McClellan Committee dominated the nation's headlines. Many of the public hearings were televised, and millions of viewers who might have paid only cursory attention to newspaper accounts observed the behavior of various trade union leaders as they testified before the Committee.[21] The investigation culminated in the Labor Management Reporting and Disclosure Act of 1959, usually referred to as the Landrum-Griffin Act or the LMRDA.

In its declaration of findings, Congress stated that "there have been a number of instances of breach of trust, corruption, disregard of the rights of individual employees, and other failures to observe high standards of responsibility and ethical conduct . . ."[22] In attempting to cope with these problems the authors of the Landrum-Griffin Act were dealing with two broad issues: (a) democracy in the labor movement, and (b) corruption and racketeering in trade unions.

The Seven Titles of the Landrum-Griffin Act

The provisions of the Act are covered by seven rather detailed titles:

A bill of rights for union members. Title I specifies that every union member is entitled to equal rights and privileges. Union members, under this section of the law, are guaranteed freedom of speech and assembly. They are protected against increased dues and initiation fees except when approved by a majority vote by a secret ballot and individual members are given the right to sue a union if aggrieved. The law does specify that the union member must "exhaust reasonable hearing procedures" within the union before going to court. A four month time limit is placed on the union review of his case. The union member is also protected against improper disciplinary action; he cannot be expelled (except for nonpayment of dues) until specifically charged in writing of a violation of union rules. He must also be given time to prepare his defense and given a "full and fair hearing."

[21] For a readable account of the events leading to the establishment of the Committee, as well as a concise summary of its activities, see Robert F. Kennedy, *The Enemy Within,* New York: Harper and Brothers (1960).
[22] Public Law 86-257, 86th Congress (September 14, 1959), p. 1.

Union reporting. The reporting provisions of the Landrum-Griffin Act are covered by Title II. Each union must file a copy of its constitution and bylaws with the Secretary of Labor. It must submit a report covering initiation fees, dues, qualifications and restrictions on membership, benefit plans and disciplinary procedures. An annual report of the union's assets and liabilities must also be filed with the Secretary of Labor.

Every union officer is required to file a detailed annual report of any personal financial dealings he might have had with employers of the members of his union. This is obviously an effort to discourage unscrupulous union leaders from selling out the rank and file. Employers must also report financial transactions with unions except for the routine transactions between banks or other financial institutions and the labor organizations or officers included among their clients.

Title II of the Landrum-Griffin Act also repealed the sections of the Taft-Hartley Act dealing with the filing of fiscal information and eliminated the requirement that union officers must take an oath that they are not members of the Communist Party.

Trusteeships. Union trusteeships were originally designed to permit national or international unions to control improperly managed local unions. There have been cases, however, of the abuse of trusteeships by national or international union officers. Trusteeships have been arbitrarily imposed by such officers to thwart local autonomy or to gain control over local funds.

Under Title III of the LMRDA, trusteeships may be established only under the constitutional provisions and bylaws of a national or international union with the sole purpose of correcting corruption or financial malpractice. A union which has imposed a trusteeship over one of its locals must report this information to the Secretary of Labor and it must continue to report on the status of the trusteeship twice a year until the affairs of the local have been turned back to its own officers.

Elections. Congress has tried to ensure the democratic operation of unions through Title IV of the Landrum-Griffin Act. This calls for elections at the national or international level at least every five years. At the local level elections must be held at least every three years. The law goes on to specify in some detail how such elections are to be conducted. Union funds, or employer contributions, cannot be used to promote the candidacy of any person. Notices must be mailed to each member in good standing at least fifteen days before an election and each member in good standing is entitled to one vote. Complaints of improper election procedures must be investigated by the Secretary of Labor. If he finds the complaint to be justified the Secretary can bring civil suit against the union; if the court agrees that the election was improperly conducted it will be nullified. A new election will then be held under the supervision of the Secretary of Labor.

Financial safeguards. Title V provides stringent penalties for any union officer or employee found guilty of misuse of union funds. It requires the bonding of all union officers and employees, and imposes limitations upon loans of union funds. This section prohibits members of the Communist Party or convicted felons from holding union office for a period of five years following the termination of party membership or release from prison. It also strengthens the provisions of the Taft-Hartley Act designed to prevent various kinds of payments by employers to union officers.

Miscellaneous provisions. Title VI of the LMRDA is a catch-all dealing with a variety of matters. The most significant section is that dealing with "extortionate picketing" which is outlawed by this Act. Fines up to $10,000 and imprisonment up to 20 years are provided for persons convicted of picketing for the purpose of personal profit or enrichment. Most of the other sections under this title deal with administrative procedures. One section, however, makes it unlawful for a union to expel a member for attempting to exercise his rights under the Act.

Amendments to the Taft-Hartley Act. In the view of one authority on labor law, the first six titles of the Landrum-Griffin Act constitute all that the sponsors of the bill had in mind as a result of the McClellan Committee investigation. In his view the remainder of the Act—Title VII—"proved to be a miscellany of uncoordinated, halfbaked, and politically contrived amendments to the 1947 NLRA."[23] It attempted to settle the issue of federal versus state jurisdiction in marginal cases and it amended the Taft-Hartley Act to permit those economic strikers not entitled to reinstatement to vote in elections conducted by the National Labor Relations Board for a period of one year from the beginning of a strike.

The most important sections under this title, however, are those which attempt to close the loopholes in the secondary boycott pro-

[23] Charles O. Gregory, *Labor and the Law,* New York: W. W. Norton and Company, (second revised edition with 1961 supplement, 1961), p. 576.

visions of the Taft-Hartley Act. The Landrum-Griffin Act is more specific than Taft-Hartley in its ban on "hot cargo" agreements. The law declares it to be an unfair labor practice for a union to force an employer into such an agreement. As in the Taft-Hartley Act, exemptions are provided for subcontractors in the construction and in the apparel and clothing industries. Further limitations on secondary picketing are also implied by this part of the law although their significance will only be known after they have been tested in court cases. Organizational and recognition picketing, for example, are declared to be unfair in certain situations.

Most of Title VII was the result of an attempt to tighten up the provisions of the Taft-Hartley Act dealing with secondary pressures including the controversial matter of "hot cargo" clauses. One section, however, amended the Taft-Hartley Act to permit modified hiring hall agreements in the construction industry. The closed shop is still outlawed—although in fact it has continued to operate in many parts of the country. But a modified form of union security is now permitted which is a tacit recognition by Congress that hiring halls serve a useful purpose in labor markets characterized by intermittent employment with workers attached to an industry or occupation rather than to specific employers. The Landrum-Griffin Act is careful to specify, however, that the modified hiring hall arrangement is not to conflict in any way with the state "right-to-work" laws permitted by the Taft-Hartley Act.

THE IMPACT OF LANDRUM-GRIFFIN ON UNIONS AND COLLECTIVE BARGAINING

The Landrum-Griffin Act was an outgrowth of the McClellan investigation which revealed that a few unions had been tainted by corruption. Implicit in a number of its provisions is the assumption that union abuses can be traced to a lack of union democracy. Indeed, one sympathetic interpreter of the law has stated that: "A major purpose of the [act] is to insure that labor organizations are democratically controlled . . . the entire structure of the act emphasizes democratic self-correction rather than governmental action."[24] Has the Act achieved this purpose? Are unions more democratic now than they were before the new law was passed? The Landrum-Griffin Act has not been on the books long enough to permit any but the most tentative judgments about its eventual impact. Up to now the evidence has been mixed.

[24] John L. Holcombe, "Union Democracy and the LMRDA," *Labor Law Journal* (July 1961), p. 597.

Some unions have modified their election and disciplinary procedures since the Act was passed, and it is a fair inference that the law provided the stimulus for these changes.[25] During its first two years the Bureau of Labor Management Reports investigated nearly 600 cases of alleged election violations. Many of the violations were of a technical nature. Most of these cases were closed following investigation and voluntary compliance by the union with the corrective action ordered. In only a handful of cases has it been necessary for the Bureau to institute court action.[26] It is apparent that steps have been taken to implement the technical election provisions of the Act. The effects of the Act on the *outcomes* of union elections are not easy to determine, and some doubts have been expressed about the effectiveness of the LMRDA in those cases where compliance has not been voluntary.

One critic of the Act feels that the courts "have been reluctant to discard the doctrine of noninterference in the internal affairs of 'voluntary' organizations."[27] The legislative history of the law indicates clearly that there was no intent to require unions to modify admission requirements. Unions with restrictive membership provisions have not been affected by the law, and many would argue that such unions can scarcely be considered to be democratic.

It is evident that Congress considered the problem of union democracy "to be one of protecting members from autocratic officers."[28] There are obvious examples of unions dominated by strongly-entrenched leaders and there is no evidence that the LMRDA has changed this. Moreover, the framers of the Act did not include provisions to protect some union officers from others. The officers of unions were conceived of as a tightly-knit group acting in concert which, it should be noted, is far from the case in a number of unions.

The notion that the rank and file must be protected from autocratic officers was also given expression in the provision that individual members have the right to sue a union for improper disciplinary action. However, the member must exhaust all internal remedies before turning to the courts. An even more serious limitation is that

[25] *Ibid.*, p. 599, and David A. Swankin, "Influence of the LMRDA on Constitutional Discipline Provisions," *Monthly Labor Review* (May 1963), pp. 491–492.
[26] Holcombe, *op. cit.*, pp. 600–601.
[27] Linda Rosenberg, "Interpretive Problems of Title I of the Labor-Management Reporting and Disclosure Act," *Industrial and Labor Relations Review* (April 1963), p. 405.
[28] *Ibid.*, p. 409.

if a member brings suit against a union under the "bill of rights" sections of the Act there are no provisions for the payment of his court costs if his suit is successful. It has been suggested that this is one reason why so few cases of this kind have reached the courts.[29] Few workers are in a position to finance litigation, particularly if it is to be carried to Courts of Appeal.

What of the provisions covering secondary pressures and organizational or recognition picketing? The evidence to date suggests that the Landrum-Griffin Act has tightened up the Taft-Hartley provisions against secondary boycotts. In particular, the question of the legality of "hot cargo" clauses, which remained in doubt following Taft-Hartley, has been settled. Such clauses are now unenforceable. This does not mean that unions will not try to develop a substitute form of secondary pressure. In the opinion of one author, "unions will manage to live with the closed secondary boycott loopholes, as they have since 1947."[30]

The circumstances under which organizational and recognition picketing will be permitted will not be determined until a number of cases have been tested before the National Labor Relations Board and the courts. One important case, *Curtis Brothers, Inc.,* was decided by the NLRB in 1957. In this case the Board decided that recognition picketing was an unfair labor practice under the Taft-Hartley Act. The Court of Appeals, however, set aside the Board's order and the Supreme Court, after passage of the Landrum-Griffin Act, upheld the Court of Appeals. This is not the end of the matter, however. Some Circuit Courts have agreed with the 1957 NLRB decision, others have disagreed. It will be some time before the various circumstances under which organizational or recognition picketing will be permitted are clarified. Despite its decision in the 1960 Curtis case, the Supreme Court has implied that changes brought about by the Landrum-Griffin Act "will go far to render organizational and recognition picketing unlawful."[31]

CONCLUSIONS

The Taft-Hartley Act was designed to "equalize" the rights, duties and obligations of unions and employers. When the Wagner Act was passed, unions were weak and many members of Congress felt that union growth should be encouraged to offset the power of large

[29] *Ibid.,* p. 427.
[30] Boaz Siegel, "The Impact of the Labor-Management Reporting and Disclosure Act of 1959 on Collective Bargaining," *Labor Law Journal* (July 1960), p. 589.
[31] Gregory, *op. cit.,* p. 578.

corporate employers. But as unions grew in numbers and in strength, there was mounting concern about the power they wielded. Unions fought passage of the Taft-Hartley Act and many union leaders continue to denounce it to this day. Some unions have been particularly critical of state "right-to-work" laws—a by-product of the Taft-Hartley Act, and some union officers claim that the "freedom of speech" provision has added to their difficulties. It is not easy, of course, to decide what is and what is not coercion and intimidation.

It is difficult to determine precisely what effect the Taft-Hartley Act has had upon union growth. Except for the spurt in membership between 1950 and 1956, unions have not grown since the Taft-Hartley Act was passed. For a time, many union leaders attributed the failure of unions to expand entirely—or almost entirely—to this law. More recently, however, an increasing number of union spokesmen have included the Taft-Hartley Act as one of several factors contributing to the stagnation of American trade unionism. Also, after their unsuccessful attempt to unseat Senator Taft when he ran for re-election to the Senate, union leaders have moderated their demands for repeal of the law. By and large, they have continued to criticize the law but have tried to eliminate what they consider to be its worst provisions by amendment rather than outright repeal. Whether they like it or not, union leaders have learned to live under the Taft-Hartley Act.

The Landrum-Griffin Act deals with the internal affairs of trade unions. It was the result of a lengthy investigation which revealed that some union officers had sadly abused their positions of trust, and that some unions either through membership apathy or dictatorial control at the top were not operated in a democratic manner. The Landrum-Griffin Act was designed to require a certain amount of public disclosure of union practices and public accounting of union funds. There are provisions with the obvious intent of making unions "more democratic." There has been little objection to these provisions, but there is also little evidence to date that unions have become more democratic as a result of the law.

It has often been observed that most organizations to which American citizens belong are run by a handful of members. There are "activists" in all sorts of organizations—religious, fraternal, political, and social. These are the members who attend all meetings and who speak up on all issues; it is largely from their ranks that officers are elected. The degree of participation varies considerably among organizations, to be sure, but in most organizations a majority of the members are content to let others make the decisions. This seems to be especially true of trade unions whose members often have the attitude that their officers are paid to take care of union affairs, and so long as the officers "deliver the goods" most rank and file members are not active participants in union affairs. As Sumner Slichter pointed out, however, this is more often an expression of satisfaction with the state of affairs than of dissatisfaction. Many union leaders have exhorted their members to attend meetings more often and to take a more active interest in union matters, but the rank and file have been largely unresponsive. They continue to leave union decisions in the hands of their officers and the minority of activists who regularly attend union meetings.

REFERENCES

BOOKS

Barkin, Solomon, *The Decline of the Labor Movement,* Santa Barbara, California: Center for the Study of Democratic Institutions (1961).

Bernstein, Irving, *et al.,* eds., *Emergency Disputes and National Policy,* New York: Harper and Brothers (1955).

Gregory, Charles O., *Labor and the Law,* New York: W. W. Norton and Company (revised edition, 1949), and (second revised edition, 1961).

Horowitz, Morris A., *Manpower Utilization in the Railroad Industry,* Boston: Northeastern University, Bureau of Business and Economic Research (1960).

Jacobs, Paul, *Dead Horse and the Featherbird,* Santa Barbara, California: Center for the Study of Democratic Institutions (1962).

Shister, Joseph, *et al.,* eds., *Public Policy and Collective Bargaining,* New York: Harper and Brothers (1962).

Shultz, George P., and John R. Coleman, *Labor Problems: Cases and Readings,* McGraw-Hill (1953).

The Taft-Hartley Act After Ten Years: A Symposium, Industrial and Labor Relations Review, Vol. 11 (April 1958).

U.S. Department of Labor, *State "Right to Work" Laws,* Washington, D.C.: Bureau of Labor Standards, Bulletin 204 (May 1959).

United Steelworkers of America, *The 1959 Steel Strike,* Pittsburgh: International Affairs Department, Pamphlet No. PR-112 (no date).

ARTICLES

Holcombe, John L., "Union Democracy and the LMRDA," *Labor Law Journal* (July 1961), pp. 597–604.

Kuhn, James W., "Right-to-Work Laws—Symbols or Substance?", *Industrial and Labor Relations Review,* Vol. 14 (July 1961), pp. 587–594.

Rosenberg, Linda, "Interpretive Problems of Title I of the Labor-Management Reporting and Disclosure Act," *Industrial and Labor Relations Review,* Vol. 16 (April 1963), pp. 405–427.

Siegel, Boaz, "The Impact of the Labor-Management Reporting and Disclosure Act of 1959 on Collective Bargaining," *Labor Law Journal* (July 1960), pp. 579–590.

Simler, Norman J., "The Economics of Featherbedding," *Industrial and Labor Relations Review,* Vol. 16 (October 1962), pp. 111–121.

Slichter, Sumner H., "The Taft-Hartley Act," *Quarterly Journal of Economics,* Vol. LXIII (February 1949), pp. 1–31.

———, ——— — "Revision of the Taft-Hartley Act," *Quarterly Journal of Economics,* Vol. LXVII (May 1953), pp. 149–180.

Swankin, David A., "Influence of the LMRDA on Constitutional Discipline Provisions," *Monthly Labor Review,* Vol. 86 (May 1963), pp. 491–496.

Chapter 9 Social Security and the Protection of Labor Standards

During the New Deal and Fair Deal administrations, a number of laws were passed to provide workers with a minimum of protection against the vicissitudes of the market place and the problems associated with aging in an industrial society. Other laws were passed to provide for minimum labor standards. A number of federal agencies were established to administer these programs. While extreme conservatives have been critical of social legislation, it has won widespread public acceptance. Unions have generally supported such legislation wholeheartedly and have often urged that it be expanded. Conservatives, and even some moderates, have recommended caution in the expansion of social legislation but they have not suggested that we turn back the clock; that we try to return to an age when each man was required to provide for all of his needs or to turn to private charity in the event of unforeseen hardships.

SETTING LABOR STANDARDS ON PUBLIC CONTRACTS

The first federal law to establish basic labor standards was the Davis-Bacon Act of 1931. This Act is limited in scope; it covers direct federal construction projects including the repair or alteration of public facilities, on all contracts of more than $2,000. The Secretary of Labor determines wage rates to be paid in a locality, usually the prevailing union rates in the area. Workers paid less than the established wages may file a claim with the Comptroller General who is authorized to withhold funds from the contractor to settle such claims. If contract funds are insufficient, individual workers may sue the contractor for the difference under The Miller Act of 1935.

Violators of the Davis-Bacon Act may not be awarded further government contracts for three years, and existing contracts are cancelled with the contractor obligated to bear any extra costs incurred. Under a series of laws starting with the Housing Act of 1937, construction workers on federally-aided housing, highway, school, hospital and airport programs are covered by provisions similar to those in the Davis-Bacon Act.

The Walsh-Healey Public Contracts Act of 1936 is broader than the Davis-Bacon Act but is still limited in scope. It has been amended several times, and the following provisions are those which have applied since the latest amendment was made in 1952. The Public Contracts Act sets basic labor standards for all work performed on United States government contracts amounting to $10,000 or more. The Secretary of Labor determines the prevailing minimum wage in an industry and all workers employed on government contracts must be paid this wage or more. The minimum applies to all employees, except office and custodial workers, who are connected in any way with the manufacture of materials under a government contract. Industry minima are generally set by the Secretary after a public hearing.

The Walsh-Healey Act also sets basic hours of work. The standard work day is eight hours and the standard work week is forty hours. Overtime is permitted but must be paid at the rate of time and one-half. The law prohibits child labor (boys under sixteen and girls under eighteen) and forbids the use of convict labor. It also regulates conditions under which work may be performed on government contracts. Work cannot be done under conditions which are unsanitary, hazardous, or otherwise dangerous to the health or safety of employees. The law also prohibits homework, i.e., all work under a government contract must be performed on the premises of the manufacturer.

Every government contractor must display a copy of the Public Contracts Act in special poster form. Contractors are also required to maintain special records which may be inspected by representatives of the Wage and Hour and Public Contracts Divisions of the U.S. Department of Labor. There are certain exemptions under the Walsh-Healey Act, for example, some contracts involving transportation by common carrier, utility services, perishable agricultural products, rentals, or seasonal services, are exempt from the provisions of the law. In any case where it can be shown that the operation of the Act will impair the conduct of government business, the Secretary of Labor is authorized to make exceptions. Exceptions to the minimum wages are also permitted in the case of learners or apprentices, and under certain circumstances in the case of handicapped workers.

The Walsh-Healey law applies to all manufacturers or regular dealers in the articles called for under the contract. In general, it does not apply to subcontractors. But under certain conditions, where the prime contractor manufactures only part of the article required, secondary contractors are also covered by the law. If a contractor violates any term of the Act, his contract may be cancelled with any additional costs involved charged to the contractor. Any firm convicted of violating the Walsh-Healey Act may not be granted a governmental contract for at least three years following the original breach of contract. Since 1952, when the law was last amended, court review of alleged violations is permitted.

The Secretary of Labor has some leeway in setting minimum rates. The minima on a specific contract may apply to a locality or they may be nationwide. In industries such as textiles where competition is nationwide, national minima are set. Following the 1952 amendment to the Walsh-Healey Act, the Secretary's freedom to set industrywide minima was challenged in *Mitchell v. Covington Mills*. A district court ruled that the minima on a specific contract could apply only to a given locality. This decision was reversed by a court of appeals, however, and the Supreme Court upheld the latter decision in 1956. This reaffirmed the principle that the Secretary of Labor can set industrywide minima in cases where competition is nationwide.

The President's Committee on Government Contracts, established by Executive Order, requires all contracting agencies dealing with the federal government to provide employment without regard to race, religion, color, or national origin.

THE FAIR LABOR STANDARDS ACT OF 1938

This Act, often referred to as the Wage and Hour law, was passed in June 1938. Like the Walsh-Healey Act it has been amended several times, and the following description is based on the most recent amendments.

The federal wage-hour law is administered by the Administrator of Wage and Hour and Public Contracts Divisions of the U.S. Department of Labor. It is much broader than the Walsh-Healey Act since it establishes minimum wages, overtime provisions, and child-labor standards which apply to all employees engaged in interstate commerce.

The law provides for minimum wages which are uniform throughout the United States, with exceptions in the case of Puerto Rico and the Virgin Islands where lower rates may be set by special industry committees representing labor, management and the public. Workers must be paid at time and one-half for all work in excess of forty hours during a given work week. A minimum age of sixteen is established for general employment while in hazardous occupations, the minimum age is eighteen years. For certain occupations, where work is performed outside of school hours, the minimum age is fourteen. The Act applies to all workers covered by the interstate commerce clause whether employed in a factory, office, or at home. As in the case of the Walsh-Healey Act, exceptions may be made in the case of learners, messengers, apprentices, and handicapped workers.

There is also a "white collar" exemption in the case of executives, administrative, or professional personnel. Local retailing activities and "outside salesmen" are exempted. Numerous other workers, including seamen, taxicab and bus drivers, employees of small newspapers, small lumbering concerns, small telephone exchanges, and fishing or fish processing concerns, are not covered by the law.

Most of the exemptions apply to workers who earn more than the statutory minimum wage but whose jobs often require them to work more than eight hours on certain days and perhaps more than forty hours in a certain week. The exemptions represent an attempt by Congress to avoid fitting all workers into a legal strait jacket. The objective of the law is to eliminate substandard wages particularly in areas where workers have few alternative job opportunities. A single employer in an area—a monopsonist in the terminology of economics—could easily exploit his workers in the absence of legal protection. While such employers might not be numerous, Congress wished to protect workers from downward wage pressure in such circumstances.

Generally speaking, all work in excess of forty hours in a given work week must be paid at one and one-half times the regular hourly rate. Special provisions are made in the case of workers employed at piece rates and for workers who do two or more kinds of work at different hourly or piece rates. Where the nature of jobs requires irregular hours, Section 7(b) of the Act permits payment to be made on the basis of contract arrangements.

Some workers are paid partly "in kind" which generally means board, room, or both. Under such circumstances, an employer may deduct the "reasonable cost" of furnishing his workers board, lodging, or other facilities but he is not expected to make a profit on such services. The law does not require that workers receive the statutory minimum "free and clear." If, for example, workers agree to the deduction of union dues or charitable contributions these may be made under the terms of the Act even if the result is that take-home pay drops below the statutory minimum.

The law also prohibits "oppressive" child labor; that is, employment of workers between the ages of fourteen and sixteen in most occupations; workers must be at least eighteen if the jobs involved are particularly hazardous or detrimental to health. The Act specifically lists a fairly large number of such jobs in mining, manufacturing, lumbering, and other occupations where the operation of machinery is involved. Exemptions to the entire law are made in the case of youngsters in school doing non-hazardous part-time work.

Unlike the Walsh-Healey Act, the Fair Labor Standards Act permits home work in certain industries such as jewelry and some parts of the apparel and garment industries. But the same provisions which apply to factory work also apply to home work under these conditions.

There are no particular reporting provisions under the Fair Labor Standards Act, and employers are not required to keep any specified set of records. The law does require each employer to keep reliable records which clearly reflect the wages, hours, and other conditions and practices of employment in his establishment.

In case of violations, employees may sue for the amounts by which they have been underpaid, or upon the request of workers, the Secretary of Labor may bring suit against an employer to recover the amounts of underpayment. The government may also bring action on its own initiative against any person who willfully violates the Fair Labor Standards Act if there is evidence of such violation. If convicted, the employer may be fined up to $10,000, and for a second conviction may be imprisoned for as much as six months. The Secretary of Labor may also seek injunctions in Federal

District Courts to restrain employers from violating the Act. The law prohibits the discharge of or discrimination against workers who have filed complaints or participated in other proceedings under the Act.

The Fair Labor Standards Act has been a controversial piece of labor legislation since its enactment. Although numerous Department of Labor studies have shown that only a small minority of employers have been affected each time the minima have been raised, there is a general hue and cry when Congress proposes to further increase the prevailing minimum. In general, the statutory minimum is well below the prevailing hourly wages of workers in most business establishments in most areas. As noted earlier, the law was designed to protect those workers who do not have alternative employment opportunities, and to prevent the fairly rare unscrupulous employer from depressing wages to substandard levels in areas where there might be considerable unemployment. Staunch conservatives, however, have generally been critical of the Fair Labor Standards Act on the grounds that it is an interference with the free market. Except when the minimum is being revised upward, however, the Fair Labor Standards Act is quite widely accepted as part of a broader policy designed to provide minimum standards of hours and earnings for all workers covered by the law.

The most recent amendment was made in 1961 and it provides for a gradual increase in the minimum to $1.25 an hour; it also broadened the coverage of the Act to include slightly more than three and one-half million workers, mostly in retail and service establishments, who formerly were excluded from its provisions. Since September 1963, the new minimum has applied to all workers previously covered by the law. An additional year was allowed for raising the minimum of the newly-covered workers to $1.25 an hour. There are still a great many workers—those employed in strictly *intra*-state activities—who are not covered by the law, but most states have laws which provide for minima, generally lower than the federal minimum, covering these workers.

THE SOCIAL SECURITY ACT OF 1935

This is one of the most comprehensive pieces of social legislation to come out of the New Deal. It provides for two nationwide systems of social insurance: one protects wage earners and their families against the unexpected loss of income due to unemployment

CHART 9–1
HOW THE SOCIAL SECURITY LAW WORKS

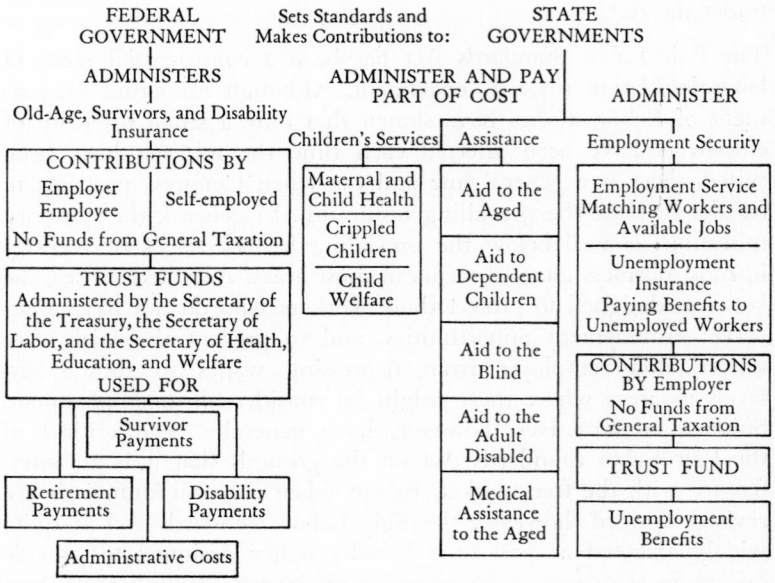

Source: Chart taken from publication of the U.S. Department of Health, Education and Welfare, Social Security Administration, 1963 OASI–81

and the other provides a system of payments upon retirement or the disability or death of the family breadwinner. Programs covering old-age, disability, and survivors insurance—all operated through a federal system—are administered by the Social Security Administration. Unemployment insurance, to be discussed in the next section, is a joint federal-state program administered by a separate agency. In addition, the Social Security Act provides for public assistance—again on a federal-state basis—to needy old people, needy dependent children, the needy blind, and the needy permanently and totally disabled. Grants are also provided to the states for maternal and child-health services and other child-welfare programs, including services for crippled children, to supplement state and local public and private funds used for such purposes. The administrative setup of the social security program is illustrated by Chart 9-1.

Old-age and Survivors Insurance

This is a nationwide social insurance program which provides pensions to retired or disabled workers. Retirement benefits are determined by the age at which retirement begins and the individual's average yearly earnings after 1950; disability benefits are determined by the worker's average yearly earnings between 1950 and the time he became disabled. Wives of retired workers are also entitled to payments depending upon the wife's age and the worker's average annual earnings.

The Social Security Act has been amended a number of times since it was first passed in 1935. Originally, for example, retirement benefits could be claimed only at age 65; in 1956, however, women became eligible for retirement payments at age 62. The law was amended again in 1961 to permit men to retire at this age. Benefit payments are scaled down, of course, if covered workers choose to retire before reaching the age of 65. A worker is entitled to his full social security payment, after retirement at age 65, if he earns no more than $1,200 a year, and he is entitled to full benefits after age 72 regardless of earnings.

Benefits are paid to all persons, or to their dependents and survivors, who have become insured by working in covered employment. Almost all gainful work is now covered. Federal government employees who have their own retirement program and self-employed doctors of medicine are not covered by the law. Almost all other workers are covered including the self-employed if they choose to come under the terms of the Act.

A worker becomes eligible for social security by being employed a certain number of covered quarters. A covered quarter is defined as a calendar quarter after 1936 in which the employee received at least $50 in wages or at least $100 of self-employment income. Once a worker has earned credits for forty quarters in covered employment he is fully insured for life, and his dependents are then entitled to survivors insurance in the event of his death. There are three kinds of benefits: retirement, disability, and survivor.

Retirement Benefits

Payment is not automatic. When a worker reaches retirement age and wishes to collect his social security, he must file a claim for benefits at the nearest social security office. There are currently 540 district offices through which claims may be filed or if necessary the worker can apply directly to the Washington office. The maximum monthly benefit which a retired worker and his family may receive is equal to 80 per cent of his average monthly earnings, or $200, whichever is less.

Survivor Benefits

Survivor benefits may be claimed by the widow of an insured wage earner. At the time of death, the widow of the fully insured worker receives a lump sum payment which may be equal to three times his monthly benefit but may not be more than $255. If the widow is under 62, she is entitled to a monthly payment equal to three-fourths of the primary insurance amount. If she has one child under 18, she is entitled to an additional benefit of the same amount, and benefits of one-half the primary insurance amount for other children under 18. If the insured worker does not leave a widow or children, dependent parents of retirement age are entitled to benefits.

Disability Insurance Benefits

A new type of protection became available to workers and self-employed persons as the result of a 1956 amendment to the Social Security Act. This provides protection against the loss of earnings as the result of disability. After a waiting period of six months, a totally disabled worker who is both fully and currently insured becomes eligible for payments. He must have been employed at least half of the forty quarters prior to his disability. Applicants for disability payments are first referred to the state rehabilitation agency. If the worker refuses rehabilitation services he is not eligible for payments. If he participates in the rehabilitation program, however, he is eligible for benefits, which continue for a year after he is re-employed if he begins to do gainful work again.

The latest schedules of monthly payments for retirement, disability and survivors insurance are given in Table 9-1. If a man elects to retire at 62 instead of 65 his monthly payment is reduced 20 per cent. His wife's payment starting at age 62 will be one-fourth less than the amount she would receive starting at 65. The table also shows that payments under survivors insurance depend upon the insured worker's average earnings. Supplements are provided for widows under 62 with children.

Who Bears the Cost of Social Security?

Wage earners and their employers share the cost of old-age disability and survivors insurance by paying special taxes. Self-employed persons pay a tax on the basis of net earnings reported on their income tax forms. Taxes are now paid on wages up to $4,800 a year. The schedule in force from 1963 to 1965 calls for equal deductions of 3⅝ per cent from employers and employees; the self-employed

TABLE 9-1
MONTHLY RETIREMENT AND DISABILITY INSURANCE PAYMENTS

Average Yearly Earnings After 1950	Retirement Benefit at 65 or Later, or Disability Benefit	Retirement Benefit for Worker, Starting at Age—			Wife of Retired Worker Starting at Age—			
		62	63	64	62	63	64	65
$800 or less	$40.00	$32.00	$34.70	$37.40	$15.00	$16.70	$18.40	$20.00
1,200	59.00	47.20	51.20	55.10	22.20	24.60	27.10	29.50
1,800	73.00	58.40	63.30	68.20	27.40	30.50	33.50	36.50
2,400	84.00	67.20	72.80	78.40	31.50	35.00	38.50	42.00
3,000	95.00	76.00	82.40	88.70	35.70	39.60	43.60	47.50
3,600	105.00	84.00	91.00	98.00	39.40	43.80	48.20	52.50
4,200	116.00	92.80	100.60	108.30	43.50	48.40	53.20	58.00
*4,800	127.00	101.60	110.10	118.60	47.70	53.00	58.30	63.50

SCHEDULE OF SOCIAL SECURITY TAX RATES

Years	Employers Per Cent	Employees Per Cent	Self-Employed Per Cent
1961	3	3	4.5
1962	3⅛	3⅛	4.7
1963–65	3⅜	3⅜	5.4
1966–67	4⅛	4⅛	6.2
1968 and after	4⅜	4⅜	6.9

MONTHLY SURVIVORS INSURANCE PAYMENTS

Average Yearly Earnings After 1950	Widow, Widower, 62 or Over or 1 Aged Parent Alone	Widow Under 62 and One Child	Widow Under 62 and Two Children
$ 800	$ 40.00	$ 60.00	$ 60.00
1,200	48.70	88.50	88.50
1,800	60.30	109.60	120.00
2,400	69.30	126.00	161.60
3,000	78.40	142.60	202.40
3,600	86.70	157.60	236.40
4,200	95.70	174.00	254.00
4,800	104.80	190.60	254.00

* Because earnings of $4,800 cannot be credited for any year before 1959, benefits shown on this line will not generally be payable for a few years to come.

Source: U.S. Department of Health, Education, and Welfare, Social Security Administration.

CHART 9–2
HISTORY OF THE SOCIAL SECURITY LAW
PASSED IN 1935

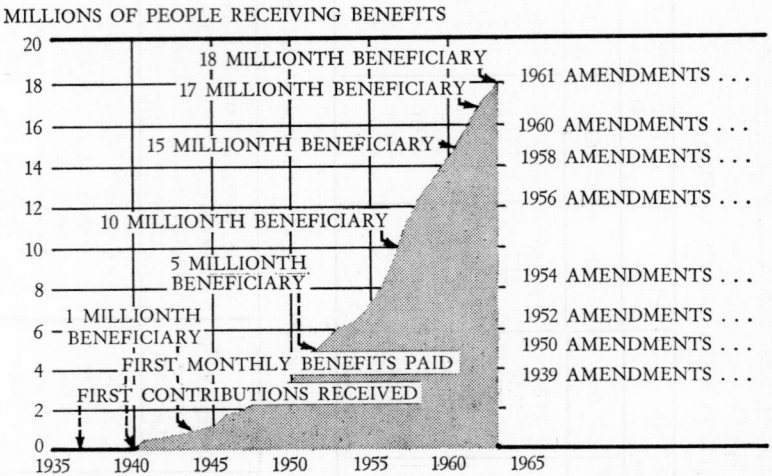

1961 AMENDMENTS . . . Reduced benefits to men at age 62; larger percentage to aged survivors; minimum benefit levels increased.

1960 AMENDMENTS . . . Benefits to disabled workers of any age; less work required.

1958 AMENDMENTS . . . Payments to dependents of disability beneficiaries; benefits increased 7%.

1956 AMENDMENTS . . . Benefits to disabled workers age 50 to 65; reduced benefits to women at 62; more workers covered.

1954 AMENDMENTS . . . Benefits increased; more workers covered; disabled workers' benefit rights protected.

1952 AMENDMENTS . . . Benefits increased 12.5%.

1950 AMENDMENTS . . . Benefits increased 77%; coverage extended to 10.5 million workers.

1939 AMENDMENTS . . . Survivor benefits added to program.

Source: Chart taken from publication of the U.S. Department of Health, Education and Welfare, Social Security Administration, 1963 OASI–83

deduction amounts to 5.4 per cent. The schedule is to be stepped up in 1966, and again in 1968, to the amounts shown in Table 9-1. Every employer is required to give each worker a receipt for the social security tax deducted once a year or if and when the worker leaves his job. Each covered worker has a social security number and the Social Security Administration maintains a separate account for every individual covered.

The Social Security program is the largest system of insurance in the United States. The number of beneficiaries has increased rapidly since 1940, as indicated in Chart 9-2, and this growth will continue as more covered workers reach retirement age. The Social

Security Act was strongly resisted by conservatives in Congress, but now that the law is on the books, it has found widespread acceptance. Some insurance companies were fearful before the law was passed that the Act might interfere with the private insurance business. However, the benefits paid under the law are relatively modest, and insurance companies have urged covered workers to supplement their retirement and survivors insurance with private plans. The Social Security program is designed to provide a *minimum* of protection for survivors of fully covered workers, and a *minimum* of retirement income for those workers who are fully insured when they leave the active labor force.

UNEMPLOYMENT COMPENSATION

During the Great Depression of the 1930's unemployment was widespread and protracted. In 1932 and 1933 about one-fourth of the civilian labor force were jobless and at no time between 1931 and 1940 did unemployment drop below 14 per cent of the civilian work force. When Congress passed the Social Security Act in 1935 it provided for a joint federal-state system of unemployment insurance. This system was merged with a public employment service program which had been enacted in 1933. The federal government's participation in these programs is under the administration of the Bureau of Employment Security of the United States Department of Labor. Each state has a cooperating Division of Employment Security which carries out the state's responsibilities and supervises administration of the programs at the local level. The two programs—the employment service and unemployment insurance—are handled by different departments in the state agency, but there is close coordination between them. The objective of the overall program is to place workers who lose their jobs in new employment. But if this cannot be done immediately, workers are entitled to unemployment compensation.

The unemployment compensation program has had an interesting side effect which undoubtedly was not anticipated by members of Congress when the law was passed. There have been four pronounced recessions in the American economy since the end of World War II. During each of these recessions, industrial production has dropped, and this has generally been accompanied by a decline in construction activity. When the level of unemployment rises, the Employment Service cannot find jobs for many of the unemployed—there simply are not that many job vacancies during recession periods. These workers then become eligible for unemployment compensation which permits them to maintain consumption spending at higher levels than would be the case if they had to rely on savings alone. Thus millions of dollars are pumped into the economic system from unemployment insurance funds and this helps sustain the level of consumption in the face of a drop in production. After a time, inventory accumulations—an important cause of downturns—begin to be depleted. Factory production is stepped up again, and building activity picks up once more.

The unemployment insurance program has become one of the most important, if not the most important, of the "built-in stabilizers" which have helped reverse each of the postwar recessions within a relatively short time and have started a new cycle of recovery. The American economy is undoubtedly much more stable—in terms of employment and production—than it would be in the absence of a system of comprehensive unemployment compensation.

The United States Employment Service

The United States Employment Service, in cooperation with state agencies, attempts to find jobs for all applicants. It also supervises state programs to see that they conform to the federal laws. It provides state agencies with technical assistance, and supervises the program of referring labor from one area to another. To a limited extent it serves as a nationwide clearinghouse which attempts to match idle workers with vacant jobs.

Unemployed workers may obtain information about job opportunities, both in their own communities and elsewhere, at one of 1,800 full-time or 2,000 part-time local offices. Employers who have job vacancies may list these with the local office, and the local office staff attempts to refer the best qualified applicants to the vacant jobs.

The local offices provide counselling and testing services, and they attempt to find jobs for new entrants to the labor force, older workers, the physically handicapped, and members of minority groups. Special services to veterans were also provided as part of the Servicemen's Readjustment Act of 1944.

The Bureau of Employment Security regularly publishes labor market information in a monthly bulletin. The state employment offices cooperate with local economic development organizations and with other groups interested in stimulating economic activity in their respective states and communities. The state agencies have also cooperated with groups seeking federal assistance under the Area Redevelopment Act of 1961 to be discussed in Chapter 22.

The public employment service has been only moderately successful in its efforts to establish a nationwide clearinghouse for unemployed workers. This is not because of a lack of effort or initiative on the part of the administrators of this agency. There are thousands of private employment agencies in the United States which also seek to find jobs for unemployed workers on a fee basis. Many of the private agencies view the public employment service as a subsidized competitor and the existence of private agencies has made it somewhat more difficult for the public employment service to develop a unified program of job placement.

Many employers feel that the best qualified workers will be obtained through private employment agencies. Larger establishments typically maintain their own employment offices where they accept job applicants "off the street" and hire only those whom they consider the best qualified. Some employers thus feel that marginal workers who always find it difficult to obtain employment will turn to the public employment service. On a statistical basis this cannot be so. During recessions, when hundreds of thousands of workers become unemployed, practically all those eligible for unemployment compensation will register with the local employment office. If there are job vacancies to which the unemployed workers can be referred they must accept suitable employment or be denied compensation. Thus not all workers referred by the Employment Service are marginal. Many are able, efficient, and highly desirable workers, but not all the latter are searching for new and permanent jobs.

Many workers who are cyclically unemployed expect to be called back to their old jobs. They might accept employment with other employers on a temporary basis, but when their original employers call them back they will generally return to their own jobs where they have built up seniority and other fringe-benefit rights. This poses a continuing problem. Employers are often aware that the workers who come to them during recessions will return to their regular employers except on the somewhat rare occasions when the job openings they have filled are superior to their regular jobs. This has contributed somewhat to the employers' "image" of the employment service as an agency which is attempting to place marginal workers.

The efforts of local employment offices to find jobs for handicapped persons, older workers, and members of minority groups, have also made some employers shy away from the public employment services. To a large extent, however, this image is the result of widespread public misunderstanding about the nature of job applicants referred by the public employment service. As a general rule, the local employment office will refer the best qualified applicant for each job vacancy. An effort is made, however, to avoid discrimination on the basis of sex, age, color, creed, or national origin. Each month thousands of well qualified workers are placed in productive employment through the efforts of the public employment service. As more and more employers find that they can obtain good workers through the local employment office the effectiveness of the public employment service may be expected to increase. The state agencies can be particularly effective in helping new entrants to the labor force find jobs for which they are qualified. Through programs of testing and counselling, those entering the labor force for the first time can be helped to find the jobs for which they are best suited. This will not mean the end of private employment agencies. Many unemployed workers will continue to register with private agencies and many employers will continue to use their services. There is room for both types of placement services in a large and diversified economy in which the task of matching qualified workers and job openings appears to be of increasing importance.

The Unemployment Compensation Program

One outgrowth of the Social Security Act of 1935 was a comprehensive system of unemployment insurance based on a joint federal-state program. Each one of the fifty states has enacted an unemployment compensation law. All state laws must meet certain federal standards established by the Social Security and Federal Unemployment Tax Acts.

Basically, unemployment insurance is designed to tide workers over periods of temporary unemployment. Compensation is not granted automatically to all unemployed workers. Before an unemployed worker can receive unemployment compensation he must have been employed on a job covered under his state's unemployment insurance law for a specified period. He must also be able and willing to work, and his unemployment must be entirely involuntary.

Federal minimum standards have been established by the federal laws upon which the joint federal-state programs are based. If these standards are met, the federal government pays the costs of administering the state unemployment insurance laws, and permits employers to credit state contributions against the federal tax imposed by the Federal Unemployment Tax Act.

When a worker is laid off temporarily, or loses his job through no fault of his own, he reports to his local employment security office. There he files a claim for unemployment compensation. This does not begin immediately, but if he cannot be placed in another suitable job, payments begin after a brief waiting period. As long as he is unemployed—and drawing compensation—the worker must report to his local employment office regularly, usually every week. He will continue to draw compensation until he returns to his old job, until suitable new employment is found for him, or until he exhausts his benefit rights.

If the unemployed worker is referred to a job he must be willing to investigate it. If he refuses a job, and the local employment service considers it "suitable" employment, he may be disqualified for further compensation. The worker has the right of appeal, however, and his case will be considered by a board of review. If the board upholds the local office's determination further compensation will be denied. If the board disagrees that the job available was "suitable" his compensation will be restored.

There is wide variation in state unemployment insurance laws. Maximum weekly benefit amounts differ from state to state and this is also true of the maximum weeks an unemployed worker can draw benefits. The amount of wages or employment during a base period required to qualify for benefits also varies from state to state. In some states only those workers employed by firms with four or more employees during twenty weeks of the year are covered. In other states, however, the law covers firms with a single employee. Some workers are generally excluded from state unemployment compensation programs. These include: (a) railroad workers who are covered by the Federal Railroad Unemployment Insurance Act, (b) agricultural workers, (c) domestic workers, (d) state and municipal workers, (e) casual laborers, and (f) workers employed by nonprofit organizations.

In general, a worker will be disqualified for state unemployment compensation if he quits his job voluntarily, without good cause, or if he was discharged for misconduct in connection with his work. In most states, compensation is not granted if the worker is out of a job because of a labor dispute in his plant. As indicated above, he will be refused compensation if he is not willing to accept an offer of suitable alternative employment.

There are provisions to protect the benefit rights of workers, however. For example, a worker cannot be denied unemployment insurance benefits if he refuses to accept new work because the job is open due to a labor dispute, or if as a condition of accepting a job he must resign from or refrain from joining a bona fide trade union. To be considered "suitable" the new job must also provide wages, hours, and conditions of work substantially similar to those which he enjoyed in his previous employment. Special provisions have been made to provide partial unemployment benefits to workers whose wages and hours have been substantially reduced as the result of a cutback in the normal work week.

The employment service has done much to improve the operation of the labor market. And unemployment compensation has helped stabilize the economy. This does not mean, however, that the nation's unemployment problem has been solved. The employment service cannot create jobs; it can only direct idle workers to reported job vacancies. Unemployment compensation has been effective only in mitigating the effects of relatively short-term unemployment.

Since 1958, the United States has been faced with a "new" unemployment problem which will be discussed in detail in Chapter 22. Briefly, this is the problem of persistent unemployment throughout the business cycle. The unemployment rate has fluctuated within fairly narrow limits, but at no time between 1958 and early 1964, when this was written, did the seasonally-adjusted unemployment rate drop below 5.3 per cent of the civilian labor force. Also, there was an increase in "long-term" unemployment which is generally defined as unemployment lasting more than 26 weeks in the course of a year.[1]

Because of this persistently high level of unemployment, there has been a strain on the unemployment insurance funds of some states. On two occasions the federal government has provided extended unemployment benefits to workers who had exhausted their benefit rights under state programs, and who were still unemployed. In 1958, the Temporary Unemployment Compensation (TUC) program was put into effect. Extended unemployment compensation

[1] As will be noted in Chapter 22, some authors define "long-term" unemployment as that lasting 15 weeks or more.

in this case was based on repayable loans from the federal government to the states. In 1961, under the Temporary Extended Unemployment Compensation (TEC) program, the federal government provided additional funds to the states for this purpose. The TEC program, however, did *not* require the states to repay the federal funds advanced.

The increase of long-term unemployment since 1958 has led to suggestions for longer benefit periods under the federal-state program, and bills have been introduced into Congress which would provide for continuing federal supplemental payments when they are needed. Others have suggested, however, that this is not the answer to the problem. What we need, according to this view, is a more effective employment policy which would reduce the need for a system of extended unemployment compensation.[2] These issues will be considered in detail in Chapter 22.

Financing Unemployment Compensation

Social security taxes are levied equally on employers and employees. In general, this is not true of unemployment compensation taxes. Except in three states (Alabama, Alaska and New Jersey), unemployment compensation funds are built up from taxes levied on employers only. Under the Federal Unemployment Tax Act, which is part of the Internal Revenue Code, all employers of four or more workers must pay an unemployment insurance tax based on the first $3,000 earned by a worker in a calendar year. Individual states may increase the tax base and some have done so in recent years.

Unemployment tax rates vary widely from state to state. They are influenced by variations in unemployment among the states and by differences in state laws. Some states provide more liberal benefit payments than others, and the duration of benefits also varies from state to state. As a result of these differences, average employer tax rates among the states ranged from 0.5 per cent to 3.1 per cent in 1960.

Most states provide for some form of *experience rating*. Under this system of tax assessment, an employer's tax depends upon the extent to which he has been able to stabilize employment. Experience rating schemes have been criticized by some writers. Employers in stable activities, such as the trades and services, might

[2] For a discussion of the issues involved see Philip Booth, "Unemployment Insurance and the Challenge of the 1960's," *Proceedings,* 14th Annual Meeting, Industrial Relations Research Association (December 1961), pp. 173–175.

enjoy low rates through no effort on their part. Other employers pay high rates because of the vagaries of the marketplace despite their efforts to stabilize employment. Thus experience rating might not be a fair method of allocating the social costs of unemployment.[3]

The Railroad Unemployment Insurance Act

This act, which is administered by the Railroad Retirement Board, provides unemployment compensation and sickness benefits to qualified railroad workers under a uniform nationwide system. The fund from which payments are made is based on a payroll tax on all carriers. The amount of the tax varies from one-half to three per cent of wages depending upon the balance in the fund. The Act contains qualifications similar to those which apply to the federal-state unemployment insurance program. For example, a railroad worker will not be paid unemployment benefits if he is out of work because of a strike which violates the Railway Labor Act or the rules and practices of his union. He will also not be paid benefits if he leaves his work voluntarily without good cause, or fails to comply with instructions from the Board to apply for work or to report to an unemployment office.

State Workmen's Compensation Laws

All states now have laws which provide for payments to workers for injuries on the job or for illness directly related to work. The earliest state laws go back to 1911, much earlier than the other forms of social legislation discussed in this chapter. As is true of unemployment compensation legislation, there is much variation among the states. In general, however, workmen's compensation laws are either compulsory or elective. In states which have compulsory legislation, every employer subject to the state act is required to arrange for compensation for workers who are disabled as a result of an accident or injury. In states which have elective laws, the employer is not required to participate in the workmen's compensation program. But if he chooses not to participate, the employer places himself in legal jeopardy. In the latter case, an injured employee may obtain compensation only by suing for damages. More than half of all state laws are compulsory.

In states where employers are required to participate in the workmen's compensation program, or in those states where the law permits them to do so, covered employers must either obtain insurance or provide proof that they can carry their own risks. The

[3] For further discussion see Charles A. Myers, "Experience Rating in Unemployment Compensation," *American Economic Review* (June 1945), pp. 353–354.

latter is known as self-insurance. Self-insurance programs require approval by the state agency administering workmen's compensation, and generally require the posting of a bond to guarantee that payments can be made.

Some states require employers to insure through a state fund while others permit private companies to compete with the state program. The latter states also permit qualified employers to establish their own funds. Generally speaking, workmen's compensation laws provide payments for all work-connected injuries or illnesses so long as these are not due to the willful misconduct or gross negligence of the worker. Compensation is generally based upon a percentage of weekly wages and this varies considerably from state to state. This is also true of the terms and periods of payment and of qualifications for complete coverage. In general, workmen's compensation ceases when the worker is fully recovered and is able to return to his job or to seek new employment. There are also varying provisions among the states for payments to workers who are partly disabled as a result of job-connected injuries or illnesses.

Federal legislation has been enacted to provide workmen's compensation for specific classes of workers. The Longshoremen and Harbor Workers' Compensation Act of 1927 covers practically all maritime workers except masters or members of the crew of a vessel. The principal workers covered are longshoremen and ship repairmen while working on board a vessel. This law provides benefits to workers for accidental injuries on the job, and for occupational diseases arising out of their employment. Compensation is based on the average weekly wage of the insured worker. If a worker is totally disabled, either temporarily or permanently, he will be paid benefits at the rate of two-thirds his weekly wage up to a maximum of $54 a week. There are also provisions for the payment of permanent partial disability compensation; and burial expenses, up to a maximum of $400, are provided for workers who lose their lives in connection with their employment. Although there are limits on the amount a worker can receive in the form of partial disability payments, all necessary medical costs are covered by this law and the employer is required to arrange for medical care. There is no limit either on the cost or period of treatment. In 1941, the Defense Base Act extended the Longshoremen and Harbor Workers' Compensation Act to the employees of all private employers on defense bases and to all employees on public works outside the continental United States.

CHILD LABOR LAWS AND OTHER MEASURES TO PROTECT LABOR STANDARDS

There are various laws, at both the state and federal levels, which prohibit child labor, regulate industrial homework, and limit the hours of work for women. As early as 1853, seven states had laws limiting the hours of work for children. It was not until 1917, however, that a federal child labor law was passed, and the Supreme Court declared this law to be unconstitutional in less than a year. Further efforts to enact federal legislation stimulated the states to take action, and today every state has a child labor law. In 1938, the Fair Labor Standards Act established minimum ages for employment in industries engaged in interstate commerce and the constitutionality of this law was upheld.

Industrial homework is not a serious problem in the United States today, although this could not have been said a generation ago. There are still a few industries which engage in this practice to some extent, however, and 21 states have laws which either prohibit or regulate industrial homework. Finally, 43 states and the District of Columbia have laws regulating the hours of work for women. Some of these also require rest periods. In 21 states and Puerto Rico there are laws which either prohibit night work or regulate the conditions under which women may work after specified evening hours.[4]

VOCATIONAL TRAINING AND REHABILITATION

A number of agencies, both at the federal and state levels, deal with such matters as job training and worker education. At the federal level, these activities come under the Bureau of Apprenticeship and Training, the Office of Vocational Rehabilitation, and the Vocational Division of the U.S. Office of Education. There are counterpart agencies within the states which deal with job training, education and rehabilitation.

The Bureau of Apprenticeship and Training of the U.S. Department of Labor was established to aid in the training of wage earners. Its purpose is to improve the opportunities for promotion through a program of training for workers in industry. A Federal Committee on Apprenticeship, made up of representatives of employers, labor and the government, has been established to help the Bureau attain its objectives.

[4] For further details on the history and present status of laws to protect labor standards see U.S. Department of Labor, *Growth of Labor Law in the United States,* Washington: Bureau of Labor Standards (1962).

Basically, the Bureau sets up standards for approved apprenticeship programs. These provide for schedules of work processes, organized instruction under proper supervision, and a progressively rising wage schedule as the apprentice completes his training. In cooperation with other bureaus of the Department of Labor, the Bureau of Apprenticeship and Training tries to anticipate occupational changes and to stimulate the training of workers in those occupations which it expects to be in short supply.

The Vocational Division of the U.S. Office of Education promotes vocational education and training under a federal-state-local plan. The plan is the result of the Smith-Hughes and George-Bardon Acts which provide about $30 million annually to the states for vocational training. Funds are distributed on the basis of population and may be used for almost any purpose, including research, which will stimulate vocational training.

Local schools carry out the programs under state supervision, and the latter must be approved by the U.S. Office of Education. Grants are available to provide full-time pre-employment training for youngsters preparing to enter the labor market, and evening classes are conducted for apprentices and others over sixteen years of age.

The Office of Vocational Rehabilitation, which is in the Department of Health, Education and Welfare, provides services to civilian men and women of working age whose ability to obtain employment or to hold a job has been impaired through a mental or physical handicap regardless of cause. Services include medical, surgical, and psychiatric treatment, as well as hospitalization, occupational and physical therapy. This agency also provides vocational counselling and training, financial aid during the period of rehabilitation, and job placement. Some of these services are conditioned upon the economic circumstances of the applicant. The objective is to return to useful employment workers who would be unable to hold a job without such training and medical treatment.

Services are also provided to management for the retraining of injured workers. The basic program goes back to 1920, but a 1954 amendment to the law increased appropriations to permit states to step up their rehabilitation activities. This amendment also provided grants to institutions which train therapists, social workers, psychologists, rehabilitation counsellors, and others who can participate in the program. Another law passed in 1954—the Medical Facilities Survey and Construction Act—provides federal grants for the construction of rehabilitation facilities such as chronic disease hospitals, nursing homes, and diagnostic and treatment centers.

While such programs of vocational training and rehabilitation are generally not widely publicized, they serve a useful purpose. Not every worker can be trained to become a skilled worker, and not every disabled worker can be helped—through rehabilitation and therapy—to hold a productive job. But those who can be helped benefit enormously both in an economic sense and psychologically. As part of its broad scheme of providing a minimum of security to the vast majority of workers, the federal government has not overlooked those who would find it most difficult to obtain new employment, as the result of an occupational injury or work-connected illness.

CONCLUDING COMMENTS

Over the past three decades a fairly comprehensive system of social insurance has been built up in the United States. Conservatives have strongly opposed this trend and claim that it has led to a "welfare state."[5] One of their major objections is that social security in the United States is compulsory. Another complaint is that protection against the vicissitudes of the market is likely to encourage indolence and malingering among workers. Critics of social insurance are not numerous, however, and few seriously suggest that our present system be scrapped. Such criticism can serve a useful purpose if it leads to more effective administration of the programs which make up our system of social security.

There are no doubt abuses of unemployment compensation. Some workers may draw benefits illegally, but this usually involves the collusion of an employer. Similarly, individuals may draw workmen's compensation to which they are not entitled by faking injuries. In any society there will be some who are out "to beat the system." But it would scarcely make sense to gear social policy to the behavior of a lazy or dishonest minority. The answer to these problems lies in improved administration, and in stiffer penalties for those who draw social insurance benefits illegally.

There are other problems, such as those involving coverage and adequacy of benefits, which can only be mentioned in a general introductory discussion of social insurance. The emotionally-charged issue of medical care—especially for the aged—is one of these.

[5] For one exposition of this point of view see William F. Buckley, Jr., *Up From Liberalism,* New York: Hillman Books (1961), pp. 186–201.

Similarly, the adequacy of benefits under the various social security programs is one of those thorny problems which cannot be resolved to everyone's satisfaction since, as Richard Lester has noted, "adequacy is a relative matter."[6] There are more technical problems involving the impact of social insurance on worker mobility, the effects on interstate competition of widely-varying state programs, the financing of social insurance under conditions of rising prices, and the shifting and incidence of taxes levied under social insurance schemes. Discussion of these would go beyond the scope of an introductory volume. They are mentioned to indicate the dynamic nature of social insurance. Any suggestion that we have found final answers to these problems would be misleading in the extreme.

It might be well, however, to conclude this discussion by attempting to place the American program in perspective. The United States has not been a pioneer in social legislation. Indeed, it has been suggested by a number of writers that we lag about a generation behind Great Britain and the democratic countries of western Europe whose social insurance programs are far more comprehensive than ours. American workers enjoy higher wages and, in general, more liberal fringe benefits than those in other countries. At the same time they are more susceptible to the threat of unemployment. While substantial progress has been made in providing worker security, our basic philosophy has been one of insuring a *minimum* of security for the aged, the disabled, the unemployed, and the surviving members of families who lose their primary breadwinners.

REFERENCES

BOOKS AND PAMPHLETS

Becker, Joseph M., S.J., *The Adequacy of the Benefit Amount in Unemployment Insurance,* Kalamazoo, Michigan: W. E. Upjohn Institute for Employment Research (1961).

Buckley, William F., Jr., *Up From Liberalism,* New York: Hillman Books (1961).

Lester, Richard A., *The Economics of Unemployment Compensation,* Princeton: Princeton University Industrial Relations Section (1962).

Our Developing Social Security System: The First Twenty-Five Years (a symposium), *Industrial and Labor Relations Review,* Vol. 14 (October 1960).

U.S. Department of Labor, *Growth of Labor Law in the United States,* Washington: U.S. Government Printing Office (1962).

——— ——— — ———, *Annual Digest of State and Federal Labor Legislation,* 1961–1962, Bureau of Labor Standards, Bulletin 253 (1963).

[6] Richard A. Lester, *The Economics of Unemployment Compensation,* Princeton: Princeton University Industrial Relations Section (1962), p. 25.

Worker Security in a Changing Economy (a symposium), *Monthly Labor Review,* Vol. 86 (June 1963).

ARTICLES

Barcus, Norman, "Problems of Financing an Adequate Unemployment Insurance Program in the Next Decade," *Proceedings,* 14th Annual Meeting, Industrial Relations Research Association (December 1961), pp. 152–164.

Blum, Fred H., "The Social and Economic Implications of the Fair Labor Standards Act: An Interpretation in Terms of Social Cost," *Proceedings,* 9th Annual Meeting, Industrial and Labor Relations Research Association (December 1956), pp. 167–183.

Booth, Philip, "Unemployment Insurance and the Challenge of the 1960's," *Proceedings,* 14th Annual Meeting, Industrial Relations Research Association (December 1961), pp. 165–177.

Brodie, Abner, "The Adequacy of Workmen's Compensation as Social Insurance," *Wisconsin Law Review* (January 1963), pp. 57–91.

Burns, Eveline M., "Social Insurance in Evolution," *American Economic Review,* Vol. XXXIV (March 1944), pp. 199–211, reprinted in Francis S. Doody, ed., *Readings in Labor Economics,* Cambridge, Massachusetts: Addison-Wesley Press (1950), pp. 455–467.

Myers, Charles A., "Experience Rating in Unemployment Compensation," *American Economic Review,* Vol. XXXV (June 1945), pp. 337–354, reprinted in Doody, *op. cit.,* pp. 430–447.

Slavick, Fred, "Ability of the Federal-State Unemployment Insurance System to Provide Benefits in Times of Recession," *Proceedings,* 14th Annual Meeting, Industrial Relations Research Association (December 1961), pp. 178–193.

Slichter, Sumner H., "The Impact of Social Security Legislation Upon Mobility and Enterprise," *American Economic Review,* Vol. XXX (March 1940), pp. 44–60, reprinted in Doody, *op. cit.,* pp. 413–429.

Somers, Herman M., "Some Issues in the Improvement of the Federal-State Unemployment Insurance System," *Proceedings,* 12th Annual Meeting, Industrial Relations Research Association (December 1959), pp. 92–103.

———, ——— —, and Anne R. Somers, "Unemployment Insurance and Workmen's Compensation," *Proceedings,* 9th Annual Meeting, Industrial Relations Research Association (December 1956), pp. 120–144.

Tolles, N. Arnold, "American Minimum Wage Laws: Their Purposes and Results," *Proceedings,* 12th Annual Meeting, Industrial Relations Research Association (December 1959), pp. 116–133.

Weiss, Harry, "Economic Effects of a Nationwide Minimum Wage," *Proceedings,* 9th Annual Meeting, Industrial Relations Research Association (December 1956), pp. 154–166.

PART 3

the structure, government, and objectives of trade unions

PART 3

the structure, government, and objectives of trade unions

Chapter 10 Trade Union Structure

Most trade unions in the United States belong to the AFL-CIO which claimed a membership of 13.5 million in 1962. The organizational structure of the Federation seems complex but for an organization of this size it is fairly streamlined. Basically, the Federation is made up of 130 national and international unions and of 332 local unions which are affiliated directly with the AFL-CIO. It will be convenient to consider first the structure of the Federation, which is shown in Chart 10-1, then that of the national or international unions. There are also state and local bodies which perform specific functions and these will be discussed separately.

THE STRUCTURE OF THE AFL-CIO

The highest governing body of the Federation is the *Convention*, which meets every two years to determine basic policies. There are also provisions in the constitution for special conventions which can be called at any time to consider specific problems.

Each national or international union is entitled to send delegates to the convention. The number of delegates is determined by the per capita dues paid to the national or international unions by their local union organizations. Other organizations affiliated with the AFL-CIO are entitled to one delegate each.

The Executive Council

Since the convention meets at two year intervals, it is necessary to have a governing body to deal with issues and problems which arise between conventions. The Executive Council consists of the Federation's president, the secretary-treasurer, and twenty-seven vice presidents. All members of the Executive Council are elected by majority vote at the convention. The Council is required to

CHART 10–1
STRUCTURAL ORGANIZATION OF THE AMERICAN FEDERATION OF LABOR AND CONGRESS OF INDUSTRIAL ORGANIZATIONS

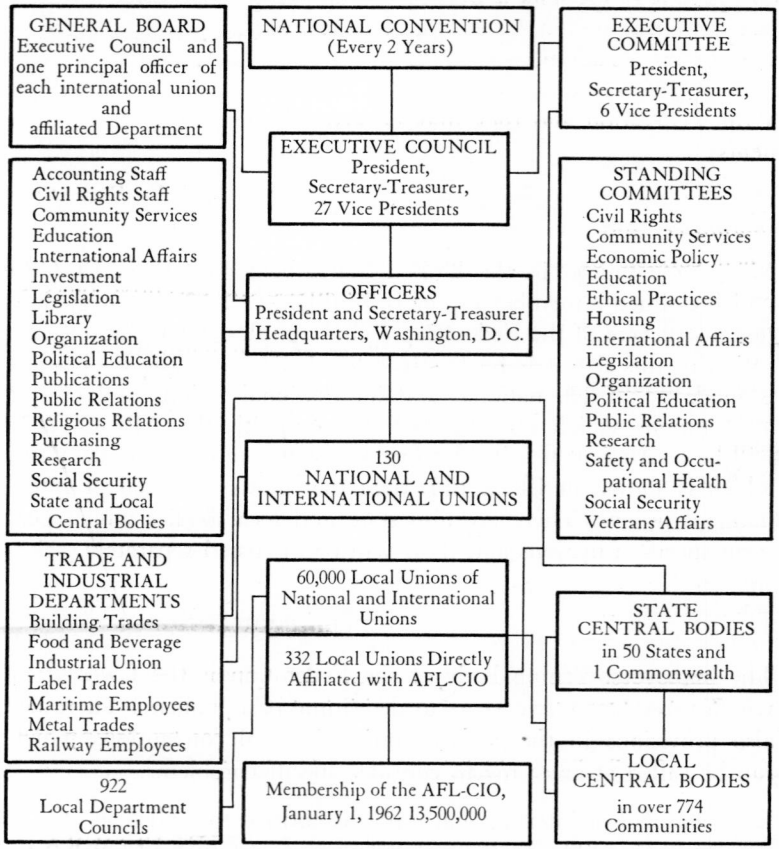

Source: Chart taken from publication of the American Federation of Labor and the Congress of Industrial Organizations

meet at least three times a year, and it may meet at more frequent intervals if the need arises.

The Executive Officers

Although it is up to the Executive Council to see that policies voted by the convention are carried out, an organization as large as the AFL-CIO must have a headquarters and executive officers to deal with day-to-day problems. The elected executive officers who are responsible for the regular supervision of affairs of the Federation are the president and secretary-treasurer. Currently, the president is George Meany, and the secretary-treasurer is William F. Schnitzler.

The president appoints a number of *Standing Committees* which deal with such matters as economic policy, ethical practices, legislation, public relations, civil rights, and a wide variety of other matters. The standing committees report to the executive officers of the Federation and they may be given a wide range of assignments.

There are two other official bodies in the Federation: the *Executive Committee* and the *General Board*. The *Executive Committee* which consists of the president, secretary-treasurer, and six vice-presidents meets every two months to advise the executive officers on all basic policy matters. The *General Board*, consisting of the Executive Council, one principal officer of each national or international union, and one officer representing each affiliated department is required to meet at least once a year to consider any policy questions which might be referred to it by the officers of the Executive Council.

Finally, the national or international unions are divided into trade and industrial departments. The most important department is the Industrial Union Department, made up largely of unions formerly affiliated with the CIO. There are other departments for unions in the building trades, the metal trades, maritime employees, and railway employees. The sixth department—the Union Label and Service Trades Department—was established to promote consumer interest in union-made products and union services by urging the purchase of only those which bear the union label.

THE FEDERATION STAFF

A body as large as the AFL-CIO requires the services of a large number of specialists such as accountants, lawyers, and public relations personnel. The staff of the Federation is divided into fourteen departments with each department head responsible to the executive officers of the Federation. There are staff specialists who deal with such routine matters as accounting, purchasing, and library affairs. Other staff specialists are concerned with civil rights, community services, education, international affairs, and legislation.

Organizational matters, political education, public relations, and the publication of union magazines and papers are also part of the Federation's headquarters structure. The Federation maintains a substantial research staff, which serves the executive officers and assists others on the headquarters staff in their relations with unions, employers, the government, and the public. The AFL-CIO also maintains specialists in the field of social security both to assist union members in routine matters and to work with legislative and other groups in the AFL-CIO in proposing changes in legislation.

AFFILIATED ORGANIZATIONS

In addition to the trade and industrial departments to which many of the national or international unions belong, the structural organization of the AFL-CIO includes state and city central bodies and local department councils.

There is a state central body—usually called the AFL-CIO State Council—in each of the fifty states and in Puerto Rico. The state bodies are made up of representatives of the local unions in each state. Their principal function is to advance the state-wide interests of organized labor and to represent trade unions on state legislative matters. The state central bodies do not report directly to the officers or Executive Council of the AFL-CIO. They are tied in with the trade and industrial departments through the local unions which they represent. Each state body has its own elected officers some of whom function on a full-time basis but some of whom also hold office in a national or international union.

At the bottom of the structural pyramid there are almost nine hundred local central bodies which have been formed at the community level by the local unions which are affiliated with the AFL-CIO directly or through a national or international union. These organizations deal primarily with local civic and community problems or with other matters strictly of a local nature. There are also more than nine hundred local department councils made up of representatives of the local unions which are affiliated both with a national or international union and with one of the trade and industrial departments. As is true of the local central bodies, the local department councils deal primarily with community matters of concern to the members of the unions which they represent.

THE NATIONAL AND INTERNATIONAL UNIONS

It will be recalled that one of the conflicts between the Knights of Labor and the trade unions was over the question of where decision-making authority should be located. The Knights wanted "one big union" with the headquarters making all major decisions. But the trade unions at that time wanted to be the guardians of their own destinies and the latter philosophy won out in this struggle. From the beginning of the A.F. of L., the locus of trade union power has moved steadily toward the national union headquarters. There is, of course, some variation among national unions. There are unions in which the locals have a great deal to say about collective bargaining and other matters, but it is a fair generalization to say that more often decision-making authority resides with the national union officers. From the beginning of the A.F. of L., the federation has had little, if anything, to say about collective bargaining or other matters directly affecting the members of a national or international union. This is consistent with the principle of autonomy—one of the basic principles on which the A.F. of L. was founded.

Each national union has its elected officers, its executive boards or councils, and staff specialists to advise the officers, to prepare union publications, and to deal with other matters of a technical or specialized nature. The headquarters staff of national or international unions vary greatly in size and degree of specialization. Some of the smaller national unions operate with very little staff assistance. But the larger unions—such as the United Auto Workers and the Steelworkers—have fairly large staff setups.

Some of the larger national unions are organized along regional lines. The regional representatives are generally staff men directly responsible to the national union president, and their function is to assist locals in the administration of agreements and in the solution of day-to-day problems as they arise. They also provide liaison between the local unions in a particular part of the country and national headquarters.

A further link between the local unions and national headquarters —often working through a regional organization—is the Business agent or the International Representative. These are the field officers of the national union who work with locals in a relatively small area to see that contracts are being administered properly, that dues are transmitted to the national headquarters, and in some cases that grievances are settled which are not of sufficient gravity to be referred to a higher level in the union organization.

To some extent the structure of the national union perpetuates the centralization of power in the national headquarters. The president of a national union will try to surround himself with staff members who are loyal to him and who are in broad agreement with his basic views on collective bargaining and other union matters. These staff members handle the national union's publicity and they also deal with the local unions which make up the national organization. The job security of staff members depends upon the way they perform. They are employees of the national union, not elected union officials. The national president will see to it that any staff member who does not go along with the national union's (i.e., the president's) policies will not hold his position too long.

This is not to imply that the presidents of national unions are dictators. Some come very close, but others are closely attuned to the desires of the rank and file. Even with the support of a strong and loyal staff, an unpopular national union president can be voted out of office. There are sporadic instances of rank and file revolt, although it is rare indeed for the president of a national union to be turned out of office. This is not because the president has an iron grip on his members, but generally because the rank and file—while not necessarily approving of every action of the president—are generally satisfied with the union's policies and with the union's accomplishments for its members.

THE LOCAL UNION

The broad base upon which American trade union organization rests is made up of thousands of local unions. Some are craft locals made up of members of a particular occupational group with a strong common bond. Such locals do not deal with a single employer; indeed, the members of the local may move from employer to employer as one job is finished and other jobs open up. Other locals belong to industrial unions. Their membership is far more heterogeneous. The locals of some industrial unions may also deal with several employers, but some of the larger locals—in the steel and auto industries, for example—may be made up of the employees of a single concern.

The officers of the local union are unpaid, and there is far more turnover of local union officers than at any other level of the trade union organization. At the very bottom of the trade union hierarchy—but of critical importance to the success of the administration of labor-management agreements—are the shop stewards. A local which deals with a number of small companies will generally have a shop steward in each company. It is his duty to see that the terms of the agreement are respected, to accept grievances from workers, and wherever possible to settle these on the spot. In some industrial union locals which deal with a single employer, there will be a number of shop stewards assigned to various departments in a plant. A good shop steward can do much to minimize grievances. If his working relationship with management is good, the shop steward can keep minor grievances from becoming major issues and he can do this while protecting the rights of the workers he represents without antagonizing the foremen with whom shop stewards usually deal. A contentious shop steward, however, can turn an amicable relationship into one marked by excessive petty bickering over minor details.

In 1962, the AFL-CIO reported approximately 60,000 local unions which belonged to national or international unions. An additional 332 local unions were affiliated directly with the Federation. In some ways the directly-affiliated local union is an anachronism. It dates back to the pre-1935 period before the split between the old A.F. of L. and the CIO took place. At that time a number of "federal" local unions were established. These locals were organized along industrial lines, but they were not affiliated with industrial unions. The original object was to organize the workers who were not bound together by a common occupational tie with the idea that ultimately they would be funneled into appropriate craft locals. They function in much the same way as the locals belonging to national or international unions, except that their officers report directly to AFL-CIO headquarters.

In many communities, most locals affiliated with the AFL-CIO belong to the local central labor organization. The same locals are likely to be represented on the state central labor bodies and some of them will also belong to local department councils.

The greatest variation in the trade union movement comes at the local union level. Some local unions are well organized and are very active while others do very little. Their officers collect dues and transmit the appropriate amounts, per capita, to national union headquarters. Shop stewards process routine grievances and the affairs of the local are handled in a generally lackadaisical manner. Meetings when they are held are poorly attended, and there is little rank and file enthusiasm for trade union activities in general. But there are other locals in which the membership is active, and often militant. In the United Auto Workers, for example, some locals wield considerable influence. The wishes of the rank and file get a respectful hearing at national headquarters and the local officers may take an active part in the collective bargaining process.

By and large, however, the affairs of local unions are managed by a handful of "activists." This is not because the organization involved is a trade union since the same is true of many other kinds of organizations which engage in political, economic, social, religious or other activities. Trade unions are sometimes singled out for criticism because the rank and file do not take a more active interest in their affairs, yet if the critics were to take a careful look at other organizations they would find that much the same is true. The typical union member is content to let the officers of the local, and the paid officers of his national union, handle affairs so long as things are going satisfactorily. When crises arise—as they do from time to time—the rank and file can generally be counted on to take an active interest in union matters until the problem which precipitated the crisis is settled to their satisfaction.

INDEPENDENT NATIONAL UNIONS

Not all national or international unions are affiliated with the AFL-CIO. The largest union in the country—the Teamsters—has been an independent union since it was expelled from the AFL-CIO following the investigation of the McClellan Committee. The United Mine Workers is also an independent national union. At one time it was affiliated with the old A.F. of L. Following the split the Miners became a spearhead in the formation of the CIO but John L. Lewis, the egregious leader of the Miners at the time it left the A.F. of L., soon fell into disagreement with the other leaders of the CIO which he then abandoned. Since that time the United Mine Workers has continued to function as an independent union. A number of smaller national unions were expelled from the CIO because of the left-wing tendencies of their leaders. These unions such as the Mine, Mill and Smelter Workers, and the United Electrical Workers have operated as independent national unions since that time.

The structure of an independent national or international union is very similar to that of the national unions which make up the AFL-CIO. Because the center of power in American trade unionism is found in the national union headquarters, the operations of most independent national unions seem not to have been impaired by their lack of affiliation with the AFL-CIO. Some of the independent national unions have lost members in recent years because of the left-wing stigma attached to their leaders. When the United Electrical Workers was expelled from the CIO, for example, a rival union was formed within the federation known as the International Union of Electrical Workers (IUE) which soon attracted a majority of the workers in the electrical machinery industry. Since the ouster of the UE and the formation of the IUE there has been "dual unionism" in this industry which, in the opinion of some, has weakened the bargaining position of both.

LOCAL INDEPENDENT UNIONS

One type of labor organization remains to be discussed. It should be noted that this segment of the American labor movement has led to controversy among labor economists, some of whom doubt that all of the organizations involved may be considered as bona fide trade unions. These are the local independent unions which are those labor organizations whose members are employed in a single plant or company and who are not affiliated with any national union or with the AFL-CIO. Local independent unions are also considered to be free of employer control or domination, directly or indirectly.[1] Troy distinguishes between local independent unions and company unions. The latter are considered to be company *dominated* unions, and these have been illegal since the Wagner Act was passed.

Not everyone would agree with Troy's distinction. Professor Philip Taft, for example, acknowledges that many local independent unions function as bona fide labor organizations while others do not. "Many independents," he writes, "cannot be regarded normally as part of the labor movement . . ."[2] In his opinion, many local independent unions "are either employer dominated or influenced by racket organizations whose chief aim is the victimization of the workers they organize."[3]

Troy has developed a series of "tests of legitimacy" and feels that most local independent unions pass this test—that they are legitimate trade unions and part of the American labor movement. Professor Taft, however, questions some of the criteria developed by

[1] Leo Troy, "Local Independent Unions in the American Labor Movement," *Industrial and Labor Relations Review* (April 1961), p. 331.
[2] "Local Independent Unions in the American Labor Movement," *Industrial and Labor Relations Review* (October 1961), p. 105.
[3] *Ibid.*, p. 102.

Troy and argues that since company dominated unions are illegal per se that all local independent unions must give the *appearance* of bona fide trade unions. It is important to emphasize that both Troy and Taft agree that some local independent unions are entirely legitimate and are accepted by the rest of the American labor movement as such. They disagree on the number of such organizations which should be considered as legitimate trade unions.

In compiling information on union membership, the U.S. Department of Labor sends questionnaires only to all unions affiliated with the AFL-CIO, and to all unaffiliated unions known to be interstate in scope.[4] Since local independent unions are, by definition, *intra*-state in character, their members are not included in the estimates of total union membership. Thus neither the number of local independent unions nor their membership figures are reported. Troy has estimated, however, that "there are probably about 2,000 in the United States with an estimated membership of 1.5 million."[5] In his opinion, there has been a significant increase in the number of local independent unions since 1939. He also believes there has been a substantial gain in membership in these organizations during this period.

THE SIZE AND COMPOSITION OF TRADE UNIONS

In 1960 there were 184 national or international unions, of which 134 were affiliated with the AFL-CIO. Fourteen of these unions accounted for more than half of all organized workers in the United States. This concentration of membership in a few large unions has long been characteristic of the American trade union movement. Two of the unions in the top ten—the Teamsters and the United Mine Workers—are independents; all of the others are affiliated with the AFL—CIO.

The size distribution of American unions in 1960 is summarized in Table 10-1. The distribution, in finer detail, is shown graphically on Chart 10-2. The curved line is the actual distribution of unions and union membership. The "line of equal distribution" shows the distribution as it would be if all unions had the same number of members.

[4] See *Directory of National and International Labor Unions in the United States*, 1959, Bulletin No. 1267, U.S. Department of Labor, Bureau of Labor Statistics (December 1959), p. 7.

[5] Troy, p. 331.

TABLE 10-1
DISTRIBUTION OF UNIONS AND MEMBERS BY SIZE OF UNION, 1960

Number of Members Reported	Unions		Membership	
	Number	Per Cent	Number (thousands)	Per Cent
400,000 or more	10	5.4	8,174	45.3
200,000 to 400,000	11	6.0	3,191	17.7
50,000 to 200,000	53	28.8	5,241	29.0
10,000 to 50,000	47	25.5	1,213	6.7
under 10,000	63	34.3	218	1.2

Source: *Directory of National and International Labor Unions in the United States, 1961,* U.S. Department of Labor, Bureau of Labor Statistics, Bulletin No. 1320 (March 1962), p. 49.

The chart indicates that 60 per cent of all union members—excluding those in local independent unions—belong to 10 per cent of the nation's unions. About one-third of all unions account for 90 per cent of total membership. Slightly more than one-fourth of all unions, excluding the local independents, have fewer than 5,000 members each. Collectively, these small unions include less than one per cent of total membership. The organizations which have

CHART 10–2
SIZE DISTRIBUTION OF UNIONS, 1960

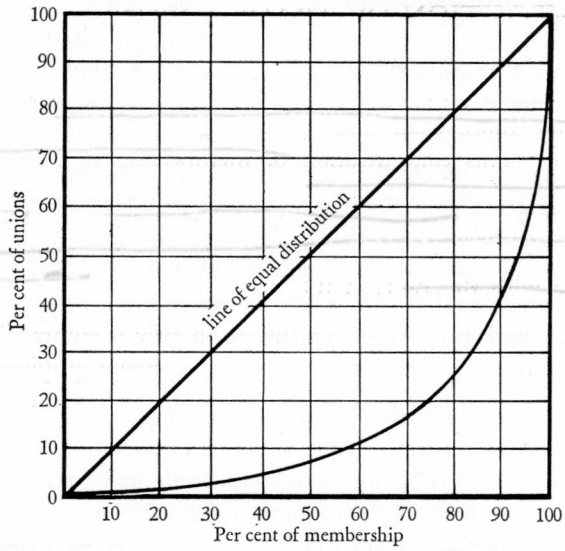

Department of Labor, Bureau of Labor Statistics, Bulletin No. 1320 (March 1962), p. 49.
Source: *Directory of National and International Labor Unions in the United States, 1961,* U.S.

done much to shape the "image" of trade unionism in America are the giants—the Teamsters, Steelworkers, Autoworkers, Machinists and Carpenters. At the other end of the spectrum are dozens of small unions representing workers in a wide variety of industries and occupations, yet the public rarely hears of these organizations or of their activities.

Trade union members are predominantly male. In 1960, it was estimated that about 15 per cent of all union members were women. Only about one out of seven women in the labor force belonged to a trade union. About 20 per cent of all women union members were in the garment and apparel industries; other unions with substantial female membership are in the textile, communications, electrical and transportation equipment industries, and in retail trade and service occupations.

Most union members are production workers. The U.S. Department of Labor has estimated that only about 2.2 million union members out of a total of slightly more than 18 million in 1960 were in so-called white collar occupations. Almost two thirds of all unions reported that they had either no members in white-collar occupations or a negligible number.

The Industrial Distribution of Membership

Slightly less than half (47.6 per cent) of all union members in 1960 were employed in manufacturing industry. Trade unionists in nonmanufacturing activities accounted for 46.4 per cent of the total in the same year. The remaining 6 per cent were in federal, state or local government employment. Two major nonmanufacturing activities—contract construction and transportation—accounted for almost twenty-seven per cent of all union members in 1960. The trade and service sectors combined included nearly 12 per cent of total union membership. Elsewhere in nonmanufacturing—excluding mining and quarrying which are highly organized—union organization is not widespread.

The degree of organization in manufacturing varies widely. The metal working industries—steel, autos, transportation equipment, for example—are heavily organized and accounted for 23 per cent of all union members in 1960. Some nondurable goods industries, such as the garment and apparel trades, are fairly well organized, but in others, such as textiles and chemicals, unions have not been able to sign up a majority of workers in the industry.

REFERENCES

BOOKS

U.S. Department of Labor, Bureau of Labor Standards, *Directory of National and International Labor Unions in the United States, 1961,* Bulletin No. 1320 (March, 1962).

ARTICLES

Taft, Philip, "Local Independent Unions in the American Labor Movement," *Industrial and Labor Relations Review,* Vol. 15, No. 1 (October 1961), pp. 102–106, and "Reply" by Leo Troy, pp. 106–110.

Troy, Leo, "Local Independent Unions in the American Labor Movement," Industrial and Labor Relations Review, Vol. 14, No. 3 (April 1961), pp. 331–349.

Chapter 11 Trade Union Government

Before the rapid growth of unions in the mid-1930's there was relatively little public interest in the ways in which trade unions were administered. Union membership was not widespread. As Sumner H. Slichter put it, ". . . some pioneer trade unionists who battled valiantly to build unions before the days of the Wagner Act . . . were brought up to regard unions as private clubs."[1] Today, however, unions are regarded by some as quasi-public institutions since where there are union shop agreements a worker must remain a union member in good standing as a condition of employment. As early as 1947, Slichter estimated that 11,000,000 jobs could be held only by men who remained in good standing in their unions.[2] Because the livelihood of so many union members is tied directly to their standing in a union, the ways in which unions are governed have come under close scrutiny in recent years. A number of scholars have made careful investigations of trade union government, but the results of these studies are not easy to interpret.

Are trade unions democratic organizations? If not, is there some way they can be made to function in a democratic manner? Or is there any reason to expect that democracy will flourish in trade unions? None of these questions can be answered by a simple yes or no. It is generally agreed that in some respects unions should be democratic. They should not practice discrimination, for example, and the rank and file members should be protected from arbitrary disciplinary action by union officers. But beyond this, some scholars

[1] Sumner H. Slichter, *The Challenge of Industrial Relations,* Ithaca, New York: Cornell University Press (1947), p. 123.
[2] *Ibid.,* p. 101.

feel, it is futile to expect unions to function in the manner of the old New England town meeting. Following a careful study of trade union government, C. Peter McGrath concluded that American labor unions have become businesslike organizations. The successful union, in his view, is essentially nondemocratic. "However unpleasant the reality, democracy is as inappropriate within the international headquarters of the UAW as it is in the front office of General Motors."[3] Moreover, McGrath did not single out the UAW and General Motors for criticism, he believes that this conclusion applies widely throughout American labor and business organizations.

Others have pointed out that while we insist upon democracy in government we do not expect all the organizations to which we belong to function in a democratic manner. Even college professors would resist having classroom matters decided by popular vote. Those who demand simple answers to even the most complex problems will find little comfort in the conclusions regarding union democracy reached by scholars who have made meticulous studies of trade union government and administration. There are wide variations in union policies. Yet in spite of this, some generalizations can be made about trade union government.

UNION ADMISSION POLICIES

Most unions admit properly qualified workers without regard to race, creed, or politics, and relatively few exclude members through excessive initiation fees. But apprenticeship rules may be effective barriers to persons seeking membership in some unions and there are a few cases where "fraternal" approval of all applicants for membership can be used for discriminatory purposes. A significant number of unions, for example, exclude women. Slichter pointed out that a number of national unions had excluded negroes through constitutional provisions or by their rituals; others discriminated against negroes by establishing separate "Jim Crow" locals.[4] Even before the Civil Rights Act of 1964, however, some unions had become concerned about the problem of racial discrimination and were taking steps to eliminate it. After the Civil Rights bill became law

[3] C. Peter McGrath, "Democracy in Overalls: Futile Quest for Union Democracy," *Industrial and Labor Relations Review,* Vol. 12, No. 4 (July 1959), p. 525.
[4] *Ibid.,* pp. 102–103. For a lucid account of barriers to Negro membership in some skilled craft unions see Ernest Dunbar, "Black Men White Unions," *Look* Magazine (December 17, 1963), pp. 43ff.

there were increasing pressures on other unions to put an end to discriminatory practices.[5]

There have been times when union locals have restricted the entry of new members for economic purposes. Some locals have an informal rule, for example, that new members will not be admitted while members in good standing are involuntarily unemployed. National union officers generally oppose such practices, however, particularly in areas where there are nonunion shops. Once refused admission—for any reason—a worker will rarely regard unions with a kindly eye. Even if there were absolutely no restrictions on membership—if the doors were wide open to all—the issue of union democracy would not be completely settled since there would still be problems involving the election of officers, the determination of basic policies, and the thorny problem of union discipline. Perhaps it is as unreasonable to expect a union with hundreds of thousands of members to follow strictly democratic procedures as it is to expect the executives of a large corporation to poll all stockholders before company decisions are made.

THE DETERMINATION AND EXECUTION OF UNION POLICIES

In a recent study of seventy international unions, with a combined membership of almost 16 million, Leo Bromwich found that "all the unions in the sample designate the convention as the supreme body of the organization . . ."[6] But who selects delegates to the conventions? Who appoints convention committees? And who presides over the convention? The fact that grass roots organizations are represented at a national convention does not in itself guarantee that democracy is at work.

The selection of delegates is of crucial importance since in most cases the officers of the union are elected by the convention.[7] Most union constitutions specify the intervals at which conventions are to be held. Generally, conventions are held every two years, al-

[5] See, for example, "How Well Can Unions Keep Pledge on Bias?", *Business Week* (November 24, 1962), pp. 54–56; and "NLRB Cracks Down on Union Bias," *Business Week* (July 11, 1964), p. 50.

[6] Leo Bromwich, *Union Constitutions,* New York: The Fund for the Republic (1959), p. 38.

[7] One of the few notable exceptions is the International Typographical Union where national officers are elected by popular vote. This union is unique in a number of other respects, however, including its two party system which generally results in lively pre-election contests for office. For an excellent and detailed discussion of this union see Seymour Martin Lipset, Martin Trow and James Coleman, *Union Democracy,* Garden City, New York: Doubleday and Company, Inc. (1962).

though some unions hold conventions only at five-year intervals. There have been times when conventions have been skipped entirely; during one period, for example, the Tobacco Workers allowed thirty-nine years to elapse between conventions.[8]

The selection of delegates is of critical importance if all factions in a national or international union are to be represented at the convention. As Bromwich points out: "Most of the rules for representation in the convention are clear, quantitative, and precise. They permit little opportunity for sharp practices or crafty pre-convention maneuvers. The differences which exist among the various unions largely reflect varied approaches to the problem of reconciling the interests of larger locals with those of the smaller ones in the distribution of convention power."[9]

More than a third of the unions which Bromwich studied have a graduated scale of representation which tends to favor smaller locals. The United Auto Workers constitution provides a typical example: it specifies that each local union shall have one delegate for 200 members or less, one additional delegate for the next 300, and an added delegate for each additional 800 members.

Most constitutions also contain rules for the election of delegates to national conventions. Some of these rules are precise while others are quite vague. Some call for nominations at one time and elections at a later date with prior notification of all members; others set a date for elections and do not provide for prior nominations. Still other constitutions state that delegates are to be elected without specifying how, when, or where, and there are some which have no provisions at all for the election of convention delegates. The constitution of the United Textile Workers, for example, requires only that each delegate establish his claim to a seat at the convention by credentials duly signed by the president and secretary of the local union.

THE CONVENTION COMMITTEES

The selection of delegates by democratic procedures does not guarantee democracy in a trade union. The various committees which run conventions can, if they wish, exert considerable control over procedures. Credential committees, for example, play an important part in settling disputed elections. Resolutions committees typically transmit policy statements from locals to the convention, and can

[8] Slichter, *The Challenge of Industrial Relations,* p. 104.
[9] Bromwich, *Union Constitutions,* pp. 10–11.

determine the priority of issues to be discussed thus controlling the direction of the convention. Appeals committees handle grievances against local union officers. Convention committees, in brief, wield considerable power in determining what is to be discussed, and when it is to reach the floor for discussion. In his survey of union constitutions, Bromwich found that "in the majority of cases, control of the committees is in the hands of the union president, and there is no real rank-and-file check on his power. In 49 of the 70 unions, the committees are simply appointed by the president. In another 11, the executive board has this job . . ."[10] Since he controls the convention committees, the union president is in an excellent position to manipulate the convention if he wishes to do so.

There is a lack of precision in union constitutions about the ways in which resolutions are to be handled. Generally, an officer of the national or international union is assigned the task of listing resolutions prior to the convention, but he is usually permitted considerable discretion in deciding how this is to be done. An even greater shortcoming in some union constitutions is the absence of specific and unambiguous rules for reporting out resolutions. The resolutions committee appears to have considerable power to decide what is and what is not to be reported out.

Once resolutions have reached the floor of the convention, debate is generally conducted according to established rules and decisions are made by majority vote. There are a few exceptions to this general rule. Some unions require a two-thirds majority for passage of a resolution. By and large, however, if resolutions reach the floor they are decided by a simple majority of the delegates.

It must be emphasized that the existence of procedural weaknesses in some union constitutions with respect to convention procedures does not mean that union officers and convention committees abuse their power. All that can be said is that in many national and international unions the opportunity for such abuses exists.

Union constitutions can, of course, be amended, but the rules for constitutional amendments again range from the precise and detailed to the ambiguous. Some unions permit the conventions themselves to alter the constitution while others call for discussion of proposed amendments at the convention with a final decision to be made by a referendum. There is again no evidence of widespread rigging of constitutional amendments in national or inter-

[10] Bromwich, *ibid.*, p. 13.

national unions. The possibility exists, however, for unscrupulous officers to do so in some unions if they are so inclined.

THE UNION OFFICERS

Basic union policies are determined by conventions, but the execution of these policies is in the hands of union officers. Theoretically, the executive board is charged with the responsibility of executing policy and the president, as chief executive officer, is subject to the board. In practice, however, the powers granted to national or international union presidents are very broad while the powers granted to executive boards tend to be much more diffuse. The union president handles decisions on a day-to-day basis, while executive boards meet only at stated intervals or at the call of the president.

In typical cases, the union president has authority to appoint or suspend staff members and other employees. He also may exercise considerable control over union funds and may have the authority to approve or disapprove of strikes by locals.

Important grievances may also be handled by the president or by other national officers selected by the president. He also typically selects national representatives who provide liaison between the national union, regional headquarters, and the locals. Most national union presidents exercise considerable control over conventions, over the appointment of staff members and union employees, over union funds, and over union publications. The typical union president surrounds himself with able staff assistants who keep him informed of conditions in the industry or industries with which he must deal; help him in making important policy decisions, and regularly keep his views exposed to the rank and file. The capable union leader—and most of them have demonstrated their capability—thus becomes a knowledgeable professional. Once in a position of power, the union president is difficult to dislodge. There have been notable instances—in the Teamsters and Steelworkers, for example—of sizeable rank-and-file revolts but these are rarely successful. The president has the weight of national headquarters on his side, and it is difficult for dissident members to air their views beyond a specific local.

This does not mean that the president can be indifferent to the wishes of the rank and file. He must be able to "deliver the goods" to the satisfaction of most members. Machinery does exist for the removal of presidents if a majority of the rank and file wish to make a change, but there have been few cases where national or international presidents have been voted out of office. Once at the helm, the chief executive officers of national unions typically remain in control until death or retirement.

ELECTION AND RECALL

A minority of national unions provide for the election of officers by a referendum vote. The outstanding example is the International Typographical Union which has become famous for its two-party system which ensures that the members can change officers annually if they wish to do so.

In the ITU, members announce their candidacy for office in the union's *Journal*. Each local nominates one candidate for each office from the published list; the five candidates for each office with the largest number of local union votes become eligible for election. All candidates are required to publish their reasons for seeking office and arguments in support of their candidacy in the union's periodical. Elections are conducted annually with appropriate safeguards at the polls.

Other unions use the referendum method but none has worked out such precise procedures as those followed by the ITU. A majority of unions—more than three-fourths of those studied by Bromwich, for example—elect officers at conventions.

Nominating procedures are far from precise in most union constitutions and there are some which specify no rules at all. Most unions which elect officers at conventions do not provide for nomination and election at separate times and few provide for the supervision of elections by representatives of candidates or by a neutral body.

In most unions, election procedures give an advantage to those in office. This does not mean that union elections are rigged but a president whose position is in jeopardy is in a position to make the decisions on the timing of nominations and elections. He will undoubtedly see that little time elapses between the two. Since his views are usually well known to the rank and file, an extended period between nominations and elections could give the opposition time to consolidate its forces.

In some of the older unions which formerly belonged to the A.F. of L. the president has the power to remove any international officer and there is no appeal from his decision. Where there are provisions for appeal, this is generally to the executive board which, in the typical union, is controlled by the president.

Among the industrial unions which formerly belonged to the CIO, the presidents are not allowed to remove international officers without appeal. Yet in some of these unions the executive board has the authority to suspend international officers, and there are no provisions for appeal. Where the president or executive boards have authority to suspend officers this authority is not limited to specific causes. The same broad authority is generally given to officers or executive boards to revoke the charters of local unions.[11]

The ability to control elections and the power to suspend officers makes it difficult for dissidents in a union to gain support for their positions. This is not entirely accidental. One thing which trade union leaders stress in their speeches and articles is the need for *union*. Workers, they maintain, must present a united front if the union is to realize gains for the rank and file. Unions are not debating societies and if their leaders often develop the attitude that "papa knows best" this is often justified. Few rank and file members are in a position to see union problems in the same broad setting as their national or international officers.

A few unions—although a distinct minority—provide for control over officers through recall provisions. Generally, a single local may initiate a recall petition. If a specified percentage of locals support the petition, the officer whose recall is being demanded is required to answer the charges. A rival candidate is selected to run against the accused officer and a referendum vote is held to determine if he is to be removed. Only a minority of nationals or internationals provide for recall. In practice it has not been used at all, but this does not mean that it could not be used. Some unions retain at least the right to get rid of national or international officers if they fail to act in the interests of the rank and file.

DISCIPLINING UNION MEMBERS

It has been said that the issue of union government which attracts the greatest attention, and which arouses the most fear, is that of union discipline.[12] The question of union discipline is not a simple one. On the one hand, unions must protect themselves against

[11] Slichter, *op. cit.*, pp. 108–109.
[12] See Philip Taft, *The Structure and Government of Labor Unions,* Cambridge, Massachusetts: Harvard University Press (1954), p. 243.

agents of employers or outside political groups intent upon sowing the seeds of dissension among the rank and file. At the same time if unions are to make more than a show of democracy members who are disciplined must have some protection against the arbitrary action of union officers.

A number of union constitutions permit members to be disciplined for rather vague offenses. These include "slandering an officer," "creating dissension," "undermining the union or working against its interests," "action which is dishonorable or might injure the labor movement," and "circulating written material dealing with trade union business without permission of the general executive board."[13] What protection does the individual union member have against disciplinary action for such vague and nebulous offenses? Most unions provide for appeal procedures of one kind or another. But the critical question is: How effective are these procedures?

Bromwich feels that "there are a significant number of unions which do not set forth careful disciplinary procedures."[14] The major weakness is in the selection of review boards. In his survey Bromwich found that twenty-six unions, with a membership of more than 5.5 million, called for establishment of a review board by the local executive board. In eight other cases such boards are appointed by presidents of the local unions. It is not likely, however, if the member has been disciplined for criticizing local union leaders that his review board will be entirely unbiased.

Other unions provide for the election of trial or review boards by the membership of the local, or the local meeting itself becomes a trial board. Such provisions, it would appear, should lead to the impartial judgment of workers subject to local union discipline. But even some unions noted for their democratic and responsible practices do not have clear-cut provisions for the unbiased review of disciplinary cases. A few unions, however, have developed procedures for guaranteeing a fair trial to members subject to union discipline. The outstanding examples are those developed by the International Typographical Union, the United Automobile Workers, and the Upholsterers.

The ITU constitution provides for a democratically-elected trial committee to hear disciplinary cases. If the decision goes against the union member he has the right of appeal. The first appeal is to

[13] Sumner H. Slichter, *op. cit.*, pp. 110–111, quoted from Philip Taft "Judicial Procedures in Labor Unions," *Quarterly Journal of Economics* (May 1945), pp. 370–385.

[14] Bromwich, *op. cit.*, p. 33.

the international executive council, but there are provisions for further appeals to the convention and ultimately to the courts. In the case of international officers, discipline is administered by a trial board made up of the presidents of the five largest locals and the decision of this board can be appealed to the next convention. The disciplinary procedures of the United Automobile Workers roughly parallel those of the ITU. But the UAW has gone a step farther by providing for an "outside" review board made up of seven well-known public figures who have no connection with the union. The Upholsterers Union provides for a similar independent public review system.

In all cases, a disciplined union member may have ultimate recourse to the courts. Yet in cases where disciplinary measures are upheld by outside review boards it is highly unlikely that an aggrieved member would take his case to court.

Some students of trade union government have argued that except in the ITU, the UAW, and the Upholsterers, the rights of disciplined union members are not strongly protected. On the other hand, Professor Philip Taft, who has made exhaustive studies of trade union government, points out that even in unions noted for their autocratic government, such as the United Mine Workers, there have been many appeals against discipline. He feels that "rights of members and their protection in the union seems, on the whole, adequate."[15] Clark Kerr has also said that "a good deal more democracy exists in unions than . . . outside observation would indicate."[16]

Unions cannot function as simple "town meeting democracies" without endangering their cohesiveness. There undoubtedly have been instances where individual union members have not received the full justice to which they are entitled but in the overwhelming majority of cases disciplined members have had an opportunity for review of their cases. Despite the fact that in many local unions review boards cannot always be considered unbiased, there is always ultimate recourse to the courts. As Professor Taft has observed, much of the concern about union discipline is without foundation. The issue has undoubtedly been greatly overplayed. A few instances of abuse do not form an adequate basis for criticizing union disciplinary procedures as a whole.

[15] Taft, *op. cit.*, p. 245.
[16] Clark Kerr, *Unions and Union Leaders of Their Own Choosing*, New York: The Fund for the Republic (December 1957), p. 10.

THE AFL-CIO ETHICAL PRACTICES CODES

Leaders of the American labor movement have recognized that as trade unions have matured, opportunities have developed for unscrupulous union officers to capitalize on their positions of power to their personal advantage and to the detriment of the labor movement as a whole. In response to this, the AFL-CIO, at its 1955 convention and through subsequent action by the Executive Council, set up six codes of ethical practices as guides to its member unions. These codes deal with the following issues:

I. Local union charters
II. Health and welfare funds
III. Racketeers, crooks, Communists and Fascists
IV. Investments and business interests of union officials
V. Financial practices and proprietary activities of unions
VI. Union democratic processes

The first code was directed primarily against "paper locals." Such locals have been established by racketeers, in collusion with employers, to forestall the organization of legitimate unions. In the language of the AFL-CIO, racketeers have also used such charters as "hunting licenses" to invade the jurisdictions of other national unions. To prevent these practices, Code I specifies that national unions should issue local charters only upon "application by a group of bona fide employees eligible for membership in the union within the jurisdiction covered by the charter."[17]

The second code specifies that no union official is to receive fees or salaries from funds established for health, welfare or retirement programs, nor should the union official have "any compromising personal ties" with agencies—such as insurance carriers or brokers—doing business with the welfare plan. This code also calls for auditing and full disclosure of welfare funds, and for the selection of insurance carriers through competitive bids. Unions are urged to remove violators of the code from office.

The third code urged all affiliated unions to prevent racketeers, crooks, Communists, Fascists, or representatives of other totalitarian agencies, from holding office. The fourth attempts to prevent conflicts of interests such as would arise if a union official had a substantial interest in the firms of employers with which he deals. The fifth code urges all unions affiliated with the AFL-CIO to

[17] Sar A. Levitan (ed.), *Government Regulations of Internal Union Affairs Affecting the Rights of Members,* Selected readings prepared for the Subcommittee on Labor, Committee on Labor and Public Welfare, U.S. Senate, 85th Congress, Second Session, Washington: U.S. Government Printing Office (1958), p. 151.

follow sound accounting practices. There are specific provisions covering union purchases, loans and investments, and contracts for the purchase or sale of goods or services which could lead to the benefit of a union officer.

The final code in the series urges that each member of affiliated unions be given the right to full and free participation in union self-government and fair treatment in the application of union rules and law. There are specific provisions dealing with union conventions, the election of officers, and the conduct of meetings.

It should be noted that many of the provisions of the ethical practices codes are also covered by the Landrum-Griffin Act, passed September 14, 1959. The last of the codes was adopted by the AFL-CIO Executive Council, on May 23, 1957. Thus some time before Congress provided legal measures for the control of internal union affairs, the AFL-CIO had noted that there were problems in some of its affiliated unions and had set up standards for dealing with these problems which it hoped all unions would meet.

LABOR CORRUPTION AND RACKETEERING

The vast majority of American unions are led by men whose honesty and integrity are above question. Members of the community might not always approve of either their objectives or their methods. And there are times when union leaders appear to place the welfare of their members above that of the community as a whole. As Philip Taft has pointed out, however, "such conduct does not indicate venality or corruption even though it might not be, from the point of view of many, socially desirable."[18]

There have been instances of the corruption of union leaders, the infiltration of bona fide unions by racketeers, and the establishment of bogus local unions by racketeers intent upon the victimization of businessmen and the public. Some union leaders have not been able to resist the abuse of power. They are not unique in this respect. The crooked politician, the embezzling financier, and the shady or dishonest businessman are not—unhappily—unknown in our society. This is not to suggest that because corruption is found elsewhere it can be tolerated in the labor movement. The honest citizen will oppose corruption wherever it is found. There has been particular indignation about labor corruption, however, because of

[18] Philip Taft, *Corruption and Racketeering in the Labor Movement,* Ithaca, New York: New York State School of Industrial and Labor Relations, Bulletin 38 (February 1958), p. 1.

the idealistic foundation upon which trade unionism rests. Revelations of labor corruption evoke much the same reaction as that which follows the exposure of malfeasance in public office.

Labor corruption, in the minority of unions where it is found, runs the gamut from outright criminal activities—such as embezzlement of union funds and the acceptance of bribes or kickbacks—to what many might regard as simply "sharp" business practices. The latter include collusive agreements with employers to create monopolies, and the acceptance of loans from employers. Such loans are generally made on terms favorable to the labor leader since the employer who lends money to a labor leader, at a lower rate of return than he could obtain elsewhere, is looking for some other form of payment. This might come in the form of a substandard contract or "sweetheart" agreement. Payoffs also have been made to corrupt union leaders as "insurance" against organizing campaigns, strikes or other legitimate union activities.

The growth of union health and welfare funds in recent years has provided a lush field for the enrichment of a few ingenious but dishonest labor leaders. Insurance policies, with high premiums and skimpy benefits, have been placed with friends of the labor leader in return for a consideration. Union funds have been invested in enterprises in which labor leaders have had an interest—sometimes as silent partners. Such investments, it should be noted, usually have not been the kind that an honest investment counselor would recommend.

There have been a few instances in the past where labor leaders have sought alliances with racketeers to protect their organizing activities. They found, however, that once established such alliances were not easy to break off, and some unions ended up by becoming the prey of underworld elements whose "protection" they had earlier sought. A more frequent phenomenon, however, has been the invasion of legitimate unions by thugs and gangsters. Following repeal of the 18th Amendment, and the loss of revenue from bootlegging, some underworld elements in Chicago moved into the labor-management field. The waterfront unions in New York were long under the domination of racketeers who victimized employees and employers alike.[19] Extortion, pilferage, murder, and other criminal activities, on a scale that probably will never be fully known, were the result of complete domination of the New York waterfront by underworld elements.

[19] *Ibid.*, pp. 12–13.

As Philip Taft has noted, corruption and racketeering are not new to the American labor movement. More than half a century ago Congress appointed the United States Industrial Commission to investigate labor problems. This Commission found evidence of extortion in the Chicago building trades. Shortly after this investigation there were revelations of illicit activities on the part of labor leaders such as Sam Parks of the New York building trades, Skinny Madden of the Chicago Steamfitters, and Robert P. Brindell of the New York Dock and Pier Carpenters' union.[20]

It is significant that the members of some unions have continued to support labor leaders even after their corrupt activities have been exposed. Sam Parks, for example, was re-elected to his office as head of the Housesmiths' Union of New York while serving a term in Sing Sing for arranging collusive agreements and selling strike insurance.[21] This has always puzzled outside observers but it is a reflection of the mores of our society. If corrupt labor leaders have continued to "deliver the goods" for the rank and file, the latter have appeared to be unwilling to pass judgment on the morals of their officers.

The latest and most widely publicized revelations of labor corruption resulted from the investigation of the Senate Select Committee on Improper Activities in the Labor or Management Field—the McClellan Committee. This investigation extended over a period of almost three years. As noted earlier, one result was the Landrum-Griffin Act of 1959. In 1956, the Ethical Practices Committee of the AFL-CIO had recommended to the Executive Council that the Allied Industrial Workers, the Laundry Workers and the Distillery Workers should "show cause" why they should not be expelled because of corrupt influences in the administration of welfare funds. And at the December 1957 convention, the Teamsters, the Bakery Workers, and the Laundry Workers were expelled on charges of domination by corrupt influences. Thus the leaders of the AFL-CIO were taking steps to renovate the House of Labor just as the McClellan Committee hearings were getting under way.

The McClellan Committee hearings ran to many thousands of pages, and only some of the major findings can be given here. Further details can be obtained from the Committee's interim

[20] *Ibid.*, pp. 4–9.
[21] *Ibid.*, p. 6.

reports.[22] And a dramatic account of the complete investigation is given in Attorney General Robert F. Kennedy's *The Enemy Within*.[23]

The Committee found evidence of corruption in a number of unions, including the Hotel and Restaurant Workers, the Sheet Metal Workers, the Mail Deliverers, the Bakery and Confectionery Workers, two locals of the Amalgamated Meat Cutters and Butcher Workmen of North America, and the United Textile Workers.[24] But the union and official most intensively investigated were the International Brotherhood of Teamsters and its president, James R. Hoffa. The *Second Interim Report* of the McClellan Committee listed 19 topics covered by the inquiry involving the Teamsters, Hoffa, and other officers of the union, and one section of this report dealt entirely with alleged malfeasance in the administration of Teamster insurance plans. Since the end of the McClellan hearings, Hoffa has been tried on a number of charges; he has been cleared of some and found guilty of others. As this was written he had appealed all adverse decisions, and continued to exercise effective control over the Teamsters.

Dave Beck, president of the Teamsters at the start of the McClellan hearings, and a powerful and respected man before his exposure, was completely destroyed as a labor leader by the investigation. He was subsequently convicted by a federal court of income tax evasion. The Teamsters elected Hoffa to succeed Beck. Both Hoffa and the Teamsters were under a cloud of suspicion at the time of his election, but under a consent decree, he was permitted to take office and a board of monitors was appointed by the court to supervise his and the union's activities. Hoffa refused to accept the monitors' recommendations, however, and there is little evidence that they inhibited his activities in any way.

Following the McClellan Committee investigation, a number of labor officials were indicted by federal courts on charges ranging from perjury to extortion and embezzlement. A few were convicted while others were acquitted, usually because of insufficient evidence to support the charges against them.

[22] For excerpts of the *First Interim Report* (March 1958), see *Monthly Labor Review* (May 1958), pp. 518–520. Somewhat more extensive excerpts of the *Second Interim Report* (August 1959) are given in *Monthly Labor Review* (September 1959), pp. 981–991.

[23] Robert F. Kennedy, *The Enemy Within,* New York: Harper and Brothers (1960); also published in paperback edition, New York: Popular Library (1960). Page references are to the latter edition.

[24] The United Textile Workers, a relatively small union, should not be confused with the Textile Workers Union of America which has not been touched by scandal.

Leaders of the AFL-CIO and of the many unions untouched by scandal were disturbed, perhaps more than anyone else, by the revelations of corruption in a handful of unions.[25] They realized that the entire labor movement would suffer from guilt by association, at least in the eyes of some. This was cogently expressed by a group of foreign labor officials, members of a mission from the International Labour Office: "Even though the inquiries of the McClellan Committee only covered a tiny minority of the unions operating in the United States, and even though the proved facts only relate to a very small number of cases, some mud has nevertheless stuck to the American trade union movement as a whole."[26]

The McClellan Committee hearing dealt largely with corruption and racketeering in the labor movement. But the Landrum-Griffin Act—an outgrowth of the McClellan investigation—attempts to deal with two distinct issues: one of these is union corruption and racketeering, the other is the lack of union democracy. Few would question the social desirability of legislation aimed at the elimination of labor corruption and racketeering. However, in the Landrum-Griffin Act Congress assumed that union democracy can be legislated. Many union officials, and some observers outside the labor movement, have serious doubts that this is so.

VOLUNTARY VERSUS LEGISLATIVE CONTROL OF INTERNAL UNION AFFAIRS

Two broad issues of union government have been discussed in this chapter. One deals with internal union affairs—the control of corruption, and the establishment of sound procedures for the administration of union financial affairs. The matter of "conflict of interest" is also involved in this connection. The other issue is that of trade union democracy.

One would expect almost unanimous agreement that all means—whether voluntary or legislative—should be used to ensure that union affairs are conducted honestly, with appropriate auditing and disclosure, and that union officials should not allow themselves to get into compromising positions where their integrity as union leaders is open to question. The only dissenters from this point of view would be the crooks or racketeers against whom the Ethical Practices Codes and some provisions of the Landrum-Griffin Act

[25] Kennedy, *op. cit.*, p. 204.
[26] *The Trade Union Situation in the United States,* Report of a Mission from the International Labour Office, Geneva: ILO (1960), p. 89.

are aimed. It is not likely that every vestige of corruption can be eliminated but every effort should be made to do so. Trade unions are not private clubs. In many ways they are quasi-public institutions. Some union leaders might bridle at public regulation of internal union affairs; however, the honest union official has nothing to fear. If regulation makes it more difficult for crooks and racketeers to subvert trade unions to their own selfish ends the entire labor movement will gain.[27]

On the issue of union democracy, however, the matter is much less simple. There is considerable disagreement about the extent of democracy in trade unions, part of which stems from a lack of agreement on the meaning of democracy. Sumner Slichter has pointed out, for example, that it is not easy to answer the question: Are unions democratic? If democracy means rank and file participation, unions might not be considered very democratic. Professional leaders decide most policy matters at the national level, yet Slichter distinguished between rank and file participation and *influence*. He felt that the influence of rank and file members is great—far out of proportion to their participation. Although there is little competition for offices at the national level, the leaders must be responsive to the wishes of the rank and file. Union constitutions generally contain provisions for turning out officers if the rank and file should become disaffected.

On specific matters—such as voting rights, union discipline and appeal procedures, the selection of convention delegates, etc.—there is wide variation among unions. Many labor scholars feel that there is considerable room for improvement in a number of national and international unions. But how is this improvement to be achieved? Can it be legislated? Jack Barbash, who has had a long career both as a trade union staff official and as an educator, feels that: "It is a serious mistake to work on the theory that union democracy can be instituted through legislation where it does not now exist."[28] This does not mean that Barbash is opposed to all legislation regulating union affairs. His views on union democracy, quoted above, were written before the Landrum-Griffin Act was passed, and at that time, he indicated his support for certain kinds of labor legislation—specifically of the disclosure type—which

[27] Many union officials have indicated their satisfaction with the reporting and disclosure sections of the Landrum-Griffin Act. See the *New York Times* (November 18, 1962); and George Strauss, "The Shifting Power Balance in the Plant," *Industrial Relations* (May 1962), p. 73.

[28] Jack Barbash, "Union Democracy," in Levitan, *Government Regulation of Internal Union Affairs Affecting the Rights of Members, op. cit.*, p. 135.

would ensure responsibility in the handling of union funds. But when it comes to such matters as union elections, and protection of the rights of individual members, Barbash is inclined to place the "greatest reliance on the preservation and strengthening of the democratic processes of the labor movement on the labor movement itself."[29]

Many unions have gone to great lengths in their efforts to increase rank and file participation in union affairs. By and large these efforts have been unsuccessful. Only a minority of rank and file members will give up part of their leisure time to attend union meetings. This is not a matter of indifference; rather it indicates that the rank and file are generally satisfied with the way local and national union officers are conducting union affairs. Slichter's comment on this is revealing: "If one asks whether unions give their members what they want, the proper answer is that for most unions the question is irrelevant. The great majority of the members do not have much opportunity or desire to consider and discuss alternative policies. Hence they are not to be regarded as making a choice. The proper question to ask is: 'Do the members like what they get?' The answer to that question is usually: 'Yes.' "[30]

REFERENCES

BOOKS

Bromwich, Leo, *Union Constitutions,* New York: The Fund for the Republic (1959).

Chamberlin, Edward H., *et. al., Labor Unions and Public Policy,* Washington: American Enterprise Association (1958).

International Labour Office, *The Trade Union Situation in the United States,* Geneva: ILO (1960).

Kennedy, Robert F., *The Enemy Within,* New York: Harper and Brothers (1960); paperback edition, New York: Popular Library (1960).

Kerr, Clark, *Unions and Union Leaders of Their Own Choosing,* New York: The Fund for the Republic (1957).

Levitan, Sar A., (ed.), *Government Regulation of Internal Union Affairs Affecting the Rights of Members,* Selected Readings prepared for the Subcommittee on Labor of the Committee on Labor and Public Welfare, U.S. Senate, 85th Congress, Second Session, Washington: U.S. Government Printing Office (1958).

Lipset, Seymour Martin, *et al., Union Democracy,* Glencoe, Illinois: The Free Press (1956); paperback edition, Garden City, New York: Anchor Books, Doubleday and Company (1962).

Slichter, Sumner H., *The Challenge of Industrial Relations,* Ithaca, New York: Cornell University Press (1947).

[29] *Ibid.,* p. 137.
[30] Slichter, *op. cit.,* p. 114.

Taft, Philip, *The Structure and Government of Labor Unions,* Cambridge, Massachusetts: Harvard University Press (1954).

——— ———, *Corruption and Racketeering in the Labor Movement,* Ithaca, New York: New York State School of Industrial and Labor Relations, Bulletin 38 (1958).

United Auto Workers, *A More Perfect Union, UAW Public Review Board* (1957).

ARTICLES

Dunbar, Ernest, "Black Men White Unions," *Look* Magazine (December 17, 1963), pp. 43ff.

McClellan Committee, "First Interim Report," (excerpts), *Monthly Labor Review* (May 1958), pp. 518–520; "Second Interim Report," (excerpts), *Monthly Labor Review* (September 1959), pp. 981–991.

McGrath, Peter, "Democracy in Overalls: The Futile Quest for Union Democracy," *Industrial and Labor Relations Review,* Vol. 12 (July 1959), pp. 503–525.

Taft, Philip, "The Responses of the Bakers, Longshoremen and Teamsters to Public Exposure," *Quarterly Journal of Economics,* Vol. LXXIV (August 1960), pp. 393–412.

Chapter 12 Trade Union Philosophy and Objectives

Earlier chapters discussed the rise of the American labor movement, the laws governing labor-management relations, the structure and government of trade unions. Before turning to a discussion of the various issues involved in collective bargaining it might be well to look at the broad objectives of trade unions. What are the goals of American unions? How do they seek to accomplish their objectives? Has the basic philosophy of the American labor movement changed over time, and if so in what direction? How do trade union attitudes in the United States compare with those found in the democracies of Western Europe? These questions cannot be answered in fine detail within the scope of this chapter, but a broad framework can be developed which should contribute to a better understanding of the collective bargaining process.

THE DISTINCTIVE IDEOLOGY OF AMERICAN LABOR UNIONS

Trade unions in the United States differ in a number of ways from their counterparts in other democratic countries. The character of the labor movement in each country has been determined to a large extent by the environment in which stable trade unionism emerged. The trade unions which finally took root in the United States—after almost a century of experimentation—were of the pragmatic variety referred to as "business unions." While there were numerous radical and reform ideas in the United States during the nineteenth century, none was able to attract a large following. The leaders of the early A.F. of L. recognized the failure of reform groups to appeal to the American imagination—including that of the working man—and out of this developed the formula which led to the growth of craft unionism in this country. Until fairly recent times conditions in Europe were quite different from those in the United States, and these conditions led to a distinctly different type of labor movement.

What are some of the characteristics of western European society which helped shape a kind of trade unionism quite different from that with which we are familiar in this country? Because of the feudal background of most western European countries, there was—until recent times—a great deal of social stratification. In the United States, by way of contrast, there has been considerably more social mobility. Thus workers in western Europe felt themselves to be part of a working class from which there was little hope of escape short of emigration. Property qualifications for voting also kept most workmen from active political participation. The standard of living in most western European countries was also well below that of the United States; there was no opportunity to escape to an open frontier, and there was little opportunity to become an independent businessman.

Because of class consciousness, lack of political participation, and limited mobility, European workers became strongly ideological.[1] Workers did not join trade unions simply to improve their economic status. There was a close connection between trade unions and political parties and a worker's political ideology would determine the union of his choice. Thus workers employed in a single plant might belong to different unions. They were not bound together by job consciousness. Indeed, workers at the same bench might often be divided by a wide ideological gap. Each political party—the Socialists, Communists, Anarchists, Social Democrats, and various religious parties—had its own trade union. A worker might move from job to job, or even change occupations, without changing his union affiliation. Ideological conflicts among the various political parties of western Europe often prevented workers from forming a united front when seeking concessions from employers. Thus the trade union movement in many western European countries remained fragmented. In terms of numerical strength, union growth might have appeared impressive, but European unions were able to accomplish much less for their

[1] Morris Weisz, "Labor Ideology and Practice in Europe and the U.S.," *Monthly Labor Review* (March 1958), pp. 265–269.

members—in terms of wages, hours, and working conditions—than their numerically weaker American counterparts.

The founders of the A.F. of L. saw the weakness of such fragmentation, and insisted that a common *job interest* would bind workers together effectively. While union membership grew slowly in the United States, during the early years of the A.F. of L., the workers who joined unions were able to win solid gains. Meanwhile their European counterparts were less interested in collective bargaining than in political maneuvering, and by dissipating their energies along broad fronts they made limited gains in any direction.

There was little kinship between American and European leaders, especially before the Second World War. European labor leaders were critical of their American counterparts. They spoke scornfully of business unionism in the United States and were critical of American labor leaders for their lack of ideology. At the same time, trade union leaders in America were often openly scornful of the failure of European trade unions to improve the economic lot of their members.

The failure of politically-oriented European unions to make substantial progress despite their numerical strength helped solidify the conviction of the leaders of the A.F. of L. that their form of union organization was superior. It is quite possible that the relative weakness of European unions were due more to *fragmentation* than to political orientation. But the founders of stable trade unionism in America were convinced that political alliances of any kind were dangerous. The only way to get ahead, in their minds, was through a show of economic strength.

THE LEFT-WING CHALLENGE

The principle of no political entanglements in the American labor movement did not go entirely unchallenged. Until our entry into World War I there was a highly vocal and well-organized group within the A.F. of L. which insisted that business unionism was not the ultimate answer to the problems of American labor. This group insisted that organized labor would eventually have to wrest control of the economy from the owners of property. Various Socialist groups at different times tried to gain control of the A.F. of L., but like their European brethren, the Socialists in this country could not unite under a common banner.

The Socialist-Labor Party

One of the splinter groups which was impatient with the stated goals of the A.F. of L. was the Socialist Labor Party founded in 1876. When Daniel De Leon became the leader of this party in 1889 he was determined that the party would slowly take over the growing A.F. of L. At one time De Leon was a teacher of mathematics, and later of international law, but he gave up his academic career to lead the Socialist Labor Party and to carry on an unremitting attack against Samuel Gompers and other leaders of the A.F. of L.

The Socialists managed to gain control of the Central Labor Federation of New York and petitioned for a charter in the A.F. of L. But at the 1890 Convention this was refused. Following this, the Socialists attempted to "bore from within." Following their rejection at the 1890 Convention, the Socialists gained some strength in the ranks of organized labor. Their propaganda campaign was aided by the depression of the early 1890's, and the failure of the A.F. of L. to grow under adverse economic conditions. The Socialist minority in the craft unions agitated strongly for political action, and urged the Federation to adopt a program for the nationalization of industry. Their campaign came to a head at the Denver convention of 1894. Because of widespread unemployment, and general political unrest, a majority of the unions represented at the convention had endorsed the Socialist program. A number of planks in the convention's platform that year had a Socialist tinge. For a time it appeared that the A.F. of L. was about to depart from its policy of no political involvement, in a very extreme way. The most controversial part of the program was Plank 10 which called for "collective ownership by the people of all the means of production and distribution." Acceptance of this plank would have meant repudiation of business unionism and adoption of an outright Socialist program.

The debate over Plank 10 raged for five days, and was finally defeated only after a number of parliamentary maneuvers by the anti-Socialists at the convention. This they accomplished by introducing a number of palpably ridiculous amendments to Plank 10 which in the general confusion the delegates voted down. Another motion calling for independent political action by the Federation was defeated by a relatively close vote. The advocates of business unionism won. However, it was close and the Socialists continued to carry on their criticism of the job-conscious craft unionism of the A.F. of L. until their program fell apart after our entry into the First World War. After the Denver convention, however, there was a split in the ranks of the Socialist Labor Party. While both groups continued to denounce A.F. of L. leaders they could not again unite in a common attack.

Meanwhile, two new Socialist movements were started in the Middle West, one led by Eugene V. Debs and the second by Victor Berger. Eventually these two groups came together and united with a splinter group which had left the Socialist Labor Party. In 1901 they met to form the Socialist Party of America which, among other things, declared its intention of organizing the workers of America—and those in sympathy with the working class—with the ultimate objective of collective ownership of the means of production. The new Socialist Party was less doctrinaire than the De Leon group had been, but it was rejected as completely by the A.F. of L. as had been the earlier more radical group. Efforts to bore from within were continued although the Socialists were not again to become the threat they had been in 1894.

When World War I broke out in Europe the leaders of socialism in the United States joined their counterparts in Europe in denouncing the war effort. They urged workers in all countries to refuse to bear arms and thus sought to abort the war in its early stages. But this was not a popular cause in the countries then at war and it soon became unpopular in the United States. While Socialist parties and Socialist trade unions became active in Europe after the end of World War I, membership in the various Socialist parties in this country dwindled to the point where they became inffective even as protest groups.

The Victory of Voluntarism

The philosophy adopted by the A.F. of L. after the defeat of the Socialist threat has been called "voluntarism." This was the notion that workers should rely exclusively on trade unions to promote their interests as wage earners. No positive aid from the government was to be sought or accepted—as a matter of fact government assistance was to be rejected.[2]

The advocates of voluntarism wanted no help from government even in the form of social legislation. The only concession they would make was to support legislation which would have guar-

[2] David J. Saposs, "Voluntarism in the American-Labor Movement," *Monthly Labor Review*, U.S. Department of Labor, Bureau of Labor Statistics, (September 1954). See also, Michael Rogin, "Voluntarism: The Political Functions of an Antipolitical Doctrine," *Industrial and Labor Relations Review* (July 1962), pp. 521–535, and the discussion of the "A.F. of L. settlement" in Chapter III.

anteed the rights of workers to organize, and the protection of trade unions from outside interference. They also favored legislative enactment of the eight-hour day. But as late as 1931, the A.F. of L. Convention refused to endorse legislation which would have provided unemployment insurance. Prior to this the A.F. of L. had supported various forms of legislation, but most of this was of a negative character. The Federation supported legislation to restrict immigration, and other legislation designed to remove legal impediments to organization and effective strike action. The third type of legislation which the Federation supported was that to provide standards for the employment of women and children.[3]

By 1954, however, the year before the merger with the CIO, the A.F. of L. had clearly departed from its earlier philosophy of voluntarism. At that convention the Federation adopted a ten-point program for government action which included a declaration that the "resumption of full production and full employment is the overriding objective of national policy."[4] As Douty pointed out, while the Federation had "not lost faith in the value of collective bargaining for improving the worker's lot, it [had] elevated government, and hence politics, to something approaching an equal role."

TRADE UNIONS AND POLITICAL ACTION

The philosophy of voluntarism in the American Labor movement had disappeared long before the 1954 Convention of the AFL. Even before the advent of the CIO, the A.F. of L. had made a few minor concessions, such as supporting unemployment insurance. But the real break with the past, marked by active trade union participation in politics, came after the CIO had become a going organization.

During the early days following the AFL-CIO split, the A.F. of L. leaders continued to insist upon the necessity of keeping out of partisan politics. The CIO also claimed in principle that it would support all candidates for political office whose views it favored, but in practice most of these candidates turned out to be members of the Democratic Party. There were times, indeed, during the early years of the split when the two federations openly supported opposing candidates, especially in primary elections.

[3] See H. M. Douty, "The Seventy-Third Convention of the AFL," *Monthly Labor Review*, U.S. Department of Labor, Bureau of Labor Statistics (November 1954).
[4] *Ibid.*

For a brief time after 1936, leaders of unions in both federations cooperated to form Labor's Non-Partisan League which supported the candidacy of President Roosevelt for re-election. But by 1938, A.F. of L. leaders had left the League and some denounced it strongly. On the other hand, by 1944, the CIO had made it clear that it intended to continue to play an active part in political campaigns and in that year it established its Political Action Committee (PAC). The PAC worked hard to support candidates of its choice.

The A.F. of L. did not follow the CIO's lead until after the Taft-Hartley Act was passed in 1947. Among other things, this law restricted the political activity of labor unions by prohibiting the use of union funds for political contributions. This act forced the A.F. of L. to set up an organization structurally independent of the federation if it wished to make political contributions. The result was Labor's League for Political Education (LLPE). Both Labor's League for Political Education and the Political Action Committee obtained their funds by direct contribution from union members instead of from general union funds. It is somewhat ironical that the Taft-Hartley Act which sought to restrict the activities of unions in a number of ways actually stimulated labor participation in political action. The CIO had already been committed to a program of political education, but the A.F. of L. set up its political arm only after the Taft-Hartley Act had forced the Federation to take a stand on participation in political campaigns.[5]

Following the AFL-CIO merger, in 1955, the merged federation established a new political arm, the Committee on Political Education (COPE). While there were some difficulties in establishing the Committee, as there were in working out other details of the merger, these were eventually ironed out and the trade union movement in the United States has continued to participate actively in political campaigns.

What are the political goals of trade unions? Would the nation's union leaders like to gain political control of the country? At times it has been asserted that the ultimate goal of union leaders is the establishment of a Labor Party either through the capture of the Democratic Party or the establishment of a new and independent political force. However, there is no evidence to support this contention. Indeed, there is considerable evidence to the contrary. Union leaders have repeatedly insisted that they have no intention

[5] See Edwin L. Witte, "The New Federation and Political Action," *Industrial and Labor Relations Review* (April 1956), pp. 409–414.

of changing established political relationships. They actively support candidates who tend to be sympathetic toward trade union views.

There are certain objectives which union leaders would like to see realized, such as greater stability of employment and more rapid economic growth with workers sharing in the gains of increased productivity. But union leaders insist that they will seek these goals by supporting candidates in the two major political parties. Most often they have supported "liberal" members of the Democratic party but this has not been universally true. Some union leaders have been outspoken in their support of Republicans. While unions are much more active in political affairs than they were a quarter of a century ago they have departed much less from Samuel Gompers' dictum of "reward your friends and punish your enemies" than many critics of trade unions would have us believe.

It is worth recalling that the rapid growth of trade unions came at a time when a liberal administration and a liberal Congress were pushing through a number of social and economic reforms. Most union leaders actively supported these reforms and were openly associated with the liberal cause. But some students of organized labor feel that as unions have prospered their leaders have tended to become increasingly conservative. Indeed, it would be surprising if the outlook of labor leaders did not change as the environment in which they operated has been altered. As Neil Chamberlain has pointed out, the dominant theme of trade unionism during the nineteenth century was that of reform of the wage system.[6] With the rise of the A.F. of L., the trade union movement tried to find its place in a political system which it accepted. Events of the 1930's led to explosive growth and the rise of a number of militant and politically-oriented labor leaders. However, as the trade union movement has grown in size and has become more secure in its position much of this militancy has been replaced by complacency.[7]

FROM MILITANCY TO MATURITY

In what ways have trade unions changed? And what are some of the causes of changes in the philosophy of union leaders? Some

[6] Neil W. Chamberlain, *Labor,* New York: McGraw-Hill Book Company (1950) p. 52.
[7] *Ibid.*

aspects of this question were examined by Will Herberg.[8] Herberg began his analysis by noting the dual nature of modern trade unions: on the one hand businesslike service organizations, and on the other, vehicles for expressing the needs of workers for social recognition and democratic self-determination. In Herberg's view, the dual nature of unions leads to a fundamental conflict of purpose and orientation. As service organizations, modern unions require efficient administrations similar to those of business enterprises. This leads, according to Herberg, to the development of union bureaucracy and a corresponding weakening of union democracy. Yet democratic self-expression is the essence of a successful mass movement.

In the early days of trade unionism, according to the Herberg thesis, the "idealistic, democratic, emancipatory aspect is dominant."[9] But as unions grew and became firmly entrenched in our political-economic system, the service aspect of unionism overwhelmed the earlier idealistic orientation. The very size of unions and the need for the development of an efficient administrative setup made it impossible for the "grass roots" democracy of early trade unionism to survive. Moreover, the founders of trade unionism—crusaders motivated by a desire for reform—were eventually displaced by paid professionals. This development, in Herberg's view, was inevitable, but it might have been speeded up by the search for power on the part of some labor leaders.

What Herberg has described is a shift in the locus of power from local to national unions as the American trade union movement passed through successive stages in its development. This shift has been noted in earlier chapters and the point to be stressed here is the change in the *outlook* of labor leaders as this evolution has progressed.

A later study by Richard Lester carries Herberg's analysis a great deal farther.[10] Lester pointed out that during the period of rapid union growth the leaders of the labor movement were motivated by a "missionary spirit." The zest for organization was not limited to professional union leaders; it was shared by many rank and file members who worked hard during the organizing campaigns

[8] Will Herberg, "Bureaucracy and Democracy in Labor Unions," Reprinted from *Antioch Review* (Fall, 1943) in Joseph Shister, ed., *Readings in Labor Economics and Industrial Relations,* New York: J. B. Lippincott Company (2nd ed., 1956), pp. 114–122.
[9] *Ibid.*, p. 115.
[10] Richard A. Lester, *As Unions Mature,* Princeton, New Jersey: Princeton University Press (1958).

following 1935. There was also a great deal of rivalry during the time when the A.F. of L. and the CIO were competing for members, and this contributed somewhat to the militant attitudes of union leaders at that time.

But missionary zeal is hard to maintain. As unions became large organizations, their leaders had to devote an increasing proportion of their time to the problems of administration. Sizeable staffs were recruited and the work of staff members had to be supervised. After a union has succeeded in organizing a substantial proportion of an industry, or a specific occupational group, the outlook of its leaders is bound to change. They are less concerned with organizing the unorganized workers than with administering the organization they have helped create. This often leads to changes in behavior both at the bargaining table and in other respects. In general, unions become less vigorous and much less militant. Union leaders are anxious to demonstrate their responsibility, and this leads to a moderation of demands in collective bargaining—particularly after the major goals of the unions have been achieved. During the formative stages of a union—when its future is far from secure—its leaders will naturally be greatly concerned with the survival of the organization. However, as unions achieve a degree of stability there is growing interest in the *mutual survival* of the union and of the employers with which it deals.[11]

Some writers who have noted the gradual shift in the philosophy and outlook of union leaders have adopted a mildly critical tone. They imply that union leaders have become soft, and as a consequence the labor movement has lost its dynamism. But others feel that such changes are to be expected. It is hard to maintain enthusiasm at fever pitch for any cause unless there are recurring crises to be faced. Once the larger unions had become established, and had reached many of their announced goals, the nature of their problems changed. And as the problems they dealt with changed the behavior patterns of union leaders also were altered. It is hard to see how it could have been otherwise in some of the larger craft and industrial unions. Given the structure of the American labor movement these unions do not go outside their industry or occupational groups in search of members after they have achieved considerable success in organizing the workers within their jurisdictions.

[11] See E. Wight Bakke, *Mutual Survival the Goal of Unions and Management,* New Haven: Yale University Labor and Management Center (1946), pp. 17–18.

There are some who look back to the period of union militancy with nostalgia. But others, such as Bakke, have noted that there is a delicate balance in the relationship between powerful unions and powerful management. If either side concentrates on individual survival, and does so by attacking the other side vigorously, Bakke believes that the result would be disastrous to both parties. In Bakke's view: "The result of failure to work out the means of *mutual survival* will not be the elimination of one by the other, but the elimination of both as free institutions by public regimentation."[12]

ATTITUDES OF THE RANK AND FILE

A great deal has been written about the changing attitudes of labor leaders as trade unions have matured. This is not surprising. Union leaders are relatively few in number and their behavior can be analyzed from the outside; that is, by examining their demands at the bargaining table and by reading their speeches and other publications. It is not necessary to ask union leaders how they feel about certain issues, and how these feelings have changed over time. Their attitudes are a matter of public record. It is much more difficult to get at the attitudes of union members, yet there can be little doubt that these also have changed as unions have grown in size and strength.

The apathy of American union members has often been noted and commented upon. However, during the early days when a union is being formed there must be at least a hard core of "activists" willing to do much of the hard work associated with organization. For unions to win organizational elections at least a majority in the bargaining unit must give the union their active support. Even during this phase, however, American union members appear to be basically non-ideological. As the position of the union becomes secure, most of the rank and file are inclined to leave union affairs in the hands of their paid leaders. They are also likely to become less interested in the political blandishments of their leaders as expressed in union publications.

The interdependence of political and trade union action, a dominant characteristic of European trade unionism, is clearly lacking in the United States. Trade union members often demonstrate a strong independence in their political behavior while at the same time remaining staunchly loyal to their unions. The presidential cam-

[12] *Ibid.*, p. 82.

paigns of 1952 and 1956 illustrate this. In both campaigns, most trade unions strongly supported Adlai Stevenson, but it is evident that many union members cast their votes for Dwight Eisenhower. It is undoubtedly a fair generalization that most rank and file union members in the United States have always been non-ideological. There are frequent references to the "labor vote," but the evidence strongly suggests that there is much less bloc voting among union members than is popularly believed.

Rank and File Attitudes toward Employers

Richard Lester has noted that as unions have moved into positions of security, demands at the bargaining table have been moderated. There might have been inflammatory speeches during organizing campaigns in which employers were described in very unflattering terms, but once unions have achieved recognition and union security, relations between union leaders and employers become at least polite if not completely amicable.

How do the rank and file view their employers? If unions are to succeed the members must have some degree of allegiance to the union. Does this mean that they have little or no allegiance to their employer? Although there has been relatively little research done on these important questions, studies to date indicate that support of a union does not mean hostility toward an employer. The most comprehensive research on this issue has been conducted by Father Theodore V. Purcell of Loyola University who concluded that the vast majority of workers in the situation which he studied had *dual* allegiance to their union and their employer.[13] This study revealed that nearly three-fourths of the workers in a large meat-packing plant felt a sense of allegiance to *both* their employer and their union. An even larger proportion (88 per cent) of the shop stewards—the lowest rung of union officialdom—indicated their loyalty to both company and union.

Another study conducted by the Institute of Labor and Industrial Relations at the University of Illinois led to similiar findings. It showed that "men feeling positive allegiance to the company feel similarly about their union."[14] Professor Stagner believes that "it

[13] Theodore V. Purcell, "Dual Allegiance to Company and Union—Packing House Workers, A Swift-UPWA Study in a Crisis Situation, 1949–1950," *Personnel Psychology* (March 1954), pp. 48–58. A more extended treatment of the research summarized in this article is given in his book *The Worker Speaks His Mind on Company and Union,* Cambridge, Massachusetts: Harvard University Press (1954).
[14] Ross Stagner, "Dual Allegiance as a Problem in Modern Society," *Personnel Psychology* (March 1954), p. 46.

is virtually certain that disputes between company and union will arise, but it is not clear that such disputes must be accompanied by hostility, or must lead to the extermination of one side or the other."[15]

The studies of rank and file attitudes toward union and management have been cross-section studies; that is, they have revealed worker attitudes at a particular time. Unfortunately, data are not available to show what changes there have been in these attitudes from the beginning of a union-management relationship, or an organizing campaign, to a later period when the union is well established and the collective bargaining relationship has been stabilized. However, workers would not join a union unless they felt somehow that their employers were not doing as much for them as they should, and in many cases they no doubt feel a strong sense of grievance against management. There must be, in brief, some degree of worker dissatisfaction before a union can be organized. If wages, hours, and working conditions improve after a union has organized a company, many of the earlier causes of dissatisfaction will be removed.

It is entirely possible—although this conjecture cannot be supported by empirical evidence—that the successful organization of a company by a union can lead to a stronger sense of allegiance to the company than was felt in pre-union days. This is unquestionably the case where unions and management have worked out a system of cooperation acceptable to both parties. Some arrangements of this kind will be discussed in a later chapter, and the evidence in the cases to be examined clearly supports the view given above.

CONCLUSIONS

The outlook of union leaders has changed as trade unions have moved through successive stages of development. The early attempts at reform unionism did not win a large following. The narrow preoccupation of the early craft unions was not conducive to growth. The explosive growth of the 1930's led to a great deal of militancy; yet as unions have matured there is evidence of growing complacency.

Rank and file union members have shown a considerable amount of independence in their political behavior. The scanty evidence available indicates quite strongly that union members do not regard

[15] *Ibid.*, pp. 46–47.

their employers with hostility, but feel a sense of allegiance to both their employers and their union.

Modern trade unions have departed from the earlier A.F. of L. principle of no political involvement. While the political activities of trade unions has been stepped up in recent years there is no evidence to support the view that American union leaders seek political power as such. Indeed, despite the establishment of structurally independent political organizations, American trade unions have continued to rely on economic strength to achieve their goals. Political action in American unions remains a relatively small part of their total activity. They are, as they have been virtually from the outset, institutions for the conduct of collective bargaining. In the chapters which follow, this central activity of American trade unions will be examined in considerable detail.

REFERENCES

BOOKS AND PAMPHLETS

Bakke, E. Wight, *Mutual Survival the Goal of Unions and Management,* New Haven: Yale University Labor and Management Center (1946).

Institute of Labor and Industrial Relations, *Labor-Management Relations in Illini City,* Two Vols., Champaign, Illinois: University of Illinois (1953, 1954).

Lester, Richard A., *As Unions Mature, an Analysis of the Evolution of American Unionism,* Princeton, New Jersey: Princeton University Press (1958).

Miernyk, William H., *Trade Unions in the Age of Affluence,* New York: Random House (1962).

Millis, Harry A., and Royal E. Montgomery, *Organized Labor,* New York: McGraw-Hill Book Company (1945).

Purcell, Theodore V., S.J., *The Worker Speaks His Mind on Company and Union,* Cambridge, Massachusetts: Harvard University Press (1954).

U. S. Department of Labor, Bureau of Labor Statistics, "New Attitudes in Labor-Management Relations," BLS Bulletin No. 1145—*American Labor and the American Spirit,* Washington: U.S. Government Printing Office.

ARTICLES

Douty, H. M. "The 73rd Convention of the AFL," *Monthly Labor Review,* U.S. Department of Labor, Bureau of Labor Statistics (November 1954).

Herberg, Will, "Bureaucracy and Democracy in Labor Unions," *Antioch Review,* Volume 3, Fall 1943, Reprinted in Joseph Schister, ed., *Readings in Labor Economics and Industrial Relations,* New York: J. B. Lippincott Company (2nd ed., 1956).

Purcell, Theodore V., S.J. "Dual Allegiance to Company and Union—Packing House Workers, A Swift UPWA Study in a Crisis Situation, 1949–1952," *Personnel Psychology,* Vol. 7 (March 1954), pp. 48–58.

Rogin, Michael, "Voluntarism: The Political Functions of an Antipolitical Doctrine," *Industrial and Labor Relations Review,* Vol. 15, No. 4 (July 1962), pp. 521–535.

Saposs, David J., "Voluntarism in the American Labor Movement," *Monthly Labor Review,* U.S. Department of Labor, Bureau of Labor Statistics, (September 1954).

Stagner, Ross, "Dual Allegiance as a Problem in Modern Society," *Personnel Psychology,* Vol. 7 (March 1954), pp. 41–47.

Weisz, Morris, "Labor Ideology and Practice in Europe and the U.S.," *Monthly Labor Review,* U.S. Department of Labor, Bureau of Labor Statistics (March 1958).

Witte, Edwin E., "The New Federation and Political Action," *Industrial and Labor Relations Review,* Vol. 9 (April 1956), pp. 406–418.

PART 4

collective bargaining—processes and issues

Chapter 13 The Negotiation of Labor-Management Agreements

As noted in the last chapter, trade unions in the United States have relied largely on collective bargaining for achieving their goals. What is the nature of the collective bargaining process? What issues are negotiated by unions and management? Have there been significant changes in collective bargaining as the trade union movement has grown and matured? These and a number of other questions concerning collective bargaining will be considered in this and the following four chapters.

Collective bargaining was practiced, at least in isolated cases, long before the A.F. of L. was founded. Vernon Jensen has shown that "although a name had not yet been found for union-management negotiation the practice of collective bargaining was already evident by the middle of the nineteenth century."[1] Moreover, in Jensen's opinion, "the beginnings of collective bargaining reveal it as a process conceived in the best heritage of our democratic traditions. It is founded not in radicalism or necessarily in militance, but in the desire to be conciliatory, fair, and businesslike."[2]

The objective of collective bargaining is a labor-management agreement. Equally important is the day-to-day administration of this agreement. But a sound agreement provides for most situations which are likely to come up before it expires, and instances of labor disputes when an agreement is in existence are fairly rare. "Wildcat strikes"—those which occur during the life of an agreement—occur

[1] Vernon H. Jensen, "Notes on the Beginning of Collective Bargaining," *Industrial and Labor Relations Review*, Vol. 9 (January 1956), p. 232.
[2] *Ibid.*, p. 234.

only infrequently and are frowned on by unions and management alike.

What is the nature of the collective bargaining agreement? It is generally referred to in the press, and in popular discussions, as a *contract*. It is misleading, however, to think of a labor-management agreement as a counterpart of the typical business contract. If business contracts are not lived up to by the parties signing them, the aggrieved party has recourse to the courts; in fact, a substantial body of contract law has evolved to settle such business disputes. There are a few instances in which unions and managements have made their agreement into a legal contract, usually by having one party make a nominal payment to the other. But these are not typical of the vast majority of labor-management agreements in the United States.

In an effort to sharpen the distinction between business contracts and labor-management agreements, some writers have resorted to various analogies. The labor-management agreement is sometimes compared with international treaties. The treaty, it is hoped, is something that the nations signing it can live with. If for some reason they cannot, diplomatic relations between the countries are ruptured, and it is possible that a third country might even enter the picture and try to settle differences between the disputants. If the two countries cannot settle their differences, even with the aid of a third party, the result might be open warfare. Analogous behavior can often be found between unions and management.

Another analogy that is sometimes used is that of the marriage agreement. This is clearly not the same thing as a business contract. If two businessmen sign a contract and one of the parties fails to live up to its terms, the case usually ends up in the courts. Once the judge has made a settlement it is not likely that the two parties will do business again. But disagreements can also arise in the happiest of marriages. It is not usual, however, for a husband who has become upset with his wife to threaten to haul her into court unless she mends her ways. And a wife displeased with the behavior of her husband does not as a rule try to reform him by threatening a lawsuit. Differences of opinion have to be ironed out if the two parties are to live together. The marriage can break up, and the two parties go their ways just as the businessmen who had a dispute over a property contract. But the important thing is that every minor disagreement in a marriage does not lead to its dissolution. The two parties must learn to settle their grievances and live together afterwards. It is this which is stressed by the writers who use the analogy of the marriage agreement in trying to explain collective bargaining. There are disputes between unions and management; there can be much table pounding, shouting, threats and abuse. But once the storm and fury is over and the issue has been settled, the two parties must be able to live together and work together in reasonable harmony if the goals of the union and management are to be realized.

THE CONTENT OF LABOR-MANAGEMENT AGREEMENTS

The earliest agreements on record were nothing more than lists of wages to be paid to the various occupational groups covered. Today, however, there is tremendous variation in labor-management agreements. Some are relatively brief documents consisting of a few pages, while others are lengthy documents, usually presented in the form of printed booklets.

The language of an agreement is important. A good agreement tends to avoid legalistic jargon and yet it must be carefully worded lest the misinterpretation of a phrase lead to a dispute completely unforeseen by either the union or management. Perhaps the best way to illustrate the coverage of an agreement is to consider a single hypothetical example. It must be remembered, however, that while such an example may be reasonably "typical" no two agreements are exactly alike in scope and coverage.

Recognition and Specification of Bargaining Units

Most agreements begin by specifying that the company recognizes the union as the sole representative of its workers within the bargaining unit covered by the agreement. In some cases the bargaining unit will be an occupational group, in others it will be the plant, and in others the entire company. There are companies which have agreements with more than one union—in some cases with several. Each agreement, therefore, must carefully specify the workers covered.

Form of Union Security

If the union has been able to negotiate a union shop agreement, the terms under which all workers in the bargaining unit are to become members will be spelled out. A typical union shop agreement indicates that the company is free to employ whomever it wishes, but all workers, as a condition of employment, must become members of the union generally within a period of thirty days. Some agreements also specify that the company will deduct union dues from the paycheck of each union member. This is known as the "checkoff." Some unions, however, prefer to collect dues directly from the workers, and in this case the contract contains no checkoff provision.

The Rights and Duties of Employers

Most agreements contain provisions indicating the rights of employers. A typical provision will show that the employer has the right to determine what and how much is to be produced, and where production is to take place. Some agreements are quite specific that the union will have nothing to say about the company's activities in the product market.

Wages

This is one of the most important provisions of a collective bargaining agreement. If there is to be a wage increase, the agreement specifies the amount. In some cases wages are not negotiated on an annual basis, but an agreement is reached to increase wages by a specified amount or percentage at different stages. In some cases deferred increases are spelled out in the agreement. Some agreements contain provisions for wage reopening during the contract period. This means that all other provisions are to be unchanged during the life of the agreement, but that—as of a given date—if either party wishes to do so the wage provision may be reopened for negotiation.

Some agreements also contain provisions for revision of existing rates on particular jobs. Such revision is usually associated with a change in work method or work load often as the result of a technological change. The wage section of a typical collective bargaining agreement may also contain provisions dealing with reporting time, shift premiums, equal pay for women doing the same work as men, the rates applicable when employees are transferred from one job to another, and payment for waiting time or travel time. In some industries and occupations wages are specified on an hourly basis, in others there are piece rate systems. Agreements in such cases typically contain provisions dealing with basic piece rates and incentive pay.

In recent years a number of agreements have provided for cost-of-living adjustments in wages as prices change. Such "escalator" clauses usually indicate that basic wages will be increased (or decreased) at stated intervals, depending upon the changes that have taken place in the Consumer Price Index published monthly by the Bureau of Labor Statistics.

Hours of Work and Overtime Pay

The basic work day and work week are generally spelled out in a labor-management agreement. Under the Fair Labor Standards Act, there must be premium pay for overtime work. But in a specific case, the basic work week might be less than the 40-hour standard established by law. In such cases, the agreement will contain provisions for overtime pay. There will also be agreement on holiday pay. And some agreements indicate that workers are to be paid when absent from the job to perform civic duties, such as jury duty.

Vacation Pay

Most agreements also specify the number of days of paid vacation to which workers are entitled. Vacation pay is generally a function of length of service. As a worker gains increasing seniority with the company he will be entitled to a longer paid vacation.

Technological Change

This is often one of the most complex provisions in a labor-management agreement. Most agreements specify that management has the right to make technological changes such as the installation of new and better machinery or basic changes in production methods. Many agreements, however, contain a provision that the union must be consulted before such changes are made. The union is generally interested in the effects of the change on employment and wage rates. If workers are to be displaced by the change, the agreement often contains provisions for the orderly reassignment of the displaced workers to new jobs. It is not unusual for the agreement to specify that reassigned workers will not suffer a reduction in earnings while learning a new occupation. This problem is also covered by another set of provisions dealing with seniority to be discussed below.

Severance Pay

Some agreements provide for lump-sum payments to workers who lose their jobs because of a plant shut-down, technological change, or the curtailment of activities which will displace some workers permanently. Severance pay usually depends upon the length of service with the company. While severance pay provisions are relatively new, it is likely that more and more agreements will contain such provisions in the future due to growing concern about unemployment as the result of structural changes in the economy.

The Grievance Procedure

It would be impossible in most cases for those who draft a labor-management agreement to foresee all of the possible problems that might come up during its life. Thus a quasi-judicial procedure must be established to protect the individual worker. If during the life of an agreement the worker feels that he has been the victim of unjust treatment in one way or another he may file a grievance. The details of grievance procedure will be discussed in a later chapter since this is one of the most important parts of a successful labor-management agreement. It provides the "safety valve" which insures that the broad provisions of the agreement will be met by both parties while still allowing for the careful treatment of individual cases.

Arbitration

The final stage of most grievance arrangements is arbitration. Since there are a number of ways in which arbitration can be handled, all of which will be discussed in a later chapter, each labor-management agreement must specify how arbitration is to take place. Most agreements which contain an arbitration clause indicate that the decision of the arbitrator will be final and binding on both parties.

Seniority

The seniority section in a typical labor-management agreement is likely to be one of its most comprehensive and complex. It will usually specify seniority districts and seniority lists. Some agreements call for probationary periods, and almost all indicate the relationship between seniority, layoffs, and recalls. The seniority section of the agreement also contains provisions dealing with promotions, transfers, leaves of absence, and the termination of seniority and employment. In some agreements provisions are made for "super" seniority. This usually applies to shop stewards or other union officials.

Fringe Benefit Provisions

Fringe benefits have become increasingly important in labor-management agreements since World War II. They deal with such matters as group life, accident, and health insurance; supplementary unemployment insurance; pension and other retirement programs.

Discharge Cases

Companies usually reserve the right to discharge a worker for "cause." This will vary greatly from case to case. Usually an agreement specifies that a worker can be discharged for insubordination, shirking on the job, or violating safety rules. Workers can also be discharged, in most cases, for excessive absenteeism, drunkenness, fighting, or otherwise violating the rules of the company which the union has agreed to observe. The worker who feels he has been unjustly discharged almost always has the right to appeal through the grievance procedure.

Miscellaneous Provisions

Many agreements also contain provisions dealing with such matters as the use of bulletin boards, the company's policy with respect to military service, the payment of shop stewards for performing union duties on company time, and a wide variety of other matters some of them relatively minor in character. Most agreements conclude with a statement spelling out the terms of the agreement.

CRITERIA USED IN WAGE NEGOTIATIONS

The preceding section shows that labor-management agreements cover a wide variety of issues, many of which have nothing to do with wages. But wages, hours, and conditions of employment are still basic. Hours and conditions of employment can be dealt with in a relatively straightforward manner. This is not to imply that there cannot be disputes, particularly over hours. In recent years there have been growing demands for a reduced work week. Some unions, such as the Rubber Workers and the International Brotherhood of Electrical Workers, have succeeded in incorporating reduced work weeks in some agreements. Shorter hours are often demanded by unions which have been losing members; in an effort to bolster their membership they seek to share the work available in an industry or occupation. While this demand can cause considerable disagreement, the issue itself is not complex. The union will demand a reduction in hours and the company may be unwilling to grant a reduction without a corresponding drop in pay. The issue will then be settled by a show of economic strength.

The negotiation of wages is a fairly complicated matter. As a general principle, unions want to win wage increases for their members. Yet different unions will use different arguments in seeking wage increases, and the same union might employ different arguments under varying conditions. In the following section we will consider briefly some of the major criteria used by unions seeking wage increases and some of the criteria used by management in resisting demands for wage increases.

CRITERIA USED BY UNIONS IN SEEKING WAGE INCREASES

The actual reason why a given union seeks a specified wage increase is not always easy to determine. It is not unlikely that at times rivalry among union leaders influences their wage demands. We can only speculate about such matters, however. The actual reasons may or may not coincide with the criteria used in wage negotiations. A number of years ago, Professor Slichter discussed some of the criteria used in negotiating wage changes. We will consider briefly the following: (1) changes in the cost of living, (2) maintenance of take-home pay in the face of reduction of hours, (3) changes in productivity, (4) the ability of the employer to pay, (5) the effects of higher or lower wages upon purchasing power and employment, and (6) wages paid in other industries or places.[3]

Unions with built-in escalator clauses do not need to seek wage increases as the result of rising prices, but most labor-management agreements do not contain such clauses. During a period of rising prices, unions often indicate that part of a wage increase which they are seeking is to compensate for the loss of purchasing power due to rising prices. As will be noted later, this is not the only reason that unions seek wage increases even when prices are going up. But if the Consumer Price Index has gone up by a significant amount during the life of an agreement, the union is almost certain to emphasize this fact when negotiating basic wages for the next agreement.

Union leaders have often been criticized for using the cost-of-living criterion in seeking wage increases. Editorial writers, for example, point out that such wage increases will be self-defeating since employers will only raise their prices. If all unions seek wage increases on these grounds there will be a general rise in the price level, and non-union firms will have to follow the lead of those dealing with unions if they are to avoid labor difficulties in their own concerns. It is often argued that workers would gain far more if instead of

[3] See Sumner H. Slichter, *Basic Criteria Used in Wage Negotiations*, The Chicago Association of Commerce and Industry (1947), pp. 8–9.

seeking wage increases to compensate for higher prices they could work toward the reduction of prices. Then, it is argued, not only would organized workers gain but all consumers would be better off.

Many union leaders are quick to concede that this would indeed be the case. But as some have pointed out they are not able to negotiate prices with employers since price setting is generally an employer prerogative. In the absence of any control over prices, they argue, union leaders must seek higher wages if their members are not to suffer a drop in real income during a period of rising prices.

There have been times when unions have not attempted to win wage increases, but have instead sought to maintain average pay in the face of a reduction in hours. This happened in a number of cases following the end of World War II. Under wartime conditions many workers earned premium pay, but when the emergency had passed hours were cut back to the normal work week. Union leaders then sought increases in hourly (or piece) rates which would result in the same take-home pay despite the cut in hours.

Improvements in Productivity

Technological change—a broad term used to describe improvements in products and production processes—has been the major force contributing to rising real per capita income in the United States. Union leaders have argued that the nation's workers should share in the fruits of technological progress and they have frequently supported demands for wage increases by pointing to changes in productivity.

The use of this criterion is closely tied to the broader issue of income distribution. The way in which gains from productivity should be shared among workers, the owners of capital, and consumers, is a matter of continuing controversy. The issues involved are not simple. They will be considered in detail in later chapters dealing with the theory of wage determination and productivity. A few of the major questions involved might be noted here, however. Which measure of productivity should the union use in seeking a wage increase? Should it be the increase in productivity in the company with which the union is bargaining? If so, should all workers get proportionate increases? Would industry—or even economy-wide—averages be more appropriate? To what extent have increases in productivity been due to the greater efficiency of workers, and to what extent are they the result of better management or equipment? As Professor Slichter has shown, the consequences of wage increases geared to productivity changes depend to some extent upon the causes of productivity gains.[4]

Ability to Pay

Unions have frequently supported demands for wage increases by the ability of employers to grant these increases. If profits in an industry are high compared with other industries—or within the same industry compared with earlier time periods—union leaders have often argued that wage increases could be granted without price increases or at least without proportional price increases. In some cases it has almost seemed that the union and management were bargaining over profits rather than wages. Union leaders in this country have repeatedly asserted that they are not opposed to the profit system. However, they contend that companies should not earn "excessive" profits, and when profits are at a relatively high level, this criterion is frequently used in support of demands for wage increases.

Effects of Wage Increases upon Consumer Purchasing Power and Employment

At times, union leaders have tried to justify demands for wage increases by asserting that higher wages are needed to maintain or increase the purchasing power of consumers. The same argument is often used when the level of unemployment is relatively high. If consumers had more money to spend, union leaders maintain, the demand for services and goods would be increased, and this in turn would permit businesses to expand their output and consequently increase their demand for labor.

Wages Paid in Other Industries or Places

Unions often support demands for wage increases by referring to the higher wages paid by other industries, or to higher wages in the same industry in other areas. The average level of wages varies considerably from region to region in the United States. And there is a surprising amount of wage diversity even within a local labor market area. Industry and area wage averages are affected to some extent by differences in product-mix and in industry-mix. It would be surprising if there were not considerable diversity in average wages from place to place, even within a given industry, since the various companies which make up an industry differ from each

[4] *Ibid.*, pp. 22–24.

other in a number of ways. In general, however, unions have sought to achieve uniformity of wages within industries, at least for similar occupations. And in regions where wages are low, unions have argued that the average level should be more nearly in line with the averages prevailing in relatively high-wage areas.

The various criteria used by unions in seeking wage increases are not entirely independent and a given union will not rely on the same criteria all the time. Conditions in the economy as a whole, as well as in specific industries and occupations, will frequently determine the basis upon which unions seek wage increases. Unions have sometimes been accused of a lack of consistency in arguing for higher wages but since economic conditions change over time, the union will use the arguments that seem most compelling at the time it is asking for a wage increase. While each of the criteria by itself may be debatable—else there would be no need to bargain over wages—union leaders could scarcely be expected to use the same arguments in support of wage increases time after time in view of changes in economic conditions between bargaining sessions.

CRITERIA USED BY EMPLOYERS IN RESISTING WAGE DEMANDS

Several of the criteria used by unions in seeking wage increases are also used by management in resisting such demands. Obviously, however, management looks at the other side of the coin in formulating its arguments.

Increases in the Cost of Living

When unions ask for wage increases because the Consumer Price Index has been rising, management often objects on the grounds that wage increases will lead to further price increases with no net gain for union members. Management accepts, in brief, the "cost-push" theory of inflation. And at the bargaining table management often claims that it must keep the consumer in mind—that in resisting the union's demands for wage increases it is not only thinking of the good of the company, but the good of society as well. Needless to say, members of the "general public," that is, those not involved in the labor dispute, often feel sympathetic toward this position especially during a period of rising prices, and this criterion has been used quite frequently by management in recent years to resist demands for wage increases.

Changes in Productivity

Management often points out that increases in productivity are not the result of greater labor effort, but stem from improved products and production processes. If these gains are to be sustained, management argues, a substantial part of the company earnings will have to be plowed back into new equipment. In most cases, management is willing to concede that workers should share in gains resulting from productivity increases. The issue boils down to the *amount* of increases which should go to the workers of a particular company. There are a few cases—the United Auto Workers-General Motors agreement is an outstanding example—where an "annual improvement factor" is computed. This forms the basis of wage increases due to productivity gains. It is assumed that some of the gains from productivity will go to consumers, some to stockholders, and that some will be used to improve plant and equipment in the company.

Inability to Pay

Just as unions frequently seek wage increases because they claim the company is *able* to pay, management often resists the wage increase on the grounds that it is *unable* to pay higher wages and to continue to operate at the level of profits needed to remain in business.

Effects of Wages on Costs and Employment

While unions use the "purchasing power" argument in support of wage demands, management looks at the cost side of the picture in resisting these demands. It is frequently claimed by management that if higher wages are granted the increase in cost will lead to a drop in employment. The economic model used in support of this argument is a highly simplified one which ignores many of the dynamic changes which occur in the real world. Yet conservative groups in particular have warned unions that persistent demands for wage increases will only result in labor's "pricing itself out of the market." In specific bargaining situations management will use the same argument, and insist that if it grants the wage increase demanded it can do so only by sacrificing jobs.

Wages Paid in Other Industries or Places

While unions generally press for wage uniformity, management generally objects to this criterion. Company spokesmen will point out they cannot be concerned with wages in other industries or other areas—that they can only look at their own books in making wage decisions. At times company spokesmen accuse union leaders of trying to "whipsaw" the wage level; that is, they claim that unions are not actually interested in wage uniformity, but only in pushing wages up as far and as fast as they can. Spokesmen for a specific company might argue, for example, that the union wants to push its wages above the average and then use this to bring wages in other concerns "into line" with the higher wages it had initially negotiated.

The Threat of Foreign Competition

A new criterion has been widely used in recent years by companies faced with increasing competition from abroad. This is a variant of the "ability to pay" criterion. Management has argued that if unions insist on pushing up the wage level, a greater share of the market will be taken over by foreign producers and that this must ultimately lead to the displacement of American workers.

Objectively, one cannot argue that either side is right or wrong in its choice of criteria. Bargaining implies give and take. Each side must be expected to muster the arguments which it feels will be most convincing, and each side will try to appeal to a wider audience than those around the bargaining table. In recent years, the negotiation of major agreements in our basic industries has generally been preceded by a considerable amount of publicity issued by both parties. The publicity campaigns are stepped up if negotiations break down and a strike results. Each side tries to sway public opinion in support of its point of view in the hope that this will help break down the resistance of the other party at the bargaining table. It is difficult to assess the effectiveness of these publicity campaigns. It is possible that this publicity makes settlement more difficult at times since if one or both of the parties announce publicly that there will be no retreat from a fixed position, it is more difficult to make concessions without losing face.

In a free society, the public statement or arguments in support of—or in resistance to—wage demands is no doubt all to the good. The public is, after all, interested in the outcome and those not associated with the dispute might be interested in evaluating the arguments of both sides. Collective bargaining would undoubtedly proceed more smoothly, however, if neither side insisted that it would *never* back down on a specific issue. Something obviously has to give if a deadlock is to be broken and nothing appears to be gained from such adamant statements which are typically followed by the kinds of compromises needed to end a labor dispute.

THE THEORY OF COLLECTIVE BARGAINING

The theory of collective bargaining cannot be separated entirely from the theory of wage determination which will be discussed in a later chapter. In this section we will consider briefly some of the theories which have focused more on the bargaining process itself. Our later discussion will deal with the more abstract theories of wage determination which have been developed both for non-unionized and unionized economies.

In recent years there has been a rapid development of theories of bargaining associated with problems of strategy and conflict. Some of these, however, have little or nothing to do with the collective bargaining process. Our attention will be limited to those which have been concerned with bargaining between organized labor and management.

CHAMBERLAIN'S THREEFOLD CLASSIFICATION OF COLLECTIVE BARGAINING

One of the earliest attempts to develop a systematic and fairly general classification of collective bargaining theories was made by Neil W. Chamberlain in 1951.[5] Chamberlain labeled his three categories: (a) the marketing theory, (b) the governmental theory, and (c) the managerial theory. These will be considered briefly.

The Marketing Theory

The marketing theory is relatively simple. According to this view, collective bargaining is a method of selling and buying labor services. The objective is to establish a price for labor just as in a simple economy higgling in the marketplace determines the price for products. This theory might have been a useful explanation of collective bargaining in its earliest stages. The first unions were organized to develop schedules of rates at which workers in specific trades would be available to employers. If alternative workers were not available, the employers would have to meet this price. If other workers could be obtained, however, employers would not pay the posted prices. Conditions in the labor market, in brief, would determine the effectiveness of such a wage policy. As collective bargaining began to deal with a growing number of issues, however, other theories were evolved to explain the more complex process.

[5] Neil W. Chamberlain, *Collective Bargaining,* New York: McGraw-Hill (1951), Chapter 6.

The Governmental Theory

The rudiments of this view of collective bargaining were given by William Leiserson in 1922.[6] Basically, this view regards the union-management relationship as a governmental system in industry. The collective bargaining agreement is the constitution, and management is viewed as the executive branch of government. The negotiating committees which amend the basic agreement as conditions change constitute the legislative branch, while the grievance procedure for the settlement of disputes within the framework of the agreement is likened to the judicial branch of government.

This theory emphasizes the continuing and dynamic nature of collective bargaining in an effort to show how differences of opinion in the work place can be settled by the same procedures which result in the enactment, amendment, and interpretation of laws in a democratic society. The governmental arrangement is viewed as a representative one. Everything must proceed according to a set of established rules. Just as it is possible for governments to break down in times of crisis, however, those involved in labor-management relationships can also resort to a show of force.

The Managerial Theory

According to this view, collective bargaining is involved primarily with business decisions. The union participates in some of these decisions; hence it shares in some aspects of the managerial function.

Most union leaders have strongly denied that they have an interest in "taking over the front office," that is, they deny that they are interested in the process of managerial decision-making. But the existence of a union imposes limitations on management's ability to make decisions unilaterally. Many of the decisions made jointly by unions and management must necessarily affect the conduct of a company's business. Thus regardless of the disclaimers made by some union leaders, there is a certain amount of sharing of some management functions when collective bargaining takes place.

The three views of collective bargaining proposed by Chamberlain are not mutually exclusive. Collective bargaining does deal with economic issues of the kind focused upon by the marketing theory. Some aspects of collective bargaining may also be viewed from the political side as is done in the governmental theory. And it cannot

[6] See W. M. Leiserson, "Constitutional Government in American Industry," *American Economic Review,* Supplement (1922). See also, Joseph Shister, "Collective Bargaining" in *A Decade of Industrial Relations Research, 1946–1956,* New York: Harper and Brothers (1958), p. 27.

be denied that collective bargaining leads to decision-making—with both parties involved in the decisions—which is the orientation of the managerial theory.

Chamberlain's threefold view of collective bargaining emphasizes the complexity of this process in a free society. It is a useful classification of some of the *elements* involved in collective bargaining, yet it is primarily a method of observing the collective bargaining process. It does not provide us with analytical tools which would contribute to an understanding of the forces at work both at the bargaining table and within the organizations which must meet to hammer out an agreement.

As Carl Stevens has pointed out, most research on collective bargaining has been descriptive; it has lacked analytical focus.[7] Theories of conflict and strategy have developed rapidly in recent years, but as Stevens has noted, there has been relatively little effort to relate these theories to collective bargaining situations. Two theories which apply to a variety of bargaining or conflict situations will be considered briefly in this chapter. A number of theories more specifically concerned which wage determination will be discussed in Chapter 19.

THE THEORY OF GAMES AND COLLECTIVE BARGAINING

The theory of games deals with involved situations such as might be encountered by the military in which strategy on one side of a conflict must take into account the most probable countermoves of the opposition. Game theory is much too complex to be considered in detail in this book but some of its elements can be illustrated by borrowing from an example developed by J. D. Williams in his lucid and entertaining introduction to game theory, *The Compleat Strategyst*.[8]

The example concerns two campers—a man and his wife—planning a trip into the mountains. The husband likes high altitudes while his wife is partial to lower elevations. The mountains are crisscrossed by a network of roads—four running north and south, and four running east and west. All of the roads go through peaks and valleys. The husband would prefer to camp on one of the peaks and his wife in one of the valleys; the problem is how to find a camp-

[7] Carl M. Stevens, "Strategy and Collective Bargaining Negotiations," *Annual Proceedings*, Industrial Relations Research Association (1960), p. 122.

[8] J. D. Williams, *The Compleat Strategyst* (a RAND Publication), New York: McGraw-Hill (1954), pp. 24–27. This example has been used with permission of the Rand Corporation and McGraw-Hill.

site high enough to satisfy the husband and low enough to satisfy the wife. To simplify the problem they agree to camp at a junction where one of the north-south roads crosses one of the east-west roads. The problem can be solved by setting up a table of altitudes at each of the intersections. This is called a *payoff matrix,* and the hypothetical table developed by Williams is shown below.

MATRIX A

Wife ▼

Husband ►

	1	2	3	4
1	7	2	5	1
2	2	2	3	4
3	5	3	4	4
4	3	2	1	6

The husband's strategy will be to read across each row and pick that row with the *highest* minimum (this is called the *maximin*). The wife's strategy will be to read down each column and pick the one with the *lowest* maximum (this is called the *minimax*). In the simple contrived example it will be noted that the husband will select Row 3 and the wife Column 2. Fortunately for the success of this camping trip, and the continued harmony of the hypothetical marriage, two of the roads will intersect at an altitude of three thousand feet—the lowest altitude which the husband would be willing to accept and the highest which his wife will agree to. Such a fortunate intersection in the theory of games is known as a *saddle point,* and the common value at this intersection is known as the *value of the game.*[9]

Not every payoff matrix will yield the neat solution given above. For example, if we interchange the numbers in Row 3–Column 2 and Row 4–Column 3 we will get the new matrix given below. If we go through the same procedure, that is, inspect each row to find its minimum, and select the greatest of these, then go down each column to find its maximum and select the one with the smallest of these, we will find that there are two intersections (Row 2–Column 2 and Row 4–Column 2). But both of these will

[9] *Ibid.,* pp. 27–66.

MATRIX B

Wife ▼

Husband ►	1	2	3	4
1	7	2	5	1
2	2	2	3	4
3	5	1	4	4
4	3	2	3	6

be at a lower altitude than the husband is willing to accept and they will also be less than the highest altitude which the wife is willing to accept. This would not be a satisfactory solution to either, and they would probably call off the camping trip.

This very brief and highly simplified excursion into game theory suggests that this analytical framework could be applied to collective bargaining. If in the example above we substitute the union for the husband's position, and management for the wife's position, and assume that their strategies deal with wages, we would obtain the same results. The union wants to get the highest wage possible and management the lowest. *Thus if we assume that there is a payoff matrix,* the union would select the row with the highest minimum; management would select the column with the lowest maximum. This would be the saddle-point solution to the problem.

Carl Stevens has attempted to develop a theory of collective bargaining within the game-theory framework. He does not suggest that there would be a single payoff matrix, but rather a series of these which he refers to as the *game-variant sequence.* There might be one matrix which applies while negotiations are going on up to a strike deadline, for example, and another which applies after this deadline has passed. Moreover, one of the parties might not *try* to reach a solution before the strike has occurred hoping to alter the conditions inside the matrix during the strike.

This is an intriguing approach to the theory of collective bargaining which might lead to important developments as the theory of conflict and strategy is itself refined and further developed. At present there is some doubt that the game-theory approach could deal with more than the simplest of bargaining situations. D. W. Irwin, in commenting on the effort by Stevens to apply this approach to collective bargaining has questioned that game theory "is sufficiently developed to cope with the infinite varieties of actual negotiations."[10] In an earlier article Stevens himself had suggested that "the game-theory format is essentially inappropriate to the analysis of negotiation . . .", and that a solution in game theory depends upon a known or arbitrarily assumed payoff matrix. The objective of the exchange of information during negotiations, however, "is to change the negotiators' perception of the values comprising the payoff matrix."[11]

This does not mean that the game-theory approach to collective bargaining is without value. No one has suggested that the two parties to negotiations would sit down and try to construct an actual matrix with appropriate numbers in each of the cells, and that these numbers would be juggled until a saddle-point solution could be achieved. This is about as far fetched as suggesting that each of the two parties feed all of the data in support of their respective positions into electronic computers, then allow the computer to manipulate the data until it reached a solution acceptable to both. While it no doubt has its limitations, the game-theory approach with its *emphasis on strategy* could lead to a better understanding of the collective bargaining process.

The negotiation of a labor-management agreement is a highly complex process. Many factors are involved, and some of these cannot be quantified. However the rapid development of powerful analytical tools in recent years has stimulated research on many kinds of decision-making processes. Many kinds of complex business problems handled by rules-of-thumb in the past can now be solved much more quickly and precisely by using the tools of management science and operations research. It might be much harder to apply these techniques to the collective bargaining process, yet it would be premature to conclude that the use of such high-powered methods will not eventually lead to a better understanding of the forces at work when labor-management agreements are being negotiated.

[10] *Annual Proceedings,* Industrial Relations Research Association (1960), p. 159.
[11] Carl M. Stevens, "On the Theory of Negotiation," *Quarterly Journal of Economics* (February 1958), pp. 96–97. In his book *Strategy and Collective Bargaining Negotiation,* New York: McGraw-Hill (1963), Stevens makes only limited reference to the concept of a payoff matrix. See, however, pp. 79–82, 89–90 and Appendix II. For an excellent account of a variety of game-theory bargaining analyses, see Robert L. Bishop, "Game-Theoretic Analyses of Bargaining," *Quarterly Journal of Economics* (November 1963), pp. 559–602.

FELLNER'S THEORY OF BILATERAL MONOPOLY

A highly abstract treatment of collective bargaining was developed by William Fellner in his celebrated article "Prices and Wages under Bilateral Monopoly."[12] A complete treatment of his theory requires the use of somewhat advanced economic concepts, but the essence of his argument, and his major conclusion, can be given in a somewhat simplified form.

The basic postulate of Fellner's theory is that under collective bargaining labor-management relations typically contain elements of bilateral monopoly. "Labor representatives have some monopoly power because the trade agreements set the conditions on which labor may be employed by an enterprise or by a group of enterprises; and managements frequently have some monopsony power because employment by other enterprises is not typically a *perfect* substitute for the given employment, as viewed from the standpoint of the worker."[13] A monopsony is the counterpart on the buyer's side of the market of a monopoly on the seller's side.

Fellner also assumes that the union makes a choice between higher or lower wages on the one hand and more or less employment on the other. Figure 13-1 illustrates the situation where a union wants to achieve the highest wage rate it can get regardless of the number of workers which can be employed at this wage.

There is an upper limit (W_{max}) above which wages cannot go and similarly there is a lower limit (W_{min}) below which they cannot fall in this particular bargaining situation. The upper limit is set by the top of the average value of product curve (AVP). If wages were pushed above this level the firm would go out of business. The lower limit is determined by other employment opportunities for this firm's workers, or it could be the minimum wage established by government order.

Between the upper and lower limits, the actual wage will be determined by the relative bargaining power of the employer and the union. For example, if the company's bargaining power is relatively strong, the best wage the union might be able to obtain is indicated by W_1. And the intersection of this wage line with the marginal value of product curve (MVP) shows the quantity of employment at that wage (E_1). If, however, the union has considerable bar-

[12] William Fellner, "Prices and Wages under Bilateral Monopoly," *Quarterly Journal of Economics* (August 1947), pp. 503–532.
[13] William Fellner, *Competition Among the Few*, New York: Alfred A. Knopf (1949), p. 252.

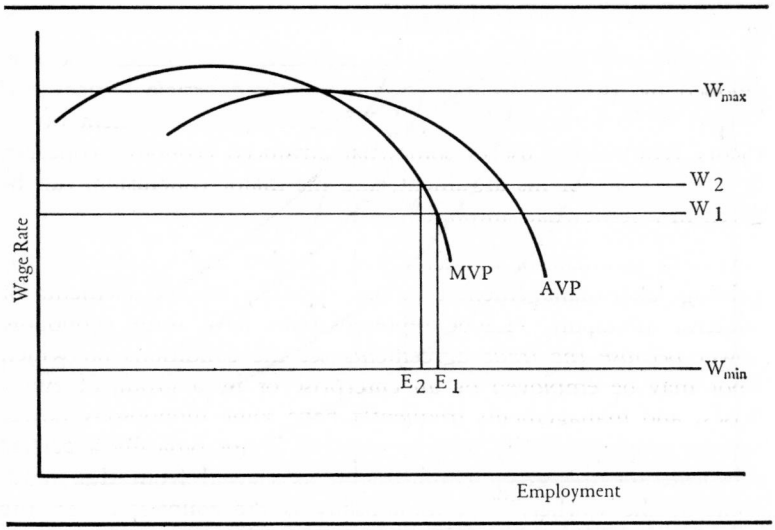

FIGURE 13–1

gaining power it might push wages up to W_2, and in this case employment would drop back to E_2. The situation described above assumes that the union negotiators are able to choose *freely* between the wage levels they can negotiate, and the number of workers who will be employed at each wage level. But this would be true only in somewhat unusual circumstances. A powerful union leader who could convince his members that those who remained employed would be better off at the highest wage he could negotiate might be able to consider higher wages and lower employment as perfect substitutes. But most union leaders would have to recognize that wages and employment are *imperfect* substitutes. This situation is illustrated by Figure 13-2.

The lines marked I_1, I_2, etc. are called *indifference curves*. The family of these curves makes up an indifference *map*. Each of these curves describes the relationship between wages and employment that would be acceptable to the rank and file under different circumstances. Again we see that there are maximum and minimum levels within which the negotiated wage must fall. And in this case —because of the shape of the indifference curves—the highest wage which the union could negotiate would be given by the point of tangency between the marginal value product curve (MVP), and the highest indifference curve which touches the MVP. In Figure

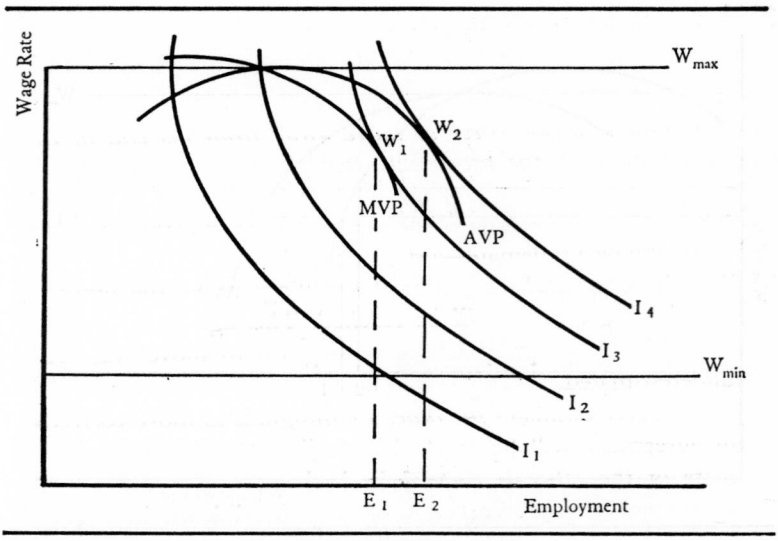

FIGURE 13–2

13-2 this is shown by the point W_1. The number of workers employed at that wage is shown by E_1 on the horizontal axis. This case assumes that the union is in a position to bargain over wages only and to accept the level of employment which will be forthcoming at that wage.

It is also conceivable, however, that a union could negotiate an agreement which specified *both* a wage level and a certain amount of employment. This would be called an "all-or-none contract." Under these circumstances, the maximum bargaining power of the union would be at the intersection of the average value of product curve (AVP), and the union's indifference curve tangent to AVP. In Figure 13-2, this wage is shown by W_2, and the volume of employment associated with that wage is given by E_2 on the horizontal axis. This shows that if the union is in a position to negotiate an all-or-none contract, it can achieve both higher wages and greater employment than if it is able to bargain over wages only.

Within the upper and lower limits which he has described, Fellner concludes that the actual wage rate to be negotiated will be *indeterminate,* that is, it will depend upon the relative bargaining power of the two parties. Moreover, this bargaining power will depend in part upon the ability of each party to correctly estimate the reactions of the other.

If we assume that each party starts from his own end of the bargaining range (W_{max} for the union, and W_{min} for the employer) Fellner draws the following conclusions:

The willingness of one party to move away from his end of the range depends upon the probability that the other party will *not* move.

(a) If each party overestimates the willingness of the other to move, there will be a stalemate—a strike will result.

(b) If each party underestimates the willingness of the other to move an agreement will be reached. This agreement will be favorable to the party whose willingness to move was *most* underestimated.

(c) If one party estimates the other's willingness to move correctly, an agreement will be reached regardless of whether the estimate of the other is correct. In both cases (b) and (c) an agreement will be reached without a breakdown in negotiations. What this agreement will be cannot be determined until the bargaining is over, and it depends largely upon the ability of one party or the other to correctly assess reactions to its proposals and its moves.[14]

COLLECTIVE BARGAINING AS A SYSTEM OF "INDUSTRIAL JURISPRUDENCE"

How useful are the theories of collective bargaining discussed in the preceding section? Because some bargaining theories use concepts which have no measurable counterpart in the real world, the non-theorist is likely to be critical of the high degree of abstraction involved. But this is not a justifiable criticism of the theories as such. All theories deal with abstractions. Perhaps the only relevant question is: Are they useful? If they help us understand the bargaining process by focusing attention on some aspects which might otherwise be ignored, the answer will be affirmative. But there are some who judge the usefulness of a theory solely in terms of its ability to predict outcomes. In this respect, we are far short of the mark—no theory has been developed to date which permits us to predict in advance the outcome of a particular bargaining situation. This is so even if we consider the wage bargain only, and in the real world collective bargaining deals with many issues other than wages.

[14] For further discussion of this type of bargaining theory, see Allan M. Cartter, *Theory of Wages and Employment,* Homewood, Illinois: Richard D. Irwin, Inc. (1959), especially pp. 87–115.

Sumner H. Slichter has noted that collective bargaining has two principal aspects. First, collective bargaining is a method of price-making; that is, of arriving at wage rates. But at the same time, collective bargaining is "a method of introducing civil rights into industry . . . of requiring that management be conducted by rule rather than by arbitrary decision." By developing the institution of the state, we have developed a body of law and procedures for administering laws. "Similarly, laboring men, through unions, formulate policies to which they give expression in the form of shop rules and practices . . . When labor and management deal with labor relations analytically and systematically . . . it is proper to refer to this system as *industrial jurisprudence*."[15]

The most complex theory of collective bargaining developed to date deals only with its first aspect—that of wage determination. In the earliest days of collective bargaining this was no doubt the major issue. But as unions have grown and become an increasingly important part of our political and economic lives, collective bargaining has expanded to deal with many issues other than the determination of wage rates. It is true that many fringe benefits involve a cost to the employer and a return to union members, current or deferred, and matters such as these can be subsumed under the general heading of "wages." But unions and management bargain about other matters which cannot be related so directly to costs or returns. For this reason, even the most "general" theory of collective bargaining would be in fact only a partial theory.

We will return to the important question of wage determination in a later part of the book. In the next chapter, some of the major non-wage aspects of collective bargaining will be considered, including issues which involve labor costs and returns to the workers as well as some issues which deal largely with "industrial jurisprudence." The latter involves the joint negotiation of work rules and practices. It is what Slichter referred to as the introduction of civil rights into industry.

REFERENCES

BOOKS

Cartter, Allan M., *Theory of Wages and Employment,* Homewood, Illinois: Richard D. Irwin, Inc. (1959).

Chamberlain, Neil W., *Collective Bargaining,* New York: McGraw-Hill (1951).

[15] Sumner H. Slichter, *Union Policies and Industrial Management,* Washington, D.C.: The Brookings Institution (1941), p. 1, italics added.

Davey, Harold W., *Contemporary Collective Bargaining,* Englewood Cliffs, New Jersey: Prentice-Hall, Inc. (second edition, 1959).

Dunlop, John T., and James J. Healy, *Collective Bargaining,* Homewood, Illinois: Richard D. Irwin, Inc. (revised edition, 1953).

Fellner, William, *Competition Among the Few,* New York: Alfred A. Knopf (1949).

Slichter, Sumner H. *Union Policies and Industrial Management,* Washington, D.C.: The Brookings Institution (1941).

———, ——— —, *Basic Criteria Used in Wage Negotiations,* Chicago: The Chicago Association of Commerce and Industry (1947).

Stevens, Carl M., *Strategy and Collective Bargaining Negotiation,* New York: McGraw-Hill (1963).

Subcommittee on Labor and Labor-Management Relations, Committee on Labor and Public Welfare, *Factors in Successful Collective Bargaining,* 82nd Congress, 1st Session, Washington: U.S. Government Printing Office (1951).

Williams, J. D., *The Compleat Strategyst* (A RAND Publication), New York: McGraw-Hill (1954).

ARTICLES

Bishop, Robert L., "Game-Theoretic Analyses of Bargaining," *Quarterly Journal of Economics,* Vol. LXXVII (November 1963), pp. 559–602.

Fellner, William, "Prices and Wages Under Bilateral Monopoly," *Quarterly Journal of Economics,* Vol. LXI (August 1947), pp. 503–532.

Schelling, T. C., "An Essay on Bargaining," *American Economic Review,* Vol. XLVI (June 1956), pp. 281–306.

Shister, Joseph, "Collective Bargaining," *A Decade of Industrial Relations Research,* 1946–1956, New York: Harper and Brothers (1958), pp. 26–63.

———, ——— "The Role of the State in Collective Bargaining," *Proceedings of the Twelfth Annual Industrial Relations Conference,* McGill University, Montreal, Canada (September 1960), pp. 1–20.

Slichter, Sumner H., "The Economics of Collective Bargaining," *Proceedings of the University of California Institute of Industrial Relations* (1948 and 1949), pp. 30–45.

———, —, ———, "Economics and Collective Bargaining," *Economics and the Policy Maker* (Brookings Lectures, 1958–1959), pp. 117–139.

Stevens, Carl M., "On the Theory of Negotiations," *The Quarterly Journal of Economics,* Vol. LXXII (February 1958), pp. 77–97.

———, —, ———, "Strategy in Collective Bargaining Negotiations," *Annual Proceedings,* Industrial Relations Research Association (1960), pp. 122–138.

Wagner, Harvey M., "Advances in Game Theory," *American Economic Review,* Vol. XLVIII (June 1958), pp. 368–387.

Chapter 14 Nonwage Issues in Collective Bargaining

The list of contract provisions in the last chapter indicates that collective bargaining deals with much more than the determination of wages. Increasingly, collective bargaining has dealt with the "total package" of wages and employee benefits. However, the negotiation of extensive employee benefits is a fairly recent phenomenon.[1] In this chapter we will discuss the payments typically referred to as "fringe benefits." We will also consider supplemental pay practices designed to stabilize employment, and one of the most important issues in collective bargaining in recent years, namely, that of "work rules" or job practices. Not all supplemental benefits are the result of negotiations; some have been granted unilaterally by employers. In this chapter, however, we will be concerned with the nonwage issues involved in collective bargaining.

Certain kinds of employee benefits are not of recent origin; some insurance schemes, for example, were negotiated before World War I. But the greatest impetus to the negotiation of employee benefits came during World War II. During the war the Wage Stabilization Board and the Office of Price Administration cooperated to keep wages and prices from rising at a time of acute shortages of manpower and materials. But as the war progressed and labor shortages became critical in some areas, many employers were more than willing to go along with union demands for bene-

[1] Such payments are referred to by most writers as "fringe benefits," but the authors of a recent comprehensive study have eschewed this term. "Payments that aggregate twenty percent of total payrolls," they assert, "are decidedly more than incidental." See Sumner H. Slichter, James J. Healy, and E. Robert Livernash, *The Impact of Collective Bargaining on Management,* Washington, D.C.: The Brookings Institution (1960), p. 422.

fits with *deferred* payments. This made jobs more attractive in their establishments without creating upward pressure on the wage level. Moreover the War Labor Board did not object to such agreements. As a result, unions were able to negotiate a number of comprehensive health, welfare and pension programs. Subsequently, various other kinds of payments for time not worked—such as vacation and holiday pay—were negotiated.

PAYMENT FOR TIME NOT WORKED

A survey conducted by the National Industrial Conference Board shows a wide variety of "time off with pay" practices.[2] Some of these are relatively minor since not all workers are covered: examples are payment for summer military training, jury duty, time off for illness in the family, medical appointments, or to get married. Others are relatively important, and these will be considered in some detail.

Vacation and Holiday Pay

Before World War II, only about one-fourth of the organized workers received paid vacations and in most cases the maximum was one week.[3] By 1953, however, 99 per cent of the manufacturing companies and 97 per cent of the nonmanufacturing companies in the National Industrial Conference Board sample granted paid vacations. The length of paid vacations has also been increasing. A study by the Bureau of Labor Statistics shows that in 1949 only one-third of the agreements which it reviewed provided more than two weeks of vacation pay. By 1957, however, more than two-thirds provided for at least three weeks and 20 per cent for four weeks or more.[4] Virtually all agreements provide that workers are entitled to vacation pay only after a stated period of service, but as paid vacations have been lengthened there has been a tendency to reduce the length of service requirement. Along with vacation pay, unions have negotiated an increasing number of paid holidays. The National Industrial Conference Board found that only 3 per cent of the manufacturing firms in its sample did *not* grant paid holidays, while only 5 per cent of the nonmanufacturing companies followed this practice. In 1939, by way of contrast, only 14 per

[2] National Industrial Conference Board, *Fringe Benefit Packages,* Studies in Personnel Policy, No. 143 (1954), pp. 8–9.
[3] Slichter, *et al., op. cit.,* p. 426.
[4] *Paid Vacation Provisions in Major Union Contracts,* 1957, Bulletin No. 1233, U.S. Department of Labor, Bureau of Labor Statistics (June 1958).

cent of a much larger number of companies surveyed provided paid holidays.[5]

Holiday pay practices vary considerably. Relatively strong unions which have succeeded in establishing satisfactory wage scales and which have won many other demands, are likely to press harder for paid holidays than weaker unions which are still striving to push up their basic wage rates. There is also some variation from state to state. Only a minority of unions have succeeded in negotiating eight or more paid holidays and fewer than half of all agreements in effect in 1958 provided for seven.[6] Some agreements also call for holiday pay when the holiday falls on a Saturday. This practice is more prevalent in manufacturing than nonmanufacturing firms.

In general, nonmanufacturing firms appear to be somewhat more liberal than manufacturing firms in granting "minor" payments for time not worked. This applies to payment on election day, when on jury duty, for keeping medical appointments, and similar payments for time not worked. On the other hand, factories appear to be more liberal in granting payment during lunch periods and wash time than nonmanufacturing establishments. Severance pay —a lump sum payment when a worker is separated from his job prior to retirement—is growing in importance. In 1953, however, fewer than half of the firms in the National Industrial Conference Board's sample made such payments.[7]

PREMIUM PAY PRACTICES

Before the Fair Labor Standards Act was passed in 1938, it was not typical for workers to be paid at premium rates for overtime. The law now specifies that workers are to be paid at the rate of time and one-half for all hours in excess of forty in *each* work week. But in some industries unions have negotiated standard work weeks of less than forty hours and premium pay in these industries begins as soon as the standard number of hours agreed upon has been reached. The law does not specify how the hours are to be spread throughout the week; it only indicates that each work week must stand alone—that there may be no averaging of hours worked over two or more weeks. Many agreements call for premium pay for work on Saturdays or Sundays—even if this falls within the forty-hour limit and some call for premium pay on the sixth or seventh

[5] Slichter, *et al., op. cit.*, p. 431.
[6] *Ibid.*, p. 432.
[7] *Fringe Benefit Packages* (1954), pp. 8–9.

day worked as such. It is also typical for workers to be paid at premium rates if they are required to work on holidays.

Approximately three-fourths of the manufacturing firms included in the National Industrial Conference Board's survey provide for shift differentials. Fewer than one-third of the nonmanufacturing firms in the sample follow this practice, however. Generally speaking, shift differentials are not large. There is a tendency for third-shift differentials to be slightly above those called for on second-shifts. Studies by the Bureau of Labor Statistics indicate that there has been a growing trend toward payment of shift differentials in manufacturing, but that this has been proceeding much more slowly in nonmanufacturing.

Shift practices vary widely from industry to industry and any summary statement would be quite unrepresentative. Industries, such as steel, which operate round the clock tend to have standard shifts with premium payments in terms of cents per hour. Other industries generally operate on a single-shift basis, although a second shift might be added if there is a sudden upsurge in production and some industries work only one shift, but vary hours as necessary in order to meet production schedules. It is only in those industries where second and third shifts are fairly common that premium pay for such work is important.

A substantial majority of agreements covering manufacturing firms and roughly half of those in nonmanufacturing establishments provide for call-in pay or reporting pay which means that workers are paid extra if they have to be called to the job rather than reporting at a scheduled time, or workers who report and find that there is no work for them that day are paid something for reporting.

HEALTH, WELFARE AND SECURITY BENEFITS

Pension plans are the best example of employee benefits with deferred payments which were given a stimulus by the wage freeze of World War II. There was also a rapid spread of various insurance programs during the war and this has continued since then. Insurance programs of various kinds were included in labor-management agreements as early as 1911, and many companies, with or without union agreements provided some form of pension before World War II. But the rapid spread of such programs started when employers took the initiative in setting up benefit plans during the war years, and when unions compensated for their inability to negotiate higher wages by seeking—and generally winning—pensions upon retirement.

Health, welfare and security programs are not as widespread as vacation and holiday pay but the evidence indicates that both pension and insurance programs have been growing in importance. By 1953, more than three-fourths of the manufacturing companies and 87 per cent of the nonmanufacturing firms in the National Industrial Conference Board sample granted pensions. Some pension plans are based on length of service and a worker's earnings while with the company; some call for amounts to supplement Social Security payments up to a specified maximum; others are entirely independent of Social Security payments.

Attitudes toward pensions vary widely. In some of the newer growth industries, where the average age of workers is quite low, unions have not pressed too hard for pension plans. But the reverse is true in industries where the average age of workers is relatively high. Some companies have been willing to negotiate fairly generous pension programs—and others to grant them unilaterally—recognizing that this is one way to cut down on labor turnover. Others have resisted them strongly, Slichter and his colleagues noted that "employers clearly took the initiative in establishing benefit plans . . . [but] were more reluctant to begin pension plans because of their long-term cost implications and because of large past-service obligations."[8]

Although the rapid spread of pension plans started more than twenty years ago, a relatively small proportion of workers are now drawing pensions under negotiated programs. As the ratio of pensioners to active workers increases, the cost of pension programs will go up and this will undoubtedly cause management to seek review of present programs. But as a growing number of workers covered by present plans approach retirement age, unions will no doubt be urged to expand and broaden pension programs. While pensions have not been a major bargaining issue in recent years, it is likely that there will be more interest in them—on both sides of the bargaining table—in the future. There are a number of questions which are not yet fully resolved. For example, private plans are generally not vested in the individual worker. Thus older workers will be reluctant to change jobs after they have built up a substantial stake in a pension with a given firm. Also, it has been

[8] Slichter, *et al.*, *op. cit.*, p. 402.

suggested that the spread of private pension plans may tend to discourage some firms from hiring older workers.[9]

Insurance

Provisions covering a wide variety of life, accident, sickness and hospitalization insurance show up most frequently in labor-management agreements. In general, a larger proportion of manufacturing than nonmanufacturing firms have such provisions but the differences are not large. Somewhat less widespread are provisions covering maternity and medical benefits. Paid sick leave, and supplements to workmen's compensation, are also found in a substantial number of labor-management agreements, with a larger proportion of nonmanufacturing than manufacturing agreements providing such benefits.

Bonuses

More than a third of the firms included in the National Industrial Conference Board's 1954 Fringe Benefit Study paid year-end and military-leave bonuses. A smaller proportion—5 to 6 per cent—granted long-service bonuses or subsidized worker savings programs. There is considerable diversity in bonus plans and it is difficult to generalize about them.

Some year-end bonuses depend upon the firms' earnings and are a form of profit sharing. About 10 per cent of the manufacturers and 13 per cent of the nonmanufacturing companies in the NICB sample had formal profit-sharing arrangements. The best known union-management profit sharing scheme, based on the Scanlon Plan, will be discussed in a later chapter. There are cases where profit-sharing plans have been instituted unilaterally by the company. Many of these were designed to keep unions out of the company, and in general this objective has been realized. Because of this, some union leaders take a dim view of profit sharing. They point out that what the company gives unilaterally the company can take away; and for rather obvious reasons, union leaders prefer to negotiate the worker's share of earnings.

THE COST OF EMPLOYEE BENEFITS

Employee benefits have become an important part of the "total package" negotiated by unions since the end of World War II and there is evidence that benefit costs as a per cent of payrolls have

[9] Robert Tilove, "Employee Benefit Plans," *A Decade of Industrial Relations Research, 1946–1956*, New York: Harper and Brothers, (1958), p. 161.

been rising. The most comprehensive studies of the cost of fringe benefits have been conducted by the U.S. Chamber of Commerce. The number of respondents to the Chamber's biennial surveys has varied but a sample of identical firms included in its surveys from 1947 to 1957 shows that benefit outlays as a per cent of payroll rose from 15 per cent to almost 24 per cent over this 10-year period. While allowance must be made for some sampling error, the relative magnitude and long-run trend of fringe benefit costs have not been seriously disputed.[10] Because of the growing importance of employee benefits, wage rates as such are no longer an accurate indicator of either labor costs or the returns to workers. It is necessary to consider both of these in terms of the total wage and fringe benefit package.

GUARANTEED ANNUAL WAGES AND SUPPLEMENTARY UNEMPLOYMENT PAYMENTS

For a brief time—in 1955 and 1956—there was a flurry of activity in contract negotiations involving supplementary unemployment compensation. Most stories in the press discussed the unions' demands for a "guaranteed annual wage" although that is not what unions were seeking at the time nor is it what some unions eventually negotiated. It should be noted that long before this some companies had adopted guaranteed annual wage plans on their own initiative; notable among these are the Procter and Gamble plan adopted in 1923, and the Hormel and Nunn-Bush plans started in the early 1930's.

Guaranteed Annual Wages

The notion of annual wage guarantees is not a new one, although only a very small minority of unions have negotiated such agreements. The first guaranteed annual wage was negotiated by the Wallpaper Craftsmen and the National Wallpaper Company in 1894. Between then and 1921, about 15 similar plans were negotiated in the wallpaper industry and between the Brewery Workers Union and various brewers in the Philadelphia area. The total number of workers covered was relatively small, however, and this new union demand made little headway or little impression outside the few firms involved. The issue was revived during the Great Depression, however, and a provision of the Fair Labor Standards Act (Sec. 7) exempted from overtime pay requirements employers who had a union agreement to provide employment on an annual

[10] See Slichter, *et al., op. cit.*, p. 425.

or semi-annual basis. Few firms, except some in highly seasonal industries, have taken advantage of this provision, however.

During the Second World War, the United Steel Workers tried to negotiate a guaranteed annual wage. The War Labor Board denied their request but recommended that the issue be studied. Such a study, referred to as the Latimer Report after its author, Murray W. Latimer, was subsequently made and published in 1947.[11] The Latimer Report viewed guaranteed wage plans favorably, and recommended that they be tied to our program of unemployment insurance. There was little response to this, however. A survey made by the Bureau of Labor Statistics in 1952 showed that fewer than one per cent of all collective bargaining agreements contained a wage guarantee provision.

Supplementary Unemployment Payments

Actually, not many unions were seeking the kind of guaranteed annual wages that have been established by some firms in seasonal industries such as shoe manufacturing and meat packing. In an industry with fairly predictable annual demand but with wide seasonal swings, it can be to the advantage of both workers and management to agree on a fixed number of weeks of employment per year. In the somewhat unlikely event that the company cannot provide this much employment it still agrees to pay the workers for a stated number of weeks. By carefully planning its production, the company can estimate its labor requirements quite closely. It is not faced with the inconvenience and added cost of laying off workers during slack seasons, and recalling (or trying to recall) them when business picks up seasonally. Given such circumstances a guaranteed annual wage works well. Most of the older guaranteed annual wage programs are in seasonal industries, but they have not spread to other industries, and with few exceptions union leaders have not tried to achieve the guaranteed annual wage. In non-seasonal industries unions have pressed for employer-financed supplementary unemployment compensation.

Under our Federal-State system of unemployment compensation, unemployment insurance benefits are determined by state legislators. During the early years of the unemployment insurance program, average benefits amounted to almost 45 per cent of the wages earned during the base periods used to compute benefit amounts. But average wages have gone up steadily, and while

[11] Office of War Mobilization and Reconversion, *Guaranteed Wages,* Washington, D.C.: U.S. Government Printing Office (1947).

there have been increases in unemployment benefits they have lagged far behind the increase in wages. By 1955, for example, average unemployment benefits amounted to about one-third of the average base period wage level.

Union leaders insisted that because benefits had lagged behind the rising wage level they were inadequate. Most favored liberalization of payments under the Federal-State unemployment insurance program but some went beyond this and began to press for supplemental unemployment payments by industry. This became one of the most widely-publicized bargaining issues of the mid-1950's.

Union spokesmen argued that employer-financed supplements to unemployment compensation would help stabilize the economy by maintaining purchasing power during periods of recession. Employers countered with the argument that by raising labor costs supplementary unemployment compensation would be self-defeating—it would simply contribute to more unemployment. Commenting on this issue early in 1955, Sumner H. Slichter pointed out that supplementary unemployment compensation in the automobile industry—which would increase the total benefits of unemployed workers to about two-thirds of their straight-time weekly earnings—would be roughly equivalent to a 5 per cent wage increase. And, he noted, there would have been relatively little alarm about a demand for a wage increase of this magnitude.[12]

Slichter did not favor the guaranteed annual wage, largely because he felt it would have injurious effects upon weak firms during recession periods. In his opinion a far more desirable objective—and one which he thought both unions and management should support—would be to increase unemployment insurance benefits. He suggested that unemployment benefits should amount to about 50 per cent of average wages. Slichter felt this objective would have a number of advantages over negotiated supplementary unemployment payment plans; among other things, it would pool risks without imposing any hardship upon weak firms. However demands for supplementary unemployment agreements persisted and in 1955 a number of plans were negotiated.

Supplementary unemployment compensation programs were negotiated in the automobile, the farm equipment, can manufacturing, and flat-glass industries in 1955. A similar plan covering workers in the merchant marine also went into effect that year and there

[12] Sumner H. Slichter, "Guaranteed Annual Wage—A Dubious Approach to a Desirable Objective," *Barron's* (April 11, 1955).

were scattered agreements with other firms in durable-goods manufacturing industries. The following year, supplementary unemployment compensation plans spread to the basic steel industry and to the "Big Four" rubber manufacturing firms. By the end of 1956, about two million workers were covered by such plans. The debate over supplementary unemployment compensation—usually under the misnomer of guaranteed annual wages—continued. Yet as Slichter and a few others had predicted, supplementary unemployment compensation did not spread widely after the initial plans had been accepted by some companies.

Two kinds of supplementary unemployment plans were negotiated: the *savings* plan and the *insurance* plan.[13] *Savings* plans were instituted in the glass industry. Under this type of plan each worker has a personal account to which the employer contributes. Payments by the employer to the individual accounts are considered as part of wages. If a worker is temporarily laid off because of slack business or illness he may draw on his account. Typically, a ceiling is imposed on the account and once the company's contribution has reached this amount the payments are stopped—or perhaps diverted to other fringe benefits such as vacation pay. Slichter has pointed out that "the savings plans are fundamentally a conventional economic device; it is simply a way by which all employees automatically save a part of a wage increase. And there is no new fundamental economic issue."[14]

The *insurance* plan of supplementary unemployment compensation was the one adopted by most unions and companies which negotiated such programs outside the flat-glass industry. Under the savings plan the employer contributions are considered as part of wages and employers are required to pay the unemployment insurance tax on these contributions. Under insurance plans, however, the employers' contributions are considered as part of welfare costs and are non-taxable. The plans which were finally negotiated in the automobile and other industries were somewhat more limited in coverage and scope than those which the unions had said they would initially seek. The first plan adopted was negotiated by the United Auto Workers and the Ford Motor Company and it set the pattern for others which followed. Under this plan, coverage is limited to workers who have a certain amount of seniority with the company. Supplementary compensation payments do not begin

[13] Sumner H. Slichter, "SUB Plans—Their Economic Impact," *Management Record*, National Industrial Conference Board (February 1956).
[14] *Ibid.*

until a one-week waiting period has elapsed. Payments are limited to a maximum of 26 weeks. More important, payments are also limited by the position of the trust fund and the number of "credits" held by each worker. The company contribution, which was set at five cents per hour worked by each employee subject to the plan, continued until the trust fund reached a stated maximum. Benefit payments were not made from this fund during the first year following the agreement.

There were several legal obstacles to be overcome before supplementary unemployment compensation plans became operative. First it was necessary to obtain state rulings on the integration of supplemental payments and unemployment insurance. Union leaders regard supplemental unemployment payments as deferred wages—something which the worker has earned and to which he has a right. But if they are "wages," as this word is used in most state unemployment laws, can unemployed workers legally draw unemployment benefits? Since most state laws relate benefits to the employment status of a worker, however, the majority of states which took action on this question permitted supplemental payments while an unemployed worker was drawing unemployment compensation. By the time the initial one-year waiting period had been reached, it was clear that this legal obstacle had been successfully hurdled.

It was also necessary for the Internal Revenue Service to decide whether supplementary unemployment benefits were "wages" for tax purposes. The Service ruled that the worker who received such benefits had to include them in his total income for tax purposes, and also that such payments were business costs deductible from company income taxes. Finally, the Wage and Hour and Public Contracts Divisions of the U.S. Department of Labor ruled that companies need not contribute to supplementary unemployment compensation trust funds on the basis of overtime earnings. Since such payments are to an irrevocable trust fund they are exempt under Sec. 7 (d) (4) of the Fair Labor Standards Act. With the legal obstacles out of the way fairly early in 1956, the plans were set to go into operation after the initial one-year waiting period.

There was still considerable concern about what these plans might do to the economy. Some argued that workers would prefer compensated idleness to employment, but as Slichter pointed out, the negotiated plans—based on 1955 unemployment compensation rates —provided total payments which amounted to only about two-thirds of average earnings. He doubted seriously that workers would be willing to forego one-third of their income for the sake of an extended "paid vacation." On the other hand since Slichter did not expect the plans to spread widely, he doubted that they would contribute much to economic stability.[15] Subsequent events have tended to bear out his prediction; the major plans were negotiated in 1955 and 1956, and few new plans have been negotiated since then.

WORK RULES

During the early days of collective bargaining, union demands were largely limited to wages, hours, and working conditions. The latter dealt principally with such matters as workers' safety and sanitation. Subsequently, as earlier sections in this chapter have indicated, the emphasis was shifted to employee benefits. This was one of the most important aspects of collective bargaining for a decade or more following the end of World War II. In recent years, however, there has been a further shift in emphasis in the negotiation of agreements. One of the most important matters in collective bargaining since about 1955 has been the broad issue of work rules, and labor-management disputes over work rules and working conditions have been far more numerous in recent years than over any other issue in collective bargaining. In 1960, for example, two-thirds of the man-days idle due to work stoppages resulted from disputes over working conditions. In the same year, disputes over union organization accounted for only 15 per cent while disputes over wages and hours accounted for 14 per cent.[16]

Work rules are one of the inevitable results of the system of "industrial jurisprudence" which has emerged under collective bargaining in the United States. Work rules cover a wide variety of matters such as work schedules, work speeds, and production methods. Rules have been evolved covering machine assignments, assembly-line speeds, time standards and work quotas under incentive systems, crew sizes, and various work methods; other rules govern the introduction of new machinery or other technological changes, the transfer of workers following technological change, and the impact of such changes on worker earnings.

Few issues in collective bargaining are as complex as those dealing with work rules and few have led to as much public misunder-

[15] *Ibid.*
[16] U.S. Department of Labor, Bureau of Labor Statistics, *Analysis of Work Stoppages, 1960,* Bulletin No. 1302 (September 1961), p. 6.

standing. Such issues as wage increases, holiday and vacation pay, and the hours to be worked before overtime pay is started are fairly straightforward. They can be understood by anyone, although there can be disagreement over them. But many are puzzled by the union position when union leaders insist on having something to say about work assignments, job transfers, retraining, and similar matters which many have long and loudly insisted are employer prerogatives. Does this mean that unions are trying "to take over the front office?" Is it an attempt on the part of union leaders to take an active part in the management of businesses? Union leaders insist that this is a misinterpretation. They readily acknowledge that work rules limit management's freedom to take unilateral action but work rules are not negotiated, they assert, to interfere with the management of the firm. The entire program of work rules, as Slichter put it, represents the unions' attempt to introduce civil rights into the work place.

Adding to the complexity of the work rules issue are the frequent charges that such rules lead to "make-work" or "featherbedding" practices. These have become emotionally-charged words. Their injection into debates over attempts by either party to make—or to change—work rules have usually led only to further confusion about this area of collective bargaining which has been growing in importance in recent years.

How did the practice of negotiating provisions dealing with work rules come into collective bargaining? And what has been the general attitude of unions and managements toward these rules? Perhaps better than anything else, work rules illustrate the evolutionary nature of the collective bargaining process. It is not at all likely that the early unions looked forward to a time when they would have an important voice in such matters as machine assignments, job transfers, the pace of assembly lines, and similar matters which are now frequently the subject of negotiations. Yet as the position of unions became more secure, their members became increasingly interested in job security.

The principle of seniority was introduced into collective bargaining fairly early and is now incorporated in most agreements. Some work rules are closely tied to the seniority system, and are designed to protect the security of workers when they become older and find it more difficult to obtain new employment if laid off. Other work rules were developed as protection against employer "speedups" and deal with such matters as machine assignments and the general pace of the job. Among the most important work rules are those designed to protect the worker against sudden and unexpected technological change. It is these—more than any others—which have led to the charges of featherbedding and make-work.

Many rules governing working conditions—such as those concerned with safety, sanitation, and such matters as heating and lighting—appear to make sense to all concerned. The worker gains added peace of mind if safety hazards are removed and the employer's liability is also diminished. A worker who can concentrate on his job in reasonable physical comfort is likely to be more productive than one who is too hot, too cold, cramped or otherwise uncomfortable. Good working conditions generally stimulate productivity, and both labor and management benefit from this. The big disagreement—and the one which the public appears to have the greatest difficulty in understanding—comes over rules which appear to have an effect upon output.

In popular discussions, no distinction is made between "make-work rules" and "featherbedding" but students of industrial relations often make such a distinction. One classification, developed by Morris Horowitz, is discussed here.[17] Under the general heading of "make-work" rules, Horowitz includes the following:

1. Regulating the number of men per machine or per crew. This would include work rules and practices which limit the number of workers on a single task or a specific machine.
2. Stand-by crews. This includes all rules which require the employment of workers regardless of need.
3. Requiring time-consuming methods of work or requiring that unnecessary work be done.
4. Limiting daily or weekly output, or the speed of work.
5. Requiring that work be performed by a specific craft or occupation. This category includes rules which specify in detail the work of each craft or occupation on the job and penalize employers for any error in assignment.

Under the general heading of "featherbedding" rules, Horowitz includes the following:

1. Requiring the payment of extra compensation for no extra work.
2. Requiring the payment of compensation for time spent not working, or for work not performed.

[17] Morris A. Horowitz, *Manpower Utilization in the Railroad Industry—An Analysis of Working Rules and Practices,* Boston: Northeastern University, Bureau of Business and Economic Research (1960), pp. 6–7.

3. Wage guarantees. This includes rules which guarantee a specific minimum amount of compensation per unit of time, regardless of the amount of work performed in that time.

There can be some overlapping—that is, some rules could fall in either category or partly in both. On the whole, however, work rules which impinge in some way upon output or productivity can be classified under one or the other of these main headings. It is important to emphasize that not all work rules are of the "make-work" or "featherbedding" varieties. There are rules which call for work-sharing during slack times, for example, and these must be clearly distinguished from make-work or featherbedding rules since they do not directly increase the cost to the employer. There are many other work rules which protect the security of workers without impinging on output and productivity, and there are some rules which deal with the installation of machinery—or more generally with worker adjustment to technological change—which may or may not have make-work effects. These are of particular interest since it is such work rules that have been at issue in a number of major labor-management disputes in recent years.

Work Rules and Technological Change

More than two decades ago, Sumner H. Slichter made a careful study of union policies toward technological change. His findings are still relevant today.[18] Slichter classified union policies toward technological change into three broad categories: (1) the policy of obstruction, (2) the policy of competition, and (3) the policy of control.

The policy of obstruction, Slichter points out, can be nothing more than a temporary expedient. By preventing the adoption of new processes in organized plants, unions can slow down the rate of technological change. However, if the industry is only partly organized non-union plants can adopt the innovations and increase their competitive advantage over unionized plants. Even in highly organized industries, obstruction can only delay—not halt—the installation of new machines or processes. Union leaders have long recognized that obstructionist tactics cannot succeed in the long run. Thus most unions, instead of obstructing technological change, have either tried to compete with it or to control it.

[18] Sumner H. Slichter, *Union Policies and Industrial Management,* Washington, D.C.: The Brookings Institution (1941), pp. 201–281. For a more recent discussion, which includes union acceptance and encouragement of technological change, see Slichter, Healy and Livernash, *Impact of Collective Bargaining,* pp. 342–371.

At times unions have tried to compete with technological change by liberalizing work rules. When the development of automatic machinery has threatened jobs, some unions have made concessions to employers such as permitting them to operate second or third shifts and accepting cuts in piece rates. This policy might be adopted if there have been substantial job displacements in an industry or if there is a surplus of workers in a particular craft or occupation. Rarely do union leaders believe that the policy of competition can halt technological change. On the other hand it can slow down the rate at which machines are introduced, and if concessions are made to employers it can increase the amount of employment on a temporary basis. The hope is that older workers can be kept on the job until they reach retirement age. Then, through gradual attrition, the number of workers in the craft or occupation can be reduced, and younger workers can adapt to the changes without fear of mass unemployment.

The policy of competition, like that of obstruction, is a short-run expedient. Most union leaders recognize this and in dealing with technological change they lean toward the policy of control. "In general terms, the policy of control simply means that the union seeks to make working conditions and wages on the jobs created by the new technique a matter of agreement between employers and the union."[19] Provisions dealing with the control of technological change vary widely from industry to industry and even among the companies within an industry. In general, unions try to see that workers displaced from a job through technological change are reassigned to other jobs without loss of earnings. Because there is always a great deal of turnover, with new workers being hired even in declining industries, it is hoped that displaced workers can be absorbed without interfering with the efficiency of the company and without loss to themselves. Slichter believed that the policy of control tended to "promote a more effective utilization of the nation's labor force by requiring employers to transfer and train older employees who otherwise would be laid off."[20] The policy of control has an advantage over other union tactics since it does not slow down the rate of technological change and thus does not interfere with output or improvements in productivity. But it does impose limits on the employer's freedom to lay off workers displaced by machines. The employer, who will gain from the in-

[19] Slichter, *Union Policies*, p. 241.
[20] *Ibid.*, p. 279.

creased productivity of the new method, is asked to help bear the cost of technological change. Moreover the union insists on its right to protect the job security of its members—particularly where this does not lead to interference with technological progress.

The issue of work rules will be considered further in the concluding section of this book. Before leaving the discussion for the present, however, it is worth repeating that all work rules do not impinge upon output or productivity. As Jack Stieber has pointed out, even "so-called make-work rules, featherbedding and other restrictive practices may, on investigation, turn out to have a sound basis. Like so many other issues which seem to be quite clear on the surface, there are usually two sides to the argument over specific make-work practices."[21] Stieber quotes, with approval, Slichter's attitude toward the complex issue of work rules:

> It is not always easy to determine when a union is "making work." There are some clear cases, such as those in which the union requires the work to be done twice, but the mere fact that the union limits the output of men, or controls the quantity of the work (with effects upon output), regulates the size of crew or the number of machines per man, or prohibits the use of labor-saving devices, does not in itself mean that the union is "making work." In such cases it is necessary to apply a rule of reason and to determine whether the limits are unreasonable. Opinions as to what is reasonable are bound to differ, but failure to apply a rule of reason would be to accept the employers' requirements, no matter how harsh and extreme, as the proper standard.[22]

Specific practices of flagrant featherbedding are often spotlighted in popular discussion of the work-rules issue. No objective student would deny that there are instances where work practices have led to increases in labor costs or to restrictions of output. The extent of actual "make-work" or "featherbedding" practices has undoubtedly been exaggerated, however. As Slichter showed more than two decades ago, unions do not as a general rule try to obstruct technological change or to impose uneconomic work rules on employers. There are exceptions to this but they should be recognized as exceptions rather than the general rule. Finally, it should be noted that unions have often encouraged employers to make technological changes when the competitive position of a plant or even of an entire industry has been threatened.[23]

[21] Jack Stieber, "Non-wage aspects of Collective Bargaining," *Business Topics*, Graduate School of Business Administration, Michigan State University (Spring 1960), p. 31.
[22] Slichter, *op. cit.*, pp. 165–166.
[23] Slichter, Healy and Livernash, *op. cit.*, pp. 355–361.

REFERENCES

BOOKS

Chamberlain, Neil W., *Labor,* New York: McGraw-Hill Book Company, Inc. (1958).

Gitlow, Abraham L., *Labor Economics and Industrial Relations,* Homewood, Illinois: Richard D. Irwin, Inc. (1957).

Horowitz, Morris A., *Manpower Utilization in the Railroad Industry—An Analysis of Working Rules and Practices,* Boston: Northeastern University, Bureau of Business and Economic Research (1960).

National Industrial Conference Board, *Fringe Benefit Packages,* Studies in Personnel Policies, No. 143 (1954).

Slichter, Sumner H., *Union Policies and Industrial Management,* Washington, D.C.: The Brookings Institution (1941).

———, ——— —, James J. Healy and Robert Livernash, *The Impact of Collective Bargaining on Management,* Washington, D.C.: The Brookings Institution (1960).

ARTICLES

Simler, Norman J., "The Economics of Featherbedding," *Industrial and Labor Relations Review,* Vol. 16 (October 1962) pp. 111–121.

Slichter, Sumner H., "Guaranteed Annual Wage—A Dubious Approach to a Desirable Objective," *Barron's* (April 11, 1955).

———, ——— —, "SUB Plans—Their Economic Impact," *Management Record,* National Industrial Conference Board (February 1956).

Stieber, Jack, "Non-Wage Aspects of Collective Bargaining," *Business Topics,* Graduate School of Business Administration, Michigan State University, (September 1960).

Thole, Henry C., and Charles C. Gibbons, *The Guaranteed Annual Wage in Business Stabilization,* Kalamazoo, Michigan: The W. E. Upjohn Institute for Community Research (June 1955).

U.S. Department of Labor, Bureau of Employment Security, *Background Information on Impact of Automation and Technological Change on Employment and Unemployment,* Washington, D.C.: (September 1961).

U.S. Department of Labor, Bureau of Labor Statistics, *Analysis of Work Stoppages in 1960,* Washington, D.C.: Bulletin No. 1302 (September 1961).

Chapter 15 The Prevention or Settlement of Disputes

Most labor-management agreements—perhaps 90 per cent or more—are negotiated quietly and peacefully. But labor peace does not make headlines; labor-management warfare does. The labor disputes with which most of us are familiar are those which occur when negotiations break down and a strike results. But thousands of disputes, most of a minor nature, are settled under the terms of existing agreements. The general public does not know when such disputes occur or how they are resolved. But the day-to-day administration of labor-management agreements is one of the most important, although little-known, aspects of collective bargaining. It is important to distinguish between the two major types of labor disputes: (1) those which occur during the lifetime of an agreement, and (2) those which take place when the negotiation of a new agreement breaks down.

Two other species of disputes should be mentioned. The first is the unauthorized or "wildcat" strike which takes place during the life of an agreement. Such strikes are usually spontaneous eruptions and they are generally settled quite promptly. Responsible union leaders do not condone wildcat strikes. And unions in general are anxious to avoid them since this is scarcely a good form of public relations. The second kind of dispute—the jurisdictional dispute—involves disagreement between two unions, neither of which may have a specific grievance against the employer. Such disputes—to which the employer is an unwilling third party—are frowned upon by many union leaders. The AFL-CIO, for example, has tried to minimize jurisdictional disputes and a number of unions have taken steps for the peaceful settlement of jurisdictional rivalry. We will return to the issue of jurisdictional disputes later in this chapter. But for the present we will concentrate on the major types of disputes, the methods that have been developed to avert disputes, and the techniques for the settlement of disputes if they cannot be averted. Sometimes, we will see, disputes can be settled only by a show of force.

THE GRIEVANCE PROCEDURE[1]

One of the most important parts of the labor-management agreement is the grievance procedure. This is the safety valve built into the agreement to prevent every minor difference of opinion from mushrooming into a major dispute. Even the most carefully worked-out agreement cannot provide for every conceivable contingency. Some grievances are of a personal nature—they do not relate to the agreement as such, but if labor and management are to work together, and to live together, there must be a method for settling the many day-to-day disputes that are bound to occur. It was not always so. In the early days of collective bargaining strikes occasionally erupted without warning, and it was because of this that grievance procedures were developed as collective bargaining matured.

The earliest grievance procedures were evidently negotiated by the International Typographical Union and various publishers with which it dealt. Perhaps the best known early grievance machinery was that developed as part of the Star Island Agreement of 1903 in the flint glass industry. The steps for the settlement of grievances in this agreement closely parallel those which are commonly followed today.[2] Another famous early grievance arrangement resulted from a spontaneous walkout which took place in the Hart, Schaffner and Marx garment shops in 1911. Discussing this strike, Joseph Schaffner, the head of the firm, pointed out that just a few days before the walkout he had commented to a friend on the satisfactory state of his industrial relations. When the workers walked out management's original reaction was one of bewilderment. The employers could not find out what was wrong. Finally, they discovered there was no single cause; the walkout had resulted from the accumulation of a great many grievances some of which, taken alone, would have been quite minor. The strike was settled and steps were taken to establish a grievance system to avoid a repetition in the future. Gradually, out of these and other experiences,

[1] This section draws heavily upon John A. Lapp, *How to Handle Labor Grievances*, New York: National Foreman's Institute, Inc. (1945).
[2] Lapp, *ibid.*, pp. 15–16.

grievance procedures were negotiated in a growing number of agreements. Today, a labor-management agreement without a grievance procedure is the exception and a very rare exception at that.

Types of Grievances

A catalogue of the thousands of grievances which are settled every year would be an imposing document. But most grievances may be classified under three main headings. These are:

1. Grievances arising from the interpretation of the meaning of words and phrases in labor-management agreements.
2. Grievances resulting from the application of the provisions of agreements in individual cases, including discipline and discharge cases.
3. Grievances affecting individuals or groups of workers which arise out of the day-to-day work environment, and not from causes covered by the labor-management agreement.[3]

The number of grievances processed every year runs into the thousands. But only a small proportion of serious cases become major issues. Many grievances arise out of purely personal relationships. If a foreman comes to work with a chip on his shoulder he will be lucky to get through the day without offending some of the workers under his direction. The same is true of individual workers. But all grievances—real or imagined—can impair a sound labor-management relationship unless promptly settled.

Other grievances result from job assignments, changes in rates of pay, discipline or discharge, and a wide variety of other matters covered by the agreement. If a worker feels that he has not been treated justly he is free to file a grievance which typically goes through the steps described in the following paragraphs. Also, disputes occasionally arise over the meaning of the language in an agreement. In this case, the language in question will usually be changed when a new agreement is negotiated, but there must be some method of settling differences in interpretation during the life of an existing agreement.

Types of Grievance Procedures

The following steps are typical of a wide variety of grievance arrangements:

STEPS

1. Shop steward and foreman,
2. Chief steward and personnel officer,

[3] *Ibid.*, p. 28.

3. Grievance committee,
4. Business agent and general manager,
5. Arbitration.

A worker with a grievance first goes to his shop steward. The latter will listen to the grievance and decide whether it is bona fide or an unwarranted gripe. If he feels that the grievance has merit he fills out a grievance form, carefully noting the time and the place and all other relevant facts. The shop steward then goes to the foreman in charge of the aggrieved worker—usually asking the worker to accompany him. Possibly the shop steward and the foreman can settle the grievance on the spot. Perhaps nothing more is called for than an apology or an indication that there has been a simple misunderstanding. It is likely that under such circumstances the grievance form will be destroyed and not become a matter of record.

But if the grievance cannot be settled at this stage it will be turned over to the grievance committee which meets at stated intervals. The committee, which ordinarily is made up of an equal number of representatives of the union and management, reviews all grievances before it at each of its meetings. Some they will agree to settle while others may result in a deadlock. These grievances are then turned over to the union's business agent and the general manager, with the stipulation that they be settled within a stated time. Some of the grievances which cannot be settled by the committee will be disposed of by the business agent—who represents the national union—and the general manager. Others must go to arbitration.

Large companies which deal with large local unions will often have so many grievances that a full-time umpire is retained by the two parties to settle those matters which cannot be handled by the first four steps of the grievance machinery. There are cases where the work load is so heavy that two or more umpires must be retained. In practically all cases, the parties will agree in their contract to abide by the decision of the umpire or arbitrator. An essential part of a successful grievance machinery is some provision for final and binding settlement.

The machinery described above is typical of that found in many labor-management agreements. There are some variations. In a few cases, for example, grievances go directly from the foreman to a shop or plant grievance committee; in other cases, where a single union deals with an association of employers, a joint committee will be established to investigate all grievances. Any which cannot be settled will be sent to an impartial umpire or a tripartite board with an impartial chairman.

Ground Rules for the Settlement of Grievances

Most large unions provide their shop stewards with manuals. Among other things, these handbooks tell the stewards how to handle grievances. Typical is the *Shop Steward's Manual* issued by the International Association of Machinists.[4] The IAM *Manual* describes the grievance procedure, quoting the relevant passages from some of its agreements. It then suggests ways by which the shop steward should go about enforcing these contract provisions. Among the "tips on relations with management" which the manual contains are the following: (1) abide by contract rules, (2) make sure that it is a just grievance, (3) get all the facts, (4) write it down, and (5) use a positive, friendly approach.

The shop steward is also exhorted to be a good listener and to disagree amiably; to try to settle at the first stage, to avoid empty threats, and to stick to the facts. If the grievance is settled successfully he is told not to gloat or brag about his victories over management. Finally, he is urged to get to the roots of the problems from which grievances grow.

The Role of the Shop Steward and the Foreman

A workable labor-management agreement will be written in language which will minimize the number of disputes over interpretation, but the best contract in the world will not minimize grievances unless the foremen and shop stewards are understanding. This is the point of immediate contact between union and management. Good foremen and able shop stewards will, of course, protect the rights of management and workers. But they can also work together to settle minor grievances satisfactorily and thus avoid the time consuming—and sometimes costly—process of carrying every grievance all the way to the final step of the procedure.

An obstreperous foreman, or a self-seeking shop steward, can do much to keep labor-management relations in a state of constant turmoil. Usually this will not last. Someone higher up the ladder —in the company, the union, or both—will usually find out what is behind a steady flow of grievances. But until this is done, and appropriate steps taken to correct the matter, the work atmosphere

[4] Research Department, International Association of Machinists, *Shop Steward's Manual,* Washington, D.C. (September 1948).

can be charged with tension, and at times serious disputes can erupt. But the shop steward and foreman must work within the broader framework of union and management policies, and these too at times can magnify rather than minimize the problem of grievance settlement.

A company which decides to adopt a tough attitude toward the union might insist that every grievance—however slight—go all the way to arbitration. In such cases labor-management relations will be constantly strained, and union and management representatives will maintain a constant air of hostility. Nothing short of a change at the top—replacement of the union business agent or international representative, or the appointment of a new personnel officer—can change such an environment. But there have been cases where such changes have led to a re-evaluation of the entire grievance procedure. Companies have found that they were processing grievances, perhaps at the cost of hundreds of dollars, involving a fraction of this amount. A careful screening of grievances has shown that enormous savings result if only those involving some new principle are processed.

If there is to be steady progress toward minimizing grievances, both unions and management must keep careful records of all grievances and their disposition. If each grievance is classified, and if the entire grievance picture is reviewed at periodic intervals, each side can notice any trends which are developing. If impartial umpires make a majority of awards to the union or to management over some specific issue, the parties might want to consider carefully before sending the next grievance all the way through the machinery. If the two parties are interested in working out and maintaining the best day-to-day relations of which they are capable they will carefully study the pattern of grievances and the pattern of settlements. As with other phases of collective bargaining, the development of a successful grievance machinery—satisfactory to both parties—is generally an evolutionary process.

ARBITRATION

There are two general types of arbitration. The first—and by far the most important—is *grievance arbitration*. Grievance arbitration is carried on under an existing agreement. In almost all cases, the decision of the arbitrator is final and binding although in reaching his decision the arbitrator is limited by his interpretation of the language of the agreement. He must decide the grievance within this framework; he is not permitted to bring in principles or facts other than those introduced by the parties. He can, however, refer to earlier decisions in similar cases. As in the common law, precedent plays an important part in grievance arbitration.

The second kind of arbitration which is used quite infrequently is called *contract arbitration*. There are some cases when the negotiation of a new agreement reaches a deadlock. Perhaps the two parties can agree on most of the provisions of the new agreement, but neither party is willing to budge on one or a few issues. In such cases—although it must be repeated that this is fairly rare—an arbitrator will be called in to render a decision on the disputed issues. We will consider grievance arbitration first and then turn to a brief discussion of contract arbitration.

Types of Arbitration Arrangements

Some labor-management agreements call for a permanent arbitrator or impartial umpire. The two parties must agree on the arbitrator before the agreement is signed and it is typical for the agreement to specify that all grievances decided by the arbitrator will be final and binding. Whatever the decision, each party agrees to abide by it. This is usually accompanied by a no strike and no lockout pledge.

Other agreements provide for *ad hoc* arbitrators. The agreement might specify that an arbitrator will be called in to handle each case that arises, or it might call for the selection of an arbitrator after a certain number of cases have accumulated. To obtain arbitrators the parties might turn to the American Arbitration Association which keeps a list of approved arbitrators and can notify the disputants of arbitrators available in a specific area. In other cases the parties will turn to universities, to priests or other clergymen to decide their cases. The major qualification of an arbitrator—however he is selected—is that he must be impartial.

A third variation is the three-man arbitration board. Such boards are typically made up of a union representative, a management representative, and an impartial member. In some cases only the impartial member, who serves as chairman, has a vote; in other cases all three members vote although the deciding vote is almost invariably cast by the impartial member. As with single arbitrators, tripartite boards may be either permanent, i.e. for the life of an agreement, or they may be selected on an *ad hoc* basis.

One advantage of the impartial umpire, or permanent arbitrator, is that the umpire becomes well acquainted with the company and the union whose disputes he must settle. Many grievances involve technical matters, such as machine assignments, job transfers, the determination of piece rates or incentive pay, and similar matters of a technical nature. If the arbitrator is familiar with the conditions in the company and if he is familiar with earlier cases which might serve as precedents, he might be able to expedite matters and render decisions in a fairly short time. One disadvantage of permanent arrangements is that the arbitrator might attempt to settle many cases by "splitting down the middle." Most agreements which call for permanent umpires specify that either party can terminate the arbitrator's appointment at its discretion. If too many cases go to one party or the other, the "permanent" arbitrator's appointment might be terminated rather quickly.[5]

In some cases the parties might feel that an *ad hoc* arbitrator will render more impartial decisions. It is likely that if an arbitrator is called in to settle a single case he will not be particularly concerned about the distribution of prior decisions. But the selection of an *ad hoc* arbitrator can be a time-consuming process. The parties might find it difficult to agree on a candidate who is mutually acceptable. Meanwhile, the grievance remains unsettled until the arbitrator is selected, hearing dates are arranged, the case is heard, and the decision is rendered. *Ad hoc* arbitrators—often university professors—have other duties, and the hearings and other details of arbitrations might have to await their pleasure.

There are advantages and disadvantages to both permanent and *ad hoc* arrangements, and the parties can only decide on the basis of experience which arrangement will work best in each case. Generally, permanent arbitrators are found in agreements involving fairly large companies and large unions where the accumulation of grievances would make it impracticable for the two parties to select *ad hoc* arbitrators for each case.

Type of Arbitrators

In addition to his impartiality, a successful arbitrator must be a judicious person. He must have a good working knowledge of labor law, he must know something about economics, and he must have a good background in the field of industrial relations. It is also helpful if the arbitrator is familiar with the industry or industries

[5] See, for example, Harold W. Davey, *Contemporary Collective Bargaining*, Englewood Cliffs, N.J.: Prentice-Hall, Inc. (second edition, 1959), p. 139n.

in which he works. No effort will be made to develop a detailed classification of various kinds of arbitrators, but one useful distinction might be drawn. There are some arbitrators who are willing to render judgment on every case that is brought to them. Such arbitrators feel that their expert knowledge permits them to render sounder decisions than could be reached by the two parties through continued negotiations. Other arbitrators, however, adopt a different view. They feel that it might be relatively easy to render an award in many cases. But at the same time they feel that the two parties will be able to live and work together in greater harmony if they can settle disputed issues themselves. Such arbitrators will decide particularly difficult cases. However, if they feel that more will be gained by refusing to make an award they will remand the case to the two parties. Representatives of the union and management will then try to hammer out an agreement knowing that if they fail a second time the case can be returned to the arbitrator.

In some situations arbitration is a continuation of the day-to-day collective bargaining process. There are other cases, however, where arbitration is clearly a judicial process. About the only general statement that can be made about arbitration is that it is essentially a flexible process which tends to adapt to changing labor-management relationships.[6]

Arbitration is not something that is particularly new in collective bargaining. It has been going on for several decades. But as R. W. Fleming has recently put it: "Arbitration is still in its swaddling clothes."[7] Arbitration procedures have remained much more flexible than courtroom procedures. As Fleming has noted: "An important characteristic of arbitration is its flexibility in resolving practical problems. Hopefully, this characteristic will assure application of traditional standards of fairness without the imposition of excessive legalisms adopted wholesale from courtroom procedures . . ."[8] Most impartial students of the collective bargaining process would agree with these sentiments.

A successful grievance procedure will include a series of deadlines for the handling of individual cases. Usually, a time is specified for each step in the process. The advantages of a quick settlement are evident. Once a decision is reached the person who filed the griev-

[6] See John T. Dunlop and James J. Healy, *Collective Bargaining,* Homewood, Illinois: Richard D. Irwin, Inc. (revised edition, 1953), p. 84.
[7] R. W. Fleming, "Some Problems of Due Process and Fair Procedure in Labor Arbitration," *Stanford Law Review,* Col. 13, No. 2 (March 1961), p. 251.
[8] *Ibid.*

ance must accept it. If there are continued delays the worker with the grievance is likely to feel that he is being by-passed, and might feel resentful toward both the company and the union. Much the same is true of arbitration. The advantages of fairly prompt decisions are widely recognized. As Arthur Ross has pointed out, however, there has been a tendency for the arbitration process to become more time-consuming. He found that over a ten-year period ending in 1956, the average time between the filing of grievances and arbitration awards increased by more than one-half, and had reached more than two hundred days. This he attributes to increasingly elaborate and formal arbitration procedures, delays in the selection of *ad hoc* arbitrators, the overloaded dockets of permanent umpires, and that he considers to be a tendency toward too much arbitration.[9] Ross feels that in many cases there has been "a dangerous trend toward reliance on technicality, reminiscent of the old system of strict pleadings under the common law . . ."[10] In his view, there has been a tendency for arbitration to lose some of its flexibility which, as noted earlier, most students of industrial relations consider to be one of the virtues of the arbitration process.

Contract Arbitration

Contract arbitration is much less widespread than grievance arbitration. It is one thing for the two parties to agree to have an outsider settle differences of interpretation of *existing* labor-management agreements. It is quite another for them to bring in a disinterested party to break a deadlock during negotiations. There are times, however, when the two parties can agree on most of the provisions being negotiated, but perhaps are deadlocked on one or two. Occasionally, under such circumstances, an arbitrator or an arbitration board might be agreed upon, and the parties will agree to abide by his decision. It must be emphasized that arbitration of this kind is fairly rare, and probably is on the decline.

Why do labor and managements object to the arbitration of part of a new agreement when most successful relationships make extensive use of grievance arbitration? In part, the answer is that such arbitration has not been notably successful in the past. Many union leaders believe that arbitration boards are likely to be biased against the union or its position. And employers object to arbitration of wage matters, for example, because in their view the arbitrators are likely to "split the difference" so that the union is bound to

[9] Arthur M. Ross, "The Well-Aged Arbitration Case," *Industrial and Labor Relations Review*, Vol. 11, No. 2 (January 1958), pp. 262–268.
[10] *Ibid.*, p. 268.

gain something while the employer is bound to lose. Also, some employers oppose such arbitration because they believe it is an improper delegation of managerial responsibility to someone outside the company.[11] Since, in general, neither labor nor managements are favorably inclined toward contract arbitration, it is not surprising that few deadlocks are settled in this way. If necessary, the parties believe, the deadlocks can be broken by a show of force—by a strike.

Compulsory Arbitration

Practically every time there is a major labor dispute the issue of compulsory arbitration is raised. Editorial writers and others will insist that regardless of how the two parties feel about it the public must be protected against the disruption of economic activity. A few legislators also become exacerbated during major labor disputes and revive the issue of compulsory arbitration. But fortunately for the state of industrial relations in our society, cooler heads have prevailed. We have had one experience with compulsory arbitration which illustrates some of the dangers of this approach.

In 1920, the Kansas Legislature enacted the Kansas Industrial Court Act. This law set up a Court of Industrial Relations which had the authority to investigate labor-management disputes in specified industries, "and, after proper hearing *and trial,* to issue orders compelling adherence to its findings."[12] Both strikes and lockouts were prohibited by law in the industries affected by this act.

A case could be initiated by either party under the Kansas Act, or the court could intervene on its own initiative. Thus the Court of Industrial Relations had greater power than our civil courts which must wait until someone sets a suit in motion. Either party could appeal the findings of the court—as in the case of civil suits—with decisions going up to the Kansas Supreme Court. During its brief life the Court of Industrial Relations handled a number of labor disputes but there was little satisfaction with its decisions. The Act was declared to be unconstitutional, and in conflict with the Fourteenth Amendment, by the United States Supreme Court in *The Charles Wolfe Packing Company vs. The Court of Industrial Relations* in 1923. Among other things, the Supreme Court noted that the Kansas Act "curtails the right of the employer, on the one hand, and of the employee, on the other, to contract about his

[11] Neil W. Chamberlain, *Collective Bargaining,* New York: McGraw-Hill Book Company, Inc. (1951), p. 94.

[12] John A. Lapp, *Labor Arbitration,* New York: National Foremen's Institute, Inc. (1946), p. 10, italics added.

affairs. This is part of the liberty of the individual protected by the guaranty of the due process clause of the Fourteenth Amendment."[13] After this experience, no other state attempted to provide for compulsory arbitration of labor-management disputes.

One objection to compulsory arbitration, which has been voiced by both labor and management, is that there is no assurance that an industrial court will be impartial in judging labor disputes. Few doubt that our civil courts are impartial in handling most decisions which come before them. Such decisions, however, generally involve relatively private matters while a major labor-management dispute becomes a public matter. Many persons tend to react emotionally to labor-management disputes and this could apply to the judges of an industrial court as well as to laymen. Another objection is that the members of an industrial court will lack the expertise needed to rule fairly on a wide range of labor-management disputes involving many occupations and industries. Grievance arbitration works well because the arbitrators selected jointly by both parties must know something about the industry and the occupations involved. But the members of an industrial court would have to be experts on *all* industries and occupations. It would be difficult to find anyone with these qualifications. Finally, to be successful, an industrial court would have to have greater powers than the civil court. It would have to be able to initiate action and not wait for one or the other parties to submit their dispute. There is general reluctance to grant a court such sweeping power and authority. Labor unions have solidly opposed any repetition of the Kansas experiment and similar opposition has been expressed by the National Association of Manufacturers and the United States Chamber of Commerce.[14] Labor and management agree, however, that where a third party can help in breaking a deadlock this is desirable as long as the two parties remain completely free to seek or not to seek assistance.

MEDIATION AND CONCILIATION

Strictly speaking, conciliation means an effort by a third party to keep negotiations going between labor and management in the face of an impending breakdown whereas mediation implies more active participation in the bargaining process. But this distinction has broken down. Conciliation is now defined as an "attempt by a third party to help in the settlement of disputes between employers

[13] Cited by Lapp, *ibid.*, p. 12.
[14] *Ibid.*, pp. 13–14.

and employees through interpretation, suggestion, and advice. In practice, conciliation is synonymous with mediation."[15]

There is a certain amount of grievance mediation in the United States, some of a formal and some of an informal character. There are cases where an arbitrator attempts to mediate a dispute under an existing agreement rather than issuing an award. This is most likely to occur in a relationship which uses a permanent umpire. Typically, however, while such mediation may precede arbitration it does not preclude the latter.[16] Generally, those who support grievance mediation are of the opinion that voluntary agreement is superior to an enforced award. This undoubtedly is the major argument in favor of grievance mediation. As noted in our earlier discussion of grievance arbitration, one type of arbitrator tries to remand as many cases as possible to the two parties on the assumption that they will be able to live and work together better if they work out their own differences. Such arbitrators would subscribe to the notion that they should attempt to mediate whenever possible.

There is one difficulty involved in grievance mediation, however. If a permanent umpire has attempted to mediate a dispute and fails he should not then arbitrate the same issue. There is an old maxim in arbitration circles that: "An arbitrator may mediate but a mediator should never arbitrate." Thus if the umpire has at one point served as a mediator he should step aside if the issue must go on to arbitration. The reasoning behind this is that in his efforts to mediate a difference of opinion the arbitrator has undoubtedly found some middle ground on which he thinks agreement can be reached. This is likely to affect his decision as an arbitrator.

Compared with arbitration grievance mediation has certain advantages in that it can save both time and money as well as lead to fundamental improvement in the long-run relationship between the two parties. On the other hand, it has been pointed out that unsuccessful grievance mediation lengthens the time between the filing of a grievance and its ultimate disposition through arbitration. Evidently labor and managements have not been greatly impressed by the advantages of pre-arbitration grievance mediation since relatively few agreements contain provisions calling for this procedure.[17]

[15] U.S. Department of Labor, Bureau of Labor Statistics, *Glossary of Current Industrial Relations Terms,* Washington (May 1960), p. 5.
[16] See William H. McPherson, "Grievance Mediation Under Collective Bargaining," *Industrial and Labor Relations Review,* Vol. 9, No. 2 (January 1956), p. 201.
[17] *Ibid.,* p. 212.

Mediation and conciliation are the most important means of settling differences of opinion on *new* agreements short of a show of economic strength. At times, collective bargaining is accompanied by a great deal of bluster and much publicity. Both labor and management may publicly take adamant positions, and indicate that they will *never* give in unless the other side makes certain concessions. Having adopted this posture it is not easy to back down. But an outsider can then enter the picture—much like the *deus ex machina* in an old Greek drama—and resolve the disputed issue short of a strike.

There is no standard pattern of operations in mediation and conciliation. Each mediator must develop his own techniques. In general, however, the process works somewhat as follows. Since the two parties have reached a deadlock in face-to-face meetings, the first step is generally to separate them. The mediator then sits down with one party and listens to all of its arguments; he weighs and evaluates this position, then repeats the process with the other party. Perhaps at this stage he is able to see areas of agreement which the two parties have overlooked in the heat of negotiations. Then begins a process of going back and fourth from one party to the other. He can perhaps encourage a modest amount of "horse trading"—elicit some concessions from both sides. If successful, he will slowly broaden areas of agreement and at the same time narrow the areas of disagreement. Perhaps at some point he is able to say to each of the parties that they no longer have an issue at dispute. If he can convince them of this they can be brought together and settlement can be reached—usually with an appropriate amount of fanfare and publicity.

The mediator must remain completely detached throughout the proceedings. He must be a good listener; he must avoid legalism, and above all he must be sincerely interested in the peaceful settlement of the dispute. At the same time a good mediator will also know when his efforts are hopeless; at this point he will bow out of the argument gracefully and let the two parties slug it out on their own terms.

Among other things, the Taft-Hartley Act provided for a Federal Mediation and Conciliation Service. If a dispute, involving interstate commerce, should threaten to cause a substantial interruption in business activity the Service may enter the dispute by making available its facilities of conciliation, mediation, and voluntary arbitration. The Service has no power to compel settlement. But in certain types of disputes, the parties have a statutory obligation to "participate fully and promptly in such meetings as may be undertaken by the Service under this Act for the purpose of aiding in the settlement of a dispute." Thus the Federal Mediation and Conciliation Service is involved in all major disputes, although it must be emphasized that it has no power to compel settlement. The Service avoids involvement in minor disputes or in grievance disputes. It will supply a panel of qualified arbitrators upon request from which the parties can make a selection. In general, however, the Federal Mediation and Conciliation Service was set up to prevent the breakdown of collective bargaining over *new* agreements.

It is difficult to measure the effectiveness of mediation and conciliation. There are outstanding cases in which it is known that mediation has averted a strike and led to a settlement acceptable to both parties. It is impossible to say whether or not such agreement would have been reached without the aid of the mediator. Most students of labor-management relations would undoubtedly agree that the mediator plays an important part in collective bargaining, and that many deadlocks would result in a strike without the intervention of an effective mediator. As Arthur S. Meyer, himself an exceptionally successful mediator, put it: "Labor disputes are exhausting processes and the mediator, like the participants, will think of nothing so much as of a settlement, any settlement, for according to the conventions of the game, each settlement is a victory and there is little to choose between one and the other. Catalysis is the guiding principle and peace the constant objective."[18] But despite the best efforts of the two parties—and of mediators—agreement cannot always be reached. When this happens, any remaining differences of opinion are settled by economic force—by a strike.

"CONTINUOUS" COLLECTIVE BARGAINING

In general, collective bargaining has become a fairly formal procedure in the United States. Each party prepares its case prior to contract negotiations and there is little direct communication between the parties until they meet at the bargaining table. Agreement is reached, if possible, without the intervention of a third party. If the parties become deadlocked a mediator or conciliator might enter the picture in an effort to avert a dispute. When

[18] Arthur S. Meyer, "Function of the Mediator in Collective Bargaining," *Industrial and Labor Relations Review*, Vol. 13, No. 2 (January 1960), p. 165.

negotiations break down the parties resort to a test of economic strength to force an eventual agreement. Until recently, collective bargaining has been a discrete process. Bargaining over each new agreement has been viewed as a separate conflict to be resolved by negotiations or a strike.

There has been a change in this pattern in recent years, however, in a number of industries faced with difficult bargaining situations. Unions and management in these industries have started to experiment with what can be called *continuous collective bargaining*. Essentially, this consists of the appointment of committees to carry on discussions between formal bargaining sessions. These committees usually represent only the unions and managements involved and some are not empowered to make recommendations. Others, however, provide for third-party participation—what Hildebrand has called the use of "informed neutrals" to engage in "voluntary private fact-finding with recommendations."[19]

Following the 116-day steel strike of 1959, the United Steelworkers of America and the major steel companies established a Human Relations Committee in an effort to avoid a repetition of this long and costly dispute. The 1963 negotiations resulted in a contract which both sides praised as "the best ever." And the Human Relations Committee was given a great deal of credit for the agreement.[20] The Human Relations Committee does not include informed neutrals. The objective is to reach agreement on recommendations prior to contract expirations. Similar committees have been set up in the auto and rubber industries. Unlike the HRC, however, these committees are for discussion purposes only—they are not expected to make recommendations.

A different approach has been followed by the Kaiser Steel—United Steelworkers study committee. This committee includes expert neutrals and it has the power to make recommendations. It was this committee which worked out the "Kaiser formula" for the division of gains from increasing productivity between workers and the company.[21] Another example of a tripartite study committee is the one established by the Armour agreement of 1959 for the purpose of studying the effects of automation and the

[19] George H. Hildebrand, *The Use of Informed Neutrals in Difficult Bargaining Situations,* Ithaca, New York: New York State School of Industrial and Labor Relations at Cornell (October 1961), pp. 6–14.
[20] "Steel Without Strikes," *Business Week* (June 29, 1963), pp. 25–26. See also, *Business Week* (November 3, 1962), pp. 51–52.
[21] "Splitting Costs Cuts," *Business Week* (December 22, 1962), p. 20.

liquidation of obsolete plants. It was also expected to recommend a program which would minimize the impact of these changes on displaced workers.[22]

It is much too early to assess the long-run consequences of these new developments in collective bargaining. Where it has been tried, "continuous" collective bargaining has produced some impressive results. The problems faced by labor and management in industries which have experienced rapid technological change and heightened competitive pressures do not lend themselves to easy solutions through crisis bargaining under deadline conditions. Patient examination of the issues leading to joint agreement on major changes in advance of contract expirations has worked well in a few cases. Further successes of study committees and the use of informed neutrals could alter the traditional pattern of collective bargaining as it has been practiced until recent times.

WORK STOPPAGES

When all else fails, labor and managements settle their disputes by resorting to a strike or a lockout. Strikes and lockouts are forms of economic warfare. The history of labor-management relations in the United States is dotted with many bitter and violent strikes. Some of the early strikes in the coal and steel industries led to violence and bloodshed. Perhaps the blackest mark in the history of industrial relations was the Ludlow Massacre which occurred during the Colorado coal strike of 1913–1914. Several women and children were killed in the encounter between the state militia and the miners and a number of miners were killed before this strike was finally settled. There was also a good deal of violence during the organizational strikes that followed the resurgence of trade unionism after 1935. The famous "Battle of the Bridge" when the United Auto Workers were trying to organize the Ford Motor Company is a case in point. It was perhaps less than a coincidence that the photographers representing a well-known pictorial news magazine were present to record the affair. In recent years, however, there have been fewer large-scale organizational strikes, and as labor-management relations have stabilized violence has diminished. Strikes involving violence and bloodshed are quite rare today.

The history of work stoppages is summarized succinctly in Chart 15-1. The number of work stoppages reached an all-time peak in

[22] Hildebrand, *op. cit.*, p. 9.

CHART 15–1
TRENDS IN WORK STOPPAGES

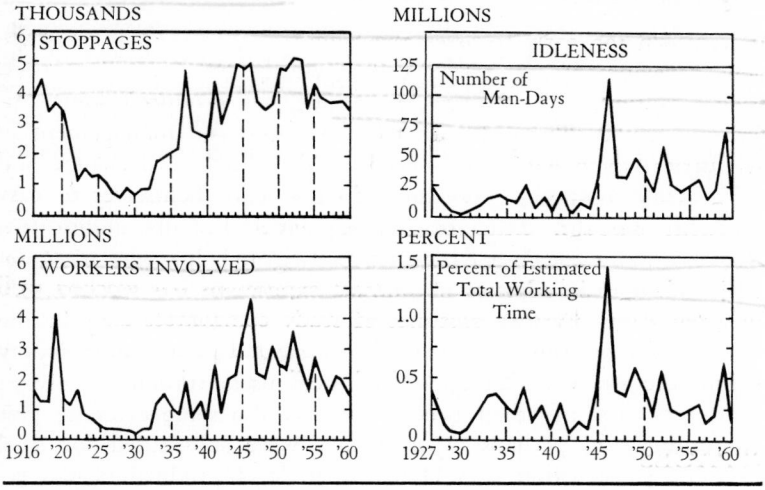

Source: *Analysis of Work Stoppages 1960*, U.S. Department of Labor, Bureau of Labor Statistics, Bulletin No. 1302 (September 1961), p. 2.

1952, a year in which there were more than 5,000 strikes. But the largest number of workers—4.6 million—were out on strike in 1946. There has been a downward trend in the number of strikes since 1952 and an even more pronounced drop in the number of workers involved since 1946. Because there are substantial increases in the labor force from year to year, there have been even more pronounced declines in the number of man-days idle due to work stoppages, and the per cent of working time lost as the result of strikes. The latter figure is of particular interest. Because of the widespread publicity given to major strikes, the public is often inclined to believe that they have a crippling effect upon our economy. But in 1946—the worst year of strike activity since 1927—time lost due to strikes averaged about 1.4 per cent of estimated total working time. In 1961, idleness due to strike activity amounted to slightly more than one-tenth of one per cent of estimated total working time.[23]

Can we conclude from the above figure that our economy produced about one-tenth of one per cent less in 1961 than it would have in the absence of strikes? Some economists would answer this

[23] *Analysis of Work Stoppages 1961*, U.S. Department of Labor, Bureau of Labor Statistics Bulletin, No. 1339 (October 1962), p. 7.

question in the negative, pointing to what has been called the "offset factor" in labor disputes. A stripped-down version of the theory of the offset factor is as follows: Few industries operate at peak capacity all the time, but in anticipation of a strike, management can begin to step up production months in advance of the strike deadline. The extra production is added to inventory to be used during the course of the strike. Thus, some would argue, strikes might not cost the economy anything in terms of production.[24]

The theory of the offset factor has a great deal of plausibility. If a strike runs longer than either side anticipated, however, the pre-strike buildup of inventories might not be sufficient to exactly offset production lost during the strike. During the long steel strike of 1959, for example, certain types of steel were in short supply before the strike ended and some steel users turned to foreign producers to satisfy their needs. There is also some evidence that aluminum, and perhaps other metals, were substituted for steel in some construction uses. Thus when steel production was resumed some markets were permanently lost to the steel industry. It is not likely that imports and the substitution of aluminum for steel had significant lasting effects on steel production. These matters are mentioned, however, to indicate the difficulty of measuring with great precision the impact of strikes upon our economy. Yet when we recognize that the time lost due to strikes is a tiny fraction of total working time, and also take into account the offsetting influence of pre-strike inventory buildups, it seems safe to conclude that industrial disputes have not seriously retarded economic growth. This is not an attempt to minimize the seriousness of strikes, nor to suggest that strikes are something which we can simply ignore. Companies involved in strikes can and do suffer losses of revenue. And striking workers are often forced to deplete their savings accounts, and frequently to go deeply into debt, before they are able to return to their jobs. At the same time those who suggest that strikes should be outlawed—usually through compulsory arbitration—fail to recognize that the alternative they suggest could be more damaging to a free society than time lost due to work disputes. Both labor and management insist on the right to settle their differences through a show of economic force

[24] For extended discussion of the theory of the offset factor, with specific application to coal production, see: C. L. Christenson, "The Theory of the Offset Factor: The Impact of Labor Disputes Upon Coal Production," *The American Economic Review,* Vol. XLIII (September 1953), pp. 513–547, and Christenson, "The Impact of Labor Disputes on Coal Consumption," *The American Economic Review,* Vol. XLV (March 1955), pp. 79–112.

if this becomes necessary. They insist on the "right" to strike so long as this does not jeopardize the health, welfare, or the security of our society.

What are the major issues which have led to strikes since the end of World War II? Between 1947 and 1959, 73 per cent of all time lost due to work stoppages resulted from strikes over wages, hours, and supplementary benefits. By 1960, idleness due to these causes had dropped to 55 per cent. From the end of World War II until 1960, 20 per cent of idleness due to strikes was the result of efforts by unions to obtain union security or to strengthen their bargaining position. By 1960, less than 2 per cent of time lost was due to disputes over these issues. But as noted earlier, there has been a growing tendency for labor and management to fail to reach agreement on negotiations involving work rules or working conditions. During the period 1947–1959, less than 5 per cent of time lost due to work stoppages was the result of disputes over working conditions. In 1960, however, more than 18 per cent of man-days idle resulted from disputes over working conditions. And it is likely that a growing proportion of disputes in the future will involve work rules and working conditions.

The type of strike which leads to the greatest amount of public indignation is the one based upon interunion or intraunion disputes. This category includes strikes resulting from union rivalry, sympathy strikes, and jurisdictional disputes. It is worth noting, however, that between 1947 and 1960, all strikes involving interunion or intraunion matters accounted for less than one per cent of total man-days idle due to work stoppages and there has been a tendency for strikes of this kind to decline in importance in recent years.

The sectors of the economy which are most highly organized are manufacturing, mining, construction, transportation, and public utilities. It is not surprising, therefore, that more than half of all strike activity is in manufacturing and that the nonmanufacturing sectors mentioned above account for a disproportionate share of strike activity. Although unions have made some headway in organizing the trades and services, strike activity in these areas has been negligible. This is partly because "white collar" unions are not strong, and therefore not overly militant; it is also partly a matter of simple statistics. Most workers in the trades and services are unorganized so that the strike activity of a small minority—expressed as a percentage of the total—will necessarily appear to be small.

The declining trend of time lost due to strikes indicated by Chart 15-1 shows that collective bargaining has become an increasingly peaceful process. At the same time, however, there has been a tendency for strikes to last longer than they did in the past. The average duration of strikes is a statistic which must be interpreted cautiously. One major dispute which lasts for an extended time can have an appreciable effect on the average. But even when this is taken into account it seems that while we have had fewer strikes in recent years they have tended to last longer than in the past. The proportion of strikes which lasted a month or longer was higher in 1959 than in any year since 1948 and this proportion increased in 1960; the number of strikes lasting three months or longer in 1959 and 1960 exceeded the number in any year since 1947.

CONCLUSIONS

As collective bargaining has matured in the United States labor and management have developed ways of settling day-to-day differences of opinion without resort to work stoppages. The development of grievance machinery provided an essential "safety valve" for dealing with the problems of individual workers within the terms of existing agreements. Most grievance arrangements today terminate in arbitration with both parties accepting the arbitrator's decision as final and binding. Less frequently, arbitration is also used for the final settlement of issues upon which the two parties fail to agree during negotiations. In some cases, a strike is ended without all issues settled. In about one-fourth of such cases in 1960, arbitration was agreed upon to settle the unresolved issues.

Mediation and conciliation play an important although unmeasurable part in contract negotiations. But there are cases where even with the aid of mediators agreement cannot be reached and work stoppages result. The few statistics quoted in this chapter indicate that time lost due to strikes involves only a tiny fraction of total working time. While there has been a tendency for strikes to run longer than in the past, time lost due to strikes, as a proportion of total working time, has declined significantly since the end of World War II.

The development of "continuous" collective bargaining in a few industries has no doubt contributed to the favorable strike record of recent years. If this practice spreads to other industries, a growing proportion of agreements could be reached without resort to economic warfare. It is not likely, however, that strikes or lockouts will become obsolete—at least in the foreseeable future. While there are general expressions of indignation when major strikes occur, and while the hardship suffered by those directly involved should not be minimized, it must be emphasized that the vast majority of all labor-management agreements negotiated each year are settled peacefully. While collective bargaining has become more and more of a peaceful process, both labor and management reserve the right to settle their differences on the economic battleground if there seems to be no other way to reach a solution. Students of industrial conflict seem to agree that so long as the health, welfare, and safety of society are not jeopardized by strike activity the right to strike, if this becomes necessary, remains one of the essential freedoms of a democracy.

REFERENCES

BOOKS AND PAMPHLETS

Alexander, Kenneth, "Strikes in Manufacturing," *The Quarterly Journal of Economics,* Vol. LXXVI (February 1962), pp. 122–144.

Chamberlain, Neil W., *Collective Bargaining,* New York: McGraw-Hill Book Company, Inc. (1951).

Cohen, Sanford, *Labor in the United States,* Columbus, Ohio: Charles E. Merrill Books, Inc. (1960).

Davey, Harold W., *Contemporary Collective Bargaining,* Englewood Cliffs, New Jersey: Prentice-Hall, Inc. (second edition, 1959).

Dunlop, John T. and James J. Healy, *Collective Bargaining,* Homewood, Illinois: Richard D. Irwin, Inc. (revised edition, 1953).

Hildebrand, George H., *The Use of Informed Neutrals in Difficult Bargaining Situations,* Ithaca, New York: New York State School of Industrial and Labor Relations of Cornell University (October 1961).

International Association of Machinists, *Shop Stewards' Manual,* Washington, D.C. (September 1948).

Kornhauser, Arthur, Robert Dubin and Arthur M. Ross, *Industrial Conflict,* New York: McGraw-Hill Book Company, Inc. (1954).

Lapp, John A., *How to Handle Labor Grievances,* New York: National Foremen's Institute, Inc. (1945).

———, ——— —, *Labor Arbitration,* New York: National Foremen's Institute, Inc., (1946).

Slichter, Sumner H., James J. Healy and E. Robert Livernash, *The Impact of Collective Bargaining on Management,* Washington, D.C.: The Brookings Institution (1960).

U.S. Department of Labor, Bureau of Labor Standards, *Federal Labor Laws and Agencies,* Bulletin 123 (revised, January 1957).

U.S. Department of Labor, Bureau of Labor Statistics, *The Dimensions of Major Work Stoppages 1947–59,* Bulletin No. 1298 (June 1961).

U.S. Department of Labor, Bureau of Labor Statistics, *Analysis of Work Stoppages 1960,* Bulletin No. 1302 (September 1961); *Analysis of Work Stoppages 1961,* Bulletin No. 1339 (October 1962).

ARTICLES

Christenson, C. L. "The Theory of the Offset Factor: The Impact of Labor Disputes Upon Coal Production, *"The American Economic Review,* Vol. XLIII (September 1953), pp. 513–547.

———, — —, "The Impact of Labor Disputes on Coal Consumption," *The American Economic Review,* Vol. XLV (March 1955), pp. 79–112.

Fleming, R. W., "Some Problems of Due Process and Fair Procedure in Arbitration," *Stanford Law Review,* Vol. 13, No. 2 (March 1961), pp. 235–251.

McPherson, William H., "Grievance Mediation in Collective Bargaining," *Industrial and Labor Relations Review,* Vol. 9, No. 2 (January 1956), pp. 200–212.

Meyer, Arthur S., "Function of the Mediator in Collective Bargaining," *Industrial and Labor Relations Review,* Vol. 13, No. 2 (January 1960), pp. 159–165.

Ross, Arthur M. "The Well-Aged Arbitration Case," *Industrial and Labor Relations Review,* Vol. 11, No. 2 (January 1958), pp. 262–271.

———, ——— —, "Changing Patterns of Industrial Conflict," *Proceedings of the Twelfth Annual Meeting,* Industrial Relations Research Association, pp. 1–24.

Chapter 16 The Structure of Collective Bargaining

In earlier chapters the process of collective bargaining, the content of labor-management agreements, methods of dispute settlement, and the result of failures to reach agreement were discussed. In this chapter we will be concerned with the *variety* of bargaining relationships. Much of what the public hears about collective bargaining involves the giants of industry and organized labor. When the United Auto Workers start negotiations with General Motors —or the United Steel Workers with the United States Steel Corporation—the progress of their negotiations is widely reported in the press and by other news media. Thousands of negotiations involving smaller companies and smaller unions are virtually unnoticed, however. Actually, there is such a variety of bargaining relationships that it is somewhat difficult to generalize about them.

What is the size distribution of American unions? And what is the size distribution of the employers with whom they deal? To what extent do unions deal with individual companies? To what extent do they negotiate with more than one employer at a time? We hear much about "industrywide" collective bargaining and the power of "labor monopolies." To what extent do unions deal with entire industries at one time? What lies behind the charge that while business monopolies are prohibited by law "labor monopolies" enjoy legal immunity and are permitted to flourish? Finally, how do unions behave in industries which include many firms—a few of which are large and powerful but the vast majority of which are relatively small? These are some of the issues discussed in this chapter. Much of the discussion is descriptive; it is based upon statistical analysis of the size of unions and employer units. But some will deal with issues where the winds of controversy blow strong. In considering these issues an effort will be made to present both sides of the debate.

TYPES OF BARGAINING RELATIONSHIPS

As collective bargaining developed in the United States various types of bargaining structures evolved. Most of the changes were gradual as employers and unions adapted to changes in economic circumstances and to shifts in relative bargaining power. The bargaining structures we find today are the result of efforts by the two parties to find the best arrangements both for contract negotiation and the day-to-day administration of agreements.

On the employer's side, "bargaining units" range from a single employer with one or more plants to associations which in some cases cover virtually an entire industry. On the union's side, the employee unit may consist of an industrial or craft union, but bargaining can take place at the local, regional, or national levels. At times, several unions work together through a trades department or other special bargaining combination.

Employer bargaining units fall into two broad categories. These are: (1) the single-employer unit, and (2) the multi-employer bargaining unit. Single-employer units vary from purely local agreements between a union and a small employer with one plant to agreements between a union and a giant corporation with many plants located in a number of regions.

Multi-employer bargaining units are even more varied. In some cases one union will deal with a large number of small employers. Frequently under such circumstances *form* agreements are used. These are identical agreements signed by different employers often with very little bargaining involved. Such agreements are likely to be found where there are a large number of small competing firms in a relatively restricted geographic area, in the trucking industry, for example.

Another type of multi-employer bargaining takes place between a union and an association of employers. Most industries have an association or institute which serves as a clearing house for information and which performs many functions that have no bearing upon collective bargaining. But there are some cases in which trade associations also serve as bargaining units for member employers. In other cases, employers band together in bargaining associations which deal with unions but do not perform the information gathering and disseminating functions of the trade association. Finally, there are some purely bargaining associations made up of employers engaged in various kinds of business activity. The sole purpose of the latter associations is to deal with unions either as advisers to the employers who belong to the group, or directly in negotiations. There are also some cases—although these are rather rare—in which a number of employers negotiate jointly with a union without setting up a formal association.

The most recent study of employer bargaining units, conducted early in 1956, was based on more than 1,700 major agreements covering 1,000 or more workers.[1] This study showed that 68 per cent of all agreements, covering 57 per cent of all workers involved, were of the single-employer type. Thus only about one-third of all agreements, covering about 43 per cent of all workers involved, were of the multi-employer variety. There was considerable variation from industry to industry and from region to region, however.

In some industries—such as ordnance, chemicals, and rubber products—all agreements were with single employers; on the other hand, all agreements in the construction industries were of the multi-employer variety. Multi-employer agreements are also characteristic of the apparel industry where such agreements outnumber those of the single-employer type about twenty to one. In transportation, excluding railroads and airlines, about four out of five agreements are of the multi-employer variety. Single agreements, however, predominate in such industries as autos, steel, and the machinery industries. Multi-employer agreements in the durable goods industries are relatively rare.

In manufacturing as a whole, about 80 per cent of all agreements covering 82 per cent of union members were with single-employer bargaining units in 1956. In nonmanufacturing, however, almost 60 per cent of agreements—including 74 per cent of covered workers—were of the multi-employer variety. Only two nonmanufacturing industries—communications and the electric and gas utilities—have no multi-employer agreements at all. But telephone companies, radio stations, and the electric and gas utilities, are purely

[1] "Characteristics of Major Union Contracts," *Monthly Labor Review,* U.S. Department of Labor, Bureau of Labor Statistics (July 1956), pp. 805–811. This BLS study supports the findings of two earlier surveys although there are minor differences due, no doubt, to sampling variations. See "Employer Unit in Collective Bargaining," *Monthly Labor Review* (December 1950), and *The Employer Bargaining Unit,* BLS Report No. 1 (February 1953).

local or regional businesses. It is understandable that such businesses would deal directly with unions rather than attempting to form associations for bargaining purposes. Perhaps the extreme of multi-employer bargaining (excluding construction where there appears to be no other kind) is reached on the railroads. There were only three railroad labor-management agreements included in the 1956 study. One of these was with a single employer, but it covered only 36,000 workers. The other two were multi-employer agreements, and they covered 1,125,000 workers.

The above discussion shows that there is no single pattern of collective bargaining which applies in all cases. The major characteristic of collective bargaining by industry or type of employer is its diversity. There is also a great deal of variation by region. An earlier study by the Bureau of Labor Statistics showed that in 1951, 72 per cent of all interstate and interregional agreements were of the single-employer type.[2] In the South, more than 90 per cent of all organized workers were governed by single-employer agreements, while on the Pacific Coast 71 per cent of the organized workers were in unions which had multi-employer agreements. These represent the extremes. The distribution of agreements in other regions ranged in between. Except for the Pacific Coast, however, where more than two-thirds of all workers are covered by multi-employer agreements, the single-employer agreement predominates.[3]

The Size Distribution of Bargaining Units

The number of agreements involved declines as the size of the union bargaining unit increases. In 1956, for example, there were more than 1,000 agreements which covered between 1,000 and 2,500 workers. But collectively, these agreements covered only slightly more than 1.5 million workers. At the other extreme, there were nine agreements covering 100,000 workers or more and in the aggregate these agreements covered almost 2.4 million workers. The size distribution of employer bargaining units ranges from the very small to the very large. It could scarcely be otherwise in an economy made up of a large number of relatively small firms and a small number of industrial giants. In a study based on 1953 data, Professor Neil Chamberlain showed that more than two-

[2] *The Employer Bargaining Unit,* BLS Report No. 1, U.S. Department of Labor, Bureau of Labor Statistics (February 1953).

[3] For an interesting discussion of multi-employer bargaining on the West Coast see Clark Kerr and Lloyd H. Fisher, "Multi-employer Bargaining: The San Francisco Experience," *Insights Into Labor Issues,* edited by Richard A. Lester and Joseph Shister, New York: The Macmillan Company (1948), pp. 25–61.

thirds of all organized workers were in firms with a thousand or more employees. As an interesting sidelight, his study showed that almost 90 per cent of all single-employer bargaining units had fewer than 500 employees while about three-fourths of all multi-employer units fell in this size category.

TABLE 16–1
DISTRIBUTION OF BARGAINING UNITS BY SIZE, 1953

Employee size group	Per cent of all single-employer units	Per cent of all multi-employer units	Per cent of workers covered in all units
1–49	36.6	19.6	1.7
50–99	17.8	15.8	2.8
100–499	34.1	41.2	18.0
500–999	5.9	11.0	10.9
1,000–2,999	4.1	8.0	18.1
3,000–9,999	1.1	3.3	18.1
10,000–99,999	0.3	1.0	22.5
100,000 & over	–	0.1	7.9

Source: Neil Chamberlain, "The Structure of Bargaining Units in the United States," *Industrial and Labor Relations Review*, Vol. X (October 1956), pp. 10–11.

The Size Distribution of Unions

Employer bargaining units include many small firms and a few giants which employ more than 100,000 union members. On the union side there is a similar variation in size. For example, in 1960, about one-fourth of all unions had fewer than 5,000 members. Almost two-thirds ranged between 5,000 and 200,000 members, and only slightly more than 11 per cent of the nation's 184 national and international unions reported membership in excess of 200,000. Only three unions—the Teamsters, the Steelworkers, and the United Auto Workers—had more than a million members. But these three unions accounted for almost 21 per cent of total membership and the 21 largest unions in the nation accounted for about two-thirds of all union membership.[4]

The American economy is made up of thousands of enterprises. The great majority of these are quite small but many industries are dominated by a few large firms. In some industries—autos, steel, rubber, and meatpacking, for example—there are either a handful of firms, or a few large firms accounting for most of the industry's output and a larger number of small firms each of which accounts for a fractional part of total production. Similarly, on the

[4] See Harry P. Cohany, "Membership of American Trade Unions, 1960," *Monthly Labor Review*, U.S. Department of Labor, Bureau of Labor Statistics (December 1961), pp. 1301–1302.

union side, there are many small unions and a few giants. Hundreds of collective bargaining relationships involve small unions and small employers. In other cases small unions deal with large employers, and some small employers deal with large unions. The point to be emphasized is the *diversity* of collective bargaining relationships. In the aggregate the "small" bargaining relationships involve millions of workers and thousands of firms.

The Duration of Agreements

There was a time when many collective bargaining agreements were negotiated for one year. But the 1956 BLS study showed that this is no longer true. It also revealed considerable variation in the duration of agreements. There were a few agreements, covering a small number of workers, which were for less than one year, while about 1 per cent of the surveyed agreements were of indefinite duration. The latter agreements, however, covered about 15 per cent of all workers represented in collective bargaining. Most agreements were for a period of two years. But about 65 per cent of all agreements were for two years or more. About one out of five agreements, covering 27 per cent of all workers represented, were negotiated for periods of three years or longer.

One should not conclude that there is a trend toward agreements of longer duration. During the early 1950's, a number of five-year agreements were signed between large unions and large employers. These typically contained escalator, or cost-of-living clauses, and some included an annual improvement factor granting automatic wage increases geared to productivity gains. But there has been a tendency in recent years for management to ask for agreements of shorter duration and in some cases, at least, unions have not balked at this request. It is likely that unions and management will continue to experiment with agreements of varying duration. There will undoubtedly be times when some agreements will be lengthened and there will be other times when the parties will decide to reopen negotiations at more frequent intervals. Just as there is considerable variation in the size of employer bargaining units, and in the size of trade unions, there is no standard pattern for the length of agreements.

PATTERN BARGAINING

The most prevalent type of collective bargaining, as the previous discussion has indicated, is that which results in an agreement with a single employer. But this does not mean that all single-employer agreements are entirely *independent* of one another. Multi-employer agreements tend toward uniformity—at least within an industry and in a given geographic area. Indeed, one reason employers band together for collective bargaining purposes is to achieve a certain degree of uniformity in their relations with labor unions. Unions do not object to this; indeed, most unions favor it. Competing employers are willing to accept uniform agreements—or agreements which tend toward uniformity—so that a relatively strong union will not play off one employer against another. Unions have long insisted that vigorous competition in the product market should not be at the expense of workers. Thus if they can achieve a degree of uniformity in the agreements they negotiate with various employers they have to a certain extent "taken labor out of competition."

But what of single-employer agreements? Will not each employer strive for the most favorable agreement from his point of view? Will he not, that is, try to keep his labor costs to a minimum? And where unions deal with one employer at a time, will they not try to obtain the most beneficial contract from the union's point of view in each case?

There was a time—and this is still true under some circumstances—when a favorite union tactic was to "whipsaw" employers. The union would pick one employer and drive a hard bargain. Once the agreement had been signed, the union would use this in its efforts to bring the wages and fringe benefits of other employers "into line." At the next round of negotiations, another employer might be selected and the process would be repeated. Whipsawing, as well as the desire of small employers to meet large unions on more favorable terms, played an important part in the development of multi-employer bargaining.

In many industries unions have long since abandoned such tactics. They still negotiate with one employer at a time but in some of the largest industries, where employers deal with large and powerful unions, a new approach has been developed known as *pattern bargaining*. What this means, in brief, is that the union negotiates an agreement with one company in an industry expecting that identical or closely similar agreements will be signed with other employers in the same industry. In recent years pattern bargaining has tended to move beyond the confines of a single industry.

There is a certain amount of rivalry among unions—especially large industrial unions. And if one large union reaches an agreement with a major employer in an industry it is likely to set a pattern for other unions to follow in other industries. Thus in certain industries—even though the typical bargaining unit is the single employer—there is a greater tendency toward uniformity of agreements than would result if each set of negotiations were entirely independent of all other negotiations.

A single craft union will often deal with a large number of employers. Thus it is no accident that there is no single-employer bargaining between the building trades unions and construction firms employing a thousand or more workers. The union will negotiate with a bloc of employers at a time and the conditions resulting from the negotiations must be met by all employers. Multi-employer bargaining is a fairly old practice in some craft unions.

With the rise of industrial unionism after 1935, however, pattern bargaining spread. It is to be found in most oligopolistic industries, that is, those industries—such as steel, autos, meat packing, and rubber—in which a few large firms account for most of the industry's output. But pattern bargaining is not limited to oligopolistic industries. It is practiced in some highly-competitive industries such as those manufacturing garments, apparel, and textile products. In 1956, for example, single-employer agreements in textiles outnumbered multi-employer agreements by more than three to one, but many of the single-employer agreements were of the pattern variety.

Oligopoly and Pattern Bargaining

The terms "oligopoly" and "monopoly" are sometimes used interchangeably in popular discussion, although it is not correct to do so. Strictly defined, a monopoly is a single seller of a product or service for which there is no close substitute. If the demand for the product is relatively inelastic, i.e. if an increase in price is accompanied by a less than proportionate decline in purchases, the firm can increase its total revenue by raising prices and curtailing output. This is precisely what a profit-maximizing monopolist will do. By definition, he has no competitors, thus he is free to set his price and output at the levels which will maximize his profits.

non-price competition

In an oligopolistic market, however, there will be not one but a few large sellers. There is a tendency for firms in oligopolistic markets to avoid price competition, but they engage in many other kinds of competition such as aggressive advertising and merchandising, quality improvements, and production innovations which will lower their costs without disturbing the price level. Each firm in the oligopolistic market is aware of the fact that if it tries to cut prices its rivals will follow suit and no one will gain. Its management also knows that if it raises prices, independently of cost changes which affect all firms in the market, its rivals are likely *not* to follow this lead, and this firm would then lose customers and revenue. This situation is referred to by economic theorists as *mutual dependence recognized*. But while there is an absence of price competition in oligopolistic markets there are many other kinds of competition. Unlike the monopolist who curtails output in order to dispose of his production at the price he has set, each oligopolist is anxious to sell as many units as possible at the ruling market price.

There is a world of difference between these two situations, as most economists have recognized for many years. The behavior of oligopolistic firms in product markets has had a significant influence on their relationships with trade unions. It is not surprising that pattern bargaining has become fairly common in industries which are predominantly oligopolistic in character. At the same time, there has been a tendency for some writers to exaggerate the extent to which unions have been able to negotiate uniform agreements with all firms in industries which are predominantly oligopolistic.

Does the practice of pattern bargaining lead to uniform wage and fringe benefit settlements in oligopolistic industries? This is not a simple question to answer. First of all, the concept of a "pattern" in collective bargaining has not been clearly defined.[5] There would be no problem of definition if all companies involved in pattern bargaining started with the same absolute level of wages and fringe benefits. This is not the case, however. Pattern bargaining is largely a post-World War II phenomenon, and the wage and fringe benefit "package" varied considerably from company to company at the time pattern bargaining became more or less the standard practice in some of our larger industries. Another way to view the pattern, therefore, is to consider the *change* in wages and fringe benefits negotiated. One could say that there is a pattern if the wages and fringe benefits in the "key" bargain were followed quite closely in all other bargains throughout the industry. The ideal would be to measure both. But as Levinson has pointed out

[5] See Harold M. Levinson, "Pattern Bargaining: A Case Study of the Automobile Workers," *The Quarterly Journal of Economics*, Vol. LXXIV (May 1960), p. 297.

"any attempt to compare absolute levels among varied firms raises extremely difficult problems of differences in employee-mix, differences in incentive versus hourly earnings, differences in the job content of similar job classifications, and a host of others."[6] Thus in practice, the term "pattern" typically denotes the major *changes* in wages and fringe benefits negotiated during the "key" bargain. In his analysis of pattern bargaining in the automobile industry—one that is frequently used to illustrate the concept of pattern bargaining—Levinson found that there is much less uniformity than is popularly believed.

Levinson studied the results of collective bargaining in 85 automobile firms in the Detroit metropolitan area—not including the "Big Three" firms of Ford, General Motors, and Chrysler. If pattern bargaining led to uniformity of wage and fringe benefit changes, one would expect the bargains in these 85 firms to follow the settlements in the "Big Three." In fact, however, Levinson found that "only 26 per cent of the companies, employing 40 per cent of the employees in the sample, followed the pattern . . ."[7] A minority of firms had reached settlements above the pattern while firms employing about 98 per cent of the workers covered by the sample had reached settlements below the pattern. In general, there was a tendency for the larger firms in the sample to follow the pattern than for their smaller counterparts.

Levinson's study is, of course, limited to one industry and one area. But it strongly suggests that pattern bargaining does not lead to uniform wage and fringe benefit changes, contrary to a fairly widespread belief. Some discussions of pattern bargaining imply that as soon as the "key" bargain has been settled all other companies in an industry will follow suit. It is true that in some oligopolistic industries, the leading firms will settle on similar if not identical terms. But even in such oligopolistic industries as steel and autos, unions deal with hundreds of smaller firms. Levinson's study suggests that in such cases there can be significant departures from the pattern established by the major firms.

Pattern Bargaining in Highly Competitive Industries

At the other end of the spectrum—in terms of market structure—are the aggressively competitive industries in our economy. Some industries—such as textiles, shoes, and apparel—are made up of a large number of firms, no one of which accounts for a substantial

[6] *Ibid.*
[7] *Ibid.*, p. 299.

share of the industry's total output. Some firms in these industries produce "specialty" products, and thus enjoy a considerable degree of control over the prices they charge, but most of them sell relatively homogeneous products in an open market where prices are determined by the forces of supply and demand. Although there are often a few large firms even in highly competitive industries, they are not in the same position as the dominant firms in such industries as steel, autos, and meat packing. They too must sell at open market prices.

Characteristically, within an industry—whether it is oligopolistic or aggressively price competitive—there will be variations in cost from firm to firm. One might expect that in price competitive industries, therefore, unions would try to negotiate agreements on the basis of "what the traffic will bear." But even in price competitive industries one can find evidence of something which approximates pattern bargaining. Some textile negotiations, for example, are conducted with associations of employers. The results of these negotiations tend to set a pattern for other firms in the industry. In the apparel industry, the "form" contract is not uncommon. The same contract is presented to a large number of employers either through an organization of employers or on an individual basis. Such agreements also tend to set a pattern throughout the industry. But as in oligopolistic industries, there are departures from these patterns. The practice of pattern bargaining has not led to uniformity of changes in wages and fringe benefits either in oligopolistic or price competitive industries—although there undeniably has been a *tendency* in this direction. The picture of pattern bargaining sketched by some writers has been misleading. The union is often portrayed as a monolithic giant which having decided what it is going to get forces all companies to fall into line. There is obviously some basis for this line of argument—unions have *tried* to obtain uniform agreements wherever possible. But union leaders are realists; they recognize that not every firm in an industry will be able to settle on the same terms and there is evidence that they have been willing to accommodate themselves to differences among firms in reaching workable agreements.

MULTI-EMPLOYER BARGAINING IN THE BASIC STEEL INDUSTRY

For many years the agreement between the United Steelworkers of America and the United States Steel Corporation set the pattern of bargaining in this oligopolistic industry. But negotiations were held with each company one at a time. Evidently U.S. Steel—which is also generally considered to be the "price leader" in the industry—did not particularly relish the position it occupied in collective bargaining. "There was an indication as early as 1947 that U.S. Steel considered itself a reluctant dragon so far as its leadership role was concerned."[8] Before 1947, the steel union was not strong enough to bargain on a multi-employer basis. After that year it began to press hard toward this goal but it was almost a decade before multi-employer bargaining became firmly established in the industry.

In 1956, twelve major companies arranged to have a committee of four represent them in bargaining on major issues. A similar four-man industry committee conducted negotiations for the industry in 1959 and it is likely that this committee approach will continue. Since 1959, the union has negotiated with a committee representing eleven major companies, with a separate arrangement for Kaiser Steel.

In addition to the dozen giants which account for most of the nation's steel output, there are probably more than 200 smaller firms which are considered to be part of the industry. Whenever possible, it appears that the union tries to apply the terms negotiated with the major firms to the smaller companies, and to see that local agreements do not conflict with the provisions of the basic settlement. But there are still extensive variations in wage-fringe benefit packages among the smaller firms in the industry.[9]

The union favors this approach to collective bargaining in basic steel. Although it might lose certain tactical advantages by giving up the ability to "whipsaw" one company at a time, union leaders evidently feel that there is more to be gained from a uniform settlement on basic issues when facing the dominant firms in the industry. Moreover, management, which at one time was reluctant to engage in such bargaining, evidently feels that the position of the industry is strengthened if it faces the union *en bloc* rather than having each company try to negotiate the most favorable terms.

[8] *Collective Bargaining in the Basic Steel Industry,* Washington: U.S. Department of Labor (January 1961), p. 87.

[9] Late in 1962, for example, the United Steel Workers negotiated a special agreement with Kaiser Steel which provided a fund to ease the transition to other jobs for steelworkers displaced by automation or other forms of technological change. This was a result of the activities of the Kaiser Steel-USW study committee discussed in Chapter 15.

In recent years bargaining between the steel union and the eleven companies with which it negotiates the basic agreement has come to be viewed as perhaps the most critical in the country. If a "non-inflationary" settlement is reached with the steel industry on a peaceful basis this is usually considered as a harbinger of industrial peace and "moderate" union demands. The steel industry occupies a critical position in our economy. It is the supplier of raw materials to a wide variety of industries and its price policy undoubtedly affects—directly or indirectly—the prices of a wide range of commodities. The United Steel Workers of America is also one of the most powerful industrial unions in the nation and its demands undoubtedly have considerable influence on those formulated by unions dealing with other industries.

"INDUSTRY-WIDE" BARGAINING AND THE "LABOR MONOPOLY" ISSUE

One of the most persistent themes in discussions of collective bargaining is that of so-called industry-wide bargaining and "labor monopolies." It is often alleged by those who hew closely to the conservative line that while we have outlawed business monopoly, labor monopolies are permitted to flourish. Labor monopolies, it is further argued, pursue their objectives through some form of "industry-wide" collective bargaining.

The Opponents of "Labor Monopoly"

The attack on "labor monopoly" has been spearheaded by two major business organizations—the National Association of Manufacturers and the U.S. Chamber of Commerce. The NAM has said:

> Monopoly power may be described as a position of power by an individual or group to control the supply and fix the price of needed goods and services. On this basis, there can be no doubt that certain international unions possess monopoly powers in some of the basic industries in the United States. They virtually control the labor supply of these industries and have proved on many occasions their ability to dictate the terms on which the services of labor are available to produce the goods and services the nation needs.[10]

The NAM goes on to say that there are numerous cases in which "employers and their employees must accept the terms fixed by the international unions; the members of the local union and the local

[10] *Monopoly Power as Exercised by Labor Unions,* New York: National Association of Manufacturers (no date), p. 5.

bargaining agents have nothing to say about these terms."[11] The cause of all this, in the view of the NAM, is the legal immunity of trade unions from the antitrust laws. What is the cure advocated by those who accept this rather extreme view of union power? It is the decentralization of collective bargaining, more specifically, the limitation of collective bargaining to local unions and individual companies.

As noted in an earlier chapter, the center of power in the American trade union movement is the national or international union. This is particularly so in many of the large industrial unions and it is not an accident. The complexity of collective bargaining in modern industrial society requires that unions retain staffs of experts to assist their officers in preparing for negotiations. Large companies, too, have their staffs of experts. Collective bargaining has become much more than a matter of table pounding, threats, and counter-threats. The organizations which claim that unions are "labor monopolies" and which "want to bring them under the anti-trust laws" are well aware of this. If the national union could be prevented from participating in collective bargaining the advantage in negotiations would shift to the side of employers. Indeed, there would be no point in having a national union headquarters if all collective bargaining had to be conducted at the local level.

There have been numerous efforts to pass Federal laws which would bar multiple-employer bargaining or so-called industry-wide collective bargaining. When the Taft-Hartley Bill was being debated, for example, a House Bill (H.R. 3020) which would have prohibited multiple-employer bargaining was passed with a substantial majority, and a similar bill, sponsored by Senator Ball, came within a single vote of being passed in the Senate.

This was a very close call indeed for the kind of collective bargaining which has become widespread in the United States. Despite rejection by the Congress which enacted the Taft-Hartley Act, over President Truman's veto, similar bills have been introduced into virtually every succeeding session of Congress. The National Association of Manufacturers has continued to call for "real bargaining at the local level and an end to the domination of bargaining by international unions."[12] Those espousing this point of view have had at times the support of well-known scholars. For example, Roscoe Pound, an eminent legal scholar, has written that "the

[11] *Ibid.*
[12] *Monopoly Power as Exercised by Labor Unions,* p. 30.

employers have no immunities and the statutes as to collective bargaining put the employers in the hands of the unions."[13]

Not everyone who has expressed concern about the "labor monopoly" problem would go as far as the NAM in limiting collective bargaining. Edward H. Chamberlin, a distinguished economic theorist, has frequently argued that labor unions have monopoly power.[14] Yet he has said: "There has been a great deal of discussion as to whether the antitrust laws should be applied to labor . . . Some partial application is surely possible, but the particular body of law associated with antitrust has actually been developed with reference to product markets, and it would seem on the face of it that the structure and functioning of product markets on the one hand and of labor markets on the other, differ in so many ways that a fresh start may be called for to meet the problems of the latter."[15] Fritz Machlup has argued that outlawing "industry-wide" collective bargaining *without at the same time outlawing "industry-wide" unions* would be ineffective.[16] Nonetheless, he is emphatic in his belief that there is a considerable amount of business monopoly in our economy and if "labor monopolies" are to be abolished, their counterparts on the business side should be abolished also.

Reservations About the Application of Antitrust Laws to Trade Unions

Most of the economists who have expressed concern about the monopoly power of trade unions would be classified as "conservatives." Commenting on this, Archibald Cox, a noted lawyer and President Kennedy's Solicitor General has said: "Much of the support for legislation subjecting unions to the antitrust laws doubtless stems from organized anti-unionism, but too many friends of labor are concerned by some aspects of the problem to condemn these questions through guilt by association."[17] But after a careful analysis of cases involving unions and the antitrust laws Cox concludes that "a case can be made out for applying the Sherman Act only to those union imposed restraints which fall

[13] Roscoe Pound, "Legal Immunities of Labor Unions," *Labor Unions and Public Policy,* Washington, D.C.: American Enterprise Association (1958), p. 168.
[14] See, for example, Edward H. Chamberlin, "Labor Union Power and the Public Interest" in *The Public Stake in Union Power,* Philip D. Bradley (ed.), Charlottesville, Virginia: University of Virginia Press (1959), p. 3.
[15] Edward H. Chamberlin, "The Economic Analysis of Labor Union Power," *Labor Unions and Public Policy,* Washington: The American Enterprise Association (1958), pp. 32–33.
[16] Fritz Machlup, "Monopolistic Wage Determination as Part of the General Problem of Monopoly," *Wage Determination and the Economics of Liberalism,* Washington: Chamber of Commerce of the United States (1947), pp. 80–81.
[17] Archibald Cox, "Labor and the Antitrust Laws—A Preliminary Analysis," *University of Pennsylvania Law Review,* Volume 104 (November 1955), p. 252.

in the category [of] tampering with the product market for the sake of sheltering employers from competition otherwise than by organizing the employees of competitors and regulating their labor standards."[18] This view has also been advanced by Douglas C. Brown who feels that unions should be subject to the antitrust laws if they are engaged in the restraint of trade in product markets, but that unions should *not* be subject to the antitrust laws when their activities are limited strictly to the labor market.[19]

Strong Opposition to the Application of Antitrust Laws to Unions

One would expect union spokesmen to oppose laws limiting the role of national and international unions in collective bargaining. Supreme Court Justice Arthur J. Goldberg, while serving as General Counsel for the Industrial Union Department of the AFL-CIO, wrote: "The truth is that those who make the 'labor monopoly' charge are not really concerned with competition or its negative counterpart monopoly. Their real goal is the weakening of unions and especially those unions which they believe are too strong."[20]

Not all opposition to the drive to bring unions under the antitrust laws has come from the ranks of organized labor. It is obvious that most Congressmen and Senators have not been convinced of the merits of the arguments advanced by those who wish to outlaw multiple-employer bargaining, area-wide bargaining, or "industry-wide" bargaining. The numerous bills to limit collective bargaining to local unions and individual employers have been sharply criticized in the halls of Congress. In a strongly-worded speech entitled "Don't 'Pulverize' Labor,"[21] Representative F. D. Roosevelt, Jr., of New York, was sharply critical of a bill introduced by Representative Lucas (H.R. 2545) which would have outlawed multi-employer bargaining. In Roosevelt's view, such a law would have led to the destruction of national unions. Roosevelt indicated the difficulties that would be involved in administering a law which would effectively restrict collective bargaining to a single employer and a local union. He also denied that multi-employer bargaining had adverse effects on small businesses and suggested that since unions must keep the ability of small businesses to pay in mind when negotiating multi-employer agreements, their demands—

[18] *Ibid.*, p. 280.
[19] Douglas V. Brown, "Labor and Antitrust Laws," *American Bar Association Proceedings* (August 1955), p. 23–29.
[20] Arthur J. Goldberg, "Labor and Antitrust," Pamphlet reprinted from *IUD Digest*, Washington: Industrial Union Department AFL-CIO (no date), p. 6.
[21] *Congressional Record* (February 19, 1953).

across the board—might be more moderate than would result if the unions approached each employer in terms of his specific ability to pay. Thus far the arguments against the application of anti-trust laws to trade unions—except when the latter engage in restraint of trade in product markets—have been persuasive, but this remains one of the major controversial issues in the arena of labor law.

COLLECTIVE BARGAINING WITH "MARGINAL" FIRMS

The issue of multi-employer, or so-called industry-wide, collective bargaining has been widely publicized. Because of this, many no doubt have an exaggerated notion of the extent to which it is practiced. As noted earlier in this chapter, however, most workers are covered by agreements negotiated with individual employers. Multi-employer bargaining, where it takes place, is very important especially if it is of the "pattern setting" variety but this should not obscure the fact that most negotiations are between unions and individual companies.

To what extent are unions willing to recognize the wide variations in costs of production and profitability that exist among individual companies? This is not a simple question to answer. As an ideal goal, many unions would like to see complete uniformity of wages and fringe benefits throughout the industries or occupational groups they represent. But union leaders are too realistic to assume that complete uniformity can be achieved.

There is evidence that when it is necessary to do so some unions will take into account the competitive position of a company—particularly a smaller company—and reach a settlement below the pattern established elsewhere in the industry. Such union behavior is not widely publicized, and for rather obvious reasons. If it became well known that unions are willing to make concessions, the precedent could be a damaging one—especially when the unions are dealing with the dominant firms in an industry. From a public relations point of view it might be desirable for the union to let it be known that it is willing to reach "reasonable" settlements with smaller companies which will permit them to stay in business. But this would conflict with the stated goal of some unions; namely, uniform industry-wide conditions.

It should be noted that even in oligopolistic industries, a certain amount of "price nibbling" among smaller firms is tolerated by the industrial giants; that is, smaller companies can at times depart from the prevailing price in an industry without inviting retaliation from the dominant firms. After all, if the dominant firms account for, say, 80 to 90 per cent of the market, how can such price nibbling damage them? Similarly, even if they are aware of it, the larger firms in an industry might tolerate departures from basic labor-management agreements, although such settlements cannot depart too far from the basic agreements.

All too little is known about the extent to which powerful national unions will permit departures from basic agreements in dealing with smaller firms. In this regard, a 1957 study by A. Howard Myers is revealing. It shows that when small companies are confronted with a crisis—especially if there is the threat of liquidation which would mean the loss of jobs—unions have been willing to make substantial concessions to the employers involved, at least on a temporary basis. Where unions have been convinced that a small firm could not survive an agreement based upon the industry pattern, they have been willing to settle for less in terms of wages and fringe benefits. At least this is what Myers found in a limited number of cases. But there are limits to which such departures from national patterns can be tolerated. "The national unions cannot allow local self-determination to undermine nation-wide gains or to weaken its national bargaining position. If the sole road to marginal plant labor relations depended upon the destruction of the national union's standards, the union could neither make such exceptions nor allow a local to approve them, even if such concessions were indispensable to the local's survival."[22] And at times, unions have made such concessions knowing that this would not prevent the ultimate liquidation of the firm, but hoping that the day of reckoning could be put off. This is not necessarily shortsightedness. It does not mean that the union hopes that somehow the company can be strengthened but the gradual loss of jobs has less of an impact than sudden liquidation.

There is also some evidence that in crisis situations the employees of marginal firms will exert considerable pressure on their union leaders to "go easy" on the company during negotiations.[23] Again, this is not so much because the workers think that by moderating their demands the company can be made to survive. It is often

[22] A. Howard Myers, *Crisis Bargaining,* Boston: Northeastern University, Bureau of Business and Economic Research (1957), p. 71.

[23] See Irwin L. Herrnstadt, "The Reaction of Three Local Unions to Economic Adversity," *The Journal of Political Economy,* Vol. LXII, (October 1954), pp. 425–439.

motivated by the desire to stretch out the period of time during which a company gradually goes out of business.

It would be helpful if we had a great deal more information about negotiations between unions and small companies. Available studies suggest that under multi-employer collective bargaining there has been a tendency toward uniformity of wages and fringe benefits, but this is only a tendency. There are significant variations from national patterns even in those industries where we have been told "industry-wide" collective bargaining is practiced. The major agreements with the dominant firms clearly reveal the tendency toward greater uniformity. But the evidence available suggests that outside this widely-publicized area of collective bargaining there is much more diversity than is commonly believed.

CONCLUSIONS

Most organized workers operate under agreements negotiated between their unions and single employers, but roughly 40 per cent are covered by multi-employer agreements. It is the latter which are emphasized in discussions of collective bargaining. Multi-employer bargaining is behind the widely-publicized "labor monopoly" issue, and has led to repeated demands that—for practical purposes—big unions be broken up into little ones.

There is evidently an exaggerated notion of the extent of multi-employer and so-called industry-wide collective bargaining. This is not surprising. We have a tendency to generalize, and in viewing complex social and economic situations, it is sometimes easy to generalize unwarrantably. Multi-employer bargaining, and the tendency toward uniformity of agreements, must be recognized. They are an important part of the labor-management scene and a significant reflection of the changing structure of collective bargaining in this country. At the same time, the tendency toward uniformity should not obscure the great diversity of collective bargaining arrangements and the wide variations in collective bargaining practices that exist in this country.

REFERENCES

BOOKS AND PAMPHLETS

American Enterprise Association, *Labor Unions and Public Policy,* Washington, D.C. (1958).

Bradley, Philip D., ed., *The Public Stake in Union Power,* Charlottesville, Virginia: University of Virginia Press (1959).

Chamber of Commerce of the United States, *Wage Determination and the Economics of Liberalism,* Washington, D.C. (1947).

Committee for Economic Development, *The Public Interest in National Labor Policy,* New York (1961).

Myers, A. Howard, *Crisis Bargaining: Management-Union Relations in Marginal Situations,* Boston: Northeastern University, Bureau of Business and Economic Research (1957).

National Association of Manufacturers, *Monopoly Power as Exercised by Labor Unions,* New York (no date).

United States Department of Labor, *Collective Bargaining in the Basic Steel Industry,* Washington, D.C. (January 1961).

Wolman, Leo, *Industry-wide Bargaining,* Irvington-on-Hudson, New York: The Foundation for Economic Education (1948).

———, ——, *Labor Monopoly,* New York: National Association of Manufacturers (1955).

ARTICLES

Alexander, Kenneth, "Strikes in Manufacturing, 1947–1957," *Quarterly Journal of Economics,* Vol. LXXVI (February 1962), pp. 122–144.

Brown, Douglas V., "Labor and Antitrust Laws," *American Bar Association Proceedings* (August 1955).

Chamberlain, Neil, "The Structure of Bargaining Units in the United States," *Industrial and Labor Relations Review,* Vol. X (October 1956).

Cox, Archibald, "Labor and the Antitrust Laws—A Preliminary Analysis," *University of Pennsylvania Law Review,* Vol. 104 (November 1955), pp. 252–284.

Goldberg, Arthur J., "Labor and Antitrust," Reprinted from *IUD Digest* (no date).

Herrnstadt, Irwin L., "The Reaction of Three Local Unions to Economic Adversity," *The Journal of Political Economy,* Vol. LXII (October 1954), pp. 425–439.

Kerr, Clark, and Llyod H. Fisher, "Multiple-Employer Bargaining: The San Francisco Experience," *Insights Into Labor Issues,* Richard A. Lester and Joseph Shister, eds., New York: Macmillan (1948).

Levinson, Harold M., "Pattern Bargaining: A Case Study of the Automobile Workers," *The Quarterly Journal of Economics,* Vol. LXXIV (1960), pp. 296–317.

Roosevelt, F. D., Jr., "Don't 'Pulverize' Labor," *Congressional Record* (February 19, 1953).

Seltzer, George, "The United Steelworkers and Unionwide Bargaining," *Monthly Labor Review,* Vol. 84 (February 1961), pp. 129–136.

U.S. Department of Labor, Bureau of Labor Statistics, "Employer Units in Collective Bargaining," Serial No. R.2013, Reprinted from the *Monthly Labor Review* (December 1950).

U.S. Department of Labor, Bureau of Labor Statistics, *The Employer Bargaining Unit,* BLS Report No. 1 (February 1953).

U.S. Department of Labor, Bureau of Labor Statistics, "Characteristics of Major Union Contracts," *Monthly Labor Review,* Vol. 79 (July 1956), pp. 805–811.

Chapter 17 The Stages of Collective Bargaining

Collective bargaining in the United States has been an evolutionary process. The legal requirement forcing businessmen to bargain with trade unions, under certain circumstances, came as a shock to many of them. It is not surprising that they were less than happy with this development and that they approached the bargaining table prepared to do battle with the representatives of their workers. As John A. Stephens, vice president of industrial relations in the U.S. Steel Corporation in 1955 put it:

> We have made substantial progress since the early years of our union relationship. Those early years were difficult. I don't mean that the present are not difficult, too, but we do have improved relationships. We then learned, and continue now to learn, that man has an almost infinite capacity for disagreement and that decency, good will, and understanding cannot be induced by law or discipline alone. The relationship some years ago was, of course, new on both sides. Adjusting to it required time, patience, tolerance, integrity of character . . .[1]

Economic historians have long found it convenient to analyze economic change in terms of stages[2] and it is equally convenient to analyze the development of collective bargaining in the United States in the same way. It must be pointed out, however, that not all relationships go through the stages to be described in the following section, and individual collective bargaining relationships do not always move in the same direction. At times there is retrogression when it appears that the two parties have lost ground in their efforts to live and work together. By and large, however, collective bargaining relationships tend to move along the same path—from an early stage of resistance to a later stage of acceptance.

[1] John A. Stephens, "Evolution of Labor Relations in U.S. Steel" in Neil W. Chamberlain, *Source Book on Labor,* New York: McGraw-Hill (1958), p. 50.
[2] One of the most recent—and best known—is the approach developed by W. W. Rostow in *The Stages of Economic Growth,* Cambridge: Cambridge University Press (1960).

THE STAGES OF COLLECTIVE BARGAINING

Open Warfare

Before 1935, many companies resisted trade unionism by any means at their disposal. Some firms maintained their own police forces, and members of these forces did not object to the rough handling of union organizers if they came on or near the premises. In the steel, coal, and automobile industries, for example, there were numerous instances of violence, this was played up at times in the press as class warfare. While this designation was less than accurate, it was a form of warfare.

The use of physical force did not disappear entirely after 1935 although—given the temper of the times—it became less widespread. More than a quarter of a century after the Wagner Act became law, there are many companies which continue to resist organization. Physical violence is still used occasionally to restrain union organizers, but more often management relies on more subtle techniques. There are cases where other elements in the community —the local police, the press, and even in some cases the ministry—have allied to discourage union organization in a community. Employers in some small communities which are just beginning to industrialize often maintain a discreet silence since they know that the local press, other businessmen in the community, and various community leaders will effectively discourage the activities of union organizers. And they know that overaction on their part would be a violation of the Taft-Hartley Act which could lead to lengthy litigation, and eventually to an organization election.[3]

Union leaders recognize such opposition as a form of warfare, and carefully plan their campaigns to break opposition to the union. They avoid violence and concentrate on a form of psychological warfare in their efforts to sign up a majority of the members of a company or plant before requesting a National Labor Relations Board election.[4]

The stage of open warfare—which has been at times marked by bitter resistance to unionism in unorganized companies—can be brief or it can last a long time. But where there has been total op-

[3] For a carefully documented account of tactics used by anti-union employers see: *Almost Unbelievable . . . The Story of an Industry, the Union and the Law,* New York: Textile Workers Union of America (1961).

[4] An exception should be noted in the case of the small handful of unions which have been associated with racketeers. They have often used "goon squads" of strong-arm men to bring both recalcitrant workers and employers into line. See Robert F. Kennedy, *The Enemy Within,* New York: Harper and Brothers (1960).

position to organization on the part of management, the scars of this stage of the relationship can last a long time even after a company has been successfully organized.

Grudging Recognition

Under the law, if a majority of workers in the bargaining unit vote to be represented by a union, management must recognize the union and bargain collectively with its representatives. But especially in cases where recognition has followed a long period of warfare between the union and management, the early relationship is likely to be a strained one to say the very least. Management will make it clear that it did not want to recognize the union but was forced to do so. Bargaining during this stage of the relationship is often quite hectic. There is much table pounding, much talk of prerogatives and of legal obligations. If the management has fought hard to keep a union out of the plant or company it is not likely to give in gracefully once recognition has been forced upon it by a majority vote. There is often a feeling of resentment against the workers who voted for the union, and there is even greater resentment against the "outsiders"—the representatives of the national or international union—with whom management must deal. An interesting example of this stage of collective bargaining is given by Shultz and Coleman involving an actual bargaining relationship between a company, which has been given the fictitious name of the Lennox Corporation, and the union with which it dealt.[5]

In the Lennox Case, management objected to the union because it allegedly introduced a leveling influence into the work group and deprived management of the flexibility it needed to run the business. In addition, it was charged that the union leaders were personally difficult to get along with and that they insisted upon introducing extraneous issues into plant-level bargaining. In this case the top management of the company felt that the collective bargaining relationship would not survive—that the union was not there to stay. The only reason the union won elections in the company's five plants, top management believed, was that lower management was not effectively practicing the personnel policy laid down at the top. Its objective was to hold the union at bay until such time as new supervisors could be trained to implement what top management firmly believed was a sound personnel

[5] "Holding the Union at Bay: The Lennox Case," in George P. Shultz and John R. Coleman, *Labor Problems: Cases and Readings*, New York: McGraw-Hill (1953), pp. 125–133.

policy which would eventually wean workers away from their loyalty to the union.

Under such conditions a collective bargaining relationship cannot stand on solid ground—it is similar to an armed truce. During this stage of the relationship, the union must engage in hard bargaining to retain the loyalty of the workers it has signed up. And management's anti-union position is generally played up by union leaders to bolster the solidarity of the rank and file. It is made perfectly clear to the workers involved that the company is out to "get" the union, and that if this happens the workers will once again be at a complete disadvantage. It is also pointed out that union activists will be subject to retribution if the union is driven out of the plant. The stage of grudging recognition is essentially unstable. Either the union will be able to convince management that it is there to stay, and that management had better adopt a reasonable attitude toward it, or the management view will prevail and workers can be convinced that it is in their best interests to vote for decertification at the next NLRB election. More often than not, union leaders are able to convince management that the union is not going to be dislodged, and the relationship moves on to the next stage.

3. *Accommodation or Willing Recognition*

During the period of grudging recognition there is likely to be a feeling of ill will on both sides of the bargaining table. But anger is an emotion that is difficult to sustain. Either there will be a blowup and the relationship will fall apart, or the ill feeling will gradually subside and the two parties will begin to work together on a more amicable basis. This is partly due to changes in personal relationships. Gradually management recognizes that it can work with the union. As the leadership of the local union begins to feel more secure some of the early antagonism toward management will begin to disappear. Collective bargaining becomes a process of give and take. There is a greater amount of information sharing, the parties become somewhat less adamant in their bargaining positions, and the general process of accommodation begins to take place. The settlement of grievances may become more informal and flexible than during the earlier stage of grudging recognition and earlier personal animosities may disappear.[6]

[6] For an interesting example of accommodation see: Frederick H. Harbison and King Carr, *Causes of Industrial Peace Under Collective Bargaining: The Libbey-Owens-Ford Glass Company and the Federation of Glass, Ceramic, and Silica Sand Workers of America,* Washington: National Planning Association (1948), partly reprinted in Shultz and Coleman, *op. cit.,* pp. 133–150.

Many bargaining relationships no doubt do not go beyond the stage of accommodation. But at this stage the two parties have learned to work and live together. Management no longer seeks to alienate the loyalty of workers to their union. The union gives up its attack on management *per se* and concentrates on issues and problems. At this stage of development, collective bargaining has become stabilized. There can be strong differences of opinion, and even occasional strikes, but the relationship is one that is likely to endure. There can still be a great deal of hard bargaining under such conditions. But the two parties want to reach agreement; they are no longer interested in attempting to destroy each other. The periods of warfare and armed truce are over and both labor and management are interested in finding a formula which will lead to their mutual survival.[7]

Acceptance

There are many labor-management relationships which do not go beyond the stage of accommodation or willing recognition. There are other cases in which management comes to accept the union completely. There is a difference between recognition and acceptance although it is partly one of degree. A collective bargaining relationship reaches the stage of acceptance when a company would not be willing to give up its relationship with the union even if it had an opportunity to do so. To the uninitiated this might seem highly improbable. Even if a relationship is of the best, it might be argued, wouldn't management still prefer to avoid dealing with a union? The answer to this question will often be yes. But there are other cases in which it would be no.

Once the leaders of a union feel that they and the union have been completely accepted by management the whole collective bargaining relationship is changed. It is no longer a contest. Both sides recognize that they stand to gain from working together. The day-to-day relationship between shop stewards and foremen is an easy one. Problems are often settled informally, and there may be considerable consultation between union and management representatives.

Union leaders, secure in their position, can develop an interest in the efficiency of the company. The union can help maintain discipline; absenteeism, tardiness, and careless work habits can be discouraged by local union leaders. There is no reason at this stage of a relationship for carrying on an unremitting attack on manage-

[7] See E. Wight Bakke, *Mutual Survival The Goal of Unions and Management,* New Haven: Yale University Labor and Management Center (1946).

ment. Instead, the union can point out to rank and file workers that everyone stands to gain if the overall productivity of the company can be improved.

Complete acceptance of a union does not mean the end of hard bargaining. What it does mean is that both sides argue from the conviction that what they demand—or are willing to give—will serve the best interests of all concerned. Acceptance of the union does not mean—as some have implied—the "sharing" of management. Management continues to run the company and the union to represent its workers. Union leaders and management will not always see eye to eye. It is possible for negotiations to break down and strikes to result even where the union is fully accepted. But when the stage of acceptance has been achieved, such strikes are conducted without acrimony or bitterness. Once the issues have been resolved the two parties are able to resume their relationship on the former basis.

It is likely that a considerable number of collective bargaining relationships in the United States have reached the stage of acceptance. This is, of course, a highly stable kind of relationship. Once an agreement has been reached management knows that the union will make every effort to live up to the terms of the contract, and the security of the union is reflected in good work habits, high worker morale, and little or no bickering over relatively unimportant issues.

Union-Management Cooperation

Acceptance of the union is undoubtedly the terminal stage in most labor-management relationships in the United States. There are a number of cases of union-management cooperation, however, which go beyond the stage of acceptance. In this section union-management cooperation will be discussed in general terms. In a later section of this chapter one particularly successful approach to cooperation will be discussed in greater detail.

Union-management cooperation is not something entirely new in collective bargaining.[8] There is evidence that cooperative arrangements have been spreading although slowly. Union-management cooperation exists wherever the two parties work *jointly* on one or more phases of the labor-management relationship. In some cases this might simply be the joint determination of piece rates. At the

[8] For a discussion of several experiments in union-management cooperation during the 1920's and 1930's, see Sumner H. Slichter, *Union Policies and Industrial Management,* Washington, D.C.: The Brookings Institution (1941), pp. 393–571.

other extreme, however, joint committees might be established to discuss all problems relating to production, sales, and distribution.

In some cases, union-management cooperation is accompanied by profit sharing, but this is not a necessary condition for cooperation to exist. The difference between the stage of acceptance and the stage of cooperation can now be made somewhat more explicit.

During the stage of acceptance, collective bargaining proceeds along traditional lines. The union formulates a set of demands and management formulates a set of counter proposals. Then an agreement is negotiated. There is considerable give and take at the bargaining table with each side recognizing the good faith of the other. And the day-to-day administration of the agreement, once it is signed, can be highly informal and flexible. But the identity of management and the identity of the union are clearly maintained. The relationship is friendly, and there is a strong spirit of cooperation on both sides. However there is no *formal* arrangement for the two parties to settle issues or to approach problems on a *joint* basis. Once joint committees are set up the relationship has moved into the stage of union-management cooperation. The objective of such joint action is to increase the efficiency of the company. As Joseph Shister has put it: "Union-management cooperation will be said to exist when the union and the management in question, through joint action, attempt to reduce the unit costs of production."[9] Shister points out that union-management cooperation should not be confused with industrial peace. Cooperation cannot exist without industrial peace, but industrial peace can and does exist without joint action by labor and management to improve efficiency.

In general, union-management cooperation is an outgrowth of adversity. The company involved finds itself in a difficult competitive situation which can be due to a number of factors—poor management in the past, the growth of new forms of competition, or the impact of a sudden recession, for example. If union leaders and management are on good terms when adversity strikes, it is not unusual for them to discuss the situation. Out of such discussions have grown a number of formal plans for cooperation.[10]

Union-management cooperation may lead to temporary action or to a permanent arrangement. In some cases, for example, unions and employers have jointly hired outside experts to analyze the com-

[9] Joseph Shister, "Union-Management Cooperation: An Analysis," *Insights Into Labor Issues,* Richard A. Lester and Joseph Shister, eds., New York: The Macmillan Company (1948), p. 87.
[10] *Ibid.,* pp. 87–91.

pany's problems and recommend a course of action. In other cases —notably in the garment industry—the union provides expert help by sending its business agents and technicians into a company to help improve its efficiency. These approaches fit the definition of union-management cooperation since they involve joint action, but they do not lead to permanent arrangements. In other cases, however, the union and the employer set up one or more joint committees to encourage worker suggestions for the improvement of operations or for the continuing study of production problems. Such programs are intended to be of a continuing nature, and often are incorporated in the labor-management agreement.[11]

Does union-management cooperation mean the end of collective bargaining? Do the identities of the union and the company become submerged in a common enterprise? Is union-management cooperation a form of collusion in which the two parties look after their own interests without regard to the effects on consumers? The answer to all three questions is an emphatic no. There are enough cases of union-management cooperation on record to support the conclusion that the companies and unions involved maintain their identities, and continue to perform their respective functions as in the days before the cooperative schemes were established. It is possible that the emphasis in collective bargaining has shifted somewhat from the negotiation of agreements to the day-to-day administration of these agreements. But the establishment of joint committees does not preclude the possibility of disagreement or even of strikes, although it must be admitted that the latter are fairly rare where cooperative relationships have been established.

It is particularly important to distinguish between union-management cooperation which is associated with efforts to reduce unit costs of production, and union-management collusion. There have been—and undoubtedly still are—instances of the latter. In the case of craft unions, the union can agree to deal only with certain employers and the employers in turn to hire only union members. The objective might be to restrict production and raise prices with obvious benefits to management and workers, but at the expense of consumers. Such collusion can be effective only in local market areas, however, and both parties run the risk of prosecution under the antitrust laws if they practice such collusion. The objectives are quite different in the two cases. Collusion is illegal and it is detri-

[11] See Sumner H. Slichter, James J. Healy, and E. Robert Livernash, *The Impact of Cooperative Bargaining on Management,* Washington, D.C.: The Brookings Institution (1960), p. 845.

mental to consumers. Union-management cooperation is quite legal, and if it results in improved efficiency it leads to benefits for management, workers, and the consumer.

It is worth repeating that relatively few labor-management relationships reach the cooperative stage; the terminal stage for most relationships will be that of acceptance. There are very few instances in which formal schemes of union-management cooperation have evolved in the absence of economic adversity. It is only when a company—and the jobs of its workers—are threatened that the two parties appear to be willing to work jointly towards a solution of their common problems. Labor-management cooperation is still more an exception than the rule even when a company is in serious jeopardy. In most cases the company, if it cannot solve its problems unilaterally, goes out of business, and its workers are faced with the problem of finding new jobs. But in the relatively limited number of cases where union-management cooperation has been tried it seems to have worked well. In a later discussion, however, we will consider some of the limitations of this approach to collective bargaining and the operation of a business.

THE CAUSES OF INDUSTRIAL PEACE

Labor-management conflict is as old as the institution of trade unionism, and there is a voluminous literature dealing with clashes between organized workers and the owners or managers of capital. In the late 1940's, however, Clinton S. Golden—a former union official who had served as a United States labor representative abroad—remarked at a meeting of the National Planning Association: "In my opinion, the time has come when, instead of looking into the causes of conflict that we know and hear so much about, we ought to try to discover *how much peace there is* and *what makes peace*."[12] Mr. Golden's suggestion was quickly adopted by the NPA, and in 1947 the Committee on the Causes of Industrial Peace under Collective Bargaining was established with Mr. Golden as chairman. For the next six years the NPA sponsored a series of case studies in a wide variety of manufacturing enterprises extending across the nation. Each case was unique in some respects but there were also a number of points of similarity. The case studies reveal the diversity of conditions under which industrial peace can be achieved. But they also reveal that there are basic causes of industrial peace, common to all of the cases. These causes, listed in

[12] From the "Background Statement" by Clinton S. Golden included in each of the *Causes of Industrial Peace Series* published by the National Planning Association.

the final report on this interesting and enlightening investigation, are:

1. There is full acceptance by management of the collective bargaining process and of unionism as an institution. The company considers a strong union an asset to management.
2. The union fully accepts private ownership and operation of the industry; it recognizes that the welfare of its members depends upon the successful operation of the business.
3. The union is strong, responsible, and democratic.
4. The company stays out of the union's internal affairs; it does not seek to alienate the workers' allegiance to their union.
5. Mutual trust and confidence exists between the parties. There have been no serious ideological incompatabilities.
6. Neither party in bargaining has adopted a legalistic approach to the solution of problems in the relationship.
7. Negotiations are "problem-centered"—more time is spent on day-to-day problems than on defining abstract principles.
8. There is widespread union-management consultation and highly developed information-sharing.
9. Grievances are settled promptly, in the local plant whenever possible. There is flexibility and informality within the procedure.[13]

It should not be inferred that the cases studied by the National Planning Association are unique, or that the case studies are exhaustive. The NPA sought to present a representative sample of outstandingly peaceful relationships—not a complete listing of them. The conditions discussed in the case studies can also be found in many other situations which have not received the same amount of publicity. And it is likely that the widely-publicized case studies helped further industrial peace in a number of other situations.[14]

The case studies leave some questions unanswered. Can peaceful labor-management relations weather severe economic crises? What happens when labor-management peace continues for a long time? How do the employees view these peaceful relationships? Is industrial peace possible only when the environment is favorable? And what is likely to happen when the favorable environment changes?[15] These questions have not been fully answered. And it

[13] Charles A. Myers, "Conclusions and Implications," *Fundamentals of Labor Peace—A Final Report,* Washington, D.C.: National Planning Association (December 1953), pp. 93–94.
[14] *Ibid.,* pp. 100–101.
[15] *Ibid.,* pp. 103–105.

has been suggested that follow-up studies, after a considerable lapse of time, might shed some light on them.

The authors of the case studies did not suggest that the companies and unions they investigated had found a magic formula for ensuring labor-management peace at all costs. It seems likely, however, that where peaceful relationships have been worked out—where the company fully accepts the union, and where the union fully accepts private ownership and operation of the company—that the two parties would be better able to weather adversity than if they remained in a state of armed truce. The NPA case studies have made an important contribution to our understanding of the causes of industrial peace. Subsequent investigation will no doubt be needed to see how these relationships have weathered the effects of time and changing economic conditions.

PROFIT-SHARING AND UNION-MANAGEMENT COOPERATION

Profit-Sharing as an Anti-Union Device

It should not be supposed that profit-sharing and union-management cooperation are synonymous. Indeed, profit-sharing is often used as a device to keep unions out of a company. It is difficult to estimate the number of profit-sharing plans in the United States, but only 38 per cent of the companies belonging to the Council of Profit Sharing Industries in 1957 had recognized trade unions.[16]

Where profit-sharing and union-management agreements are found in conjunction, it is likely that the labor-management relationship is a mature one and that the two parties have worked out a successful formula for living and working together. American unions, in general, have not tried to negotiate profit-sharing plans. Thus where a company has recognized a union and also operates a profit-sharing plan it is likely that management has taken the initiative in working out the latter arrangement.

Profit-Sharing and Union-Management Cooperation—the "Scanlon Plan"

As noted earlier, cooperation exists only where there is *joint* action by the union and management to improve efficiency. There can be cooperation with or without profit sharing. In a number of cases, however, unions and managements have developed profit-sharing

[16] Joseph B. Meier, ed., *Profit Sharing Manual,* Council of Profit Sharing Industries (1957 edition), pp. 408–414 and 448–450. There were 159 members of the Council in 1957; of these, 60 had agreements with unions.

schemes which are based upon formal programs of union-management cooperation. The most famous of these is undoubtedly the "Scanlon Plan," named after the man who developed this unique form of labor-management cooperation the late Joseph N. Scanlon.

The originator of the Scanlon Plan was an unusual man—a one-time prizefighter, cost accountant, steelworker, local-union president, research director of the United Steelworkers of America, lecturer at the Massachusetts Institute of Technology, and labor relations consultant to a large number of enterprises. The scheme of labor-management cooperation which Scanlon developed will perpetuate his name in the annals of industrial relations.

What is the essence of the Scanlon Plan? Those who worked most closely with Scanlon in the development of this unique scheme of labor-management cooperation stress one thing—worker participation. In the words of one of Scanlon's closest collaborators. "This plan doesn't mean giving people a 'sense of participation'; workers don't want that. This plan means giving them real participation."[17]

One way to look at the Scanlon Plan is to consider it as a *group incentive* scheme, that is, individual workers are not rewarded for the suggestions they make—a very common procedure in many companies which have no form of labor-management cooperation. Instead, under the Scanlon Plan, every worker in the company benefits from gains in productivity. There is no distinction between "production" and "non-production" workers. Office workers, maintenance workers, production workers—everyone in the company—shares in the bonuses which are an integral part of the group incentive program under the Scanlon Plan.

In a typical Scanlon Plan situation, bonuses are determined by a ratio of total payroll to the sales value of what was produced by that payroll. The ratio is computed for some agreed-upon historical period, and then becomes the basis for computing extra dividends to workers in the form of bonus payments.

The ratio is used to determine a "normal" labor cost. In any month when actual labor costs are below this norm the difference between the two constitutes the bonus pool. Before payment is made, however, some part of the pool is set aside against possible deficit months in which the labor cost exceeds the norm. In many cases the bonus

[17] Frederick G. Lesieur, "What the Plan Isn't and Is," in Frederick G. Lesieur, (ed.), *The Scanlon Plan,* New York: John Wiley and Sons, Inc.—The Technology Press of M.I.T. (1958), p. 39.

is split with 25 per cent going to management, and 75 per cent going to the workers in the company.[18]

Thus far two aspects of the plan have been discussed—worker participation and the bonus scheme. But how are productivity gains actually achieved? The answer in its broadest sense has already been implied—gains in productivity result from worker suggestions. But there must be some system for processing these suggestions, and this is achieved through the establishment of joint union-management committees. There may be several kinds of committees such as screening committees which examine all worker suggestions and production committees which discuss actual operations.[19] Such joint committees epitomize union-management cooperation.

Union-management cooperation under the Scanlon Plan does not mean that management has ceased to operate the company or that the union has stopped representing its workers. What it does mean is that the two parties jointly solve problems which increases the company's productivity and from which both parties then benefit. The plan will not succeed if either party approaches it in a half-hearted way. The unions and companies which have adopted the Scanlon Plan have become enthusiasts.

The Scanlon Plan has been adopted by several dozen companies in a wide variety of industries. But the curious might raise the question: "If the Scanlon Plan has worked so well in the companies which have adopted it, why hasn't it spread throughout manufacturing industry?" This is not an easy question to answer. It does seem significant that the Scanlon Plan has been limited to small and medium-sized companies.[20] Not all of these companies are single-plant units; some are multiple-plant firms. But the plan has not been adopted by any of the nation's industrial giants. This suggests that the sort of environment in which the plan has worked is one where workers and management have a fairly close relationship. There is much less specialization in the small and medium-sized concern than is found in the large corporation with its numerous departments and management hierarchy. Thus one limitation on the spread of the Scanlon Plan appears to be the size of

[18] Elbridge S. Puckett, "Measuring Performance Under the Scanlon Pan," in Lesieur, *The Scanlon Plan*, p. 66. For a specific example of how the ratio is computed see pp. 67–73 of this article. See also, Russell W. Davenport, "Enterprise for Everyman," reprinted from the January 1950 issue of *Fortune*, as pp. 17–33 of *The Scanlon Plan*.
[19] George P. Shultz, "Worker Participation on Production Problems," *Personnel* (November 1950), p. 5, reprinted in Lesieur, *op. cit.*
[20] George P. Shultz, "Variations in Environment and the Scanlon Plan," in Lesieur, *op. cit.*, p. 101.

firm. It seems to be best adapted to those situations in which it is physically possible for workers and management to sit down together to discuss problems of mutual concern.

But there are thousands of firms in the small and medium-sized categories which have not adopted the Scanlon Plan or some variation of it. Why? One possible answer is that it calls for a considerable amount of "give" on both sides. Management undoubtedly has to be the first to unbend. Workers could easily be sold on the merits of union-management cooperation if they could anticipate additional monetary gains through bonus payments. But union-management cooperation involves the yielding of prerogatives by management. It is likely that the managers of many concerns feel that they know more about operating the company than the workers so why should they sit down with the latter to discuss production problems? Others might feel that they can tap worker ingenuity through a simple scheme of worker suggestions with bonuses paid directly to those workers whose suggestions are adopted. Such managers might feel that they are tapping the reservoir of worker experience, and yet the workers are kept at arms length. Management makes all the decisions and the workers do not actually participate in running the firm.

There are no doubt other reasons why the Scanlon Plan has not spread. One of the important characteristics of our economic and social system is its diversity. It is not likely that any single scheme will be embraced by all businessmen or unions, yet the record of the Scanlon Plan remains an impressive one. Many of the companies which have adopted it were in serious financial difficulty before they elected to try union-management cooperation. Others were not in difficulty, but they realized substantial gains in productivity once the plan was put into effect. There have been a handful of cases in which the Plan failed, but these few failures can be explained. In some cases the Scanlon Plan was conceived as a substitute for collective bargaining. Where this attitude has been found the plan has not worked.[21] In other cases either management or the workers decided to try the plan without being fully convinced of its merits. It appears that a complete commitment is required if the plan is to succeed and where this commitment has been made there have been no failures.

The Scanlon Plan is not, of course, foolproof. If the major product of a company is rendered obsolete by technological change—or some

[21] Schultz, *op. cit.*, p. 107.

other outside disturbance—and the company is not in a position to adapt to some other type of production, the Scanlon Plan alone could not guarantee success. The plan is not a substitute for good management or for good union leadership. But where the combination of good management and sound union leadership is found, and where the two parties are willing to engage in union-management cooperation without reservation, the evidence strongly suggests that the Scanlon Plan is more than a scheme for achieving mutual survival. It is a stimulus to growth and prosperity shared by management and workers alike.

CONCLUSIONS

The stages of collective bargaining discussed in this chapter are useful in helping analyze labor-management relations in a wide variety of situations. Not all relationships go through these stages. Some never go beyond the stage of grudging recognition and there are numerous cases where managements have succeeded in keeping unions out of the company by one means or another. In most situations, however, when a union is recognized there is gradual progress at least to the stage of accommodation. Complete labor-management cooperation and aggressive resistance to unionism are still extremes in the spectrum of labor-management relations. Also, progress is not always in one direction. There have been cases where management has accommodated itself to the union, and the relationship has appeared to be on a sound footing. But then for one of a number of reasons—a change in management or union leadership, for example—the relationship deteriorates and goes back to the status of an armed truce. There are even some cases where workers vote to give up their union affiliation. By and large, however, labor-management relations in the United States have been evolutionary. The general pattern has been one of movement from resistance to the union, to recognition, and gradually to acceptance. There is no assurance that this trend will continue. In a later section we will consider some changes in management attitudes toward trade unions as our economy has prospered, and some of the changes in unions themselves as we have moved into the age of affluence.

REFERENCES

BOOKS

Bakke, E. Wight, *Mutual Survival the Goal of Unions and Management,* New Haven: Yale University Labor and Management Center (1946).

Causes of Industrial Peace Under Collective Bargaining, Washington, D.C.: National Planning Association, Case Studies 1–13, 1948–1953.

Harbison, Frederick H., and John R. Coleman, *Goals and Strategy in Collective Bargaining,* New York: Harper and Brothers (1951).

Lesieur, Frederick G., ed., *The Scanlon Plan . . . A Frontier in Labor-Management Cooperation,* New York: The Technology Press of M.I.T. and John Wiley and Sons, Inc. (1958).

Meier, Joseph B., ed., *Profit Sharing Manual,* Council of Profit Sharing Industries (1957 Edition).

Shultz, George P., and John R. Coleman, *Labor Problems: Cases and Readings,* New York: McGraw-Hill Book Company, Inc. (1953).

Slichter, Sumner H., *Union Policies and Industrial Management,* Washington, D.C.: The Brookings Institution (1941).

———, ——— —, James J. Healy, and E. Robert Livernash, *The Impact of Collective Bargaining on Management,* Washington, D.C.: The Brookings Institution (1960).

ARTICLES

Chamberlain, Neil W., "Collective Bargaining and Union-Management Cooperation," Chapter 18, *Collective Bargaining,* New York: McGraw-Hill Book Company, Inc. (1951), pp. 415–442.

Myers, Charles A., "Conclusions and Implications," *Fundamentals of Labor Peace—A Final Report,* Case Study No. 14, Causes of Industrial Peace in the Collective Bargaining Series, Washington, D.C.: The National Planning Association (1953).

Shister, Joseph, "Union-Management Cooperation: An Analysis," Richard A. Lester and Joseph Shister, eds., New York: The Macmillan Company (1948), pp. 87–115.

PART 5

labor economics: the labor market and wage determination

Chapter 18 The Labor Force and the Labor Market

LABOR AND THE PROCESS OF PRODUCTION

In primitive society man lived by the sweat of his brow. He had nothing but the most rudimentary tools to work with and this was reflected in his standard of living which was abysmally low. It was only after man had learned to accumulate capital—in the form of primitive tools and labor-saving devices—that he began to experience a rising standard of living. As civilizations evolved some men became owners of capital and others remained workers. But most members of society find it necessary to work for a living; only a small minority are able to live on the fruits of past capital accumulation.

There are many kinds of work. Some jobs are stimulating and interesting while others are dull, repetitive and monotonous. Some jobs pay well, others pay poorly. Some kinds of work require many years of training, others are essentially unskilled. It does not follow, however, that the highly trained are always well paid, although it is generally true that those without skills—in honest occupations—are poorly paid.

There must be some mechanism for determining how workers are allocated to the various sectors of an economy and for determining how much they will be paid for the work they do. Thus it makes sense to talk about a labor market just as it does about product markets, although there are important differences between them. In this and the following chapters we will be concerned with the economics of the labor market; with the demand for and the supply of workers, with wage determination under union and nonunion conditions, with productivity, and with the distribution of income.

Each of these topics could occupy a book several times the length of this one and we can deal with them only in a summary way, but an effort will be made to cover the rudiments of the major areas of labor economics.

POPULATION AND LABOR FORCE

There were approximately 180 million persons living in the United States in 1960, and there had been an enormous upsurge—roughly 30 million—in population during the 1950's. This rapid growth is expected to continue, and to reach about 208 million by 1970.[1] Population is heavily concentrated along the Atlantic Seaboard, in the Great Lakes States, and along the Pacific Coast, but the vast area which includes the Central and Mountain States is also filling up. The center of population—an abstract measure which defines a point at which the United States would be balanced if it were a flat plane—has been steadily shifting westward. The American economy must feed, clothe, and provide for the other material wants of this large and rapidly growing number of persons. And, of course, not everyone in the population is actively employed. Only about 73 million persons—or 40 per cent of the total population—were included in the labor force in 1960. And fewer than 70 million, including the armed forces, were employed.

Labor Force Measurement

The labor force in the United States is defined as the noninstitutional population fourteen years of age and over. Those in schools, hospitals, prisons, and other institutions—regardless of age—are not considered to be part of the active work force. A profile of the labor force is given in Chart 18-1 based on 1955–1960 averages to minimize the effects of the swings in economic activity called the business cycle.

The average noninstitutional population fourteen years of age and over during this period came to slightly more than 121 million persons. Of these, about 71.2 million—or 59 per cent—were in the *total* labor force. It is customary to subtract the members of the armed forces—who numbered slightly more than two and one-half million during this period—since they are not available for civilian employment. After this adjustment, the *civilian* labor force during the latter half of the 1950's averaged about 68.3 million, or 56 per cent of the noninstitutional population. The civilian labor force is

[1] *Manpower Challenge of the 1960's,* Washington: U.S. Department of Labor (no date), p. 4.

CHART 18–1
THE LABOR FORCE, 1955–1960 AVERAGES
(in thousands)

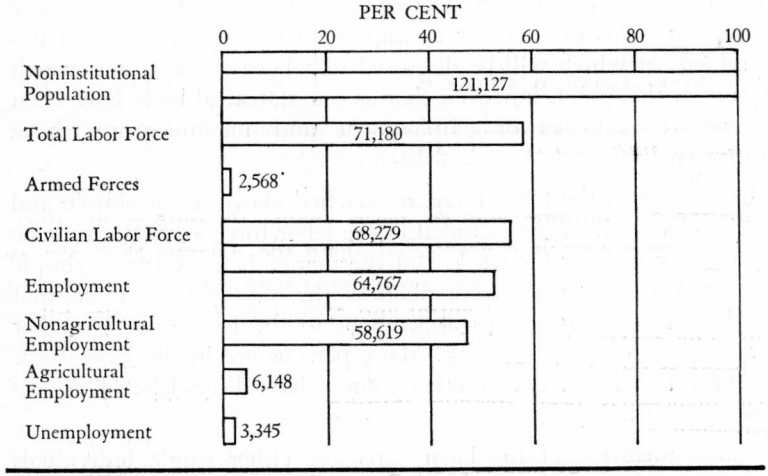

Source: *Economic Report of the President* (January 1962), p. 230.

defined as the number of persons who are employed plus those who are unemployed but looking for work. Chart 18-1 shows that about 53 per cent of the noninstitutional population consisted of employed persons and the vast bulk of these were in nonagricultural employment. Farm workers accounted for only slightly more than 6.1 million persons. An average of slightly more than 3.3 million were unemployed during this period.

Since 1790 the federal government has conducted a census of the population at ten-year intervals, and for more than two decades the government has made monthly estimates—based on carefully designed sample surveys—of the labor force. The decennial census reports provide thoroughly detailed information about the *occupational status* of the work force while the monthly report on the labor force emphasizes labor-force attachment.[2] The object of the labor force surveys is to determine the total number of persons employed and the number out of jobs but seeking work. The first labor force

[2] Joseph Scherer, "Labor Force: Concepts, Measurement, and Use of Data," *The Journal of Business of the University of Chicago,* Vol. XXXI (January 1958), p. 39. See also A. J. Jaffe and C. D. Stewart, *Manpower Resources and Utilization,* New York: John Wiley and Sons, Inc. (1951), p. 448; and *Measuring Employment and Unemployment* by the President's Committee to Appraise Employment and Unemployment Statistics, Washington: U.S. Government Printing Office (1962). For an excellent and detailed historical account, see Stanley Lebergott, *Manpower in Economic Growth,* New York: McGraw-Hill (1964).

surveys were conducted by the Works Progress Administration toward the end of the Great Depression. In 1942, the Bureau of the Census began to make these surveys on a regular basis with the results published by the U.S. Department of Labor. There are some complexities involved in the measurement of employment and unemployment which will be discussed in a later chapter. It is worth noting at this point, however, that as our statistical tools have been sharpened estimates of employment and unemployment have improved.

The concept of the labor force as sketched above seems simple and straightforward. To be included in the labor force a person must be at work or looking for work. But the matter is not quite as simple as that. Some persons are members of the *regular* labor force, that is, they have a continuous attachment to the labor force whether working or looking for work. Many persons are in the labor force at some times and not at others; these have been labeled as *secondary* workers.[3]

Regular members of the labor force are either single individuals who must support themselves or heads of families who must support not only themselves but their dependents. Secondary workers are primarily women who move into and out of the labor force as work becomes available to them and as they are impelled to do so by economic or other reasons. Most workers in the labor force, by far, have a regular attachment. There is no question about the status of such workers. It is not easy, however, to estimate the proportion of workers in the labor force with a less than permanent attachment, although it should be noted that those in this category are a relatively small minority.

There are advantages to an "elastic" labor force. At times of emergency, such as during World War II, we have been able to call upon millions of additional workers who would not normally be employed or seeking jobs. Even in the absence of emergencies, it is advantageous to employers—and to the economy as a whole—to have a flexible supply of labor. There are many women who are pleased to have an opportunity to be employed some of the time, but because of family responsibilities or other reasons would not wish to have a full-time job year in and year out.[4] As will be

[3] Richard C. Wilcock, "The Secondary Labor Force and the Measurement of Unemployment," *The Measurement and Behavior of Unemployment,* National Bureau of Economic Research, Princeton, New Jersey: Princeton University Press (1957), p. 167.

[4] Thomas A. Mahoney, "Factors Determining the Labor-Force Participation of Married Women," *Industrial and Labor Relations Review,* Vol. 14 (July 1961), pp. 563–577.

noted in a later chapter, however, the existence of secondary labor force members contributes somewhat to the problems involved in obtaining accurate estimates of unemployment.

The Part-Time Work Force

Not everyone who has a job works full-time. In 1960 about 82 per cent of all workers employed in nonagricultural industries were at work full-time (35 hours a week or more), while about 11 per cent worked part-time (1 to 34 hours) on a voluntary basis. An additional 3 per cent worked part-time on a temporary basis for noneconomic reasons; the remaining 4 per cent worked on a part-time basis for economic reasons. About half of the latter indicated that they usually worked full-time while the remaining half usually worked part-time. As might be expected, a considerably larger proportion of men (87 per cent) work full-time than women (71 per cent). Only six per cent of employed male workers had part-time jobs for voluntary reasons, compared with 21 per cent of employed women.

Some jobs lend themselves more than others to part-time work. For example, part-time workers are most likely to be found in sales work, private household work, or service work excluding household employment. On the other hand, very few craftsmen or operatives choose to work on a part-time basis. Those in these occupations who are found to be working part-time usually indicate that this is for economic reasons, and that they prefer to work on a full-time basis.[5]

The authors of a comprehensive study of part-time employment concluded that: "Part-time employment has been growing faster than full-time, and this trend can be expected to continue. By 1970 there will probably be nearly 16 million part-time workers, but only a little more than half of them are likely to be voluntary part-time workers in non-farm industries."[6] There has been a significant increase in the number of workers who have been able to find only part-time jobs although they would prefer full-time employment. But the "bulk of the growth in part-time employment in the last five years can be traced to a rise in the number of workers who desire part-time jobs and the commensurate growth of industries adaptable to the use of a part-time labor supply."[7]

[5] Robert L. Stein and Jane L. Meredith, "Growth and Characteristics of the Part-Time Work Force," *Monthly Labor Review* (November 1960), p. 1172.
[6] *Ibid.*, p. 1175.
[7] *Ibid.*

CHART 18–2
CIVILIAN LABOR FORCE, TOTAL EMPLOYMENT, AND GROSS NATIONAL PRODUCT
Seasonally Adjusted, Quarterly Averages

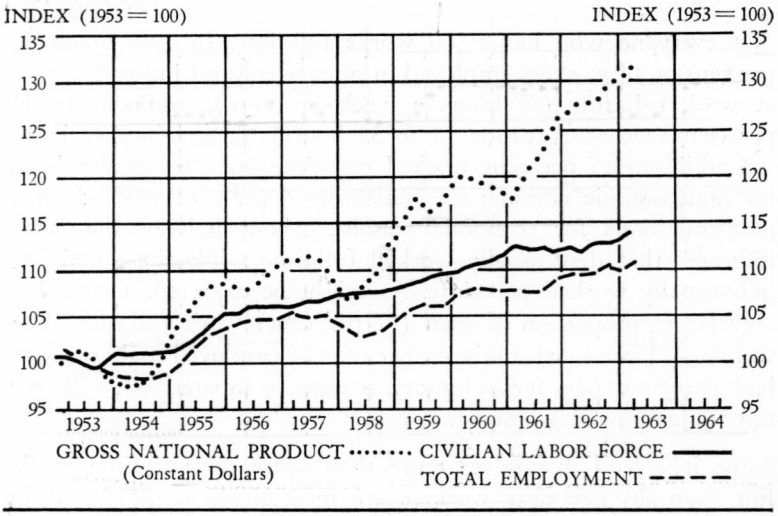

Source: Chart taken from publication of the United States Department of Labor, Bureau of Labor Statistics. Beginning January 1960 data include Alaska and Hawaii

RECENT TRENDS IN THE CIVILIAN LABOR FORCE

Recent trends in the civilian labor force may be shown by a series of charts prepared by the Bureau of Labor Statistics. The first of these, Chart 18-2, shows trends since 1953 in the civilian labor force and in Gross National Product (the dollar value of all goods and services produced) in constant prices. Changes in total employment are also given on this chart. GNP has increased at a more rapid rate than the labor force indicating substantial gains in productivity. At the same time, total employment has gone up less than the labor force which means that many of those in the labor market have been unable to find jobs.

The pattern of employment also changed substantially during this decade. As Chart 18-3A indicates, there was a decline in the number of workers engaged in the production of goods with the sharpest drop in agriculture. But there was also a modest drop in the number of workers employed in the durable-goods sector of manufacturing. Employment in the remaining sectors shown in Chart 18-3A remained fairly stable.

CHART 18–3A
EMPLOYMENT IN GOODS-PRODUCING INDUSTRIES
Monthly 1953 to Date

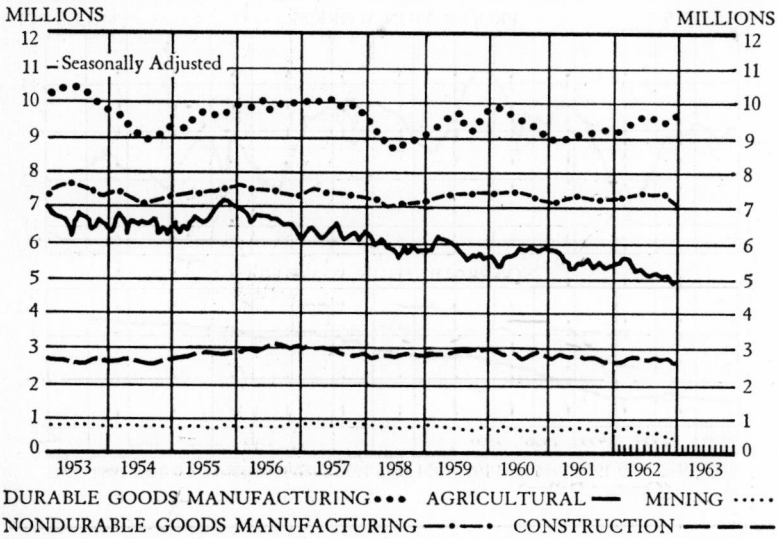

Source: Chart taken from publication of the United States Department of Labor, Bureau of Labor Statistics. Latest Data: December 1962

There was a pronounced shift in employment within the manufacturing sector as shown by Chart 18-3B. There was a drop in the number of production workers which was just about offset by the rise in nonproduction workers. Fewer hands are now required to turn out a growing volume of goods as an increasing amount of work is done by machines—often directed by electronic computers. However, a growing number of nonproduction workers—such as office employees and salesmen—are needed as output increases.

Finally, Chart 18-4 shows recent trends in the service-producing industries. Employment in federal government agencies was quite stable during the 10 years covered by this chart and there was a slight decline in transportation and public utilities. Employment in finance, and in the trade and service sectors rose, however. The strongest upsurge was in state and local government employment as a result of expansion of the public school system, including public higher education, and the expansion of other institutions providing services at the state and local levels.

CHART 18–3B
PRODUCTION AND NONPRODUCTION WORKERS IN MANUFACTURING
Seasonally Adjusted

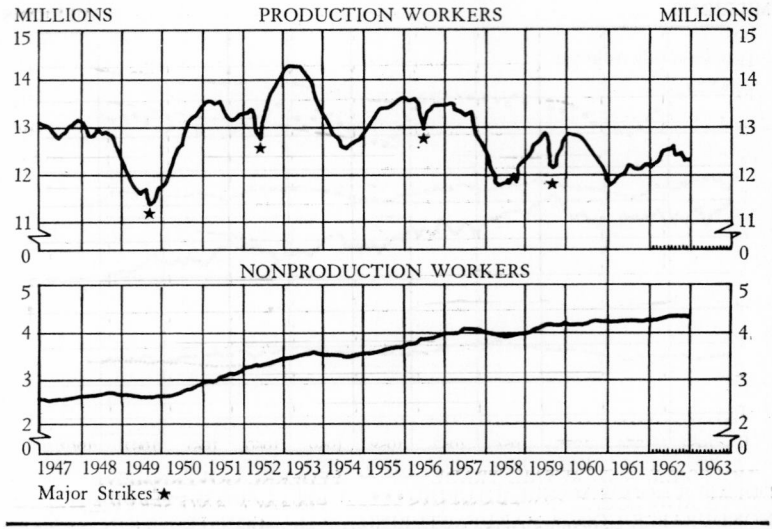

Source: Chart taken from publication of the United States Department of Labor, Bureau of Labor Statistics. Latest Data: December 1962

The Occupational Distribution of the Labor Force

The occupational distribution of the labor force has changed remarkably since the turn of the century. In 1900, for example, farm workers accounted for about 38 per cent of the employed civilian labor force; by 1950, this had dropped to 12 per cent. Meanwhile, the percentage of craftsman, operatives, and laborers (except farm and mine) had increased from 45 per cent to 52 per cent and there was an even sharper increase of white-collar workers, from 18 per cent to 37 per cent. Service workers in private households dropped from 5 per cent to 3 per cent, during this period, while service workers in other occupations increased from 4 per cent to 8 per cent.[8] These trends continued during the 1950's. In 1955, the number of white-collar workers matched those in manual occupations for the first time. There has been a further shift since then (see Chart 18-5). Employment in professional, managerial, trade and service occupations is expected to show a further rise and the number of farm workers

[8] *Occupational Trends in the United States, 1900 to 1950,* Bureau of the Census (1958), p. 7.

CHART 18–4
EMPLOYMENT IN SERVICE-PRODUCING INDUSTRIES
Monthly 1953 to Date

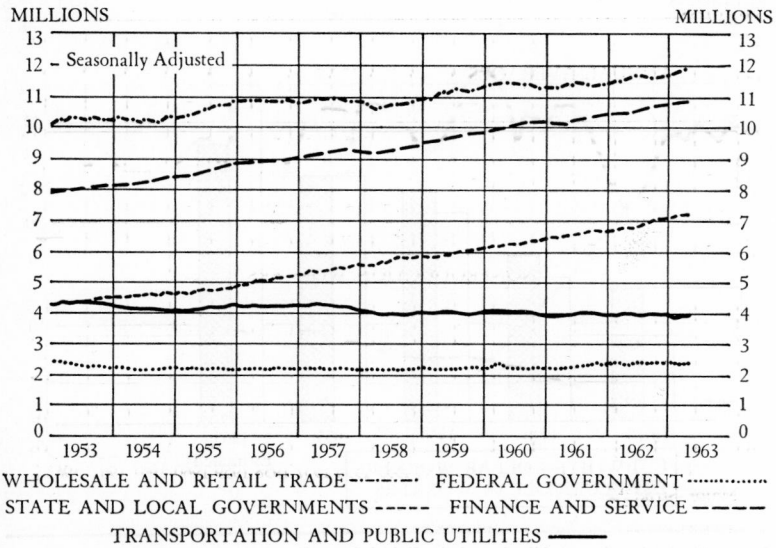

Source: Chart taken from publication of the United States Department of Labor, Bureau of Labor Statistics. Latest Data: May 1963

is expected to continue its slow decline.[9] The pattern of shifting occupations, with projections to 1965, is summarized in Chart 18-6.

These trends reflect the continued shift from agriculture to industry, the rapid expansion of research and development activities, the increasing size and complexity of business organizations requiring a growing amount of paper work, and an upsurge in the demand for educational and medical services. The key to these shifts—the factor which permits a more rapid rise in service-producing than in goods-producing occupations—is technological progress which leads to steady gains in productivity.[10] This will be discussed in detail in Chapter 21.

THE LABOR MARKET

The labor force constitutes the supply of workers in the labor market. We have noted that this supply is anything but homo-

[9] *Manpower Challenge of the 1960's*, p. 10.
[10] Robert L. Stein and Herman Travis, "Labor Force and Employment in 1960," *The Monthly Labor Review* (April 1961), p. 352.

CHART 18–5
EMPLOYMENT OF WHITE COLLAR AND BLUE COLLAR WORKERS
1910, 1940, 1950, 1955, and Estimated 1965

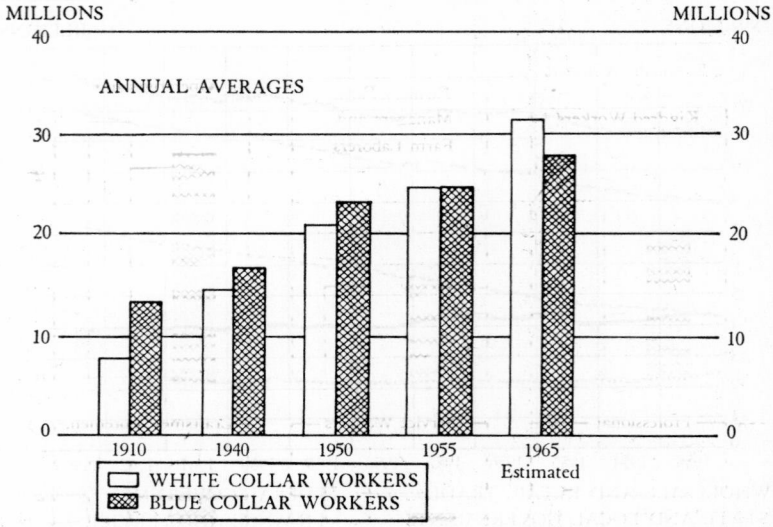

Source: Chart taken from publication of the United States Department of Labor, Bureau of Labor Statistics. Data for 1955 and 1965 not exactly comparable with earlier years.

geneous. While it is made up predominantly of full-time workers, many in the labor force choose to work on a part-time basis. There is also movement into and out of the labor force under changing economic conditions. And we do not fully understand all the forces which motivate persons to seek employment at different times and under different conditions.[11]

The supply of labor takes into account only half of the market equation, however. It is also necessary to look at the demand side. It should be noted at the outset that the labor market is far more complex than product markets. It makes little difference whether a potato is sold in California or in Maine and while the buyer and seller of the potato will both be concerned about its price, what happens to the potato after the transaction is of little consequence to the seller. This is not true of human beings. In a free society we stress the worth of the individual. Not everyone can be employed in the job of his choice; not everyone can earn as much money as he

[11] See Clarence D. Long, *The Labor Force Under Changing Income and Employment*, National Bureau of Economic Research, Princeton, New Jersey: Princeton University Press (1958).

CHART 18–6
EMPLOYMENT FOR MAJOR OCCUPATIONAL GROUPS
Actual 1955 and Estimated 1965

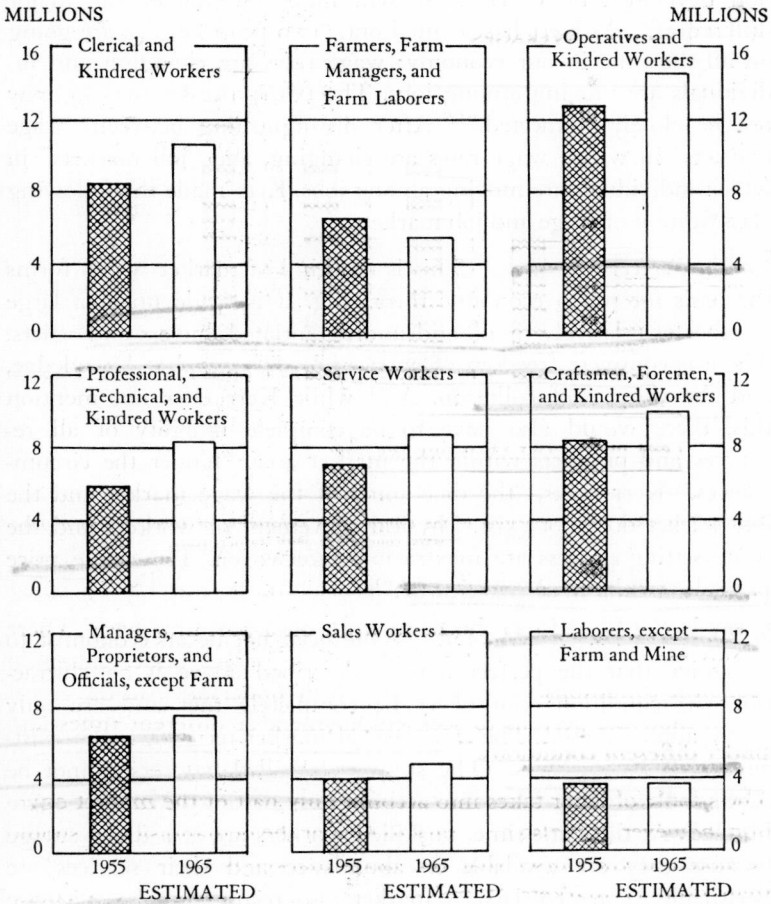

Source: 1955–U.S. Bureau of the Census, *Monthly Report on the Labor Force*. 1965–Projections by U.S. Bureau of Labor Statistics. Chart taken from publication of the United States Department of Labor, Bureau of Labor Statistics

would like, but whatever his occupation or his monetary reward, each individual feels that he is entitled to decent treatment and that the dignity of his person must be respected. Thus the simple models used to describe the operation of product markets can serve only as rough guides to a discussion of labor markets.

The Wage Market and the Job Market

Up to now we have referred to *the* labor market. But this is an oversimplification. In the real world there are many kinds of labor markets; while all of these cannot be discussed, a useful classification developed by Clark Kerr will indicate some of the major differences.[12] As Kerr has pointed out, "two processes . . . are going on all the time in our economy: wage rates are changing and individuals are moving among jobs. The two processes may or may not be closely connected."[13] After distinguishing between "wage markets" in which wage rates are changing, and "job markets" in which individuals are moving among jobs, Kerr made the following classification of wage and job markets:

1. *The Perfect Market.* This is the kind of market which forms the basis for much economic theorizing. It is made up of a large number of relatively small, and undifferentiated, buyers and sellers. There is complete freedom of entry and exit, complete knowledge, and the absence of collusion. And while Kerr does not mention this, there would also have to be complete mobility of all resources and products within the market area. "Under the circumstances," Kerr notes, "the dichotomy of the wage market and the job market does not exist. Physical movement of workers and the wage setting process are inextricably interwoven. The single price prevails and the market is cleared."[14]

ABSTRACTION

2. *The Neo-Classical Market.* One need not be an economist to recognize that the perfect market described above is an abstraction; its conditions can never be completely met and are only rarely approximated. The neo-classical market recognizes the existence of "imperfections." The supply of skilled workers cannot be expanded suddenly because it takes time for a worker to acquire his skill. At the same time, unskilled workers are at a disadvantage because they are available in abundance and their services are perishable. The neo-classical market also recognizes the existence of unions, but these are assumed to be "only sufficiently strong to offset market imperfections introduced by combinations, formal or informal, of employers."[15] Workers within each skill classification are presumed to be relatively homogeneous.

[12] Clark Kerr, "Labor Markets: Their Character and Consequences," *American Economic Review,* Papers and Proceedings, Vol. XL (May 1950), pp. 278–291.
[13] *Ibid.,* p. 278.
[14] *Ibid.,* p. 279. Kerr cites a description of such a perfect labor market in J. R. Hicks, *The Theory of Wages,* New York: The Macmillan Company (1935), pp. 4–5.
[15] *Ibid.,* p. 280.

In spite of the imperfections which it recognizes, the neo-classical model assumes that the market is what determines wages and the allocation of resources approaches the optimum in the long run. Thus while neither the wage market nor the job market make the instantaneous adjustments assumed in the perfect market, they are still closely related; indeed, they remain inseparable.[16]

3. *The Natural Market.* In the neo-classical model it is assumed that wages will tend toward equality for workers in a given skill classification. But there is an abundance of evidence that in the real world this equality of wages is not found. A characteristic of actual labor markets is wage diversity rather than wage uniformity. During World War II, when the War Labor Board collected volumes of wage data, it was found that within local labor markets, especially where there was no collective bargaining, there was a wide dispersion of wage rates. Contrary to a widespread belief that wage differentials are offset by "fringe benefits," the latter were found to "reinforce rather than offset the rate inequalities."[17]

In the natural market, the typical worker has a very limited view of the market as a whole, and unless he is unemployed or just entering the labor force, he is not "actively in the market." The workers' knowledge of the labor market may be limited to his own plant or office and other jobs about which he has general information. Workers do not regularly weigh the advantages of the jobs they hold against other alternatives and employers are not constantly hiring and firing workers in an effort to find the greatest bargains in the labor market.

In the natural market there is a fairly clear distinction between the "wage market" and the "job market." Wages are not set entirely by the free influence of competitive forces, and they do not tend toward equality. Also, resources are not necessarily used to their best advantage.

4. *The Institutional Market.* The institutional market is one in which the policies of unions, employers, and the government have more to do with wage movements than free competitive forces. Indeed, the objective of policies developed by all three—unions, employers, and the government—is to limit the free operation of the forces of supply and demand. Under these circumstances the wage market and the job market operate in two separate orbits.

[16] An outstanding economist in the neo-classical tradition was Alfred Marshall. See his *Principles of Economics*, New York: The Macmillan Company (8th edition, 1938).
[17] Kerr, *op. cit.*, p. 280.

Institutional policies—rather than the market—set the upper and lower limits of wages, and these clearly reduce the mobility of labor.

Uniform wages are often found for a given grade of workers in the institutional market, but this is because of the influence of institutions—notably unions, and to some extent government. It is not a result of the interaction of demand and supply. Demand and supply cannot be ignored, of course, but their influences is considerably curtailed by policies of unions, employers, and the government.

ABSTRACTION

5. *The Managed Market.* The managed market—like the perfect market—does not exist in the real world. The objective of the managed market would be to tie wage setting and worker movement more closely together than they are in the natural or institutional market. This would be accompanied by the imposition of state controls, of one kind or another, on wage setting, the allocation of labor, or perhaps both.

The long-run trend in the United States has been toward the institutional labor market but collective bargaining and government intervention have not eliminated wage diversity. Where unions have an influence on wages there is a tendency toward uniformity within a craft, or for given grades of labor within an industry, but there is still a great deal of wage diversity among labor markets. Occupational wage surveys conducted by the Bureau of Labor Statistics show that for identical occupations there are substantial variations in wages from community to community. The effects of institutional policies on the *general* level of wages are also debatable at best. Some writers feel that unions have succeeded in "raising" wages, but others believe that the wage level is about what it would have been in the absence of trade unions. We will consider this matter further in the following chapter which is concerned with wage determination.

Structured and Unstructured Labor Markets

Another useful way to view labor markets is to consider those which are *structured,* and those which are *unstructured* or "structureless."[18] Phelps has defined an unstructured labor market as one which "contains few, if any, established institutions by means of which people obtain market information, move into and out of

[18] See Lloyd H. Fisher, "The Harvest Labor Market in California," *Quarterly Journal of Economics* (November 1951); Clark Kerr, "The Balkanization of Labor Markets," *Labor Mobility and Economic Opportunity,* Cambridge, Massachusetts: The Technology Press of M.I.T.—John Wiley and Sons, Inc., (1954); and Orme W. Phelps, "A Structural Model of the U.S. Labor Market," *Industrial and Labor Relations Review,* Volume 10 (April 1957).

jobs, qualify for advances in rank or pay, or identify themselves with any type of organization . . ."[19] An extreme example of an unstructured labor market is the harvest labor market of California. This is so, according to Fisher, because there are no unions, the workers are unskilled, payment is by unit of product, little capital equipment is used, and relations between the worker and his employer are transitory and impersonal. In such a labor market payment is usually in cash and while rates will vary greatly over time they tend to be uniform at any moment within a local labor market area.[20]

According to Clark Kerr, some structure can be introduced into a labor market without institutional rules. This is so because some workers are more highly skilled than others; skilled crafts exist even without craft unions. But the degree of structure is increased as the labor market becomes institutionalized. In such markets institutional rules limit the movement of workers, they affect hiring policies, and often they are the deciding factor in wage determination.

Phelps has distinguished three main types of structured labor markets. First, there is the market for public employees which is highly structured by legislation and administrative rules. The second type is the non-union labor market in the large firm where the rules are laid down by the personnel or industrial relations department. Finally, there is the labor market in which rules are negotiated by unions and formalized in the labor-management agreement.[21] Phelps has estimated that at least one-third of the nation's workers are employed in unstructured labor markets. About one-fourth of the nation's workers belong to trade unions and are thus in structured labor markets. This means that the remainder of the labor force—about 40 per cent—is in non-union structured labor markets.

Within the three broad types of structured labor markets there are many compartments, that is, many barriers to mobility. Each labor market is actually made up of an intricate network of sub-markets. These sub-markets can be considered as "noncompeting groups," to use a term originated by J. E. Cairnes many years ago, but not in the same sense that Cairnes used this term.[22]

[19] Phelps," A Structural Model of the Labor Market," p. 406.
[20] Fisher, "The Harvest Labor Market in California," pp. 470–471.
[21] Phelps, "A Structural Model of the Labor Market," p. 407.
[22] J. E. Cairnes, *Political Economy,* New York: Harper (1874). See also Kerr, "Balkanization of Labor Markets," pp. 93–94.

Cairnes viewed the various socio-economic classes—unskilled manual workers, white-collar workers, and professional workers, for example—as noncompeting groups. But as Kerr has pointed out there are many other barriers to mobility than the socio-economic status of workers. Differences in skill, the workers' lack of knowledge of the labor market, the individual preferences of employees, and the attitudes and policies of employers—plus the fact of space and the cost of travel—impose barriers to mobility which cut down noncompeting groups greatly in size.

Even within a single labor market, unskilled workers do not compete with skilled craftsmen and skilled workers in one occupation do not compete with skilled workers in others. The result is an extremely complex interlacing of sub-markets each of which is governed by its own institutional rules, customs, legislation, or administrative procedures.

The geographic extent of sub-markets also varies considerably. Skilled craftsmen, for example, are often not attached to any particular employer and their movement need not be restricted to a particular community. A skilled carpenter, for example, might work part of the year in New York City and part of the year in Miami, Florida. Similarly, a highly-skilled auto mechanic may move around the country virtually at will. The operator of a spinning frame in a textile mill might find it difficult to locate another job, however, if he loses the one he has or if he quits voluntarily to search for other employment.

It is not easy to define the boundaries of labor markets or the sub-markets within a given area. The labor market for some workers is national in scope while the mobility of some workers is highly restricted.[23] The extent of a market depends in part upon a worker's education and skills. Highly trained professionals—engineers and physicists, for example—are likely to find suitable employment in many different localities. Such workers are likely to be willing to move to another job which holds promise of being more interesting or which pays better. The same is true of highly-skilled craftsmen; electronic technicians, and glass blowers, for example, have been in short supply in recent years. While job opportunities for them can be restricted to areas where the electronics industry is located, they have a number of choices. They can work in New England, the Great Lakes region, or southern California, and there need be little

[23] See Robert L. Raimon, "Interstate Migration and Wage Theory," *The Review of Economics and Statistics* (November 1962), pp. 428–438.

concern about finding employment except perhaps during short stretches of cyclical decline in economic activity.

Workers without these skills—machine tenders, assemblers, clerks, and others who do not have skills in relatively short supply—find it much less easy to move about. The boundaries of their labor markets are likely to be restricted to an area within commuting distance of their homes. Age is also an important factor in the mobility of labor. In general, younger workers tend to be more mobile than their older counterparts in the labor force.[24]

One further characteristic should be noted about some types of structured labor markets. The skilled craftsmen, it has been pointed out, is able to move from employer to employer and many have no permanent attachment to a single employer throughout their work careers. But workers who are not members of a craft union do not have the same degree of mobility, partly because of hiring practices which restrict the lateral movement of workers from company to company.

Many establishments—especially middle-sized and large concerns—recruit their work force through "hiring jobs." These jobs are generally open only to new entrants to the labor force. Even at the hiring level, new workers might be hired for a probationary period, but if they survive this—and perform effectively on the job—their job security increases with seniority. Promotion in such companies is from within. As workers retire, or leave the firm for other reasons, their places are filled by someone on a lower rung of the seniority ladder. It is quite rare in many companies for a worker to be brought in above the level of a hiring job.

In a broader sense, Kerr speaks of "ports of entry" in institutional labor markets.[25] It is through these ports of entry that workers enter a labor market, or are rejected and must turn elsewhere for employment. The typical port of entry outside the skilled crafts, is the "hiring job" in the large concern. There are also ports of entry to the skilled crafts. Some crafts insist upon a fairly long period of apprenticeship. Not all workers are willing to go through a long period of training even for the reward of fairly steady work at relatively high pay once the apprenticeship has been completed.

These are only some of the factors which stratify labor markets and break them up into smaller sub-markets. They illustrate the point

[24] *Ibid.*, p. 429.
[25] Kerr, "Balkanization of Labor Markets," p. 101.

that when we talk about *the* labor market we are oversimplifying. Our economy is made up of a great network of labor markets, and the latter are further divided into sub-markets of workers who belong to essentially noncompeting groups.

Empirical Research on Labor Mobility

Since the end of World War II there have been a number of studies of labor mobility based on interviews with workers—both employed and unemployed.[26] The results of some of these studies, with references to several others, have been summarized by George P. Shultz.[27]

Voluntary movement, it has been found, depends upon the existence of alternative job opportunities. However, workers in the typical labor market have "only fragmentary and imperfect knowledge about alternative jobs in the community, if indeed they have any knowledge at all.[28] They appear to know relatively little about wages and working conditions in other companies even within the local labor market area. Workers in smaller communities appear to be better informed than their counterparts in larger towns. To some extent, however, this depends upon the worker's satisfaction with his present job. Lack of information about other jobs among employed workers often is due to the fact that they are not interested in seeking employment elsewhere. As a worker accumulates seniority, his interest in other jobs appears to diminish.

These studies also revealed that job satisfaction depends upon a great many factors. One of the most important is the steadiness or security of employment; others include wage rates, working conditions, relationships with fellow workers, the interest of the work performed, and the degree of independence or control the worker has over his job. These factors are not necessarily listed in the order of their importance. Indeed, some studies have shown that workers place relatively little emphasis on wages as a source of job satisfaction.[29]

Workers who are dissatisfied with their jobs will, of course, quit under certain circumstances and often they will do this when there

[26] Some of these are: Lloyd G. Reynolds and Joseph Shister, *Job Horizons,* New York: Harper (1949); Lloyd G. Reynolds, *The Structure of Labor Markets,* New York: Harper (1951); Charles A. Myers and George P. Shultz, *The Dynamics of the Labor Market,* New York: Prentice-Hall (1951); and William H. Miernyk, *Inter-Industry Labor Mobility,* Boston: Northeastern University, Bureau of Business and Economic Research (1955).

[27] George P. Shultz, "Recent Research on Labor Mobility," *Proceedings,* 4th Annual Meeting, Industrial Relations Research Association (December 1951), pp. 1–9.

[28] *Ibid.,* p. 5.

[29] *Ibid.,* p. 8.

is no alternative job lined up. This is especially true if the worker has not been with the firm for a great length of time, if the general level of employment is high, and if his responsibilities will permit him to spend some time between jobs.

Much of the labor turnover in our economy is concentrated among young, short-service workers. When labor market conditions are favorable, a young worker might "shop around" for some time before settling down to a steady job. His ability to do this, of course, depends upon the state of balance in the labor market. If there is a high level of unemployment even the young worker will be less likely to quit his job—without an alternative lined up—than he will if the labor market is fairly tight and the newspapers are filled with want ads. There are also drifters or floaters who never seem to stay with one job for any great length of time. As Sumner H. Slichter pointed out, a high turnover rate may be caused by many workers changing jobs occasionally, or by a small proportion of the work force changing jobs many times during the year.[30] Thus a large number of workers moving into and out of "hiring jobs" can lead to a relatively high turnover rate, but even then the majority of workers will not be changing jobs.

Recent research on the mobility of *involuntarily unemployed* workers has also indicated that they are much less mobile than many economists appeared to believe in the past. Among the involuntarily unemployed are the highly mobile drifters who do not appear to be able to hold a job. They might perform well for a time but after a while they fail to meet work standards or refuse to accept plant discipline. When fired from a job such a worker will naturally move elsewhere in search of employment. But these workers are far from typical. Most workers are anxious to perform well and to advance at least within the limits of their capabililties.

Many capable workers are displaced from their jobs through the liquidation of a mill or factory, the shutdown of a mine, the depletion of resources or—in more recent times—by automation or other forms of technological change. The experience of these unemployed workers is of major interest since they constitute a much larger part of the unemployed than do the job drifters. The problem of unemployment in general is discussed more fully in Chapter 22. Here we are concerned only with a summary of findings about the mobility of displaced workers since recent

[30] Sumner H. Slichter, *The Turnover of Factory Labor,* New York: D. Appleton and Company (1919), pp. 10–44.

studies have raised some doubts about earlier views of the operation of the labor market.

The typical view, until fairly recent times, was that involuntary unemployment resulting from the large-scale displacement of labor would result in one of two things, or perhaps both in combination. First, it was assumed that as the level of unemployment in a labor market rose, wages would fall. This was supposed to attract new employers to the community to absorb the displaced workers and as unemployment declined wages would be bid up again. Another assumption was that the displaced workers would readily migrate to other areas where job opportunities were more plentiful. It was usually assumed that both types of movement would take place. Some workers would migrate, and some businesses would relocate to the communities with high-level unemployment, until equilibrium had been achieved again. Those who subscribed to such views accepted the classical or neo-classical versions of labor market behavior at face value.

But recent studies of displaced workers have revealed that many of them at least are highly immobile.[31] The studies show that a large proportion of the displaced workers do not move out of the community even in the absence of alternative jobs locally. As a result, some communities have had high-level unemployment for long periods of time—in some cases for a decade or more—following massive layoffs due to the liquidation of plants or the shutdown of mines.

The immobility of these workers is not the result of apathy or inertia. They want to work and many would gladly move if they felt they could find employment elsewhere. But when a plant is closed or a mine is shut down workers in all age groups are affected. The relatively young, short-service worker will move elsewhere in search of employment—especially if he is without family responsibilities—while those who are close to retirement age might make no effort to find new employment. But most workers affected by shutdowns of this kind fall somewhere between these extremes. They do not simply pack up and move—especially those who are middle-aged or older—because they are aware of the hiring practices which have become common in American industry. Many of them recognize that they are too old for the hiring jobs in large concerns, and those with family responsibilities might not be able to support their dependents on the pay they would earn in hiring jobs—even

[31] Myers and Shultz, *Dynamics of Labor Market* (1951), and Miernyk, *Inter-Industry Labor Mobility* (1955).

if these were available to them. They know that the "ports of entry" are closed to them. They remain in the community in the hope that job opportunities will improve or they may commute to nearby communities in search of employment. Often such shutdowns occur during periods of recession, however, and the workers involved have little opportunity to find any other kinds of employment until general economic conditions improve. Even then many of them are able to obtain only relatively unskilled jobs in one of the unstructured labor markets where there are no ports of entry, but where the pay is generally low and where there is little or no job security. The even more serious plight of those who find no jobs at all will be discussed in Chapter 22.

CONCLUSIONS

In this chapter we have described briefly the labor force and the labor market. The labor force is defined as that part of the non-institutional population fourteen years of age and over which is employed or actively seeking work. But this definition overlooks some of the complexities involved. It is important to distinguish between the primary and the secondary members of the labor force and to recognize that there is a significant amount of movement into and out of the labor force at all times. The labor force is far from fixed; it is constantly in a state of flux. It expands and contracts in response to changes in economic conditions in the short-run while long-run labor participation rates vary with income, hours of work, technological change, and changes in the demand for educational, medical and similar services.

The labor market is far more complex than product markets. Several models of the labor market were examined briefly, and a distinction was made between structured and unstructured labor markets. The classical and neo-classical models of the labor market do not distinguish between wage markets and job markets. But the natural, institutional, and managed labor market models recognize that wage determination and labor mobility are not as closely related as economists believed they were in the past.

The classical labor market is a fair description of unstructured labor markets in the real world. Yet when we recognize that most workers are employed in structured labor markets it is necessary to turn to the institutional model as a more realistic framework for analysis. Here we find that wage determination and labor mobility are both affected by institutional rules, legislation, or administrative procedures.

Foreign observers of the American scene have often commented on the high degree of labor mobility in this country. Compared with other countries there is undoubtedly a great deal of movement of workers in the United States but such movement is not as general as was often assumed in an earlier day. Much of the mobility of labor is concentrated among the relatively young, short-service workers in the economy. Some of it is accounted for by the highly skilled workers and professionals who tend to be more mobile than those with less education or training. Employed workers who do not fall into this category tend to be relatively immobile. They do not shop around for other jobs but concentrate on accumulating seniority as a means of protecting their present job security. The involuntarily unemployed worker is also less mobile than was often believed in the past. Again the relatively young will move to other areas in search of new employment, but those who are middle-aged or older are much less mobile; they may be unemployed for long stretches of time if displaced from their jobs through a shutdown.

Finally, we noted that there is not a single labor market in the United States. When we classify labor markets in fairly broad terms, there are many sub-markets within each whether we view the labor market geographically, industrially, or in terms of occupation.

REFERENCES

BOOKS

Bancroft, Gertrude, *The American Labor Force: Its Growth and Changing Composition,* New York: John Wiley and Sons, Inc. (1958).

Bureau of the Census, *Occupational Trends in the United States, 1900–1950,* Working Paper No. 5, Washington, D.C.: U.S. Department of Commerce (1958).

Clague, Ewan, Walter J. Cooper and E. Wight Bakke, *After the Shutdown,* New Haven: Yale University, Institute of Human Relations (1934).

Cooper, Sophia, *Interim Revised Projection of U.S. Labor Force, 1965–75,* Special Labor Force Report No. 24, U.S. Department of Labor, Bureau of Labor Statistics (1962).

Economic Report of the President, January 1962, Washington, D.C.: U.S. Government Printing Office (1962).

Jaffe, A. J., and Charles D. Stewart, *Manpower Resources and Utilization, Principles of Working Force Analysis,* New York: John Wiley and Sons, Inc. (1951).

Lebergott, Stanley, *Manpower in Economic Growth,* New York: McGraw-Hill (1964).

Long, Clarence D., *The Labor Force Under Changing Income and Employment,* National Bureau of Economic Research, Princeton, N.J.: Princeton University Press (1958).

Miernyk, William H., *Inter-Industry Labor Mobility,* Boston: Northeastern University, Bureau of Business and Economic Research (1955).

Myers, Charles A., and W. Rupert Maclaurin, *The Movement of Factory Workers,* New York: John Wiley and Sons, Inc. (1943).

Myers, Charles A., and George P. Shultz, *The Dynamics of the Labor Market,* New York: Prentice-Hall (1951).

President's Committee to Appraise Employment and Unemployment Statistics, *Measuring Employment and Unemployment,* Washington, D.C.: U.S. Government Printing Office (1962).

Reynolds, Lloyd G., and Joseph Shister, *Job Horizons,* New York: Harper and Brothers (1949).

———, ——— —, *The Structure of Labor Markets,* New York: Harper and Brothers (1951).

Slichter, Sumner H., *The Turnover of Factory Labor,* New York: D. Appleton and Company (1919).

U.S. Department of Labor, *Manpower Challenge of the 1960's* (no date).

ARTICLES

Barry, Carol A., "White Collar Employment: Trends and Structure," *Monthly Labor Review* (January 1961), pp. 11–18.

———, ——— —, "White Collar Employment: Characteristics," *Monthly Labor Review* (February 1961), pp. 139–147.

Kerr, Clark, "Labor Markets: Their Character and Consequences," *American Economic Review,* Papers and Proceedings, Vol. XL (May 1950), pp. 278–291.

———, ———, "The Balkanization of Labor Markets," *Labor Mobility and Economic Opportunity,* Cambridge, Massachusetts: The Technology Press of M.I.T.–John Wiley and Sons, Inc. (1954), pp. 92–110.

Lampman, Robert J., "New Facts and Interpretations in Labor Market Analysis," *Industrial and Labor Relations Review,* Vol. 10 (January 1957), pp. 297–311.

Levine, Louis, "Unemployment by Locality and Industry," *The Measurement and Behavior of Unemployment,* National Bureau of Economic Research, Princeton, New Jersey: Princeton University Press (1957), pp. 325–388.

Mahoney, Thomas A., "Factors Determining the Labor-Force Participation of Married Women," *Industrial and Labor Relations Review,* Vol. 14 (July 1961), pp. 563–577.

Palmer, Gladys L., "Contrasts in Labor Market Behavior in Northern Europe and the United States," *Industrial and Labor Relations Review,* Vol. 13 (July 1960), pp. 519–532.

Phelps, Orme W., "A Structural Model of the U.S. Labor Market," *Industrial and Labor Relations Review,* Vol. 10 (April 1957), pp. 402–423.

"Population Changes and Prospects," *Economic Report of the President,* January 1957, Washington: U.S. Government Printing Office (1957), pp. 85–98.

Raimon, Robert L., "Interstate Migration and Wage Theory," *The Review of Economics and Statistics,* Vol. VLIV (November 1962), pp. 428–438.

Rees, Albert, "The Meaning and Measurement of Full Employment," *The Measurement and Behavior of Unemployment,* National Bureau of Economic Research, Princeton, New Jersey: Princeton Press (1957), pp. 13–62.

Scherer, Joseph, "Labor Force: Concepts, Measurement, and Use of Data," *The Journal of Business of the University of Chicago,* Vol. XXXI (January 1958), pp. 38–62.

Shultz, George P., "Recent Research on Labor Mobility," *Proceedings,* Fourth Annual Meeting, Industrial Relations Research Association (1951), pp. 1–9.

Stein, Robert L., and Jane L. Meredith, "Growth and Characteristics of the Part-Time Work Force," *Monthly Labor Review* (November 1960), pp. 1166–1175.

Stein, Robert L. and Herman Travis, "Labor Force and Employment in 1960," *Monthly Labor Review* (April 1961), pp. 344–354.

Wilcock, Richard C., "The Secondary Labor Force and the Measurement of Unemployment," *The Measurement and Behavior of Unemployment,* National Bureau of Economic Research, Princeton, New Jersey: Princeton University Press (1957), pp. 167–210.

Chapter 19 Wage Determination ——Theory and Policy

Economists have long been interested in the theory of distribution—that is, in the development of abstract models to help explain the complicated process by which the total product of a society is divided among the factors of production: land, labor, capital and the entrepreneur. Thus wage theory is at the heart of labor economics.

In a review of the history of wage theory, John T. Dunlop, suggested that it can be divided into three broad periods: (1) The *classical* period extending into the 1870's, (2) a second period extending through the 1920's called the *neo-classical* period, and (3) the *contemporary* period.[1]

CLASSICAL WAGE THEORY

During the classical period, one of the most widely-held views about wages was that of the *wage fund*. The classical period was one of rapid economic growth, no appreciable rise in real wages, and substantial differences in the level of real wages among countries. Although the Industrial Revolution was underway long before the end of the classical period, agriculture was still the major occupation. Under these circumstances, in Dunlop's words: "The wage-fund apparatus seems congenial . . . as it still does to the broad features of many under-developed countries."[2]

1870's

[1] John T. Dunlop, "The Task of Contemporary Wage Theory," George W. Taylor and Frank C. Pierson, eds., *New Concepts in Wage Determination,* McGraw-Hill (1957), p. 117. See also his article with the same title in John T. Dunlop, ed., *The Theory of Wage Determination,* London: Macmillan (1957), p. 4.
[2] Dunlop in Taylor and Pierson, *New Concepts,* p. 118.

In the short run, according to the classical formulation, the labor supply is fixed and the amount which employers decide to spend on wages is also fixed. The sum of the individual amounts of all employers makes up the wage fund. The wage fund doctrine was not very sophisticated; it did not, for example, go into the complexities of variations in wage rates. According to this theory, if the average wage rate were set too high, some workers would have to remain unemployed while if the average were too low, employers could not attract all the workers they needed. Hence, market forces would bring the average wage to the level which would just "clear the market." Employers in the aggregate would be able to attract as many workers as they needed and the wage rate would not be so high that some workers would be without jobs.

In the long run, however, the size of the wage fund could change. If the wage fund increased—and average wages rose—this would lead to an increase in population and thus to an increase in labor supply. The competition of workers for available jobs would then tend to depress the average level of wages again. In the long run, wages would tend toward the subsistence level. This was the essence of Ricardo's "iron law of wages," and of the Malthusian theory of population growth. The wage fund theory ignored the possibility that population *and* wages might rise together since it failed to take into account gains in productivity. As the sophistication of economists increased, and as they observed that the amount of a nation's total product which could be paid to labor did not remain fixed, the doctrine of the wage fund had to be scrapped. It was replaced during the neo-classical period by the more elegant marginal productivity theory.

NEO-CLASSICAL WAGE THEORY

1920's

The marginal productivity theory of distribution cannot be credited to any single economist. Versions of it were developed independently by the British economists, Jenons, Wicksteed, and Marshall. Other versions were developed by western European economists such as Walras and Barone, and J. B. Clark in this country.[3] Originally, the marginal productivity theory was thought to apply only to economies which operated under conditions of perfect competition. By definition, this would exclude any economy in which trade unions have any effect upon wage determination.

[3] Allan M. Cartter, *Theory of Wages and Employment,* Homewood, Illinois; Richard D. Irwin (1959), p. 11.

But as late as 1932, J. R. Hicks, an eminent economic theorist wrote: "The same forces which determine wages in a free market are still present under regulation; they only work rather differently . . ."[4] At the time Hicks wrote, unions were not strong in the United States but they were an economic force which could not be ignored in Great Britain. But Hicks was of the opinion that, in the aggregate, workers could not receive more than the total value of the marginal product of labor:

> The only wage at which equilibrium is possible is a wage which equals the value of the marginal product of the labourers . . . in this way the demand for labour of each employer is determined; and the total demand of all employers is determined from it by addition. Since in equilibrium it is necessary that the total demand should equal the total supply, the wage must be that which just enables the total number of labourers available to be employed. This must equal the value of the marginal product of the labourers available.[5]

The theory of marginal productivity appeared at a time when the rate of population growth began to slow down as urbanization proceeded rapidly in western Europe and in this country. And it was at this time that there was a great upsurge in industrialization. There was a growing amount of government intervention through factory legislation. While the central interest of economists continued to be the theory of distribution, there was less interest in the question of how the total product was to be distributed among social classes than in the forces which would determine returns to each of the factors of production. In a free market, it was assumed, each factor would receive a return proportional to its contribution to output—given the existing conditions of demand and supply. Until the Great Depression dispelled the illusion, it was generally supposed that the wage rate which would be equal to the marginal productivity of labor would be one which would tend toward equilibrium, that is, the wage level would settle at a point where there would be no unemployment, and at which employers in the aggregate could obtain all the labor they needed.

As the theory of marginal productivity became more refined, it was pointed out that wages are not *determined* by labor's marginal product. It was argued only that once a wage rate was determined, marginal productivity would indicate how much labor would be employed at the prevailing wage.[6] Thus as Dunlop has pointed out,

[4] J. R. Hicks, *The Theory of Wages,* London: Macmillan (1932), p. vi.
[5] *Ibid.,* p. 8.
[6] Dunlop, in Taylor and Pierson, *New Concepts,* pp. 122–123, and Cartter, *Theory of Wages and Employment,* p. 23.

marginal productivity did not provide a complete theory of wages, "but only a statement of the demand side."[7]

Once the argument had been accepted that marginal productivity did not determine wages, but that at a given level of wages marginal productivity would determine employment, some writers attempted to reconcile the regulation of wages by unions with the marginal productivity principle. But is it not possible that unions can extract more than the marginal product of labor from an employer? J. R. Hicks answered this question in the negative. A union will be willing to go on strike to increase wages—up to a point. And an employer will be willing to accept a strike rather than grant a wage increase above a certain level—again up to a point. Once a new wage is determined, and all other adjustments have been made, the new wage will equal the marginal product of labor.

Hicks summarized his theory of industrial disputes in Figure 19-1 below.

Hicks constructed a schedule of wage rates set against various expected strike lengths for the union and the employer. The union's resistance curve drops sharply for an expected strike of moderate length, indicating that above a certain wage rate the union is not willing to take a long strike. Below that rate, however, the union's resistance curve drops much more slowly indicating that the workers will be willing to strike for an extended period of time rather than accept a wage less than OW in Figure 19-1. Similarly, the employer's concession curve rises rapidly to point P on Figure 19-1, and more slowly beyond that point. The point P—at the wage OA—indicates the highest wage which the union can obtain through skillful negotiation.[8]

G. L. S. Shackle has recently criticized Hicks' assumption that the union's resistance curve slopes continuously downward to the right. This indicates that the lower the wage rate the longer a union would be willing to stay out on strike. Shackle presented a modification of Hicks' diagram shown in Figure 19-2. Shackle has not changed the shape of the employer's concession curve. But the union's *inducement curve,* as Shackle has termed it, slopes *upward* to the right. This indicates that the union will accept a longer strike the higher the wage rate it seeks. According to Shackle, an employer would be willing to grant a wage of y_A rather than accept a strike longer than x_A.

[7] Dunlop, p. 122.
[8] J. R. Hicks, *The Theory of Wages,* p. 143.

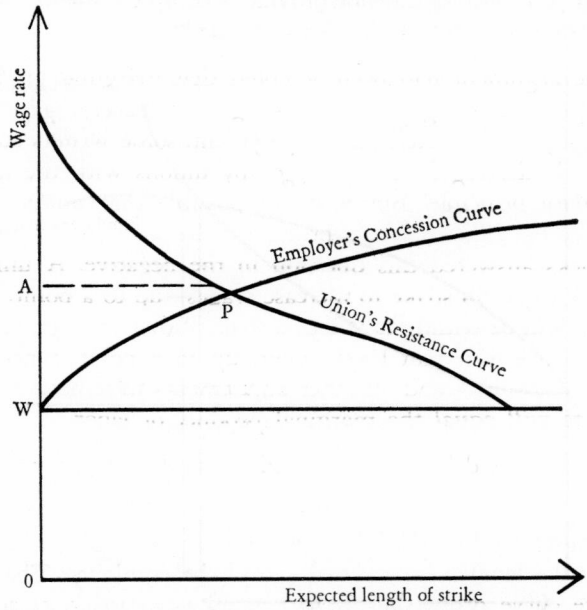

FIGURE 19–1

Source: J. R. Hicks, *The Theory of Wages*, London: The Macmillan Company, Ltd. (1935), p. 143. Reprinted by permission of the publisher.

According to both Hicks and Shackle, if the two parties knew the shapes of each other's schedules, agreement on wages would be reached at the point of intersection. Given such knowledge there would be no strike. Negotiations would result in a wage given by the intersection of the two schedules.

The theory of industrial disputes developed by Hicks, and Shackle's modification of it, are highly abstract. They might have been included in the section on collective bargaining theory in Chapter 13. They are discussed here, however, to illustrate some of the efforts made by modern economists to reconcile the existence of unions with the marginal productivity theory of distribution. According to Hicks, "the number of labourers which an employer will prefer to take on is that number which makes his profits the maximum, and that number is given by the equality of wages to the marginal product of the labour employed."[9] This is so, Hicks and his followers would argue, whether the employer deals with a union or not.

[9] *Ibid.*, p. 9.

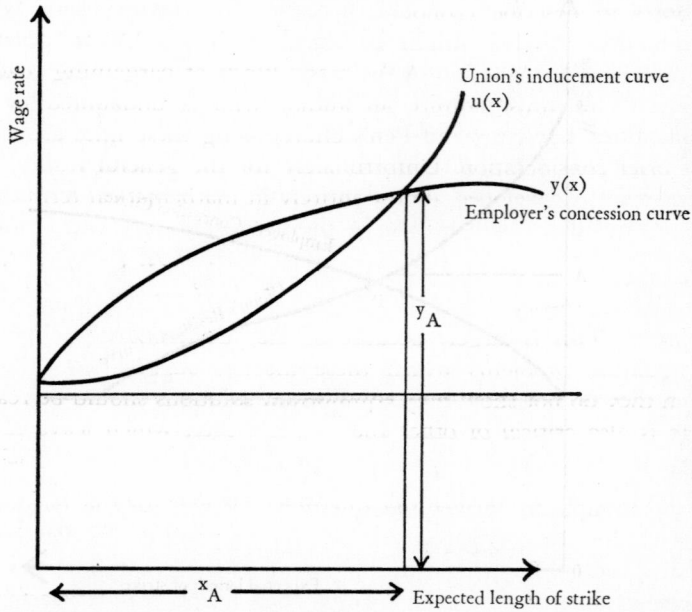

FIGURE 19–2

Source: G. L. S. Shackle, "The Nature of the Bargaining Process," in John T. Dunlop (editor), *The Theory of Wage Determination*, London, Macmillan and Company, Ltd. (1957), p. 302. Reprinted by permission of the publisher.

BARGAINING THEORY

In a perfect market—made up of many small producing units with complete mobility of all factors of production—the equality of wages and the marginal product of labor would be realized. These conditions are not found in advanced industrial societies, however. As a result, many economists have criticized the theory of marginal productivity as a complete explanation of the process of wage determination in an economy where wages are determined by bargaining rather than by impersonal market forces. Some representative theories of wage determination under bargaining will be discussed briefly in this section.

Pen's "General" Theory of Bargaining

Most economists tend to be somewhat skeptical of theories that claim to be general. A completely general theory is one which would apply to all cases and at all times. Critics of such theorizing point out that as economic and social conditions change earlier efforts to describe economic processes in abstract terms become outmoded. Also, it might be asked, is it possible to develop a generalized explanation of the many kinds of bargaining that take place? One must admire an author who is undaunted by such difficulties, however, and Pen's efforts along these lines are worthy of brief consideration. Unfortunately for the general reader, Pen's argument is developed almost entirely in mathematical terms. Some of its full flavor will be lost in the brief summary which follows.

Pen is critical of the theory developed by Hicks, and also of Zeuthen's theory which is discussed briefly farther on in this chapter. This is largely because of the "determinate" solutions to bargaining problems which these theories suggest. According to Pen they do not show *why* equilibrium solutions should be reached. He is also critical of other theories, however, which leave the impression that bargaining solutions must be "indeterminate."

Pen attempts to answer the question: "What are the factors that determine the [wage] result of the bargaining?"[10] Pen admits that if more than one variable is involved—for example wages and a pension scheme—his theory provides a much less satisfactory explanation of the bargaining process.[11] And in the real world, it should be noted, collective bargaining usually deals not with two but with a wide range of matters some of which do not involve wages or labor costs at all.

Each party, Pen assumes, will derive a certain satisfaction if bargaining leads to a certain wage rate. Pen calls this *ophelimity*—a term suggested by Vilfredo Pareto as a substitute for *utility*. What each party wants to do, in brief, is to maximize its *ophelimity*. And if the wage demanded by the union is greater than that which management is ready to grant there is a bargaining problem.

One interesting feature of Pen's theory is the recognition that psychological factors are involved in the bargaining process; these he calls the *ludic*[12] elements behind each party's ophelimity. The will to win in any kind of contest; the fear of "losing face," or the desire to improve one's status are examples of Pen's ludic elements.

Recognizing that a form of satisfaction is to be maximized—and that there are non-economic as well as economic elements involved

[10] J. Pen, "A General Theory of Bargaining," *American Economic Review* (March 1952), p. 27.
[11] *Ibid.*, pp. 41–42.
[12] The word is derived from the Latin *ludere*—to play a game.

in this satisfaction—the bargaining problem, in Pen's view, becomes a power problem. The next question is: What determines bargaining power?

The fundamental element in the power struggle, according to Pen, is the *mutual* dependence of the two parties. Because of this mutual dependence, there will be upper and lower limits to the wages which can be reached through negotiation. The upper limit is called management's net contract ophelimity and the lower limit is the union's net contract ophelimity. Between these limits there is a range of wages that could be negotiated. Up to this point, Pen's theory is similar to Fellner's analysis of collective bargaining under bilateral monopoly discussed in Chapter 13.

Pen then introduces what he calls a *risk valuation function*. In his theory this is a measure of the satisfaction (or dissatisfaction) which either party derives from the simple fact that a risk is involved in collective bargaining. If either side holds too firm, a strike might result. The question is how far can each side push the other without inducing an actual conflict. Finally, Pen introduces what he calls the *correspection function*—a term which he borrowed from an earlier treatment of bargaining by Schumpeter. This is a function which relates the actual net contract ophelimity of *management* and the risk valuation of the *union*. Somewhere along this function —which Pen views as a downward sloping curve, like the demand curve in elementary economic theory—the two parties will arrive at a wage agreement.

If each of these relationships is considered as a mathematical function, Pen views the bargaining process as a series of efforts by each of the two parties to shift the other's functions. Each side starts with a satisfaction which it wishes to maximize. Management must keep in mind its cost and profit situation, and how changes in the wage level will effect its balance sheet. The union must consider the morale of the workers. The possibility of a conflict—with the costs which this will involve—must be kept in mind by both parties. Pen implies that each party might begin negotiations with somewhat exaggerated claims recognizing that "horse-trading" will be involved before a solution is reached.

Pen concedes that it would be impossible to measure precisely the ophelimities and risk valuations involved. Thus the theory cannot be tested empirically. But he feels that his theory indicates the factors which determine the outcome of negotiations, and while these factors cannot be measured—at least at present—"they make the result of the bargaining determinate . . ."[13] In terms of wage bargaining only, therefore, Pen disagrees with Fellner that the solution to a bargaining problem must be indeterminate; that it can only be specified in terms of upper and lower limits.

Other Theories of Bargaining

G. L. S. Shackle has developed a theory of bargaining strategies based on probabilities. These probabilities he refers to as "potential surprise."[14] He assumes that the values of potential surprise can be compared by means of indifference maps similar to those used by Fellner. And given their respective indifference maps, the two parties can make rational choices among the strategies available to them.

F. Zeuthen was the first to use the risk evaluation approach to a theory of bargaining.[15] Zeuthen reasoned that bargaining is a process under which each side compares possible advantages and disadvantages at each step of the proceedings. The advantages are the economic gains which would accrue to either party as the result of a favorable settlement; the disadvantages are due to the possibility of a breakdown in bargaining which would result in a strike. Agreement will be reached, according to Zeuthen, when the maximum risks of the two parties are equal.

More recently, Harvey Wagner has examined the three major approaches to bargaining theory:[16] (1) bilateral monopoly, (2) risk evaluation; and (3) the theory of games. Wagner has developed an interesting variation of the bilateral monopoly theory in which he stresses the uncertainty aspects involved. This uncertainty stems from the imperfect knowledge each party has about the strategy which the other party will adopt. Wagner does not appear to be greatly impressed by the risk evaluation approach followed by Zeuthen, Pen and others. In his view, these theories assume knowledge of certain quantities which could not be known until the bargaining process had been completed.

Wagner also develops a bargaining theory using the game theory framework. The theory he uses is of the "non-zero-sum" type, that

[13] *Ibid.*, p. 39.
[14] G. L. S. Shackle, *Expectation in Economics,* Cambridge: Cambridge University Press (1949), pp. 101ff.
[15] F. Zeuthen, in *Problems of Monopoly and Economic Warfare,* London (1930). See also his *Economic Theory and Method,* Cambridge, Massachusetts: Harvard University Press (1955), especially the chapter on "Economic Warfare," pp. 286ff.
[16] Harvey M. Wagner, "A Unified Treatment of Bargaining Theory," *Southern Economic Journal,* Vol. XXIII (April 1957), pp. 380–397. See also the debate between J. C. Harsanyi and Wagner in the April 1958 issue of this journal.

is, losses to management, when an agreement is reached, are not necessarily equal to the union's gains. He also assumes that collective bargaining is a "non-cooperative game." This type of game assumes that there is no direct communication between the parties. Each side decides upon a strategy, then informs an "umpire" of its choice. The umpire in turn informs each side of the result of the two strategies adopted. An interesting feature of this theory is the conclusion that under certain circumstances the parties might not *want* to reach agreement, but might prefer a strike. Earlier theories of bargaining showed the conditions under which labor and management would reach agreement. Wagner shows both the case where the parties will reach agreement, and the case where a strike will result. He also agrees with Fellner that the results of bargaining must remain indeterminate except in the case where an "umpire" would be involved as a go-between in the bargaining process; that is, a bargaining situation where a mediator or conciliator is called in to help the two parties reach an agreement.

The above discussion shows that economists using the tools of conventional economic analysis have reached a variety of conclusions about the forces which determine wages and the results of the bargaining process. The stripped-down versions given here are simplified. In their original forms, most of these theories are presented in mathematical terms. Despite their sophistication, however, they do not come to grips with the broad spectrum of problems involved in actual wage determination. They deal with the forces determining a single wage rate. This has led some labor economists to question their relevance to collective bargaining in the real world. A different approach to the problems of wage determination will be considered in the following paragraphs.

CONTEMPORARY WAGE THEORY

During the classical period, the question which concerned wage theorists was: How is the total product of the economy divided among social classes? During the neo-classical era the emphasis was shifted to distribution among the factors of production. As Dunlop has noted, these questions are of relatively little contemporary interest. Emphasis has now shifted to the general level of money wages, the level of real wages, and the structure of wage rates. The questions asked today are: How do unions affect wages? What effect do wage increases have on efficiency? Are wages determined more by economic forces or by the political considerations of union leaders? As will be noted in later discussions, there are no precise answers to these questions, and there may never be. The fact that these questions are still asked, however, shows that they deal with matters that are important to all of us. Both the wage fund and marginal productivity theories provided simple answers. But both were based on simplifying assumptions which have little relevance to the world around us. As we have learned more about wages, through the availability of a growing body of statistical data, the one fact which stands out starkly is the complexity of the wage structure. How does contemporary wage theory attempt to answer the questions raised above given the tremendous diversity in wage rates and wage patterns which we observe?

From an economic point of view, a wage rate is a special kind of price. Thus a theory of wages is a specialized part of a more general theory of prices. The central concepts in price theory are demand and supply. As noted in earlier sections, however, both the wage fund and the marginal productivity theories failed to take into account the supply side of the price equation. In the earlier formulations the amount of labor supplied depended upon the labor force, and the labor force depended upon population growth. Wage rates were then determined by social custom or institutional rules. In Dunlop's words, ". . . the pivotal task of wage theory is to formulate an acceptable theory on the supply side."[17]

A further weakness of early wage theory—insofar as it has any relevance for the real world—was the emphasis on a single wage rate. Attention was centered on the wages of unskilled laborers. The wages of all other workers, it was argued, could then be translated into terms of this lowest common denominator. In the absence of statistical data against which to test wage hypotheses, this might not have been a bad first approximation. But the characteristic which stands out most in any empirical study of wages is *diversity* rather than uniformity. Contemporary analysts have concentrated on this aspect of wages in their efforts to provide a systematic explanation of *wage structure*.

Job Clusters and Wage Contours

In an effort to develop a manageable yet realistic framework for the explanation of wage structure, John T. Dunlop has developed the concepts of "job clusters" and "wage contours."

A *job cluster* is defined as "a stable group of job classifications or work assignments within a firm (wage-determining unit) which

[17] Dunlop, in Taylor and Pierson, *New Concepts*, p. 128.

are so linked together by (1) technology, (2) the administrative organization of the production process . . . or (3) social custom that they have common wage-making characteristics."[18] The wage rates for the jobs within a cluster are more closely related than are the rates outside the cluster.

Within a single firm or plant there may be a number of job clusters. Highly skilled machinists and pattern makers, for example, could constitute a job cluster in one type of plant, machine tenders or operatives might make up another cluster, and the plant maintenance workers might comprise a third.

Generally, each job cluster contains one or more *key rates*. The key rate might be regarded as the rate within a job cluster from which all other rates fan out. It could be the most typical rate in the cluster, it could be the highest, or it could be the lowest. The key rate is typically the critical rate in collective bargaining. In the short run, at least, the relationship of rates within a job cluster may be regarded as given. Thus if a key rate is increased by ten cents an hour, proportionate increases would ordinarily be granted to workers paid at other rates within the job cluster.

Job clusters and key rates are part of the *internal* wage structure of an employment unit—the firm, a plant, or an office. But there is also a great deal of variation in wages from firm to firm, industry to industry, and locality to locality. When we step outside a single bargaining unit and view this array of wage rates we are observing the *external* wage structure.

The way in which the internal wage structure is established will be considered in a later section dealing with job evaluation. Now, however, we will consider the external wage structure in terms of Dunlop's concept of the wage contour.

A *wage contour* is defined as "a stable group of wage-determining units (bargaining units, plants, or firms) which are so linked together by (1) similarity of product markets, (2) resort to similar sources for a labor force, or (3) common labor-market organization (custom) that they have common wage-making characteristics."[19]

The wage rates for given occupations in a particular firm are more closely related to the rates paid by some firms than to others. According to Dunlop a wage contour has three dimensions. These are: (1) a particular group of occupations or job clusters, (2) a

[18] *Ibid.*, p. 129.
[19] *Ibid.*, p. 131.

sector of industry, and (3) geographical location. Thus a given wage contour is defined in terms of both the product market and the labor market. The firms included in a specific contour may be located in a single labor market area, within a specific region, or they may be scattered over the country as a whole. Finally, while the boundaries of some wage contours may be rather clearly defined, it is difficult if not impossible to discover the boundaries of others.

The wages of carpenters in a metropolitan area make up one type of wage contour. If the area is highly organized, as is true of most metropolitan areas, all carpenters doing a specific type of work might be earning the same rate of pay. This is so regardless of the size of the firms which employ them. But the wages of carpenters vary significantly from one community to another even within the same region. This is an example of a wage contour with a rather clearly defined boundary which is that of the local labor market area. Other wage contours, however, can be nation-wide. In the steel industry, for example, there has been a trend toward the equalization of wage rates by occupation without respect to locality. This is an example of an occupational-industrial wage contour which is independent of geographic location. As a final example we might consider the wages of machinists who work in a wide variety of industries which blanket the industrialized section of the country. While the wages of machinists will not be identical from firm to firm, or from region to region, the wages of machinists are more closely related to each other than they are to other wage rates. This is an example of an occupational wage contour. A wage contour is not specifically confined to a given industry or a given locality, but each wage contour is confined to some range of skills, occupations, or job clusters.

In the case of organized workers, each wage contour contains one or more *key settlements*. The key settlements in wage contour might be the key rates in the job clusters of the dominant firm in an industry. This firm might be outstanding because of the share of the market it commands, or because of the firm's leadership in industrial relations.

The twin concepts of job clusters and wage contours are effective devices for explaining the *interdependence* of wages in modern industrial society. The focal point of the internal wage structure in each employment or bargaining unit is the key rate. And the key settlements within specific wage contours are interrelated. This does not mean that there is a tendency toward uniformity either of key rates or key settlements. But recognition of the existence of key rates and key settlements permits us to understand better the wide diversity of wage rates while at the same time recognizing that individual wage rates are not determined in a vacuum but are related to one another. Both key rates and key settlements are affected by a host of economic forces.

Wage determination is the process of price-setting in the labor market. But wage contours cannot be divorced from the *product* market. Indeed, one of the most powerful forces affecting a specific wage contour is the nature of the product markets served by the firms in a given contour. In an industry where prices are administered—where there is an absence of price competition—key rates and key settlements might tend to be remarkably close together, if not actually uniform, regardless of the location of firms. In highly competitive industries—such as cotton textiles—there have been remarkably persistent wage differentials from region to region. But within each region key rates or key settlements tend to be close to one another. In the latter case, the firms in each region make up the wage contour.

Dunlop cites the example of the wages of Boston motor truck drivers to illustrate his concept of wage contours.[20] Within a given metropolitan area, the hourly rates of the highest-paid teamsters were almost twice as high as those at the bottom of the wage scale. The drivers of trucks delivering magazines, newspapers, and oil, for example, earned a great deal more than the drivers of trucks hauling waste paper, laundry, or scrap iron. The wages of drivers of oil trucks make up one wage contour while the wages of drivers of laundry trucks make up another. Each of these, as Dunlop notes, is a reflection of the product market. Within the specific contour the wage rates of competing firms tend to be close together if not identical, but there are wide variations from contour to contour.

An earlier generation of economists might have dismissed such wage differentials as the result of "imperfections" in the market place. If there were greater knowledge, mobility, and an absence of institutional pressures on wages, a nineteenth-century economist might have argued that such differences would eventually tend to disappear. But economists today recognize that there are wide dif-

[20] *Ibid.*, p. 135. See also, *Union Wages and Hours: Motortruck Drivers and Helpers*, U.S. Department of Labor, Bureau of Labor Statistics, Bulletin No. 1356 (May 1953). An excellent study of wage variation within local labor markets, covering a number of occupations, has been made by H. M. Douty, "Sources of Occupational Wage and Salary Rate Dispersion Within Labor Markets," *Industrial and Labor Relations Review* (October 1961), especially pp. 70–71.

ferences among product markets. Some product markets are vigorously price competitive, and in others prices are administered. Some industries or lines of business are made up of many small firms with limited capital requirements, others are dominated by a few industrial giants each of which is a multi-million dollar concern. The differences among product markets are not temporary. They are an integral part of our system of economic organization. Similarly, the differentials among wage contours are not transitory. They are not due to lack of knowledge, lack of mobility, or to other alleged "imperfections." They are a result of the blending of economic forces in labor markets and product markets, and while they are not fixed for all time such differentials are remarkably persistent.

THE INTERNAL WAGE STRUCTURE

Within a firm wage rates are associated with job clusters, each of which contains one or more key rates. But how are these key rates determined? The state of the labor market has a great deal to do with the determination of some key rates. Unskilled workers, for example, have generally been available in relatively ample numbers. And the forces of supply and demand have had a great deal to do with determining the wage rates of "common" labor. Custom, on the other hand, has been an important determinant of wages for highly skilled workers. Long apprenticeships have limited the supply of some craftsmen and as a result they have always earned relatively high wages.

Custom and institutional rules—including union rules—still play an important part in determining wages within a plant or a company. With the rise of industrial engineering, however, systematic techniques for the development of internal wage structures made their appearance. The application of these techniques is known as *job evaluation.*

Job Evaluation

There are four basic systems of job evaluation. In an introductory textbook we cannot go into the intricacies of any of these methods but they can be described briefly.[21] The four basic systems are:

1. *The ranking method* which compares job against job as a whole.
2. *The classification method* which provides for established arbi-

[21] For further details see Solomon Barkin, "Wage Determination: Trick or Technique," *Labor and Nation* (June-July, 1946), reprinted in Joseph Shister, ed., *Readings in Labor Economics and Industrial Relations,* Philadelphia: Lippincott (second edition, 1956), pp. 263–268.

trary job grades with definitions and requires all jobs to be slotted into these pre-established grades, as in the case of civil servants.

3. *The point system* which provides for a comparison of the jobs against a given list of job factors (which may vary from ten to fifteen in number). Each job factor is assigned a number of point values.
4. *The factor comparison method* which compares job against job on the basis of given job elements.[22]

The simplest type of job evaluation is the ranking method under which no effort is made to measure specific factors involved in the job such as skill, responsibility, training, and experience, or such negative factors as job hazard or the unpleasantness of work. In a relatively small plant, for example, skilled craftsmen would be paid the highest wage, and the individual firm might have relatively little control over their rates. At the bottom of the scale, cleanup men and other unskilled workers might also have their wages determined by forces outside the plant. The availability of an ample supply of such workers might dictate the wage they are to receive. All other jobs will be ranked between these extremes and the wages associated with each job might be determined by fairly rough rules of thumb.

The remaining three types of job evaluation, however, depend upon a more complicated process. The classification, or civil service, method is fairly well known.[23] Job grades are established on the basis of skill, education, responsibility, and other similar factors. Rate ranges are assigned to each of these classifications. A worker may move up the promotional ladder from one classification to another, each time starting at the bottom of the range and working his way to the top. The initial determination of the rate ranges might depend to a considerable extent upon market influences. The ranges could also be determined on the basis of wage surveys which have played an important part in the development of internal wage structures in recent years. Again, however, no effort is made to assign specific weights to each of the factors associated with the job.

Under the point system and the factor comparison method, the various requirements associated with each job are arrayed. Weights are assigned to each of these factors. There is no single method of determining these weights, but once the weights are determined,

[22] *Ibid.*, p. 263.

[23] It should be noted that this method is not limited in its application to civil service jobs.

a "wage curve" is developed and related to the weighted factors. The points assigned to each job are then added up. The jobs with the largest number of points are paid the rates at the top of the wage curve; those with the smallest number of points fall at the bottom of the curve.

In the early days of job evaluation some enthusiasts believed they had discovered a "scientific" method of wage determination which was independent of all subjective evaluations. Efforts to determine wages by quasi-mathematical or statistical methods were not warmly received by workers, however, and in recent years there have been few claims that job evaluation is a method for precisely determining the "right" wage rate for each job. Even the early enthusiasts recognized that they had to take market forces into account—as well as past practices—in arriving at a workable set of wage rates. As unions increased in power and began to play a more important part in wage determination, further adjustments had to be made in many job evaluation systems. While job evaluation is still widely used today few claim that it is a "scientific" technique for wage determination.

Some Union Views of Job Evaluation

Union spokesmen have differing opinions about job evaluation. For example, Solomon Barkin, formerly a textile union staff official, feels that job evaluation has made several contributions to the process of collective bargaining. This is so, in his view, because job evaluation has stressed the need for a formal system of job rates instead of personal rates; it has reduced the number of different rates within a plant and it has provided a rational basis for differentiating rates for jobs. It has also reduced differences in wage rates by reason of sex, religion, race, or color. But some managements, in what Barkin considers to be "monopolistic and semi-monopolistic unorganized industries," have used job evaluation as a substitute for collective bargaining. Furthermore, some of the factors used in merit rating under such systems—cooperation and loyalty, for example—can be used to promote anti-union ends. Thus, Barkin concludes, the "job evaluation technique is a management tool."[24] He goes on to point out that unions have always favored a simple job rate structure with clearly defined job descriptions. In his opinion, however, these goals can be achieved in a much more satisfactory manner through collective bargaining than by means of formal job evaluation.

[24] Barkin, *op. cit.*, p. 268.

A contrary view has been expressed by William Gomberg who at one time was associated with the International Ladies Garment Workers Union. Gomberg states that "the basic concepts of job evaluation were used by trade unionists long before these ideas were formalized into a systematic body of thought."[25] Workers, Gomberg believes, are "far more keenly interested in how much they receive compared to what some of their fellow workers in other occupations are receiving than in any absolute level of wages for the whole factory."[26] Thus job evaluation provides at least a rough measuring rod for establishing rational relationships in rates of pay. Gomberg is as critical as Barkin of certain job evaluation techniques—notably the National Metal Trades Job Evaluation Plan—particularly if they are based upon *fixed* weights assigned to various factors. But on the whole, he believes, the problem which job evaluation presents to collective bargaining is "not so much how to fight it as a management tool, but rather how to reshape it into a more useful collective bargaining instrument."[27]

Much of the controversy surrounding job evaluation has diminished in recent years. As Livernash has pointed out, the way in which job evaluation is administered is of extreme importance. "If the management constructs the evaluation plan and brings the finished product to the union with an insistence upon accepting the placement of jobs virtually without criticism, the plan may well, if accepted, usher in a period of unrest and bitterness leading to its destruction."[28] But if management develops a job evaluation plan as a means of establishing a basic rate structure, and if it is willing to negotiate adjustments in the plan with the union, the technique can be introduced without leading to conflict. "Job evaluation does not necessarily create nor alleviate conflict, but there is no issue in job evaluation that cannot be resolved to the mutual satisfaction of both labor and management."[29]

The Internal Wage Structure and the Labor Market

Even in the absence of a union, few companies are in a position to establish an internal wage structure without reference to market

[25] William Gomberg, "A Collective Bargaining Approach to Job Evaluation," *Labor and the Nation* (November-December, 1946), reprinted in Joseph Shister, *Readings in Labor Economics and Industrial Relations,* p. 268.
[26] *Ibid.,* p. 269.
[27] *Ibid.*
[28] Edward R. Livernash, "Wage Administration and Production Standards," W. S. Woytinsky and Associates, *Wages and Employment in the United States,* New York: Twentieth Century Fund (1953), p. 338.
[29] *Ibid.,* p. 339.

influences. And where there is a union, job evaluation must take place within the framework of collective bargaining unless there is to be continuing strife and unrest. As Clark Kerr and Lloyd H. Fisher pointed out, "sound wage structures are subject to the forces of internal logic and of external environment *both at the same time* . . ."[30] In the opinion of these authors, job evaluation programs which attempt to establish relative rates within a plant, independently of other considerations, do not go far enough. In their words:

> A job description and job evaluation plan, where collective bargaining prevails, must coexist with the labor agreement. The two are related, not only (1) through the union security provisions of the contract as they influence the political situation of the union, and (2) through the grievance machinery and its adequacy for handling the volume of cases normally incident to the introduction of a plan, but particularly (3) through the seniority clauses. A job evaluation plan sets up a wage structure, while seniority clauses affect the flow of employees through this structure. The two must be compatible.[31]

The internal wage structure does not exist in a vacuum. Whether management alone determines what the wage rates for each job in a plant will be, or whether these are the result of bargaining between unions and management, the internal wage structure cannot be isolated from influences outside the plant or the company. While job evaluation can lead to an orderly system of wage rates the technique cannot be used without reference to external forces. Kerr and Fisher put it succinctly when they state that: "A job evaluation plan must be devised and administered with one eye always on the market."[32]

Wage Incentives

Both job evaluation and collective bargaining tend to produce uniformity of rates for the same job in a given work environment. But workers may be paid either on an hourly basis or on the basis of some incentive plan. Where hourly rates are in effect—whether negotiated or unilaterally installed by management—the trend is toward uniformity of payment for the same kind of work. On assembly lines or in other machine-paced operations, the output of workers on identical jobs is the same. The worker must either

[30] Clark Kerr and Lloyd H. Fisher, "Effective Environment and Administration of Job Evaluation," *Harvard Business Review* (May 1950), p. 77.
[31] *Ibid.*, p. 86.
[32] *Ibid.*, p. 91.

keep up with the pace set by the machine or he cannot continue to hold his job. Under such circumstances hourly rates tend to be negotiated or—in the absence of unions—to be administered by management. There are other types of jobs in which the worker's daily output is determined by his skill, dexterity, and effort. In jobs of this kind, the worker is often paid by the piece or according to some other incentive plan. As Livernash has pointed out, incentive-pay methods are typically associated with "short-cycle, repetitive, standardized, worker-paced" operations.[33]

Typically, incentive-pay methods are based on a standard or "normal" daily output. The least efficient and ambitious worker in the plant is expected to produce a minimum number of units in the average working day and for this he will be paid a basic hourly wage. Workers who can produce more than the minimum standard, however, earn more for each unit of output. It is important under such circumstances that the work also meet basic production standards. This means that the output of each worker must be inspected, and unsatisfactory work returned to him to be redone without compensation. But the worker who is able to meet production standards satisfactorily can earn substantially more than the minimum daily wage in incentive-pay plants.

There are pressures, however, which hold the output of even the most efficient workers within limits. For example, an "eager beaver" in a plant might be able to produce twice as much as the minimum daily standard. But if he does this consistently, and particularly if he seems to do it with ease, the industrial engineers in the plant might begin to think that there is too great a spread between the output of the most efficient worker and the minimum standard. They might then restudy the job with a view to increasing the minimum daily standard without a corresponding increase in compensation. This is the essence of what unions refer to as the "speedup." Unions have consistently and vigorously opposed anything which they consider to be an effort to speed up the plant's operations without adding to worker income. Hence, social pressures operate to keep the spread between minimum daily standards and the maximum output of individual workers within what the workers consider to be reasonable limits and these pressures operate whether or not there is a union in the plant.

[33] E. R. Livernash, "The Internal Wage Structure," George W. Taylor and Frank C. Pierson, eds., *New Concepts in Wage Determination,* New York: McGraw-Hill (1957), p. 167.

THE EXTERNAL WAGE STRUCTURE

Actual determination of wage rates—or the internal wage structure—in a plant or company is far more complex than one would be led to believe by some of the earlier theories of wage determination. The notion of marginal productivity has a beautiful logical consistency. Those who continue to be impressed by the theory of marginal productivity insist that workers cannot be paid more than the value of the marginal product of labor. But they are inclined to view labor as a homogeneous factor of production, and they overlook many of the pressures and forces which operate on the wage structures of plants and companies in the real world.

The factors which *determine* wages in a plant or company are many and complex. The output of some workers is fixed by the pace of the machines they operate. The output of others varies with worker skill and effort. In some cases the internal wage structure is installed and administered entirely by management. In others it is the result of collective bargaining. In still others it may be the joint product of formal job evaluation and collective bargaining.

Internal wage structures are far from simple yet there is an orderliness which shows that they are not determined randomly or by caprice. Dunlop's description of wage structures as depending upon key rates, wage contours, and key settlements, lacks the neatness and precision of the theory of marginal productivity. But it is an important step toward the explanation of diversity in the wage structure as well as of regularities. The notions of key rates, wage contours, and key settlements also provide a nexus between the internal wage structures of individual plants or companies and the external wage structure.

The internal wage structure of a plant or company—which at first glance might appear to be a disorderly maze of different wage rates—is the essence of simplicity compared with the wage structure of the nation, a region, or of a single labor market area. The internal wage structure ranges from the top rates paid to highly skilled workers to relatively low rates for those who perform menial tasks. This can be explained in terms of market forces even if one conveniently chooses to ignore all other factors which impinge upon wages. Highly skilled workers are in scarce supply while workers with no skills at all are relatively abundant. In a highly developed economy there is a considerable need for skilled workers, while unskilled workers are needed only for janitorial and similar tasks. This is a result of an increasing reliance upon machines, materials-handling devices, and various other forms of mechanical rather than human energy. Thus one should not be particularly surprised to discover that in the internal wage structure of a plant or company there is a grading of wages upward from unskilled to skilled jobs.

When we turn to the external wage structure, however, the diversity of rates is often bewildering. We find that skilled workers in some industries receive a great deal more than skilled workers in others, and that there are even significant variations in the rates paid to unskilled workers. At the extremes, the average hourly earnings of unskilled workers in "high pay" industries may be significantly greater than the average hourly earnings of semiskilled or even of skilled workers in "low-pay" industries.[34] How do we explain the diversity of wages so characteristic of the inter-industry wage structure? This is a much easier question to ask than to answer. Many economists—both labor economists and general economists—have attempted to explain the variations in the inter-industry wage structure but the result has been more controversy than agreement.

One participant in the controversy, John T. Dunlop, has said:

> The inter-industry variations in wages over substantial periods are to be explained in terms of these factors: changes in productivity and output, the proportion of labor costs to total costs, the competitive conditions in the product market for the output of an industry, and the changing skill and occupational content of the workforce of an industry.[35]

Significantly, Dunlop does not include unionization as one of the forces affecting inter-industry wage structure. In a later study, however, Joseph Garbarino adds unionization to the factors earlier listed by Dunlop as affecting the inter-industry wage structure.[36] Garbarino's conclusion received support from a study by Ross and Goldner published at the same time.[37] This matter will be discussed in the following chapter which contains a more extended discussion of the impact of unions on wages and income distribution.

In the last chapter we noted that in a "structureless" labor market there is a tendency for wages to be the same. Not all unorganized

[34] See Sumner H. Slichter, "Notes on the Structure of Wages," *The Review of Economics and Statistics* (February 1950), p. 83.

[35] John Dunlop, "Productivity and the Wage Structure," in *Income, Employment and Public Policy,* Essays in honor of Alvin H. Hansen, New York: W. W. Norton and Company (1948), p. 362.

[36] Joseph Garbarino, "A Theory of Inter-Industry Wage Structure Variation," *Quarterly Journal of Economics* (May 1950), p. 305.

[37] Arthur M. Ross and William Goldner, "Forces Affecting the Inter-Industry Wage Structure," *Quarterly Journal of Economics* (May 1950), pp. 266–281.

labor markets are "structureless," however. A recent survey of unorganized workers in a metropolitan labor market revealed substantial variations. "The actual rates paid for similar work even within a given community tend to be rather persistently dispersed over a range larger than would be expected under competitive conditions.[38] The authors of this study feel that wages for non-union workers are responsive to market forces. But the market they studied was far from "perfect" as this term is used in economic theory. The tendency toward uniformity noted by Fisher in his study of the harvest labor market of California is not found in all non-unionized labor markets.

CONCLUSIONS

In this chapter we have distinguished between *internal* and *external* wage structures. It is obvious that labor markets are far more complex than product markets. In a given product market there is a tendency toward uniformity of prices after allowance is made for differences in quality for products which can be substituted for one another. But outside of some "structureless" labor markets, the outstanding characteristic of wage rates is their *diversity*. Within a plant or company which does not use incentive-pay methods, workers doing identical work will usually be paid at the same rate.[39] Wages within a firm tend to be related to differences in skill levels.

The external wage structure is far more complex. The average earnings of unskilled workers in some industries are higher than those of semiskilled or possibly even of some skilled workers in other industries. It appears that wages are not related in a simple functional manner to one or a few easily observable factors. This we might have suspected from our earlier discussion of labor markets which were found to be more complex than product markets.

The fact that there is such diversity in wage rates does not mean that there is a lack of order in the labor market, however. Economists are not in complete agreement about the relative importance of factors causing inter-industry wage variation but they agree that wage rates are not the result of random causes. Various economic and institutional forces affect wages in a variety of ways. Differences

[38] George P. Shultz, Irwin L. Herrnstadt, and Elbridge S. Puckett, "Wage Determination in a Non-Union Labor Market," *Proceedings,* 10th Annual Meeting of the Industrial Relations Research Association (September 1957), p. 4.

[39] There are cases in which female workers are paid less than males for similar or identical work. Since enactment of the Equal Pay Act of 1963, however, employers subject to the Fair Labor Standards Act are forbidden to discriminate on the basis of sex. See Public Law 88–38, enacted June 10, 1963.

in productivity, the proportion of labor cost to total cost, competitive conditions in product markets, and skill or occupational requirements, all have a bearing upon the external wage structure. What about the influence of unions on the wage level and wage structure? Raising this question again opens the door to controversy. It will be considered in some detail in the following chapter.

REFERENCES

BOOKS

Cartter, Allan M., *Theory of Wages and Employment,* Homewood, Illinois: Richard D. Irwin, Inc. (1959).

Dunlop, John T., *Wage Determination Under Trade Unions,* New York: Augustus M. Kelley, Inc. (1950).

———, ——— —, ed., *The Theory of Wage Determination,* Proceedings of a Conference Held by the International Economic Association, New York: St. Martin's Press (1957).

Hicks, J. R., *The Theory of Wages,* London: Macmillan and Company (1932).

Shackle, G. L. S., *Expectation in Economics,* Cambridge: Cambridge University Press (1949).

Taylor, George W. and Frank C. Pierson, eds., *New Concepts in Wage Determination,* New York: McGraw-Hill Book Company, Inc. (1957).

U.S. Department of Labor, *Union Wages and Hours: Motortruck Drivers and Helpers,* July 1, 1962 and Trend 1936–62, Bureau of Labor Statistics, Bulletin No. 1356 (May 1963).

Zeuthen, F., *Economic Theory and Method,* Cambridge, Massachusetts: Harvard University Press (1955), especially Chapter 57, "Economic Warfare," pp. 286ff.

ARTICLES

Barkin, Solomon, "Wage Determination: Trick or Technique," *Labor and Nation* (June-July, 1946), reprinted in part in Joseph Shister, ed., *Readings in Labor Economics and Industrial Relations,* New York: J. B. Lippincott Company (second edition, 1956), pp. 263ff.

Douty, H. M., "Some Problems of Wage Policy," *Monthly Labor Review* (July 1962), pp. 733–741.

———, — —, "Sources of Occupational Wage and Salary Rate Dispersion Within Labor Markets," *Industrial and Labor Relations Review* (October 1961), pp. 67–74.

Dunlop, John T., "Productivity and the Wage Structure," *Income Employment and Public Policy,* Essays in honor of Alvin H. Hansen, New York: W. W. Norton and Company, Inc. (1948), p. 362.

Garbarino, Joseph, "The Theory of Interindustry Wage Structure Variation," *Quarterly Journal of Economics* (May 1950), pp. 282–305.

Gomberg, William, "The Collective Bargaining Approach to Job Evaluation," *Labor and the Nation* (November–December, 1946), reprinted in part in Joseph Shister, ed., *Readings in Labor Economics and Industrial Relations,* New York: J. B. Lippincott Company (second edition, 1956), pp. 268ff.

Haley, Bernard F., "Value and Distribution," Howard S. Ellis, ed., *A Survey of Contemporary Economics,* Philadelphia: The Blakiston Company (1948), pp. 1–48.

Kerr, Clark and Lloyd H. Fisher, "Effect of Environment and Administration on Job Evaluation," *Harvard Business Review* (1950), pp. 77–96.

Lester, Richard A., "Results and Implications of Some Recent Wage Studies," Richard H. Lester and Joseph Shister, eds., *Insights Into Labor Issues,* New York: The Macmillan Company (1948), pp. 197–237.

Livernash, Edward R., "Wage Administration and Production Standards," W. S. Woytinsky and Associates, *Wages and Employment in the United States,* New York: Twentieth Century Fund (1953), pp. 330–344.

Pen, J., "A General Theory of Bargaining," *American Economic Review* (March 1952), pp. 24–42.

Ross, Arthur M. and William Goldner, "Forces Affecting the Interindustry Wage Structure," *Quarterly Journal of Economics* (May 1950), pp. 254–281.

Shultz, George P., Irwin L. Herrnstadt and Elbridge S. Puckett, "Wage Determination in a Non-Union Labor Market," *Proceedings,* Tenth Annual Meeting of the Industrial Relations Research Association (September 1957), pp. 1–13.

Slichter, Sumner H., "Notes on the Structure of Wages," *The Review of Economics and Statistics* (February 1950), pp. 80–91.

Wagner, Harvey M., "A Unified Treatment of Bargaining Theory," *Southern Economic Journal* (April 1957), pp. 380–397.

Chapter 20 The Economic Consequences of Trade Unions

p. 379 Summary

THE IMPACT OF UNIONS ON WAGES AND PRICES

As Chart 20-1 shows, earnings in manufacturing, a highly-organized sector of the economy, have increased more rapidly than prices since the end of World War II. If the average layman were asked: "Do you think that unions have affected these wage changes?" he would no doubt view the questioner with wonder, then answer "yes." It is widely believed by union leaders, by businessmen, and by the public at large, that unions are *supposed* to have an impact on wages. Otherwise, one might ask, why would unions exist?

There is less agreement among economists about the effects of unions on wages and prices, however. Some agree with the generally-accepted view that unions have an influence on wages. Others believe that the effects of unionism on wages and prices have been exaggerated. Some of these views will be examined in the first part of this chapter. We will consider the impact of unions on wages under two main headings; first, their impact on the wage *level*, then their effect on the wage *structure*.

Unions and the Level of Wages

We will not attempt in this brief section to review the voluminous literature on unions and wages. Instead, some representative views will be examined. A fair sampling has been given by Clark Kerr.[1]

[1] Clark Kerr, "The Impacts of Unions on the Level of Wages," *Wages, Prices, Profits and Productivity,* New York: The Fifteenth American Assembly, Columbia University (June 1959), pp. 92–94.

CHART 20–1
TREND OF EARNINGS IN MANUFACTURING, AND CONSUMER PRICE INDEX

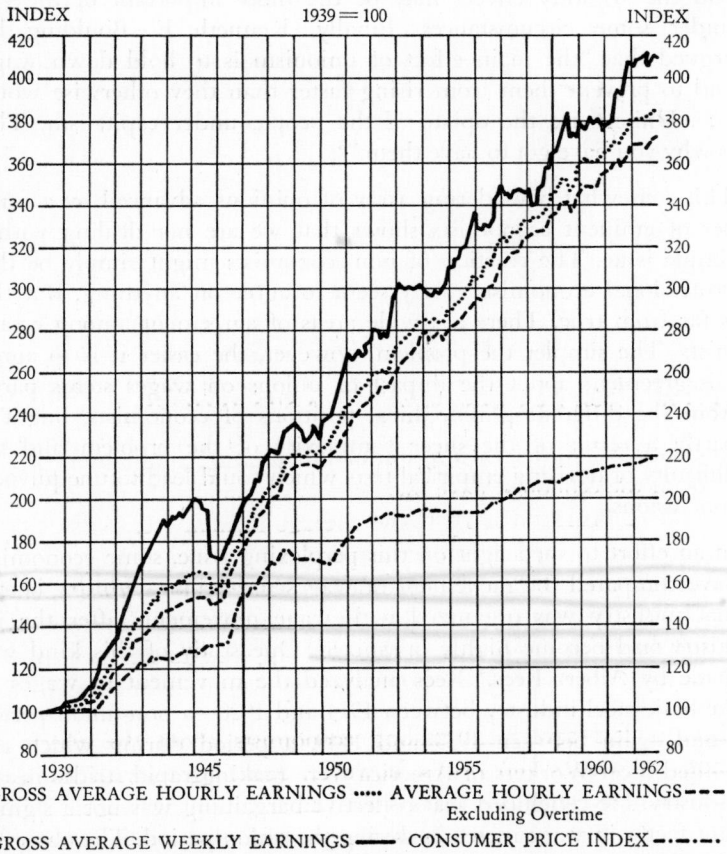

Source: Chart taken from publication of the United States Department of Labor, Bureau of Labor Statistics. Latest Data: November 1962

On the one hand, Kerr notes, such economists as Charles E. Lindblom and Edward H. Chamberlin believe that union pressure on wages definitely leads to inflation. Others, such as Sumner Slichter and A. P. Lerner, have argued that unions are only one of *several* causes of inflation. Moving along the spectrum, Lloyd G. Reynolds states that "collective bargaining does not have as much impact on the money wage level as has sometimes been suggested." While Walter A. Morton believes that "unions are a minor factor affecting inflation and may retard it as well as augment it."[2] Milton Friedman has claimed that unions have both a "rigidity effect" and an "upward-pressing effect." But the two largely offset one another, and the "rigidity effect" may be the more important of the two under some circumstances. Finally, Kenneth E. Boulding has argued that "the main effect of unionism is to hold down wages and to prevent them from rising faster than they otherwise would . . . Unions are the opiate of the people under capitalism. That is why you have got to have them."[3]

This somewhat bewildering array of opinions advanced by a number of eminent economists shows that we are not dealing with a simple issue. The reaction of non-economists might simply be that professional economists rarely seem to agree on anything. But this is far from true. There are wide areas of agreement among economists. The simpler the problem, however, the easier it is to agree. Disagreement about the impact of unions on wages stems partly from the different philosophical positions of economists, but it is partly a result of the sheer complexity of the problem and the difficulty of devising empirical tests which could lead to unequivocal conclusions.

In an effort to shed light on this perplexing issue, some economists have compared the movement of wages in a given industry before that industry was organized with wage movements after the industry had become highly organized. One study of this kind was made by Albert Rees.[4] Rees analyzed the movement of wages in the basic steel industry between 1914 and 1920—a non-union period —and again between 1939 and 1949, a period during which the United Steel Workers of America were making rapid strides in the industry. He concluded that collective bargaining was not a significant factor in wage increases during the union period. The observed wage increases, in his view, were caused by a tremendous increase in the demand for steel with an accompanying increase in the demand for steelworkers.

Rees feels that under conditions of full employment, and in the absence of unions, wages would be determined largely by the demand for and the supply of labor. Under collective bargaining, he claims, the cost of living becomes more important than labor market forces. Rees does not deny that wage increases are negoti-

[2] *Ibid.*, pp. 93–94.
[3] *Ibid.*, p. 94.
[4] Albert Rees, "Post-War Wage Determination in the Basic Steel Industry," *The American Economic Review* (June 1951), pp. 389–404.

ated by unions under inflationary conditions. He concludes, however, that "Negotiated wage increases are one of the most visible manifestations of inflation, but their visibility should not be confused with causation."[5] This conclusion was buttressed by a statistical analysis which showed that the percentage gain in steelworkers' wages from 1939 to 1948 was smaller than that during the earlier non-union period. Also, Rees observed, the percentage increases in steel wages since the industry has been organized have often been smaller than the relative increases in the earnings of non-union workers during the same time. From his own and other studies, Rees concluded that "there is considerable evidence that in the United States collective bargaining tends to retard wage increases when strong inflationary pressures are present."[6]

Several years later the relationship between unionism and the earnings of steelworkers was examined by Professor Lloyd Ulman, using a different analytical approach. Under conditions of rising prices, he concluded, the steelworkers' union has exerted upward pressure on wages instead of retarding wage increases.[7] Rees remained unconvinced, however, and replied to Ulman "that collective bargaining is not among the causes of rapid inflation."[8]

Many other economists have addressed themselves to this question.[9] The lack of agreement among economists about the effects of unions on the level of wages underscores the difficulty of testing various hypotheses by empirical methods. As Robert Ozanne has said, some economists imply that "our elaborate collective bargaining process is little more than a superstitious ritual, resembling perhaps the fertility dances of primitive peoples," at least as far as its effect on wage levels and income distribution is concerned.[10]

After comparing wage movements during the period 1923–29, and again during 1947–55, Ozanne concluded that real hourly earnings of production workers in manufacturing rose more than twice as rapidly during the unionized period than in the earlier non-union period. He also feels that "wage movements in the union period

[5] *Ibid.*, p. 404.
[6] Albert Rees, "Wage Levels Under Conditions of Long-Run Full Employment," *The American Economic Review*, Papers and Proceedings (May 1953), p. 452.
[7] Lloyd Ulman, "The Union and Wages in Basic Steel: A Comment," *American Economic Review* (June 1958), p. 426.
[8] "Reply," *Idem.*, p. 433.
[9] For a partial listing see Melvin W. Reder, "The General Level of Money Wages," *Proceedings*, Third Annual Meeting, Industrial Relations Research Association, p. 14.
[10] Robert Ozanne, "Impact of Unions on Wage Levels and Income Distribution," *Quarterly Journal of Economics* (May 1959), p. 178.

show surprising independence of the market demand for labor."[11] In his view, collective bargaining is more than a ritual. Ozanne believes that unions had a significant impact on wages long before they had organized a substantial part of the labor force. After a careful analysis of wage movements in a single company—the McCormick Harvesting Machinery Company—from 1862 through 1897, Ozanne concluded that "small craft unions had a wage impact grossly underestimated by their numbers as a percentage of the labor force." He also feels that "labor historians may have significantly underestimated union influence in the latter half of the nineteenth century."[12]

One development in collective bargaining has received relatively little attention in the discussions of the impact of unions on the wage level. This is the automatic wage adjustment or "escalator clause" incorporated into many labor-management agreements during the 1950's. Joseph Garbarino, one of the few economists to consider the effects of escalator clauses, has concluded that "automatic wage adjustment systems probably add to the inflationary potential of wage policy (at least so long as they are partial in coverage)."[13]

It seems unlikely, in view of the statistical difficulties involved, that labor economists and other students of industrial relations will reach agreement on the impact of unions on the wage level. In part this might be due to the fact that many have tried to generalize too broadly. After noting various contradictory opinions Clark Kerr had the following to say:

> . . . I should like to suggest that all of them are right and all of them are wrong. All of them are right to the extent that they suggest that some kinds of unions could have the suggested effects under some kinds of circumstances. All of them are wrong, to the extent they suggest (and some of them do not) that their conclusions are the universal rule. The only universal rule is that there are all kinds of unions operating under all kinds of circumstances and they can have all kinds of effects. But it should also be added that kinds and circumstances and effects can be related—at least to a certain degree. Truth is more likely to emerge from studying the impacts of the unions, than "the impact of the union."[14]

[11] *Ibid.*, p. 195. See also, Robert R. France, "Wages, Unemployment, and Prices in the United States, 1890–1932, 1947–1957," *Industrial and Labor Relations Review* (January 1962), pp. 187 and 190.

[12] Robert Ozanne, "Union Wage Impact: A Nineteenth Century Case," *Industrial and Labor Relations Review* (April 1962), p. 375.

[13] J. W. Garbarino, "Economic Significance of Automatic Wage Adjustments," Harold W. Davey, *et al.*, eds., *New Dimensions in Collective Bargaining*, New York: Harper and Brothers (1959), p. 172.

[14] Clark Kerr, "The Impacts of Unions on the Level of Wages," p. 94.

Unions and the Wage Structure

There is obviously little agreement about the impact of unions on the level of wages. What is the attitude of students of labor economics toward the question: Have unions affected the *structure* of wages? As noted in the last chapter, the major characteristic of wages in the United States is their diversity. There are substantial variations in wages among industries and regions. Even for similar or identical occupations wages are far from uniform *within* a given labor market area. One of the stated goals of some unions is the elimination of wage differentials—at least among workers doing the same job in a given industry. Some of the stronger unions, such as those in the steel and meatpacking industries, have been quite successful in achieving equal pay for similar work regardless of location. Wage differentials have been remarkably persistent, however. Yet one is hard pressed to find agreement among economists about the impact of unions on the *general* wage structure of the United States.

Reynolds and Taft, for example, feel that "collective bargaining clearly makes for reduction of wage differentials among firms competing in the same product market."[15] In their view, however, it is the pressure of competition in the product market which is the decisive factor causing a tendency toward wage uniformity. Thus *within a single industry,* Reynolds and Taft conclude: ". . . the effect of union efforts to reduce wage differentials among rival producers appears to be moderately favorable—not so completely beneficial as unions sometimes allege, but sufficiently so to warrant a positive score for collective bargaining."[16] The impact of unions on the *intra*-industry wage structure—at least in highly organized industries—has been to introduce a tendency toward uniformity of pay for similar or identical occupations.

But what of the *inter*-industry wage structure? Some industries have become highly organized while others have successfully resisted trade unionism. Have wages increased more rapidly in the highly organized unions? And if so, can we conclude that unions have affected the inter-industry structure of wages? As noted in the last chapter, Dunlop attributes inter-industry variations in wages to changes in productivity and output, the proportion of labor cost to total cost, competitive conditions in the product market, and changing skill and occupational requirements. In his

[15] Lloyd G. Reynolds and Cynthia H. Taft, *The Evolution of Wage Structure,* New Haven: Yale University Press (1956), p. 175.
[16] *Ibid.,* p. 179.

analysis Dunlop gives "no distinctive place to the role of labor organization."[17] While he concedes that the influence of unions on the structure of wages cannot be ignored, he concludes that the role of unionization has been neither distinctive nor uniform.[18]

Arthur Ross has argued, however, that "real earnings in the highly organized industries have increased to a greater extent than have those in the less organized industries."[19] Trade unions have had an impact on the wage structure, in his view, and this has been in the direction of widening inter-industry differentials. Strong unions have been successful in pushing wages up in some industries while weaker unions have not been able to achieve the same effect in other industries.

In a later study, Ross and Goldner concluded that "unionization is a source of wage advantage, which operates most effectively under facilitating environmental circumstances."[20] These authors feel that unions have been able to push wages up in expanding industries, particularly in those dominated by a few large and profitable firms. This view has been supported by Garbarino who has said that "while wage behavior is the result of the operation of a large number of factors . . . the variables of productivity, concentration, and unionization will be capable of explaining the major portion of differential movements."[21]

There has been relatively little debate about the effects of unionism on the *intra*-industry wage structure. Where unions have succeeded in organizing a substantial part of an industry they have been able to eliminate wage differentials among firms in that industry.[22] But there is much less agreement about the effects of unions on the *inter*-industry wage structure. Some writers believe that unions have had little if any effect while others feel that strong unions have pushed wages up in highly-organized industries while weak unions have been less successful in doing so in partly-organized industries.

[17] John T. Dunlop, "Productivity and the Wage Structure," *Income, Employment and Public Policies,* Essays in honor of Alvin H. Hansen, New York: W. W. Norton (1948), p. 360.
[18] *Ibid.*
[19] Arthur Ross, *Trade Union Wage Policy*, Berkeley, California: University of California Press (1948), p. 117.
[20] Arthur M. Ross and William Goldner, "Forces Affecting the Inter-Industry Wage Structure," *Quarterly Journal of Economics* (May 1950), p. 281.
[21] Joseph Garbarino, "A Theory of Interindustry Wage Structure Variation," *Quarterly Journal of Economics* (May 1950), p. 305.
[22] In a later section this conclusion will be modified somewhat since the elimination of inter-firm differentials in some industries has been limited to particular regions.

This lack of agreement again stems from the statistical difficulties involved. All of the authors involved in the debate over the impact of unions on the wage structure agree that wages are affected by a number of forces. The difficulty stems from their inability to disentangle these forces and to assign relative weights to each. Few would care to argue that wages in highly-organized industries (such as steel and autos) have not increased more rapidly than those in partly-organized industries such as textiles. But there are many other differences between the highly-organized and the partly-organized industries, including differences in market structure, the degree of internal competition, productivity, susceptibility to foreign competition, and various other factors which could impinge upon wages. It is likely that unless someone is able to devise a statistical method for measuring each of these forces with precision, economists will continue to have differences of opinion about the impact of unions on the inter-industry wage structure.

What of skill differentials? Have unions widened or narrowed the gap between the wages of skilled and unskilled workers? It should come as no surprise by this time that there are differences of opinion on this score. Some writers have argued that the effect of unions on skill differentials has been neutral;[23] others disagree. While Reynolds and Taft are of the opinion that unions have had only a slight effect on occupational differentials, they conclude that: "to the extent that unionism has had any net effect on occupational differentials, this has almost certainly been in the direction of narrowing them."[24]

Jack Stieber has pointed out that "occupational earnings differentials . . . have narrowed substantially in steel during the past 50 years much as they have in most other industries."[25] While he insists that the relative earnings differentials between skilled and unskilled workers in basic steel have not been maintained—as some other writers have implied—Stieber is careful to avoid the conclusion that the narrowing in skill differentials in this industry has been the result of union policy. Indeed, he points out the different pressures that exist within the union on this issue. Low-wage workers prefer across-the-board increases which would continue

[23] Clark Kerr, "Wage Relationships—The Comparative Impact of Market and Power Forces," John T. Dunlop, ed., *The Theory of Wage Determination,* New York: St. Martin's Press (1957), p. 179; and William Goldner, "Labor Market Factors and Skill Differentials in Wage Rates," *Proceedings,* Tenth Annual Meeting, Industrial Relations Research Association, pp. 8–9.

[24] Clark Kerr, "Wage Relationships," *op. cit.,* p. 185.

[25] Jack Stieber, "Occupational Wage Differentials in the Basic Steel Industry," *Industrial and Labor Relations Review* (January 1959), p. 167.

the trend of narrowing differentials between unskilled and skilled workers. But the higher-skilled (and higher-paid) workers favor increases which will maintain differentials rather than narrowing them.

On balance, there is less disagreement about the effects of unions on occupational or skill differentials than there is about the impact of unions on the inter-industry wage structure. Even those authors who accept the view that there has been a narrowing of skill differentials are of the opinion that this has not been the result of an egalitarian union philosophy. In part at least the narrowing has been due to the action of various economic forces rather than conscious union policy.[26]

Geographic Wage Differentials

Geographic or inter-area wage differentials are among the most persistent in the United States. In general, wage rates tend to be high in the heavily industrialized Middle Atlantic, Great Lakes, and Pacific Coast states. They tend toward the average in New England and some of the Midwestern states and wages taper off to their lowest levels in the South. But the geographical wage structure is far more complex than the above summary statement suggests.

The general wage level in New England, for example, is close to the national average. But wages in some industries in New England are higher than they are in other regions, while the reverse is true for other industries. There is also a considerable amount of wage variation *within* as well as among regions. In general, wages tend to be lower in small communities than in larger metropolitan areas. It is not uncommon for wages in a small community in a high-wage *region* to be lower than wages in a large community in a low-wage region. The wage structure may be viewed in a number of ways: industry by industry, occupation by occupation, and area by area. Any way it is viewed, however, the wage structure is complex but in some ways the geographical wage structure is the most complicated of all.

How have unions affected the geographical wage structure? Are variations in geographical wage contours associated with variations in union strength? This question can be answered with a qualified affirmative. In general, we find a higher degree of unionism in high-wage than in low-wage areas. But we cannot simply conclude

[26] See Richard Perlman, "Forces Widening Occupational Wage Differentials," *The Review of Economics and Statistics* (May 1958), p. 110.

that unions *cause* wages to be high in some areas while the absence of unions causes wages to be low elsewhere. There are some regions —New England is an example—where unions are relatively strong but where wages are not high. The geographical wage structure is affected by many economic forces. Wages in each region are influenced by the rate of population growth, and by the expansion or contraction of industrial and other forms of economic activity. Other factors which have a bearing on a region's wage level are its "industry-mix," the degree of competition within its industries and no doubt the degree of unionism. These factors cannot be isolated in any way which will show the relative influence of each.

Geographical wage differentials have been remarkably persistent. But wide variations in wages within regions tend to weaken somewhat the significance of *average* wage levels on a geographical basis. Reynolds and Taft are of the opinion that "unionism appears thus far to have had only a slight effect on geographical differentials; and this effect has not always been in the same direction."[27] Some unions have adopted the policy of equal pay for equal work regardless of location. And the influence of these unions has been in the direction of narrowing inter-regional differentials. Other unions, however, have deliberately maintained inter-regional wage differentials in an effort to obtain what the traffic will bear in each region. And in some industries, unions have succeeded in organizing the firms in some regions while they have met with relatively little success in others. The textile industries provide examples of the latter situation. Textile mills in the North are predominantly organized, while only a minority of workers in the South belong to unions. While North-South textile wage differentials have narrowed in recent years this has been largely a reflection of the weakness of unions in the organized regions rather than an indication of growing strength in the predominantly unorganized South.

The Overall Impact of Unions on the Wage Structure

Perhaps it will be useful at this point to summarize the preceding discussion of the impact of unions on the wage structure. This has been done by Reynolds and Taft who note the following: Unions have had an important impact on *interpersonal* wage differentials. Where they have succeeded in organizing firms they have insisted on an impersonal wage structure. Wage rates are to be attached to *jobs* not individuals.

[27] Reynolds and Taft, *Evolution of Wage Structure*, p. 182.

Unions have also had a significant impact on *interfirm* differentials where the firms are members of a single competitive group. This seems to be the case both in product markets where there is a high degree of price competition and in those markets where prices tend to be administered.

The impact of unions on *geographical* or inter-area wage differentials has been relatively slight. In some industries, inter-regional differentials have been largely or entirely eliminated. In others, while inter-regional differentials have been narrowed they have not been eliminated, and in some industries, unions have pursued a policy of maintaining inter-regional differentials.

The impact of unions on *occupational* differentials has also been relatively slight. Whatever influence unions have had has been in the direction of narrowing differentials. In recent years, however, there has been a tendency for occupational differentials to be maintained, and in some cases there has been a slight widening.

Although this is one of their more debatable conclusions, Reynolds and Taft are of the opinion that the impact of unions on *inter-industry* differentials has been relatively minor. If there has been an effect, they believe, it has been in the direction of widening inter-industry differentials.[28]

Reynolds and Taft feel that "the friends of trade unionism as well as its critics have tended to overestimate its actual effects on the wage structure . . . fears that complete unionization will bring seismic disruption of the wage structure do not seem to be well founded . . . countries with the strongest union movements appear to have a wage structure which is more orderly and defensible than the wage structure of countries where unionism has been weak."[29]

The Economic Consequences of Geographical Wage Differentials

Most economists in the United States would probably agree that complete uniformity of wages is an idle dream of egalitarian reformers. Within reasonable limits, occupational wage differentials can be defended on the grounds that higher-skilled workers must undergo extensive periods of training and they should be rewarded for this. Also, not everyone has the natural aptitudes needed to do skilled work, thus market forces alone would tend to maintain occupational differentials. In a market economy, inter-industry differentials are also likely to persist. The ratio of labor cost to

[28] *Ibid.*, pp. 193–194.
[29] *Ibid.*, pp. 193–195.

total cost varies widely from industry to industry. Some industries require relatively little capital investment and these tend to be price competitive. Others require huge investments and in these prices are often administered. In general, wages are lower in labor-intensive than in capital-intensive industries.

In an economy where market forces determine the allocation of resources, some industries are bound to pay higher wages than others. And even within an "industry," as Dunlop has noted in his discussion of wage contours, there will be substantial variations among workers with the same job titles. While some union leaders have talked at times as though they would like to see such differentials eliminated, their actions indicate that they are rarely troubled by occupational and inter-industry differentials.

There has been somewhat more controversy about geographical wage differentials, however. Some economists have roundly condemned unions for their efforts to eliminate geographical wage differentials even within a single industry and they have been equally critical of public policy—notably minimum wage legislation—which in their view interferes with the free market allocation of resources. These economists, in the classical tradition, believe that wage differentials play an important role in economic development. Low wages in some regions, they assert, will attract capital to those regions and speed up their industrialization. At the same time, workers in low-wage regions will be encouraged to migrate to relatively high-wage regions. In the long-run, this will tend to bring about a more efficient allocation of resources than would be the case if inter-regional wage differentials were eliminated.

Other economists, however, have tended to question this line of reasoning. They have indicated that labor cost is only one of the determinants of industrial location. And they are doubtful that labor is sufficiently mobile to eliminate geographical differentials through the process of inter-regional migration, even over fairly long periods of time.[30]

Regardless of how economists feel about them, and despite efforts by some unions to eliminate inter-regional wage differentials, the

[30] For a criticism of union and government interference with geographical wage differentials see John V. Van Sickle, "The Southeast: A Case Study in Delayed Industrialization," *American Economic Review* (May 1951), pp. 384–393; and "Regional Aspects of the Problem of Full Employment and Fair Wages," *Southern Economic Journal* (July 1946), pp. 35–46. For the contrary view that "low wages appear to be less influential in industrial location and expansion than is popularly believed," see Richard A. Lester, "Southern Wage Differentials: Developments, Analysis, and Implications," *Southern Economic Journal* (April 1947), p. 387.

latter have been remarkably persistent. But as noted earlier, the *average* wage level in a region tells us relatively little. There are wide variations around these averages. Some regions are "high wage" regions for some industries and "low wage" regions for others. Some industries which are highly unionized pay essentially the same wage for similar occupations in all regions. There is no simple and direct relationship between average geographical wage levels and the movement of industry.

Some industries are relatively footloose, and plants in these industries are often attracted to low labor-cost areas. Other industries, however, must locate with respect to raw materials or markets and cannot be induced to locate in a particular area simply because wages there are low. Locational economics has long been a neglected subject but there have been rapid advances in recent years. As we have learned more about the forces which determine the location of industry—both those which cause some industries to be migratory, and the ones which contribute to the relative immobility of others—some of the furor about geographical wage differentials has subsided. The controversy is revived, however, when unions announce that they are going to step up organizational activities in areas where they have made little headway in the past or when Congress prepares to debate the issue of raising the statutory minimum wage.

UNION WAGE POLICY AND EMPLOYMENT

What effect have unions had upon employment? Have unions won wage increases only at the cost of the jobs of some of their members? In establishing their wage *policies* have unions taken into account the potential "employment effect?" The "law of demand," as we learn it in our first course in economics, tells us that buyers will take more of a good at low than at high prices; that is, demand curves slope downward to the right. If the demand for labor is viewed in terms of such a schedule, one might conclude that there is a simple and direct relationship between employment and wages. And some evidently think this is the case. They point out, for example, that as the coal miners became strongly organized and pushed wages up employment in this industry fell. Or they point to the New England textile industry and note that as unions became strong in this region and wages rose, much of the industry relocated to the South where unions made much less headway. But the relationship between wages and employment in these cases cannot be explained in terms of a simple demand curve. The latter is a timeless schedule while the events we have described occurred over fairly long periods of time.

Examples can also be cited of highly organized industries—such as shipbuilding, aluminum, aircraft, and electrical machinery—where wages and employment have increased together.[31] Evidently the wage-employment relationship is somewhat more complex than that between the price of a commodity and the quantity of that commodity demanded at any moment of time. In the final analysis, the demand for labor is a *derived* demand. Both wages and employment depend upon conditions in the product market; upon changes in labor supply (including hours worked), and upon changes in productivity.[32]

This is not to deny that wages can influence employment, but only to indicate that the connection between them is not a simple and direct one. If wages are pushed up rapidly management might have an incentive to substitute capital for labor—as in the bituminous coal industry since the end of World War II—and this indeed has an employment effect. But it takes time for the employment effect to be realized. It is possible, if not always easy to work out in practice, for a reduction in labor requirements to be geared to normal turnover—to retirement rates and voluntary quits—so that declining employment in an industry *need not* lead to unemployment. As will be noted in the following chapter, however, rapid technological progress in recent times has often resulted in substantial unemployment.

In determining their wage policies do unions take the employment effect into account? What is it that trade unions try to maximize? Assuming that they know the relationship between wages and employment, Dunlop suggests that union leaders might direct wage policy toward a number of goals. For example, the wage policy of a particular union might be designed to achieve:

1. The largest possible wage bill for a particular segment of the economy regardless of whether all wage earners are employed.
2. The largest possible wage bill from a segment of the economy including funds from the public support of the unemployed.
3. The largest *private* payroll to employed workers, deducting from their wage income an amount to pay out-of-work benefits to unemployed members.

[31] See Ross and Goldner, "Forces Affecting the Interindustry Wage Structure," pp. 274–275.
[32] *Ibid.*, p. 269.

4. The maximization of employment even if this means a smaller total wage bill than the union is able to achieve.
5. The highest average wage income for each unit of labor affiliated with the union.[33]

The policy which a given union will pursue depends upon conditions in the labor and product markets. A union might pursue one set of goals under certain labor and product market conditions, but it can alter these goals as underlying market conditions change.

Finally, not everyone would agree that unions try to maximize anything. Arthur Ross, for example, has stated that: "The union is not a business enterprise selling labor. It is a political institution representing the sellers of labor, and there is no necessary reason to assume that it will automatically or mechanically behave in the same fashion as a profit maximizing business enterprise."[34] He goes on to conclude that "the volume of employment associated with a given wage rate is unpredictable before the fact, and the effect of a given rate upon employment is undecipherable after the fact."[35]

Dunlop views the trade union as an institution responding to economic forces. Ross, however, emphasizes the political nature of trade unions, and suggests that union wage policy is determined by the pressures operating on the union's leadership. The union leaders try to reconcile various pressures—to achieve a compromise among them—rather than seeking to maximize wages, employment, or some combination of the two.[36] Other writers have jumped into the fray. After a detailed analysis of the wage behavior of a number of unions in various industries, Shultz and Myers concluded that "some unions, faced with a particular set of labor market and product market conditions, do take into account the probable effect of wage demands on the level of employment for their membership."[37] These situations, the authors contend, are not at all unusual except in periods of full employment and rising prices. Where there is strong competition in the product market, and where an industry is not completely organized, Shultz and Myers maintain that unions must take into account the employment effect in establishing their wage policy.

[33] John T. Dunlop, *Wage Determination Under Trade Unions,* New York: Augustus M. Kelly, Inc. (1950), pp. 32–40.
[34] Arthur M. Ross, *Trade Union Wage Policy,* Berkeley and Los Angeles: University of California Press (1948), p. 22.
[35] *Ibid.,* p. 80.
[36] *Ibid.,* pp. 11–12.
[37] G. P. Shultz and C. A. Myers, "Union Wage Decisions and Employment," *American Economic Review* (June 1950), p. 379.

The Dunlop-Ross debate over the determinants of union wage policy has led to a voluminous literature on the subject.[38] Much of the discussion has been concerned with the relationship between wages and employment without explicit reference to prices. During the latter half of the 1950's, however, there was a tendency for wages, prices, and unemployment to rise together. This shifted the emphasis of economic analysis from a simple wage-employment relationship to the more complex wage-price-*unemployment* relationship.[39]

Demand-Pull versus Cost-Push Theories of "Inflation"

Whether union leaders are responsive to internal (political) or external (economic) pressures, it is widely believed that they will take advantage of favorable labor market conditions in formulating wage demands. Support for this view is found in an elaborate statistical analysis by A. W. Phillips, a British economist. After analyzing changes in wage rates and unemployment in Great Britain from 1861 to 1957, Phillips concluded that "there is a clear tendency for the rate of change of money wage rates to be high when unemployment is low and to be low or negative when unemployment is high."[40] When the labor market is tight, this study suggests, employers will bid up wages in an effort to attract workers from one another, and unions will not be reticent about seeking wage increases. But when there is substantial unemployment in the economy wages will rise only slightly. If the level of unemployment is particularly high union leaders might even be willing to accept wage cuts.

One of the puzzling economic phenomena in the United States since 1955, however, has been the coexistence of "creeping unemployment" and "creeping inflation." The price level has edged upward, but this has not been due to a tight labor market. Indeed, prices and unemployment have gone up together. This has brought a new dimension into the analysis of the wage-employment relationship. During the latter half of the 1950's economists were con-

[38] For a partial list of books and articles dealing with the topic see M. W. Reder, "The Theory of Union Wage Policy," *Review of Economics and Statistics* (February 1952), p. 34.

[39] The unemployment problem will be touched on only briefly here. It is discussed in considerable detail in Chapter 22.

[40] A. W. Phillips, "The Relation Between Unemployment and the Rate of Change of Money Wage Rates in the United Kingdom, 1861–1957," *Economica* (November 1958), p. 290. Robert R. France has suggested, however, that "wage increases under trade unions are less sensitive to high unemployment than under non-union conditions." See his "Wages, Unemployment, and Prices in the United States," *op. cit.*, p. 190.

cerned about the interaction among wages, employment *and* prices.

As is often the case there was a tendency for economists—and others—to split into opposing camps. Some attributed rising prices to "cost-push," others insisted with equal vigor that it was due to "demand-pull." Those who accepted the cost-push explanation of rising prices often associated it with rising labor costs resulting from union-negotiated wage increases. Those who accepted the demand-pull explanation of rising prices, however, asserted that "there was too much money chasing too few goods" in the economic system. The period following the end of World War II was cited as an example of the latter situation. Paul Samuelson and Robert Solow asserted that "most economists are now agreed that [the] first postwar rise in prices was primarily attributable to the pull of demand that resulted from wartime accumulations of liquid assets and deferred needs."[41]

But others insisted that the rise in prices was due to upward pressure on costs. Wage increases, it was frequently claimed, exceeded gains in productivity. Those who argued in this vein concluded that unions had been the primary cause of inflation in the American economy since the end of World War II. And some drew the further conclusion that by over-pricing jobs, unions were also responsible for the rising level of unemployment.

The investigation of changes in wages and unemployment in Great Britain by A. W. Phillips influenced the thinking of a number of American economists. The view is still rather widely-held that there is a fairly close connection between the forces causing prices to rise and the forces causing unemployment. Thus, we have been told, we are faced with a choice. If we insist upon a low level of unemployment, we must accept a fairly rapid rise in prices. But if price increases are to be held within bounds we must pay for this with a higher level of unemployment.[42] This argument seems to give at least tacit support to the "cost-push" theory of inflation.

Not all economists have been willing to accept these conclusions, however. It has been pointed out, for example, that unions negotiate wages for fewer than one-third of the workers in our economy and that prices have gone up slowly in heavily-organized industries

[41] Paul A. Samuelson and Robert M. Solow, "Analytical Aspects of Anti-Inflation Policy," *American Economic Review* (May 1960), p. 177.
[42] See Samuelson and Solow, *ibid.*, pp. 192–193.

CHART 20–2
CONSUMER PRICE INDEX
Selected Groups

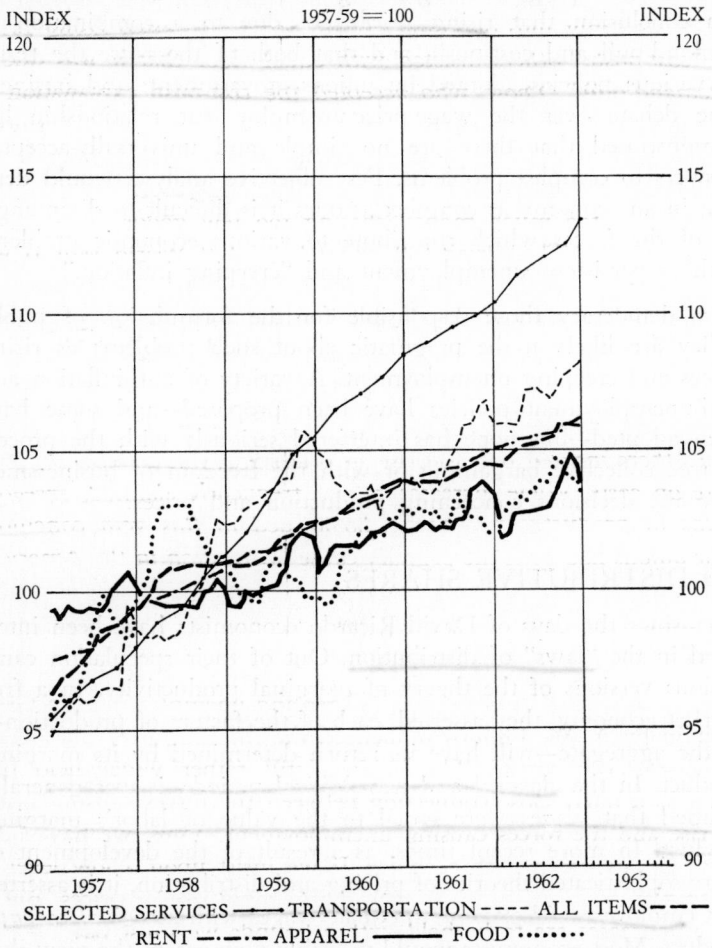

Source: Chart taken from publication of the United States Department of Labor, Bureau of Labor Statistics. Latest Data: December 1962

while they have increased rapidly in the largely unorganized trade and service sectors (see Chart 20-2). One group of well-known economists has insisted that "the evidence that collective bargaining has caused inflation is far from conclusive."[43] Others have

[43] *The Public Interest in National Labor Policy,* by an Independent Study Group, New York: Committee for Economic Development (1961), p. 119.

contended that a variety of forces influence the price level, and that it is unfair to lay all of the blame on trade unions.

As the debate progressed a growing number of economists accepted the conclusion that rising prices are due to a combination of demand-pull and cost-push, and that both of these are the result of various policies adopted by unions, government, and business. The debate over the wage-price-unemployment relationship has demonstrated that there are no simple and universally-accepted answers to complex problems. Few objective analysts would deny that in an economy as complex as ours it is difficult to disentangle all of the forces which contribute to various economic problems such as persistent unemployment and "creeping inflation."

In a democracy those responsible for the formulation of public policy are likely to be pragmatic about such problems as rising prices and creeping unemployment. A variety of anti-inflation and anti-unemployment policies have been proposed—and some have been adopted—but none has interfered seriously with the process of free collective bargaining or with the freedom of businessmen to make decisions concerning production and prices.

UNIONS AND DISTRIBUTIVE SHARES

Ever since the days of David Ricardo economists have been interested in the "laws" of distribution. Out of their speculation came various versions of the theory of marginal productivity. In a free market economy, they asserted, each of the factors of production—in the aggregate—will have its return determined by its marginal product. In the classical and neo-classical periods, it was generally claimed that wages were equal to the value of labor's marginal product. In more recent times, as a result of the development of more sophisticated theories of pricing and distribution, it is asserted that employers will attempt to equate wages with marginal *revenue* product. Most economists would probably now accept the view that the theory of marginal productivity does little to explain what *determines* wages. But there is still strong support for marginal productivity as the basis for a general theory of distribution. This raises the interesting question: Can trade unions affect distributive shares?

A number of analysts have answered this question in the negative. Whatever else unions have been able to do, it is argued, they have not been able to alter the share of total income going to labor as a whole. In the early 1930's, Paul H. Douglas published the results of empirical studies conducted over a number of years which showed that labor's share of the national income had been fairly constant.[44] These studies were conducted at a time when unions were relatively weak in the United States, however, and one could not conclude from them that unions have been unable to affect distributive shares.

In *The Theory of Wages,* J. R. Hicks argued that the relative share of national income going to labor could be altered but this would result from the introduction of labor-saving inventions rather than the direct action of trade unions.[45] More recently, other scholars have concluded that unions cannot affect labor's share through collective bargaining. Allan Cartter has said, for example: "There is scanty evidence that unions . . . possess the power to raise general *money* wages above what they would have been in the absence of unionism, much less real wages or labor's share of total income."[46] And more recently, Professor Sidney Weintraub has concluded that "over time, *the share of wages in the total of business income remains almost constant.*"[47] Weintraub goes on to conclude that "over short periods of time during which productivity scarcely changes, *each rise in money wages will be translated into price increases.*"[48] The relative shares going to labor and to other factors of production will thus remain unchanged.

wages ↑
prices ↑

There has been some opposition to this view, however. Robert Ozanne has argued that while labor's share remained relatively constant before unions had achieved significant power in the United States, this share has increased since the end of World War II. At the same time, he has said, the share of profits before taxes was increasing during the non-union period, but has remained relatively stable during the union period.[49] Ozanne does not explicitly state that unions have affected distributive shares but his analysis suggests this conclusion. Clark Kerr, who has a skillful knack for dissecting broad generalizations, has suggested "that a certain kind

[44] Paul H. Douglas, *Real Wages in the United States, 1890–1925,* Boston: Houghton Mifflin Company (1930); and *The Theory of Wages,* New York: The Macmillan Company (1934).
[45] J. R. Hicks, *The Theory of Wages,* London: Macmillan and Company (1932), pp. 121–134.
[46] Allan M. Cartter, *Theory of Wages and Employment,* Homewood, Illinois: Richard D. Irwin, Inc. (1959), p. 167.
[47] Sidney Weintraub, "A Law that Cannot be Repealed," *Challenge* (April 1962), p. 17.
[48] *Ibid.,* p. 19.
[49] Robert Ozanne, "Impact of Unions on Wage Levels and Income Distribution," *Quarterly Journal of Economics* (May 1959), p. 195.

of trade-unionism under certain conditions will have no effect; that a certain kind of trade-unionism under certain conditions will raise labor's share; and . . . a certain kind of trade-unionism under certain conditions will reduce labor's share."[50] Kerr's ultimate conclusion, however, is that trade unionism in the United States has had relatively little effect on labor's share of national income. By supporting a full employment policy trade unions have tended to *reduce* labor's share. But at the same time, unions have effectively raised the wages paid by some employers who have been temporarily unable to recapture profits. When these forces are balanced off against one another, Kerr suggests, trade unionism has done relatively little to alter the total share of income going to labor as a whole.[51] Kerr has also stated that "labor's share of income, industry by industry, has fared no more favorably in unionized industries than in non-union."[52]

One final note will conclude our discussion of the impact of unions on distributive shares. Given our present state of knowledge perhaps we cannot answer the question: "Can unions affect distributive shares?" Even those who have argued that labor's share of national income is *relatively* constant have indicated that there has been a *slight* increase in the share going to all employees. But there are many statistical difficulties involved in the precise measurement of income distribution. We do not, for example, have a satisfactory breakdown between wages and salaries. There are even greater conceptual difficulties. As Robert Solow has pointed out, "an unknown fraction of society's capital takes the form of the improvement of human abilities and skills.[53] That is, workers today spend a greater part of their lives in education and training than was the case a half century ago. How much of their earnings should then be considered as a return on this investment, and how much as a reward for physical or mental effort? These questions cannot be answered by means of statistical analysis, but this does not mean that they can be ignored.

Few economists deny that the share of national income going to all workers has been *relatively* constant; that the effect of unions

[50] Clark Kerr, "Trade Unionism and Distributive Shares," *American Economic Review* (May 1954), p. 281.

[51] Kerr notes that in Great Britain wage earners have gained at the expense of salaried workers, and that full employment in Great Britain has led to a smaller reduction in the share of wages than in the share of income going to all employees, i.e., wage and salary workers combined. *Ibid.*, p. 291.

[52] *Ibid.*, p. 288.

[53] Robert M. Solow, "A Skeptical Note on the Constancy of Relative Shares," *American Economic Review* (September 1958), p. 630.

upon the distribution of income in the United States has not been great. As Solow has noted, however, perhaps the question of distributive shares is far more complicated than has been assumed by those who simply measure the percentages going to "labor" and to other factors of production without taking into account changes in skill distributions, educational attainment, and other changes which make the work force today vastly different from that of a half century ago.

REFERENCES

BOOKS

Cartter, Allan M., *Theory of Wages and Employment,* Homewood, Illinois: Richard D. Irwin, Inc. (1959).

Dunlop, John T., *Wage Determination Under Trade Unions,* New York: Augustus M. Kelly, Inc. (1950).

———, ed., *The Theory of Wage Determination,* New York: St. Martin's Press (1957).

Hicks, J. R., *The Theory of Wages,* London: Macmillan and Company (1932).

National Labor Policy, by an Independent Study Group, New York: Committee for Economic Development (1961).

Reynolds, Lloyd G., and Cynthia H. Taft, *The Evolution of Wage Structure,* New Haven: Yale University Press (1956).

Ross, Arthur M., *Trade Union Wage Policy,* Berkeley and Los Angeles: University of California Press (1948).

ARTICLES

Dunlop, John T., "Productivity and Wage Structure," *Income, Employment and Public Policy,* Essays in Honor of Alvin H. Hansen, New York: W. W. Norton and Company, Inc. (1948), pp. 341–362.

France, Robert R., "Wages, Unemployment, and Prices in the United States, 1890–1932, 1947–1957," *Industrial and Labor Relations Review* (January 1962), pp. 171–190.

Garbarino, Joseph W., "A Theory of Interindustry and Wage Structure Variation," *Quarterly Journal of Economics* (May 1950), pp. 282–305.

———, "The Economic Significance of Automatic Wage Adjustments," *New Dimensions in Collective Bargaining,* New York: Harper and Brothers (1959), pp. 154–175.

Goldner, William, "Labor Market Factors and Skilled Differentials in Wage Rates," *Proceedings,* Tenth Annual Meeting, Industrial Relations Research Association, pp. 1–10.

Kerr, Clark, "Trade-Unionism and Distributive Shares," *American Economic Review* (May 1954), pp. 279–292.

———, "The Impacts of Unions on the Level of Wages," *Wages, Prices, Profits and Productivity,* Fifteenth American Assembly, Columbia University (June 1959), pp. 91–108.

Lester, Richard A., "Southern Wage Differentials: Developments, Analysis and Implications," *Southern Economic Journals* (April 1947).

Meyers, Frederic, "Unions, Anti-trust Laws and Inflation," Reprint No. 87, University of California (1959).

Morton, Walter A., "Trade Unionism, Full Employment, and Inflation," *American Economic Review* (March 1950), pp. 13–39.

Ozanne, Robert, "Impact of Unions on Wage Levels and Income Distribution," *Quarterly Journal of Economics* (May 1959), pp. 177–196.

Perlman, Richard, "Forces Widening Occupational Wage Differentials," *The Review of Economics and Statistics* (May 1958), pp. 107–115.

Phillips, A. W., "The Relation Between Unemployment and the Rate of Change of Money Wage Rates in the United Kingdom, 1861–1957," *Economica* (November 1958), pp. 283–299.

Reder, Melvin W., "The General Level of Money Wages," *Proceedings,* Third Annual Meeting, Industrial Relations Research Association, p. 1–17.

———, "The Theory of Union Wage Policy," *The Review of Economics and Statistics* (February 1952), pp. 34–45.

Rees, Albert, "Wage Levels Under Conditions of Long-run Full Employment," *American Economic Revew* (May 1953), pp. 451–457.

———, "Postwar Wage Determination in the Basic Steel Industry," *American Economic Review* (June 1951), pp. 389–404.

Reynolds, Lloyd G., "Wage-Push and All That," *American Economic Review* (May 1960), pp. 195–211.

Ross, Arthur M., and William Goldner, "Forces Affecting the Interindustry Wage Structure," *Quarterly Journal of Economics* (May 1950), pp. 254–281.

Samuelson, Paul A., and Robert M. Solow, "Analytical Aspects of Anti-Inflation Policy," *American Economic Review* (May 1960), pp. 177–194.

Shultz, G. P., and C. A. Myers, "Union Wage Decisions and Employment," *American Economic Review* (June 1950), pp. 362–380.

Solow, R. M., "A Skeptical Note on the Constancy of Relative Shares," *American Economic Review* (September 1958), pp. 618–631.

Stieber, Jack, "Occupational Wage Differentials in the Basic Steel Industry," *Industrial and Labor Relations Review* (January 1959), pp. 167–181.

Ulman, Lloyd, "The Union and Wages in Basic Steel: A Comment," and "Reply," by Albert Rees, *American Economic Review* (June 1958), pp. 408–433.

———, "Collective Bargaining and Inflation," *California Management Review* (Spring 1960), pp. 51–58.

Van Sickle, John V., "Regional Aspects of the Problem of Full Employment and Fair Wages," *Southern Economic Journal* (July 1946), pp. 35–46.

———, "The Southeast: A Case Study in Delayed Industrialization," *American Economic Review* (May 1951), pp. 384–393.

Weintraub, Sidney, "A Law that Cannot be Repealed," *Challenge* (April 1962), pp. 17–19.

Chapter 21 Productivity

THE MEANING AND MEASUREMENT OF PRODUCTIVITY

One of the basic concepts of the theory of mechanics is *efficiency*, which is defined as the ratio of the energy output to the energy input of a machine. The corresponding concept in economics is *productivity*, defined as the ratio of output to one or more of the inputs used in production. The object of the measurement of productivity is to determine how efficiently resources are being used.

The concept of productivity is one of the most important in economic analysis. We noted in an earlier chapter that the theory of marginal productivity is an important part of the broader theory of distribution. But the concept of productivity is not only at the heart of distribution theory; it is basic to our understanding of the process of economic growth, and in recent years it has played an increasingly important part in discussions of labor-management relations.

Economic growth is best measured in terms of increases in *real output per capita*.[1] George J. Stigler put it well when he said:

> We may, as a rule, view an increase in output per worker as evidence of economic progress whether it stems from improvements in labor or improvements in the cooperating resources. A general increase in output due to improvements in the productivity of labor is an unmixed blessing if it comes from better training, better minds and better physiques: we are in effect adding to the hands that run our economic system without—as the classical economists sometimes believed necessary—adding to the mouths that consume its product. Similarly, increases in output per worker achieved by increasing the quantity or improving the quality of cooperating resources imply that we have extended

[1] See W. W. Rostow, *The Stages of Economic Growth*, Cambridge: Cambridge University Press (1960), p. 34.

our mastery over nature or over ignorance: we can live better without working harder.[2]

The most widely used measure of productivity is *output per man-hour*. It is important to emphasize, however, that this is not a measure of labor efficiency. Rather, it is a simplifying statistical device used to express all inputs in terms of a single denominator—the man-hours involved in production. When output is measured in physical terms and all inputs are expressed in terms of man-hours, a ratio may be derived to construct a productivity index. Some base period is selected and set equal to 100. Increases, or decreases, in productivity can be measured from this base.[3]

A more general measure of productivity is

$$\frac{\text{Output}}{\text{Input of Labor and Input of Other Resources}}$$

Generally, as a matter of convenience, the "other resources" (materials, capital equipment, management, etc.) are lumped together under the heading of "capital."[4]

The concepts described above are straightforward enough but the measurement of productivity is far from a simple matter. Thousands of man-hours of research and computation have gone into efforts to measure productivity—for specific industries or sectors, or for the economy as a whole—by private and government agencies. But specialists in the measurement of productivity are far from satisfied with the results. The National Bureau of Economic Research—one of the outstanding private research organizations in the United States—has published a number of volumes dealing with the meaning and measurement of productivity.[5] The Bureau of Labor Statistics of the U.S. Department of Labor has a productivity division which is concerned with the continuous study and measurement of productivity. It has published indexes of real product per man-hour for the economy as a whole and specific indexes of productivity for a wide range of manufacturing and non-manufacturing industries. "Because of serious difficulties in measuring

[2] George J. Stigler, *Trends in Output and Employment,* New York: National Bureau of Economic Research, Inc. (1947), p. 42.

[3] See John W. Kendrick, "Productivity, Costs and Prices: Concepts and Measurements," *Wages, Prices, Profits and Productivity,* New York: The American Assembly, Columbia University (1959), pp. 38–39.

[4] Stigler, *op. cit.,* p. 49.

[5] Probably the most impressive of these is John W. Kendrick, *Productivity Trends in the United States,* Princeton, New Jersey: Princeton Press (1961). See also, *Output, Input and Productivity Measurement,* Princeton, New Jersey: Princeton University Press (1961).

CHART 21–1
INDEXES OF REAL PRODUCT PER MAN-HOUR IN THE TOTAL PRIVATE ECONOMY, AGRICULTURE, AND NONAGRICULTURE, 1909–1962
Post-World War II Period Based Primarily on BLS Man-Hours

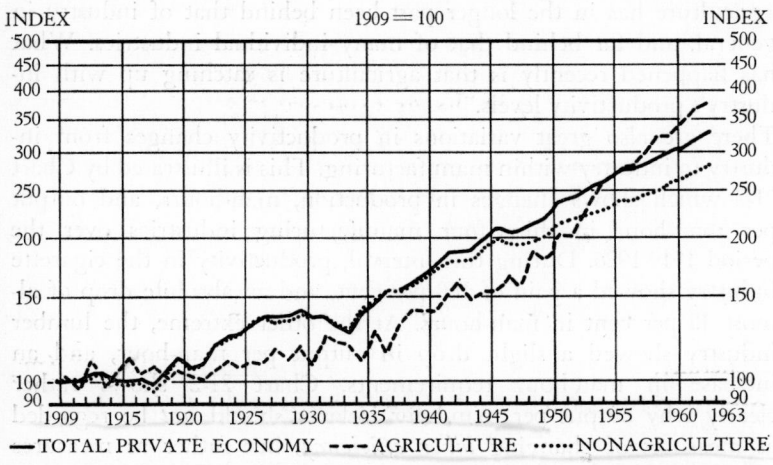

Source: Chart taken from the United States Department of Labor, Bureau of Labor Statistics.

the output of government which is neither priced nor reported in physical units, the broadest measure appropriate for productivity measurement is the real gross *private product.*"[6]

Trends in Output per Man-Hour

The productivity indexes published by the Bureau of Labor Statistics are expressed in terms of output per man-hour. Chart 21-1 shows trends in productivity, covering the period 1909-1962, for the total private economy and for the agricultural and nonagricultural sectors.

During this fifty-three year period, real output per man-hour in the total private economy increased about 225 per cent. Output per man-hour in agriculture began to increase more rapidly than the corresponding measure for the nonfarm sector during the 1930's and there has been a particularly strong upsurge in farm productivity since 1947.

The measurement of changes in productivity from a common base requires careful interpretation. The word to emphasize in this

[6] John W. Kendrick, "Productivity, Costs and Prices: Concepts and Measurements," *op. cit.*, p. 39.

connection is *changes* in productivity. As Ewan Clague, the Commissioner of Labor Statistics, has noted: "It is true that agriculture has forged far ahead since 1947, but this does not show that the *level* of productivity on farms is ahead of the level in nonfarm industry. On the contrary, the level of output per man-hour in agriculture has in the longer past been behind that of industry in general, and far behind that of many individual industries. What has happened recently is that agriculture is catching up with industry's productivity levels."[7]

There are also great variations in productivity changes from industry to industry within manufacturing. This is illustrated by Chart 21-2 which shows changes in production, man-hours, and output per man-hour in thirty-four manufacturing industries over the period 1919-1926. During this interval, productivity in the cigarette industry showed a gain of 160 per cent, and an absolute drop of almost 40 per cent in man-hours. At the other extreme, the lumber industry showed a slight drop in output per man-hour, and an increase in man-hour requirements. Chart 21-2 shows rather clearly why output per man-hour indexes should *not* be regarded as measures of changing *labor efficiency,* but rather as measures of changes in *total* efficiency. To a large extent the increases in productivity in the cigarette, chemical, iron and steel, motor vehicle, and other industries clustered at the top of Chart 21-2, resulted from the substitution of mechanical for human effort. This is a process which has been going on since the beginning of the Industrial Revolution and it is the *major* cause of gains in productivity. There are, of course, other factors to be considered. The skill and efficiency of labor has improved in many industries during this period, and the same can be said of management.

Improved management alone can lead to significant gains in output per man-hour even if other things remained unchanged. Similarly, if the health, stamina, training and morale of the workforce—either in a specific industry or in the economy as a whole—improve significantly over time, output per man-hour will go up. But the greatest gains in productivity—and these often come in fairly short spurts over limited periods of time—result from the introduction of new and improved machinery. When power-driven looms replaced hand looms, for example, there was unquestionably an increase in productivity although human effort was reduced.

[7] Ewan Clague, "Interpreting Productivity Measurements and Their Application to Economic Problems," paper presented before the American Marketing Association-American Farm Economic Association, Washington, D.C. (December 30, 1959), mimeographed, p. 10.

CHART 21–2
PER CENT CHANGE IN OUTPUT PER MAN-HOUR
PRODUCTION, AND MAN-HOURS, 1919–1926
34 Manufacturing Industries

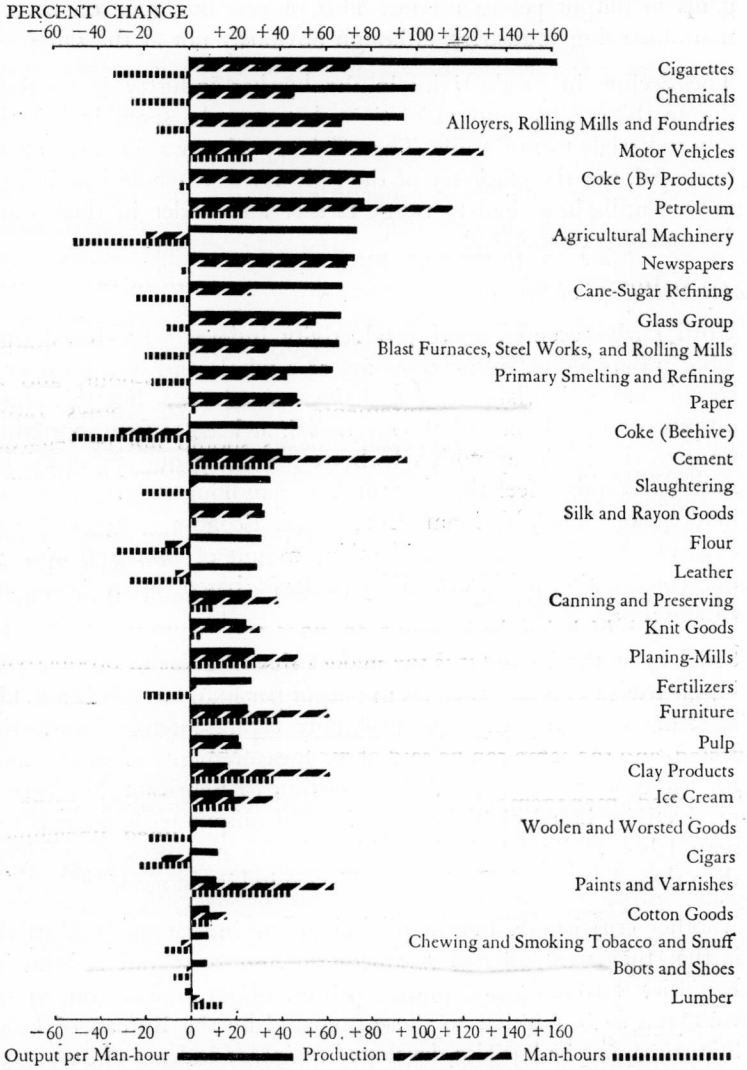

Source: Chart taken from publication of the United States Department of Labor, Bureau of Labor Statistics.

When the early power looms were replaced by automatic looms, which could operate for hours without stopping, there was a further gain in productivity. And in recent years the introduction of high-speed "weaving machines" have resulted in further sharp gains in output per man-hour. This process has gone on in most manufacturing industries, although obviously not at the same rate.

The decline in productivity in the lumber industry is no doubt due to the greater amount of time that must be spent in bringing raw materials to saw mills. The efficiency of saw mills as such has increased, but the efficiency of the industry as a whole has dropped as saw mills have had to range farther and wider in their search for suitable raw materials.

Combining Labor and Capital Inputs

Until fairly recently, most productivity indexes were based upon labor inputs alone. In the economy as a whole and in a number of specific industries, labor is one of the major inputs. For this reason output per man-hour indexes are useful, at least as first approximations to the efficiency with which we are using our resources. But some economists feel that output per man-hour indexes alone are inadequate. The National Bureau of Economic Research, for example, has devoted a considerable amount of time and effort to the construction of productivity indexes based upon labor and capital inputs combined.

Scholars at the National Bureau feel that the omission of capital inputs leads to an upward bias in output per man-hour indexes. This is rather obviously the case in highly capital-intensive industries. But they feel that this is also true of measurements of productivity for the economy as a whole.[8] According to Fabricant, "indexes of productivity based on the comparison of output with the input of both labor and tangible capital are better measures of efficiency than those based on labor input or the capital input alone."[9]

Another criticism of output per man-hour indexes of productivity is that they treat all man-hour inputs as homogeneous. John W. Kendrick has computed output per man-hour indexes on an unweighted basis (similar to those prepared by the Bureau of Labor Statistics), but he has also developed *weighted* indexes of output per man-hour. For weighting purposes he has translated the compensation of labor into average hourly earnings. The logic of using the

[8] Solomon Fabricant, *Basic Facts on Productivity Change,* New York: National Bureau of Economic Research, Inc., Occasional paper 63 (1959), pp. 6–8.
[9] *Ibid.,* p. 8.

average hourly earnings as a weight for man-hours is that higher paid workers contribute more to productivity than lower paid ones.

Kendrick has computed similar unweighted and weighted indexes of capital productivity. The weights used in this case are rates of return on investment. This implies that capital which earns a high rate of return is being utilized more efficiently than that which earns relatively less.[10] The separate indexes have been combined into a general index of productivity based upon both capital and labor inputs. The results of these exhaustive and painstaking studies, covering the period 1889-1957, are summarized in Table 21-1.

TABLE 21–1
AVERAGE RATES OF INCREASE IN PRODUCTIVITY, PRIVATE DOMESTIC ECONOMY, 1889–1957

	Average annual percentage rate of change		
	1889–1957	1889–1919	1919–1957
Physical output per man-hour (*unweighted*)	2.4	2.0	2.6
Physical output per man-hour (*weighted*)	2.0	1.6	2.3
Physical output per unit of tangible capital (*weighted*)	1.0	0.5	1.3
Physical output per unit of labor, and capital combined (*weighted*)	1.7	1.3	2.1

Source: Solomon Fabricant, *Basic Facts on Productivity Change*, p. 10. Reprinted by permission of the National Bureau of Economic Research.

The unweighted index of output per man-hours shows the most rapid rate of increase. During the 69-year period, the unweighted index of physical output per man-hour showed an average annual increase of 2.4 per cent. When weighted in terms of hourly earnings the annual rate dropped to 2 per cent. And when labor and capital inputs are combined there is a further drop to 1.7 per cent. It is also interesting to note that all of the indexes show a slower rate of increase during the period 1889-1919. There was a notable acceleration in productivity during the years 1919-1957. This is shown graphically on Chart 21-3. The scale along the left-hand side of this chart is a logarithmic or ratio scale on which equal vertical distances represent equal percentage changes. The index plotted at the top of Chart 21-3 has a considerably steeper slope than the one

[10] John W. Kendrick, *Productivity Trends in the United States*, pp. 32–35.

CHART 21–3
INDEXES OF PRODUCTIVITY IN THE UNITED STATES, 1889–1957
Estimates for the Private Domestic Economy

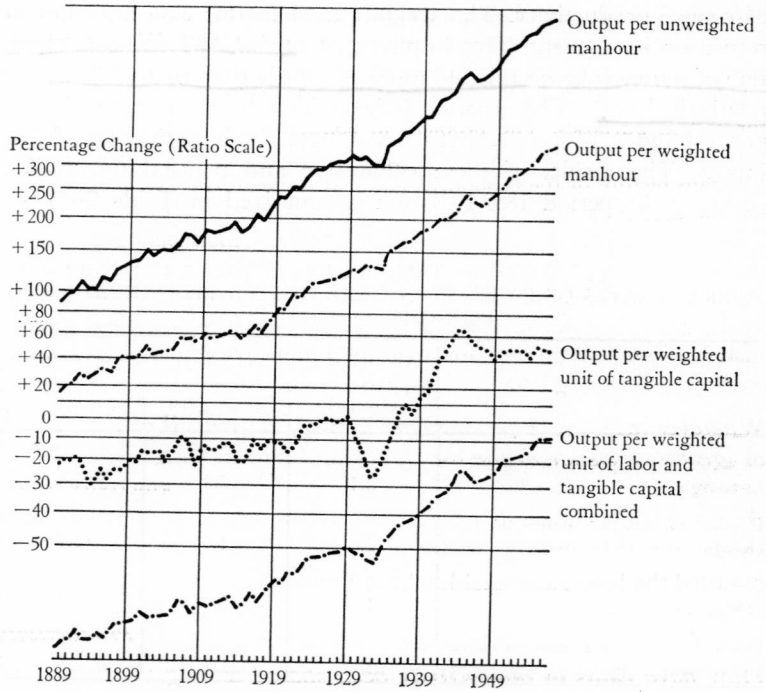

Source: Solomon Fabricant, *Basic Facts on Productivity Change,* Occasional Paper 63, National Bureau of Economic Research, Inc. (1959), p. 13. Reprinted by permission.

at the bottom. The index labeled "Output per Weighted Unit of Labor and Tangible Capital combined" shows only about 72 per cent as much increase as the "Output per Unweighted Man-Hour" index. This is what spokesmen for the National Bureau of Economic Research mean when they say that output per man-hour indexes have an "upward bias."

Representatives of the Bureau of Labor Statistics—which continues to publish indexes of output per man-hour—are aware of the criticism of these indexes which has been made by other agencies notably the National Bureau of Economic Research. Ewan Clague, Commissioner of Labor Statistics, has commented on the debate over the measurement of productivity as follows:

We in the Bureau of Labor Statistics have, of course, examined the implications of the readjustment of the productivity index to allow for capital investment. We recognize clearly that productivity gains usually require capital investment, which becomes a cost that must be met in the long run. On the other hand, a measure of output per unit of total input is not necessarily the *one best* measure of productivity. We can repeat what we have said on many previous occasions, namely, that there is a whole family of productivity statistics, each with its own significance for certain purposes. The problem in connection with productivity statistics is not that any of them is right or wrong, but that each presents a certain picture of the economy. The real problem consists in determining the uses to which each of these should be put. A comparison of the United States rate of progress with the Soviet Union may require one statistic; a comparison with average hourly earnings may require quite a different statistic. And the development of a balanced rate of growth in the United States may require still another. It is for these reasons that it is most important for users of productivity statistics to know what they are using.[11]

Whatever measure of productivity is used, the overall picture is one of greater efficiency in the use of resources in the long run. Indexes of out-put per man-hour show faster gains in productivity than those which combine labor and capital inputs. But as Chart 21-4 shows, whether indexes of labor productivity or total productivity are used the long-run trend has been upward.

Productivity and Earnings

How have gains in productivity been shared among the factors of production? In the last chapter we discussed various attitudes toward the hypothesis of the "constancy of relative shares." Some economists are of the opinion that the percentage share of national output going to labor has been *relatively* constant. Others have indicated their doubts about this, although even the skeptics would not deny that within limits there has been relatively little change in the division of total output among the factors of production. It is interesting to note, therefore, that between 1914 and 1939 "real" average hourly earnings (money earnings adjusted for changes in the cost of living, increased at about the same rate as output per man-hour (Chart 21-5). There were times during this period when real earnings rose more rapidly than output per man-hour but at other times the reverse was true. This strongly suggests that in the long run there is a fairly close relationship between gains

[11] Ewan Clague, "Productivity—What it is and How it is Measured," Paper presented to the Chicago Association of Commerce and Industry (May 26, 1959), mimeographed, pp. 16–17.

CHART 21–4
INDEXES OF PRODUCTIVITY IN FIVE MAJOR INDUSTRIAL DIVISIONS
Estimates for 1889–1957 or 1889–1953

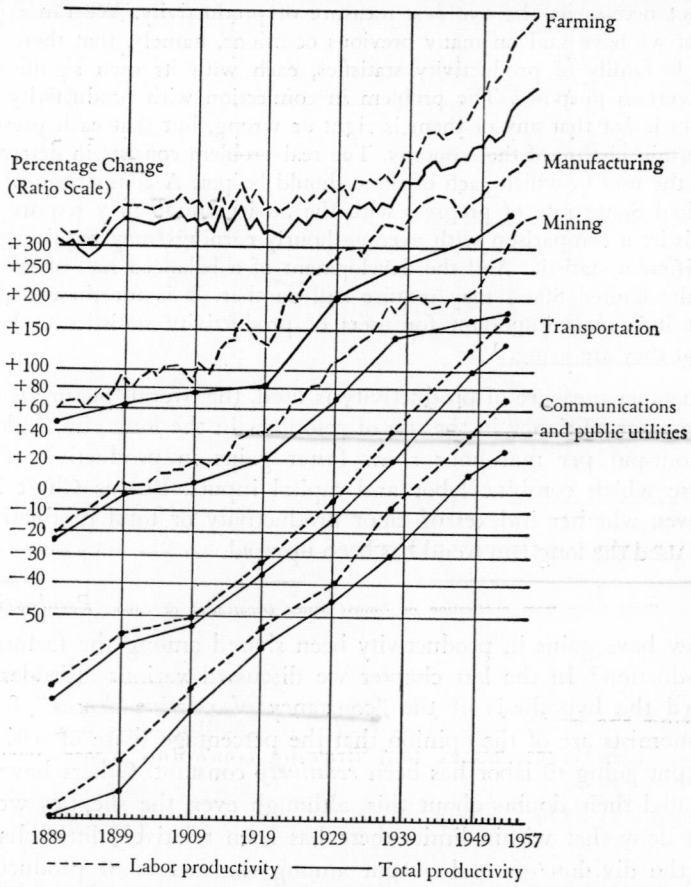

Source: Solomon Fabricant, *Basic Facts on Productivity Change*, Occasional Paper 63, National Bureau of Economic Research, Inc. (1959), p. 24. Reprinted by permission.

in productivity and increases in "real" earnings. This does not necessarily mean that there is an inexorable law relating earnings and productivity and it does not "prove" the constancy of relative shares. What it does indicate—and this should come as no surprise—is that in the long-run increases in returns to labor depend upon gains in productivity.

CHART 21–5
OUTPUT PER MAN-HOUR AND "REAL" HOURLY EARNINGS
MANUFACTURING 1914–1939
1939 = 100

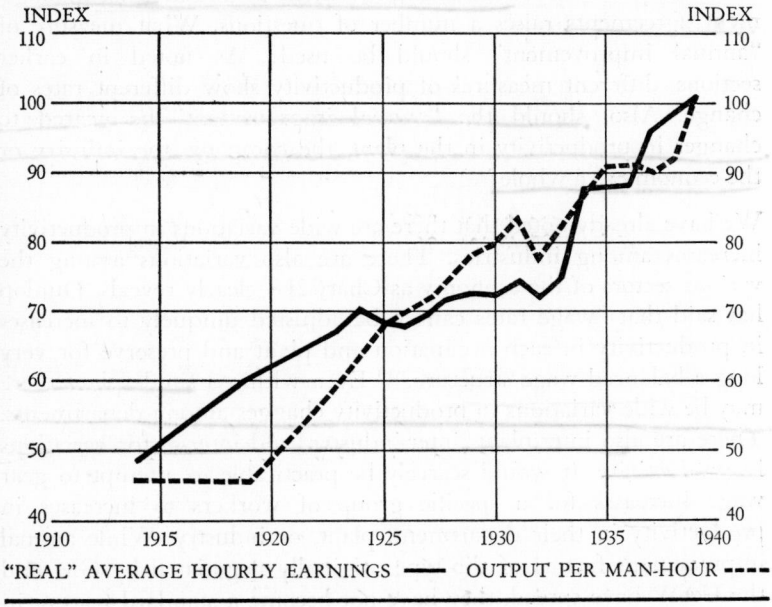

Source: Chart taken from publication of United States Department of Labor, Bureau of Labor Statistics.

Productivity and Collective Bargaining

During the early days of collective bargaining most negotiations dealt with wages, hours, and working conditions. Later, various kinds of "fringe benefits" were incorporated in labor-management agreements. The agreement signed by General Motors and the United Automobile Workers in May 1948 explicitly recognized the relationship between gains in productivity and wage increases. It provided for sharing the returns from increased productivity between capital and labor. Since then a number of collective bargaining agreements have included similar provisions. The GM-UAW agreement provided for an annual improvement factor—that is, an automatic increase in wages—based upon gains in productivity. The section of the agreement dealing with this stated:

The annual improvement factor provided herein recognizes that a continuing improvement in the standard of living of employees depends upon technological progress, better tools, methods, processes and equipment, and a cooperative attitude on the part of all parties in such progress. It further recognizes the principle that to produce more with the same amount of human effort is a sound economic and social objective.[12]

The incorporation of annual improvement factors in labor-management agreements raises a number of questions. What measure of "annual improvement" should be used? As noted in earlier sections, different measures of productivity show different rates of change. Also, should the "annual improvement" be geared to changes in productivity in the plant, the company, the industry or the economy as a whole?

We have already noted that there are wide variations in productivity increases among industries. There are also variations among the various sectors of the economy as Chart 21-4 clearly reveals. Dunlop has said that "wage rates cannot be adjusted uniquely to increases in productivity in each occupation and plant and preserve for very long a balanced wage structure."[13] Even within a single plant there may be wide variations in productivity changes among departments. There are also inter-plant, inter-industry, and inter-sector variations in productivity. It would scarcely be practicable to attempt to gear wage increases for a specific group of workers to increases in productivity in their department, plant, or industry. While annual improvement factors of the type originally negotiated by GM and the UAW have spread, they have not become a standard feature in labor-management agreements. Where they are used there has been a tendency to gear automatic wage increases to average gains in productivity in the economy as a whole or—since agriculture is generally regarded as a special case—to increases in productivity in the non-farm sector of the private domestic economy.

UNION ATTITUDES TOWARD PRODUCTIVITY

One of the driving forces behind increases in productivity is technological change. And there was a time when workers were fearful of technology. During the early days of the Industrial Revolution in England when skilled hand weavers were being displaced by machines, there was a violent reaction. Although the workers at this time were unorganized, a movement developed to halt the spread of machine production. The members of this move-

[12] Quoted by Ewan Clague in "Prices, Wages and Productivity," paper presented before the *Labor Relations and Arbitration Conference,* University of California (May 25, 1959), mimeographed, p. 14.

[13] J. T. Dunlop, "Productivity and the Wage Structure," *Income, Employment and Public Policy,* Essays in honor of Alvin H. Hansen, New York: W. W. Norton and Company, Inc. (1948), p. 342.

ment were called Luddites, after a member of the group named Ned Ludd, and they attempted to safeguard the jobs of craftsmen by smashing the new machines. They accepted the "lump of labor" theory and felt that if machines did the work laborers would have to go unemployed. Needless to say, while their efforts led to serious social unrest in some British factory towns, they were unable to halt the march of technology.

Even in a much later age workers have been concerned with the possible effects of technological change upon employment. When unions consisted predominantly of skilled craftsmen they tried at times to protect their jobs from the encroachment of machine production. Sumner Slichter has listed the following union policies toward the introduction of machinery:

1. The policy of *obstruction* in which unions attempted to prevent the introduction of new machines into union shops.
2. The policy of *competition* under which organized workers made concessions to their employers in an effort to make them competitive with non-union employers using machine methods.
3. The policy of *control* under which unions permit the introduction of machinery, but seek to control the men who operate the machines, and possibly the rate at which machinery is introduced.[14]

Although a number of efforts were made to obstruct the introduction of machinery, or to compete with new machines, neither of these policies was successful. The march of technology seemed inexorable and where unions attempted to obstruct it the result was the destruction of the union rather than the machines. The policy of control, however, has been somewhat more successful and in its broadest sense this policy is followed by some unions today.

Union attitudes toward productivity have changed since the rise of widespread industrial unionism in the United States. Individual workers might be concerned about the possible loss of employment due to technological change as in the past. But as industrial unions grew "they became preoccupied more with the responsibility of securing economic gains rather than fastening their controls on a specific job."[15] Some of the earlier craft unions attempted to main-

[14] Sumner H. Slichter, *Union Policies and Industrial Management,* Washington, D.C.: The Brookings Institution (1941), p. 201. In a later study Slichter and his associates noted that some unions have actively encouraged technological change. See Sumner H. Slichter, James J. Healy and E. Robert Livernash, *The Impact of Collective Bargaining on Management,* Washington, D.C.: The Brookings Institution (1960), pp. 355–361.

[15] Solomon Barkin, "Trade-Union Attitudes and Their Affect Upon Productivity," *Industrial Productivity,* Industrial Relations Research Association (1951), p. 110.

tain the demand for craftsmen by limiting output and the speed of work, by insisting upon time-consuming methods, and at times by regulating the number of men who could be assigned to a job.[16] But industrial unions not only accepted the inevitability of technological change, they actively encouraged such change. The philosophy of the leaders of industrial unionism was that rapid gains in productivity would lead to higher per capita income; the latter, in turn, would stimulate demand. As the demand for goods and services increased, the demand for labor would also go up. The leaders of industrial unionism hoped that rapid industrial growth would lead both to steady improvement in real income and a tendency toward full employment.

The craft unions had lived through good times and bad. But during the early days of the A.F. of L. the notion was widespread that "good jobs"—and this meant jobs for skilled workers—were scarce. Hence union leaders felt that they were serving the best interests of their members when they engaged in restrictive practices and opposed technological change. The rapid growth of industrial unionism in the United States started midway through the worst depression this country has ever known. As industrial unions grew in size and strength they witnessed a slow rise in income and gains in employment. World War II convinced many leaders of industrial unionism that economic expansion was the best guarantee of steady improvement in the condition of organized labor. Thus the industrial unionist became strongly productivity-conscious. Far from restricting output or opposing technological change, leaders of the industrial unions urged business to step up its rate of investment in order to increase its efficiency. This was not because of an altruistic interest in business—it was because the leaders of industrial unionism hoped to capture a steady share of the gains resulting from increased productivity.

Even the productivity-conscious industrial unions were concerned about the potential impact upon specific workers—or groups of workers—when there were sudden changes in technology. While encouraging technological change, which would lead to gains in productivity, the unions wanted to be kept informed of impending change. And they wanted to have a say in the transfer of workers displaced by machines, the establishment of production standards when new processes were developed, and the negotiation of wage rates on new jobs. Some unions negotiated provisions which permitted management to make technological improvements without

[16] *Ibid.*, p. 111.

consulting the union but they reserved the right to file grievances if they felt that individual workers had been adversely affected, and these at times called for final determination of disputed issues by an impartial arbitrator. Other unions negotiated provisions calling for consultation prior to the installation of new machinery. The object again was not to restrain management, but to ensure that individual workers or groups of workers did not bear the entire cost of technological change.

At times some managements have complained that such rules—although seemingly innocuous—actually have restrained technological progress. In their opinion, management always takes a risk when a new machine is installed. The union contract permits the installation of new equipment but the union retains its right to participate in the setting of rates and job standards and in the transfer of affected workers. Under these circumstances, those who subscribed to this point of view allege that management cannot be certain that it will gain as a result of the change. The union response to this line of argument is that workers are entitled to a *share* of the gains resulting from increased productivity. And if the job security of workers can be protected, through transfer and the maintenance of their old rates of pay, worker morale will be improved, and this in itself will be a stimulus to improvement in productivity.

Finally, some union spokesmen have recognized that upward pressure on labor costs has been an important stimulus to technological change. According to Barkin, "the sluggishness of management, which neither competition nor profit seeking seemed fully to overcome, is frequently partially corrected by the pressure from the recurrent demands for improvements in labor benefits."[17] Some might view this line of argument as an apology by trade unionists for their incessant demands for wage increases and expanded fringe benefits, but this view has been shared by many not connected with the trade union movement. Sumner H. Slichter, for example, frequently stated that trade unions provided an important stimulus to management to improve its operations, and that this led to gains in productivity. Others have noted that by pushing the economy toward full employment unions have encouraged more complete utilization of the existing labor supply, and this in itself leads to gains in productivity for the economy as a whole.[18]

[17] *Ibid.*, p. 22.
[18] See, for example, Clark Kerr, "Productivity and Labour Relations," *Productivity and Progress*, Sidney, Australia: Angus and Robertson (1957), p. 19.

AUTOMATION

Shortly after the end of World War II a new development began to take place in a number of advanced industrial countries which was to have an enormous impact upon productivity at least in specific sectors of the economy. This process—which has led to a considerable amount of controversy—is called *automation*. Some writers insist that automation is nothing new; it is simply a continuation of developments that can be traced back to the beginning of the Industrial Revolution. Others, however, disagree with this view. The latter position has been succinctly put by Shultz and Baldwin:

> Today, people are calling every conceivable kind of technological change "automation." This is riding fashion too hard, because there are still thousands of technological changes occurring every week which have nothing at all to do with automation. The term is not a synonym for technological change; it is instead a particular kind of technological change that has gathered momentum since the second World War.[19]

This view is also expressed in a recent publication of the U.S. Department of Labor which provides a concise definition of automation: "... automation refers to the use of machinery—computers, transfer devices, and automatic mechanisms—to control and regulate industrial processes and to speed up compilation of data in offices. Technological change includes not only automatic devices but also all other types of equipment and procedures which tend to increase and speed up the production and distribution of goods, materials, and services and to reduce manpower requirements per unit of output."[20]

There is a voluminous, and rapidly growing, literature on automation. The topic can be touched on only briefly in this chapter. There are several types of automation and it is not easy to tell in all cases where to draw the line. One type—often referred to as "Detroit automation" consists of linking together a series of separate manufacturing operations. This is usually considered to be a form of automation since the product is typically "untouched by human hands," but Shultz and Baldwin prefer to call it "continuous automatic production."[21] In general, automation is thought of as

[19] George P. Shultz and George B. Baldwin, *Automation a New Dimension to Old Problems*, Washington, D.C.: Public Affairs Press (1955), p. 1.
[20] *Impact of Automation and Technological Change on Employment and Unemployment*, Washington, D.C.: U.S. Department of Labor, Bureau of Employment Security, BES No–R–206 (September 1961), p. 1.
[21] Schultz and Baldwin, *op. cit.*, p. 3.

a process which is largely controlled by computers and various types of mechanisms which permit "feedback" control. Feedback control in its broadest sense, means that the process is subject to self-regulation. One of the simplest examples of a "closed feedback loop" is provided by the thermostat found in conventional home heating systems. Once the thermostat is set it maintains temperature within certain limits automatically. When the temperature drops below that set on the thermostat a switch is actuated which starts a furnace or boiler. As heat is pumped into the house the temperature rises and the thermostat again actuates a switch turning off the heat. It is a "closed loop" because it is a self-contained unit—a simple yet efficient self-correcting mechanism. In automatic production processes high speed electronic computers are linked to various kinds of electronic sensing devices which maintain production within pre-established tolerance limits. There are numerous examples of industrial automation of this type. They are found in a wide variety of manufacturing industries, and in these industries they have had an important impact on productivity.

A third development is sometimes referred to as "office automation," but is more frequently called *electronic data processing*. In banks, insurance companies, and in other enterprises which handle tremendous volumes of routine paper work, electronic computers record data and make calculations with previously unheard of speed. Computers have also been tied in with the telephone system permitting almost instantaneous transmission of data facilitating the centralization of record keeping and the rapid compilation of statistical data from widely scattered geographical sources.

The Effects of Automation on Employment and Productivity

The advent of automation in its various forms set off a lively controversy which is far from over. Indeed, since we are still in the early stages of what some have called the Second Industrial Revolution it is likely that this controversy will continue for some time. The first steps toward the automation of production processes proceeded fairly slowly, and they were made at a time of relatively full employment. The initial job displacements were relatively minor. But in specific plants there were enormous gains in productivity without any increase in labor requirements. This led to some concern, and in the late 1940's and early 1950's a few books and articles began to appear forecasting widespread unemployment as automation spread. One of the first authors to take this pessimistic point of view was Norbert Wiener, an eminent mathematician who contributed to the development of the high-speed digital computer. In his book *The Human Use of Human Beings* Wiener suggested the possibility of massive unemployment as automation spread: ". . . remember that the automatic machine, whatever we think of any feelings it may have or may not have, is a precise economic equivalent of slave labor. Any labor which competes with slave labor must accept the economic conditions of slave labor. It is perfectly clear that this will produce an unemployment situation in comparison with which . . . the depression of the thirties will seem a pleasant joke."[22] At the time that he made this dire prediction, Professor Wiener also gave an amazingly accurate forecast of the types of industries and offices in which automation would take place.[23] A few years later some of the views advanced by Wiener were echoed by labor leaders as they began to see isolated instances of layoffs due to automation.

Business spokesmen, however, tended to view the spread of automation as a benign influence and to label those who suggested that the new development would lead to unemployment as alarmists. Essentially, their argument was that automation is a continuation of the Industrial Revolution. They cited the lessons of history to support their views that industrialization had *created* not destroyed jobs. They recognized that specific workers were at times displaced by machines, but insisted that these workers were absorbed in new employment—and that the new jobs were often created by the labor-saving machines.[24]

In response to this argument, those who suggested that automation might lead to substantial unemployment pointed out that during the early stages of industrialization changes occurred slowly, and that even under these conditions specific groups of workers were often adversely affected by change. But automation has proceeded rapidly. It has rendered some skills obsolete and has eliminated or drastically reduced the need for unskilled labor in a number of industries. Finally, it has been suggested, the old argument that workers displaced by machines can find jobs in factories building the machines applied only to a day when machines themselves were quite simple. In a highly automated industrial society, it is

[22] Norbert Wiener, *The Human Use of Human Beings,* Garden City, New York: Doubleday and Company, Inc. (second edition, revised, 1954), p. 162.
[23] *Ibid.,* pp. 158–159.
[24] For several representative views see *Impact of Automation and Technological Change on Employment and Unemployment,* p. 2.

often claimed, much of the work of constructing new machines will be done by machines themselves.[25]

The spread of automation is no longer a matter of speculation. It is found—in varying degrees—in such large-scale industries as steel, autos, rubber, and oil refining. And the spread of electronic data processing in large offices has been equally rapid. New developments in computer technology and the application of this technology to production and various office processes is continuing at a rapid pace. Some of the effects are clearly observable. Automation has led to significant increases in productivity in specific plants and offices. While it has not led to general unemployment it has contributed to *localized* unemployment in some steel and auto-producing centers and perhaps elsewhere. This has led to a revival of pessimism reminiscent of Norbert Wiener's early pronouncements.[26] A newer view is that the effects of automation can be controlled but that this will require increasing cooperation among various groups including business, government, organized labor, and education if the harmful effects of automation are to be mitigated and society is to benefit from the new technology.

Because of the fairly high turnover rate in many large offices, and because electronic data processing spread at a time of relative shortage of unskilled office workers, the employment effects of office automation have not been as noticeable or dramatic as those in some manufacturing industries. But it is too early in this development to suggest that office automation might not eventually lead to the actual displacement of labor as it has already done, for example, in the steel and auto industries.

There is further evidence of growing concern about the potential impact of automation on employment. It has become a collective bargaining issue in a few cases, and is almost certain to be an increasingly important issue in labor-management negotiations in the future. A number of unions and managements have commissioned studies of the employment effects of automation in specific circumstances.[27] The Armour Committee, of which Clark Kerr, an eminent labor economist and educator was chairman, has made an

[25] See William H. Miernyk, "Men, Machines and Electronic Brains," *The Commercial and Financial Chronicle* (August 4, 1955), p. 9.

[26] See, for example, Donald N. Michael, *Cybernation: The Silent Conquest,* Santa Barbara, California: Center for the Study of Democratic Institutions (1962).

[27] For a list of some of these studies see *Progress Report of Automation Committee* formed under agreements September 1, 1959 by Armour and Company and United Packing House, Food and Allied Workers (AFL-CIO) and Amalgamated Meat Cutters and Butchers Workmen of North America (AFL-CIO), pp. 8–10.

important contribution to our knowledge about the impact of automation on employment. After a careful investigation of the Armour Company experience, as well as that of a number of other companies and unions, the committee concluded:

> The experience of working together in looking at the problems of automation during the past year-and-one-half has convinced all members of the Committee of one thing: Only through a coordinated approach in which public policy and private action mutually reinforce one another can the employment problems of technological change be met. *Collective bargaining by itself cannot fully solve these problems.*[28]

The evidence to date seems to support a number of conclusions about automation. Automation has already led to significant gains in productivity in individual plants and offices. Its potential for further gains in productivity is enormous. But while automation has had a favorable impact on productivity it has created problems. The problem which has attracted most attention to date is that of localized unemployment. This will be discussed in further detail in the following chapter. The early view that automation would be an unmixed blessing—and that its effects on employment would all be favorable—has not been supported by recent events. There is growing recognition that we cannot rely on either collective bargaining or the labor market itself to solve the problems which automation has engendered. The labor market does not operate as smoothly as many have often assumed and workers displaced from some occupations are not immediately absorbed into others. There are other effects of automation which have received relatively little attention to date but which will undoubtedly require further study in the future. The entire structure of the labor force will be affected as automation spreads. Demands for new skills will be created. Other types of labor will become redundant and there will be a growing need for retraining and more vigorous placement efforts if full employment is to be achieved. There will also no doubt be psychological and sociological effects which cannot be fully anticipated at the present time.[29] Not only will automation have further effects upon productivity, but future developments will unquestionably influence labor-management relations, education, and in many ways the entire cultural fabric of industrial society.

[28] *Ibid.*, p. 10. Italics added.

[29] See Bernard Karsh, "The Meaning of Work in an Age of Automation," *Current Economic Comment* (August 1957), pp. 3–13; and William A. Faunce, "Automation and Leisure," *Automation and Society*, H. P. Jacobsen and J. S. Roucek, eds., New York: Philosophical Library (1959), pp. 297–308.

PRODUCTIVITY AND HOURS OF WORK

Earlier in this chapter we noted that there was disagreement about the best way to measure gains in productivity, but whatever measure is employed, everyone is agreed that the long-run trend of productivity has been upward. A clear and forceful indicator of this is given by trends in hours worked and hourly earnings. The long run trends, covering slightly more than half a century, are summarized in Table 21-2.

TABLE 21–2

HOURS AND EARNINGS OF PRODUCTION WORKERS IN MANUFACTURING, 1909–1959

	1909	1959	Percent change
Average weekly hours	51.0	40.3	—21.0
Average hourly earnings	$ 0.19	$ 2.22[b]	+ 1,068
"Real" average hourly earnings (1947–49 = 100)[a]	$ 0.48	$ 1.78[b]	+ 270.8

[a] Straight time average hourly earnings adjusted for changes in the consumer price index. The latter was estimated for 1909 from partial data.

[b] Excluding fringe benefits.

Sources of data: *Historical Statistics of the United States Colonial Times to 1957, U.S.* Department of Commerce, Bureau of the Census (1960), pp. 91, 126; and *1960 Supplement to Economic Indicators,* U.S. Government Printing Office (1960), pp. 43, 46, 81.

Twenty years before the beginning of this period, in 1890, the work week for *all* workers in manufacturing averaged 60 hours. As Table 21-2 shows there had been a substantial drop by 1909. The decline continued slowly for the next two decades—as late as 1926, for example, the average work week in manufacturing was still slightly longer than 50 hours. But between 1909 and 1959, there was a reduction of 21 per cent in the average weekly hours of production workers in manufacturing. Meanwhile, average hourly earnings, without adjustment for price changes, showed more than a ten-fold increase. A much more significant measure, of course, is the increase in "real" average hourly earnings, i.e. changes in money earnings adjusted for changes in consumer prices. In terms of constant dollars, straight-time average hourly earnings increased almost 271 per cent during this 51-year period. And it must be noted that the gains in hourly earnings over this period understate gains in the *total* returns to labor since fringe benefits are excluded. Such benefits were virtually non-existent at the beginning of the period but were enjoyed—to varying degrees—by all manufacturing workers in 1959.

The increase in "real" hourly earnings is not a measure of productivity gains in manufacturing. But real wages in manufacturing could not have increased without substantial increases in productivity whether measured in terms of labor inputs or combined labor and capital inputs. Over an even longer period of time workers have enjoyed the fruits of increased productivity through a combination of greater leisure and increased earnings.

It should be noted that the decline in average weekly hours did not proceed continuously. The drop was rather slow from the 1890's until the Great Depression of the 1930's. There was a pronounced drop during the later years of the depression. The average work week was increased during World War II due to a combination of labor shortages and the demands of the war effort. Since 1946, however, there has been only a fractional decline in the average work week in manufacturing.

What forces were responsible for the reduction in hours? One of the goals of the early trade unions was a reduction in hours of work and there is evidence that union pressures contributed substantially to the reduced work week between the 1890's and the 1930's. As Kerr has noted, shorter hours "would occur anyway over time with rising productivity; but schedules of hours of work are a convention of the labour market and it takes quite a shock, like a depression or union pressure, to get them changed. They are less likely to be changed in the normal course of events than are wages."[30]

The effects of legislation should also be noted. Since 1938, when the Fair Labor Standards Act was passed, employers have had to pay penalty rates for work in excess of the standard 40-hour week. Since they earn time and one-half for overtime, many workers are pleased if they have an opportunity to work more than 40 hours a week—at least for relatively short periods of time. However, employers try to schedule production to avoid premium payments. As a consequence, since the end of World War II, the average work-week in manufacturing has been fairly close to 40 hours although specific companies, such as a number of those in the rubber industry, have adopted a shorter standard work week.

During the early 1960's there was some union pressure for further reduction in hours. Early in 1962, Local 3 of the International

[30] Kerr, "Productivity and Labour Relations," *op. cit.*, p. 18.

Brotherhood of Electrical Workers, located in New York City, negotiated a 25-hour work week.[31] Other unions, such as the Retail, Wholesale and Department Store Union, have negotiated more modest reductions in the standard work week. Still others have sought to reduce the amount of work on an annual basis by demanding longer vacations or in some cases more paid holidays. Indeed, some observers believe that in the future workers will prefer longer vacations and more paid holidays to a gradual reduction in working hours through a progressive shortening of the work day. As already noted, the average work-week in manufacturing has dropped only fractionally since the end of World War II. But a recent Bureau of Labor Statistics study of fringe benefits showed that "the average full-time worker in 1960 had 155 more hours of paid leisure than a worker had in 1940. Of that total, 48 hours resulted from six days of paid vacation and 32 from four more days of paid holidays."[32]

It seems reasonable to expect that beyond some point further reduction in the average work-week would become impracticable. While workers in the past obtained some of the gains of increased productivity in the form of a shorter work day and in a reduction of the work week from six to five days, it seems quite likely that in the future an equally significant measure will be the number of days worked per year as unions negotiate an increasing number of days off with pay.

What are the economic consequences of shorter hours? Earlier in this chapter it was stated that workers could not have enjoyed the gains in "real" income which they have received without corresponding increases in productivity. But to some extent increases in productivity were a *result* of shorter hours. When the standard work week was 60 hours excessive fatigue undoubtedly reduced the efficiency of a great many workers. Unless output is entirely paced by a machine, the output of workers is not uniform throughout the work day. The worker does not punch a time clock and immediately reach peak production if he has any control over the rate of output. During the early part of the work day there is some "warming up" time, and later in the day fatigue will impair his efficiency.

[31] This contract set off a round of controversy. Even some union leaders appeared to object to such a drastic reduction in the work week. Some employer groups, never regarded as favorably inclined toward unions, denounced the move without reservation. It has been suggested that the members of this Local were less interested in more leisure than in having premium pay for "overtime" beginning after they had worked 25 rather than 40 hours in a week.

[32] The results of this study were cited in *Business Week* (March 31, 1962), p. 83.

Thus in many factories when daily hours were cut from ten to eight, daily output per worker went up. In any work situation there is some "output optimum" length of work period.[33] While precise measurement of the output optimum might be difficult—if not impossible—this theoretical construct has a counterpart in the real world. Neither daily nor weekly output per worker will be maximized if the work day is too short. On the other hand, if the work day is long enough to impair efficiency average hourly output will also be reduced. While the optimum output length of work period will vary from occupation to occupation, and industry to industry, it seems reasonable to suppose that beyond some point the work day cannot be shortened without adverse effects upon productivity. Since workers share in the benefits of rising productivity they will not seek to shorten the work day or the work week to the point where total output will be reduced. The most probable course of events is that unions will continue to press for a combination of rising earnings and more leisure as productivity continues to increase. Except in isolated cases, however, it is not likely that they will press for substantial reductions in the work week, but will continue to negotiate more full days off with pay.

REFERENCES

BOOKS AND PAMPHLETS

American Assembly, *Wages, Prices, Profits and Productivity,* New York: Columbia University (June 1959).

Cartter, Allan M., *Theory of Wages and Employment,* Homewood, Illinois: Richard D. Irwin, Inc. (1959).

Fabricant, Solomon, *Basic Facts on Productivity Change,* Occasional Paper 63, New York: National Bureau of Economic Research, Inc. (1959).

Kendrick, John W., *Productivity Trends in the United States,* Princeton, New Jersey: Princeton University Press (1961).

Michael, Donald M., *Cybernation: The Silent Conquest,* Santa Barbara, California: Center for the Study of Democratic Institutions (1962).

National Bureau of Economic Research, *Output, Input and Productivity Measurement,* Studies in Income and Wealth, Volume 25 of the Conference on Research on Income and Wealth, Princeton, New Jersey: Princeton University Press (1961).

Progress Report Automation Committee, Armour and Company, United Packinghouse, Food and Allied Workers (AFL-CIO), and Amalgamated Meat Cutters and Butcher Workmen of North America (AFL-CIO), Chicago, Illinois (June 19, 1961).

Rostow, W. W., *The Stages of Economic Growth,* Cambridge: Cambridge University Press (1960).

Schultz, George P., and George B. Baldwin, *Automation a New Dimension to Old Problems,* Washington, D.C.: Public Affairs Press (1955).

[33] Clyde E. Dankert, "Shorter Hours—In Theory and Practice," *Industrial and Labor Relations Review* (April 1962), p. 307.

Slichter, Sumner H., *Union Policies and Industrial Management,* Washington, D.C.: The Brookings Institution (1941).

———, ———, *Technology and the Great American Experiment,* Madison, Wisconsin: University of Wisconsin Press (1957).

———, ———, James J. Healy and E. Robert Livernash, *The Impact of Collective Bargaining on Management,* Washington, D.C.: The Brookings Institution (1960).

Stigler, George J., *Trends in Output and Employment,* New York: National Bureau of Economic Research, Inc. (1947).

U. S. Department of Labor, *Impact of Automation and Technological Change on Employment and Unemployment,* Washington, D.C.: Bureau of Employment Security, BES No. 4–206 (September 1961).

University of California Western Assembly, *Wages, Prices, Profits, Productivity,* Berkeley and Los Angeles: Institute of Industrial Relations, University of California (1959).

Wiener, Norbert, *The Human Use of Human Beings* (Garden City, New York: Doubleday and Company, Inc. (second edition revised, 1954).

ARTICLES

Barkin, Solomon, "Trade-Union Attitudes and Their Effects Upon Productivity," *Industrial Productivity,* Industrial Relations Research Association (1951), pp. 110–129.

"Benefits and Problems Incident to Automation and Other Technological Advances," Report to the President from Advisory Committee on Labor-Management Policy (mimeographed, January 11, 1962).

Clague, Ewan, "Productivity—What It Is and How It Is Measured," Presented before the Chicago Association of Commerce and Industry, Chicago, Illinois (mimeographed, May 26, 1959).

———, "Prices, Wages and Productivity," Presented before the Labor Relations and Arbitration Conference, University of California, San Francisco, California (mimeographed, May 25, 1959).

———, "Interpreting Productivity Measurements and Their Application to Economic Problems," Presented to the American Marketing Association—American Farm Economic Association, Washington, D.C. (mimeographed, December 30, 1959).

———, ———, and Leon Greenberg, "Technological Change and Employment," *Monthly Labor Review* (July 1962), pp. 742–746.

Dankert, Clyde E., "Shorter Hours—in Theory and Practice," *Industrial and Labor Relations Review* (April 1962), pp. 307–322.

Dunlop, John T., "Productivity and the Wage Structure," *Income, Employment and Public Policy,* Essays in honor of Alvin H. Hansen, New York: W. W. Norton and Company, Inc. (1948), pp. 341–362.

Faunce, William A., "Automation and Leisure," *Automation and Society,* H. P. Jacobson and J. S. Roucek, eds., New York: Philosophical Library (1959), pp. 297–308.

———, ———, "Automation and the Automobile Worker," *Social Problems* (Summer 1958), pp. 68–78.

Federal Reserve Bank of Kansas City, "Average Labor Productivity as a Guide to Wage Adjustments," *Monthly Review* (March–April 1962), pp. 8–14.

Jacobson, Eugene, *et al.,* "Employee Attitudes toward Technological Change in a Medium Sized Insurance Company," *Journal of Applied Psychology* (December 1959), pp. 349–354.

Karsh, Bernard, "The Meaning of Work in an Age of Automation," *Current Economic Comment* (August 1957), pp. 3–13.

Kerr, Clark, "Productivity and Labour Relations," *Productivity and Progress,* Sidney, Australia: Angus and Robertson (1957), pp. 1–35.

Miernyk, William H., "Men, Machines and Electronic Brains," *The Commercial and Financial Chronicle* (August 4, 1955), pp. 9 ff.

Stieber, Jack, "Automation and the White-Collar Worker," *Personnel* (November–December 1957).

Chapter 22 Unemployment

PROBLEMS IN THE LABOR MARKET

The 1950's ushered in the age of affluence in the United States. All indicators of economic progress surged upward. The Gross National Product—the dollar value of goods and services produced in a given year—rose from $368.6 billion in 1950 to $554.9 billion in 1962, both measured in 1962 prices. This represented an increase of slightly more than 50 per cent. After tax per capita income, measured in 1962 prices, went up from $1,715 in 1951 to $2,060 in 1962, an increase of 20 per cent. Whether measured in aggregate terms, or on a per capita basis, the indicators of economic well-being show a strongly rising trend since the end of the second World War. But one of the paradoxes of the age of affluence has been an increase in the unemployment rate at a time when the nation has experienced unparalleled prosperity. Employment has gone up, and at a fairly rapid rate. But the level of unemployment has increased even more rapidly. The broad trends in employment and unemployment since the end of World War II are summarized in Table 22-1.

The civilian labor force rose rapidly in 1946 and 1947 as demobilization was completed and it has continued to edge up steadily, with the exception of one year since then. In 1951 there was a fractional decline in the civilian labor force due to partial mobilization for the Korean War. But during the seventeen years covered by Table 22-1, the civilian labor force registered a gain of 18.2 million members, an increase of more than one-third. Employment during this period rose from 52.8 million to 68 million—up almost 29 per cent. But at the same time, there was nearly a three-fold increase in unemployment.

These trend comparisons need some qualification. Unemployment in 1945 was abnormally low since this was the year in which World

TABLE 22–1

LABOR FORCE, EMPLOYMENT AND UNEMPLOYMENT, 1945–1962
(in thousands)

Civilian Labor Force			Employment		Unemployment		
Year	Number	Per cent change	Number	Per cent change	Number	Per cent change	Per cent of civilian labor force
1945	53,860	–	52,820	–	1,040	–	1.9
1946	57,520	+6.8	55,250	+4.6	2,270	+118.3	3.9
1947	60,168	+4.6	57,812	+4.6	2,356	+ 3.8	3.9
1948	61,442	+2.1	59,117	+2.3	2,325	— 1.3	3.8
1949	62,105	+1.1	58,423	—1.2	3,682	+ 58.4	5.9
1950	63,099	+3.3	59,748	+2.3	3,351	— 9.0	5.3
1951	62,884	—0.3	60,784	+1.7	2,099	— 37.4	3.3
1952	62,966	+0.1	61,035	+0.4	1,932	— 8.0	3.1
1953	63,815	+1.3	61,945	+1.5	1,870	— 3.2	2.9
1954	64,468	+1.0	60,890	—1.7	3,578	+ 91.3	5.6
1955	65,848	+2.1	62,944	+3.4	2,904	— 18.8	4.4
1956	67,530	+2.6	64,708	+2.8	2,822	— 2.8	4.2
1957	67,946	+0.6	65,011	+0.5	2,936	+ 4.0	4.3
1958	68,647	+1.0	63,966	—1.6	4,681	+ 59.4	6.8
1959	69,394	+1.1	65,581	+2.5	3,813	— 18.5	5.5
1960	70,612	+1.8	66,681	+1.7	3,931	+ 3.1	5.6
1961	71,603	+1.4	66,796	+0.2	4,806	+ 22.3	6.7
1962	72,011	+0.6	67,999	+1.8	4,012	— 16.5	5.6

Sources: *1962 Supplement to Economic Indicators* (1962), p. 34; and *Economic Indicators*, Joint Economic Committee (December 1963), p. 10.

War II ended. It is important to note cyclical movements in employment and unemployment over this period as well. Total employment dropped in three of the post-war years as the economy passed through recessions of varying degrees of intensity. It will be noted that unemployment is far more volatile than employment. Each time there was a relatively small drop in employment (in 1949, 1954, and again in 1958) there were relatively large increases in unemployment. Cyclical ups and downs in unemployment are not unusual in a free market economy. But a great many policy makers, trade union leaders, and economists, have been concerned about the tendency of unemployment to settle at a higher level during the recovery from each of the post-war recessions. This can be noted in the right-hand column of Table 22-1. It is illustrated even more graphically by Chart 22-1 which shows the trend in total unemployment and in long-term unemployment from 1948 to the spring of 1961. The chart shows that not only has there been a

CHART 22–1
TOTAL AND LONG-TERM UNEMPLOYED SEASONALLY ADJUSTED, JANUARY 1948–APRIL 1961

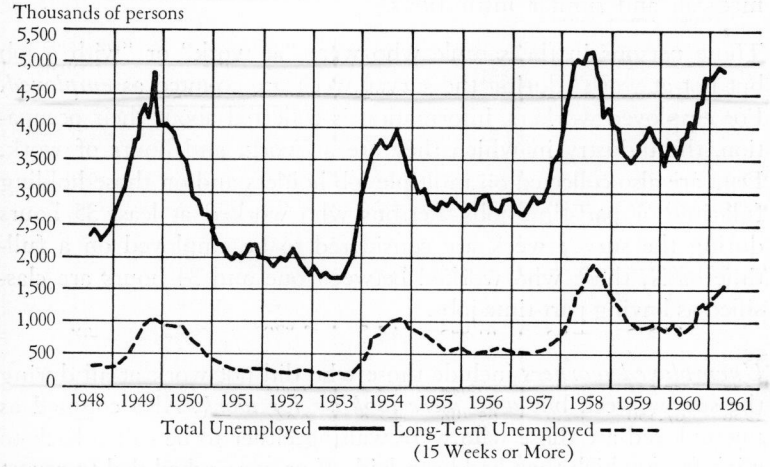

Source: Jane L. Meredith, "Long-Term Unemployment in the United States," *Monthly Labor Review*, June 1961, p. 604.

significant increase in the number of workers unemployed but for a great many there has been a substantial increase in the *duration* of unemployment.

What are the causes of "creeping unemployment" during periods of expanding employment, rising income, and increasing affluence? How can we define and measure unemployment? How does unemployment during the prosperous fifties compare with that of the depressed thirties? How has the rise in unemployment affected trade unions and the process of collective bargaining? Finally, what is being done about the problem of increasing unemployment?

DEFINITIONS AND MEASUREMENT OF UNEMPLOYMENT

The Monthly Report on the Labor Force

Information on employment and unemployment is collected by a monthly survey conducted by trained interviewers from the Bureau of the Census. The survey covers a sample of about 35,000 households in 333 areas which are considered to be a representative cross-section of all the nation's labor market areas. The population which the sample is designed to represent is the "civilian non-institutional population" made up of persons 14 years of age or older. This excludes all members of the armed forces and inmates of penal, medical, and similar institutions.

Those persons in the sample who were "at work" or "with a job but not at work" during the survey week are counted as *employed*. For employed workers, information is collected about their occupation, the industry in which they are at work, and hours of work. Data are also collected on multiple job holders and on those holding full-time or part-time jobs. Persons who worked at least 35 hours during the survey week are considered to be employed on a full-time basis; those who worked between one and 34 hours are classified as having part-time jobs.

Unemployed workers include those who did not work at all during the survey week but *who were looking for work*. Also counted as unemployed are those who were waiting either to be called back to a job from which they had been laid off or were scheduled to report to a new job within the following thirty days (and who were not in school during the survey week). Finally, workers who were temporarily ill and those who believed no jobs were available in their line of work in the community are included among the unemployed.

From this monthly sample national estimates are made by applying appropriate "blow up" factors. The sample is a revolving one, that is, the same households are not included month after month, although a complete change is not attempted every month. The sample is selected in such a way as to give every household in the nation an equal opportunity to be included in the survey.

When the data have been collected by census enumerators they are turned over to the Bureau of Labor Statistics for tabulation, analysis, and publication. The BLS publishes a measure of sampling variability known as the "standard error" which can be used to determine the upper and lower limits within which the "true" level of unemployment will fall on a probability basis. Without going into technical details, it may be noted that these limits are quite narrow. If, for example, in a specific month the BLS reports an unemployment estimate of 4 million, the chances are two out of three that the true figure lies somewhere between 3.9 million and 4.1 million. And the chances are 19 out of 20 that the true figure will fall between 3.8 million and 4.2 million.[1] Small month-to-month changes—40,000 to 50,000 for example—must be interpreted with caution. Such changes are within the limits of sampling variability and might not represent any change in the actual unemployment situation. The BLS is always careful to point this out, however. When the monthly survey of the labor force shows a small increase or decrease in unemployment—well within the limits of sampling variability—it is reported as "no change." The estimates prepared jointly by the Bureau of the Census and the Bureau of Labor Statistics have come under attack at times. But the integrity of the government agencies responsible for preparing the estimates of employment and unemployment has been staunchly upheld by professional statisticians, representatives of business, and the leaders of organized labor.[2]

THE TAXONOMY OF UNEMPLOYMENT

Unemployment may be classified in a number of ways: (a) by degree (partial or total), (b) by volition (voluntary or involuntary), (c) by duration (short-term, long-term, and very long-term), and (d) by cause (seasonal, cyclical, frictional, structural, etc.). There will always be some voluntary unemployment in a free-market economy since there is a constant turnover of workers as some quit old jobs in search of new. Such unemployment is likely to be more prevalent during good times than bad since a worker will not readily quit a job—even one he does not particularly like—at a time when other job opportunities are scarce. Some workers, especially married women in the labor force, are not interested in full-time, year-round jobs. At times they show up in the statistics as partially unemployed or temporarily unemployed workers.

Many kinds of short-term unemployment do not constitute a serious problem. But involuntary unemployment—especially if it is of relatively long duration—is a serious economic and social problem. In the minds of many economists, congressmen, and others, it has been the number one economic problem of the postwar period. The remainder of this chapter will be concerned almost entirely with involuntary unemployment, with particular emphasis on causes and proposed remedies.

[1] *Employment and Unemployment,* Hearings before the Subcommittee on Economic Statistics, Joint Economic Committee, Eighty-seventh Congress (December 18–20, 1961), p. 42.

[2] For an extended discussion of this issue see *Measuring Employment and Unemployment,* Report of the President's Committee to Appraise Employment and Unemployment Statistics, Washington, D.C.: U.S. Government Printing Office (1962).

UNEMPLOYMENT BY DURATION AND TYPE

Any attempt to develop a simple cross-classification of unemployment by duration and type will run into difficulties. This is because the two are not mutually exclusive. Some kinds of unemployment are distinctly short-term but other kinds of unemployment may be either short or long-term. One cross-classification of unemployment by duration and type is given in Table 22-2. This classification will undoubtedly not be accepted by all economists and the types of unemployment listed in the left-hand column of this table do not exhaust all the possibilities. Some other kinds of unemployment are discussed below.[3]

TABLE 22–2

TYPES OF UNEMPLOYMENT BY DURATION

	Short-term	Long-term or "Very long-term"
Casual	x	
Seasonal	x	
Frictional	x	
Initial	x	x
Cyclical	x	x
Structural	x	x
Due to inadequate demand		x

The Department of Labor defines short-term unemployment as that lasting up to 15 weeks. Long-term unemployment lasts from 15 to 26 weeks. Unemployment of 27 weeks or more is considered as "very long-term" unemployment. The various types of unemployment listed in Table 22-2 will be discussed briefly:

Casual

Some types of work are casual or intermittent. Various kinds of dock workers, for example, can only be employed when ships are available to be loaded or unloaded. The same applies to some kinds of construction workers and various other workers who cannot tell on a day-to-day basis when they will or will not be employed. Often such workers are employed on the basis of a roster and when their

[3] In a recent publication the Bureau of Labor Statistics lists 58 terms used to describe various kinds of unemployment. Many of these could be included under the seven types listed in Table 22–2, but some could not since they are not directly linked to duration. Furthermore, there is quite a bit of duplication involved in the BLS Glossary of Unemployment Terms since the authors of this report have attempted to make it a comprehensive one. See *Unemployment: Terminology, Measurement and Analysis*, Subcommittee on Economic Statistics of the Joint Economic Committee, Washington, D.C.: U.S. Government Printing Office (1961), pp. 15–22.

names come up through a process of rotation they work on a given day. These workers are often unemployed for a few days at a stretch. But so long as they remain attached to a particular hiring-hall, or other agency which will call them to work when a job is available, they would not be included in the unemployment statistics. If, by chance, such a worker should be included in the monthly survey discussed above he would be classified as "with a job but not at work." Some authors prefer to include casual unemployment under "hidden" or "disguised" unemployment to be discussed below.

Seasonal

Many types of employment are seasonal. Some shoe factories, for example, have two major "runs" a year; these usually come in the spring and the fall, and between the busy seasons some shoe workers may be unemployed for several weeks at a time. Workers in agriculture, food-processing, some kinds of construction, and workers in various service activities are often seasonally unemployed.

Frictional

Some workers are unemployed for short periods of time because their places of employment are temporarily closed down on a non-seasonal basis. There is also a considerable amount of *voluntary* unemployment which must be classified as frictional. There is always some turnover in the labor market as workers quit jobs to seek other employment. If a worker is "between jobs" and is included in the monthly survey of the labor force he would be considered as frictionally unemployed. Some workers might also be temporarily unemployed because their place of employment is closed due to a labor dispute elsewhere. Their employers cannot afford to keep them on the job if their major customers have been closed by a strike.[4]

Initial

Some youngsters step right out of school into a job, and they might never experience involuntary unemployment. But others—and this is especially true of "dropouts"—experience several spells of unemployment before finding steady work. If this unemployment lasts only a few weeks it is short-term but in many cases the new entrants to the labor force are unemployed for several months before finding steady work.

[4] There has been a considerable amount of controversy in some states over the question of whether or not striking workers should be considered as legally unemployed—at least after some period of time—and hence eligible for unemployment compensation.

Cyclical

In a free-market economy certain types of business activity—notably manufacturing and construction—are highly cyclical. The upward and downward movements of industrial production and building activity—loosely referred to as the "business cycle"—are accompanied by similar fluctuations in employment. The effects of these fluctuations are felt by other sectors of the economy, but to a lesser extent. During the 15 years from the end of World War II until 1960, for example, there were four recessions of varying intensity. During each of these recessions unemployment rose and there was a corresponding drop in unemployment as recovery got under way. Some indication of the intensity of each of the four postwar cycles can be obtained by referring back to Table 22-1. Cyclical unemployment may be either of short or long duration. Not all workers are laid off or recalled at the same time. In many establishments workers with the lowest seniority are the first to go and the last to be recalled. Cyclical unemployment for such workers might definitely be long-term; it is if they are out of work 15 weeks or longer. And some might fall in the "very long-term" category, if their spells of joblessness last more than 26 weeks. Even some relatively high seniority workers might be laid off during recessions. The chances are fairly good, however, that they will not be out of work long. If their layoff lasts less than 15 weeks they would fall in the category of the short-term cyclically unemployed.

Some authors have argued that cyclical unemployment is aggravated by the entry of "secondary workers" into the labor market during periods of recession. The thesis is that when primary breadwinners are laid off and jobs are generally unavailable for male workers, some wives enter the labor market temporarily in search of employment. If their husbands were steadily employed they would not be seeking jobs but they hope to find work of some kind to help tide their families over until the husbands are recalled to steady employment.[5]

Structural

Structural unemployment results from "once-for-all" changes in the economy. Structurally unemployed workers are not laid off; they are workers who have lost their jobs permanently. This might result from the relocation of a mill or factory, the closing of a mine

[5] This is usually referred to as the "additional worker theory." For a discussion see Richard C. Wilcock, "The Secondary Labor Force and the Measurement of Unemployment," *The Measurement and Behavior of Unemployment,* National Bureau of Economic Research, Princeton, N.J.: Princeton University Press (1957), p. 172.

or smelter, or a permanent cutback in the scale of operations of an enterprise. Some workers might also become redundant due to the introduction of automation or other forms of technological change.

The depletion of resources, shifts in demand, the development of competitive products or processes, and competition from other countries are among the causes of structural unemployment. Some of the workers who lose their jobs due to these or other causes might be fortunate enough to find new employment within a relatively short time. Relatively young workers, particularly if they do not have family responsibilities, might move to other localities where job opportunities are more promising. And even where an industry is contracting—such as the decline of the New England textile industry during the first half of the 1950's—there are some job openings due to normal turnover in the companies which remain in operation. Some workers who lose their jobs when a plant or mill is liquidated may thus find new employment in another plant or mill in the same industry. But if the industry as a whole is declining there will not be enough jobs for all displaced workers. The workers who are middle-aged or older often find it difficult, if not impossible, to move to other localities. Even if they were able to move they recognize that their age would be a barrier to reemployment. Such workers are likely to remain unemployed for long periods of time and some might never find continuous employment again; they are prematurely forced out of the labor force and the labor market.

Long-term structural unemployment is likely to be highly localized. It has been found, for example, in the declining textile areas of New England and the Middle Atlantic States. There has also been a considerable amount of structural unemployment in the coal-mining areas of Pennsylvania, West Virginia, and Southern Illinois. A number of steel and auto-manufacturing centers have had high unemployment rates in recent years and much of this unemployment is structural.

Unemployment Due to Inadequate Demand

Some economists have argued that there would be little or no long-term unemployment if the economy grew at a sufficiently rapid rate to sustain a high level of demand for goods and services. Since the demand for labor is derived from the demand for goods and services, those who subscribe to this view attribute much if not all of long-term unemployment to a slow rate of economic growth.

OTHER TYPES OF UNEMPLOYMENT

"Hidden" Unemployment

A number of writers have referred to "concealed," "disguised," or "hidden" unemployment. These terms are not always used synonymously. But collectively they refer to the under-utilization or unproductive use of labor in an economy. In some declining industries, such as coal mining, there are not enough jobs available for all the workers attached to the industry. In some locations, however, the available work is shared among a larger number of workers than would be needed to maintain operations through a system of "job rotation." Some workers might be employed for a week or two then temporarily laid off while others take their places. And there are other cases where an enterprise operates only part of a week with all of its work force idle the remainder of the time.

Another type of disguised or hidden unemployment is found in relatively poor agricultural areas. Workers might be able to eke out a bare subsistence on their jobs if relatively inefficient methods are followed. Another type of hidden unemployment is found among displaced workers who are forced to withdraw from the labor force before they would normally retire. Also, workers who are able to find part-time jobs when they would prefer full-time employment are considered by some authors to be among the hidden unemployed.

The "Unemployables"

In any sizeable labor market area some hard-to-place workers are considered to be basically unemployable. Workers with a history of mental illness often find it difficult to locate new jobs. Other workers find a lack of training or education, or language difficulties, to be barriers to employment, and some "emotionally handicapped" workers—even if they have not been treated for mental illness—find it difficult to obtain, or to retain, a job. Physically handicapped workers—even though perfectly capable of doing many kinds of work—might find the doors of employment offices closed to them. In many cases age alone is a barrier to re-employment if a worker is displaced from an earlier job. It is significant, however, that a great many "unemployable" workers found jobs and worked effectively during the World War II years of labor shortage. "Unemployability" appears to be a matter of degree; it depends as much upon conditions in the labor market as the characteristics of the workers who are rejected by employers when healthy, younger workers are available in the necessary numbers.

CHART 22–2
SEASONALLY-ADJUSTED SHORT- AND LONG-TERM UNEMPLOYMENT
QUARTERLY AVERAGES, 1953–62

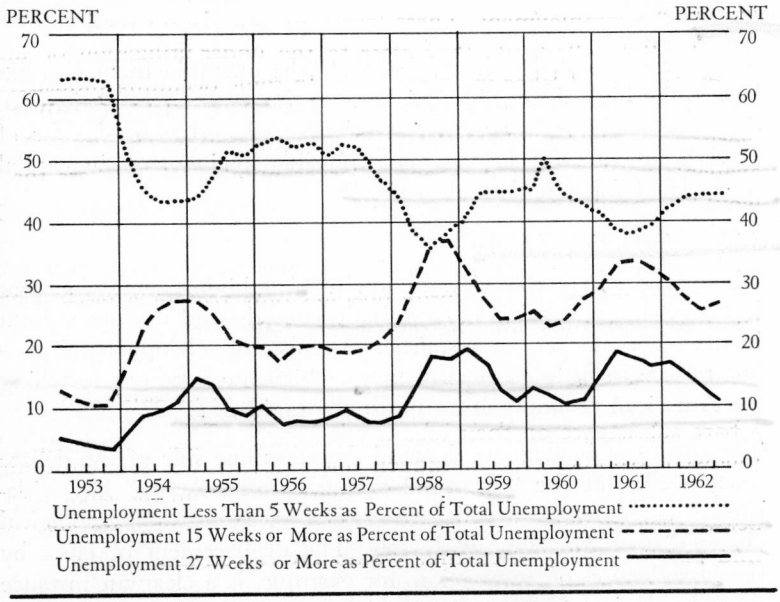

Source: Chart taken from publication of the United States Department of Labor, Bureau of Labor Statistics: Latest Data: Fourth Quarter 1962

PERSISTENT UNEMPLOYMENT IN A GROWING ECONOMY

One of the questions most hotly debated by businessmen, economists, and policy makers during the latter half of the 1950's concerned the rate of growth of the American economy. Many accepted rather uncritically the proposition that the American economy was growing "too slowly." This is not the place to discuss the various issues raised in this debate. It is sufficient for our purposes to point out that, whether or not it grew fast enough to satisfy everyone, the American economy did grow during the decade of the 1950's. As noted in Chart 22-1, unemployment also registered a marked increase during this period. Moreover as Chart 22-2 shows, there was a substantial increase in the number of long-term unemployed. Indeed, it was the existence of this "persistent unemployment" which led many to accept the hypothesis that the American economy was growing too slowly. A number of theories have been advanced in an effort to explain the increase in persistent unemployment in a growing economy. Although a certain amount of oversimplification is involved, these can be classified under two broad headings:

Inadequate Demand

Those who accept this theory feel that "the unemployment rate has been quite high since mid-1957, because the rate of growth in final demand has been low relative to the actual and normal rates of growth in potential supply made possible by increases in capital stock, labor force, and productivity."[6]

The Structural Transformation Theory

Those who accept this view maintain "that higher unemployment has been due not to inadequate final demand—and its concomitant in the labor market, an insufficient number of job opportunities—but rather, to technological changes which are currently reaching the American economy at an unusually rapid pace."[7]

The theory of inadequate demand describes one side of the debate fairly well. But the "structural transformation theory" has widespread acceptance only if one defines the term "technological changes" very broadly and loosely. The displacement of labor by the introduction of automation, for example, is a clear-cut instance of technological change. But some part of the high-level unemployment of the latter half of the 1950's has been due to changes in the location of industry, the depletion of resources, and rising imports. Shifts in demand—such as oil for coal and synthetics for natural fibers—have been due partly to changes in technology and partly to other causes. In the broad sense that changes of this kind can be considered to lead to new "production functions" they may be considered as technological. In this sense, those who recognize that part of the increase in persistent unemployment has been due to these causes might be willing to accept the structural transformation hypothesis.

It has also been pointed out that as a result of "structural change" the composition of the employed labor force has been changing quite rapidly in recent years. It was during the decade of the 1950's that white-collar workers outnumbered blue-collar or manual workers for the first time in our history, and the proportion of white-collar workers in the labor force has been growing. Some

[6] *Higher Unemployment Rates, 1957–60: Structural Transformation or Inadequate Demand,* Subcommittee on Economic Statistics of the Joint Economic Committee, Washington: U.S. Government Printing Office (1961), p. 6.
[7] *Ibid.,* p. 6.

structural transformation theorists claim that blue-collar workers displaced by technological change have been unable to shift into the growing white-collar occupations, and it is these workers, they assert, who comprise a substantial part of the persistently unemployed.[8]

Our knowledge of the characteristics of the persistently unemployed has increased in recent years due to the publication of detailed data by the Bureau of Labor Statistics. Analysis of unemployment data since 1955 shows that there are heavy concentrations among middle-aged and older workers and new entrants to the labor force (many of whom are "school dropouts"). Also, non-white workers have accounted for a disproportionate share of unemployment. Unemployment is also heavily concentrated among laborers, operatives and craftsmen in mining, construction, and manufacturing. Finally, the geographic distribution of unemployment is far from even. There have been heavy concentrations of unemployment in some of the labor market areas of New England, the Middle Atlantic States, and the Upper South.[9]

Analysis of the composition of unemployment by age, sex, occupation, industrial attachment, and geographic location reveals that the problem of rising persistent unemployment during the latter half of the 1950's is a complex one. After evaluating the two theories which were posed as alternative hypotheses of the causes of persistent unemployment, the staff of the Joint Economic Committee concluded that: "Those labor market symptoms which would indicate that the higher unemployment has been due to structural causes are almost totally absent . . . The evidence adverse to the structural transformation theory confirms the contentions of the aggregate demand theory."[10]

At least one member of the Joint Economic Committee was unwilling to accept this conclusion, however. Representative Thomas B. Curtis, in a dissenting note to the Subcommittee's report, commented that "there are many other theories or possibilities that explain the rate of unemployment since 1957 beside the two theories posed . . ."[11] Some economists have also dissented from the view that persistent unemployment in recent years has been due to

[8] *Ibid.*, p. 7.
[9] William H. Miernyk, "The Incidence of Persistent Unemployment," *Proceedings*, Twelfth Annual Meeting, Industrial Relations Research Association, Washington, D.C. (December 28, 1959), pp. 22–39.
[10] *Higher Employment Rates, 1957–60*, pp. 78–79.
[11] *Employment and Unemployment*, Report of the Subcommittee on Economic Statistics to the Joint Economic Committee, Washington, D.C.: U.S. Government Printing Office (1962), p. 19.

structural transformation *or* inadequate demand. In their view this proposition would be improved if it were rephrased to read, "structural transformation *and* inadequate demand."

Economists who have specialized in analysis of labor market problems have stressed the complexity of the problem of rising persistent unemployment. They feel that it is unwise to attempt to explain this phenomenon entirely in terms of a single cause. This could lead to undue concentration on one type of policy designed to alleviate unemployment when a many-pronged attack on the problem of persistent unemployment might be necessary.[12]

WAGES, PRICES, AND UNEMPLOYMENT

Another approach to the unemployment problem has been cast in the framework of macroeconomic (i.e. aggregative) economic theory. This approach has dealt wtih the interrelations among wages, prices, and unemployment. It was discussed in Chapter 20 where the wage-price relationship was emphasized; in the discussion which follows, the wage-price-*un*employment problem will be considered.

A. W. Phillips, whose work on unemployment and changes in money wages was cited in Chapter 20 (see pages 385–386), concluded that the statistical evidence he had marshalled supported the hypothesis that "the rate of change of money wage rates can be explained by the level of unemployment and the rate of change of unemployment . . ."[13] He goes on to say that "it seems . . . that if aggregate demand were kept at a value which would maintain a stable level of product prices the associated level of unemployment would be a little under 2½ per cent. If, as is sometimes recommended, demand were kept at a value which would maintain stable wage rates the associated level of unemployment would be about 5½ per cent."[14] Phillips was careful to emphasize the tentative nature of his conclusions. He felt that there was a need for much more research into the interrelationships among unemployment, wage rates, prices, and productivity. But his conclusions have been

[12] For a statement of this general position see Richard C. Wilcock and Walter H. Franke, *Unwanted Workers,* Glencoe, Illinois: The Free Press (1963), especially Chapter 1. For a clear statement of the reasoning behind the inadequate demand theory see Gunnar Myrdal, *Challenge to Affluence,* New York: Pantheon Books (1963), pp. 23–25. The causes of structural unemployment are discussed on pp. 12–22.

[13] A. W. Phillips, "The Relation Between Unemployment and the Rate of Money Change Rates in the United Kingdom, 1861–1957," *Economica* (November 1958), p. 299.

[14] *Ibid.,* p. 299.

accepted without serious qualification by a number of American economists.

In terms of trade union behavior, and perhaps in terms of public policy, the Phillips hypothesis suggests the following: First, rising wages play an important part in inducing "inflation" as we now refer to any sustained increase in average prices. Secondly, the community is faced with a choice. It can either have a low level of unemployment with rising prices, or it can have a relatively high level of unemployment and stable prices. In Great Britain—which has had a low level of unemployment since the end of World War II—Phillips believed that stable prices would be associated with a 2.5 per cent unemployment rate. Since stable wages, in his opinion, would produce a much higher unemployment rate—about 5.5 per cent—it is clear that Phillips accepted the proposition that modest wage increases are compatible with stable prices. The wage increases, under conditions of stable prices, would be made up by gains in productivity.

Application of the Phillips Analysis to American Conditions

A comparison of increases in hourly earnings and unemployment rates in the United States has been made by Paul Samuelson and Robert Solow.[15] These authors have also related unemployment rates to price changes as indicated by the following diagram. According to the "modified Phillips curve" which Samuelson and Solow have constructed, price stability would involve an unemployment rate of about 5½ per cent. The reduction of unemployment to 3 per cent would involve a price rise of about 4½ per cent annually. The authors do not assume that the relationship shown in Figure 22-1 is a precise one, but is based on their "best guesses." They point out that there is nothing invariant about this relationship, particularly in the long run. Various kinds of changes in the economy, or in public policy, could cause the Phillips curve to shift —hopefully downward and to the left.

COMMENTS ON MACROECONOMIC WAGE-PRICE-UNEMPLOYMENT STUDIES

The studies by Phillips, Samuelson-Solow, and a more recent study by Robert R. France,[16] reveal that the intricate interrelationships

[15] Paul Samuelson and Robert Solow, "Analytical Aspects of Anti-Inflation Policy," *American Economic Review* (May 1960), pp. 177–194.

[16] Robert R. France, "Wages, Unemployment, and Prices in the United States, 1890–1932, 1947–1950," *Industrial and Labor Relations Review* (January 1962), pp. 171–190.

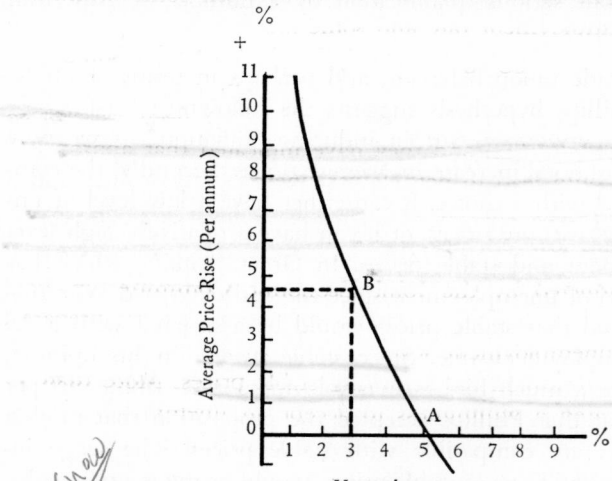

FIGURE 22–1

Source: Samuelson and Solow, *American Economic Review* (May 1960), p. 192. Reprinted by permission of the publisher.

among wage changes, price changes, and unemployment can be described statistically. But they must be interpreted with caution. Relationships such as that illustrated by the modified Phillips curve shown in Figure 22-1 are derived by a statistical technique known as regression analysis. This is a useful type of analysis for showing relationships, but a regression curve does not necessarily imply causation. That is, high prices do not necessarily "cause" unemployment. Nor does a low unemployment rate necessarily "cause" a rapid increase in prices. Also, such aggregative analyses fail to distinguish among the various types of unemployment examined earlier in this chapter. In the short-run, at least, it would be entirely possible to have a high level of *structural* unemployment which would have no direct connection with changes in either wages or prices. If, on the other hand, a high level of unemployment were due almost entirely to inadequate demand, one would expect prices and wages to be affected.

As noted earlier, some writers have attributed rising unemployment since 1957 to inadequate demand, but others have emphasized structural change as the primary cause. The issues involved are of more than academic importance. Policy makers are concerned about both price increases and unemployment. Ideally, they would like to see low unemployment rates and stable prices. But in practice it might be necessary to choose between some *minimum* acceptable unemployment rate and some *maximum* acceptable rate of price increases. Aggregative analysis of the Samuelson-Solow type suggests a close association between price increases and unemployment rates. The authors of this study have been careful to qualify their conclusions, and they have indicated that appropriate public policy could lead to both lower unemployment rates and a slower rise in prices. But some economists appear to believe that stable prices and low unemployment rates are incompatible.

A survey conducted by the Joint Economic Committee in 1958 showed that 60 per cent of a sample of economists were prepared to accept an unemployment level of more than five per cent, if necessary, as a condition for achieving stable prices. More than 13 per cent indicated a willingness to accept an unemployment rate of 7 per cent if this would lead to price stability.[17] While this sample is not necessarily representative of the thinking of all professional economists, it suggests that some at least accept the kind of relationship described by Figure 22-1 without qualification.

What kinds of policies would the two major theories of unemployment discussed in this chapter suggest? The theory of inadequate demand indicates a need for more rapid economic growth. It calls for a policy designed to stimulate investment and consumption and other measures to increase the demand for goods and services. This policy would assume that if sufficient demand for goods and services could be generated the derived demand for labor would also be increased and unemployment would decline.

If unemployment is primarily structural, however, a different set of policies would be called for. Structural unemployment exists because the labor market is not a "perfect" one; that is, workers displaced from jobs in one industry or one part of the country do not readily move to other jobs in other industries or other parts of the country. Thus a policy designed to cut down on structural unemployment would be one which attempted to improve the operation of the labor market.

Fortunately, it is not necessary to choose one approach to the exclusion of the other. Efforts to stimulate economic growth are entirely compatible with policies designed to improve the operation of the labor market. In general, policy makers in the United States, in recent years, have been eclectic. They have inaugurated programs

[17] *Economic Policy Questionnaire,* Tabulation of Replies Submitted to the Subcommittee on Economic Stabilization of the Joint Economic Committee (December 1958), p. 3.

to stimulate economic growth, and they have also taken steps to make the labor market operate more effectively.

EMPLOYMENT POLICIES

During World War II, involuntary unemployment in the nation virtually disappeared. In 1944, for example, the unemployed amounted to slightly more than one per cent of the civilian labor force. This was in sharp contrast to the years of the Great Depression. In the worst year, 1933, one out of four members of the civilian labor force was unemployed. Even during the war years, however, there was concern about a resurgence of unemployment following the end of hostilities. This concern was shared by the governments of many democratic nations. Articles 55 and 56 of the United Nations Charter pledged these nations to the maintenance of full employment. The governments of all advanced democratic societies now have full employment policies; the policy of the United States was embodied in the Employment Act of 1946.

The Employment Act of 1946

The American full employment policy consists essentially of a brief and fairly general statement of principle. The declaration of policy states that:

> . . . It is the continuing policy and responsibility of the Federal Government to use all practicable means . . . to coordinate and utilize all its plans, functions, and resources for the purpose of creating and maintaining, in a manner calculated to foster and promote free and competitive enterprise and the general welfare, conditions under which there will be afforded useful employment opportunities, including self-employment, for those able, willing, and seeking to work, and to promote maximum employment, production, and purchasing power.

The law also provided for the establishment of the Council of Economic Advisers, and the Joint Committee on the Economic Report now known as the Joint Economic Committee. The act contains no specific provisions for dealing with high-level unemployment. In principle, however, the act pledges the government to take whatever steps are necessary to insure adequate job opportunities for all. Essentially, the Congress which framed this act was thinking in terms of the mass unemployment of the 1930's which was due to inadequate aggregate demand. At the time the law was passed there was relatively little evidence of structural unemployment. Indeed, the law does not deal with the causes of unemployment, hence it does not prescribe specific remedies for eliminating unemployment if and when it should appear.

During the 1950's it became increasingly evident that something more than a statement of principle was needed. Of particular concern to many congressmen was the problem of chronic, localized unemployment. During a decade of economic growth and relative prosperity the nation was dotted with a number of communities with high-level unemployment. Unemployment in some of the depressed areas was caused by the out-migration of industry. In others it stemmed from shifts in demand. As automation progressed rapidly in some industries, thousands of additional workers joined the ranks of the structurally unemployed in still other depressed areas.

As early as 1955 legislation was introduced to provide aid for the nation's depressed areas.[18] But the first bills introduced were not passed. Other bills were introduced into later sessions of Congress, and eventually two of these passed the House and the Senate. Both bills were vetoed by President Eisenhower, however. The issue of depressed areas was an important one in the national election campaign of 1960 and the first piece of major legislation to be signed into law by President Kennedy, on May 1, 1961, was one designed to provide Federal assistance to depressed areas.

The Area Redevelopment Act of 1961

In its Declaration of Purpose, this Act states that ". . . the Federal Government, in cooperation with the States, should help areas of substantial and persistent unemployment and underemployment to take effective steps in planning and financing their economic redevelopment. . . Under the provisions of this Act new employment opportunities should be created by developing and expanding new and existing facilities and resources rather than by merely transferring jobs from one area of the United States to another."[19]

The Act is administered by an Area Redevelopment Administrator in the Department of Commerce. An advisory board made up of secretaries of various departments and an advisory committee made up of representatives of labor, management, and the public were established to assist in the administration of the new program.

Communities with unemployment ranging from 50 per cent above the national average in three out of four years to twice the national

[18] For a discussion of the early proposed legislation see William H. Miernyk, *Depressed Industrial Areas—A National Problem,* Washington, D.C.: National Planning Association (1957), pp. 43ff.
[19] Public Law 87–27, 87th Congress (May 1, 1961), p. 1.

average in one out of two years are eligible for assistance under the Act. The law provides for loans to local development groups both for the construction of business facilities and public facilities. For certain types of public facilities, outright grants may be made under the law. Technical assistance is also provided to local redevelopment organizations, and funds are provided for the development of a modest re-training program to help workers displaced from their old occupations find employment in new and expanding occupations.

The Manpower Development and Training Act of 1962

It has long been recognized that technological change can lead to the displacement of labor. But until fairly recently it was assumed that workers displaced by machines would be able to find new employment through the normal operation of the labor market. Research on labor mobility, particularly during the 1950's, showed that the transfer from declining to expanding occupations is not always an easy one. Young workers are fairly mobile, both geographically and occupationally, but workers who are middle-aged and older who lose their jobs due to a once-for-all change often find it difficult to locate new jobs which they are qualified to hold. In the Manpower Development and Training Act, Congress recognized that there were shortages of trained personnel in many occupational categories at a time when the "skills of many persons have been rendered obsolete by dislocations in the economy arising from automation or other technological developments, foreign competition, relocation of industry, shifts in market demands, and other changes in the structure of the economy . . ."[20]

Under the Area Redevelopment Act a relatively small number of workers were granted retraining and subsistence payments for a period of sixteen weeks. The early experience under this Act was encouraging, and this undoubtedly contributed to the decision by Congress to expand the retraining program.

The Retraining Act is administered jointly by the Secretary of Labor and the Secretary of Health, Education and Welfare. They are assisted by a national advisory committee made up of representatives of labor, management, agriculture, education and training, and the public in general. The Department of Labor compiles data on skill requirements, the occupational outlook, job opportunities, labor supply, and employment trends. The objective is to train displaced workers for occupations in which demand is greater than

[20] Public Law 87–415, 87th Congress (March 15, 1962), p. 1.

supply. Eligible trainees may receive subsistence payments and training for as much as a full year, and the Act makes provisions for on-the-job training where this "involves reasonable progression." Such training is supplemented by classroom instruction when necessary. A 1963 amendment permits training for youths, beginning at age 17, and basic education for illiterate older workers.

The Secretary of Health, Education and Welfare arranges for training facilities with state vocational and educational agencies. In states where such agencies are inadequate for the purpose, the Secretary is authorized to provide needed training by making contracts with public or private educational or training institutions.

Federal Legislation and Structural Unemployment

Both the Area Redevelopment Act and the Manpower Development and Training Act recognize that in a highly complex industrial economy the worker who becomes structurally unemployed may find it difficult or impossible to find new employment without assistance. Although these laws provide Federal funds for area redevelopment and retraining they require a considerable amount of state and local participation. They are, in brief, a cooperative effort between the Federal government and the respective states involved to reverse the upward trend in persistent unemployment.

Conservative groups opposed this legislation, especially the Area Redevelopment Act. The opposition was based largely on the grounds that this legislation would be an unwarranted broadening of the scope of Federal government activities since—given time—the labor market itself would solve the unemployment problem. At the same time staunch conservatives argued that high wages were a cause for unemployment, and that unions would have to stop exerting upward pressure on the wage level if they were interested in seeing jobless workers return to productive employment.

The argument that the labor market will solve the unemployment problem without government interference is based on an economic theory as old as this nation. The economic model involved is a very simple one. It assumes a direct functional relationship between wages and employment, a high degree of labor mobility, and an economy in which all markets are perfectly competitive. It is doubtful that the economic conditions upon which such a model is based ever prevailed; they certainly do not exist in complex modern industrial society. The Area Redevelopment Act and the

Manpower Development and Training Act recognize that market forces alone will not keep unemployment to a minimum in a society such as ours. At the same time the object of both pieces of legislation is not to interfere with the labor market, but to make it operate more effectively. Some workers are highly mobile but others are not. Thus efforts are being made to redevelop communities where local unemployment rates have been well above the national average for extended periods of time. Meanwhile, the Manpower Development and Training Act is designed to encourage the occupational mobility of labor by training workers to fill current and projected job openings.

LABOR MARKET LEGISLATION IN OTHER COUNTRIES

The United States was not the only advanced industrial nation to experience high-level unemployment before the second World War. As noted earlier, virtually all of the countries in the free world had adopted full employment policies by the mid-1940's. A number of nations have taken vigorous steps to implement these policies, and as a consequence have avoided the problem of "creeping unemployment."

The British Full Employment Policy

Even during the depression years of the 1930's the British government was taking steps to combat unemployment. Efforts were made to encourage the development of new industry in areas of above-average unemployment. But at a time when unemployment was widespread, due to inadequate total demand, these efforts were not highly successful. By the late 1930's, however, the British government had appointed a commission to study the unemployment problem intensively. This commission concluded that the unemployment problem was not a local matter—as many still believed at that time—but was national in character. A successful attack on high-level unemployment, the members of the commission concluded, would require active participation by the national government. Before an employment policy could be developed and put into effect, however, the second World War intervened. As in other nations which participated in the conflict, the unemployment problem quickly disappeared to be replaced by one of labor shortages.

During the war years, however, Parliament continued to discuss the employment situation in the postwar world and out of this discussion came a policy which pledged the British government to take all necessary steps to prevent the resurgence of mass unemployment. Unlike the American Employment Act of 1946, however, which is a statement of principle rather than a guide for action, the British policy statement contained recommendations for specific action. Wartime experience had adequately demonstrated that if the total demand for goods and services could be maintained at a high level the demand for labor would also be high. And the government pledged itself to maintain the level of demand necessary to sustain full employment.

As a result of the prewar investigation, however, Parliament also recognized that the maintenance of adequate demand was only part of an effective full employment policy. Unemployment is not distributed evenly among industries, areas, or occupations. Recognizing this, the British Parliament set up the framework for a program designed to deal specifically with heavy concentrations of unemployment. This was to be done by restraining the growth of new industry in heavily congested areas, and by the use of government influence to encourage the growth of such industry in labor-surplus areas. A number of laws were passed, beginning in 1947 and culminating in the Local Employment Act of 1960, to accomplish these objectives.

The British full employment program provides for some retraining, and also for some financial assistance to workers able and willing to move from areas of labor surplus to other areas where job opportunities are more plentiful. In general, however, the British approach has been one of encouraging the redevelopment of labor surplus areas—the same philosophy which underlies the Area Redevelopment Act in this country. The British government uses somewhat more stringent measures than have been suggested in this country, however. Before new industrial buildings can be constructed in Great Britain, a permit must be obtained from the Board of Trade. This agency is roughly the counterpart of the U.S. Department of Commerce, but it has a great deal more administrative authority than this or any other agency in the United States. By denying permits to industrialists who wish to expand in congested areas—and indicating that such permits would be granted for construction in labor surplus areas—the Board of Trade has effectively steered a substantial number of factories to communities with high-level unemployment. In addition, the British program provides for loans and grants for redevelopment activities. Finally, the Board of Trade need not wait until unemployment in a community becomes serious before taking action. If the Board is convinced that economic changes in an area will lead to a substantial number of layoffs in the near future it can begin to take action immediately to encourage the expansion of other job-creating activities in the area.

Swedish Labor Market Policy

Sweden is another industrial nation which has adopted an aggressive full employment policy. The emphasis in Sweden is somewhat different from that in Great Britain. The agency which administers the Swedish policy is the Swedish Royal Labor Market Board. To some extent the Board has been concerned with redevelopment activities in areas of high-level unemployment, but, in general, the Swedish approach has been one of encouraging occupational and geographical labor mobility.

Occupational mobility is encouraged by means of a retraining program. In a dynamic economy the skills and experience of some workers will be rendered obsolete by economic change, while at the same time other changes might lead to a shortage of workers with other skills. Through a system of vocational retraining, the Swedish government has attempted to keep a balance between skill requirements and skill availability in the labor market. If there is a surplus of textile workers and a shortage of metal workers, for example, the textile workers are retrained to work in machine shops, steel mills, and similar establishments. While undergoing retraining the workers receive subsistence payments, if necessary, to supplement unemployment compensation.

Geographic labor mobility has been encouraged in Sweden in a rather unique way. The Labor Market Board recognized that one obstacle to movement for many workers was the lack of suitable housing. As a result, the government provided a supply of prefabricated houses. If there is a shortage of workers and a shortage of housing in some locations, and a surplus of workers elsewhere, the prefabricated houses are erected in the labor shortage area. Workers who wish to move to these areas to accept new jobs are given travel grants. Family subsistence payments are also available if it is necessary for the worker to be separated from his family for some time. With the availability of prefabricated houses, however, long separations are rarely necessary. As economic development proceeds in the labor shortage areas private housing is constructed. At some point the prefabricated houses are no longer needed and they can then be dismantled and stored or sent to other areas where they are needed. The combination of retraining and a policy of providing workers with temporary housing in labor shortage areas has led to a relatively high degree of labor mobility in Sweden.

Full Employment Programs Elsewhere in Europe

The economic development of Western Europe is far from even. Some countries, such as the Federal Republic of Germany, are highly industrialized. Others, such as Italy, Spain, and Greece, lack sufficient industry to generate effective full employment. In recent years, however, there has been a considerable amount of labor mobility across national boundaries in Western Europe. In general, the movement has been from the labor-surplus countries into those which have had a shortage of labor. Workers from Italy, Spain, and Greece are granted temporary permits to accept employment in Western Germany. There has been a persistent shortage of many kinds of workers in Western Germany, and employers in need of workers can recruit temporary employees in other countries with which Western Germany has signed agreements to permit such recruiting. The workers do not permanently change their country of residence, and there has been a fairly steady flow of workers back and forth among the countries involved. Not everyone would consider this to be the ideal solution to unemployment but as a temporary expedient it seems to have worked well. Workers from other countries have contributed to the rapid redevelopment of Western Germany. At the same time, temporary employment has been provided to thousands of workers from other nations and they have had the added advantage of on-the-job training in many cases which has made them more effective workers when they returned to their own countries.

The Results of European Labor Market Policies

It is difficult to make international comparisons of unemployment directly. The United States, Canada—and in recent years Sweden—estimate unemployment on the basis of sample surveys. Most other nations, however, count only the *insured* unemployed. But the rate of insured unemployment is also regularly measured in the United States and on this basis—which permits more direct comparison—unemployment rates in the United States and Canada have been substantially higher than those in Great Britain and the countries of Western Europe since the early 1950's.[21]

[21] President's Committee to Appraise Employment and Unemployment Statistics, *Measuring Employment and Unemployment,* Washington: U.S. Government Printing Office (1962), pp. 233–270.

CHART 22–3
RATES OF UNEMPLOYMENT, 1951–62
Unadjusted

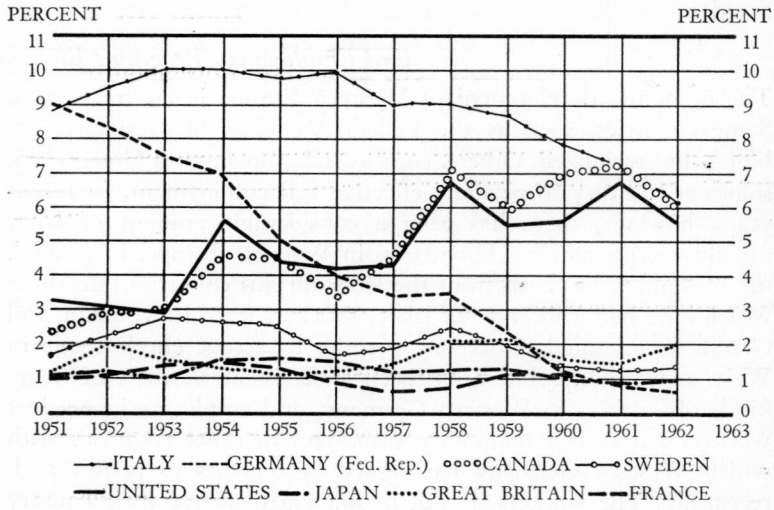

Source: Chart taken from publication of the United States Department of Labor, Bureau of Labor Statistics. Latest Data: 1962

There are other factors which must be taken into account when comparing unemployment rates. Some nations—such as Austria, Belgium, the Netherlands, Norway, and Sweden—are very small, comparable in size to some of the larger states in this country. In addition, the population of these countries is more homogeneous than that of the United States in terms of cultural and ethnic backgrounds. There is undoubtedly less resistance to movement from one community to another, if this is necessary to find employment, than is often found in this country. Other countries, such as the Federal Republic of Germany, France and Great Britain, suffered extensive wartime damage. Their industrial facilities had to be rebuilt and their economies revitalized. This called for the full utilization of all available workers. But even after these factors are taken into account there is strong evidence that Great Britain and the western European nations have come much closer to effective full employment than have the United States and Canada (see Chart 22-3) and to some extent this is due to differences in labor market policies.

Until recently the United States had no program for the redevelopment of depressed areas or for the retraining of displaced workers. Such programs have been in existence in Great Britain and some of the western European countries since the end of World War II. Indeed, to some extent the policies adopted in the United States in the early 1960's—the Area Redevelopment Act and the Manpower Development and Training Act—were patterned after earlier programs which have been in successful operation in other democratic countries for a number of years.

The United States is probably more strongly committed to a free market system than most other democratic nations and this thinking extends to labor markets as well as product markets. The philosophy behind this commitment to the market place is one of attempting to maximize individual freedom. But there has been growing recognition in recent years that labor markets do not function in the same way as commodity markets. Workers are not homogeneous. There is a vast difference between a temporarily unemployed skilled craftsman and a semi-skilled or unskilled factory worker who has been displaced by a once-for-all change. Some kinds of workers respond to changes in the labor market more easily than others. Some kinds of workers are more mobile, geographically and occupationally, than others. Each year, thousands of youngsters—untrained for any occupation—pour into the nation's labor markets. Many experience several years of intermittent unemployment before finally locating jobs which are more or less steady. Some academic economists have recognized the complexity of the labor market but others have not. As a consequence the issue of how to solve unemployment has been widely debated. But whatever the views of scholars, government policy in recent years has been turning in the direction of improving the operation of labor markets by area redevelopment, by retraining, and by an intensified effort on the part of the United States Employment Service to match idle workers with available jobs. The experience of democratic nations in Western Europe which have long recognized that workers often need help in finding employment or re-employment augers well for the success of a labor market policy in this country designed to achieve the same ends.

UNEMPLOYMENT AND COLLECTIVE BARGAINING

Trade unions have been affected by the rising level of persistent unemployment in a number of ways. Some unions have seen their membership decline as workers have been displaced by one or more kinds of structural change. Declining membership scarcely provides a strong base for collective bargaining. Employers can use the argument that further wage increases will only accelerate the rate of decline in unemployment. Whether or not they accept such arguments at face value, some union leaders cannot ignore the fact of high-level unemployment when preparing for and conducting negotiations.

A number of union leaders have responded to the rising level of unemployment by asking for a shorter work week. Their objective is to share the available jobs among all workers attached to an industry. The shorter work week, these union leaders assert, should not lead to a cut in take-home pay. The typical management response has been that a shorter work week would simply lead to higher costs, and thus possibly to a decline in sales with no net gain in employment in the long run. Government officials opposed a shortening of the work week during the early 1960's since in their view this might slow down the rate of economic growth.

The relationship between shorter hours on the one hand, and costs, prices, and the rate of economic growth on the other is not a simple one, however. If shorter hours were accompanied by an upsurge in productivity—as they have been at times in the past—employment and output could increase together. The net addition to the total wage bill would add to the stream of personal income and to a higher level of consumer spending. If hours were shortened without a substantial gain in productivity; however, upward pressure on costs could lead to higher prices, and to a decline in demand. The immediate effects of a shorter work week cannot be predicted since they will depend to some extent upon other changes that take place in the economy. It should be noted that the length of the work week has declined sharply in the United States during the past half century without creating the disturbing effects which some predict if there is a further decline. It should also be noted, however, that in recent years workers have sought added leisure more in terms of paid holidays and paid vacations than a further reduction of the average work week.

One large local union—Local No. 3 of the International Brotherhood of Electrical Workers—succeeded in negotiating a 25-hour work week early in 1962. Harry Van Arsdale, the leader of this local, said that the object of the shorter work week was to increase jobs. Critics of the union have insisted that the real object was to increase pay since premium rates would start after 25 hours rather than the 30-hour standard which the latest agreement replaced. Whatever the objective, the success of this powerful local in reducing its standard work week did not set off a chain reaction in other unions. Most demands for a shorter work week in recent years have been for a reduction from 40 to 35, but even these demands have not met with success.[22]

Critics of organized labor have taken issue with union leaders who have sought a shorter work week. They claim that this would not cure the unemployment problem. And some insist it is the unions themselves which have caused the problem of rising unemployment by exerting upward pressure on labor costs. Their position is that if unions could be weakened the labor market itself would cure the unemployment problem. Many union leaders have exercised restraint in negotiating wage increases when unemployment was at relatively high levels. But despite this restraint unemployment continued to rise. This has encouraged union leaders to seek other avenues for solving the unemployment problem. As Jack Barbash has said:

> The point is that workers are losing jobs and you can't expect the unions to take it lying down. Nor is there any evidence that surrender of the unions would result in a more efficient management performance. The evidence is to the contrary. The management performance has increased in efficiency precisely because it has been confronted with the challenge of the unions.[23]

Union leaders deny that they have been responsible for creating unemployment. They have pointed out that various kinds of structural changes in the economy—including automation and other forms of technological progress—have permitted substantial increases in output with reduced labor requirements in many industries. While they have supported the government programs for area redevelopment and retraining, they have insisted that more aggressive efforts will have to be made if the unemployment problem is to be solved. And for this reason they have continued to insist that shorter hours might be necessary if available work is to be spread among all workers who are actively in the labor market.

THE ECONOMIC CONSEQUENCES OF HIGH-LEVEL UNEMPLOYMENT

In a free market economy unemployment cannot be eliminated. Some kinds of work are seasonal and workers in seasonal occupations are idle part of the year. There is also a certain amount of

[22] See "Retreat on Shorter Hours," *Business Week* (September 23, 1961), pp. 111–114.
[23] J. Barbash, "The Union Response to Technological Change," *Changing Patterns in Industrial Relations*, Montreal: McGill University, Industrial Relations Centre (1961), p. 99.

frictional unemployment in a free-market economy. And while the business cycle has been dampened in recent years it has not been eliminated, so that from time to time there is a certain amount of cyclical unemployment which would probably be hard to eliminate completely. The major unemployment problem in a free-market economy is that associated with inadequate total demand, structural change, or a combination of both. The object of full employment policy is to eliminate, or at least to minimize, unemployment due to the latter causes.

Those who have objected to government programs to minimize unemployment stress the costs associated with these programs. But unemployment is far from costless. The unemployed worker is not adding to the nation's output of goods and services but he does continue to consume. To help tide workers over short spells of unemployment, the Employment Security Program was established in the late 1930's. Unemployment insurance payments now amount to billions of dollars annually. Such payments reached an all-time high of about $4.4 billion in 1961. The most ambitious program to improve the operation of the labor market yet suggested in the United States—the Manpower Development and Training Act of 1962—called for appropriations of $435 million to be spent over a three-year period. The disproportion between the amount spent on unemployment insurance benefits and the amounts which have been allocated for programs to reduce unemployment is striking. If average weekly insured unemployment could be cut in half—not an unreasonable goal for a highly productive industrial economy—unemployment insurance benefits would also be roughly halved. If unemployment insurance benefits were reduced, unemployment compensation taxes levied on employers would also be cut. And if one to two million workers could be transferred from the ranks of the unemployed to the productively employed there would be a substantial increase in the nation's output of goods and services.

It is fairly easy to construct a balance sheet which shows—roughly at least—the high cost of unemployment and the economic gains which would accrue to the nation if total employment were increased. But there are hidden costs which cannot be expressed in dollar terms. The displaced worker who is unable to find new employment feels frustrated and rejected. He cannot understand why he is unable to find work in a society in which he sees all around him the evidence of growing affluence. The unemployed worker does not want relief; he wants the independence and dignity that go with productive labor—whatever the nature of his job. Thus there are social and psychological costs associated with high-level unemployment as well as the more easily perceived economic costs.

The problem of persistent unemployment—particularly that resulting from structural changes in the economy—is not likely to be a temporary one. Technological change will displace other workers. Increasingly the American economy is becoming integrated into an international economy encompassing all the nations of the free world; various changes in the international economy will have different kinds of employment and unemployment effects upon the American economy. It will be necessary to cope with new unemployment problems in areas, industries, and occupations other than those which have been affected thus far. There is a strong likelihood that vigorous efforts will be required to make the labor market function more effectively than it has in the recent past.

REFERENCES

BOOKS

Joint Economic Committee, *Employment and Unemployment,* Hearings before the Subcommittee on Economic Statistics, Eighty-seventh Congress (December 18–20, 1961), Washington, D.C.: U.S. Government Printing Office (1962).

———, *Employment and Unemployment,* Report of the Subcommittee on Economic Statistics, Washington, D.C.: U.S. Government Printing Office (February 2, 1962).

———, *Higher Unemployment Rates, 1957–60: Structural Transformation or Inadequate Demand,* Subcommittee on Economic Statistics, Washington, D.C.: U.S. Government Printing Office (1961).

———, *The Structure of Unemployment in Areas of Substantial Labor Surplus,* Study Paper No. 23, Washington, D.C.: U.S. Government Printing Office (1960).

———, *Unemployment: Terminology, Measurement and Analysis,* Subcommittee on Economic Statistics, Washington, D.C.: U.S. Government Printing Office (1961).

Miernyk, William H., *Depressed Industrial Areas—A National Problem,* Planning Pamphlet No. 98, Washington, D.C.: National Planning Association (1957).

Myrdal, Gunnar, *Challenge to Affluence,* New York: Pantheon Books (1963).

President's Committee to Appraise Employment and Unemployment Statistics, *Measuring Employment and Unemployment,* Washington, D.C.: U.S. Government Printing Office (1962).

Studies in Unemployment, Prepared for the Special Committee on Unemployment Problems, U.S. Senate, Washington: U.S. Government Printing Office (1960).

U.S. Department of Labor, *Family Characteristics of the Long-Term Unemployed,* Bureau of Employment Security, TEUC Report Series No. 1 (January 1962).

U.S. Department of Labor, *Who Are the Unemployed?,* Bureau of Labor Statistics (April 1961).

Wilcock, Richard C., and Walter Franke, *Unwanted Workers,* Glencoe, Illinois: The Free Press (1963).

ARTICLES

Barbash, J., "The Union Response to Technological Change," *Changing Patterns in Industrial Relations,* McGill University Industrial Relations Centre (1961).

Clague, Ewan, "Employment and Unemployment," Submitted to the Joint Economic Committee for Hearings on January 1961 Economic Report of the President (mimeographed February 9, 1961).

Dankert, Clyde E., "Shorter Hours—In Theory and Practice," *Industrial and Labor Relations Review* (April 1962), pp. 307–322.

France, Robert R., "Wages, Unemployment, and Prices in the United States, 1890–1932, 1947–1957," *Industrial and Labor Relations Review* (January 1962), pp. 171–190.

Groom, Phyllis P., "Retraining the Unemployed," *Monthly Labor Review* (August 1961), pp. 823–828.

Long, Clarence D., "Prosperity Unemployment and Its Relation to Economic Growth and Inflation," *American Economic Review* (May 1960), pp. 145–161.

Meredith, Jane L., "Long-Term Unemployment in the United States," *Monthly Labor Review* (June 1961), pp. 601–610.

Miernyk, William H., "British and American Approaches to Structural Unemployment," *Industrial and Labor Relations Review* (October 1958), pp. 3–19.

———, "The Incidence of Persistent Unemployment," *Proceedings,* Twelfth Annual Meeting, Industrial Relations Research Association (December 28, 1959).

Phillips, A. W., "The Relation Between Unemployment and the Rate of Change of Money Wage Rates in the United Kingdom, 1861–1957," *Economica* (November 1958), pp. 283–299.

Samuelson, Paul A., and Robert M. Solow, "Analytical Aspect of Anti-Inflation Policy, *American Economic Review* (May 1960), pp. 177–194.

Wilcock, Richard C., "The Secondary Labor Force and the Measurement of Unemployment," *The Measurement and Behavior of Unemployment,* National Bureau of Economic Research, Princeton, N.J.: Princeton University Press (1957), pp. 167–210.

PART 6

manpower management— the state of the american labor movement

Chapter 23 Manpower Management

THE EARLY DAYS OF PERSONNEL MANAGEMENT

Manpower management has always been an important part of the overall managerial function. But the attitudes of employers toward workers have changed drastically over time. Early business managers worked on the assumption that most workers were inherently lazy and had to be driven to their tasks. During the *laissez-faire* period of capitalism, when the philosophy of Social Darwinism was widely accepted, the successful businessman was usually viewed as one who had fought his way to the top in the struggle for the survival of the fittest. Employees were accustomed to authoritarian employer attitudes. In mills and factories, hours were long and the work was hard; supervisors were expected to maintain strict discipline. They were given the responsibility for maintaining output and this responsibility was backed up by unlimited authority to hire and fire.

During the "open shop" era, early in the present century, the attitude of many managements toward unions was clear-cut—keep them out and you'll have no problems with them. Union organizers were often blacklisted during this period, and the "yellow dog" contract was commonplace. The authority of management in the work place was absolute. And it was widely believed that the continued efficiency of our industrial system depended upon the maintenance of this authority.

Needless to say, American workers did not respond favorably to authoritarian management. Worker morale was rarely high. To some early students of management this in itself was a threat to efficiency. If workers could be induced to increase their productivity both labor and management would benefit. This was the philosophy underlying the development of *scientific management.* To this end, Frederick Taylor—originator of the movement—and his successors developed a variety of techniques which they believed would lead to increased efficiency. These techniques included time and motion studies, improved cost accounting, and the optimum utilization of the workers' energies and skills.[1]

By the time scientific management came on the scene the trade union movement was firmly established in this country. Moreover, union leaders were unalterably opposed to the techniques introduced into industry by Taylor, Gantt, Gilbreth, Bedaux and other developers of "efficiency systems." Union leaders regarded scientific management as a "speedup"; the objective, in their view, was to increase output for the benefit of management—not to provide higher wages for labor. Where unions were able to organize workers they fought scientific management and often with at least moderate success. But large segments of manufacturing industry remained unorganized until the late 1930's and until then personnel policies were determined entirely by management.

The Rise of Paternalism

The threat of unions and the philosophy of scientific management brought about a considerable change in personnel policies in many companies. The 19th-century notion that workers had to be driven to their tasks was superseded in many companies by the idea that workers must be urged to *cooperate* with management for the common good of all. During the 1920's, as discussed in an earlier chapter, many "company unions" were formed. And even in many cases where company unions were not formed the dominant personnel philosophy was that of paternalism.

Paternalism, as the term implies, is the philosophy that "papa knows best." A corollary idea is that everyone in the enterprise is laboring for the common good. Efforts are made to keep worker morale high and to win the loyalty of workers to the company and its management. Where paternalism has succeeded, authoritarian management has given way to benevolent management. Commands are replaced by exortation and it is important to make each worker feel that he "belongs." Paternalism brought with it a few modest and low-cost fringe benefits. The company picnic, loans to tide workers over periods of extreme hardship, and perhaps modest dis-

[1] For a lucid discussion of the philosophy of scientific management see Daniel Bell, *The End of Ideology,* Glencoe, Illinois: The Free Press (1960), pp. 226–229.

counts to employees who buy a firm's products are all part of the efforts to weld workers and management into a "company family."[2] Paternalism, where it is practiced, is viewed askance by union leaders. They argue that however well workers are treated by management all decisions are unilateral. Even under paternalism the worker who incurs the displeasure of his boss has no recourse—he can be fired without notice. In some cases, paternalistic labor relations appeared to work well—at least for a time, and this particular offshoot of scientific management made a partial contribution to the changing image of the worker. Even in enterprises where management was definitely not paternalistic, worker incentives were slowly replacing older authoritarian methods for maximizing worker output.

The Rise of Human Relations

The next phase in the evolution of manpower management, and one which some writers feel is not yet completed, was the development of the human relations approach. This concept is usually associated with the work of Elton Mayo who was Professor of Industrial Research at Harvard.[3] The basis of Mayo's approach to human relations was an effort to understand motivation. What is the worker striving for? Is he interested only in maximizing his income? Mayo thought not. "In the place of the older theories of motivation, Mayo developed an image of man as a creature of sentiment, whose overriding desire was to stand well with his fellows."[4] Thus the human relations approach involves the application of large doses of psychology to labor-management relations. This approach remains a controversial one but it has made a contribution to a new view of the worker by management. It has also led to a great deal of research on worker motivation and the sources of worker satisfaction.[5]

The human relations approach to industrial relations has its defenders and its critics. Those who support the use of various psychological techniques in programs to improve worker morale stress the intangible benefits of "recognition of the worker as an individual." But the critics of the human relations approach often regard it as a

[2] This is written in the present tense since paternalism as a philosophy of manpower management is far from extinct.
[3] See Elton Mayo, *The Social Problems of an Industrial Civilization,* Boston: Graduate School of Business Administration, Harvard University (1945).
[4] Reinhard Bendix, "Managers, Workers, and Ideas in the U.S.," in Conrad N. Arensberg, *et al.,* eds., *Research and Industrial Human Relations,* New York: Harper and Brothers (1957), p. 12.
[5] See Harold L. Wilensky, "Human Relations in the Workplace: An Appraisal of Some Recent Research," in Arensberg *et al., op. cit.,* pp. 25–50.

means for the manipulation of workers by management for their own ends, namely, increased profits. Some of its severest critics consider this approach as a sophisticated form of paternalism. In spite of the controversy which surrounds the human relations approach to manpower management, however, few would deny that it has had an important impact upon personnel policies and industrial relations techniques.

THE PROFESSIONALIZATION OF INDUSTRIAL RELATIONS

In the 19th century the owner of an enterprise was generally its manager, and while the owner of a large firm might have a number of assistants he rarely delegated much authority. The rise of the large corporation changed all this, however. In the first place there was a separation of ownership and control. By the 1920's—with a few notable exceptions—the large corporations of this country were owned by investors who had little to do with their operations; they were run by professional managers. The efficient operation of the sprawling industrial giants found in most of our industries led to increasing specialization. The hierarchy of management tended to follow that of a military organization; it was divided into "line" and "staff" officers. As in a military unit, the line officers are the decision-makers, and they rely upon staff officers for technical advice and guidance in making their decisions.

Prior to 1935, the department of personnel or industrial relations rarely occupied an important place in the corporate structure. The major functions of the department in most cases were recruiting workers and keeping unions out of the enterprise. There were relatively few manpower specialists. The Department of Industrial Research had been organized at the Harvard Graduate School of Business Administration as early as 1926 to "organize and direct research concerned with workers and their work in an industrial plant . . ."[6] But there was virtually no academic interest in such fields as labor economics or personnel administration. At that time the authority of employers was largely unchallenged and except in companies whose managements had adopted a paternalistic philosophy there was relatively little interest in worker attitudes.[7]

[6] Elton Mayo, "The Social Problems of an Industrial Civilization," in Herbert G. Heneman, Jr. and John G. Turnbull, eds., *Personnel Administration and Labor Relations,* New York: Prentice-Hall, Inc. (1952), p. 29.

[7] See Douglas V. Brown and Charles A. Myers, "The Changing Industrial Relations Philosophy of American Management," *Proceedings* of the Ninth Annual Meeting, Industrial Relations Research Association (December 1956), pp. 3–4.

THE IMPACT OF UNIONS ON PERSONNEL ADMINISTRATION

The resurgence of unionism in 1935, and its rapid growth during the following decade, led to a series of remarkable changes in personnel administration and labor relations. After the Wagner Act was passed, and its constitutionality upheld, some of the tactics formerly used by companies to keep unions at bay could no longer be employed. Also as industrial unions swept through the manufacturing sector of the American economy along a broad front, more and more companies were faced with the problem of dealing with union negotiators.

Initially, many managements were completely unprepared for this new development. They were forced by law to recognize and bargain with unions if a majority of their workers voted for representation, but there was nothing in their prior training or experience to prepare them for this task. Once a union had been recognized the personnel department had a great deal more to do than simply to operate a hiring office. Personnel managers were faced with the necessity of advising top management about a vast new range of problems. At first much of the brunt was absorbed by the legal departments of corporations. Company lawyers studied the new labor laws and advised management on what could and what could not be done. But excessive legalism rarely contributes to healthy collective bargaining. Out of sheer necessity management specialists in industrial relations were developed. To meet the need for specialists in personnel management and industrial relations, colleges and universities began to give courses in labor economics, labor law, personnel administration and a wide variety of other courses designed to contribute to successful manpower management.

In an earlier day the philosophy of management had been quite simple—keep unions out of the company at whatever cost. But once managements were forced by law to recognize and bargain with unions—regardless of managerial attitudes—it became necessary for company after company to learn how to live and work with a union.

LINE AND STAFF MANAGEMENT IN INDUSTRIAL RELATIONS

In a small business the function of management is direct and clear-cut. In an individual proprietorship, for example, the owner-manager makes all the decisions. If he relies on outside advice at all it will be typically to consult his accountant on such matters as taxes, depreciation, or other technical accounting details. But in larger enterprises there is specialization of management. In corporations, as noted in an earlier section, it is common to distinguish between *line* officers and *staff* management. The line officers are the decision makers and it is the function of staff officers to advise line management.

It is clearly a function of line management to make decisions concerning production, investment, the location of facilities, and the formulation of a pricing policy. But who should determine personnel or industrial relations policies? The typical view advanced by organization theorists has been that line management should also determine basic personnel policies.[8] Line management from the president down to the foreman, according to the traditional view, has complete authority to make decisions. The role of the staff is that of providing counsel and advice.

Broad personnel policy is typically determined by top management but in the day-to-day administration of this policy, decisions are often made by foremen. Indeed, prior to the mid-1930's, the foremen in some concerns had a considerable amount of authority. Prior to World War I—especially in smaller companies—"the foreman carried out virtually all personnel functions other than determining general wage changes."[9]

With the emergence of powerful unions and the spread of collective bargaining, manpower management has become increasingly complex. As Dunlop and Myers have noted, personnel policies cannot always be divorced from other policies. "The responsibility for settling grievances, for labor morale, and for the quality and amount of production cannot be bifurcated."[10] Thus top management must still accept the responsibility for setting the broad guidelines of personnel policies. As a consequence of this it is still a popular view that the role of the industrial relations director or personnel officer is to advise line management; that is, personnel relations is still widely considered to be a staff function.

Until fairly recently the role of line and staff in industrial relations had been discussed in somewhat abstract terms. There was relatively

[8] See, for example, Paul and Faith Pigors, "Who Should Make Personnel Policies?" from M.I.T. Publications in Social Science, Series 2, No. 29 (reprinted from *Personnel,* November 1950), p. 2; and John T. Dunlop and Charles A. Myers, "The Industrial Relations Function in Management," *Personnel* (March 1955), p. 4.
[9] Dunlop and Myers, *op. cit.,* p. 6.
[10] *Ibid.,* p. 4.

little empirical evidence to draw upon in testing various hypotheses about personnel management. In the mid-1950's, however, Charles Myers and John Turnbull conducted an important study of line and staff industrial relations functions in 34 firms.[11] Employment in the sample firms ranged from 500 to almost 30,000. Of the selected firms, 25 (74 per cent) engaged in collective bargaining. The firms covered a wide variety of manufacturing industries and included a modest sprinkling of non-manufacturing establishments. Most of the firms were located in New England but slightly less than one-fourth of the sample firms were located in other regions. The authors found no evidence of geographic bias.

In all of the firms studied the industrial relations director, or personnel officer, indicated "that he operated at staff capacity or, at most, in some combination of staff and line capacity." But in each case as the personnel officer went on to describe his functions, "it was clear that in a number of situations *he made the effective decisions*."[12] In one extreme case, for example, an industrial relations director who insisted that he was a staff man said that he:

> . . . made decisions on most promotions, could overrule the foreman on disciplinary action without getting higher approval . . . disciplined foremen for failing to follow established personnel policies, had rather complete discretion in negotiating the terms of a contract with the union, was sole interpreter of the union agreement for management, and handled all grievances after the first step![13]

It appears that the traditional concept of the industrial relations director or personnel manager as a *pure* staff officer is an oversimplification. Indeed, as a result of their study, Myers and Turnbull have defined a range of policies for administering the industrial relations function. These are:

1. The line handles the personnel function completely.
2. The line delegates to an industrial relations unit the responsibility for providing advice only.
3. The line formally delegates to an industrial relations department the responsibility for providing advice *and* service, with the line retaining and utilizing continuing decision-making and review authority.
4. The line formally delegates to an industrial relations department

[11] Charles A. Myers and John G. Turnbull, "Line and Staff in Industrial Relations," *Harvard Business Review* (July-August 1956), pp. 113–124.
[12] *Ibid.*, p. 114.
[13] *Ibid.*

the responsibility for making final decisions . . . subject only to *periodic* review . . .

5. The industrial relations department gets by default (or may even usurp) the decision-making authority in a given functional area.

The type 1 policy would be found only in relatively small concerns and Myers and Turnbull encountered none in their study. Indeed, they found that all but one of the non-unionized companies, and most of the unionized companies, fell into type 3. In a few of the unionized companies, however, they found evidence of the type 4 policy. For example, "in at least five cases [the industrial relations] department had extensive authority in the negotiation of the collective bargaining agreement . . ."[14]

In a majority of the cases studied, line officers decided who was to be hired, promoted, transferred, layed off or retired. In discipline and discharge cases the line again had basic authority, although in most cases, approval of the personnel department was required before discharge. In all of the companies line management had responsibility for the wage and salary program, but personnel departments had rather complete authority in administering the programs. And in such important areas as contract negotiations, interpreting agreements, and processing grievances, staff officers played an important role in the decision-making process.

In general, the amount of authority exercised by industrial relations departments was greater in large than in small firms. This is not surprising. For one thing, large companies frequently deal with large unions also staffed with specialists. On both sides of the bargaining table staff men will be selected because of their expert knowledge. Neither the line management of a large company nor the elected officers of a large union can be expected to familiarize themselves with a great mass of legal, economic, and statistical detail. As a consequence, the staff men are often the *effective* decision makers. As Myers and Turnbull conclude: "The larger the company the stronger the union pressures, the more skilled the staff, and the greater the common purpose of line and staff executives, the more logical it is to delegate to the staff the authority to make decisions in policy interpretations and to take a more active role in policy formulation."[15]

[14] *Ibid.*, p. 115.

[15] *Ibid.*, p. 124. See also, "Personnel Manager," in Herbert G. Heneman, Jr. and John G. Turnbull, *Personnel Administration and Labor Relations,* New York: Prentice-Hall, Inc. (1952), p. 17.

THE DETERMINANTS OF LABOR-MANAGEMENT RELATIONS

One need not be a specialist in labor economics or industrial relations to recognize that union-managment relations vary widely from company to company. Some firms seem to be faced with a strike—or the threat of a strike—year in and year out. Others have worked out harmonious relations with their unions. Why is this so? Are some unions easier to get along with than others? Or are labor-management relations largely the result of management attitudes? The answers to these questions are not simple. Some unions are undoubtedly more militant than others and the relative strength of unions and management is far from uniform among industries and regions. It is a common belief, however, that "top management gets the kind of labor relations it deserves."[16]

Of course, it might be argued, management could always get along with the union—by giving in to all of the union demands. But students of industrial relations are not convinced that this would lead to a good labor-management relationship. Even if it satisfied the union, management would scarcely consider this to be the ideal solution. At one extreme a "hard" approach to industrial relations can produce undesirable results because of low worker morale and a general lack of harmony. At the other extreme, a "soft" approach might lead to harmony, but also undoubtedly to indifferent performance.[17]

Management need not abdicate its responsibility in order to have good industrial relations, however. Stagner has concluded that "if it is not wholly true that management gets the kind of union it deserves, it is at least true that management attitudes play an important role."[18] Stagner goes on to point out that management has more freedom to act—and to initiate change—than does the union, and in his opinion management has more to gain from good labor-management relations than do the union officers.

Psychologists and social psychologists who have studied labor relations emphasize the importance of good worker morale in achieving good work performance. They also recognize that discipline is required on the job. Yet discipline and high morale are far from incompatible. Effective two-way communications have often been stressed as one of the ingredients of good morale. The dissatis-

[16] Ross Stagner, "Do Management Attitudes Determine Union-Management Relationships?" *Current Economic Comment* (February 1955), p. 3.
[17] Douglas M. McGregor, "The Human Side of Enterprise," *Adventure in Thought and Action,* School of Industrial Management, Massachusetts Institute of Technology (June 1957), p. 24.
[18] Stagner, *op. cit.,* p. 9.

fied worker who cannot air his grievances is likely to be an unproductive worker. This is why grievance procedures have become standard in most labor-management agreements. But effective communication is not enough to ensure harmonious labor-management relations. The management of a concern might have the highest regard for its workers; it might also have effective communication with both workers and unions. This alone does not guarantee a lack of labor-management conflict.[19] The basic attitude of management toward the union or unions with which it deals will still have much to do with the state of labor-management relations in a given company. This has been suggested in our earlier discussion of the stages of collective bargaining, (see Chapter 17, pp. 304–311) but that discussion was about end results. What tactics are used by management at various stages of the labor-management relationship?

MANAGEMENT ATTITUDES TOWARD TRADE UNIONS

Management attitudes toward unions cover a broad range. Some managements bitterly resent the intrusion of a union; other managements have highly cooperative relationships with unions. One interesting classification of management attitudes, and of collective bargaining tactics, has been made by Robert N. McMurry.[20] While other classifications could be developed, McMurry's is useful since it illustrates widely-diverging philosophies of labor-management relations. McMurry has identified the four philosophies he discusses by naming them after the representatives of management most closely associated with them.

Boulwareism

This approach to labor-management relations is generally attributed to Lemuel Boulware, formerly Vice-President of Employee and Community Relations of the General Electric Company. According to McMurry, wherever Boulwareism is practiced management has a rather intransigent attitude toward unions. This is illustrated by the following policies:

1. Management tends to bypass the union and communicate directly with employees on day-to-day problems.
2. Management competes with the union for its employees' alle-

[19] See Paul Pigors, "Communication in Industry: A Cure of Conflict?" *Industrial and Labor Relations Review* (July 1953), p. 508.

[20] Robert N. McMurry, "War and Peace in Labor Relations," *Harvard Business Review* (November-December 1955), pp. 48–61.

giance by attempting to convince workers that it is sincerely interested in their welfare.

3. Management follows a tough line in negotiating with the union. It will publicly state its final offer during negotiations with a deadline for acceptance and a warning that settlements beyond this deadline will not be retroactive.
4. Management communicates its offers directly to its workers and the public rather than to the union.

General Electric is a large company, and it is said to deal with at least 100 unions. Management has insisted that it is deeply concerned about the welfare of its workers but it has not gone out of its way to get along with union leaders. Boulwareism represents what economists refer to as a "take it or leave it" approach to price (or wage) setting. While the result has not led to harmonious relations between union leaders and management, General Electric has been in a sufficiently strong position to stick to its publicly-announced offers. There is little evidence of give and take at the bargaining table. Boulwareism has spread to a few companies, although this philosophy of labor-management relations has not been widely adopted. Where it has been followed, however, unions have had little success in breaking down management's intransigent attitude.[21]

Crawfordism

This approach is not as well known as Boulwareism. It was developed by Fred Crawford, President of Thompson Products Company. It is predicated on the assumption that if management does a good job of holding employees' loyalties workers will feel no real need for a union. Crawfordism has been defined by McMurry as follows:

1. It is a one-man show dominated by Mr. Crawford who has been described as a "natural leader of tremendous vitality, self assurance, and singleness of purpose who believes strongly in 'rugged individualism.' "
2. Mr. Crawford is said to be highly sensitive to his employees' needs and fulfills those needs to win their loyalty.
3. He is highly adaptable and is willing to use unorthodox means, if necessary, to achieve his goals.
4. He insists that "management must be strong" and delegates

[21] See Stephen J. Galpin, "Boulwareism," *The Wall Street Journal* (November 3, 1954); and Paul Jacobs, "The Showdown at GE," *The Reporter* (October 27, 1960), pp. 35–36.

authority to his subordinates while encouraging them to develop their own initiative.

5. He has been described as an effective showman who reduces complex economic concepts to homely parables. He also has frequent personal contacts with his workers, and maintains an effective communications setup to keep everyone informed.

The major difference between Boulwareism and Crawfordism is that the former can be used by a large company while the latter is restricted to small concerns. Both approaches contain an element of paternalism and both are based on the notion that management knows better than anyone else what is best for its workers. Where Boulwareism is practiced management attempts to deal directly with its workers, although it goes through the legal formalities of negotiations and signs labor-management agreements with unions. Where Crawfordism is practiced management attempts to win the loyalties of its workers and to convince them that unions serve no useful purpose. But management does not engage in open conflict with the union. A more subtle tactic is employed. This consists of efforts to convince workers that a union is not needed in a company where management recognizes its workers' needs and is willing to try to satisfy those needs.

Fairlessness

This approach to labor-management relations has been named after Benjamin Fairless, formerly Chairman of the Board of the United States Steel Corporation. Under Mr. Fairless U.S. Steel attempted to maintain amicable relations with its unions. The essence of this philosophy, as summarized by McMurry, is as follows:

1. Management feels that if it manifests a sympathetic understanding of the needs and problems of its unions, their members and their leaders, and implements this understanding by appropriate action, the union will respond similarly toward management's needs and problems.
2. Management limits its communications to employees to union channels or to joint company-union channels.
3. Management tackles problems realistically at the grass-roots level rather than adopting a rigid and legalistic posture in defense of its own prerogatives.
4. Management recognizes the need and value of building and maintaining cooperative relationships on a day-to-day basis.

The objective is to achieve industrial peace and a high degree of worker satisfaction by maintaining good relations with unions.

This approach to union-management relations stands in marked contrast to the two earlier approaches described by McMurry.

Studebakerism

This rather awkward term has been used by McMurry to describe the union-management philosophy developed by Harold Vance, former President, and Paul Hoffman, former Chairman of the Executive Committee, of the Studebaker-Packard Corporation. This approach is based on the notion that groups work together best when they collaborate for their mutual benefit rather than when they attempt to solve problems solely on the basis of economic power. According to McMurry, the union contract at Studebaker-Packard gave shop stewards and workers "a real measure of the control and power which the factory manager, the personnel manager, and the top foreman have in other plants."[22]

Among other things, the Vance-Hoffman approach provided the following:

1. The company has, in effect, subcontracted to the union the responsibility for keeping the assembly line running for a group piece rate.
2. The union decides the number of men to be employed on a production line, and thus determines their earnings.
3. The stewards have an important voice in the allocation of jobs through their interpretation of seniority rules.

Critics of Studebakerism have attributed the financial difficulties faced by the Studebaker Corporation to its unusually permissive labor-relations philosophy. It has been claimed, for example, that the seniority system led to virtual chaos. The critics also feel that the Studebaker management abdicated its responsibility, and failed to enforce the industrial discipline needed to achieve efficient operations. Defenders of Vance and Hoffman deny that Studebaker's permissive labor-relations policy was responsible for the company's financial difficulties. They attribute these to the competitive pressures exerted on a small company by the "Big Three" of the automobile industry.

It is worth repeating that the four philosophies described by McMurry do not by any means cover the spectrum of management attitudes toward unions. A number of years ago Harbison and Coleman studied about 100 plant-level collective bargaining situ-

[22] McMurry, *op. cit.*, p. 49. See also Daniel Katz, "Satisfactions and Deprivations in Industrial Life," *Roots of Industrial Conflict,* New York: McGraw-Hill Book Company (1954), p. 104.

ations mostly in newly-unionized manufacturing industries. While they classified these relationships into various categories ranging from "armed truce" at one extreme to union-management cooperation at the other, they also noted the great diversity in labor-management relationships. "In the mass production industries," they stated, "there are many types of union-management relations. Indeed, no two are exactly alike."[23] They considered the classification of labor-management relations which they developed as "models" or as "clustering points" on the continuum of all collective bargaining relationships in the country.

CHANGING MANAGEMENT ATTITUDES TOWARD COLLECTIVE BARGAINING

There is no simple, linear evolution of collective bargaining or of management attitudes toward unions and the collective bargaining process. While there are discernible long-run trends, there are also variations around these trends. During the latter half of the 1930's, management in this country was faced with something new. For the first time collective bargaining was a legal requirement if a majority of workers voted for union representation. Coupled with this were the problems engendered by the worst depression this country has even known. These conditions stimulated union growth. Management was scarcely prepared for the task of collective bargaining on a broad scale. Unions took the initiative at the bargaining table and they held this initiative throughout World War II although their ability to negotiate wage increases during the conflict was severely limited. They did, however, negotiate many so-called fringe benefits, and consolidated their gains in union membership.

The latter half of the 1940's was a period of considerable labor unrest characterized by rapidly rising prices and wages. Some managements attempted to eliminate the uncertainties of annual bargaining by negotiating long-term contracts. Annual improvement factors and cost-of-living or "escalator" clauses were incorporated in some agreements. But unions continued to advance new proposals in collective bargaining, and management strategy appeared to be that of fighting a delaying action.

There was a notable change in management attitudes during the 1950's, however. The union growth curve slowed down and toward

[23] Frederick H. Harbison and John R. Coleman, *Goals and Strategy in Collective Bargaining,* New York: Harper & Brothers (1951), p. 18.

the end of the decade it began to drop. Although the nation was faced with a number of economic problems—notably "creeping inflation" and persistent unemployment—the post-war period was one of general prosperity. In this environment management began to develop a tougher line toward collective bargaining. Not only have some managements adopted a firmer posture at the bargaining table, but union proposals have often been met with management counter-proposals. Viewed in broad outline, collective bargaining during the early 1960's was quite different from that of the immediate postwar period. In terms of power relationships, unions lost ground and management gained.[24]

During the period of rapid union growth concern was often expressed about the increasing power of unions. Some feared that unions would dominate the economy; one leading economist suggested that we were headed toward a "laboristic society."[25] But in a volume published after his death, Slichter repudiated the notion that our society was about to become a laboristic one. He indicated that "the rise of white-collar workers will mean a slight dilution of the strength of the trade union movement and more of a balance on the whole between unions and employers."[26] Some union leaders are also aware of the change in their power position. They recognize that the period of rapid growth is behind them[27] and this has been reflected in a tempering of their demands at the bargaining table.

THE FUTURE OF PERSONNEL ADMINISTRATION AND MANPOWER MANAGEMENT

Certain trends in the labor force can be projected for the next decade with a small margin of error. This is so because those who will enter the labor force within the next ten years have already been born. These trends suggest some of the problems which manpower managers will be faced with in the immediate future and provide the basis for informed speculation about the future of personnel management.

[24] For further discussion of this point see William H. Miernyk, *Trade Unions in the Age of Affluence,* New York: Random House (1962).
[25] See Sumner H. Slichter, "Profits in a Laboristic Society," *Harvard Business Review* (May 1949), pp. 346–361.
[26] Sumner H. Slichter, *Economic Growth in the United States: Its History, Problems and Prospects,* ed. by John T. Dunlop, Baton Rouge: Louisiana State University Press (1961), p. 187.
[27] See Solomon Barkin, *The Decline of the Labor Movement,* Santa Barbara, California: Center for the Study of Democratic Institutions (1961).

During the depression years of the 1930's the birth rate fell. Thus during the early 1950's the entry rate into the labor force also dropped. It was during this time that various forms of automation began to be introduced in manufacturing, and electronic data-processing began to be widely used in some of the larger non-manufacturing establishments such as banks and insurance companies. It is fortunate that these major technological developments occurred at a time when the labor force entry rate was relatively low. As it was, there were dislocations but these would have been far more severe if more youngsters had been looking for jobs at a time when some workers were being displaced by computers and materials-handling devices.

The birth rate rose rapidly during World War II, however, and contrary to the expectation of some demographers it has remained high throughout the postwar period. By the middle of the 1960's there will be a bulge in the number of youngsters finishing high school. Many of these will go on to higher education but others will move directly into the labor market. Rapid economic growth will be required to absorb the new job seekers without displacement of older workers. Meanwhile the "thin generation"—those born during the 1930's—will be working its way up the labor force age ladder. Thus during the latter half of the 1960's there will be a shortage of workers in the "prime age group" in the labor force while an increasing number of youngsters will be seeking employment.[28] Charles Myers suggests that the relative shortage of workers in the prime age group will require the better selection, placement, and training of workers if labor turnover is to be reduced. It is in this age group, Myers notes, that the young professionals, the skilled craftsmen, supervisors, and junior executives—all key people in any organization—are generally found.

By 1975, the "thin generation" will be in the 35–45 age group while the war babies, and those born during the early postwar period, will be moving into the labor force in increasing numbers. Meanwhile, the composition of the labor force will continue to change. White-collar workers will grow both in absolute and relative terms, while there will be slower growth in goods-producing industries. There will undoubtedly continue to be a premium on highly trained and skilled scientific and technical personnel as we move farther into the space age. Shifts in the age structure and the

[28] See Charles A. Myers, "The Challenge of the 1960's: Manpower Management," *Personnel* (May–June, 1959), MIT Reprint Series II, No. 75, (no page numbers given).

occupational composition of the work force will contribute to the problems of training, placement, and the efficient utilization of manpower.

What of the future of personnel administration? Professor Myers has reviewed some of the criticisms of personnel administration and has suggested a new orientation for this important managerial function.[29] Personnel administration has been criticized by students of management for its lack of internal cohesion. At the same time it has been criticized by union representatives, as well as by some independent scholars, as a technique for manipulating human beings.[30] In a broader context, there has been criticism of the assumptions underlying much of management's philosophy about workers; especially the assumptions that the average man is indolent by nature, lacks ambition, dislikes responsibility, is inherently self-centered, indifferent to organizational needs, resistant to change, "gullible, not very bright, the ready dupe of the charlatan and the demagogue."[31]

Improvements in Personnel Administration

Viewing these and other criticisms of personnel administration, Myers concludes that they "have hit pretty close to the mark in many organizations."[32] He has suggested some general directions which might be taken to improve personnel administration:

1) *A re-emphasis on the underlying philosophy of dealing with people in a democratic society.* Techniques of personnel administration *can* be manipulative, but they need not be. The democratic philosophy is based on a belief in the dignity of man. Myers notes that we have fallen short of the ideal upon which our political philosophy is based but it remains the foundation of our political faith and our political theory. In his view, it should also be the foundation of a sound program of personnel management.

2) *How can the organization provide those opportunities which most people seek at work?* In some organizations there are many layers of management and supervision and despite much talk about two-way communication there is relatively little of the latter. Over-

[29] Charles A. Myers, "What About the Future of Personnel Administration?" *Personnel Administration* (September–October, 1958), MIT Reprint Series 2, No. 73.
[30] *Ibid.*, pp. 5–6.
[31] Douglas M. McGregor, "The Human Side of Enterprise," *Adventures in Thought and Action,* Proceedings of the Fifth Annual Convocation, School of Industrial Management, M.I.T. (June 1957), p. 24.
[32] Myers, *op. cit.*, p. 7.

centralization of organization, in the view of some, fails to challenge the best capacities and interests of workers and lower echelons of management alike. The suggested solution is more decentralization of responsibility and authority. There are obvious limits to which this can be pushed, of course, but there is undoubtedly some optimal organizational pattern which will elicit the best work—and provide the greatest satisfaction—to all the members of an organization. Myers is of the opinion that personnel administrators should do all they can to achieve such an organizational arrangement.

3) *Is management consulting its subordinates at all levels to get their ideas and suggestions on how work can be done better and how mutual problems can be solved?* The critics of personnel administration answer this question in the negative, at least in many enterprises. In most organizations management still makes decisions and workers carry out orders. Myers points out that under the Scanlon Plan—and this could also be said of other forms of labor-management cooperation—both productivity and job satisfaction have been improved when everyone in the organization has an opportunity to contribute useful ideas. Up to now, programs of labor-management cooperation have succeeded in a number of middle-sized and relatively small establishments but they have not been adopted by large-scale enterprises. There is no logical reason why such programs of cooperation would not work in larger enterprises, however, particularly if the above recommendation for a greater amount of decentralization of authority and responsibility were carried out.

CONCLUSIONS

The management of manpower has become an increasingly important part of the total managerial function. In an earlier day, before unions became an important force in the economy, personnel policies were decided unilaterally by management. But as Sumner Slichter noted a number of years ago, one result of widespread collective bargaining was the introduction of civil rights into industry.[33] Management no longer has complete freedom of decision in matters which affect the work force.

The impact of unions on manpower management has not been limited to those firms whose managements have completely accepted

[33] Sumner H. Slichter, *Union Policies and Industrial Management,* Washington, D.C.: The Brookings Institution (1941), p. 1.

trade unionism. Even where unions have not been fully accepted—or where there is no union at all—management must take into account the reaction of workers to changes in personnel policies. Return to the authoritarian ways of the past might increase the solidarity of workers and strengthen the position of union leaders. In the case of non-union workers, it could drive them into the arms of union organizers. The influence of unions on manpower management has extended far beyond the firms they have been able to organize. It probably is not going too far to say that one of the major causes of the slowdown in union growth which occurred at the end of the 1950's was the revolution in manpower management which resulted from the rapid growth of unions during the preceding twenty-five years.

REFERENCES

BOOKS

Arensberg, Conrad M. *et al., Research in Industrial Human Relations,* New York: Harper and Brothers (1957).

Barkin, Solomon, *The Decline of the Labor Movement,* Santa Barbara, California: Center for the Study of Democratic Institutions (1961).

Bell, Daniel, *The End of Ideology,* Glencoe, Illinois: The Free Press (1960).

Harbison, Frederick H. and John R. Coleman, *Goals and Strategy in Collective Bargaining,* New York: Harper and Brothers (1951).

Heneman, Herbert G., Jr. and John G. Turnbull, *Personnel Administration and Labor Relations,* New York: Prentice-Hall, Inc. (1952).

Miernyk, William H., *Trade Unions in the Age of Affluence,* New York: Random House (1962).

ARTICLES

Brown, Douglas V. and Charles A. Myers, "The Changing Industrial Relations Philosophy of American Management," *Proceedings,* Industrial Relations Research Association (December 1956).

Dunlop, John T. and Charles A. Myers, "The Industrial Relations Function in Management," *Personnel* (March 1955), pp. 3–10.

Garbarino, Joseph W., "Bargaining Strategy and the Form of Contracts," *Industrial Relations* (February 1962), pp. 73–88.

McGregor, Douglas M., "The Human Side of Enterprise," *Adventure in Thought and Action,* Cambridge, Massachusetts: School of Industrial Management, M.I.T. (June 1957).

———, "An Uneasy Look at Performance Appraisal," *Harvard Business Review* (May–June 1957), pp. 89–94.

McMurry, Robert N., "War and Peace in Labor Relations," *Harvard Business Review* (November–December 1955), pp. 48–61.

Myers, Charles A., "What About the Future of Personnel Administration?" *Personnel Administration* (September–October, 1958), pp. 5–12.

———, "The Challenge of the 1960's: Manpower Management," *Personnel* (May–June 1959).

———, "Lessons from Abroad for American Management," *The Journal of Business of the University of Chicago* (January 1960), pp. 1–9.

Myers, Charles A. and John G. Turnbull, "Line and Staff in Industrial Relations," *Harvard Business Review* (July–August 1956), pp. 113–124.

Pigors, Paul, "Communication in Industry: A Cure of Conflict?" *Industrial and Labor Relations Review* (July 1953), pp. 497–509.

Pigors, Paul and Faith, "Personnel Policies: Plan and Purpose," *Personnel* (July–November 1950), MIT Reprint Series No. 2, No. 29.

Stagner, Ross, "Do Management Attitudes Determine Union-Management Relationships?" *Current Economic Comment* (February 1955), pp. 3–9.

Chapter 24 The Present State and the Future of American Unions

THE IMAGE OF UNION POWER

In the brief span of two decades—from 1935 to 1955—American unions grew from about 4 million to almost 17 million members. The position of unions in our society has changed radically since the early 1930's. At that time unions were predominantly of the craft variety; they had scarcely penetrated the nation's mass production industries. Their political power was limited and employers gave unions scant consideration when making business decisions. Today employers and governments must reckon with unions when major decisions are being made. As a *Fortune* writer noted a few years ago, "whether viewed as an economic, social, or political force, unionism possesses enormous power, and it is in the nature of power that, once possessed, it will be used."[1]

The growth of union power is attributed by some to government encouragement: "The extraordinary leverage of unionism on our society is not necessarily in the nature of things. On the contrary, it has been to some extent created, and then heavily buttressed, by government legislation."[2] This writer concluded, however, that "what the state has given, the state can also diminish or take away."[3] The same position has been taken by Edward H. Chamberlin, a noted economist. "Unions have achieved their present position

[1] John Davenport, "Labor Unions in the Free Society," *Fortune* (April 1959), p. 212.
[2] *Ibid.*
[3] *Ibid.*

largely through public indulgence, and if the public becomes less indulgent, union power can be curbed."[4]

Conservative writers discussing union power generally state—or at least imply—that unions have *too much* power. A commonly-held view of critics of trade unionism is that under present laws unions are free to exercise monopoly power while monopoly in business is restrained. Unions have also been blamed by many for inflation and unemployment. Some have suggested that now that they have achieved powerful positions, union leaders have developed a callous disregard for all workers except those who help maintain them in office. The problem, as those who have expressed concern about the growth of unions see it, is not the use of power but its abuse.

The abuse of union power was widely discussed a few years ago when it was the subject of an intensive congressional investigation conducted by the McClellan Committee. This investigation revealed that some union leaders had indeed taken advantage of their positions for personal gain. Others used strong-arm tactics to force relatively weak employers into line and there was evidence that some unions collaborated with underworld elements for the illicit gain of both. Many of the McClellan Committee hearings were televised; they were also given prominent attention by the press. The public was shocked by the revelations of graft and corruption. The hearings clearly established that only a small minority of American unions were tainted by corrupt leadership, and that only a few other union leaders used questionable tactics to achieve legitimate ends. But the public does not always discriminate carefully. The emphasis in the McClellan hearings, after all, was on corruption and illegal activities and the labor movement as a whole suffered in the eyes of the public as the result of the activities of a handful of union officers who were totally unrepresentative of the great mass of union leaders.

Not only has there been a tendency to generalize too broadly about the corruption of union leaders, but there has also been a tendency to generalize unwarrantably about union power. Some unions undoubtedly are stronger than the employers with whom they deal. In other labor-management relationships power is relatively evenly balanced. At times the union appears to achieve its objectives with relatively little difficulty; at other times employers appear to have the edge at the bargaining table. Market conditions, the level of unemployment, technological change in the industry involved, and

[4] Edward H. Chamberlin, "Can Union Power be Curbed?" *Atlantic Monthly* (June 1959), p. 50.

various other factors contribute to such shifting power relationships. Finally, there are other unions which are relatively weak. Unions in highly competitive industries, such as textiles and shoes, for example, have not demonstrated much power at the bargaining table.

Some unions have been able to organize only a minority of workers in the occupations they represent and such unions have typically won only modest gains for their members. If they press too hard they are likely to place the employers who recognize them at a competitive disadvantage *vis-á-vis* non-union firms. In terms of power, unions range along a spectrum. There are a few which are able to virtually dictate the terms which employers must accept. At the other extreme, some unions must constantly exercise restraint lest they play into the hands of non-union employers.[5]

THE PRESENT STATE OF THE LABOR MOVEMENT

The institution of trade unionism received a setback as a result of the McClellan hearings. But this was largely in terms of the public's attitude toward unions. Other forces have been at work, however, which have affected the growth of union membership. In 1954, for example, American union members accounted for 25.1 per cent of the nation's labor force and 35.1 per cent of non-agricultural employment. By 1962, these percentages had declined to 22.2 and 30 respectively. In absolute terms, union membership had changed only slightly during this period but the total labor force and non-agricultural employment had increased rapidly with a consequent relative decline in union strength.

Membership in some unions has increased while other unions have been faced with an absolute loss in members. This is not the result of disaffection on the part of trade unionists; it is due to various economic changes. The relocation of industry, technological advances, shifts in demand, and a changing pattern of international trade are among the forces which have eliminated many jobs formerly held by union members. At the same time, unions have met with relatively little success in organizing non-manufacturing firms and they have also made relatively little headway in organizing factory workers in the South.

How do the events of recent years square with the image of union power discussed in the introductory section of this chapter? Some

[5] See William H. Miernyk, "The Need for a New Look at Union Power," *Labor Law Journal* (November 1959), pp. 776–780.

writers have continued to stress the growing power of unions. The best statistics available, however, indicate rather clearly that the relative strength of unions has been declining for several years—something which is difficult to reconcile with the thesis of growing union power. Commenting on this, Solomon Barkin, former research director of the Textile Workers Union of America, has said:

> The anomaly of the day is that the opponents of trade unions are seeking to restrain the economic and political activities of unions at a time when their growth has been halted. Many individual unions are shrinking in size, and the membership of the total movement has declined. The proportion of union members in the total work force has also gone down. Not only are employees not joining unions in the vast numbers they once did but employers are increasingly resisting the spread of organization and are challenging the mightiest industrial unions in outright economic battle, in several instances forcing unions to withdraw economic demands and in other instances weakening and even destroying the organization.[6]

In a similar vein, A. H. Raskin, a member of the editorial board of the New York *Times,* and a respected observer of union affairs, has said:

> . . . Each day brings compelling reminders that labor strength is on the downgrade and that, like the colonial powers of Europe, its leaders may soon be presiding over the dismantling of their own empires unless they can find imaginative new approaches to the challenges thrust on them by automation, intensified foreign competition, and a dramatic shift in the composition of the work force.[7]

The loss of momentum in the trade union movement, in Raskin's view, has limited the ability of unions to win sizeable wage increases or other benefits for their members. Partly because of excess capacity—which means that industry has the ability to produce more in a given time period than can be sold—some large companies are not particularly averse to occasional strikes. Public concern over the problem of inflation has further limited the ability of union leaders to press for substantial wage increases. The philosophy of gearing wage increases to productivity gains appears to be gaining acceptance among union leaders. "Such a slide-rule system," Raskin believes, "with total increases of eight to ten cents an hour each year, will make it more and more difficult to explain to the average worker what economic service he obtains in return for his union dues."[8]

[6] Solomon Barkin, *The Decline of the Labor Movement,* Santa Barbara, California: Center for the Study of Democratic Institutions (1961), p. 5.
[7] A. H. Raskin, "The Squeeze on the Unions," *The Atlantic* (April 1961), p. 55.
[8] *Ibid.,* p. 59.

The lack of success among unions in recent years in achieving either gains in membership, or substantial economic benefits for the workers they now represent, has undoubtedly contributed to the apathy of union members. And non-members might show more interest in unions if the dynamism of the period of rapid growth could be revived.[9]

Some students of the labor movement have suggested that the decline of union strength in the late 1950's and early 1960's is a temporary phenomenon. Perhaps the strongest exponent of this view is Professor Irving Bernstein. Bernstein recognizes that unions have been faced with problems in recent years, but he appears to be unwilling to accept the conclusion that union membership has reached the saturation point or that unions have attained an "organizational plateau." In his opinion, unions are already beginning to make progress in the so-called "inpenetrable" sectors of the labor force. He feels that unions will make progress in small towns, among government employees, and in the organization of non-manual workers. He does not expect such organization to occur on a massive scale, but he does anticipate gradual growth. "The American labor movement has not saturated its organizable potential. The door is not shut, locked and bolted; it *can* be opened . . . the time for testing lies ahead. But as of now, don't count the unions out."[10]

There are differences of opinion among economists, historians, and other students of the labor movement about its short-run prospects. The majority view, however, appears to be that unions have already encountered serious difficulties, and that their problems are likely to become more severe unless there is a revitalization of the labor movement. And the latter does not seem imminent. But what do students of the labor movement have to say about the long-term future of American trade unions?

THE LONG-TERM OUTLOOK FOR AMERICAN UNIONS

Four views of the future of American unions will be examined in this section. The first considers the trade union outlook in the 1960's, an intermediate projection. The second deals with the union outlook in the late 1970's, a genuinely long-term view. The

[9] Barkin, *op. cit.*, pp. 36–52. See also, Gus Tyler, *A New Philosophy for Labor*, Santa Barbara, California: Center for the Study of Democratic Institutions (1959).

[10] Irving Bernstein, "Don't Count the Unions Out," *Challenge* (November 1961), Reprint No. 106, Institute of Industrial Relations, U.C.L.A., p. 3. See also his article, "The Growth of American Unions, 1945–1960," *Labor History* (Spring 1961), pp. 131–157.

third set of ideas relate to a period two to three decades away. Finally, the comments of a leading labor economist and labor historian about the future of the American labor movement, without specifying a particular time period, will be summarized.

Fewer Strikes and Smaller Wages Increase in the 1960's

According to Professor Oscar Ornati, in the absence of a war or a major depression "we can expect the labor relations of the 1960's to be marked by increased government participation and less frequent strikes."[11] Evidently Ornati expects the relative decline in union membership to continue. But for the unions, he concludes, this will not be an unmixed blessing. "The realization that unions do not now, and are not likely in the future, to dominate the economy of the United States helps the process of their acceptance as a permanent aspect of the American scene."[12]

In recent years, most unions have negotiated relatively modest wage increases and this is likely to continue in the immediate future. The relatively small wage increases of the 1960's, in Ornati's view, will not be due to union concern about wage-push inflation. More aggressive competition—both in domestic markets and from abroad—is expected to impose restraints upon union wage demands.

The failure of unions to grow rapidly and the likelihood of small wage increases will not necessarily mean a complete lack of vigor in the labor movement according to Ornati. He expects a greater amount of union participation in tripartite organizations at all levels of government. During the coming decade, in his opinion, unions will be represented in such government agencies as the Federal Reserve Board and "on most of the federal and state regulatory commissions as well as in other government agencies concerned with social and economic problems."[13]

Although there will be fewer strikes in the 1960's than there have been in the past, according to the Ornati thesis, this does not mean a complete absence of labor disputes. However the strikes of the coming decade will be concerned primarily with working conditions and work rules rather than wage demands. Much of the industrial conflict of the coming decade will be "rooted in disagreements over job changes." But Ornati also foresees the creation of new industry-wide agencies to cope with the problem of work rules.

[11] Oscar Ornati, "Fewer Strikes, Smaller Wage Hikes," *Challenge* (November 1960), p. 18.
[12] *Ibid.*, p. 19.
[13] *Ibid.*

Ornati is somewhat more optimistic about the future of American unions than A. H. Raskin whose ideas were discussed in the preceding section. But Ornati's is a somewhat restrained and guarded optimism. Unions will not be able to count upon a rising membership trend and substantial wage increases. But Ornati believes that union leaders will continue to play an important role in our society by channelling their energies into other directions, notably into participation in government agencies.

Collective Bargaining in the Late 1970's

A somewhat longer view of the future of unions has been taken by George W. Brooks, Director of Research and Education of the Pulp, Sulphite and Paper Mill Workers.[14] Brooks bases his analysis of the future of American unions on past trends and he emphasizes that he is making a series of *projections* rather than *predictions*. He anticipates that by 1977 there will have been a significant decrease in the number of companies and unions engaged in collective bargaining. But the companies involved will be larger than they are now and workers in each industry will be represented by a single union. Thus he foresees fewer but larger firms and unions.

Even more than today, according to Brooks, collective bargaining will be conducted by experts on both sides of the table. "The two sets of spokesmen will have had a long acquaintance with each other, and their attitudes will be marked by a real appreciation of each other's problems."[15] Brooks is not at all optimistic about the organization of office, technical and professional workers. In his view the unions of the future will still be largely limited to manufacturing and other blue-collar workers. The proportion of manufacturing workers in the labor force will continue to decline, as it has been doing for some time, and Brooks suggests that the direct and indirect labor costs attributable to workers represented by unions will also be a declining proportion of sales price. Because of this, he feels, "the economic results of . . . negotiations will be dazzling. The wages and other benefits will be far beyond the fondest imaginings of a few years ago."[16]

Finally, Brooks feels that union staff members will be much more involved in plant-level bargaining than they have been in the past.

[14] George W. Brooks, "What Will Collective Bargaining Look Like in Twenty Years?" *The Next Twenty Years in Industrial Relations,* Cambridge, Massachusetts: Industrial Relations Section, Department of Economics and Social Science, M.I.T. (1957), pp. 3–21.
[15] *Ibid.*, p. 3.
[16] *Ibid.*, p. 4.

Experts in various fields: pension plans, health and welfare funds, incentive programs, and job analysis, for example, will be employed by national and international unions to handle affairs at the plant level.

On balance, the projection made by Brooks is only mildly optimistic. He sees little union growth among white-collar workers and clearly implies that union members will comprise a declining proportion of the labor force. But largely because of this he foresees an era in which unions will once again be able to win sizeable gains in wages and benefits for their members since the additions to costs will be spread over a proportionately smaller number of workers than at present. Some labor economists might object to this conclusion by noting that there has been a tendency for non-union wages to follow union wage increases in the past as a result of so-called "tandem" wage boosts granted by employers to non-union workers following most rounds of union wage increases. It might be argued that if employers did not grant such increases in the future while unions won sizeable gains for their members, the unorganized office, technical and professional workers might see their only hope of improvement in forming or joining unions, thus stimulating another spurt of membership growth.

Unrestrained Optimism about the Long-Term Union Outlook

The most optimistic view of all deals with the union outlook in two or three decades. It has been advanced by Solomon Levine and Bernard Karsh in two recent articles.[17] Levine and Karsh "predict that in the next two or three decades the labor movement will achieve a broader membership base than it has today." And they go on to conclude that "unions will be more fully supported and more integrated into the future industrial structure than at any time before in American history."[18] The authors do not qualify this prediction, although it must be emphasized they are not talking about the immediate future but a period perhaps thirty years away. During the interim, they suggest that the transition for unions will be a painful one: "In the next two or three decades, labor relations are likely to experience severe conflicts as bargaining units are reformed, union jurisdictional lines are redrawn, leadership rivalries

[17] Bernard Karsh and Solomon B. Levine, "The Coming Revolution in Labor Relations," *Mill and Factory* (December 1960), Reprint No. 90, Institute of Labor and Industrial Relations, The University of Illinois. A more detailed account is given in Solomon B. Levine and Bernard Karsh, "Industrial Relations for the Next Generation," *Quarterly Review of Economics and Business* (February 1961), pp. 18–29.

[18] Levine and Karsh, "Industrial Relations for the Next Generation," p. 21.

are intensified, and new issues are injected into negotiations."[19] But this will be a transitional phase to a new kind of trade unionism and a new phase in American industrial relations.

The driving force of the new unionism which Levine and Karsh envisage will be what they call "a huge middle group of intellectual employees" in which they would include many of the office, technical and professional workers who have joined unions only in very small numbers up to now. But the inability of unions to organize such workers thus far "has taken place within a context of organizational structure and function which future technology in decision-making technique will make obsolete."[20] Changing technology, including what these authors call "information technology," will lead to a greater isolation between the decision-makers in business and employees, including high-level and well-educated professional and technical workers. This will lead to a growing social isolation among such workers which, according to Levine and Karsh, will stimulate them to join unions.

Levine and Karsh agree with Brooks that there will be fewer but larger unions in the future. They disagree with him, however, when it comes to the scope of such unions. Brooks foresees larger unions representing workers in a given industry while Levine and Karsh predict that the typical national union in two or three decades will be *multi-industrial*. "We predict that *process unionism* will increasingly replace our conventional industrial and occupational union structures."[21] What they are suggesting is that the organizational base for unions will not be related to a product or a specific job but rather to broadly-based production programs covering many markets and various skills. They are suggesting that some of the lines currently separating industries will break down. They imply that management will be much more concerned with processes in the future than with products and that this will force unions to alter their organizational structure to accommodate to the technologically-induced changes in business organization.

The larger unions which they foresee will have highly centralized leadership and greatly expanded staff functions. Local unions, in their view, will have less to say about union decisions than at present. But Levine and Karsh believe that they "will gain social and educational importance that will have the indirect effect of

[19] *Ibid.*, p. 19.
[20] *Ibid.*, p. 21.
[21] *Ibid.*, p. 23.

increasing the responsiveness of union officials to the members' needs and aspirations."[22]

In their view, contract negotiations will occur much less frequently than at present. In their *Mill and Factory* article, these authors suggest that by 1985 major negotiations will occur at perhaps only ten-year intervals. These negotiations will continue to deal with the traditional matters of wages, hours, fringe benefits and working conditions but in addition to this, Levine and Karsh believe, there will be bargaining over production programming, planning, innovation and investment. They go on to suggest that the major negotiations "will probe deeply into issues such as private and public consumption, education, recreation, mental health, urbanization, race relations, and perhaps even art appreciation and citizen morale."[23] Thus, according to this thesis, union leaders will participate to a large extent in management decision-making, at least during major negotiations, in the new process unionism which they envisage. Among other things, collective bargaining in the future, as these authors see it, will "fundamentally focus on the basic values at stake in the development of the economy and the relationship between life in and outside industry." Almost every management policy, they suggest, "will be subject to question, ranging from proposed capital investments to donations to charity or education."[24]

Finally, Levine and Karsh feel that government will play a much greater part in collective bargaining under process unionism than it has up to now. Government agencies, such as the departments of Labor and Commerce, will be expected to follow the course of bargaining quite closely and to provide the parties with the views of these agencies on the economic implications of various bargaining proposals.

In this new world of labor-management relations, Levine and Karsh foresee intense but relatively infrequent strikes. They suggest that during the next generation new techniques for settling disputes will be developed and that strikes and lockouts as we know them today will be largely averted. But this will not mean an end to industrial conflict. Unions and management will continue to have different sets of values and as these clash there will be conflicts. Levine and Karsh suggest that these conflicts will be relatively severe although they will not occur at frequent intervals. Also, they expect the government to take a much more direct hand in the

[22] *Ibid.*, p. 24.
[23] *Ibid.*, p. 25.
[24] *Ibid.*, p. 26.

settlement of disputes when they do occur and they expect the spotlight of publicity to be focused on such disputes in an effort to increase "legitimate outside pressure" on the parties. As they put it, "private" collective bargaining will become highly public.

The Karsh-Levine thesis might strike many students of current industrial relations as bizarre. Some might object that social scientists are not equipped to make *predictions* but should be content to make *projections* based upon one or more sets of assumptions. It requires boldness and imagination, however, to make a very long-range analysis such as Levine and Karsh have attempted. Their view of the future of industrial society and of the future of labor-management relations is based in part upon the extrapolation of past trends. But they have gone beyond this. They have tried to foresee the various kinds of changes which will be induced by new technological developments, continued shifts in the labor force, and a substantial increase in the number of professional and technical workers in the years ahead. These changes, in their view, will reverse the trend in union membership of the past few years, and lead to a resurgence of growth in unions which they believe will be radically altered in terms of structure and function.

A Final Comment on the Future of Unions

The views about the future of American unions expressed in the preceding sections cover a fairly wide range of discussion about both the short-term and the long-term outlook. Some writers, such as A. H. Raskin, appear to be relatively pessimistic about the future of American unions. At the other extreme Levine and Karsh exhibit unrestrained optimism. Forecasting of the kind these authors have engaged in is always a hazardous art. The difficulties can be realized by anyone old enough to think back a quarter of a century. How many at that time would have envisaged the kind of society we have today?

Our discussion of the future of American unions will be concluded with the remarks of Philip Taft, a distinguished labor economist and historian, taken from his presidential address to the Industrial Relations Research Association. His views are worth quoting at some length:

> Recognizing the great uncertainties which face us at many levels, it appears to me that the future of unionism in the United States is secure. While in many respects the labor movement expresses the views of the majority of workers, it has never in the United States rallied the majority of wage earners to its banner, and a safe forecast is that it will

not in the immediate future. But it will remain the largest organized group in the community for a long time to come. While there may not be any organization drives on a grand scale, there is no reason to assume that some unions will not, as in the past, gain substantial increases in members. Yet, the immediate and perhaps distant outlook is not for any drastic changes, either up or down. There are long periods in labor history when the labor movement remained stable, not increasing its numbers nor suffering severe losses. The propensity of workers to join unions changes over time and responds to changing expectations. There is no reason to assume that the unions will not be able to recruit new members, but they have not devised an effective appeal to the growing mass of white collar workers, but this may wait for a John L. Lewis.[25]

THE PROSPECTS FOR INDUSTRIAL PEACE

The preceding sections have dealt primarily with the future of the institution of trade unionism. Even the most pessimistic observers do not suggest that unions are on the way out. But the development of a "hard line" by management in some areas of collective bargaining was noted in the last chapter. What does this suggest for the future of industrial peace? Is it likely that strike activity will tend to increase or decrease in the years ahead?

Various writers who have noted the stiffening of management attitudes have also pointed out that aggregate strike activity has not been increasing. Despite recent changes in attitudes toward collective bargaining, "the long-run trend is so clearly in favor of realistic bargaining by increasingly experienced representatives that a new epic of strikes and violence can hardly be expected. It is more likely that the strike is 'withering away,' to quote Arthur Ross; and perhaps even as Dunlop has concluded, 'on balance relationships never have been better.' "[26] Milton Derber has also argued that the swing in the pendulum of bargaining power in management's favor is not likely to alter established patterns of collective bargaining: "The collective bargaining process is too firmly ingrained in our legal, political, and economic framework . . . we can expect union-management relations to fluctuate within rather narrow limits for some years to come."[27]

[25] Philip Taft, "Reflections on the Present State of the Labor Movement," *Proceedings,* 14th Annual Meeting, Industrial Relations Research Association (December 1961), p. 14.

[26] Clark Kerr, "The New Opportunities for Industrial Relations," *Arbitration and Public Policy,* Washington, D.C.: BNA Inc. (1961), Reprint No. 173, Institute of Industrial Relations, University of California, p. 4.

[27] Milton Derber, "Management and Union Rights in Industrial Establishments," *Current Economic Comment* (May 1960), p. 10.

Arthur Ross, of the University of California, has made extensive studies of industrial conflict. In his view there has been a long-run tendency for strike activity to decline. A few major industries, he has found, "account for a very substantial proportion of strike activity in the United States, although they employ only a small part of the labor force."[28] Strikes outside these major industries produce what Ross calls "the residual level of conflict." Ross indicates that there have been cycles of strike activity in the various major industries which he calls "centers of conflict." But he finds that these cycles have been declining. Strike cycles remain in such industries as basic steel, construction, electrical equipment and machinery. As a result of these strike cycles and the "residual level of conflict" the average union member in the United States loses approximately two days per year due to strike activity. If the major strike cycles which he notes would disappear, the residual level of conflict would reduce this average to about one day per union member per year. While it is not likely that this average will be achieved in the immediate future the long-run trend in strike activity has been downward and the likelihood is that this trend will continue. While no one seriously expects strike activity to disappear, the statistical evidence overwhelmingly supports Ross's hypothesis that the strike is slowly withering away.

THE ROLE OF UNIONS IN A PLURALISTIC SOCIETY

A pluralistic society may be roughly defined as one in which there are "as many power centers as possible, consistent with the effective functioning of the society."[29] Those who accept the notion that power in a democratic society should be widely diffused have consistently recognized the role which unions have played in such diffusion of power. If a balance is to be maintained in which no group dominates society a healthy and vigorous trade union movement will be required. As George Brooks has put it: "We cannot maintain unions as a standby facility."[30]

The difficulty experienced by some in attempting to evaluate the role of unions in a democracy is their inability to think in other than business terms. But as David Cole has pointed out, "collective bargaining is an important part of a social movement. It repre-

[28] Arthur M. Ross, "The Prospects for Industrial Conflict," *Industrial Relations* (October 1961), p. 66.
[29] Clark Kerr, "Managing the Managers—The Distribution of Power in American Industrial Society," in Stephen D. Kertesz and M. A. Fitzsimons, eds., *What America Stands For,* Notre Dame, Indiana: University of Notre Dame Press (1959), p. 94.
[30] Brooks, *op. cit.,* p. 21.

sents a great transformation. In place of the traditional property or proprietary concept of industry, which was reflected in the master-servant doctrine for centuries, the managements of American industry must now accept the fact of equality—equality in status and equality in the right of employees to express themselves and to insist upon how they shall work and be compensated."[31] As part of a social movement, unions have often played the role of social critics. But in the view of Sumner Slichter, "America needs a trade union movement that is strong, that demands public confidence, and that is a source of responsible and well-informed criticism of our economic institutions."[32]

In a democracy, with many centers of power, differences of opinion are bound to occur. At times these may lead to acrimonious debate or to outright disputes. But there would have been little progress in our society—economic or political—without differences of opinion. Trade unions have played an important part in the evolution of modern democracy. As Cole stated they have contributed to the shift from a master-servant relationship to one of equality of status. As Slichter noted many years ago unions introduced a system of industrial jurisprudence into industry thus broadening the base of our democratic system.

How does the contribution of American unions to the democratic process compare with those made by unions in other free nations? There may be room for debate about this but most labor scholars would rate American unions quite high in such a comparison. Some, such as Philip Taft, would give American unions the highest grade of all:

> . . . with all its faults, and it has many, the American labor movement is the most effective and therefore the best in the world. It has done more for its people; it has understood its social and economic environments, and it has a better record, yes and I include the craft unions, in supporting good causes, the oppressed abroad and the exploited at home. It is a movement of workers, officered largely by men and women risen from the ranks. It is not necessarily wiser than other segments of our society, nor are its prescriptions for change always just, equitable or desirable. Yet, it is a vigorous movement, directing its major efforts toward protecting rights on the job, it is needed if democracy is to continue and prosper.[33]

[31] David L. Cole, "The Outlook for Free Collective Bargaining," *IL-Research* (Fall-Winter 1960–1961), p. 7.
[32] Sumner H. Slichter, "New Goals for the Unions," *Atlantic Monthly* (December 1958), p. 58.
[33] Taft, *op. cit.*, p. 14.

REFERENCES

BOOKS AND PAMPHLETS

Barkin, Solomon, *The Decline of the Labor Movement,* Santa Barbara, California: Center for the Study of Democratic Institutions (1961).

Brooks, George W., *The Sources of Vitality in the American Labor Movement,* Ithaca, New York: New York State School of Industrial and Labor Relations, Bulletin 41 (July 1960).

Industrial Relations Research Association, *Power in Industrial Relations, Its Use and Abuse,* Proceedings of the Spring Meeting (May 1958), *Labor Law Journal* (September 1958), pp. 617–713.

Jacobs, Paul, *Old Before Its Time: Collective Bargaining at 28,* Santa Barbara, California: Center for the Study of Democratic Institutions (1963).

Tyler, Gus, *A New Philosophy for Labor,* Santa Barbara, California: Center for the Study of Democratic Institutions (1959).

U.S. Department of Labor, *Directory of National and International Labor Unions of the United States, 1961,* Bulletin No. 1320, Bureau of Labor Statistics (March 1962).

ARTICLES

Barbash, Jack, "What's Ahead for Labor?" Bureau of Industrial Relations, The University of Michigan, Reprint No. 20, University of Wisconsin, Industrial Relations Research Center.

Bernstein, Irving, "The Growth of American Unions, 1945–1960," *Labor History* (Spring 1961), pp. 131–157.

———, ———, "Don't Count the Unions Out," *Challenge* (November 1961).

Brooks, George W., "What Will Collective Bargaining Look Like in Twenty Years?" *The Next Twenty Years in Industrial Relations,* Cambridge, Massachusetts: Industrial Relations Section, Department of Economics and Social Science, Massachusetts Institute of Technology (November 1957), pp. 3–21.

Chamberlin, Edward H., "Can Union Power be Curbed?" *The Atlantic Monthly* (June 1959), pp. 46–50.

Clague, Ewan, "Emerging Economic Issues in Labor-Management Relations," *IL-Research* (Spring 1960), pp. 3–7.

Cole, David L., "The Outlook for Free Collective Bargaining," *IL-Research* (Fall-Winter 1960–1961), pp. 3–7.

Davenport, John, "Labor Unions in the Free Society," *Fortune* (April 1959), pp. 131 ff.

Derber, Milton, "Management and Union Rights in Industrial Establishments," *Current Economic Comment* (May 1960), pp. 3–11.

Karsh, Bernard and Solomon B. Levine, "The Coming Revolution in Labor Relations," *Mill and Factory* (December 1960), University of Illinois, Institute of Labor and Industrial Relations, Reprint No. 90.

Kerr, Clark, "Managing the Managers—The Distribution of Power in American Industrial Society," in Stephen D. Kertesz and M. A. Fitzsimons, *What America Stands For,* Notre Dame, Indiana: University of Notre Dame Press (1959), pp. 89–98.

———, ———, "The New Opportunities for Industrial Relations," *Arbitration and Public Policy,* Washington, D.C.; BNA Incorporated (1961), pp. 1–9.

Levine, Solomon B. and Bernard Karsh, "Industrial Relations for the Next Generation," *Quarterly Review of Economics and Business* (February 1961), pp. 18–29.

Miernyk, William H., "The Need for a New Look at Union Power," *Labor Law Journal* (November 1959), pp. 776–780.

Ornati, Oscar, "Fewer Strikes, Smaller Wage Hikes," *Challenge* (November 1960), pp. 18–20.

Raskin, A. H., "The Squeeze on the Unions," *Atlantic Monthly* (April 1961), pp. 55–60.

Ross, Arthur M., "The Prospects for Industrial Conflict," *Industrial Relations* (October 1961), pp. 57–74.

Slichter, Sumner H., "New Goals for the Unions," *Atlantic Monthly* (December 1958), pp. 54–58.

Solomon, Benjamin and Robert K. Burns, "Unionization of White-Collar Employees: Extent, Potential, and Implications," *The Journal of Business of the University of Chicago* (April 1963), pp. 141–165.

Taft, Philip, "Reflections on the Present State of the Labor Movement," *Proceedings,* 14th Annual Meeting, Industrial Relations Research Association (December 1961), pp. 2–14.

NAME INDEX

Alexander, Kenneth, 281, 302
Arensberg, Conrad M., 455n, 471

Bakke, E. Wight, 208n, 209, 212, 307n, 317, 342
Baldwin, George B., 408, 416
Ball, Joseph Hurst, Senator, 296
Bancroft, Gertrude, 342
Barbash, Jack, 128n, 196–197, 447, 450, 487
Barcus, Norman, 164
Barkin, Solomon, 128–129, 138, 359n, 361, 368, 405n, 407, 417, 467n, 471, 476, 487
Barone, Enrico, 346
Barry, Carol A., 4n, 343
Beck, Dave, 194
Becker, Joseph M., S.J., 163
Bedaux, Charles E., 454
Bell, Daniel, 78–80, 82n, 454n, 471
Bendix, Reinhard, 455n
Berger, Victor, 203
Bernstein, Irving, 57, 74n, 76–78, 80, 82n, 127n, 138, 477, 487
Bishop, Robert L., 235n, 241
Bloom, Gordon F., 103n
Blum, Fred H., 164
Booth, Philip, 157n, 164
Boulding, Kenneth E., 372
Boulware, Lemuel, 462
Bradley, Philip D., 301
Brandeis, Elizabeth, 69
Brandeis, Louis D., 94
Brichner, Dale J., 99
Brindell, Robert P., 193
Brodie, Abner, 164
Bromwich, Leo, 182–184, 186, 188, 197
Brooks, George W., 479–481, 485, 487
Brown, Douglass V., 98–99, 298, 302, 456n, 471
Buckley, William F., 162n, 163
Burns, Eveline M., 164
Burns, Robert K., 488

Cairnes, J. E., 335–336
Carr, King, 306n
Cartter, Allan M., 239n, 240, 346n, 347n, 368, 389, 391, 416
Chamberlain, Neil W., 206, 230–232, 240, 259, 270n, 281, 286–287, 302, 318
Chamberlin, Edward H., 99, 197, 297, 371, 473, 474n, 487
Christenson, C. L., 278n, 282
Clague, Ewan, 342, 396, 400, 401n, 404n, 417, 450, 487
Clark, J. B., 82n, 346
Cohany, Harry P., 287n
Cohen, Sanford, 281
Cole, David L., 485–487
Coleman, James, 182n
Coleman, John R., 118n, 138n, 305, 306n, 318, 465, 466n, 471
Commons, John R., 56, 69–70, 72, 74–75, 81
Coolidge, Calvin, 40–41
Cooper, Sophia, 342
Cooper, Walter J., 342
Cox, Archibald, 297, 302
Crawford, Fred, 463
Curtis, Police Commissioner, 40–41
Curtis, Thomas B., 431

Dankert, Clyde E., 416n, 417, 450
Davenport, John, 473n, 487
Davenport, Russell W., 315n
Davey, Harold W., 241, 267n, 281
Davis, Horace B., 77–78, 82n
Debs, Eugene V., 32, 34, 100, 203
DeLeon, Daniel, 34, 202–203
Derber, Milton, 484, 487
Doody, Francis S., 77n, 82n, 164
Douglas, Paul H., 389
Douty, H. M., 204, 212, 358n, 368
Dubin, Robert, 281
Dunbar, Ernest, 181n, 198
Dunlop, John T., 64, 69n, 72–74, 76–78, 81, 82n, 241, 268n, 281, 345, 347, 348n, 350, 354–356, 358, 365–366, 368, 375–376, 377n, 381, 383–385, 391, 404, 417, 458, 467n, 471, 484

Eisenhower, Dwight D., President of the United States, 126, 210, 437
Ellis, Howard S., 369
Engels, Friedrich, 60, 82n
Epstein, Albert, 75n

Fabricant, Solomon, 398–400, 402, 416
Fairless, Benjamin, 464
Faunce, William A., 412n, 417
Fellner, William, 236, 238, 241, 353–354
Fisher, Lloyd H., 286n, 302, 334n, 335, 363, 367, 369
Fitzsimons, M. A., 485n
Fleming, R. W., 268, 282
Foster, W. H., 30
Foster, William Z., 41
France, Robert R., 374n, 385n, 391, 433, 450
Franke, Walter H., 432n, 449
Frankfurter, Felix, 89
Friedman, Milton, 372

Galbraith, John Kenneth, 62, 62n, 69n
Galenson, Walter, 57
Galpin, Stephen J., 463n
Gantt, Henry L., 454
Garbarino, Joseph W., 366, 368, 374, 376, 391, 471

Gary, Elbert H., 41
George, Henry, 19
Gibbons, Cardinal, 22
Gibbons, Charles C., 259
Gilbreth, Frank B., 454
Gitlow, Abraham L., 259
Goldberg, Arthur J., 128n, 298, 302
Golden, Clinton S., 311
Goldner, William, 366, 369, 376, 377n, 383n, 391–392
Gomberg, William, 362, 368
Gompers, Samuel, 30–32, 36, 41, 81, 89, 92–93, 206
Gould, Jay, 22
Green, Nathan, 89n
Greenberg, Leon, 417
Gregory, Charles O., 87, 91n, 99, 133n, 136n, 138
Groom, Phyllis, 450

Haley, Bernard F., 369
Hansen, Alvin H., 368, 404n, 417
Harbison, Frederick H., 306n, 318, 465, 466n, 471
Hardman, J. B. S., 31n
Harris, Seymour E., 57
Harrison, William Henry, 90
Harsanyi, J. C., 353n
Hartley, Fred Allan, Jr., Representative, 53, 114, 129
Haywood, "Wild Bill," 34
Healy, James J., 242n, 256n, 258n, 268n, 281, 310n, 405n, 417
Heneman, Herbert G., Jr., 456n, 471
Herberg, Will, 207, 212
Herrnstadt, Irwin L., 300n, 302, 367n, 369
Hicks, J. R., 332n, 347–349, 351, 368, 389, 391
Hildebrand, George H., 275, 276n, 281
Hoffa, James R., 194
Hoffman, Paul, 465
Holcombe, John L., 134n, 135n, 138
Horowitz, Morris A., 119n, 138, 255, 259
Hoxie, Robert F., 66–67, 72, 81

Irwin, D. W., 235

Jackson, Andrew, 15–16
Jacobs, Paul, 119, 138, 463n, 487
Jacobsen, H. P., 412n, 417
Jacobson, Eugene, 417
Jaffe, A. J., 323n, 342
Jensen, Vernon H., 217
Jevons, W. Stanley, 346
Jones, Mother, 34

Karsh, Bernard, 81, 412n, 417, 480–483, 487–488
Katz, Daniel, 465n
Kendrick, John W., 394–395, 398–399, 416
Kennedy, John F., President of the United States, 297, 437
Kennedy, Robert F., 131n, 194–195, 197, 304n
Kerr, Clark, 63, 82n, 189, 197, 286, 302, 332, 333n, 334n, 335–337, 343, 363, 369–371, 374, 377n, 389–391, 407n, 411, 414, 418, 484n, 485n, 487
Kertesz, Stephen D., 485n
Kornhauser, Arthur, 281
Kuhn, James W., 138

Lampman, Robert J., 343
Lapp, John A., 261n, 270n, 271n, 281
Latimer, Murray W., 249
Lebergott, Stanley, 323, 342
Leiserson, William M., 231
Lerner, A. P., 371
Lescohier, D. D., 69
Lesieur, Frederick G., 314n, 315n
Lester, Richard A., 64n, 76n, 82n, 163, 207, 210, 212, 286n, 309n, 369, 381n, 391
Levine, Louis, 343
Levine, Solomon, 81, 480–483, 487–488
Levinson, Harold M., 291–292, 302
Levitan, Sar A., 190n, 197
Levy, Recorder, 87
Lewis, John L., 50, 174, 484
Lindblom, Charles E., 371
Lipset, Seymour Martin, 182n, 197
Livernash, E. Robert, 242n, 256n, 258n, 281, 310n, 362, 364, 369, 405n, 417
Long, Clarence D., 330n, 343, 450
Lucas, Wingate Hezekiah, Representative, 298
Ludd, Ned, 405

Machlup, Fritz, 297
McGrath, C. Peter, 181, 198
McGregor, Douglas M., 461n, 469n, 471
McGuire, P. J., 30
Maclaurin, W. Rupert, 343
McMurry, Robert N., 462–465, 471
McPherson, William H., 272n, 282
Madden, Skinny, 193
Mahoney, Thomas A., 324, 343
Marshall, Alfred, 333n, 346
Marx, Karl, 30, 58, 60–61, 81, 82n
Mayo, Elton, 455, 456n
Meany, George, 55, 169
Meier, Joseph B., 313n, 318
Meredith, Jane L., 325n, 344, 421, 450
Meyer, Arthur S., 274, 282
Meyers, Frederic, 391
Michael, Donald N., 411n, 416

Miernyk, William H., 212, 338n, 340n, 343, 411n, 418, 431n, 437n, 449–450, 467n, 471, 475n, 488
Mill, John Stuart, 62
Millis, Harry A., 15n, 16n, 20, 20n, 47n, 57, 67, 81, 94n, 99, 111n, 212
Mitchell, James P., 127
Montgomery, Royal E., 15n, 16n, 20, 47n, 57, 67, 81, 94n, 99, 111n, 212
Moore, Eli, 17
Morton, Walter A., 371, 391
Myers, A. Howard, 300, 302
Myers, Charles A., 158n, 164, 312n, 338n, 340n, 343, 384, 392, 456n, 458–460, 468–472
Myrdal, Gunnar, 432n, 449

Nixon, Richard M., 127
Northrup, Herbert R., 103n

Ornati, Oscar, 478–479, 488
Owen, Robert, 18
Owen, Robert Dale, 16, 18
Ozanne, Robert, 373–374, 389, 392

Palmer, A. Mitchell, 41–42
Palmer, Gladys L., 343
Pareto, Vilfredo, 351
Parks, Sam, 193
Passfield, Lord and Lady (see Webb)
Pen, J., 350–353, 369
Perlman, Richard, 378n, 392
Perlman, Selig, 57, 69–72, 81
Perloff, Harvey S., 1n
Petrillo, James C., 114
Phelps, Orme W., 334–335, 343
Phillips, A. W., 385–386, 392, 432–433, 450
Pierson, Frank C., 345n, 347n, 355n, 368
Pigors, Faith, 458n, 472
Pigors, Paul, 458n, 462n, 472
Pound, Roscoe, 296–297
Powderly, Terrence V., 22
Puckett, Elbridge S., 315n, 367n, 369
Purcell, Father Theodore V., 210, 212

Radin, Max, 99
Raimon, Robert L., 336n, 343
Raskin, A. H., 476, 479, 483, 488
Reder, Melvin W., 110, 373, 385n, 392
Rees, Albert, 93n, 344, 372–373, 392
Reuther, Walter, 55
Reynolds, Lloyd G., 338n, 343, 371, 375, 377, 379, 380, 391–392
Rezler, Julius, 77–78, 81
Ricardo, David, 388
Roberts, Owen Josephus, Justice, U.S. Supreme Court, 98
Rogers, James Thorold, 61–63, 81
Rogin, Michael, 203, 212
Roosevelt, Franklin D., President of the United States, 107, 110, 205
Roosevelt, Representative F. D., Jr., 298, 302
Rosenberg, Linda, 135n, 138
Ross, Arthur M., 73–74, 81, 269, 281–282, 366, 369, 376, 383n, 384–385, 391–392, 484–485, 488
Rostow, W. W., 303, 393, 416
Roucek, J. S., 412n, 417

Samuelson, Paul A., 386, 392, 433–435, 450
Saposs, David J., 203, 213
Scanlon, Joseph N., 247, 313–317, 470
Schaffner, Joseph, 261
Schelling, T. C., 241
Scherer, Joseph, 323n, 344
Schnitzler, William F., 169
Schumpeter, Joseph A., 352
Seltzer, George, 302
Senior, Nassau, 64
Shackle, G. L. S., 348–350, 353, 368
Shaw, Chief Justice, Massachusetts Supreme Court, 87–88
Sherman, John, Senator, 90
Shister, Joseph, 64n, 76n, 82n, 124n, 129n, 138, 207n, 231n, 241, 286n, 309, 318, 338n, 343, 359n, 362n, 368–369
Shultz, George P., 118n, 138, 305, 306n, 315n, 316n, 318, 338, 340n, 343–344, 367n, 369, 384, 392, 408, 416
Siegel, Abraham, 63, 82n
Siegel, Boaz, 136n, 139
Sikes, Earl L., 82n
Simler, Norman J., 119, 139, 259
Slavick, Fred, 164
Slichter, Sumner H., 65, 70, 126n, 127n, 139, 164, 180–181, 183n, 187n, 188n, 196–197, 224, 226, 240–241, 242n, 243n, 244n, 246, 248n, 250–254, 256–259, 281, 308n, 310n, 318, 339, 343, 366, 369, 371, 405, 407, 417, 467, 470, 486, 488
Smith, Adam, 58–61, 86–87
Solomon, Benjamin, 488
Solow, Robert M., 386, 390–392, 433–435, 450
Somers, Anne R., 164
Somers, Herman M., 164
Stagner, Ross, 210, 213, 461, 472
Stein, Robert L., 5, 325n, 329n, 344
Stephens, John A., 303
Stephens, Uriah, 22
Stevens, Carl M., 232, 234–235, 241
Stevenson, Adlai, 210
Stewart, Charles D., 323n, 342
Stieber, Jack, 258–259, 377, 392, 418
Stigler, George J., 393–394, 417
Strasser, Adolph, 30–31
Strauss, George, 196n

Sultan, Paul, 81, 124n
Summers, Clyde W., 127n
Swankin, David A., 135n, 139
Sylvis, William H., 21

Taft, Cynthia, 375, 377, 379–380, 391
Taft, Philip, 69, 175–176, 179, 187n, 188n, 189, 191, 193, 198, 483, 484n, 486, 488
Taft, Robert A., Senator, 53, 114, 137
Tannenbaum, Frank, 67–68, 69n, 82n
Taylor, Frederick, 454
Taylor, George W., 345n, 347n, 355n, 368
Teller, Ludwig, 85n, 99
Thole, Henry C., 259
Tilove, Robert, 247n
Tolles, N. Arnold, 64
Tower, Charles H., 118n
Travis, Herman, 5, 329n, 344
Trow, Martin, 182n
Troy, Leo, 175–176, 179
Truman, Harry S., President of the United States, 115, 296
Turnbull, John G., 456n, 459–460, 471–472
Tyler, Gus, 477n, 487

Ulman, Lloyd, 57, 373, 392

Van Arsdale, Harry, 446
Vance, Harold, 465
Van Sickle, John V., 381n, 392
Veblen, Thorstein, 66

Wagner, Harvey M., 241, 353–354, 369
Walras, Leon, 346
Ware, Norman, 14n, 57
Webb, Sidney and Beatrice, 64–66, 72, 82n
Weintraub, Sidney, 389, 392
Weiss, Harry, 164
Weisz, Morris, 200n, 213
Wicksteed, Philip, 346
Wiener, Norbert, 410–411, 417
Wilcock, Richard C., 324n, 344, 426n, 432n, 449–450
Wilcox, Clair, 99
Wilensky, Harold L., 455n
Williams, J. D., 232–233, 241
Wilson, Woodrow, President of the United States, 42, 91
Witte, Edwin E., 70, 205, 213
Wolman, Leo, 39n, 57, 74, 302
Woytinsky, W. S., 369
Wright, Frances, 18

Zeuthen, F., 351, 353, 368

SUBJECT INDEX

Ability to pay, 226
Agency shop, 124
Aggregate demand, 433–437
"All-or-none" contract, 238
Allied Industrial Workers, 193
Amalgamated Meat Cutters and Butcher Workmen of North America, 194
Amalgamation, 28
American Arbitration Association, 266
American Federation of Labor (A.F. of L.), 24–29, 31–32, 34–38, 40, 42–44, 49–52, 54, 105–107, 186, 200–202, 204–205, 406
  Denver convention of 1894, 202
  formative years, 31
  founders, 30
American Federation of Labor—Congress of Industrial Organizations (AFL-CIO), 3, 5–6, 55, 167–178, 190, 193, 195, 205, 298
  affiliated organizations, 170
  Convention, 167
  delegates, 167
  Ethical Practices Codes, 190, 195
  Ethical Practices Committee, 193
  Executive Council, 55, 167
  executive officers, 168
  federal local unions, 173
  federation staff, 169–170
  General Board, 168
  industrial union department, 55, 298
  Labor's League for Political Education, (LLPE), 205
  local unions, 173–174
  membership of, 5–6, 167
  research staff, 170
  standing committees, 168
  State Councils, 170
  state and local bodies, 167, 170
  structure of, 167–168
  trade and industrial departments, 169
American Federation of Labor—Congress of Industrial Organizations merger, 54–56, 205
  implementation agreement, 55
  no-raiding agreement, 54
  state and local bodies, 55
  unity committees, 54
American Federation of Musicians, 114n
American Labor Party, 16
American Labor Union, 34
American Plan, 42
American Railway Union, 32
Anheuser-Busch Company, 98
Annual improvement factor, 403–404
"Anti-Petrillo" Act (see Unlawful Practices in Radio Broadcasting Act)
Anti-Strikebreaker Law, 106
Antitrust laws and industrywide collective bargaining, 99
Apprenticeship, 21, 359
Apprenticeship rules, 181
Arbitration, 67, 101, 222, 265–271, 280
  types of arrangements, 266–267
Arbitration boards, 266
Arbitrators, 266–269, 272
  types of, 267–268
Area Redevelopment Act, 153, 437–439, 445
Area Redevelopment Administration, 437–438
Armour Committee, 411–412
Association of Iron and Steel Workers, 32
Automation, 339, 408–412, 430
  effects on employment and productivity, 409–412
  electronic data processing, 409
  and feedback control, 409
  and technological change, 408
Autonomy, 27, 171

Bakery and Confectionery Workers, 193–194
Bargaining agent, 105
Bargaining power, 73, 352
Bargaining relationships, 283–286, 288, 301
  diversity of, 288, 301
  in manufacturing, 285
  types of, 284–286
  variety of, 283, 286
Bargaining theory, 8, 350–354
  determinate solutions, 351
  indeterminate solutions, 353
  psychological factors, 351
  risk valuation, 352–353
  uncertainty, 353
Bargaining units, 284–288
  size distribution of, 286–288
Bedford Cut Stone case, 93–94
"Big Three" automobile firms, 292
Bilateral monopoly, 236, 353
Bituminous coal miners, 33
Bonuses, 247
Boston Central Labor Union, 41
Boulwareism, 462–463
Boycott, 91, 98
Brewery Workers, 28, 248
Brims case, 93–94
British Combination Acts, 61, 63
British Full Employment Policy, 440–442
  Local Employment Act of 1960, 441–442
Brotherhood of Firemen and Enginemen, 19
Brotherhood of Locomotive Engineers, 19
Bureau of the Census, 324, 421, 423
Business agent, 171, 310
Business contracts, 218
Business cycles, 74–76
Business unionism, 29, 33, 44, 61, 66, 199, 201
Byrnes Act (see Anti-Strikebreaker Law)

Call-in pay (see Reporting pay)
Capital, 60
Capital productivity, 399
Capitalism, 60–63
Carnegie Corporation, 32
Carpenters, 29–30, 98, 178
Carpenters Society of Philadelphia, 13
Charles Wolfe Packing Co. vs. The Court of Industrial Relations, 270
Child labor laws, 160
City centrals, 17, 19–20, 24
Civil Rights Act, 181
Civilian labor force, 322–323, 326, 419
Classical economists, 64–65
Clayton Act, 89, 91–92, 94–95, 97
Closed shop, 14, 17, 79, 88, 109, 115n, 116, 118, 134
Collective bargaining, 65, 67, 217, 219, 230–240, 242–258, 283–301, 303–311, 317, 351, 363, 365, 372, 374–375, 412, 479, 485
  dynamic nature of, 231
  and efficiency, 307
  with marginal firms, 299–301
  and non-wage issues, 242–258
  process of, 306
  resistance to, 304
  and small companies, 301
  specification of bargaining units, 219
  staff assistants, 479
  stages of, 303–311, 317
  structure of, 283–301
  as a system of industrial jurisprudence, 239–240
  variety of bargaining relationships, 283
  and work rules, 253–256
Collective democracy, 69
Collusion, 310
Committee on the Causes of Industrial Peace Under Collective Bargaining, 311
Committee for Industrial Organizations (CIO), 49–50
Committee on Political Education, 56, 205
Common law, 85–86
Common rule, 65
Commonwealth v. Hunt, 87–88
Communist Labor Party, 40
Communist Manifesto, 60
Communist Party, 40–41, 132–133
Company unions, 43, 47–48
  membership, 47
Compulsory arbitration, 270–271
Conciliation, 271–272, 280
Conflict of interests, 190, 195
Congress of Industrial Organizations (CIO), 50–52, 54, 72, 102, 105–107, 187, 205
  and communists, 51, 54
  Political Action Committee, 205
Conspiracy cases, 15
Conspiracy doctrine, 87–88
Consumer Price Index, 221, 224, 227, 387
"Continuous" collective bargaining, 275–276, 280
"Cooling-off" period, 126–127
Coronado cases, 92–93, 95, 97
Coronado Coal Company, 92
Corporations, 2–3, 16
Cost of production, 62
"Cost-push" theory of inflation, 227
Council of Economic Advisers, 436
Council of Profit Sharing Industries, 313
Countervailing power, 62
Craft unionism, 49
Craft unionists, 36
Craft unions, 21–22, 25, 27, 29, 31–34, 37, 49, 54, 335
Crawfordism, 463–464
Criminal conspiracy, 86

Danbury Hatters case (see *Loewe v. Lawlor*)
Davis-Bacon Act, 141
Defense Base Act, 159
Deferred payments, 243
Democracy, 7, 486
Department of Health, Education and Welfare, 160–161
Department of Justice, 106
Depressed areas, 437
Depressions, 3, 17, 19–20, 32, 39, 44, 46, 76, 103, 151, 248, 324, 347, 414, 436
  of 1857, 19
  of 1873, 20
  of 1893, 32
  of 1920, 39
  Great Depression, 3, 44, 46, 103, 151, 248, 324, 347, 414, 436
  panic of 1837, 17
  and union growth, 76
Director of Economic Stabilization, 108
Discrimination in employment for union activities, 116–117
Distillery Workers, 193
Domination of labor organizations, 116
Dual allegiance, 210–211
Dual unionism, 27–28, 36
Duplex Printing Press Company, 93

Earnings, 370–371
Efficiency, 62
Eight-hour day, 20, 204
Employee benefits, cost of, 247–248
Employers concession curve, 348–349
Employment, 326–327, 329–331, 420, 423, 435–440
  of manual workers, 330
  in manufacturing, 327
  month-to-month changes, 423

occupational distribution, 331
policies, 435–440
in service industries, 327, 329
and union wage policy, 382–385
Employment Act of 1946, 436
Employment Security Program, 448
Equilibrium of wages, 87
Equity court, 89
Erdman Act, 100–101
Escalator clauses, 220, 224, 288, 374, 466
European employment programs, 443–445
Exclusive jurisdiction, 27
Extortionate picketing, 133

Fabian socialism, 64
Factors of production, 345, 347, 350
Fair Deal, 114, 140
Fair Labor Standards Act, 142–145, 160, 244, 248, 252, 414
exemptions, 143
and minimum wages, 143
Fairlessness, 464–465
Featherbedding, 119, 254–256, 258
Federal Committee on Apprenticeship, 160
Federal Mediation and Conciliation Service, 122, 273–274
Federal Reserve Board, 478
Federal Society of Journeymen Cordwainers, 14
Federal Unemployment Tax Act, 154, 157
Federal unions, 49
Federation of Organized Trades and Labor Unions of the United States and Canada, 24
Ford Motor Company, 251, 276
Foreign competition, 229
Fortune magazine, 78, 473
Fourteenth Amendment, 270–271
Fringe benefits, 130, 242, 333
Full employment, 8–9, 372
Full employment policies, 436

Game theory (see Theory of games)
Game-variant sequence, 234
Garment industry, 310
General Counsel, NLRB, 115
General Electric Company, 462
General Motors, 228, 403
George-Bardon Act, 161
"Globe Doctrine," 106
Globe Machine and Stamping Co., 106
Greenbackism, 20
Grievance arbitration, 265–266, 271
Grievances, 173, 262–265, 267–269, 280, 312
procedures, 222, 262–263, 268–269
role of shop steward and foreman, 264–265
rules for settlement of, 264
types of, 262
Gross National Product, 326, 419
Group incentives, 314
Guaranteed annual wages, 248–250

Harvard Graduate School of Business Administration, 456
Hat Finishers, 18
Health, welfare and security benefits, 245–247
Hiring jobs, 337, 339–340
Hitchman Coal Company v. Mitchell, 94
Holiday pay practices, 244
Homestead Acts, 19
"Hot cargo" agreements, 117–118, 120, 134, 136
Hotel and Restaurant Workers, 194
Hourly earnings, 413
Hours of work, 221, 413–416
trends in manufacturing, 413
House of Representatives, 107
Housing Act of 1937, 141
Human relations, 455–456
Human Relations Committee, 275

Illegal assistance to labor organizations, 116
Immigrants, 36–37
Immobility of labor, 340, 342
Independent national unions, 174–175
Indifference curves, 237
Industrial conflict, 482, 485
Industrial democracy, 69
Industrial jurisprudence, 65, 253, 486
Industrial peace, 309, 311–313, 484–485
Industrial relations, 7–9, 456, 478
Industrial Revolution, 60, 68, 345, 404, 408, 410
Industrial unionism, 49–50, 71
Industrial unions, 54, 172, 187, 406, 457
Industrial Workers of the World (IWW), 34–37, 67
membership, 35
Industrialization, 347
Industrywide collective bargaining, 283, 295, 299, 301
Inflation, 385–388
Informational picketing, 120
Initiation fees, 119
Injunctions, 20, 42, 88–89, 93–96, 100, 125–126
Institutional economists, 64, 69
Insurance, 247
Insurance plans (see Supplementary unemployment compensation)
Internal Revenue Service, 252
Internal union affairs, 196
Internal wage structure, 362–363
International Association of Machinists (IAM), 93, 98, 178

International Brotherhood of Electrical Workers, 223, 414–415, 446
International Harvester Company, 108
International Labour Office, 195
International Ladies Garment Workers Union, 362
International Representative, 171
International Typographical Union, 186, 188–189, 261
Interstate commerce, 105–106
Ironmoulders, 18, 21, 33

Jacksonian democracy, 15
"Jim Crow" locals, 181
Job cluster, 355–357
Job consciousness, 36, 200
Job displacements, 409
Job evaluation, 359–363, 365
  administration of, 362
  basic systems, 359–360
  union views of, 361–362
Job market, 332
Job satisfaction, 338
Job security, 17
Job-territory, 71
Joint committees, 309–310
Joint Economic Committee, 431, 435–436
Jones & Laughlin case, 104–105
Journeymen cordwainers, 86
Journeymen Stonecutters Association, 18
Jurisdictional awards, 118
Jurisdictional disputes, 28, 118–119

Kansas Court of Industrial Relations, 270
Kansas Industrial Court Act, 270
Kansas and Texas Railroad, 22
Key bargain, 291–292
Key rates, 358, 365
Key settlements, 357–358, 365
Knights of Labor, 22–26, 170–171
  conflict with national unions, 23–24
  District Assemblies, 23
  Local Assemblies, 23
  membership of, 23, 26
  National Assembly, 23
Korean War, 54, 419

Labor combinations, 59
"Labor conspiracies," 15
Labor corruption and racketeering, 191–195
Labor disputes, 106, 478
Labor economics, 7–9
Labor economists, 70
Labor force, 4, 75, 322–331, 341, 420, 426
  composition of, 4
  measurement of, 322–325
  occupational distribution, 328–329
  occupational status, 323
  part-time, 325
  and population, 322
  secondary workers, 426
  trends in, 326
Labor force surveys, 323–324
Labor law, 7, 13, 85, 113–114
  evolution of, 85
  restrictive, 113–114
Labor-management agreements, 33, 172, 217–223, 261–265, 284, 288, 335
  content of, 219–223
  discharge cases, 222
  duration of, 288
  form agreements, 284
  fringe benefits provisions, 222
  grievance procedures, 261–265
  language of, 219
  negotiation of, 217–219
Labor-management cooperation, 63, 317, 470
Labor-management disputes, 14–16, 40–41, 63, 100, 107, 127, 217, 253, 260–281, 485
  Boston police strike, 40–41
  Colorado coal strike of 1913–1914, 276
  Hart, Schaffner & Marx strike of 1911, 261
  Philadelphia printers strike, 14–15
  prevention or settlement of, 260–276
  Pullman strike of 1894, 100
  steel strike of 1959, 127, 278
  "wildcat" strikes, 217, 260
  over working conditions, 253
Labor-management relations, 3, 95–99, 461–462, 482
  determinants of, 461–462
  limiting the judicial control of, 95–99
Labor-Management Relations Act of 1947, 52–53, 114–122, 124–130, 132–133, 136–137, 205, 273, 296, 304
  emergency disputes, 125
  fact-finding board, 126
  "free speech" provision, 122, 137
  non-communist affidavit, 53
  "right-to-work" provision, 53
Labor-Management Reporting and Disclosure Act, 131–136, 191, 193, 195–196
  "bill of rights" section, 136
  Bureau of Labor Management Reports, 135
  financial safeguards, 133
  union elections, 135
Labor market developments, 76
Labor markets, 99, 110, 321, 329–342, 350, 362–363, 366–367, 412, 438–439
  boundaries of, 336–337
  institutional, 333–334, 337
  and internal wage structure, 362–363
  local, 333
  managed, 334
  natural, 333
  neo-classical, 332–333

non-union, 335
perfect, 332, 350
structured, 334–335, 337
structureless, 366–367
sub-markets, 335–337, 342
unstructured, 334–335
Labor mobility, 335–336, 338–342, 438, 440, 445
empirical studies of, 338
voluntary, 338
Labor "monopolies," 99, 283, 295–299, 474
and the antitrust laws, 296–299
Labor movement, 15–18, 72
beginning of, 15–18
goals of, 72
Labor standards, 85, 141
Labor supply, 329–330
Labor turnover, 339, 411
Laboristic society, 467
Labor's League for Political Education, 55
Labor's Non-Partisan League, 205
Labour partnership, 62
Laissez-faire, 60, 86, 453
Landrum-Griffin Act (see Labor-Management Reporting and Disclosure Act)
Large-scale organizations, 2–3
Latimer Report, 249
Laundry Workers, 193
League of Nations, 39
Legal barriers to labor organization, 59
"Little Steel" Formula, 108
Living wage, 65
Local employment offices, 154–155
Local independent unions, 175–176
company dominance of, 175–176
estimated membership of, 176, 176n
estimated number of, 176, 176n
Local unions, 17, 19–21, 24, 172–174, 187
officers, 172, 174
organization of, 172–174
Localized unemployment, 411, 437
"Loco-Focos," 16
Loewe v. Lawlor, 90, 93
Longshoreman and Harbor Workers Compensation Act, 159
"Long-term" unemployment (see Persistent unemployment)
Luddites, 405
Ludlow Massacre, 276
Lump of labor theory, 405

McClellan Committee (see Senate Select Committee on Employer Activities in the Labor or Management Field)
McCormick Harvesting Machinery Co., 374
Machinists, 18, 29
Macroeconomic wage-price-unemployment studies, 433–436
Mail Deliverers, 194
Maintenance-of-Membership Agreements, 52, 109, 123
Make-work rules, 119, 255, 258
Malthusian theory of population, 346
Management, 453–454, 456–460, 466–467, 484
authority of, 453, 456
changing attitudes toward collective bargaining, 466–467
"hard line" in collective bargaining, 484
hierarchy of, 456
line and staff in industrial relations, 457–460
scientific, 454
Manpower Development and Training Act, 438–440, 445, 448
Manpower management, 453–471
Manual workers, 4, 430–431
Manufacturing earnings, 371
Marginal productivity, 346–348, 350, 355, 365, 388
Market structures, 72
Mass production, 43–44
Mass production industries, 49–50, 56
Massachusetts Institute of Technology, 314
Massachusetts Supreme Court, 87
Maximin, 233
Mediation, 101, 272–274, 280
Medical Facilities Survey and Construction Act, 161
Medieval guilds, 13
Mercantilism, 68
Merchant capitalists, 14
Mergers and consolidations, 90
Mill and Factory, 482
Miller Act, 141
Mine, Mill and Smelter Workers, 174
Minimax, 233
Mitchell v. Covington Mills, 142
Mobility of workers, 36
Molly Maguires, 20
Monopolistic practices, 90
Monopsony, 236
Monthly Report on the Labor Force, 421–423
Multi-employer agreements, 285–286, 289, 293–295
in the basic steel industry, 293–295
and pattern bargaining, 289
Multi-employer bargaining, 293–299, 301
Multi-industrial unions, 481
Multiple job holders, 422
Mutual dependence recognized, 291
Mutual insurance, 65
Mutual survival, 208–209

National Association of Manufacturers, 271, 295–296

National Bureau of Economic Research, 394, 398, 400
National Defense Mediation Board, 107
National Industrial Conference Board, 243–247
National Industrial Recovery Act, 46, 103
National and international unions, 19–21, 24, 27, 31–32, 75, 170–172, 174, 176, 296
  membership of, 75
  organization of, 170–172
National Labor Relations Act, 47–48, 52–53, 72, 104–106, 113–115, 120–121, 304, 457
  "free speech" provision, 120–121
National Labor Relations Board, 48, 104–106, 110, 112, 115, 117–122, 125, 133, 136, 304, 306
NLRB v. Curtis Brothers, Inc., 136
NLRB v. Jones & Laughlin Steel Corporation, 48
NLRB v. Virginia Electric and Power Company, 121
National Labor Union, 20–21
National Mediation Board, 102
National Metal Trades Job Evaluation Plan, 362
National Planning Association, 311–312
National Trades Union, 17, 21
National Typographical Union, 18
National War Labor Board, 52, 107–110, 112, 243, 249, 333
"Natural" wage rate, 60
Negotiations, 482
New Deal, 46, 95, 103, 114, 140, 145
New England Association of Farmers, Mechanics and Other Workmen, 16–17
No-strike pledge, 107
Non-competing groups, 335
Non-production workers, 328
Norris-LaGuardia Act, 89, 95–98, 100

Occupational mobility, 440
Office of Price Administration, 108, 242
Office of Vocational Rehabilitation, 160–161
Old Age and Survivors Insurance, 146–147
On-the-job training, 439
"One Big Union," 22–24
Open shop, 42, 109, 453
Operating Engineers, 28
Ophelimity, 351–352
Order of the Knights of St. Crispin, 21
Organizational picketing, 120, 134
Organizing committees, 50–51
Output per man-hour, 394–398
Overtime pay, 221
Owner-manager, 2

Paternalism, 454–455
Pattern bargaining, 288–293
  in highly competitive industries, 292–293
  and oligopoly, 290–291
Payoff matrix, 233–235
Pearl Harbor, 51, 107
Pension plans, 245–246
Per capita income, 419
Persistent unemployment, 156–157
Personnel administration, 9, 457, 467–470
  future of, 467–470
  suggested improvements in, 469–470
Personnel policy, 458–460
Personnel practices, 80
Philadelphia Cordwainers case, 87–88
Philadelphia Mechanics Union of Trade Associations, 16
Phillips curve, 385–386, 433–434
Pinkerton detectives, 20
Pluralistic society, 485–486
Political Action Committee, 55
Political involvement, 29
Population, 1, 422
Predatory unions, 67
Premium pay practices, 244–245
President's Committee on Government Contracts, 142
Prevailing wage, 347
Price controls, 108, 113
Price stabilization, 111
Private employment agencies, 153
Process unionism, 481
Producers and consumers cooperatives, 18, 21, 66–67
Product market, 98
Production workers, 328
Productivity, 225, 228, 288, 315, 321, 329, 375, 393–407, 413–416, 476
  annual improvement factor, 288
  changes in, 396–397
  and collective bargaining, 403–404
  combined labor and capital inputs, 398–401
  and earnings, 401–402
  general index of, 399
  and hours of work, 413–416
  meaning and measurement of, 393–394
  union attitudes toward, 404–407
  variations in, 404
Professional managers, 2
Professional and technical workers, 481, 483
Profit sharing, 309, 313–317
  as an anti-union device, 313
  and union-management cooperation, 313–317
Promotion, 337
Public employment service, 153–154, 156
Pullman Company, 32, 100
Pulp, Sulphite and Paper Mill Workers, 479

Racial discrimination, 181
Racketeers, 190
Radical unionism, 34
Railroad Brotherhoods, 103
Railroad Retirement Board, 158
Railroad Unemployment Insurance Act, 158
Railway Labor Act, 101–103, 105, 115, 158
Rationing, 108
Real average hourly earnings, 401–402, 414
Real output per capita, 393
Real wages, 19
Recognition picketing, 120, 134
"Red scare," 41
Reform movements, 18, 20, 200
Reform organizations, 16
Refusal to bargain in good faith, 116–117
Regular labor force, 324
Reporting pay, 245
Representation election, 120
Research and development, 329
Restraint or coercion, 117
Restrictionism, 65
Retail, Wholesale and Department Store Union, 415
Revolutionary unionism, 67
Ricardo's Iron Law of Wages, 346
Right of self-organization, 106
"Right-to-work" laws, 122–124, 128, 137
Rights and duties of employers, 220
Rubber Workers, 223

Saddle point, 233–234
Savings plans (see Supplementary unemployment compensation)
Scanlon Plan, 313–317, 470
Secondary boycott, 93–94, 96, 99, 118, 133, 136
Secondary picketing, 134
Secondary workers, 324
Secretary of Health, Education and Welfare, 438–439
Secretary of Labor, 132–133, 140–142, 144, 438
Senate Select Committee on Employer Activities in the Labor or Management Field, 67, 129, 131, 133–134, 174, 193–195, 474–475
Seniority, 222, 254
Servicemen's Readjustment Act, 152
Severance pay, 221
Sheet Metal Workers, 194
Sherman Act, 90–94, 297
Shift differentials, 245
Shop steward, 172–173
Shorter hours, 413–416, 446
Single-employer agreements, 285, 289
Single tax, 19
Sit-down strikes, 51
Skill differentials, 377–378
Smith Amendments, 107
Smith-Connally Act (see War Labor Disputes Act)
Smith-Hughes Act, 161
Social Darwinism, 453
Social insurance, 163
Social legislation, 85, 163
Social mobility, 200
Social reform, 31
Social Security Act, 145–148, 151
  disability insurance benefits, 148
  eligibility provisions, 147
  history of, 150
  retirement benefits, 147
  self-employed persons, 148
  survivor benefits, 148
Social Security Administration, 146, 150
Social Security payments, 246
Social stratification, 200
Socialism, 30
Socialist Labor Party, 34, 202–203
Socialist Labor and Trade Alliance, 34
Socialist Party, 34, 201, 203
Socialists, 29, 202
Socio-economic classes, 336
Speedup, 364
Standard work week, 415–416
Star Island Agreement, 261
State Divisions of Employment Security, 151
Statutory law, 85–86
Stove Founders Defense Association, 33
Strike cycles, 485
Structural transformation theory, 430
Studebaker-Packard Corporation, 465
Studebakerism, 465–466
"Super" seniority, 222
Supervisors, 115
Supplementary unemployment compensation, 248–253
Supreme Court, 91–92, 94, 98, 103, 121, 160, 271
Swedish labor market policy, 442–443
Sympathy boycott, 118
Sympathy strikes, 14, 118

Taft-Hartley Act (see Labor-Management Relations Act of 1947)
Tandem wage increases, 480
Teamsters, 28, 174, 176, 178, 185, 193–194, 287
Technological change, 221, 225, 253, 256–258, 275, 405, 407, 438, 449, 468, 481
  Armour Agreement of 1959, 275
  Kaiser formula, 275
  and work rules, 256–258
Technological developments, 36, 71–72
Technology, 66

Temporary Extended Unemployment Compensation, 157
Temporary restraining order, 96
Temporary Unemployment Compensation Program, 156
Ten-hour movement, 14, 16–17
Testing and counselling, 154
Texas and New Orleans Railway case, 102
Theories of the labor movement, 58–74
Theories of trade union growth, 74–81
Theory of collective bargaining, 230–240
  Chamberlain's classification of, 230–232
Theory of distribution, 345
Theory of games, 232–235, 353–354
Thompson Products Company, 463
Trade unionism, profile of, 3–6
Trade unions, 3–5, 9, 13–14, 17–18, 33, 37, 39, 44–45, 48, 51–52, 56, 61, 63–74, 76–77, 89–99, 105, 107, 109, 132, 135, 172, 176–178, 180, 182, 189, 192, 199–201, 204–212, 305–307, 370–391, 407, 462–467, 470–471, 473–486
  and antitrust laws, 89–99
  attitudes of rank and file, 209–211
  during colonial times, 13–14
  disaster theory, 77
  discipline, 182
  and distributive shares, 388–391
  dual nature of, 207
  early attempts at federation, 17–18
  economic consequences of, 370–391
  as economic or political organizations, 72–74
  elections, 132
  functional types, 66
  future of, 477–484
  government, 64, 180
  health and welfare funds, 192
  ideology, 199–201
  and impact on wages, 374
  industrial composition, 178
  industrial distribution of, 5, 178
  influence of, 3
  job conscious, 70
  legality of, 48
  and level of wages, 371–375
  as a leveling influence, 305
  male and female membership, 4, 178
  management attitudes toward, 462–467
  and manpower management, 470–471
  manufacturing, 178
  Marxian view of, 61
  maturity of, 206–209
  membership, 5, 33, 37, 39, 44–45, 48, 51–52, 56, 105, 107, 109, 178
  and money wage level, 371
  nature of, 71–74
  non-manufacturing, 178
  periods of rapid expansion, 76
  philosophy and objectives, 199
  and political action, 204–206, 212
  political nature of, 384
  power, 473–476
  present state of, 473–477
  recognition of, 305–307
  and relative income shares, 389–390
  response to the factory system, 67
  restrictive membership provisions, 135
  role of, 485–486
  size and composition of, 176–178
  size distribution, 3–4, 176–177
  staff members, 172
  structure and function of, 67
  and technological change, 407
  theory, 63–74
  and wage structure, 375–380
Trusteeship, 132
Trusts, 90

Unemployment, 8, 45, 151, 153, 339, 419–449
  causal factors, 434
  characteristics of, 431
  and collective bargaining, 445–447
  "creeping," 421, 440
  cyclical, 153, 420–421
  definitions and measurement of, 421–423
  disguised, 425
  duration of, 421
  by duration and type, 424
  economic consequences of, 447–449
  frictional, 448
  due to inadequate demand, 427
  involuntary, 339, 423, 425
  long-term, 424
  by occupation, 431
  persistent, 429–432
  rates, comparative, 444
  short-term, 423
  social and psychological costs, 449
  structural, 426–427, 434
  taxonomy of, 423–428
  trends of, 420, 429
  voluntary, 423
  wages and prices, 432
Unemployment compensation, 151–152, 154–157, 162, 249–250, 448
  benefits, 155
  exclusions from, 155
  experience rating, 157
  financing, 157
  and labor disputes, 156
Unfair labor practices for employers, 104, 115
Unfair labor practices for unions, 117–118
Union activities, judicial control of, 92

Union admission policies, 181–182
Union constitutions, 182n, 184, 188
Union conventions, 182–184
  committees, 183–184
  delegates, 182–183
  resolutions, 184
Union corruption, 474
Union democracy, 135, 137, 180–182, 188–189, 196, 207
Union discipline, 187–188, 196
  appeal procedures, 188
Union growth, 38–39, 49, 51, 53, 56, 69, 71–72, 74–81, 111, 466–467, 473, 483–484
  debate about, 75
  factors influencing, 78
  growth cones, 72
  and inertia, 77
  and major wars, 76
  multicausal theories of, 77
  obstacles to, 69
  resistance to, 71
  the stagnation thesis, 78
  theories of, 74–81
  wars and depressions as causes of, 76
  during World War I, 38
Union hiring hall, 115n
Union-management cooperation, 308–311
Union membership, 3–6, 74, 78–80, 128, 137, 475
  geographical distribution, 5–6
  industrial classification, 4–5
  in large enterprises, 79
  in manufacturing, 79
  "real membership," 75, 80–81
  during wartime, 79
  and white-collar workers, 79–80
Union officers, 185–187, 197, 207–208, 211
  changing outlook of, 207, 211
  election of, 186, 197
  functions of, 185
  nominating procedures, 186
  recall provisions, 187
  referendum vote, 186
  staff assistants, 185, 208
Union philosophy, 208–209
Union recognition, 219
Union repression, 86
Union resistance curve, 348–349
Union security, 108–109, 219
Union shop, 79, 109, 115n, 116, 122, 124
Union wage policy, 382–385
United Auto Workers, 173, 178, 183, 188–189, 228, 251, 276, 287, 403
United Cigar Makers, 18, 24, 30
United Electrical Workers, 174–175
United Mine Workers, 34, 50, 92, 174, 176, 189
United Nations Charter, 436
U.S. Chamber of Commerce, 248, 271, 295
U.S. Department of Labor, 141, 143, 145, 151–152, 160, 176, 178, 221, 243, 245, 249, 252, 286, 324, 326, 334, 394, 398, 400–401, 408, 415, 422–424, 431
  Bureau of Apprenticeship and Training, 160–161
  Bureau of Employment Security, 151–152
  Bureau of Labor Statistics, 221, 243, 245, 249, 286, 326, 334, 394, 398, 400–401, 415, 422–423, 431
  Wage and Hour and Public Contracts Divisions, 141, 143, 252
U.S. Employment Service, 151–152, 445
United States v. Hutchison, 97–99
U.S. Industrial Commission, 193
U.S. Office of Education, 160–161
U.S. Senate Committee on Education and Labor, 31
U.S. Steel Corporation, 41, 293–294, 303, 464
United Steelworkers of America, 171, 178, 185, 275, 287, 293, 295, 314, 372
United Textile Workers, 183, 194
University of California, 485
Unlawful Practices in Radio Broadcasting Act (Lea Act), 114
Upholsterers Union, 188–189
Uplift unions, 66
Urban-agrarian economy, 1
Urbanization, 347
Utility, 351

Vacation and holiday pay, 221, 243–244
Value of the game, 233
Vocational Division, U.S. Office of Education, 160–161
Vocational training and rehabilitation, 160
Voluntarism, 203–204

Wabash and Missouri Railroad, 22
Wage contours, 355–358, 365
Wage controls, 108, 112
Wage curve, 361
Wage determination, 8, 240, 321, 345, 358–359, 365
  and product markets, 358–359
Wage differentials, 375–382
  geographic, 378–381
  interfirm, 380
  inter-industry, 376, 380
  interpersonal, 379
  occupational, 380
Wage fund, 345–346, 355
Wage and Hour Law (see Fair Labor Standards Act)
Wage incentives, 363–364
Wage level, 8
Wage market, 332

Wage movements, 373–374
Wage negotiations, 223–229
criteria used by employers, 227–229
criteria used by unions, 224–227
Wage policy, 345
Wage-price unemployment relationship, 386–388
Wage rates, 333, 355–356, 364, 366–367
dispersion of, 333
diversity of, 355, 366–367
hourly, 364
key rates, 356
Wage stabilization, 111
Wage Stabilization Board, 242
Wage structure, 8, 355–356, 359, 365–368, 370, 375, 378–380
external, 356, 365–368
impact of unions on, 379–380
and industry-mix, 379
inter-industry, 366, 378
internal, 356, 359, 365, 367
Wage theory, 345–350, 354–359
classical, 345–346
contemporary, 345, 354–359
neo-classical, 345–350
Wage uniformity, 227–229
Wages, 62, 66, 220, 372–373
in basic steel industry, 372–373
and employment, 66
movement of, 372
Wagner Act (see National Labor Relations Act)
Wallpaper Craftsmen, 248
Walsh-Healey Public Contracts Act, 141–144
minimum wage, 141–142
standard work week, 141
War Labor Disputes Act, 110–111
Weighted output per man-hour, 398
Welfare and Pension Plans Disclosure Act, 130
Western Federation of Miners, 34–35
White collar workers, 4, 178, 328, 330, 430–431, 468
Work assignments, 118
Work rules, 242, 253–258, 478
and technological change, 256–258
and working conditions, 255
Work stoppages, 276–280
causes of, 279
inter-union disputes, 279
intra-union disputes, 279
"offset factor," 278
trends in, 277, 280
Workmen's compensation laws, 158–159, 162
Works Progress Administration, 324
World War I, 35, 37, 40, 42, 52
World War II, 52, 110–111, 123, 126, 225, 242, 245, 249, 253, 324, 333, 406, 414–415, 428, 436, 466, 468

"Yellow-dog" contracts, 42, 94, 96, 101, 453